# Lecture Notes in Computer Scienc

*Commenced Publication in 1973*
Founding and Former Series Editors:
Gerhard Goos, Juris Hartmanis, and Jan van Leeuwen

T0237973

Tommaso Di Noia   Francesco Buccafurri (Eds.)

# E-Commerce
# and Web Technologies

10th International Conference, EC-Web 2009
Linz, Austria, September 1-4, 2009
Proceedings

 Springer

Volume Editors

Tommaso Di Noia
Politecnico di Bari, Dipartimento di Elettrotecnica ed Elettronica
Via E. Orabona 4, 70125 Bari, Italy
E-mail: t.dinoia@poliba.it

Francesco Buccafurri
University of Reggio Calabria, Department DIMET
Via Graziella, loc. Feo di Vito, 89122, Reggio Calabria, Italy
E-mail: bucca@unirc.it

Library of Congress Control Number: 2009932591

CR Subject Classification (1998): J.1, H.4, H.2, H.3, K.6.5, C.3, E.3

LNCS Sublibrary: SL 3 – Information Systems and Application, incl. Internet/Web
and HCI

ISSN       0302-9743
ISBN-10    3-642-03963-4 Springer Berlin Heidelberg New York
ISBN-13    978-3-642-03963-8 Springer Berlin Heidelberg New York

Typesetting: Camera-ready by author, data conversion by Scientific Publishing Services, Chennai, India
Printed on acid-free paper      SPIN: 12736850      06/3180      5 4 3 2 1 0

# Preface

After the initial enthusiastic initiatives and investments and the eventual bubble, electronic commerce (EC) has changed and evolved into a well-established and founded reality both from a technological point of view and from a scientific one. Nevertheless, together with its evolution, new challenges and topics have emerged as well as new questions have been raised related to many aspects of EC. Keeping in mind the experience and the tradition of the past editions of EC-Web, we tried, for its 10th edition, to introduce some meaningful innovations about the structure and the scientific organization of the conference. Our main target was to highlight the autonomous role of the different (sometimes heterogeneous) aspects of EC, without missing their interdisciplinary scope. This required the conference to be organized into four "mini-conferences," each for a relevant area of EC and equipped with a corresponding Area Chair. Both the submission and the review process took into account the organization into four tracks, namely: "Service-Oriented E-Commerce and Business Processes," "Recommender Systems," "E-Payment, Security and Trust" and "Electronic Commerce and Web 3.0." Therefore, the focus of the conference was to cover aspects related to the theoretical foundation of EC, business processes as well as new approaches exploiting recently emerged technologies and scenarios such as the Semantic Web, Web services, SOA architectures, mobile and ubiquitous computing, just to cite a few. Due to their central role in any realistic EC infrastructure, security and privacy issues are widely considered, without excluding legal and regulatory aspects.

We received a broad spectrum of submissions and we are confident that the papers that were finally selected for publication and presentation will contribute to a better understanding of EC issues and possibilities in the Web 2.0 and Web 3.0 eras. We are grateful to all authors for their submissions. All papers were reviewed by at least three reviewers, either members of the Program Committee or external experts in the field. We received 61 papers and we accepted 20 of them for full oral presentation and 11 papers for short oral presentation. We received submissions from 26 countries (covering five continents), namely, Algeria, Australia, Austria, Brazil, Canada, Chile, China, Colombia, Croatia, Cyprus, Czech Republic, Denmark, France, Germany, Greece, Hungary, India, Iran, Italy, New Zealand, Romania, Serbia, Slovakia, South Korea, Spain, Taiwan, The Netherlands, Tunis, UK, USA and Vietnam.

Keynote talks further enriched EC-Web 2009. Edith Elkind gave the talk "Voting: A View Through the Algorithmic Lens" introducing recent developments in computational social choice and discussing the use of voting in practical applications. Martin Hepp in his talk "Product Variety, Consumer Preferences, and Web Technology: Can the Web of Data Reduce Price Competition and Increase Customer Satisfaction?" explained how to develop a Semantic Web enabled e-commerce application using the GoodRelations vocabulary.

We wish to thank Track Chairs Martin Hepp, Barbara Masucci, Giovanni Semeraro and Stefan Tai for their valuable contribution and support as well as all the PC members of each track and external reviewers. Our thanks also go to Roland Wagner and to Gabriela Wagner for their great support in every single step of the organization. We do not forget Amin Anjomshoaa, who supported us with ConfDriver and fixed and changed the review system according to our needs. We are very grateful to them all.

September 2009                                          Francesco Buccafurri
                                                       Tommaso Di Noia

# Organization

## Program Chairs

Francesco Buccafurri      Università degli Studi Mediterranea di Reggio
Calabria, Italy
Tommaso Di Noia      Politecnico di Bari, Italy

## Track Chairs

Service Oriented E-Commerce and Business Processes
    Stefan Tai, Karlsruhe University, Germany
Recommender Systems
    Giovanni Semeraro, Università degli Studi di Bari, Italy
E-Payment, Security and Trust
    Barbara Masucci, Università di Salerno, Italy
Electronic Commerce and Web 3.0
    Martin Hepp, Bundeswehr University Munich, Germany

## Program Committee

### Service-Oriented E-Commerce and Business Processes

| | |
|---|---|
| Marco Aiello | University of Groningen, The Netherlands |
| Christoph Bussler | Merced Systems, USA, |
| Schahram Dustdar | Vienna University of Technology, Austria |
| Holger Giese | HPI Potsdam, Germany, |
| Rania Khalaf | IBM Research, USA |
| Heiko Ludwig | IBM Research, USA |
| Ingo Melzer | Daimler Research, Germany |
| Christos Nikolaou | University of Crete, Greece |
| Thomas Sandholm | HP Labs, USA |
| York Sure | SAP Research, Germany |
| Vladimir Tosic | NICTA, Australia |
| Willem-Jan van den Heuvel | University of Tilburg, The Netherlands |
| Christian Zirpins | University of Karlsruhe, Germany |

### Recommender Systems

| | |
|---|---|
| Gianbattista Amati | Fondazione Ugo Bordoni, Italy |
| Sarabjot Singh Anand | University of Warwick, UK |
| Liliana Ardissono | University of Turin, Italy |
| Giuliano Armano | University of Cagliari, Italy |
| Paolo Avesani | Fondazione Bruno Kessler, Italy |

| | |
|---|---|
| Pierpaolo Basile | University of Bari, Italy |
| Bettina Berendt | KU Leuven, Belgium |
| Shlomo Berkovsky | CSIRO, Australia |
| Robin Burke | De Paul University, USA |
| Rayid Ghani | Accenture Technology Labs, USA |
| Marco de Gemmis | Università degli Studi di Bari, Italy |
| Alexander Felfernig | University Klagenfurt, Austria |
| Michele Gorgoglione | Politecnico di Bari, Italy |
| Dietmar Jannach | Dortmund University of Technology, Germany |
| Pasquale Lops | Università degli sutdi di Bari, Italy |
| Bhaskar Mehta | Google Inc. |
| Stuart E. Middleton | University of Southampton, UK |
| Cosimo Palmisano | Fiat Group SpA, Italy |
| Michael Pazzani | Rutgers University, USA |
| Roberto Pirrone | University of Palermo, Italy |
| Francesco Ricci | Free University of Bozen-Bolzano, Italy |
| Shilad Sen | Macalester College, USA |
| Barry Smyth | University College Dublin, Ireland |
| Carlo Tasso | University of Udine, Italy |
| Eloisa Vargiu | University of Cagliari, Italy |

## E-Payment, Security and Trust

| | |
|---|---|
| Anna Lisa Ferrara | University of Illinois at Urbana-Champaign, USA |
| Matthew Green | Johns Hopkins University, USA |
| Audun Jøsang | University of Oslo, Norway |
| Seny Kamara | Microsoft Research, USA |
| Gianluca Lax | Università Mediterranea di Reggio Calabria, Italy |
| Josè Maria Sierra | Universidad Carlos III de Madrid,  Spain |
| Allan Tomlinson | University of London, UK |

## Electronic Commerce and Web 3.0

| | |
|---|---|
| Hans Akkermans | Free University Amsterdam, The Netherlands |
| Alfredo Cuzzocrea | University of Calabria. Italy |
| Flavius Frasincar | Erasmus University Rotterdam, The Netherlands |
| Fausto Giunchiglia | University of Trento, Italy |
| Andreas Harth | DERI Galway, Ireland |
| Birgit Hofreiter | University of Vienna, Austria |
| Uzay Kaymak | Erasmus University Rotterdam, The Netherlands |
| Juhnyoung Lee | IBM Research, USA |
| Sang-goo Lee | Seoul National University, Korea |
| Andreas Radinger | Bundeswehr University Munich, Germany |
| Bernhard Schandl | University of Vienna, Austria |
| Gottfried Vossen | University of Münster, Germany |
| Peter Yim | CIM Engineering, Inc., USA |

# External Reviewers

Josè Francisco Aldana Montes
Claudio Baldassarre
Linas Baltrunas
Marco Brambilla
Steve Capell
Simona Colucci
Florian Daniel
Roberto De Virgilio
Eugenio Di Sciascio
Nicola Fanizzi
Fernando Ferri
Clemente Galdi

Christophe Guéret
Fedelucio Narducci
Cataldo Musto
Pasquale Pace
Azzurra Ragone
Davide Rossi
Michele Ruta
Jean-Claude Saghbini
Floriano Scioscia
Eufemia Tinelli
Alexander Totok

# Table of Contents

## Invited Talk

## Design and Modelling of Enterprise and Distributed Systems

## Electronic Commerce and Web 3.0

## Collaboration-Based Approaches

## Recommender Systems Modelling

## Reputation and Fraud Detection

## Recommender Systems and the Social Web

# Recommender Systems in Action

# Voting: A View through the Algorithmic Lens

Edith Elkind

Division of Mathematical Sciences
Nanyang Technological University
Singapore
eelkind@gmail.com

**Abstract.** In recent years, voting and elections have been actively studied by computer scientists, both because of their interesting algorithmic properties and due to their potential applications to the design of multiagent systems and e-commerce. In this talk, I will give an overview of several recent developments in the nascent area of computational social choice and discuss their relevance to the use of voting in practical e-commerce applications.

T. Di Noia and F. Buccafurri (Eds.): EC-Web 2009, LNCS 5692, p. 1, 2009.

# Personalized Popular Blog Recommender Service for Mobile Applications

Pei-Yun Tsai and Duen-Ren Liu

Institute of Information Management
National Chiao Tung University, Taiwan
`halohowau@gmail.com, dliu@iim.nctu.edu.tw`

**Abstract.** Weblogs have emerged as a new communication and publication medium on the Internet for diffusing the latest useful information. Providing value-added mobile services such as blog articles is increasingly important to attract mobile users to mobile commerce. There are, however, a tremendous number of blog articles, and mobile users generally have difficulty in browsing weblogs. Accordingly, providing mobile users with blog articles that suit their interests is an important issue. Very little research, however, focuses on this issue. In this work, we propose a Customized Content Service on a mobile device (m-CCS) to filter and push blog articles to mobile users. The m-CCS can predict the latest popular blog topics by forecasting the trend of time-sensitive popularity of weblogs. Furthermore, to meet the diversified interest of mobile users, m-CCS further analyzes users' browsing logs to derive their interests, which are then used to recommend their preferred popular blog topics and articles. The prototype system of m-CCS demonstrates that the system can effectively recommend mobile users desirable blog articles with respect to both popularity and personal interests.

**Keywords:** Mobile Service, Blog, Recommender System, Time-Sensitive Topic.

## 1 Introduction

Weblogs have emerged as a new communication and publication medium on the Internet for diffusing the latest useful information. Blog articles represent the opinions of the population and react to current events (e.g., news) on the Internet [1]. Most people read blogs because it is a new source of news [2]. Looking for what is the latest popular issue discussed by blogs and attracting readers' attention is an interesting subject. Moreover, providing value-added mobile services such as blog articles is increasingly important to attract mobile users to mobile commerce, to benefit from the proliferation and convenience of using mobile devices to receive information anytime and anywhere. There are, however, a tremendous number of blog articles, and mobile users generally have difficulty in browsing weblogs owing to the limitations of mobile devices such as small screens, short usage time and poor input mechanisms. Accordingly, providing mobile users with blog articles that suit their interests is an important issue. Very little research, however, focuses on this issue.

T. Di Noia and F. Buccafurri (Eds.): EC-Web 2009, LNCS 5692, pp. 2–13, 2009.

There are three stems of research regarding blogs. The first type of research focuses on analyzing the link structure between blogs to form a community [3, 4]. The research on the weblog community proposes a way to discover bursty evolution of blogspace. Through the hyperlinks between blogs, people can communicate across blogs by publishing content relating to other blogs. Nakajima *et al.* [5] proposed a method to identify the important bloggers in the conversations based on their roles in preceding blog threads, and identify "hot" conversation. The second type of research focuses on analyzing blog content. Gruhl *et al.* [6, 7] modeled the information praopgation of topics among blogs based on blog text. In addition, blog text analysis focuses on eliciting useful information from blog entry collections, and determining certain trends in the blogosphere [8]. Mei *et al.* [9] proposed a probabilistic method for modeling the most salient themes from a text collection, and discovering the distributions and evolution patterns over time and space. With analysis of tracking topic and user drift, Hayes *et al.* [1] examine the relationship between blogs over time without considering the popularity degree of topics within blogs. The last type is about user modeling in blog space. A variety of methods has been proposed to model the blogger's interest, such as classifying articles into predefined categories to identify the author's preference [10].

The preceding studies, whether focused on the analyses of hyperlinks or blog texts, were all observed from the viewpoints of bloggers. They examined the interests of bloggers and discussed which topics were widely discussed by the bloggers. The majority of previous studies ignore the roles played by the reader mass, who take browsing actions on the blog articles. Blog readers are often interested in browsing emerging and popular blog topics, from which the popularity of blogs can be inferred according to the accumulated click times on blogs. Popularity based solely on click times, however, cannot truly reflect the trend of popularity. For example, a new event may trigger emerging discussions such that the number of related blog articles and browsing actions is small at the beginning and rapidly increases as time goes on. Thus, it is important to analyze the trend of time-sensitive popularity of blogs to predict the emerging blog topics. In addition, blog readers may have different interests in the emerging popular blog topics. Nevertheless, very few researches have addressed such issues.

In this work, we propose a Customized Content Service on a mobile device (m-CCS) to recommend blog articles to mobile users. The m-CCS can predict the trend of time-sensitive popularity of blogs. First, we analyze blog contents retrieved by co-RSS to derive topic clusters, i.e., blog topics. We define a topic as a set of significant terms that are clustered together based on similarity. By examining the clusters, we can extract the features of topics from the viewpoints of the authors. Moreover, we analyze the click times the readers give to articles. For each topic cluster, from the variation in trends of click times we can predict the popularity degree of the topics from the readers' perspectives.

Second, mobile users may have different interests in the latest popular blog topics. Thus, the m-CCS further analyzes mobile users' browsing logs to derive their interests, which are then used to infer their preferred popular blog topics and articles. We scrutinize the browsing behaviors and dissect the interests of the mobile users, then modify the ranking of topic clusters according to their preferences. The filtered articles are then sent to the individual's mobile device immediately via a WAP Push service. This allows the user to receive personalized and relevant articles and satisfies the demand for instant information. The prototype system of m-CCS demonstrates that the system can effectively recommend desirable blog articles to mobile users that satisfy popularity and personal interests.

## 2   System Process Overview

Because of their dramatic growth during recent years, blogs have become a dominant medium on the Internet. In order to provide blog contents to mobile users immediately, we propose a *Customized Content Service on mobile* (m-CCS) to combine two sources, time-sensitive popular topics and personal preference pattern. This is based on the idea of social navigation [11] , i.e., everyone is interested in realizing what others like. Some research [12] has considered that observing the behavior of other users could create value for individuals, and it has already been applied extensively to large-scale websites.

In Fig. 1, the first step of our system is to get some blog articles from the Internet. The RSS mechanism is a useful way to capture the latest articles automatically without visiting each site. There is a shortage of information caused by insufficient RSS feeds subscribed to individuals, so we propose *co-RSS* method to solve this problem. The *co-RSS* process is similar to the concept of Web 2.0; anyone on the Internet can subscribe to RSS feeds. By gathering all feeds from users, RSS flocks called *crows-RSS* are formed to enrich information sources. After this preliminary procedure, the system can automatically collect attractive contents from diverse resources.

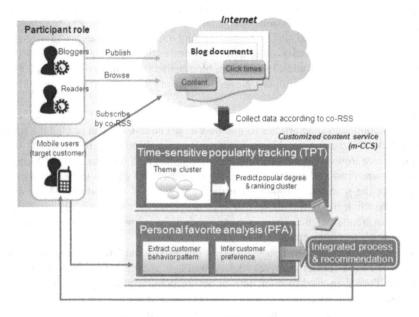

**Fig. 1.** System overview for m-CCS

We use the information retrieval technology [13] to pre-process articles which are crawled everyday from blog websites according to *crows-RSS* feeds. After extracting features of blog articles by the process of *time-sensitive popularity tracking* (TPT), m-CCS groups articles into topic clusters and automatically traces the trend of popularity. Then, m-CCS can rapidly respond to the topics that most readers may be interested in.

Since the viewable content on mobile phone screens is limited, it is particularly desirable to design a personalized service for filtering articles. The m-CCS can instantly monitor daily service transfer rates and log user viewing records to infer implicit preference of mobile users. The browsing records of users are analyzed to find behavior patterns and then the personal preferences are deducted through *personal favorite analysis* (PFA).

Finally, the system pushes the blog articles to the mobile users by integrating the above message sources, including the popular topics from the discussions of all blog articles, and the preference of readers. The m-CCS sorts out the most popular topics of the day and filters related articles based on users' implicit preference. The filtered articles are then sent to the user's mobile device via a WAP Push service. This allows users to receive personalized and relevant blog articles in real time.

## 3   Time-Sensitive Popularity Tracking Module

We identify the blog topic clusters and their popularity according to the viewpoints of writers and readers, and then trace the trend of popularity with time. Therefore, we can forecast the popularity degree for each topic cluster. In the following subsections, we will illustrate the details of the tracking process in Fig.2.

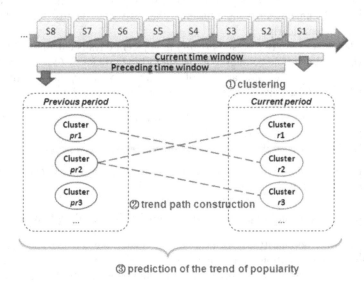

**Fig. 2.** Time-sensitive popularity tracking process

### 3.1 Forming Topic Clusters of Blog Articles

Articles in blogs are free and usually contain different opinions so that it is difficult to categorize articles into their appropriate categories which are defined by bloggers. That is to say, the existing category in a blog website is insufficient to represent the blog. In our research, we use article features derived from the pre-processing process to deal with blog articles which are published within a given time window on the Internet. The size of the time window is set as seven days. That is, all the articles posted in the past seven days will be categorized and recommended to individual users.

A hierarchical agglomerative algorithm with group-average clustering approach [14] is applied to implement the clustering step. It treats each article as a cluster first and then successively merges pairs of clusters. During the process, we calculate each cluster quality to decide whether we should stop merging or not. In this process, similarities between two articles can be calculated by means of the cosine similarity measure, as shown in Eq.1.

$$Sim(d_m, d_n) = \cos(\vec{d}_m, \vec{d}_n) = \frac{\vec{d}_m \bullet \vec{d}_n}{\|\vec{d}_m\| \cdot \|\vec{d}_n\|} \tag{1}$$

### 3.2 Constructing the Trend Path between Clusters Belonging to Adjacent Days

To reveal the path of the trend which predicts the popularity degree of current clusters, we measure the similarity between the target cluster $r$ and all the clusters $pr$ belonging to the preceding period, and then select the one with max values to construct the link with one of the preceding clusters.

As blog articles are usually composed of unstructured words, to obtain similarity between two clusters which belong to two days, we average the value of cosine similarity between documents crossing clusters. Then we can identify the differences between two clusters clearly.

The similarity between two clusters $(r, pr)$ in adjacent days is calculated by Eq. 2., where $d_i$ / $d_j$ is a blog article belonging to the set of blog articles $S_r$ / $S_{pr}$ in cluster $r$/$pr$; | $S_r$ |/| $S_{pr}$ | is the number of blog articles of $S_r$/ $S_{pr}$ and $Sim(d_i, d_j)$ denotes the cosine similarity between the articles $d_i$ and $d_j$, as mentioned in section 3.1.

$$similarity(r, pr) = \frac{\sum\limits_{d_i \in S_r} \sum\limits_{d_j \in S_{pr}} Sim(d_i, d_j)}{|S_r| \|S_{pr}|} \tag{2}$$

After the establishment of linkages, the trend of each current cluster can be derived from the preceding related cluster.

### 3.3 Acquisition of Actual Popularity Degree for Each Preceding Cluster

To help predict the popularity degree of a current cluster, we consider the click times in proportion to the attention from readers who make a topic rising and flourishing. After clustering blog articles to form topic group and constructing the trend path, the actual popularity degree for each preceding cluster can be acquired from the times the articles have been clicked in previous period. For each preceding cluster $pr$, we obtain the total click times of the articles, $CT_t(S_{pr})$, on the Internet within preceding time period, as defined in Eq.3.

$$CT_t\left(S_{pr}\right) = \sum_{d_i \in S_{pr}} ClickTimes_t\left(d_i\right) \tag{3}$$

where, $S_{pr}$ denotes the set of blog articles $d_i$ in cluster $pr$, and the actual click times for blog article $d_i$ in time $t$ can be represented by $ClickTimes_t(d_i)$. Then, the click times can be transferred to actual popularity degree, $APD_{pr}(t)$, which is a normalized value based on the maximum $ClickTimes$ over all $S_i$ in the preceding period, as follows.

$$APD_{pr}\left(t\right) = \frac{CT_t\left(S_r\right)}{Max\left\{ClickTimes_t\left(S_i\right)\right\}} \times 100\% \tag{4}$$

### 3.4  Predicting Popularity Degree of Current Cluster

The time series is a set of serial observation values by time order as in Fig 3. Forecasting mainly uses the history to respond to the development trend in the future. A standard exponential smoothing method [15] assigns exponentially decreasing weights to the previous observations. In other words, recent observations are given relatively more weight in forecasting than the older observations. Unlike traditional predictive models, it can estimate time series with a small amount of data. We modified the *double exponential smoothing* method [16] to forecast the degree of popular trend for each cluster of blog topic.

Here are the two equations associated with *double exponential smoothing*. For each cluster $r$, we use the weighted average method that combines the *actual popularity degree* (APD) and *predicted popularity degree* (PPD) of preceding period to predict the popularity degree of current cluster on the assumption that the effect of popularity degree decays as days pass, as defined in Eq.5..

$$PPD_r'\left(t+1\right) = \alpha \times APD_{pr}\left(t\right) + \left(1-\alpha\right) \times \left[PPD_{pr}\left(t\right) + b_{pr}\left(t\right)\right] \tag{5}$$

where we use cluster $pr$ at preceding time $t$ to predict the initial popularity degree of cluster $r$ at time $t+1$ which is denoted by $PPD_r'\left(t+1\right)$. For preceding cluster $pr$ at time $t$, $APD_{pr}(t)$ is the actual popularity degree as mentioned above; $PPD_{pr}(t)$ denotes the predictive popularity degree of cluster $pr$ at time $t$. The $b_{pr}(t)$ represents the trend effect for previous period. Note that the value of initial predictive popularity degree for current cluster, $PPD_r'\left(t+1\right)$, is between zero to one.

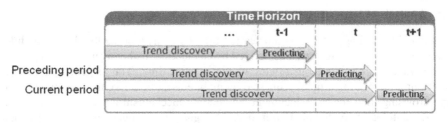

**Fig. 3.** The time series of popularity trend

We combine the difference of the predictive popularity degrees at time $t$ and at time $t$-$1$ and the trend effect at time $t$-$1$ to calculate the trend effect at time $t$ using the weighted average.

$$b_{pr}(t) = \delta \times \left[ PPD_{pr}(t) - PPD_{ppr}(t-1) \right] + (1-\delta) \times b_{ppr}(t-1) \tag{6}$$

Note that the cluster $pr$ is the preceding cluster of $r$, while the cluster $ppr$ is the preceding cluster of $pr$. The $PPD_{ppr}(t\text{-}1)$ and $b_{ppr}(t\text{-}1)$ are the predictive popularity degree and trend effect of cluster $ppr$ at time $t$-$1$ respectively. The parameters $\alpha$ and $\delta$ in Eq.5 and Eq.6 respectively are both smoothing constants between zero to one which can be decided by experts.

In the prediction model, we adopt a double exponential smoothing approach to predict the topic popularity. The double exponential smoothing approach is usually applied to analyze time series data; however, it does not consider the relation between topic clusters belonging to adjacent time periods. In our research, we concentrate on topic clusters in different time periods and construct the topic linkage from the preceding time to the current as a topic trend path with a popularity degree. Therefore, to make a link between topic clusters, the maximal similarity between adjacent clusters, i.e., current cluster $r$ and preceding cluster $pr$, as described in Section 3.2, is selected to adjust the predictive popularity degree of cluster $r$. Notably, the smaller similarity leads to the lower reliability of the prediction path between two clusters.

$$PPD_r(t+1) = PPD'_r(t+1) \times similarity(r, pr) \tag{7}$$

# 4   Personal Favorite Analysis Module

Modeling user preference is useful for many personalized services, such as recommender system [17]. In this paper, we propose a novel scheme to model the interests of users who browse blog articles in mobile device.

In our research, we extract a set of keywords to represent blog articles; then a cluster of documents which contain keyword sets is regarded as a topic. In addition, a blog article is regarded as a preference unit.

Because of the limited features of mobile devices, it is inconvenient to give explicit relevance ratings of blog documents for mobile users. We analyze browsing behavior to get individuals' favorites and thus do not require any extra user effort. First, we analyze the browsing pattern of each user to calculate user preference scores for blog articles which have been read by mobile users.

## 4.1   Analysis of User Browsing Behavior

We model browsing patterns within session time by analyzing the log data of mobile users. A user's browsing pattern is derived by calculating his/her average reading time per word for browsing blog articles within session time. The system records the browsing time of blog articles requested by mobile users to derive the session interval and browsing time for each document. A timeout mechanism is used to terminate a session automatically when a user does not give any request in a time period.

Calculating the time interval between user requests within each session could estimate the user's stick time of the article.

In order to acquire the browsing pattern for the user $u$, we analyze the browsing speed, $H_{u,s}$, to get the average reading time per word in this session $s$, as shown in Eq.8.

$$H_{u,s} = \frac{1}{|D_{u,s}|} \times \sum_{d_i \in D_{u,s}} \frac{Time_u(d_i)}{DocSize(d_i)} \qquad (8)$$

where $d_i$ is a article $i$ that the user had browsed within session $s$; $D_{u,s}$ is a set of artcles browsed by user $u$ in session $s$; and $|D_{u,s}|$ denotes the number of articles in $D_{u,s}$. DocSize($d_i$) identifies the size number of words of the article; $Time_u(d_i)$ denotes the browsing time for the user $u$ in blog article $d_i$.

After obtaining a user's current browsing behavior, $H_{u,s}$, which is viewed as the user's recent pattern within one session, we use a weighted approach to predict a user's future browsing pattern by an incremental approach, which incrementally modifies the former browsing pattern using the user's current browsing behavior. The parameters $\beta$ can be adjusted in order to set one as more important than the other. We believe that recent browsing behavior has greater effect upon the future behavior of the mobile user, so we set the parameter $\beta$ to give recent pattern more weight.

The predicted browsing pattern is calculated by using Eq.9, where $H'_{u,s}$ denotes former browsing pattern which has been accumulated till session $s$ for mobile user $u$. Then we can use the new browsing pattern at session $s$, i.e., $H_{u,s}$, to predict the future behavior at new session $s+1$.

$$H'_{u,s+1} = \beta \times H_{u,s} + (1-\beta) \times H'_{u,s} \qquad (9)$$

## 4.2 Inferring User Preference for Articles

In this step, we infer user preferences for articles based on their browsing behavior that is considered as implicit feedback information. By analyzing a user reading time on a article, we can infer how much the user has interested in the article and its corresponding preference score. If the stick time is longer than usual, we can estimate that the user has high preference level of the article. That is, the user is addicted to the article and is willing to spend more time on it.

According to the user's reading behavior in usual time, we use the user's browsing pattern mentioned in section 4.1 to estimate the browsing time for article and calculate the *Predict Browsing Time*, $PBT_u(d_i)$, to compare with *Actual Browsing Time*, $ABT_u(d_i)$, of the user. The predict browsing time $PBT_u(d_i)$ is denoted by $PBT_u(d_i) = DocSize(d_i) \times H'_{u,s+1}$, where $DocSize(d_i)$ is the size of blog document $d_i$; $H'_{u,s+1}$ means the browsing pattern for user $u$ as mentioned in Section 4.1. Then, we calculate the *preference score* (PS) for target user $u$ on blog article $d_i$ as following,

$$PS_u(d_i) = \frac{1}{1 + \frac{PBT_u(d_i)}{ABT_u(d_i)}} \qquad (10)$$

We can observe that the value of this function is in the range (0, 1), and the higher value of preference score means that user has more interest in the article.

## 5  Integrated Process and Recommendation Module

In the process of *time-sensitive popularity tracking* (TPT), we apply *modified exponential smoothing* method to provide equal ranking score of topic cluster for every mobile user. Next, we consider each user's preference in a *personal favorite analysis* (PFA) step to modify the order of topic cluster and derive the personal ranking cluster.

The different topic clusters belonging to successive days may be covered by the same articles. Once a mobile user has read one article, his/her preference score is inferred from browsing behavior and can be applied to modify the ranking score of the topic cluster in which the article is included. Therefore, cluster ranking can be modified using a user's preference scores for a certain article belonging to this cluster. We calculate the *Customized predictive popularity degree* (CPPD) as follows:

$$CPPD_{u,r} = \omega \times PPD_r + (1-\omega) \times \frac{\sum_{d_r \in D_{u,r}} PS_u(d_r)}{|D_{u,r}|} \tag{11}$$

In the formula above, we use the average *preference score* (PS) of user $u$ for those documents that have been read and contained in the target cluster $r$ to modify the *predictive popularity degree*, $PPD_r$. $D_{u,r}$ denotes the set of documents which user $u$ has browsed in cluster $r$. We adjust the value of $\omega$ to weight $PPD_r$ and the average *preference score*.

As regards those mobile users who have expressed their own preferences significantly in our system, the ranking of theme clusters provided by m-CCS would be more customized. On the other hand, if a user has very few behavior records to be analyzed, the degree of modification of topic clusters is smaller. That is, the less the browsing history of users, the less the personal ranking of clusters. The system will first recommend the more general and popular theme clusters.

**Fig. 4.** m-CCS interface to display recommended contents on mobile device

Finally, the article with high attention degree will be recommended to mobile users from the personalized ranking of theme clusters. Attention degree shows the click counter of the article on the Internet, and it also presents that readers have highly trust on the article.

After the processing above, the picked articles are transformed into XHTML for mobiles and then pushed to handsets via WAP. Because the resolution of handsets allows only scroll browsing and user time is short compared with that of PC users, the system will only push the titles of no more than ten articles (see Fig.4 ). Then users can click the title in which they are interested to view full contents.

## 6   System Architecture

We are implementing a prototype m-CCS system of the proposed mobile service based on the CHT mobile customer database stored in the MySQL database; it is developed using the Python programming language. The operating web GUI uses a Django Web Framework (see Fig.5).

This research is conducted in collaboration with CAMEO InfoTech Inc., provider of the WAP Push service for mobile phones. Currently, there are 200 000 users of Chunghwa Telecom (CHT), the biggest telecom company in Taiwan, with more than 4000 users officially subscribing to the service and paying a regular fee. Taking advantage of m-CCS, we look forward to improving customers' satisfaction by providing customized blog contents.

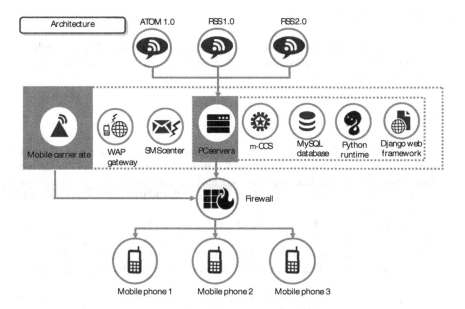

**Fig. 5.** The system architecture of m-CCS

# 7  Conclusion and Future Work

Our study suggests a new value-added service for mobile phone applications. Dispatches of customized blog contents not only enable mobile phone users to enjoy reading blog articles without time and venue limitations but also provide a proactive channel to deliver the blog articles instead of passive browses from the users.

Owing to their dramatic growth in recent years, blogs have become a dominant medium on the Internet. Although RSS feed is a common solution to receive the latest contents automatically, there are still some problems, including lack of subscriptions and overloaded information. For that reason, filtering the articles so they are suitable for each user is an important issue. In the past, studies about blogs centered on bloggers (the authors) but ignored the views of mass readers. Our study applies the co-RSS method based on the notion under Web 2.0. Our proposed m-CCS can predict the trend of time-sensitive popularity of blogs. The m-CCS is grounded on the topic clusters of the blog articles which represent the perspectives of the authors. The m-CSS also considers the aspects of the readers' click rates to trace the popularity trends of the theme clusters from the affluent blog contents. Moreover, as regards mobile phone users, the m-CCS will analyze their browsing behaviors and personal preferences to recommend their preferred popular blog topics and articles.

Our future work is to show that, with sufficiently large samples and by executing the methods proposed in this research, we can effectively increase the population of people who use their mobile phones to read blog articles, and also increase the number of blog entry views.

## Acknowledgement

This work was done in cooperation with CAMEO InfoTech Inc. The research was supported in part by the National Science Council of Taiwan under the grant NSC 96-2416-H-009-007-MY3.

## References

1. Hayes, C., Avesani, P., Veeramachaneni, S.: An analysis of bloggers and topics for a blog recommender system. In: Proceedings of the Workshop on Web Mining, 7th European Conference on Machine Learning and the 10th European Conference on Principles and Practice of Knowledge Discovery in Databases (ECML/PKDD), Berlin, Germany, vol. 7, pp. 18–22 (2006)
2. Lasica, J.D.: Weblogs: A new source of information. In: Rodzvilla, J. (ed.) We've got blog: How weblogs are changing our culture. Perseus Publishing, Cambridge (2002)
3. Kumar, R., Novak, J., Raghavan, P., Tomkins, A.: On the bursty evolution of blogspace. In: Proceedings of the 12th International Conference on World Wide Web, pp. 568–576 (2003)
4. Kumar, R., Novak, J., Raghavan, P., Tomkins, A.: Structure and evolution of blogspace. Communications of the ACM 47, 35–39 (2004)

5. Nakajima, S., Tatemura, J., Hino, Y., Hara, Y., Tanaka, K.: Discovering important bloggers based on analyzing blog threads. In: Proceedings of the WWW 2005 workshop on the weblogging ecosystem: aggregation, analysis and dynamics (2005)
6. Gruhl, D., Guha, R., Liben-Nowell, D., Tomkins, A.: Information diffusion through blogspace. In: Proceedings of the 13th International Conference on World Wide Web, pp. 491–501. ACM Press, New York (2004)
7. Gruhl, D., Guha, R., Kumar, R., Novak, J., Tomkins, A.: The predictive power of online chatter. In: Proceedings of the eleventh ACM SIGKDD international conference on Knowledge discovery in data mining, pp. 78–87. ACM Press, New York (2005)
8. Glance, N., Hurst, M., Tomokiyo, T.: BlogPulse: Automated trend discovery for weblogs. In: WWW 2004 Workshop on the Weblogging Ecosystem: Aggregation, Analysis and Dynamics (2004)
9. Mei, Q., Liu, C., Su, H., Zhai, C.X.: A probabilistic approach to spatiotemporal theme pattern mining on weblogs. In: Proceedings of the 15th international conference on World Wide Web, pp. 533–542. ACM, Edinburgh (2006)
10. Liu, K., Chen, W., Bu, J., Chen, C., Zhang, L.: User Modeling for Recommendation in Blogspace. In: IEEE/WIC/ACM International Conferences on Web Intelligence and Intelligent Agent Technology Workshops, pp. 79–82 (2007)
11. Dieberger, A.: Supporting social navigation on the World Wide Web. International Journal of Human-Computers Studies 46, 805–825 (1997)
12. Rosenfeld, L., Morville, P.: Information architecture for the world wide web. O'Reilly & Associates, Inc., Sebastopol (2007)
13. Salton, G., McGill, M.J.: Introduction to modern information retrieval. McGraw-Hill, Inc., New York (1983)
14. Jain, A.K., Murty, M.N., Flynn, P.J.: Data clustering: a review. ACM computing surveys 31, 264–323 (1999)
15. Montgomery, D.C., Johnson, L.A., Gardiner, J.S.: Forecasting and time series analysis. McGraw-Hill, New York (1990)
16. Bowerman, B.L., Richard, T.O.C.: Forecasting and time series: an applied approach. Duxbury Press (1993)
17. Paul, R., Hal, R.V.: Recommender systems. Commun. ACM 40, 56–58 (1997)

# Bargaining Agents in Wireless Contexts: An Alternating-Offers Protocol for Multi-issue Bilateral Negotiation in Mobile Marketplaces

Azzurra Ragone[1,2,3], Michele Ruta[1], Eugenio Di Sciascio[1], and Francesco M. Donini[2]

[1] SisInfLab, Politecnico di Bari, Bari, Italy
{a.ragone,m.ruta,disciascio}@poliba.it
[2] Università della Tuscia , Viterbo, Italy
donini@unitus.it
[3] Università di Trento , Trento, Italy

**Abstract.** We present an approach to multi-issue bilateral negotiation for mobile commerce scenarios. The negotiation mechanism has been integrated in a semantic-based application layer enhancing both RFID and Bluetooth wireless standards. OWL DL has been used to model advertisements and relationships among issues within a shared common ontology. Finally, non standard inference services integrated with utility theory help in finding suitable agreements. We illustrate and motivate the provided theoretical framework in a wireless commerce case study.

## 1  Introduction and Motivation

Automated negotiation mechanisms call for adopting logical languages to model advertisements allowing to perform inferences wherever is the need to go beyond plain undifferentiated goods and not only a single issue (usually price) is amenable to negotiation. OWL DL is a natural candidate for this purpose: it is one of the reference formalisms for the Semantic Web effort, with a formal logic-based semantics, much more expressive than *e.g.*, Propositional Logic, yet decidable. Indeed the formal semantics of OWL DL is based on Description Logics (DL) one. Hence, it can be useful in a number of negotiation scenarios. In this paper we present a OWL DL-based approach to multi-issue bilateral negotiation in a mobile context. Wireless agents exploit a logic-based alternating-offers protocol integrated in a mobile resource discovery layer for pervasive environments. Basically, we adapt languages and technologies from the Semantic Web vision to pervasive environments. In great detail, we propose an extension of both EPCglobal RFID standard [6] and Bluetooth Service Discovery Protocol [3] supporting formalisms for knowledge representation and enabling advanced negotiation services. Semantic-based annotations are stored on RFID tags attached to products and goods which can describe themselves to a reader gateway. It acts as front end in a possible Bluetooth-based interaction with the user PDA. Noteworthy is the feature to preserve the original code-based discovery of both Bluetooth and RFID technologies, thus keeping a legacy compatibility with basic applications. Furthermore, according to W3C recommendations for mobile applications, our approach copes with limited storage and

T. Di Noia and F. Buccafurri (Eds.): EC-Web 2009, LNCS 5692, pp. 14–25, 2009.

computational capabilities of mobile and embedded devices, and with reduced bandwidth provided by wireless links. Issues related to the verbosity of semantic annotation languages cannot be neglected. Hence, in order to make our approach sustainable in reality, we exploited a novel efficient XML compression algorithm, specifically targeted for DIG 1.1 [2] document instances. Machine understandable ontological languages are exploited to perform non-standard reasoning services integrating utility theory to find the most suitable agreements. To this aim existing relationships among issues in requests and offers and related preferences of agents (both expressed by means of logical formulas) have to be taken into account. The proposed framework has been devised for intelligent recommendation purposes in furnishings stores. Using a PDA s/he can interrogate the store software application and be able to assemble components, select colors, materials, type of shelves or drawers, complements like hangers, rails, baskets and different type of organizers. Each component is endowed with an RFID tag hosting the semantic annotation of the component itself. Hence, the customer can select his preferred configuration and so instruct his wireless software agent to negotiate with other mobile-agents running on the seller side. Each agent will encourage a specific configuration the retailer prefers to sell[1]. Main contributions of the paper are:

– *The exploitation of a logic-based approach in the negotiation process.* The availability of an ontology modeling the reference domain knowledge allows to annotate relationships among components, so ruling out components not compatible with each other. In the same way, it allows to discover similar components replacing missing ones. Moreover, inference services can be used in order to reveal conflicting information between a request and an offer ("a wardrobe with *sliding doors* w.r.t. another one with *hinged doors*"). Finally, a semantic-based approach allows the system to provide a *result explanation* of the negotiation process: for each configuration the system will show what the user has to give up w.r.t. his initial request and what is still in the configuration.
– *The exploitation of mobile technologies in supporting the semantic-based interaction between negotiating agents.* By attaching an RFID tag on each product, the retailer agent will be able to negotiate only on available goods and, on the other hand, the user agent can interact with it "from everywhere". That is, the negotiation process will happen taking into account objects actually available in a virtual shelf (if a piece has been picked-up by a customer which is still in the store it will be labeled as not available for the negotiation process). This "real time" availability is therefore taken into account in determining a set of preferred configurations the seller wants to offer.
– *An agreement smart suggestion.* The negotiation process could find an agreement (the proposed configuration) beneficial for both the retailer and the buyer, by taking into account utilities of both participants (this is a bilateral matchmaking process rather than an unilateral one, as requirements and preferences from both buyer and retailer are considered).
– *A support for non-expert users.* A user-friendly graphical interface hides any technical underlying detail (*e.g.*, logic expressions). Users equipped with their PDAs only have to drag and drop components on a canvas and set utilities (if they want) for them. Then, after the interaction with the system, they will just scroll the negotiation results.

---

[1] We assume the retailer aims at selling *e.g.*, configurations on special, like offers of the week.

HingedDoors ⊑ Shape; Oak ⊑ Wood; SlidingDoors ⊑ Shape; Birch ⊑ Wood;

HingedDoors ⊑ ¬SlidingDoors; Oak ⊑ ¬Birch; Basic_clothes_rail ⊑ Hangers;

WireBasket ⊑ Drawer; ShoeBox ⊑ Box;

ClosedWardrobe ≡ Wardrobe ⊓ ∃material ⊓ ∃basicShape ⊓ ∃shutters;

Walk_in_closet ≡ Wardrobe ⊓ ¬∃shutters;

TidyShoeBox ≡ ShoeBox ⊓ ∃material ⊓ ∀material.Plastic;

Add_on_clothes_rail ⊑ Basic_clothes_rail ⊓ ∃complement ⊓ ∀complement.(Tie_rack ⊓ Trouser_hanger)

**Fig. 1.** The ontology used in the examples

Returned configurations are ranked w.r.t. utility functions, but the user keeps the final decision; he can either choose one of the proposed configurations or simply drop out and/or start a new negotiation changing preferences.

The rest of the paper is organized as follows: next Section focuses on the adopted logical formalisms, Section 3 presents and motivates the negotiation protocol we devised and exploited and Section 4 outlines the reference communication architecture. Finally, Section 5 clarifies our settings with the aid of a toy example and conclusion closes the paper.

## 2 Semantic Annotations

In this section we briefly illustrate the semantic annotations of resources in our application. We use to annotate resources a fragment of OWL-DL, where besides owl:Class and owl:ObjectProperty, one is able to express owl:DataTypeProperty $f$ (for **F**eatures) on objects such as height, width, length and many others by means of *concrete domains*. In this paper we refer to $\mathcal{AL}(D)$ [1] subset of OWL DL. Hereafter we will use DL syntax which results more compact than OWL one. In order to model the domain knowledge and represent relationships among elements, we use an ontology $\mathcal{O}$ containing Concept Inclusion axioms of the form $A \sqsubseteq C$ and $A \equiv C$, where the concept name $A$ can appear only once on the left-had side of axioms. We restrict $\mathcal{O}$ to be acyclic, *i.e.*, the definition of $A$ should not depend on $A$ itself (see [1] for a precise definition). Using $\mathcal{AL}(D)$ it is possible to express subclass relations and disjointness relations involving concept names, *e.g.*, Birch ⊑ Wood and HingedDoors ⊑ ¬SlidingDoors. Formulas representing demands $D$ and configurations $S$, are expressed as generic OWL-DL expressions. So, an example description can be the following one:

Wardrobe⊓∀basicShape.SlidingDoors⊓∀material.Birch⊓ = 4drawers⊓ =$_{200}$ height

formally modeling this configuration: "*a wardrobe made from birch wood with sliding doors, four drawers and 200 meters high*". Notice that for what concerns numerical properties, also range expressions are allowed in the form $(f \geq n) \sqcap (f \leq m)$. In order to better explain the approach, in the rest of the paper we will refer to ontology $\mathcal{O}$ in Figure 1, where some attributes proper of a wardrobe are listed and related to each other through the ontology itself. Even though subsumption and satisfiability are basic and useful reasoning tasks in a number of applications, there are typical problems related to negotiation that call for non-standard reasoning services. For instance, suppose you have the buyer's agent $\beta$ with her **Demand** represented by the concept $D$ and the seller's agent $\sigma$ with his **Supply** represented by $S$. In case $\beta$'s request $D$ and $\sigma$'s offer $S$ are in conflict with each other with respect to the domain knowledge modeled in the ontology $\mathcal{O}$— in formulae $S \sqcap D \sqsubseteq_{\mathcal{O}} \bot$ — how to suggest to $\beta$ which parts in $D$ are in conflict with $S$ and conversely to $\sigma$ which parts in $S$ are conflict with $D$? The above question is very significant in negotiation scenarios where you need to know "what is wrong" between $D$ and $S$ and negotiate on it. In order to give an answer to the previous question and provide explanations, Concept Contraction [14] can be exploited.

**Concept Contraction** . Given two concepts $C_1$ and $C_2$ and an ontology $\mathcal{O}$, where $C_1 \sqcap C_2 \sqsubseteq_{\mathcal{O}} \bot$ holds, find two concepts $K$ (for Keep) and $G$ (for Give up) such that both $C_1 \equiv K \sqcap G$ and $K \sqcap C_2 \not\sqsubseteq_{\mathcal{O}} \bot$.

In other words $K$ represents a contraction of $C_1$ which is satisfiable with $C_2$, whilst $G$ represents some reasons why $C_1$ and $C_2$ are not compatible with each other. With Concept Contraction, both *conflicting information* in $\beta$'s request w.r.t. $\sigma$'supply can be computed and vice versa. Actually, for Concept Contraction minimality criteria have to be introduced. Following the Principle of Informational Economy [15], for $G$ we have to give up as little information as possible. In [14] some minimality criteria were introduced and analyzed. In particular, if the adopted DL admits a normal form with conjunctions of concepts as $\mathcal{AL}(D)$, $G_\exists$ *minimal* irreducible solutions can be defined [8].

## 3   The Negotiation Mechanism

Here, we outline the negotiation mechanism, taking into account the semantics of $D$ and $S$ as well as the domain knowledge modeled within an ontology in the OWL DL fragment we identified in Section 2, exploiting Concept Contraction. We start describing: the *negotiation protocol*, *i.e.*, the set of rules specifing how an agreement can be reached; the *negotiation strategy*, that specifies the actions to take by agents given the protocol [9]; the *utility function* of the agents, used to evaluate negotiation outcomes [7]. We note that the mechanism is a **one-to-many** negotiation, since the buyer's agent will negotiate simultaneously with other $m$ different agents – each one linked with a particular configuration the retail prefers to sell. Moreover, it is a negotiation with **incomplete information** as each agent knows its utility function and ignores the opponent disagreement thresholds and utility functions. Finally, as agents are **rationale** they will never accept an agreement if the agent's utility over such an agreement is smaller than disagreement thresholds[2] set by the agent before negotiation starts. The protocol is inspired to Rubinstein's alternating-offers one [10]. Our protocol, anyway, is different from that of Rubinstein; actually we consider *multi-issue negotiation*: negotiation is not on a single item (or on a single bundle of), but on many issues related with each other

---

[2] Disagreement thresholds, also called disagreement payoffs, or reservation values, are the minimum utility that each agent requires to pursue a deal [9].

through an ontology. The protocol has a finite set of steps[3]: the negotiation terminates either because the agreement has been reached or because one agent opts out. The agent who moves first is selected randomly, at each step the agent who moves has two choices: *concede* or *opt out*, while the other one *stands still*. Agents are forced to concede until a *logical compatibility* is reached between the initial request and the supply, *i.e.*, until the inconsistency sources are eliminated. At each step, amongst all the concessions allowed by the protocol, the agent choose the *minimal concession, i.e., minimal* w.r.t. the utility loss paid by the agent who makes the concession [5]. The negotiation ends either if a logical compatibility is reached or if one agent opts out (*conflict deal*). For what concerns **strategy**, if it is its turn to move, an agent can choose to **opt out** if its utility at that step is smaller than its disagreement threshold, then the negotiation ends immediately. Otherwise, it **concedes**: the concession is the *minimum possible concession*, that is the concession less decreasing its utility. Here, our main focus is not on how to compute utility functions, however we give a hint on that topic. We define an agent's **utility function** over all possible outcomes [7] as: $u^p : \mathcal{A} \cup \{Opt\} \to \Re$ where $p \in \{\beta, \sigma\}$ —$\beta$ and $\sigma$ stand for buyer and seller respectively— $\mathcal{A}$ is the set of all possible agreements, $Opt$ stands for Opt out. For what concern the buyer, she can set utilities while choosing components through the GUI, however, we point out that she *does not have to, i.e.*, she can only set utilities for components she deems very important[4]. For the retailer, instead, the utility of each agent is computed based on several parameters, that can be changed, updated, deleted over time by the retailer itself. A utility value will be coupled with each configuration and will be computed as a weighted function of *e.g.*, the real-time availability of each piece and its cost, so taking into account unsold stocks.

### 3.1 Logic-Based Alternating-Offers Protocol

For the sake of clarity, from now on we indicate the buyer's agent with $\beta$ and her potential partners (retail's agents) with $\sigma$. The first step of the protocol is the normalization of both $\beta$'s demand $D$ and $\sigma$'s configuration $S$. The normalization step substitutes $A$ with $A \sqcap C$ everywhere in a concept, if either $A \sqsubseteq C$ or $A \equiv C$ appears in $\mathcal{O}$, then considers the equivalence $\forall R.(A \sqcap B) \equiv \forall R.A \sqcap \forall R.B$ as a recursive rewrite rule from left to right. After the normalization stage, $D$ is a conjunction of elements in the form: $D = \bigsqcap_i C_i$, where $C_i$ represents issues the user is willing to negotiate on. Users can express utilities on single issues or on bundles of them. For instance, w.r.t. the previous request the buyer may set utility values on $\forall$basicShape.SlidingDoors (single issue) as well as on the whole formula $\forall$basicShape.SlidingDoors$\sqcap\exists$material$\sqcap$ $\forall$material.Birch (bundle of issue). We indicate these concepts with $P_k$ — for Preferences. To each $P_k$ will be attached a utility value $u^\beta(P_k) \geq 0$. The global utility is a suitable sum of the utilities for preferences entailed by the final agreement[5]. In

---

[3] In the following, for the sake of simplicity, we always describe an interaction between only two opposite agents; although we notice that multiple negotiations can be performed at the same time, among *one* agent and *many* candidate partners.

[4] The system will therefore work also for lazy users, unwilling to set a large number of utilities.

[5] Both agents' utilities are normalized to 1 to eliminate outliers, and make them comparable: $\sum_i u^\beta(P_k) = 1$.

particular, given a concept expression $A$ representing a final agreement, we define the final utility associated to the agent $p$, with $p \in \{\beta, \sigma\}$ as:

$$u^p(A) = \sum_k \{u^p(P_k) \mid A \sqsubseteq P_k\} \qquad u^p(Opt) = t_p \qquad (1)$$

where $t_p$ is the **disagreement threshold** of agent $p$. Summing up, before the real negotiation starts (step 0) we have a demand $D$ and a configuration $S$ such that: $D = \sqcap_i C_i$ and $S = \sqcap_j C_j$. Preferences $P_k$ (for the buyer) and $P_h$ (for the retailer) will be associated to concepts (or bundle of) $C_i$ and $C_j$. Finally, both for $\beta$ and $\sigma$ we have the corresponding **disagreement thresholds** and utility functions $t_\beta$, $u^\beta$ and $t_\sigma$, $u^\sigma$. If $D \sqcap S \sqsubseteq_{\mathcal{O}} \bot$ then demand and supply descriptions are in conflict with each other and $\beta$ and $\sigma$ need to negotiate on conflicting information if they want to reach an agreement. The negotiation will follow an alternating offers pattern: at each step, either $\beta$ or $\sigma$ gives up a portion of its conflicting information choosing the item with the minimum utility. Notice that both agents $\beta$ and $\sigma$ know $D$ and $S$, but they have no information neither on counterpart utilities nor preferences. Both $\beta$ and $\sigma$ will solve two Concept Contraction problems, computing a $G_\exists$ *minimal irreducible* solution, and rewrite $D$ and $S$ as:

$$D = G_0^\beta \sqcap K_0^\beta \qquad\qquad S = G_0^\sigma \sqcap K_0^\sigma$$

Where $G_0^\beta$ (respectively $G_0^\sigma$) represent the sources of conflict and the reason why $D$ ($S$) is in conflict with $S$ ($D$). Since we compute *G-irreducible* solutions we can normalize $G_0^\beta$ and $G_0^\sigma$, following the same procedure for $D$ and $S$, as:

$$G_0^\beta = G_{(0,1)}^\beta \sqcap G_{(0,2)}^\beta \sqcap \ldots \sqcap G_{(0,n)}^\beta = \prod_{i=1}^n G_{(0,i)}^\beta; \quad G_0^\sigma = G_{(0,1)}^\sigma \sqcap G_{(0,2)}^\sigma \sqcap \ldots \sqcap G_{(0,m)}^\sigma = \prod_{j=1}^m G_{(0,j)}^\sigma$$

In the previous formulas, indexes $(0, i)$ and $(0, j)$ represent the i-th and j-th conjunctive element in $G^\beta$ and $G^\sigma$ at round 0. Due to the structure of $D$, $S$ and $\mathcal{O}$ we have that: *for each* $G_{(0,i)}^\beta$ *there always exists a* $C_i$ *in the normalized version of $D$ such that* $G_{(0,i)}^\beta = C_i$. The same relation holds between each $G_{(0,j)}^\sigma$ and $C_j$ in the normalized form of $S$. Hence, some of $P_k$ and $P_h$ can be partially rewritten in terms of $G_{(0,i)}^\beta$ and $G_{(0,j)}^\sigma$ respectively. Since the information in $G_0^\beta$ and $G_0^\sigma$ are the reason why an agreement is not possible, then either $\beta$ or $\sigma$ will start conceding one of $G_{(0,i)}^\beta$ or $G_{(0,j)}^\sigma$ reducing their global utility of $u(G_{(0,i)}^\beta)$ or $u(G_{(0,j)}^\sigma)$, respectively. Suppose $\beta$ starts the negotiation and gives up $G_{(0,2)}^\beta = C_5$ with $P_3 \sqsubseteq_{\mathcal{O}} G_{(0,2)}^\beta$, that is, giving up $C_5$ preference $P_3$ will not be satisfied anymore. She reformulates her request as $D_1 = \sqcap_{i=1..4,6..} C_i$ and sends it to $\sigma$. Notice that since $P_3 \sqsubseteq_{\mathcal{O}} G_{(0,2)}^\beta$, the global utility of $\beta$ decreases to $u_1^\beta = \sum_{k=1..2,4..} u(P_k)$. Now, $\sigma$ is able to validate if $\beta$ really changed her request in round 0, to do so, $\sigma$ computes $\langle G_1^\beta, K_1^\beta \rangle$ solving a concept contraction problem w.r.t. the new demand $D_1$ and checks if $G_1^\beta$ is more general than $G_0^\beta$. In formulas, $\sigma$ checks if $G_0^\beta \sqsubseteq_{\mathcal{O}} G_1^\beta$ holds, in case of positive answer, then $\sigma$ knows that $\beta$ did not lie and he continues the negotiation. Otherwise he may decide to leave the negotiation (conflict deal) or ask $\beta$ to reformulate her counteroffer. If the negotiation continues, $\sigma$ computes his conflicting information w.r.t. to $D_1$ and rewrites $S$ as $S = G_1^\sigma \sqcap K_1^\sigma$ where $G_1^\sigma = \sqcap_{j=1}^m G_{(1,j)}^\sigma$. Again, for each $G_{(1,j)}$ there exists a $C_j$ in the normalized version of $S$. Hence, if $\sigma$ decides to concede $G_{(1,j)}$, his global utility decreases proportionally to the utility of $P_h$ to which $G_{(1,j)}$ belongs to. Once $\sigma$ sends his counteroffer to $\beta$, this latter is able to check if $\sigma$ lied. The process ends when one of the following two conditions holds:

**1.** the global utility of an agent is lower than its **disagreement threshold**. In this case the negotiation terminates with a conflict deal.

**2.** there is nothing more to negotiate on and the global utility of each agent is greater than its disagreement threshold. In this case the negotiation terminates with an agreement. **The agreement $A$ is computed** simply as $A = D_{last} \sqcap S_{last}$, where $D_{last}$ and $S_{last}$ are the request and the offer in the last round.

Since users can express a utility value also on bundles, whenever they concede an issue as the **minimum concession** (in term of minimum global utility decrease), the set of all the bundles in which the issue is present has to be taken into account. They choose based on the utility of the whole set. For instance, suppose the buyer sets the following preferences on a ClosedWardrobe: $P_1 = \forall$basicShape.SlidingDoors; $P_2 = \leq_{210}$ height; $P_3 = \forall$basicShape.SlidingDoors $\sqcap$ $\forall$shutters.Glass with the following utilities: $u^\beta(P_1) = 0.1$, $u^\beta(P_2) = 0.4$ and $u^\beta(P_3) = 0.5$. At the n-th step the conflicting information is:

$$G_n^\beta = \forall\text{basicShape.SlidingDoors} \sqcap \leq_{210}\text{ height}$$

Hence, $\beta$ can concede whether $\forall$basicShape.SlidingDoors or $\leq_{210}$ height. If she concedes $\forall$basicShape.SlidingDoors then her global utility decreases of $u^\beta(P_1) + u^\beta(P_3) = 0.6$, while conceding $\leq_{210}$ height her utility decreases of $u^\beta(P_2) = 0.4$ only. In this case the **minimum concession** is $\leq_{210}$ height.

Algorithm 1 defines the behavior of agents during a generic n-th round of the negotiation process. We present only the algorithm related to $\beta$'s behavior since the behavior of $\sigma$ is dual w.r.t. $\beta$'s one.

**1-4** If there is nothing in conflict between the old $D_{n-1}$ and just-arrived $S_n$, then there is nothing more to negotiate on: the agreement is reached and returned.

**5-11** If $\beta$ discovers that $\sigma$ lied on his concession, then $\beta$ decides to exit the negotiation and terminates with a conflict deal. If we want $\beta$ ask $\sigma$ to concede again it is straightforward to change the protocol to deal with such a behavior.

**13-15** If after the minimum concession, the utility of $\beta$ is less than her **disagreement threshold**, then the negotiation ends with a conflict deal.

## 4    System Architecture

Main actors of our framework are RFID transponders clung to objects, an RFID reader integrated in a hotspot able to extract tags data and wireless devices interacting with hotspot via Bluetooth. Figure 2 shows the structure of the proposed framework, which is based on a two-level architecture that embeds semantic-enhanced variants of both RFID EPCglobal standard [12] and Bluetooth Service Discovery Protocol [11]. The first one is exploited to interconnect readers and tags dipped in the environment (the

```
1  if D_{n-1} ⊓ S_n ⋢_O ⊥ then
2      agreement A reached;
3      return A = D_{n-1} ⊓ S_n;
4  end
5  if n > 0 then
6      compute ⟨G_n^σ, K_n^σ⟩ from D_{n-1} and S_n;
7      if G_{n-1}^σ ⋢_O G_n^σ then
8          σ lied;
9          conflict deal: exit;
10     end
11 end
12 compute minimum concession G_{(n-1,i)}^β;
13 if u_{n-1}^β < t^β then
14     conflict deal: exit;
15 end
16 formulate D_n deleting G_{(n-1,i)}^β from D_{n-1};
17 send D_n to σ;
```

**Algorithm 1.** The behavior of $\beta$ at step $n$

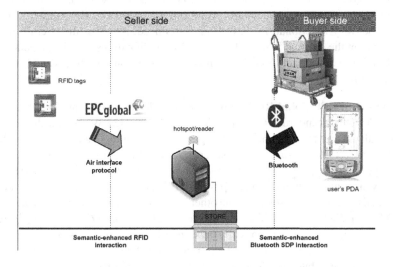

**Fig. 2.** Actors and interaction in the proposed framework

left hand side in Figure 2), the second one enables a communication between a reader and a mobile host acting as requester deployed in the wireless context (the right hand side in Figure 2). The hotspot plays a fundamental role in the whole discovery architecture as it: (i) collects descriptions and data-oriented parameters (such as price for example) referred to tags in its radio range; (ii) accepts and replies to requests received via Bluetooth taking into account resource descriptions extracted from transponders. Basically, the agreement between the buyer and seller wireless agents is reached after a progressive interaction. The negotiation protocol described above, can be seen as a common application layer interconnecting the seller and buyer side of Bluetooth SDP hosts with the final purpose of attempting a possible agreement between them. On the other hand, the seller agent also refers to objects in its radio range via the semantic-based EPCglobal protocol in order to retrieve products descriptions whose annotation are exploited in the negotiation process. In what follows basic features of the architecture layers are briefly recalled. Some details have been omitted for the sake of brevity. For a wider argumentation the reader is referred to [4].

**Semantic-based Bluetooth Service Discovery.** In [11] a framework has been proposed allowing to manage knowledge-based discovery of resources, by integrating a semantic micro-layer within the OSI Bluetooth stack at application level preserving legacy applications. Unused classes of Universally Unique Identifiers (UUIDs) in the original standard were exploited to unambiguously mark ontologies thus thinking up so called OUUIDs as Ontology Universally Unique IDentifiers. The fundamental assumption is that each resource is semantically annotated. A resource provider stores annotations within resource records, labelled with unique 32-bit identifiers. Each record basically consists of a list of resource attributes: in addition to the OUUID, there are a $ResourceName$ (a human-readable name for the resource), a $ResourceDescription$ (expressed using DIG syntax) and a variable number of $ResourceUtilityAttr_i$ attributes, *i.e.*, numerical values used according to specific applications. By adding some SDP Protocol Data Units (PDUs) to the original standard (exploiting not used PDU ID), further semantic enabled discovery functionalities have been introduced. Anyway, the overall interaction is based on the original SDP in Bluetooth. No modifications have been made to the original structure of transactions whose basic parameters, data structures and functions, have been completely saved.

**Semantic-based EPCglobal RFID standard.** We refer to RFID transponders compliant with EPCglobal standard of Class 1-Generation 2 UHF [13]. We assume the reader be familiar with basics of this technology. The practical feasibility of an advanced exploitation of RFID must take into account the severe bandwidth and memory limitations. From this standpoint two opposite questions have to be considered. First of all, due to technological advances and growing demand, passive RFID tags with greater memory amounts are expected to be available soon. On the other hand, XML-based ontological languages like OWL (http://www.w3.org/TR/owl-features/) and DIG (http://dl.kr.org/dig/) are far too verbose for a direct storage on RFID tags. In order to enable the semantic enhancements of RFID, the EPCglobal air interface protocol must provide read/write capabilities for semantically annotated product descriptions w.r.t. a reference ontology, along with additional data-oriented attributes (contextual parameters). Neither new commands nor modification to existing ones have been introduced in the proposed approach. Moreover, a mechanism is clearly required to distinguish semantic enabled tags from standard ones, so that semantic based applications can exploit the new features without interfering with legacy ones. In order to accomplish this coexistence, we extend the memory organization of tags compliant with the above standard. We exploit two bits in the EPC tag memory area currently reserved for future purposes. The first one –at $15_{hex}$ address– is used to indicate whether the tag has a user memory (bit set) or not (bit reset). The second one –at $16_{hex}$ address– is set to mark semantic enabled tags. In this way, a reader can easily distinguish semantic based tags by means of a *SELECT* command with proper values for reference parameters [12]. The following inventory step –which proceeds in the standard fashion– will skip "non-semantic" tags. The EPC standard requires the content of

TID memory up to $1F_{hex}$ bit is fixed. TID bank can be extended to store optional information, generally consisting of tag serial number or manufacturer data. Hence we use the TID memory area starting from $100000_2$ address to store a 128-bit OUUID labeling ontology the tag description refers to. In order to retrieve the OUUID stored within a tag, a reader will simply exploit a *READ* command with proper parameters. Contextual parameters (whose meaning may depend on the specific application) are stored within the User memory bank of the tag. There, we also store the semantically annotated description of the product the tag is clung to (opportunely compressed). An RFID reader can perform extraction and storing of a description from/on a tag by means of one or more *READ* or *WRITE* commands, respectively. Both commands are obviously compliant with the RFID air interface protocol.

## 5 An Illustrative Example: Looking for a New Wardrobe in a Furniture Store

To clarify our approach we present a simple example case study. Let us imagine a user entering a furniture store wishing to buy a new wardrobe. She hopes to find "*a closed wardrobe made from birch, with sliding doors equipped with glass shutters, a number of drawers between 3 and 5, at most two wire baskets, a shoe box organizer in a textile material, between 230 and 260 meters high and with rails for hanging clothes.*". Hence, she uses her PDA to run the *house planner* application. Then she starts to drag and drop components until she composes such a configuration on her PDA and sets utility values. Then her agent $\beta$ starts a negotiation, while she hopes to find, if not the dreamed wardrobe, at least a good compromise.

On the other side, consider, among others, the following configuration offered by one of the m seller agents $\sigma$ " *a closed wardrobe made from oak, with hinged doors, equipped with glass shutters, 4 drawers and 2 wire basket, equipped with Tidy shoe, a shoe box organizer, 236 meters high and with add on rails (basic rail plus tie rack and trouser hanger).*". As we have seen in Section 3 to each piece of information (component) it is associate a **utility value**, expressing relative importance of components. Agents also indicate a **threshold**, to rule out agreements less preferable than a conflict deal. Both the request $D$ and the offer $S$ can be formalized as[6]:

$$P_1^\beta = \forall \texttt{basicShape.SlidingDoors} \qquad\qquad u^\beta(P_1^\beta) = 0.35$$

$$P_2^\beta = \forall \texttt{material.Birch} \qquad\qquad u^\beta(P_2^\beta) = 0.2$$

$$P_3^\beta = \geq \texttt{3drawers} \sqcap \leq \texttt{5drawers} \sqcap \leq \texttt{2WireBasket} \qquad u^\beta(P_3^\beta) = 0.05$$

$$P_4^\beta = \forall \texttt{shutters.Glass} \qquad\qquad u^\beta(P_4^\beta) = 0$$

$$P_5^\beta = \exists \texttt{organizer} \sqcap \forall \texttt{organizer.(ShoeBox} \sqcap \exists \texttt{material} \sqcap \forall \texttt{material.Textile)} \quad u^\beta(P_5^\beta) = 0.05$$

$$P_6^\beta = \exists \texttt{complement} \sqcap \forall \texttt{complement.Basic\_clothes\_rail} \qquad u^\beta(P_6^\beta) = 0.1$$

$$P_7^\beta = \geq_{230} \texttt{height} \sqcap \leq_{260} \texttt{height} \qquad\qquad u^\beta(P_7^\beta) = 0.25$$

$$t^\beta = 0.6$$

---

[6] ClosedWardrobe $\equiv$ Wardrobe $\sqcap$ $\exists$material $\sqcap$ $\exists$basicShape $\sqcap$ $\exists$shutters is the object of the negotiation on which users express preferences, for that reason it is not part of the negotiation process.

$$P_1^\sigma = \forall \texttt{basicShape.HingedDoors} \qquad\qquad u^\sigma(P_1^\sigma) = 0.3$$
$$P_2^\sigma = \forall \texttt{material.Oak} \qquad\qquad u^\sigma(P_2^\sigma) = 0.2$$
$$P_3^\sigma = \; = \texttt{4drawers} \sqcap \; = \texttt{2WireBasket} =_{236} \texttt{height} \qquad u^\sigma(P_3^\sigma) = 0.25$$
$$P_4^\sigma = \exists \texttt{complement} \sqcap \forall \texttt{complement.Add\_on\_clothes\_rail} \qquad u^\sigma(P_4^\sigma) = 0.05$$
$$P_5^\sigma = \forall \texttt{shutters.Glass} \qquad\qquad u^\sigma(P_5^\sigma) = 0.05$$
$$P_6^\sigma = \forall \texttt{organizer.} \sqcap \forall \texttt{organizer.TidyShoeBox} \qquad u^\sigma(P_6^\sigma) = 0.15$$
$$t^\sigma = 0.5$$

$K$ and $G$ are computed for both $\beta$ and $\sigma$.

$K_0^\beta =$ ∀shutters.Glass⊓ ≥ 3drawers⊓ ≤ 5drawers⊓ ≤ 2WireBasket ⊓ ∃complement ⊓ ∀complement.Basic_clothes_rail ≥₂₃₀ height⊓ ≤₂₆₀ height
$G_0^\beta =$ ∀basicShape.SlidingDoors ⊓ ∀material.Birch ⊓ ∃organizer ⊓ ∀organizer.(ShoeBox ⊓ ∃material ⊓ ∀material.Textile)

$K_0^\sigma =$ ∀shutters.Glass⊓ = 4drawers⊓ = 2WireBasket⊓ =₂₃₆ height ⊓ ∃complement ⊓ ∀complement.Add_on_clothes_rail
$G_0^\sigma =$ ∀basicShape.HingedDoors ⊓ ∀material.Oak ⊓ ∃organizer ⊓ ∀organizer.TidyShoeBox

Now suppose that by coin tossing, $\sigma$ moves first. He starts giving up the component with the minimum utility (the TidyShoe box), which is his minimum concession. Then he computes his utility and, since it is greater than the threshold value, decides to go on with the negotiation process. In the following step we have:

$K_1^\beta =$ ∀shutters.Glass⊓ ≥ 3drawers⊓ ≤ 5drawers⊓ ≤ 2WireBasket ⊓ ∃complement ⊓ ∀complement.Basic_clothes_rail ≥₂₃₀ height⊓ ≤₂₆₀ height ⊓ ∃organizer ⊓ ∀organizer.(ShoeBox ⊓ ∃material ⊓ ∀material.Textile)
$G_1^\beta =$ ∀basicShape.SlidingDoors ⊓ ∀material.Birch ⊓ ∃organizer

$K_1^\sigma = K_0^\sigma$
$G_1^\sigma =$ ∀basicShape.HingedDoors ⊓ ∀material.Oak

At this point, $\beta$ gives up ∀material.Birch which is the preference with the minimum utility. The protocol continues until agents reach logical compatibility. A final agreement could then be:

$A =$ ClosedWardrobe ⊓ ∀basicShape.SlidingDoors ⊓ ∀material.Oak ⊓ ∀shutters.Glass⊓ = 4 drawers⊓ = 2WireBasket⊓ =₂₃₆ height ⊓ ∃organizer⊓∀organizer.(ShoeBox⊓∃material⊓ ∀material.Textile) ⊓ ∃complement ⊓ ∀complement.Add_on_clothes_rail,

with corresponding utilities $u^\beta = u^\beta(P_1^\beta) + u^\beta(P_3^\beta) + u^\beta(P_5^\beta) + u^\beta(P_6^\beta) + u^\beta(P_7^\beta) = 0.8$ for $\beta$, and $u^\sigma = u^\sigma(P_2^\sigma) + u^\sigma(P_3^\sigma) + u^\sigma(P_4^\sigma) + u^\sigma(P_5^\sigma) = 0.55$ for $\sigma$, both above the thresholds.

## 6  Conclusion

We have presented a framework for semantic-based multi-issue bilateral negotiation grounded in a mobile context. Semantic annotations describing products and good features are compressed and properly stored in RFID tags. Semantic-enhanced versions of both RFID and Bluetooth standards are so exploited to enable an infrastructure-less interaction between buyer and seller wireless negotiation agents. Hence, seller configurations are proposed based on concrete product availability and the buyer can interrogate it from everywhere aided by an intuitive GUI. Non standard inference services and utility theory have been exploited in the negotiation process to reach a suitable agreement. The complete framework has been implemented and it is currently being evaluated in the case study scenario.

## Acknowledgments

The authors thank Tommaso Di Noia for fruitful discussions, ideas and suggestions. This research is partially sponsored by *Distributed Production as Innovative System (DIPIS)* and *Telecommunication Facilities and Wireless Sensor Networks in Emergency Management* projects.

## References

1. Baader, F., Calvanese, D., Mc Guinness, D., Nardi, D., Patel-Schneider, P.: The Description Logic Handbook. Cambridge University Press, Cambridge (2002)
2. Bechhofer, S., Möller, R., Crowther, P.: The DIG Description Logic Interface. In: DL 2003 (2003)
3. Bluetooth, http://www.bluetooth.com
4. Di Noia, T., Di Sciascio, E., Donini, F., Ruta, M., Scioscia, F., Tinelli, E.: Semantic-based bluetooth-rfid interaction for advanced resource discovery in pervasive contexts. IJSWIS 4(1), 50–74 (2008)
5. Endriss, U.: Monotonic concession protocols for multilateral negotiation. In: Proc. of AAMAS 2006, pp. 392–399 (2006)
6. EPCglobal, http://www.epcglobalinc.org
7. Kraus, S.: Strategic Negotiation in Multiagent Environments. The MIT Press, Cambridge (2001)
8. Ragone, A., Di Noia, T., Di Sciascio, E., Donini, F.M.: Alternating-offers protocol for multi-issue bilateral negotiation in semantic-enabled marketplaces. In: Aberer, K., Choi, K.-S., Noy, N., Allemang, D., Lee, K.-I., Nixon, L.J.B., Golbeck, J., Mika, P., Maynard, D., Mizoguchi, R., Schreiber, G., Cudré-Mauroux, P. (eds.) ASWC 2007 and ISWC 2007. LNCS, vol. 4825, pp. 395–408. Springer, Heidelberg (2007)
9. Rosenschein, J., Zlotkin, G.: Rules of Encounter. MIT Press, Cambridge (1994)
10. Rubinstein, A.: Perfect equilibrium in a bargaining model. Econometrica 50, 97–109 (1982)
11. Ruta, M., Di Noia, T., Di Sciascio, E., Donini, F.: Semantic-Enhanced Bluetooth Discovery Protocol for M-Commerce Applications. IJWGS 2(4), 424–452 (2006)
12. Ruta, M., Di Noia, T., Di Sciascio, E., Scioscia, F., Piscitelli, G.: If objects could talk: A novel resource discovery approach for pervasive environments. International Journal of Internet and Protocol Technology (IJIPT), Special issue on RFID: Technologies, Applications, and Trends 2(3/4), 199–217 (2007)
13. Traub, K.: EPCglobal Architecture Framework. Technical report, EPCglobal (July 2005)
14. Di Noia, T., Di Sciascio, E., Donini, F.M.: Semantic Matchmaking as Non-Monotonic Reasoning: A Description Logic Approach. JAIR 29, 269–307 (2007)
15. Gärdenfors, P.: Knowledge in Flux: Modeling the Dynamics of Epistemic States. Bradford Books, MIT Press, Cambridge, MA (1988)

# A Group Recommender System for Tourist Activities

Inma Garcia, Laura Sebastia, Eva Onaindia, and Cesar Guzman

Dpt. Computer Science, Technical Univ. of Valencia
Camino de Vera s/n, 46022, Valencia, Spain
{ingarcia,lstarin,onaindia,cguzman}@dsic.upv.es

**Abstract.** This paper introduces a method for giving recommendations of tourist activities to a group of users. This method makes recommendations based on the group tastes, their demographic classification and the places visited by the users in former trips. The group recommendation is computed from individual personal recommendations through the use of techniques such as aggregation, intersection or incremental intersection. This method is implemented as an extension of the *e-Tourism* tool, which is a user-adapted tourism and leisure application, whose main component is the *Generalist Recommender System Kernel (GRSK)*, a domain-independent taxonomy-driven search engine that manages the group recommendation.

**Keywords:** Recommender Systems, Group Recommenders, Tourism.

## 1 Introduction

Recommender systems (RS) are widely used in the internet for suggesting products, activities, etc. These systems usually give a recommendation for a single user considering his/her interests and tastes. However, many activities such as watching a movie or going to a restaurant, involve a group of users. In such a case, RS should take into account the likes of all the group users by combining the tastes and preferences of all the members into a single set of preferences and obtain a recommendation as if they were a single user. This tedious and complicated task requires the group members previously agree on the way their particular preferences will be gathered together into a single group profile. In order to overcome this shortcoming, some RS take into account the interests and tastes of the group as a whole. The first task of this type of systems is to identify the individual preferences and then find a compromise that is accepted by all the group members. This is the crucial point in a group RS because how individual preferences are managed to come up with group preferences will determine the success of the recommendation.

This paper is focused on a RS for tourism. *e-Tourism* [8] is a web-based recommender system that computes a user-adapted leisure and tourist plan for both a single user and a group. The system does not solve the problem of travelling to an specific place but it recommends a list of activities that a single tourist

T. Di Noia and F. Buccafurri (Eds.): EC-Web 2009, LNCS 5692, pp. 26–37, 2009.
© Springer-Verlag Berlin Heidelberg 2009

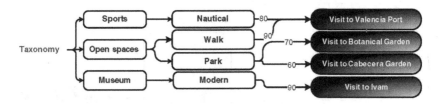

**Fig. 1.** GRSK taxonomy

or group of tourists can perform in a city, particularly, in the city of Valencia (Spain). It also computes a time schedule for the list of recommended activities taking into account the distances between places, the opening hours, etc. - that is, an agenda of activities.

The component of *e-Tourism* in charge of generating the list of activities that are likely of interest to the single user or group of users is the *Generalist Recommender System Kernel (GRSK)*, whose main aspects are explained in Section 2. Section 3 details the basic recommendation techniques used to model the individual user preferences, and section 4 introduces the techniques to compute the final group recommendations. Section 5 presents the experimental setup to evaluate our approach. Section 6 summarizes similar state-of-the-art RS and we finish with some conclusions and future work.

## 2    The Generalist RS Kernel (GRSK)

The task of the *Generalist Recommender System Kernel (GRSK)* is to generate the list of activities to recommend to a single user or to a group of users. This section describes the main aspects of the GRSK when working as a group RS.

### 2.1    GRSK Taxonomy

The GRSK behaviour relies on the use of a taxonomy to represent the user's likes and the items to recommend. It has been designed to be *generalist*, that is independent of the current catalog of items to recommend. Therefore, the GRSK is able to work with any application domain as long as the data of the new domain are defined through a taxonomy representation.

The entities in a **taxonomy** are arranged in a hierarchical structure connected through a *is-a* relationship in which the classification levels become more specific towards the bottom. In the GRSK taxonomy (an example is shown in figure 1), entities represent the **features** $(F)$ that are commonly managed in a tourism domain like 'Open Spaces', 'Museums', 'Nautical Sports', etc. as figure 1 shows. The leaf nodes of the taxonomy represent the **items** to recommend; they are categorized by the lowest-level or most specific feature in the hierarchy. The edges linking an item to a feature are associated a value to indicate the **degree of interest** of the item (activity in the tourism taxonomy) under the feature, i.e. as a member of the category denoted by the feature. An item can also be

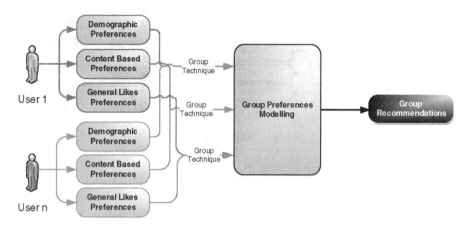

**Fig. 2.** Group recommendation process

categorized by more than one feature in the taxonomy. For instance, in figure 1, the item 'Visit to Valencia Port' is categorized as 80% of interest as 'Nautical Sport' and 90% of interest as a place for going for a 'Walk'.

Items are described by means of a list of tuples which represent all their incoming edges. Each tuple is of the form $(i, f, r)$, where $i$ is the item, $f \in F$ is a feature defined in the taxonomy and $r$ is the degree of interest of the item $i$ under $f$. Additionally, items are associated a numeric value $AC^i$ (**acceptance counter**) to represent how popular the item $i$ is among users; this value indicates how many times the item $i$ has been accepted when recommended.

### 2.2    User Information

The GRSK records a **profile** of each individual user $u$, which contains personal and demographic details like the age, the gender, the family or the country. The profile also keeps information about the **general likes** of the user, denoted by $GL^u$, which are described by a list of pairs on the form $(f, r)$, where $f \in F$ and $r \in [0, 100]$. A user profile in GRSK also contains information about the historical interaction of the user with the RS, namely the set of items the user has been recommended and his/her degree of satisfaction with the recommendation.

The first step to utilize the system is to register and make up the user profile. Whenever a person asks for a new recommendation, his/her user profile is updated to better capture his/her likes.

A **group of users** $G$ is composed of a set of users already registered in the system. The GRSK takes into account each individual user profile to return the list of recommended items to the group of users.

### 2.3    Group Recommendation Process

Figure 2 outlines the process for computing the group recommendation. Once the individual preferences of each user are modeled, they are combined to obtain

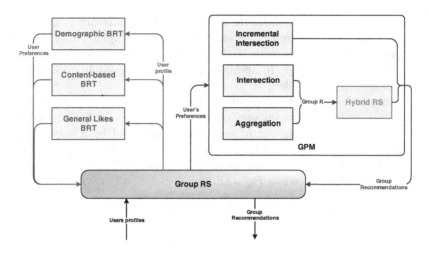

**Fig. 3.** GRSK Architecture

the group preferences by means of a group preference modelling. These group preferences are then used to retrieve the list of items to recommend (group recommendations). The individual user preferences as well as the group preferences are described by means of a list of tuples of the form $(u/G, f, r)$, where $f \in F$ and $r \in [0, 100]$.

The main components of the GRSK are shown in figure 3. The Group RS is in charge of controlling the whole recommendation process. First, users profiles are sent by the Group RS to the basic recommendation techniques (BRT) modules that produce a list of individual preferences according to each type of recommendation (demographic RS [3], content-based RS [3] and likes-based filtering [4]). The result of this phase is a set of three lists of individual preferences for each member in the group. These individual preferences are sent by the Group RS to be processed by the Group Preference Manager (GPM), which, through methods like aggregation, intersection or incremental intersection, combines the individual preferences and reports the final group recommendation. The first phase is detailed in the next section whereas the second phase is explained in section 4.

## 3 Modelling the Individual User Preferences

The first task of the Group RS is to elicit the individual preferences from the users profiles. These preferences are computed by means of three basic recommendation techniques (BRT): demographic and content-based recommendation techniques, and likes-based filtering technique. The preferences returned by each BRT are independent from each other, and they will be later used to recommend the group items.

The **demographic BRT** classifies the user $u$ into a demographic category according to his profile details. For example, a person with children is classified into a different category than a retiree as they will likely have different likes. We will call $P_d^u$ the set of preferences generated by a demographic BRT. We opted for a demographic BRT because it is able to always give a recommendation for the problem of the *new user*. In addition, it can also suggest items other than items previously recommended.

The **content-based BRT** computes a set of preferences by taking into account the items that have been previously rated by the user (historical interaction). We will call $P_{cb}^u$ the set of preferences generated by a content-based BRT. Let $f$ be a feature and $I$ a list of items described by a pair $(i, f, r^i)$ in the taxonomy. Given a user $u$ who has rated a set of items $I^u$ with a value $ur^i$, a preference $(u, f, r^u)$ is added to $P_{cb}^u$ with:

$$r^u = \frac{\sum\limits_{\forall i \in I \cap I^u} ur^i * r^i}{|I^u|}$$

The value $r^u$ denotes the interest-degree of a user $u$ for the items described under the feature $f$ among the whole set of items rated by $u$. The use of a content-based BRT will allow us to increase the user satisfaction by recommending items similar to the ones already accepted by the user. For example, if the user likes visiting museums, the system will tend recommending visits to other museums.

The **likes-based filtering module** is an information filtering technique that works with the general user likes $GL^u$ specified by the user in his profile. In this case, the set of preferences $P_{lf}^u$ is simply built as $P_{lf}^u = \{(u, f, r^u) : \forall (f, r) \in GL^u : r^u = r\}$.

## 4   Generating the Group Recommendations

Once the individual preferences are elicited from the BRT modules, the group RS sends them to the **Group Preference Manager** (GPM) to get the group preferences model (see figure 3). The GPM makes use of three disjunctive methods to construct the group preferences: aggregation, intersection and incremental intersection. These three methods differ in how the lists of individual preferences are combined.

The aggregation mechanism is a common technique that has been used in various group RS (see section 6). This technique gathers the individual preferences of all the group members to make up a single set of preferences. However, aggregating preferences does not necessarily account for the preferences of the group as a whole; the intersection mechanism is thereby introduced as a counterpoint. The intersection technique obtains a set of preferences that are shared by all the participants in the group. The risk of using this mechanism is that we might end up with an empty intersection list if the group is rather heterogeneous. Finally, the incremental intersection mechanism combines the advantages of aggregation and intersection in a single strategy.

The GPM is fed with three lists of individual preferences and builds a list of group preferences calculated with the selected disjunctive method. Individual preferences are denoted by $(P_d^u, P_{cb}^u, P_{lf}^u)$.

## 4.1 Aggregation

Aggregation gathers the individual preferences computed by the BRT modules for every member in the group $G$, and creates a single set of group preferences for each type of recommendation ($P_d^G$, $P_{cb}^G$, $P_{lf}^G$):

$$P_{brt}^G = \{(G, f, r^G) : \exists(u, f, r) \in \bigcup_{\forall u \in G} P_{brt}^u\}, \text{where } r^G = avg(r)$$

$P_{brt}^G$ is the result of aggregating the preferences returned by the BRT for at least one user in the group. The interest-degree of a group preference $r^G$ is calculated as the **average value** of the interest-degree of the users in $G$ for the feature $f$.

The three lists of group preferences ($P_d^G$, $P_{cb}^G$ and $P_{lf}^G$) are then used to obtain three lists of items to recommend. An item described under a feature $f$ is included in a list if there is a tuple $(G, f, r^G)$ that belongs to the corresponding group preference list. The three lists of items are combined by a **Hybrid RS**, which applies a mixed hybrid recommendation [3]. By handling these lists of items independently, we give much more flexibility to the GRSK because any other hybrid technique could be used instead.

The Hybrid RS returns a single list of ranked items ($RC^G$) whose elements are tuples of the form $(i, Pr^i)$, where $i \in I$ is an item to recommend, and $Pr^i$ is the estimated interest-degree of the group in the item $i$. This latter value is calculated as follows:

$$Pr^i = percentile(AC^i) + avg_{\forall f}(r^i + r^G) \tag{1}$$

where $percentile(AC^i)$ refers to the percentile rank of the acceptance counter of $i$ ($AC^i$) with respect to the whole set of items accepted by the users when recommended. The second part of the formula considers the average interest-degree in all the features that describe the item $i$ in both the taxonomy ($r^i$) and in the group preferences ($r^G$). The hybrid RS finally selects the best ranked items as the final group recommendations $RC^G$.

## 4.2 Intersection

The intersection mechanism finds the preferences that are shared by all the members in the group and make up the group preferences.

$$P_{brt}^G = \{(G, f, r^G) : \exists(u, f, r) \in \bigcap_{\forall u \in G} P_{brt}^u\}, \text{where } r^G = avg(r)$$

The final list of recommended items $RC^G$ is computed as above from the three lists $P_d^G$, $P_{cb}^G$ and $P_{lf}^G$.

Figure 4 shows an example of the recommendation process when using the aggregation and intersection mechanisms. This example is based on the taxonomy in figure 1. The table on the left shows the lists of preferences computed by each BRT. The intersection method obtains only one preference (*Nautical*

| Preferences | D | CB | LF |
|---|---|---|---|
| User 1 | (NS,90), (W,50) | (P,30) | |
| User 2 | (NS,70) | | (W,70) |
| User 3 | (NS,80), (MM,100) | (P,50) | |

NS:  Nautical Sport        P:  Park
W:  Walk                        MM:  Modern Museum

| Preferences | D | CB | LF |
|---|---|---|---|
| Intersection | (NS,80) | | |
| Aggregation | (NS,80), (W,50), (MM,100) | (P, 40) | (w, 70) |

| Items Intersection | | Items Aggregation | |
|---|---|---|---|
| Valencia Port | 210 | Ivam | 230 |
| | | Valencia Port | 200 |
| | | Botanical Garden | 170 |

**Fig. 4.** Example of group recommendation (Aggregation and Intersection)

*Sport*) because it is the only feature shared by all the group members. On the other hand, the aggregation method creates one list per BRT with the individual preferences of all the users. For example, the $r^G$ value associated with *Nautical Sport* is computed as the average of the $r^u$ values of all the group members.

When using the intersection, the system will recommend only items described under the feature *Nautical Sport*; in the taxonomy of figure 1, only one item is associated to this feature, *Visit to Valencia Port*. Assuming that *percentile* ($AC_{ValenciaPort}$) is 50, the priority of this item is computed as ($r^i$ and $r^G$ are 80): $Pr_{ValenciaPort} = 50 + avg(80 + 80) = 210$. On the other hand, when using the aggregation, all the items can be recommended; the final recommendations will depend on the priority of each item. For example, in this case, the priority of *Visit to Valencia Port* is computed as: $Pr_{ValenciaPort} = 50 + avg(80 + 80, 90 + 50) = 200$; this item is described by the features *Nautical Sport* and *Walk* with $r^i$ values of 80 and 90, respectively. The first three items in the list will be recommended, as the group has requested three recommendations. It is important to note that the *IVAM Museum* will be recommended although only one user has *modern museum* among his preferences.

### 4.3   Incremental Intersection

The preferences predicted for the group are some function of all of the known preferences for every user in the group. Social Choice theorists, concerned with the properties of voting methods, have been investigating preference aggregation for decades. A very popular work is that of Arrow [2] which demonstrates the impossibility of combining individual preferences into a single expression of social preference in a way that satisfies several desirable properties. However, there are other investigations, specifically on Collaborative Filtering RS, that show that the only possible form for the prediction function is a weighted average of the users' ratings. The Incremental Intersection (II) method is actually a weighted average of the most voted preferences among the users in the group, that is the preferences shared by the largest possible group of members.

The II method draws up a joint list for each user with the preferences computed by all the BRT. If more than one BRT returns a preference for the same feature $f$, the II builds a single preference $(u, f, r^u)$ where $r^u$ is the average interest-degree of all the preferences for $f$. The II method starts a voting process where a feature $f$ is voted by a user if there is a preference for the feature $f$ in his joint list.

| Preferences | D | CB | LF | | Preferences II | | Items recommended | |
|---|---|---|---|---|---|---|---|---|
| User 1 | (NS,90), (W,50) | (P,30) | | | (NS,80) | 3 votes | Valencia Port | 205 |
| User 2 | (NS,70) | | (W,70) | | (W,60), (P,40) | 2 votes | Botanical Garden | 170 |
| User 3 | (NS,80), (MM,100) | (P,50) | | | (MM,100) | 1 vote | Cabecera Garden | 150 |

**Fig. 5.** Example of group recommendation (Incremental Intersection)

The items to recommend will be the ones that describe the most voted features. At the first iteration, we select the features with the highest number of votes ($|G|$ votes), where the value $r^G$ associated with each feature is computed as the average of $r^u$ for all the users with preferences with $f$. Then, the items that describe these features are selected and their $Pr^i$ is computed as equation 1 shows. If there are not enough items to cover the requested number of recommendations, at the next iteration we select the features that received at least $|G| - 1$ votes, and so on. This way, we incrementally consider the features shared by the largest possible number of users in the group.

Figure 5 shows an example of the recommendation process when using the II. The preferences computed by each BRT for the group members are the same as in figure 4. In this case, we obtain several lists of preferences ordered by the number of votes of the features contained in the list. In the first iteration, only one item associated to the most-voted feature is recommended, namely *Visit the Valencia Port*. As the group has requested three recommendations, a second iteration will consider the features with at least two votes. In this case, three items are recommended, which are shown in figure 5 together with their calculated priority. It is important to remark that, unlike the aggregation method, the II does not recommend *IVAM Museum* at the second iteration because the feature that describes this item will only appear in the third iteration.

## 5  Experimental Results

This section shows the experimental results performed to compare the three methods for the elicitation of the group preferences. As we are working with our own domain, our first task was to obtain data from real users. We prepared a questionnaire with questions about general preferences, demographic data, visited places and the user's degree of satisfaction when visiting the places. The questionnaire was filled in by 60 people and these data were used to create several groups with a different number of users.

Unlike individual recommendations, when dealing with groups, the most important issue is that the recommendation is as satisfactory as possible for all the members in the group. Thus, through the experimental setup presented in this section, our intention is to analyse which of the three techniques described above obtains the best recommendations as for the whole group satisfaction.

Let $RC^u$ be the recommendation for a single user $u$, such that each element in $RC^u$ has the form $(i, u, Pr_u^i)$, where $i$ is the recommended item ($i \in I$), $u$ is the user and $Pr_u^i$ is the priority of the item $i$ for the user $u$. $Pr_u^i$ is set equal to 0 if this value is unknown for a given item $i$. Given a recommendation $RC^G$ for

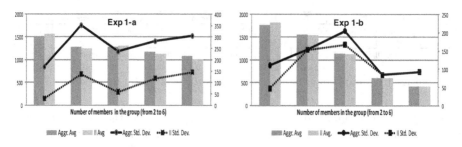

**Fig. 6.** Experiment 1: Comparison of the quality of the recommendations (II and Aggr)

a group $G$, such that $u \in G$, the **utility** of the user $u$ with respect to $RC^G$ is calculated as:

$$U_u^G = \sum_{\forall i \in RC^G} Pr_u^i$$

Thus, in order to analyse the quality of the recommendations, we consider the average and the standard deviation (dispersion) of the utility over all the group members: $\mu_G(U_u^G)$ and $\sigma_G(U_u^G), \forall u \in G$.

We executed three experiments, one per each preference elicitation mechanism, namely aggregation (Aggr), intersection (Int) and incremental intersection (II). We used groups of different size ranging from 2 to 6 members; the number of requested recommendations is set to 10 items in all cases. We also run the three experiments twice: the first batch is run with user ratings on the 30% of the items (Fig. 6 Exp-1-a), and the second one with user ratings on the 70% of the items (Fig. 6 Exp1-b). The X axis indicates the number of members in the group. Bars represent the utility on average of the recommendations obtained for each group size and elicitation mechanism. Likewise, the points in the lines determine the dispersion level for each group size and elicitation mechanism. Notice that bars are referred to the scale on the left whereas lines refer to the scale on the right. It can be observed that, in both sets of experiments, and for every group size, the utility on average is quite similar in all cases, whereas the dispersion (standard deviation) is lower in the incremental intersection than in the aggregation technique. The reason behind is that the II incrementally considers the preferences that satisfy a larger number of users whereas the aggregation recommends the most prioritized items for *at least one* member in the group, which obviously does not imply to be for *all* the group members. Therefore, we can conclude that the II obtains solutions of a similar utility as the aggregation technique but with a lower degree of dispersion, which is interpreted as all members in the group are equally satisfied.

On the other hand, in the first set of experiments (Fig. 6 Exp-1-a), the results of the II and the Int technique coincide (so we do not include the results of the Int technique), because the first intersection computed by II is enough to obtain the number of requested recommendations. However, in the second set of experiments, when the user has rated a larger number of items, it can be

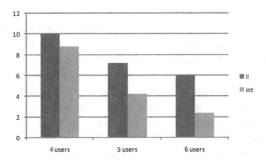

**Fig. 7.** Comparison of the number of recommendations (II and Int)

the case that the result of the Int mechanism does not cover the number of requested recommendations. A more detailed representation is shown in Figure 7, which compares the number of recommendations obtained by the II and the Int techniques in the second set of experiments for groups of 4, 5 and 6 members. It can be observed that as the number of members increases, the Int mechanism finds more difficult to return a large set of recommendations. It is in these cases when the usefulness of the II mechanism shows up, because the incremental consideration of smaller groups helps to find more suitable items to recommend. In groups of 4 members, a large number of recommendations satisfy all members in the group; in groups of 5 members and 6 members, as more users contribute to the final recommendation, the number of recommendations that satisfy all the members lessens and so the results of II and aggregation become much more similar (this effect can also be observed in Fig. 6 Exp-1-b).

We can conclude that the II mechanism obtains the best results, because it brings together the benefits of the Aggr and the Int techniques.

## 6   Related Work

Systems for recommending items to a group of two or more users in a tourist domain are particularly useful as people usually make group travels (family, friends, etc.). We will illustrate some group recommender systems for tourism such as *Intrigue*, *Travel Decision Forum* or *CATS*.

*Intrigue* [1] assists a group of users in the organization of a tour. Individual participants are not described one by one but the system models the group as a set partitioned into a number of homogeneous subgroups, and their possibly conflicting individual preferences are separately represented. *Intrigue* uses socio-demographic information about the participants and it elicits a set of preferences to define the subgroup requirements on the properties of tourist attractions, paying attention to those preferences possibly conflicting between subgroups. The group information stores a relevance value to estimate the weight that the preferences of a member should have on the recommendation. Each subgroup may have a different degree of influence on the estimation of the group preferences.

*CATS* [7] is a conversational critique-based recommender that helps a group of members to plan a skiing vacation. The recommender manages personal as well as group profiles. The individual preferences are elicited by subsequently presenting a recommendation to the user. By critiquing a recommendation, the user can express a preference over a specific feature in line with their own personal requirements. The group profile is maintained by combining the individual user models and associating critiques with the users who contributed them. The group recommendation displays information relating to group compatibility.

The *Travel Decision Forum* [6,5] uses animated characters to help the members of a group to agree on the organization of a vacation. At any given moment, at most one member is interacting with the system, the other users in the group are represented as animated characters. The system uses a character that represents a mediator, who directs the interaction between the users. Users must reach an agreement on the set of preferences (group profile) that the recommendation must fulfil. Initially, each user fills out a preference form associating a degree of interest to each preference. The individual user profile as well as the group profile contain the same set of preferences. The degree of interest of a specific group profile is calculated out of the degree of interest of each user in the group. Once the group profile has been created, all group members must agree on the group preference model. The mediator asks each member of the group in turn whether the group model can be accepted or not. Using the users critiques, the mediator reconfigures the preferences ratios, and the recommendation is done using the group preference model.

All the described recommender systems only use aggregation methods to compute the group profile. In contrast, our approach uses three different mechanisms: aggregation, intersection and incremental intersection. Another distinguish characteristic is that *e-Tourism*, instead of making recommendations that directly match the group preferences (likes), it applies a more sophisticated technique: a hybrid recommendation technique that combines demographic, content-based recommendation and preference-based filtering.

# 7   Conclusions and Further Work

*e-Tourism* is a web-based service to make recommendations about personalized tourist tours in the city of Valencia (Spain) for a group of users. The component in charge of the recommendation process is the GRSK, a taxonomy-driven domain-independent recommendation kernel. Group recommendation are elicited from the individual preferences of each single user by using three basic recommendation techniques: demographic, content-based and preference-based filtering. For each recommendation technique, we compute a list of group preferences through the application of aggregation, intersection and incremental intersection methods. Finally, constrains yield to a list of items to recommend. The evaluation of this process shows that the incremental intersection is able to work in a great variety of situations, because it brings together the benefits of the aggregation and intersection techniques.

The design of the GRSK allows us to easily add new basic, hybrid or group recommendation techniques. This is an important contribution to be able to check and measure the effectiveness of a different technique for the domain where GRSK is being applied. We are actually developing a feedback process to adapt the GRSK behaviour through consecutive interactions between the group and the system.

Finally, we are also working in the use of agreement techniques to obtain group recommendation. The members of the group are modeled as agents who attempt achieving a reconciled solution for the whole group maximizing the user satisfaction. This technique allows us to include more sophisticated user behaviours into the group.

**Acknowledgments.** This work has been partially funded by Consolider Ingenio 2010 CSD2007-00022, Spanish Government Project MICINN TIN2008-6701-C03-01 and Valencian Government Project Prometeo 2008/051.

# References

1. Ardissono, L., Goy, A., Petrone, G., Segnan, M., Torasso, P.: Intrigue: personalized recommendation of tourist attractions for desktop and handset devices. Applied AI, Special Issue on Artificial Intelligence for Cultural Heritage and Digital Libraries 17(8-9), 687–714 (2003)
2. Arrow, K.J.: Social Choice and Individual Values. Yale University Press (1963)
3. Burke, R.: Hybrid web recommender systems. In: The Adaptive Web, pp. 377–408. Springer, Heidelberg (2007)
4. Hanani, U., Shapira, B., Shoval, P.: Information filtering: Overview of issues, research and systems. User Modeling and User-Adapted Interaction 11 (2001)
5. Jameson, A.: More than the sum of its members: Challenges for group recommender systems. In: Proceedings of the International Working Conference on Advanced Visual Interfaces (2004)
6. Jameson, A., Baldes, S., Kleinbauer, T.: Enhancing mutual awareness in group recommender systems. In: Mobasher, B., Anand, S.S. (eds.) Proceedings of the IJCAI (2003)
7. McCarthy, K., McGinty, L., Smyth, B., Salamó, M.: Social interaction in the cats group recommender. In: Workshop on the Social Navigation and Community based Adaptation Technologies (2006)
8. Sebastia, L., Garcia, I., Onaindia, E., Guzman, C.: e-Tourism: a tourist recommendation and planning application. In: 20th IEEE International conference on Tools with Artificial Intelligence, ICTAI (2008)

# Personalized Location-Based Recommendation Services for Tour Planning in Mobile Tourism Applications

Chien-Chih Yu and Hsiao-ping Chang

Dept. of MIS, National ChengChi University, Taipei, Taiwan
{ccyu,ping}@mis.nccu.edu.tw

**Abstract.** Travel and tour planning is a process of searching, selecting, group-ing and sequencing destination related products and services including attractions, accommodations, restaurants, and activities. Personalized recom-mendation services aim at suggesting products and services to meet users' pref-erences and needs, while location-based services focus on providing informa-tion based on users' current positions. Due to the fast growing of user needs in the mobile tourism domain, how to provide personalized location-based tour recommendation services becomes a critical research and practical issue. The objective of this paper is to propose a system architecture and design methods for facilitating the delivery of location-based recommendation services to sup-port personalized tour planning. Based on tourists' current location and time, as well as personal preferences and needs, various recommendations regarding sightseeing spots, hotels, restaurants, and packaged tour plans can be generated efficiently. An application prototype is also implemented to illustrate and test the system feasibility and effectiveness.

**Keywords:** Mobile tourism, personalized recommendation, location-based ser-vice, tour planning.

## 1 Introduction

In recent years, due to the rapid advancement of mobile computing technologies, mobile commerce has become one of the hottest research domains. Among various m-commerce related issues, the design, development and delivery of mobile services and applications to assist on-the-move users in making mobility-related decisions is considered as a critical research topic, and therefore more research efforts devoted to this area are highly expected [1,16]. As one of the most important type of mobile services, location-based services focus mainly on providing point of interest information to mobile users based on their current positions [2,10,21]. On the other hand, as major e-commerce and e-business application functions, personalized recommendation services aim at suggesting products and services to meet users' needs and preferences [25,26]. It has been noted that, without proper system support, the integrated process of searching and filtering products, comparing alternatives, and recommending suitable selections for users can be extremely complicated and hard to be carried out. Furthermore, when taking into account the support of mobile users

T. Di Noia and F. Buccafurri (Eds.): EC-Web 2009, LNCS 5692, pp. 38–49, 2009.

with a variety of mobile devices in personalized and location-based decision making, the complexities of the problem and associated solution processes are compounded significantly, and the design and implementation issues for constructing the desired personalized mobile recommender systems become even more complex [15,20].

In the tourism management domain, mobile and wireless technologies have been pointed out as one of the most interesting areas of technological innovation for enhancing Internet applications to tourism [4]. Identified primary functions of location-based services for travelers include localization of persons and objects, routing between them, as well as search for objects such as hotels, restaurants, shops, or sights, and information about traveling conditions. Eventually, tourists are typical consumers who have strong mobility-related needs and have shown significant interests in acquiring location-based services during trips [24]. They like to make their own tour plans while on the trips, and moreover, have a high frequency in rescheduling their trips to suit the dynamically changing conditions and needs. As a key application service in tourism, travel and tour planning is a process of searching, selecting, grouping and sequencing destination related products and services including attractions, accommodations, restaurants, and activities. With more availability of comprehensive data about travelers and destinations as well as more exchanges of experiences between travelers, the location-based recommendation services based on content and/or collaborative filtering technologies attract more interests in the travel and tourism domain [14]. How to provide personalized location-based recommendation services for facilitating tour planning process inevitably becomes a critical research and practical issue in mobile tourism applications. However, existing mobile services related to personalized tour recommendation services are still very primitive. In the literature, although there are more and more mobile applications to explore position information for guiding the on-the-trip users, there is still a lack of personalization in context to meet the interests, preferences, and devices of the individual tourists [22]. Ideal personalized location-based tour planning recommendation services should be able to integrate information about tourists' preferences, needs and constraints, location and time information, destination and attraction information, as well as recommendation models and rules in order for recommending personalized tour plans in which sightseeing spots, restaurants, and. hotels are bundled to match the context and location aware conditions. Since there are very limited previous research efforts undertaking the integrated issues of personalized location-based tour plan recommendations, the objective and contribution of this paper is set to provide a system architecture and development method for efficiently and effectively guiding the design and implementation of the demanded location-based recommendation service systems to support personalized tour planning.

The rest of this paper is organized as follows. A brief literature review on location-based and personalized recommendation services is provided in section 2. The proposed functional framework, processes, models and rules for developing and delivering personalized location-based tour planning recommendation services are presented in section 3. A prototype system is illustrated and evaluated in section 4. Section 5 contains a concluding remark with future research issues.

## 2 Literature Review

Among many research works regarding personalized and/or location-based mobile services, Chen et al. (2005) propose an architecture design of an m-service portal [7]. In their proposed architecture, there are three major components, namely, list manager, profiler, and agency. List manager maintains a personalized list of pre-configured m-services specified by mobile users. Profiler is responsible for storing personal information and preferences such as information needs and message delivery preference. Agency uses intelligent agent technologies to automatically search in the web service/m-service registers to identify appropriate services that satisfy users' needs. Focusing on web service interoperation, Zhang et al. (2005) provide a framework for dynamic and personalized composition of web services [26]. Four major components specified in the framework include storages for personal preference settings, web services for inter-business cooperation, business intelligence to satisfy users' needs, and geographic displays for location-based services. Hand et al. (2006) propose a three-tier location-based development architecture that consists of client communication tier, application-tier, and geographic information system (GIS) tier [11]. The client communication tier is a protocol independent tier, where the users' location is established and where communication with the application tier occurs. The application tier performs all results-set mark-up into the appropriate output display for the user's wireless device. The geographic information system tier performs all location-based application query processing.

As for specifically applying to the tourism domain, Kakaletris et al. (2004) address the design and implementation issues for delivering location-based tourism-related content services [13]. Key points that require careful considerations include service features and procedures, content structure, quality-of-service terms, and security. By illustrating an example of generic tourist guide, Scherp and Boll (2004) emphasize on supporting the dynamic generation of personalized multimedia content in respect of the tourist's interests and preferences, current location and environment, and mobile device used [22]. Aiming at effectively coordinating and integrating disparate information and service resources anytime and anywhere, Chiu and Leung (2005) propose a ubiquitous tourist assistance system that is built upon multi-agent and semantic web technologies for providing personalized assistance and automation to the tourists with different preferences and often changing requirements during their trips [8]. Five agent clusters specified in the system architecture include tourist assistant, ontology maintenance and search, requirement/preference management, package planning, and local tour planning. Ricci and Nguyen (2007) present a critique-based mobile recommender system that lets users expressing session-specific preferences in addition to the long-term collected preferences [20]. The objective is to provide on-tour system support to mobile travelers for selecting products or services based on the integration of both types of preferences. Driver and Clarke (2008), on the other hand, point out that most research related to mobile, context-aware activity scheduling to date has focused on tourist guide applications [9]. This type of application provides the user with a static tour on a mobile device, but does not support dynamic and context-based trail management. An application framework comprising trail generation and trail reconfiguration point identification modules is then proposed for managing mobile and context-aware trails.

As can be seen, although there are several previous works addressing the design and implementation issues for delivering personalized and/or location-based tourism services, only partial solutions to the targeted context and location aware personalized tour planning and recommendation services have been provided. For efficiently and effectively integrating personalized and location aware information to support the recommendation and rescheduling of personalized tour plans, the need of an application framework and development method for directing and facilitating the service system design, implementation, and operation processes is still significant, and more in-depth exploration into this topic is required.

## 3 Personalized Location-Based Tour Planning Recommendation

The information and decision requirements for supporting personalized location-based tour planning services include (1) user profiles containing personalized preferences, needs, constraints and self-specified evaluation criteria, (2) mobile tourists' time and location information, (3) tourism related destination, attraction, and accommodation information, (4) decision associated model, knowledge, and process information. Major location-based tourism information that tourists requested includes destination-oriented information about what to see, where to eat, and where to stay overnight, etc. Specified information for sightseeing spots include tourism types and features (such as culture-archeological site, sport-ski park), sightseeing theme, opening hours, ticket price, location and map, transportation and directions, briefings and suggested visiting time, etc. Detailed accommodation information specified include hotel name, hotel class (star rating), brief introduction, hotel location (city/region/address) and map, transportation and directions, distances to point-of-interests (e.g. train stations, historical sites, city center, etc.), check-in/check-out times, available rooms, facilities, price per room per night, room availability, photos, booking services, website and contact information, and customer rating score, etc. Detailed dining and restaurant information include restaurant name, food type, location, map, transportation, opening hours, customer rating score, menu and recommended food lists, etc.

In addition to information requirements, functional requirements specified include user profile management, tourism information management, location-aware personalized recommendation of attractions (e.g. sightseeing spots, museums, restaurants, hotels) and tour plans, tour plan management, as well as map-based positioning and visualization. A few more functions required in the back end system include model base and knowledge base management, as well as ontology and case base management provided that they are used as matching techniques. The design scopes include functional architecture design, process design, user interface design, presentation design, database design, model base design, knowledge base design, as well as the ontology and case base design, etc. In the following subsections, descriptions will focus on the functional framework and recommendation process, as well as database, model base, and rule base design considerations.

### 3.1 Framework and Process for Personalized Location-Based Recommendation

Based on the results of requirement specifications, a functional framework for supporting the personalized location-based tour planning recommendation is presented in Figure 1. The core services of the personalized location-based tour planning recommendation offered to the tourists include single-typed attraction/point-of-interest recommendation and packaged tour plan recommendation. A recommended tour plan bundles and schedules a series of selected sightseeing spots, restaurants and hotel with specified sequence and suggested time-to-stay. For an example, a tourist may like to make a half day tour in a city starting from his current position and time, and based on his preference, needs, time and device constraints, as well as criteria for site selections. He would also like to be able to reconfigure his tour plan by the time he leaves a sightseeing spot or restaurant, and use his current time and location for recommending the next visit or subsequent visits with suggested visiting time.

The tourism related information services, tourism related location-based services, as well as GIS and Google map services are supportive services that allow tourists to access tourism information, tourist location information and location aware tourism site information, as well as geographical information and maps associated with tourists and tourism attractions. The core tour planning recommendation services also use these supportive services to generate content descriptions for recommended attractions or the tour plan, and display the result in the tourist's mobile device.

Based on the proposed functional framework, personalized location-based recommendation services can be generated to support tourists in making decisions that answer questions including what and where to eat for lunch or dinner? Are there any nearby interesting sightseeing spots? Are they still open and do we have enough time to visit? Where to stay for tonight? A recommended tour plan summarizes the

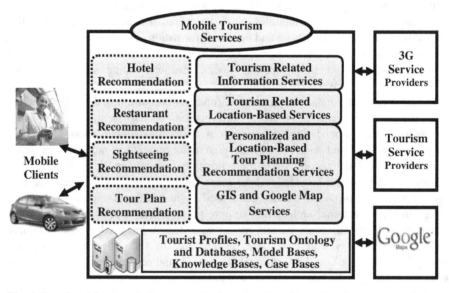

**Fig. 1.** Functional framework for personalized location-based tour planning recommendation

desired decision outcomes and organized them into a sequential process with suggested time to stay. Figure 2 depicts an example flow chart of the personalized location-based tour planning recommendation process. Once the tourist activates the location-based tour planning recommendation services, the tourist's current location is identified and current time is recorded, personal preferences and criteria are retrieved or specified online. For instance, in the example scenario, the time periods specified for lunch time and dinner time are 11:00am-14:00 pm and 18:00-21:00 pm respectively, the maximal number of visiting spots is set to be 7, and the time for ending daily activities is set to be 21:00 pm. The search ranges can also be set to, for example, 3 km for restaurants and 5km for sightseeing spots.

During the recommendation process, if the updated current time is around the lunch time or the dinner time periods, and the tourist has not eat yet, then the restaurant recommendation service is launched to locate a preferred restaurant within certain search range. If the current time is not in the eating time zones and is no later than 21:00 pm, the number of visited sightseeing spots is less than 7, and there are still nearby open unvisited sightseeing spots with sufficient visiting time, then the recommendation process continues to activate the sightseeing recommendation services. If the current time reaches the time limit 21:00 pm or the number of visited sightseeing spots reaches 7, then the hotel recommendation service is activated. Finally, the complete tour plan consists of sequentially arranged places generated from restaurants, sightseeing spots, and hotel recommendations is sent to and presented in the tourist's mobile device.

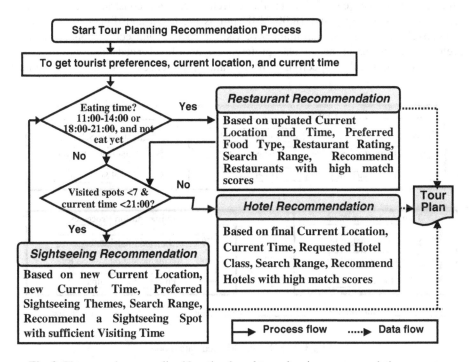

**Fig. 2.** The example personalized location-based tour planning recommendation process

## 3.2  Database, Model Base, and Knowledge Base Design

For designing and developing system database, the Object-Oriented (OO) database design approach is adopted to create the conceptual data model, and then the OO model is translated into an entity-relationship (ER) model which is further transformed into the internal relational model for physical database implementation. Figure 3 presents the OO data model in which identified objects include Tourist, Tourism Information, Tour Plan, and Recommendation Process. The Tourist object composes of Needs and Preferences (N&P), Search Range and Criteria, as well as Current Location and Time objects, and the Needs and Preferences object is further classified into Sightseeing N&P, Restaurant N&P, and Hotel N&P objects. The Tourism Information object aggregates three sub-class objects including Sightseeing Spots Information, Restaurant Information, and Hotel Information objects. The Recommendation Process object has several component objects including Process Input, Recommendation Model, Recommendation Rule, and Process Output. The Tour Plan object consists of Sightseeing Spot Selection, Restaurant Selection, and Hotel Selection objects as the components.

For model base and knowledge base design, the process modeling, decision modeling, and rule base approaches are used. Focusing on the example presented in the previous sub-section, Figure 4, Figure 5, and Figure 6 respectively illustrate the recommendation process model as well as associated decision model and rules for the hotel and sightseeing spot recommendations. The inputs to the personalized location-based tour plan recommendation process include tourist current location, the current time, search range (e.g. 3 km to the current location), constraints and criteria (e.g. 11:00am-14:00 pm and 18:00-21:00 pm as the lunch and dinner time periods respectively, 7 as the maximal number of visiting spots), sightseeing spots needs and preferences, restaurant needs and preferences, and hotel needs and preferences. For more specifically specifying needs and preferences, we take the hotel

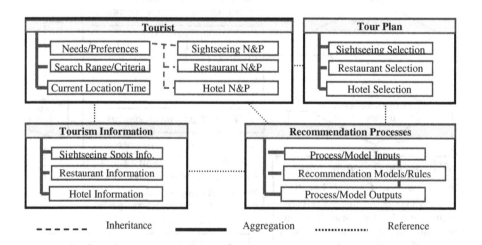

**Fig. 3.** The Object-Oriented data model

| **Tour plan recommendation process model** |
|---|

Record current location and current time
Set restaurant search range, preferred lunch and dinner food type, restaurant rating
Set sightseeing search range, preferred sightseeing theme, opening hours
Set hotel search range, preferred hotel class, room type, room rate, facility, customer rating
Set temp_time=current time
Set temp_location=current location

While loop
 If temp_time is between 11:00am and 14:00pm and lunch status=no
   or temp_time is between 18:00pm and 21:00pm and dinner status=no
   then Activate Restaurant Recommendation Service Model (temp_location, restaurant search
      range, preferred food type, restaurant rating)
   Temp_time = temp_time + suggested_eating_time
   Temp_location=location_of_recommended_place
 If temp_time<21:00pm and number_visited_site<7
   Then Activate Sightseeing Recommendation Service Model (temp_location, sightseeing search
      range, preferred sightseeing theme, opening hours)
   Temp_time = temp_time + suggested_visiting_time
   Temp_location=location_of_recommended_place
End loop

Activate Hotel Recommendation Service Model (temp_location, hotel search range, preferred hotel
   class, room type, room rate, facility, customer rating)

Output tour plan (selected sightseeing spots, restaurants, and hotel with sequence numbers)

**Fig. 4.** The tour plan recommendation process model

recommendation as an example for explanation. As a specific instance, data elements and values such as "hotel distance to the current location < = 3km", "room type = single", and "availability = yes" can be used as the matching criteria in the data retrieval step, and then, the data elements and values such as hotel distance to the current location, hotel class (3 star and above), price per room per night (less than US$150), facilities (Internet access), and customer rating score can be chosen as the hotel evaluation criteria in the ranking and selection step. Hotels with the highest total evaluation scores are ranked and presented to the tourist for selection.

The resulting output elements of a recommended tour plan include tour plan ID, sequence number of attractions/activities, types of attractions/activities (sightseeing, restaurant, hotel), attraction/activity ID, attraction/activity name, information of selected sightseeing spots (e.g. name, location, address, distance to the updated current location, sightseeing theme, suggested visiting time, etc.), information of selected restaurants (e.g. name, location, address, distance to the updated current location, food type, suggested eating time, customer rating score, etc.), information of the selected hotel (e.g. name, location, address, distance to the updated current location, hotel class, room type, room rate, check in/check out times, facilities, distance to point-of-interest, customer rating score, etc.), as well as a map showing all selected attractions with their sequence numbers. Through using the attraction/activity ID, detailed information about the recommended sightseeing spots, restaurants, or hotel can be accessed and reviewed. Similarly, sightseeing evaluation model and rules are shown in Figure 6.

| Hotel evaluation model and rules |
|---|
| Record current location<br>Set hotel search range, room type, room availability<br>Set preferred hotel class, room rate, facility, customer rating<br>Retrieve hotel distance to the current location, hotel class, room rate, facility, customer rating |
| If Hotel distance to the current location = 0, then T1 = "100"<br>  else T1 = (100-10*(Hotel distance to the current location)<br>IF Hotel class a is >= Preferred hotel class a1, then T2 = "100"<br>  else T2 = 100 – 20*(a1 – a)<br>If Room rate b is <= Specified room rate b1, then T3 = "100"<br>  else T3 = 100 –(b – b1)<br>If Facility set F contains Specified facility set F1, then T4 = "100"<br>  else T4 = 100 – 100*Count(F1-F)/Count(F1)<br>If Customer rating c is >= Specified customer rating c1, then T5 = "100"<br>  else T5 = 100 –10*(c1– c) |
| SET  HT = Sum(T1*W1,…,T5*W5)<br>  Subject to Sum(W1,..,W5) = 1<br>  where HT = total score of hotel evaluation<br>  Ti and Wi are value and weight of the ith hotel evaluation criteria, i = 1,…, 5 |

**Fig. 5.** The hotel evaluation model and rules

| Sightseeing evaluation model and rules |
|---|
| Record current location, current time, recommended and visited sightseeing spots<br>Set sightseeing search range, preferred sightseeing theme<br>Retrieve sightseeing distance to the current location, sightseeing theme, suggested visiting time |
| If Sightseeing distance to the current location = 0, then T1 = 100<br>  else T1 = 100 - 10*(Sightseeing distance to the current location)<br>If Sightseeing theme set S contains Specified sightseeing theme set S1, then T2 = 100<br>  else T2 = 100 – 100*Count(S1-S)/Count(S1) |
| SET ST = Sum(T1*W1, T2*W2)<br>  Subject to Sum(W1, W2) = 1<br>  where ST = total score of sightseeing evaluation<br>  Ti and Wi are value and weight of the ith sightseeing evaluation criteria, i = 1, 2 |

**Fig. 6.** The sightseeing evaluation model and rules

## 4   The Prototype System

A prototype system that enables the delivery of the personalized location-based tour planning recommendation services is developed. In the system environment, system and application software in the back-end server side include Windows XP, Microsoft IIS Web Server 5.1, .NET Framework 2.0, and Microsoft SQL Server 2005, as well as ASP.NET 2.0, Web Services, and Google Map API 2.0. Besides, the CHT Windows Mobile 5.0 Smart Phone Emulator is used as the client-side emulator. Figure 7 presents the prototype system environment that allows tourists to use PDAs or smartphones for accessing the web-based applications and activating desired personalized location-based recommendation services. Sightseeing spots, restaurants, and hotels can be selected, or a packaged personalized tour plan can be generated based on tourists' location-aware needs, preferences, constraints, and criteria.

In Figure 8, a few screenshots of the personalized location-based recommendation services are illustrated. From the left hand side to the right, the first screenshot shows the list of mobile tourism services including restaurant, hotel, sightseeing spot, and tour plan recommendation services, as well as user profile management services. The second screenshot displays user interactions for setting matching items and values, as well as evaluation criteria to activate the tour plan recommendation. As mentioned, these items include search range, multiple sightseeing themes, lunch food type, dinner food type, restaurant ratings, hotel class and room rate, etc.

The third screenshot presents the overview of the recommended tour plan with photos and names, sequence numbers (in red balloon), distances to the previous locations, suggested visiting time frames, and location maps of the recommended sightseeing spots, restaurants, and hotel. Clicking on these items will show enlarged

**Fig. 7.** The prototype system environment

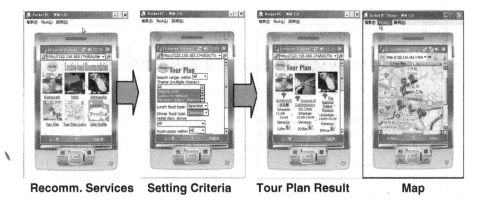

**Recomm. Services    Setting Criteria    Tour Plan Result         Map**

**Fig. 8.** The prototype system UI and output screenshots

pictures or detailed information of the corresponding places. The right hand screenshot is a Google Map display that visually spots all the recommended places.

The prototype system accessible by 3G mobile devices is evaluated by 28 recruited students who have both mobile usage and travel experience. They are asked to complete an evaluation questionnaire that consists of 22 items in 6 categories. Based on a 5-point Likert scale (1 as strongly disagree and 5 as strongly agree), the average scores of the 6 criteria including user interface and layout, functionality, ease of use, understandability, satisfaction, and intention for future use are 3.87, 4.07, 4.10, 4.45, 3.76, and 3.81 respectively with the overall average score being above 3.7. The outcome indicates positively the applicability of the proposed framework and methods.

## 5 Conclusion

In this paper, we propose a service framework, design methods, and process models for developing and delivering personalized location-based mobile tour planning recommendation services. A system prototype is built and tested to validate the feasibility and effectiveness of the proposed approach. This research integrates advanced mobile and recommendation technologies to guide and facilitate the development and delivery of powerful location-based recommendation services for supporting pre-trip and/or during-the-trip personalized tour planning that take into account tourists' location and time, needs and preferences, as well as constraints and criteria. Future research works include evaluating the operational efficiency and user acceptance of the system using real world cases, and enhancing the recommendation functions by integrating ontology mapping and case-based reasoning mechanisms.

## References

1. Anckar, B., D'Incau, D.: Value Creation in Mobile Commerce: Findings from a Consumer Survey. J. of Info. Technology Theory and Application 4(1), 43–64 (2002)
2. Barnes, S.J.: Location-based Services: The State of the Art. E-Service Journal 2(3), 59–70 (2003)
3. Berger, S., Lehmann, H., Lehner, F.: Location Based Services in the Tourist Industry. Information Technology & Tourism 5(4), 243–256 (2003)
4. Buhalis, D., Law, R.: Progress in Information Technology and Tourism Management: 20 Years on and 10 Years after the Internet—The State of eTourism Research. Tourism Management 29(4), 609–623 (2008)
5. Cardoso, J.: Developing Dynamic Packaging Systems Using Semantic Web Technologies. Transactions on Information Science and Applications 3(4), 729–736 (2006)
6. Castillo, L., et al.: SAMAP: An User-Oriented Adaptive System for Planning Tourist Visits. Expert Systems with Applications 34(2), 1318–1332 (2008)
7. Chen, M., Zhang, D., Zhou, L.: Providing Web Services to Mobile Users: The Architecture Design of an M-Service Portal. International Journal of Mobile Communications 3(1), 1–18 (2005)
8. Chiu, D.K.W., Leung, H.F.: Towards Ubiquitous Tourist Service Coordination and Integration: a Multi-Agent and Semantic Web Approach. In: Proceedings of the 2005 International Conference on Electronic Commerce, pp. 574–581 (2005)

9. Driver, C., Clarke, S.: An Application Framework for Mobile, Context-Aware Trails. Pervasive and Mobile Computing 4(5), 719–736 (2008)
10. Giaglis, G.M., Kourouthanassis, P., Tsamakos, A.: Towards a Classification Framework for Mobile Location Services. In: Mennecke, E.B., Strader, T.J. (eds.) Mobile Commerce - Technology, Theory, and Applications, pp. 67–85. Idea Group Publishing (2002)
11. Hand, A., Cardiff, J., Magee, P., Doody, J.: An Architecture and Development Methodology for Location-based Services. Electronic Commerce Research and Applications 5(3), 201–208 (2006)
12. Hawking, P., Stein, A., Zeleznikow, J., Sharma, P., Nugent, D., Dawson, L., Foster, S.: Emerging Issues in Location Based Tourism Systems. In: Proceedings of the 2005 International Conference on Mobile Business, pp. 75–81 (2005)
13. Kakaletris, G., et al.: Designing and Implementing an Open Infrastructure for Location-Based, Tourism-Related Content Delivery. Wireless Personal Communications 30(2-4), 153–165 (2004)
14. Kansa, E.C., Wilde, E.: Tourism, Peer Production, and Location-Based Service Design. In: Proceedings of the 2008 IEEE International Conference on Service Computing, pp. 629–636 (2008)
15. Kwon, Q., Shin, M.K.: LACO: A Location-based Cooperative Query System for Securely Personalized Services. Expert Systems with Applications 34(4), 2966–2975 (2008)
16. Ngai, E.W.T., Gunasekaran, A.: A Review for Mobile Commerce Research and Applications. Decision Support Systems 43(1), 3–15 (2007)
17. Niaraki, A.B., Kim, K.: Ontology Based Personalized Route Planning System Using a Multi-Criteria Decision Making Approach. Expert Systems with Applications 36(2p1), 2250–2259 (2009)
18. Puhretmair, F., Rumetshofer, H., Schaumlechner, E.: Extended Decision Making in Tourism Information Systems. In: Bauknecht, K., Tjoa, A.M., Quirchmayr, G. (eds.) EC-Web 2002. LNCS, vol. 2455, pp. 57–66. Springer, Heidelberg (2002)
19. Ricci, F., Arslan, B., Mirzadeh, N., Venturini, A.: ITR: A Case-based Travel Advisory System. In: Craw, S., Preece, A.D. (eds.) ECCBR 2002. LNCS (LNAI), vol. 2416, pp. 613–627. Springer, Heidelberg (2002)
20. Ricci, F., Nguyen, Q.N.: Acquiring and Revising Preferences in a Critique-Based Mobile Recommender System. IEEE Intelligent Systems 22(3), 22–29 (2007)
21. Sadoun, B., Al-Bayari, O.: Location Based Services Using Geographical Information Systems. Computer Communications 30(16), 3154–3160 (2007)
22. Scherp, A., Boll, S.: Generic Support for Personalized Mobile Multimedia Tourist Applications. In: Proceedings of the 2004 ACM International Conference on Multimedia, pp. 178–179 (2004)
23. Tomai, E., Spanaki, M., Prastacos, P., Kavouras, M.: Ontology Assisted Decision Making – A Case Study in Trip Planning for Tourism. In: Meersman, R., Tari, Z., Herrero, P. (eds.) OTM-WS 2005. LNCS, vol. 3762, pp. 1137–1146. Springer, Heidelberg (2005)
24. Werthner, H., Ricci, F.: E-commerce and Tourism. Communication of the ACM 47(12), 101–105 (2004)
25. Yu, C.C.: Personalized and Community Decision Support in eTourism Intermediaries. In: Andersen, K.V., Debenham, J., Wagner, R. (eds.) DEXA 2005. LNCS, vol. 3588, pp. 900–909. Springer, Heidelberg (2005)
26. Zhang, D., Chen, M., Zhou, L.: Dynamic and Personalized Web Services Composition in E-Business. Information Systems Management 22(3), 50–65 (2005)

# Do You Trust Your Phone?[*]

Aniello Castiglione[**], Roberto De Prisco, and Alfredo De Santis

Dipartimento di Informatica ed Applicazioni "R. M. Capocelli",
Università di Salerno,
Via Ponte don Melillo, I-84084 Fisciano (SA), Italy
Tel.: +39089969594
castiglione@acm.org, robdep@dia.unisa.it, ads@dia.unisa.it

**Abstract.** Despite the promising start, Electronic Commerce has not taken off mostly because of security issues with the communication infrastructures that are popping up threateningly undermining the perceived trustworthiness in Electronic Commerce.

Some Internet security issues, like malware, phishing, pharming are well known to the Internet community. Such issues are being, however, transferred to the telephone networks thanks to the symbiotic relation between the two worlds. Such an interconnection is becoming so pervasive that we can really start thinking about a unique network, which, in this paper, we refer to as the Interphonet.

The main goal of this paper is to analyze some of the Internet security issues that are being transferred to the Interphonet and also to identify new security issues of the Interphonet. In particular we will discuss about mobile phones malware and identity theft, phishing with SMS, telephone pharming, untraceability of phone calls that use VoIP and Caller ID spoofing. We will also briefly discuss about countermeasures.

**Keywords:** VoIP security, SMS security, identity theft, mobile malware, telephone phishing, telephone pharming, untraceability, caller ID spoofing, SMS spoofing, NGN.

## 1  Introduction

The Internet is a fertile ground for dishonest people: Electronic Commerce, online banking transactions and any other online operations involving confidential information give opportunities to perform fraudulent actions whose goal is mainly to steal money. The Internet poses many well known threats. One of them is that of malware (malicious software), like, for example, computer viruses. Phishing is another well known Internet threat: an attacker elicits the disclosure of private information from the victim.

---

[*] This work has been partially supported under the project *"Framework for Advanced Secure Transactions - Definizione di un'architettura di riferimento per la realizzazione di sistemi di micropagamenti"*, developed in collaboration with Telepark S.r.l. and funded by Regione Campania (Italy), in the framework of the POR Campania 2000/2006 Misura 3.17.

[**] Corresponding author.

T. Di Noia and F. Buccafurri (Eds.): EC-Web 2009, LNCS 5692, pp. 50–61, 2009.
© Springer-Verlag Berlin Heidelberg 2009

A more recent threat, which goes side by side with phishing, is that of pharming. Pharming refers to techniques that bring the user to a web server (or more generally to an Internet server) which is not the one that the user wants. Such a redirection is usually accomplished by exploiting vulnerabilities in the DNS. In a well orchestrated pharming attack, the web server to which the user is redirected looks exactly as the real one. In this situation, it is very easy to induce the victim to disclose private information. Malware can be used to perform a pharming attack. Phishing can be used, for example, to lead a victim to visit a fake bank web site. Hence, these attacks are powerful tools for dishonest people to steal money or perform other fraudulent actions. The above threats are only some of the security issues that the Internet poses to its users. It goes beyond the scope of this paper to extensively analyze Internet related security issues. Here we are only emphasizing the ones that are more relevant for the problems analyzed in this paper and that we think may threaten the spread of Electronic Commerce.

What we have said so far is fairly well known to the Internet community since these threats have been around for awhile. What people seem unaware of is that many of such issues are being transferred to the telephone networks. Nowadays, indeed, the Internet and the telephone networks are becoming more and more interconnected. This implies that many of the problems that we have discussed before also apply to the telephone networks. Furthermore, the interconnection with the Internet creates even new security issues for the telephone networks, such as identity theft and untraceability, which did not exist before (or at least were much more difficult to achieve). Since the interconnection is becoming so pervasive we like to think about a unique network, which include the Internet and the telephone networks. Such a unified network is commonly known as Next Generation Network (NGN) and we like to call it the *Interphonet*. The interconnection itself is not the unique cause of the problem. Newer mobile phones (usually called smart-phones) resemble more and more to small personal computers. This allows the possibility of spreading malware also on mobile phones. By taking advantage of all these possibilities, dishonest people can perform fraudulent actions over the Interphonet and threaten the pervasiveness of the Electronic Commerce that often rely on such new technological tools. For example, it is relatively easy to send an SMS impersonating any person or organization of which one knows the mobile telephone number. Phishing can be performed via SMS, and with SMS bulk services it is easy to reach a multitude of mobile devices. Fraudulent actions involving SMS sent via the Internet are becoming common. In particular [16] reports a successful phishing attacks. Moreover, it is possible to place a call and forge the source telephone number impersonating whoever we want. Pharming can be applied to telephone calls: a user types a telephone number on his smartphone but the call is deviated somewhere else (this requires that, before the call, the mobile device has been the target of a malware attack).

*Some related work.* There are a number of papers that have recently addressed several emerging security issues in the Internet. Very few of them specifically consider the Interphonet. In [2], Enck *et al.* analyze some aspects of the connection between the Internet and the mobile telephone networks showing how to launch a Denial of Service attack by sending a huge volume of SMS via web-based messaging portals to mobile telephone networks. Another paper [1] also consider the Denial of Service problem in the GSM network in a more general way. Security problems related to the Voice over IP service are tackled in [11] where confidentiality, integrity and availability issues are considered.

## 2    Technologies

The communication infrastructures that we are interested in are the Internet and the telephone networks (both mobile and PSTN). Until few years ago these two network infrastructures were completely separated. Nowadays, however, the interconnection is increasingly growing.

### 2.1    GSM and SMS Architecture

The *Global System for Mobile Communications* (GSM) is a standard adopted worldwide. Such a standard offers a variety of services, which, beside the obvious one of voice call, include voice mail, call handling facilities and messages. The basic one is the Short Message Service (SMS) which allows to exchange short alphanumeric messages among users, located anywhere in the world, connected to any digital cellular network. Mobile phone users can use the service by simply typing the message on the phone keypad. A message is usually delivered within few seconds if the recipient is reachable. Otherwise, a "spooling" system keeps the message until the recipient becomes available. The messages are handled, maintained and transmitted, by SMS Centers (SMSCs). SMS are injected into the mobile network essentially by submitting the message text and associated information to an SMSC. Normally a user would just compose the message text on the keyboard of the mobile device and send it to the recipient (on behalf of an SMSC) via the mobile device itself. However it is possible to inject an SMS into the network from a connection outside the wireless carrier's network. For example, one can use a web-based messaging portal using several different protocols such as SMPP (created by SMS Forum/Logica) or CIMD (created by Nokia). Since these communications are not encrypted it is possible to intercept and modify them. Once the SMSC has received the request, the content of the request is inspected and, possibly, modified in order to make it compliant with the format used by the SMSC. At this point the message becomes indistinguishable from an SMS sent by a mobile device and it is queued in order to be forwarded and delivered. Personal use of SMS is normally limited to single point-to-point messages. However it is becoming increasingly widespread the use of SMS for commercial purposes (e.g., advertising). Clearly, to have an effective impact, it is necessary to have services that allow sending a large number of messages in automated ways. Spurred by such a necessity, a number of companies are starting to provide Internet services that allow sending bulk SMS. This feature facilitates (or at least increases the chances of) phishing with SMS (see Section 3.2 and Section 3.3).

## 2.2  Voice Over IP (VoIP)

VoIP is the technology that allows "voice" to be transported over the Internet Protocol. It consists of software, hardware and industry standards. VoIP can be used to make phone calls between "something" connected to the Internet (PC, ATA, etc) and a traditional phone. In some cases, even a phone call between two traditional phones can actually use VoIP but only among "carrier" operators. For the scope of this paper, we are interested only in the fact that using VoIP one can make and receive phone calls using a PC connected to the Internet. Using VoIP, a user can get a regular phone number, with country and area codes. In order to use that number it is enough to be connected to the Internet. This implies that for VoIP is not true that a phone number tells where the user is geographically located. Currently there are many companies that, in order to foster the use of VoIP, offer VoIP numbers free of any charge and to obtain such a number it is enough to surf to an appropriate web site; registration to such web sites requires only undocumented information (like name, date of birth and address). Recently in [12] has been coined a new term ("vishing") to address the term "VoIP phishing".

## 3  Security Issues

In this section we discuss how the increasing interaction between the Internet and the telephone networks creates, makes simpler, or transfers from the former to the latter network, opportunities for dishonest users to perform fraudulent actions. Emerging Internet threats (e.g., malware, phishing, pharming) are being transferred to the telephone networks. Many of such issues are strongly interconnected and, thus, it is difficult to discern the borders between some of them.

### 3.1  Mobile Phones Malware

Malware (spyware, adware, malicious software, e.g. viruses, Trojan horses) is a widespread threat to computers connected to the Internet [8]. Less known is the analogous risk for mobile equipments. Mobile equipments can be considered safer than computers connected to the Internet because on one hand the operating systems are less known and less vulnerable and, on the other hand, the connectivity may be limited. However, newer phones increasingly resemble to computers and they run complex operating systems (e.g., Symbian OS, Windows Mobile, Apple iPhone OS, BlackBerry OS, etc.) allowing for more vulnerabilities. Newer phones can be reached through a variety of ways (e.g., Bluetooth, IrDA, Wi-Fi, GPRS, UMTS) and thus the exposure to malware is increasing. However, even with classical ways of reaching a mobile equipment (e.g. the SMS) it is possible to spread malware. Malicious SMS could be constructed to contain executable malicious code. Most SMS centers are supporting the Enhanced Messaging Service (EMS) developed by the Third Generation Partnership Project (3GPP) [10]. Such a standard extends the SMS standard to include a User Data Header (UDH) which allows to include binary data in the SMS (e.g. [3]). Mobile telecommunication companies are starting to use SMS to send executable code to their users for various reasons, such as minor phone upgrades and new applications. A user that receives an SMS from a telco has no reason not to trust the message and not to execute the code. Furthermore, using a simple WAP-Push SMS it is possible to deliver URL from which a user can download an application or a patch. However, as we will discuss in Section 3.2, it is possible to fake the identity of the sender of an SMS. Hence, the threat of receiving malware through SMS is concrete.

## 3.2   Identity Theft

In the GSM networks the identity is provided by the *International Mobile Subscriber Identity* (IMSI) and the *International Mobile Equipment Identifier* (IMEI) codes. The first one identifies the SIM card and the second one the mobile device. We remark that these two codes are not correlated and often the IMEI code is not bound to the user. The IMSI code instead, usually, is bound to the individual or organization which has bought the SIM card.

There are several degrees of identity theft. The highest level of identity theft is when one can clone both the IMSI and the IMEI codes. Cloning the IMSI codes requires physical access only for a few seconds to the user's SIM card to discover with a brute force attack the private key stored in the SIM card. Luckily, this attack is not easy to perform because on one hand it requires physical access to the user's hardware and, on the other hand, newer SIM cards are not vulnerable to brute force attacks.

In [15] it is shown how to build a private GSM network in order to impersonate an official Base Station and steal all the information needed to make a perfect clone of a GSM SIM card simply by interacting with the mobile equipment of the user under attack. We remark that it is easy to get cheap hardware to assemble a Base Station or to buy it on the Internet.

Talking about SMS, the simplest form of identity theft is to fake the real user phone number. This is possible by setting the sender field in the message header. As we have already pointed out (see Section 2.1), this is easy to do by contacting an SMSC. For example, it is possible to inject an SMS into a SMSC via a web-based messaging portal. A typical service offers a form that allows to set all the parameters of the SMS (see Figure 1). In particular, it allows to set the sender phone number to any desired string, which, obviously, can be a regular mobile phone number. Notice that, in this case, the malicious attacker is using the stolen identity only in the sense that the sender phone number appears to be the stolen one.

There exist other ways of delivering an SMS to an SMSC that can be easily found on the Internet. Another way of delivering an SMS to a SMSC is to contact it via a direct data call (e.g. with a modem). In this case the entire message needs to be correctly formatted in order to comply with the SMS standard (task that, in the previous case, is done by the web-based service). This is possible only when the SMSC accepts the incoming data call without authentication. Not long ago this was the default behavior of the SMSCs. Nowadays, however, most data calls

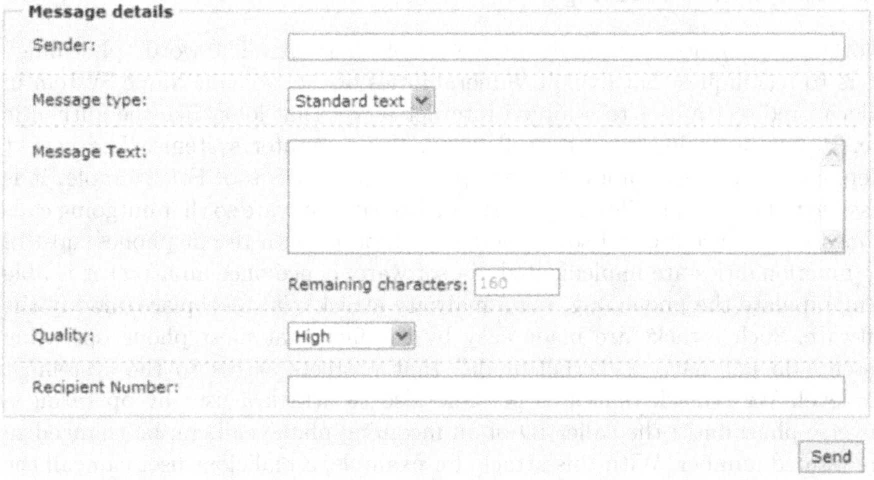

**Fig. 1.** Example of a typical web-based service for sending SMS

to SMSC are filtered and permitted only for management reason. Nevertheless, in some countries where there are old telecommunication infrastructures, all incoming calls to an SMSC are accepted.

Thanks to caller ID spoofing it is possible to mount a similar attack by placing a normal (spoofed) call (see Section 3.5).

### 3.3 Phishing with SMS

Among all the above possibilities, the one that is currently most usable is to fake the identity phone number using web-based messaging portals offered by bulk SMS service providers. This kind of identity theft can be used to perform a new kind of phishing attack [17]. This emerging problem attracts the attention of both the scientific and the economic communities. The interest of the former community is to provide technical solutions while the latter is concerned with financial losses (usually suffered by customers). Regarding possible countermeasures, many organizations, like banks, suggest not to trust any email message requesting confidential information. Phishing can be accomplished with SMS in the same way. Even expert users that would normally not trust an email message coming from a known sender, might accept the authenticity of an SMS coming from a known source. Moreover some institutions (like banks), warn their customers not to trust email, but to trust phone calls or SMS. This makes phishing with SMS easier and opens the doors to caller ID spoofing attacks. Moreover with bulk SMS services an attacker can easily reach many mobile devices. As we have pointed out before in Section 3.2, the identity of the sender of an SMS can easily be forged.

## 3.4   Telephone Pharming

Another risk connected to malware is that of pharming. The word "pharming" refers to techniques that exploit vulnerabilities of the Domain Name System in order to redirect a user to a forged Internet server that looks like the authentic one. Pharming techniques are well known for computer systems. The newest telephone technologies allow for "telephone pharming" too. For example, it is possible to hijack a mobile equipment and forge its software so that outgoing calls or messages are redirected somewhere else. Indeed, with recent phones most of the functionalities are implemented via software, hence once an attacker is able to manipulate the phone (e.g. via a malware attack), it can replace/modify the software. Such attacks are made easy by the fact that most phone operating systems do not have a "kernel mode" that protects access to the system at low level. We remark that it is possible also to attack a user by operating a "reverse pharming": the caller ID of an incoming phone call can be changed to any wanted number. With this attack, for example, a malicious user can call the victim masquerading the actual phone number (the one the attacker is using) by letting the malware change such an incoming number to any desired number. Alternatively, and quite simply, it may be used a caller ID spoofing attack to reach the same goal.

## 3.5   Caller ID Spoofing

It is interesting to show that caller ID spoofing has been around from the initial introduction of it. Such a feature was mainly used by companies accessing a Primary Rate Interface (PRI) phone line provided by carriers. Caller ID spoofing has been used, in its basic form, by changing the telephone number of all outgoing calls in order to show outside the "general" (e.g. PBX) number. Many websites that provide Caller ID spoofing are popping up on the scene. Some of them implement even other "services" that go beyond the simple spoofing of the number: call recorder, voice changer, unmasking private numbers (makes useless the caller ID blocking *67#), corporate plan, and others. There exist some implementation of spoofing software (SpoofApp) running on Apple iPhone, Google Android and RIM BlackBerry mobile platforms. The VoIP server Asterisk may also be used to forge the outgoing number of a call using a very simple PHP script (see [13]). A good compendium of the state of the art for the caller ID spoofing world is given in [14].

## 3.6   Untraceability

When talking about traceability in the Interphonet, we mean the identification of the digital equipment involved in the execution of the action. If we confine the discussion only to the classical wired telephone networks (PSTN), then traceability is not so difficult: the networks indeed know where the originating phone is located (and plugged to the wall) and telecommunication operators are required to maintain logs of all phone activities, and supply them, if required, to the law enforcement agencies. With the introduction of mobile phones, traceability of phone calls has become slightly more complicated. This is due to the fact that while in the PSTN the phone number is sufficient to identify both the customer and the physical location of the phone, with mobile networks this is not true anymore. Indeed, on one hand the mobile equipment is not bound to a physical location and on the other hand the identity of the individual who buys the service, in most cases, is not strongly verified or even not verified at all. For example, in some countries in order to buy a SIM card it is not necessary to show an identification document (e.g. driver license, passport, identification card). Even when one has to provide some proof of identity it is very easy to provide a fake one (especially considering that the documents do not have to be shown to a public officer).

With Internet, traceability means to determine an IP address. Roughly speaking an IP address is the equivalent of a phone number in the telephone networks. However there are substantial differences between these two addressing systems that render the association between the equipment and the person using it even more complicated. There are several Internet anonymizer tools which mask the real IP address. More sophisticated techniques can be used. For example, a malicious user who has physical access to a network could steal an IP address. Another possibility for malicious user over the Internet is that of performing an intrusion into someone else system and use that system to perform the wanted action. To all extents, the IP address of the violated system will appear as the originating IP address. Hence, the Internet offers much more opportunities to hide the identity behind an IP address. Using VoIP one can make phone calls from (and to) the Internet. So, the identity hiding opportunities offered by the Internet extend to the telephone networks: it is enough to make the phone call from an IP address conveniently hidden with one of the above discussed, or similar, techniques.

## 3.7  Putting Everything Together

In the previous section we have outlined several security issues by classifying them into separate kinds of attacks. We have also remarked that these attacks are strongly interconnected and malicious users exploit them together in order to perform fraudulent actions. In this section we provide an hypothetical example which involves many of the discussed security issues.

A malicious user, connected to the Internet with an IP address that cannot be tied to his real identity, subscribes, with a fake identity, to a VoIP service which provides him a telephone number. Moreover, the malicious user buys from an SMS bulk service provider the possibility of sending SMS. Notice that, even if buying such services requires a payment, in most cases the payment can be easily done without revealing the identity of the payer (e.g., with an anonymous money transfer). Mr. Bill Sphigath receives a message from his telephone mobile operator. Apparently the message contains a security patch and Mr. Bill, trusting the identity of the sender, executes the code contained in the message. However the message has been actually sent by the malicious user and the

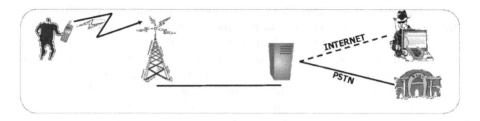

**Fig. 2.** Telephone pharming. Mr. Bill calls his bank but the call is deviated somewhere else.

attached code has installed a software module capable of deviating some outgoing phone calls (pharming); in particular, phone calls directed to Bill's bank Customer Care center. After a couple of weeks Mr. Bill receives an SMS from his bank (or a call from the telephone number of his bank). The SMS asks Mr. Bill to call the bank Customer Care because the bank needs to verify some information about his bank account. Although Mr. Bill believes the truthfulness of the message, the message has been sent by the malicious user (as well as the spoofed call apparently coming from the number of his bank). Mr. Bill, worried by the fact that the bank needs information about his account, immediately calls the Customer Care number. Because the calls to such a number are redirected to the number provided by the malicious user in the pharming attack, although Mr. Bill dials and sees on the phone display the number of the Customer Care, the call is actually redirected to the other number (see Figure 2). Such a number is the VoIP number created by the malicious user and can be physically located anywhere. Behind the VoIP number the malicious user has setup an IVR (*Interactive Voice Response*) which is used by most Customer Care, including Mr. Bill's bank, to receive customer phone calls. The IVR has been setup to "look and feel" as that of Mr. Bill's bank. The IVR service, in order to identify the user, asks Mr. Bill his bank account number and the associated personal access code. Moreover, to justify the request made to Mr. Bill, the system will inform him that he has been contacted because he should change his personal access code in order to improve the security of his account. Clearly, at this point the malicious user has both Mr. Bill's bank account and personal access code.

## 4   Countermeasures

As we have pointed out before, giving countermeasures is not the focus of this paper. Such countermeasures must rely on well-known cryptographic tools. However in this section we briefly discuss some of the actions that we can take to defend ourselves from the security threats of the Interphonet. On a non-technical side, the first and simplest countermeasure is not to trust messages (both email and SMS), especially when they require the disclosure of private information and reveal such information only after having gained a sufficient level of confidence about the interlocutor. On a technical side, we can identify two basic issues that, if solved, would address most of the security problems that arise in the Interphonet: authentication and encryption of the communication. Both are well studied and cryptographic techniques are widely available. The problem is to devise viable methods to implement them in the Interphonet in order to minimize the impact on the existing infrastructures and overcome interoperability problems.

Security issues can be tackled either solely from the endpoints or involving the network. Involving the network, however, would imply a bigger impact on the network infrastructure while a solution involving only the endpoints is entirely transparent to the network [18]. Moreover, if two users wish to achieve security goals without the help of the network cannot do otherwise. Guaranteeing security poses different problems depending on whether we are targeting SMS security or voice call security. However in both cases the endpoints must be capable of running specialized applications that use of cryptographic algorithms. This is not feasible with standard mobile equipments, whose computing capabilities are limited. However newer devices are equipped with enough powerful hardware that allows to run software that can use advanced cryptographic algorithms. For SMS, the encryption software must assure that the encrypted data should be in a form compliant with the SMS message body standard and the size of the resulting encrypted data should not be too big. The simplest authentication method is to share a secret key. Secret keys, however, have a number of well known drawbacks. Public key authentication is more suitable, although more expensive in terms of communication overhead. For SMS, the use of public key algorithms introduces the necessity of sending more than a single message between the source and the destination requiring interaction between them. It also implies charges for the recipient of the message which, for regular SMS, does not exist. If one can use (one-time) secret keys, then clearly this is the simplest solution. In such a case it is possible to include an HMAC, for example, with MD5 or SHA, using 128 or 160 bit. Another possibility is to use digital signatures schemes. A public key infrastructure and its concrete implementation for securing SMS has been presented in [21].

For voice calls it is easier to use public key cryptography because the end users must anyway interact. So, assuming that end users would have enough computing power on the mobile device, it is viable to authenticate the parties and encrypt the call [18]. Regarding the concrete security issues that arise from the use of caller ID by means of an authentication factor, a reasonable solution has been presented in [7]). Palmieri and Fiore in [9]) developed a novel hybrid framework for enhanced end-to-end security in VoIP environments by using digital signatures and encryption to enforce calling party identification, privacy, no-replay attack and non-repudiation.

It is worth noting that, even when the mobile operating system has a "kernel mode" or uses cryptographic protection to restrict certain functionality by checking digitally signed execcutable, often it is possible to bypass such constraints (see for example [20]) allowing the user to install any kind of (dangerous) software.

## 5   Conclusions

In this paper we have analyzed some new security issues that arise from the interconnection of the Internet and the telephone networks. Such security threats derive both from the interconnection of the telephone networks and the Internet and from new mobile devices which resemble more and more to small but powerful computers. We have shown how to perform several fraudulent attacks that are possible in the Interphonet. We believe that the Interphonet gives new possibilities for fraudulent attacks and thus everyone should be aware of them. The GSM standard provides three algorithms for authentication and encryption. However the solutions proposed eventually proved to be insecure. Moreover such standards were designed to protect only the communication between the Mobile Equipment and the Base Station. The remaining part of the communication is transmitted without any protection. Since in the Interphonet this communication can flow even through the Internet, privacy concerns are amplified. There are many other issues that are not discussed in this paper. We have however outlined several possible attacks that involve many of the security issues arising in the Interphonet. We believe that these problems, while well pondered for the Internet, are still undervalued for the Interphonet. It is quite obvious that the technical countermeasures must make use of cryptographic tools. At the same time, we are not sure that cryptography may overcome the intrinsic and (probably) insurmountable weaknesses deriving from the use of an open system which may be considered the Internet.

Recently [19] , the U.S. Secret Service has determined that the BlackBerry of the U.S. President did not provide the requisite security required for its continued use. Secret Service raised special concern because potential attackers could gain access to government confidential information. Although President Obama persuaded his security staff to let him keep using his smartphone, it is not clear how, exactly, the device was modified to ensure extra security.

## References

1. Bocan, V., Cretu, V.: Security and Denial of Service Threats in GSM Networks. Periodica Politechnica, Transactions on Automatic Control and Computer Science 49(63) (2004) ISSN 1224-600X
2. Enck, W., Traynor, P., McDaniel, P., La Porta, T.: Exploiting Open Functionality in SMS-Capable Cellular Networks. In: Proc. of CCS 2005, Alexandria, VA, USA, November 2005, pp. 7–11 (2005)
3. Kim, S.h., Leem, C.S.: Security Threats and Their Countermeasures of Mobile Portable Computing Devices in Ubiquitous Computing Environments. In: Gervasi, O., Gavrilova, M.L., Kumar, V., Laganá, A., Lee, H.P., Mun, Y., Taniar, D., Tan, C.J.K. (eds.) ICCSA 2005. LNCS, vol. 3483, pp. 79–85. Springer, Heidelberg (2005)
4. Lawton, G.: E-mail Authentication Is Here, but Has It Arrived Yet? IEEE Computer 38(11), 17–19 (2005)
5. Peersman, G., Cvetkovic, S., Griffiths, P., Spear, H.: The Global System for Mobile Communications Short Message Service. IEEE Personal Communications, 15–23 (2000)

6. Salam, A.F., Rao, H.R., Pegels, C.C.: Consumer-Perceived Risk in E-Commerce Transactions. Comm. of the ACM 46(12), 325–331 (2003)
7. Fujii, H., Shigematsu, N., Kurokawa, H., Nakagawa, T.: Telelogin: a Two-factor Two-path Authentication Technique Using Caller ID, NTT Information Sharing Platform Laboratories, NTT Technical Review, Vol. 6(8) (August 2008), https:// www.ntt-review.jp/archive/ntttechnical.php?contents=ntr200808le3.html
8. Thompson, R.: Why Spyware Poses Multiple Threats to Security? Communications of the ACM 48(8), 41–43 (2005)
9. Palmieri, F., Fiore, U.: Providing True End-to-End Security in Converged Voice Over IP Infrastructures. Journal of Computer & Security (in press) (January 2009), http://dx.doi.org/10.1016/j.cose.2009.01.004
10. 3$^{rd}$ Generation Partnership Project, Technical realization of the Short Message Service (SMS), Rel. 5.1.0, 3GPP Technical Specific Group Terminals (2001)
11. Internet Protocol Telephony and Voice Over the Internet Protocol, Security Technical Implementation Guide, Defense Information Systems Agency (DISA) for the U.S. Department of Defense (DOD), Version 2, Rel. 2 (April 2006), http://iase.disa.mil/stigs/stig/VoIP-STIG-V2R2.pdf
12. Griffin, S.E., Rackley, C.C.: Vishing. In: Proc. of the ACM InfoSecCD '08: Proceedings of the 5th annual conference on Information Security Curriculum Development, pp. 33–35 (2008)
13. Caller ID spoofing with PHP and asterisk (last updated 14 February 2006), http:// www.nata2.org/2006/02/14/caller-id-spoofing-with-php-and-asterisk/
14. The definitive resource on Caller ID spoofing (last updated, 20 February 2009), http://www.calleridspoofing.info/
15. Running your own GSM network, 25th Chaos Communication Congress (last updated, 29 December 2008), http://events.ccc.de/congress/2008/Fahrplan/events/3007.en.html
16. SMS phishing, Computer Crime Research Center, September 04 (2006), http://www.crime-research.org/news/04.09.2006/2221/
17. SMiShing: SMs phISHING, Wikipedia, the free encyclopedia (last updated, 1 May 2009), http://en.wikipedia.org/wiki/SMiShing
18. Castiglione, A., Cattaneo, G., De Santis, A., Petagna, F., Ferraro Petrillo, U.: SPEECH: Secure Personal End-to-End Communication with Handheld. In: Proc. of ISSE 2006, Securing Electronic Business Processes (Information Security Solutions Europe), October 2006, pp. 287–297. Vieweg Verlag (2006)
19. Harauz, J., Kaufman, L.M.: A New Era of Presidential Security: The President and His BlackBerry. IEEE Security & Privacy 7(2), 67–70 (2009)
20. Jailbreak (iPhone), Wikipedia, the free encyclopedia (last updated 29 April 2009), http://en.wikipedia.org/wiki/Jailbreak_(iPhone)
21. Castiglione, A., Cattaneo, G., Cembalo, M., De Santis, A., Petagna, F., Ferraro Petrillo, U.: An Extensible Framework for Efficient Secure SMS". Technical Report - University of Salerno

# A Multi-scheme and Multi-channel Framework for Micropayment Systems [*]

Aniello Castiglione[1], Giuseppe Cattaneo[1], Maurizio Cembalo[1],
Pompeo Faruolo[1], and Umberto Ferraro Petrillo[2]

[1] Dipartimento di Informatica ed Applicazioni "R.M. Capocelli",
Università di Salerno,
Via Ponte don Melillo, I-84084 Fisciano (SA), Italy
castiglione@acm.org, {cattaneo,maucem,pomfar}@dia.unisa.it
[2] Dipartimento di Statistica, Probabilità e Statistiche Applicate,
Università di Roma "La Sapienza",
P.le Aldo Moro 5, I-00185 Rome, Italy
umberto.ferraro@uniroma1.it

**Abstract.** In this paper we present an integrated framework for developing and running micropayment services. Our framework is multi-channel, as it allows a micropayment service to be used, at the same time, by clients using different types of communication channels. It is also multi-scheme, because it allows to have on the same server different types of micropayment schemes.

The framework has been designed in such a way to simplify the distribution and the replication of its server components across several machines, thus increasing the overall efficiency. On the client side, it includes two library of classes that can be used to run micropayment services on Java applications running on a desktop computer, in a Web browser or on a mobile phone. The framework also includes the implementation of two traditional micropayment schemes, as well as the communication modules needed to implement micropayment schemes over HTTP based and SMS based communication channels.

## 1 Introduction

*Micropayments* are a particular form of electronic financial transactions meant for the payment of very small amount of money and used in situations where the usual payment systems are impractical or very expensive with respect to the amount of moneys to be payed. From a formal point of view, we define a *micropayment scheme* as a distributed protocol where a party, the *Client User*, is interested in paying a *Vendor*. Many schemes, such as PayWord[1] require the

---

[*] This work has been partially supported under the project *"Framework for Advanced Secure Transaction - Definizione di un'architettura di riferimento per la realizzazione di sistemi di micropagamenti"*, developed in collaboration with Telepark S.r.l., and funded by Regione Campania, Italy, in the framework of the POR Campania 2000/2006 Misura 3.17.

T. Di Noia and F. Buccafurri (Eds.): EC-Web 2009, LNCS 5692, pp. 62–71, 2009.

existence of a third-party, the *Payment Service Provider (PSP)*, that is trusted by the other two parties. The PSP acts as a broker, by authorizing clients to make micropayments to vendors, and redeem the payments collected by the vendors.

The design of a micropayment system has to cope with two different, often opposite, needs. On one side, the need to guarantee the security of the parties involved in the transaction. On the other side, the need of keeping small the cost to be paid by the service operator for running the transaction. Since the introduction of micropayment schemes, dating back to the early nineties, the scientific community has been working on schemes able to achieve an optimal trade-off between these two needs, such as Tick Payments[2], NetBill[3], Millicent[4], iKP[5], NetCard[6]. At the same time, the strong interest and the considerable financial resources spent by the industry led to the implementation and the deployment of several micropayments frameworks, like *BitPass*[7], *Paystone Technologies*[8], *Digicash*[9], *Pay2See*[10], *ECash*[11], *SubScrip*[12], *NetCash*[13]. Unfortunately, the market results were far away from the expectations and most of these systems failed to survive in the long period.

Investigating the reasons behind these failures has been an interesting subject for the financial analysts, becoming soon the focal point of a deep debate in the community (see, e.g., [14,15,16]). The most commonly accepted explanation is that these systems failed mostly for sociological and economic reasons. Even if they succeeded in reducing the cost of a transaction, this remained still too high compared to the average value of the transactions, thus significantly reducing the revenue of each payment. The only scenario in which they resulted profitable was the one with a very large number of transactions per day, but unfortunately, only few companies, like PayPal [17], were able to survive thanks to the huge volume of transactions they were able to raise and process.

This trend has been changing in the last years, with a renewed interest toward this market. A Tower Group study has estimated that, in 2009, the market size for transactions implemented through micropayments will be worth $11.5 billion, in the US, and $40 billion globally, with a growth of more than 20% with respect to 2008 (see [18]).

Differently from the past, this growth is mostly due to small and medium companies and has several reasons like, for example, the decrease in the average price of a transaction because of the significant reductions, in terms of hardware and software, in the cost for implementing a micropayment service.

In addition, the mobile commerce is rapidly becoming very popular as a method to perform microtransactions. Moreover, we cite the growing interest towards the electronic purchase of inexpensive contents such as digital songs.

However, one of the most significant reason behind this success is the choice of many micropayment service providers to operate on several different markets at once, using an approach that is, case by case, tailored according to the context and to the users' needs. These new services put a particular attention to the users' experience and, often, relax some of the previous (strong) security requirements in change of a better usability. We cite, as example, the case of city transportation agencies that allow users to buy tickets by just sending a simple (unsigned) SMS message. The result is a system less secure, under certain conditions, but easier to use for end users because of the absence of very complex or cumbersome registration and/or authentication procedures. In addition, the choice to operate on several different markets allows to enlarge the consumer base, by proposing the same micropayment service to several different market segments, possibly using different communication channels.

This strategy has the important side effect that the same micropayment scheme may be well suited for a particular context (e.g., via a Web browser over the Internet) and completely inefficient or unsecure when used in a different context (e.g., when using a mobile phone over a GPRS data connection). In such a case, the optimal solution would be to use different micropayment schemes or to customize a same scheme according to the context where it will be used. The emerging need is thus two-fold. On a side, the need to run the same micropayment service in different contexts, independently from the underlying communication facilities. On the other side, the need to run in the same context several micropayment schemes at once.

## 2   Our Contribution

By taking into account the considerations made in Section 1, we designed and implemented an integrated Java based framework for developing and running micropayment services. Our framework is *multi-channel*, as it allows a micropayment service to be used, at the same time, by clients using different types of communication channels. It is also *multi-scheme*, because it allows a server to run several types of micropayment schemes at same time.

The development of new micropayment schemes is simplified in our framework by the existence of a modular architecture where the developer has just to specify, for each new scheme, how it will behave during user registration and when running the scheme. The management of the communication channels and of all the operations related to sending and receiving data is accomplished by *communication channel adapters*; these are software modules explicitly developed for dealing with a particular type of communication channel.

The interaction between the client user and the vendor is modeled after the Java Payment API standard specification defined in [19], and based on the existence of a *requestor* (i.e., the client user) and one or more *providers* (i.e., the vendors). In this specification, the provider has to offer a set of network-accessible standard functions that can be used by requesters to register themselves to the service and run transactions. Other actors can participate to a micropayment scheme as additional providers.

Finally, our framework comes with an explicit support for performing micropayments using mobile phones, as this seems to be one of the most promising market segment in this field. This support has the form of a library of Java classes and runnable by most existing mobile phones. Moreover, it also includes a communication module that can be used to implement micropayment schemes

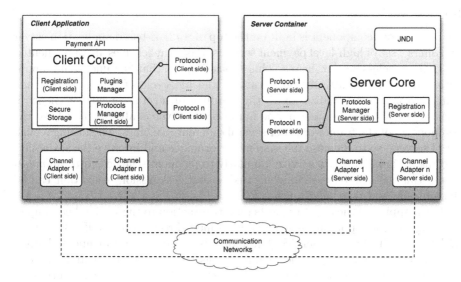

**Fig. 1.** The architecture of our framework

by means of SMS messages. A copy of the software package implementing our framework is available upon request.

## 3   The Architecture

One important requirement for our framework was *efficiency*, intended as the ability to process a very high number of transactions. We observe, to this end, that even the most optimized framework possible is inherently limited, in its efficiency, by the physical amount of computing and memory resources used to run it. For this reason, we have based the design and the implementation of our framework on the Java Platform Enterprise Edition (J2EE) architecture (see [20]). This architecture offers, at a very low cost, the possibility to organize the components of a server application in modules and distribute or replicate them over several different machines. The overall architecture, shown in Figure 1, adopts the traditional client-server paradigm and has been organized in four main components: server core, client core, micropayment protocols and communication channel adapters. The server core sits on the top of a J2EE compliant application server and is in charge of hosting the module implementing the micropayment protocols. The client core is a library of Java classes that can be integrated in any client application for performing micropayments within our framework. Micropayment protocols are the modules of our framework in charge of implementing the client-side and the server-side of micropayment schemes. Finally, the communication channel adapters provide a set of functions that can be used by clients to interact with the framework using different types of communication channels. The role of each component is explained in more details in the remaining part of this section.

## 3.1    Server Core

The server core component is built on the top of a J2EE-based application server and offers a set of high-level payment services. Payment schemes are implemented as J2EE stateless session beans. This choice implies that the underlying application server automatically takes care of the life cycle of these components, ranging from their initialization to the handling of several concurrent client requests for a scheme. Moreover, the application server is able to distribute the components of the framework over several different machines, when using a cluster of servers, so to increase the system performance and improve the scalability and the availability of the service. Similarly to payment schemes, also *communication channel adapters* are implemented as stateless session beans that can be dynamically added to the framework.

The mapping of the client requests for a transaction to the session bean implementing the corresponding scheme is performed through the JNDI [21] service. JNDI is a J2EE directory service that allows dynamic registration and look up of distributed components via their name. We assign a unique name and a unique identifier to each scheme in the JNDI directory. Whenever a client initiates a new transaction with the server, the start-up message, carrying the ID of the scheme to be used, is sent by the client to the *Protocols Manager*, a standard component of our framework. This will query the directory for the session bean implementing that scheme and return to the client the reference to this bean.

## 3.2    Client Core

The client core allows to share in a single application the support for several payment schemes and several transportation channels. It has been designed using a layered approach, shown in Figure 1.

On the top layer there is the *Payment API* module. This module offers to the client application a set of functions that can be used to choose the transportation channel, look up for a payment service, begin, conduct and close a transaction. The complexity behind these operations is completely hidden to the application and is dealt with in the lower layer of the core.

The implementation of the transaction related functions exposed by the Payment API module is provided, at a lower layer, by a set of modules featuring the client-side part of the supported micropayment schemes. All these modules have the same standard interface and are dynamically loaded in the system and initialized by means of a *Plugins Manager* that acts as a broker between the modules and the Payment API.

At this same layer, there is the *Secure Storage*: a facility that can be used by the modules implementing the micropayment schemes as a secure local storage for sensible data like cryptographic keys or other private informations. This module encrypts the data to store using a symmetric cipher (AES) with a key that can be either obtained from a passphrase specified by the user or, in the case of mobile phones, stored on the SIM card.

At the bottom layer there are the communication channel adapters. These are modules implementing a standard communication interface on the top of different communication channels. The communication interface is used by the modules implementing the micropayment schemes in order to communicate with the transaction server. The interaction between the communication channel adapters and the upper levels is mediated by a *Protocols Manager*.

The layered architecture has the advantage of simplifying the development of new modules and makes it possible to transparently integrate them in the system, without modifying the client core.

Currently, the framework offers two implementations of the client core. The first is a set of standard Java classes that can be used to perform micropayments in desktop or web browser based applications. The second is again a set of Java classes, but designed to run over mobile phones as a J2ME midlet.

## 3.3   Micropayment Protocols

Micropayment protocols are implemented in our framework as Java session beans providing, basically, two standard functionalities: *user registration* and *payment*. User registration occurs when a user needs to register for the first time to the service. Usually, the user is required to provide his credentials during this phase and obtains, as a result of the registration, some sort of security identity that will be used for the subsequent transactions. Payment occurs when the user is willing to buy, for a price that is known, a service or a product from a vendor whose identity is known.

Any scheme implemented in our framework has to provide an implementation for these two functionalities both on the server side and on the client side. Concerning the user registration phase, the vendor may decide not develop a registration protocol on his own but to use the standard one, provided with our framework and documented in Section 3.5.

This approach is general enough to allow the implementation of most part of the available micropayment schemes, including the ones involving three (user, vendor, PSP) or more actors. In this case, it is possible to model the behavior of several different actors implementing several server-side components. Notice also that the protocols implementations are independent from the underlying communication channel because all the communication adapters share the same communication interface. For this reason, when implementing a new protocol, the developer has just to code in Java the steps dictated by the protocol, without having to worry about the way data will be exchanged.

At the current stage the framework includes the implementation of the following two protocols:

*Electronic Checks.* It is a very simple payment scheme, described in [22], where the user digitally signs a piece of data that identifies the transaction and sends the resulting document to the PSP. This will in turn verify the digital signature of the received document and, if the signature has been validated, proceed with the money transfer from the user to the vendor. This is probably the simplest secure payment scheme possible and was developed to provide an upper bound on the computational cost of a transaction.

In this protocol, the user initially register himself to the system, sending his RSA public key to the PSP. When he is going to buy a product or a service from a vendor, he creates a message containing all information relating to the transaction, such as, the price to be paid and a description of the product or of the service. Then, he signs the message using his private key and sends it to the PSP, that verifies the signature and, if it is valid, authorizes the vendor to proceed with the transaction. Finally, the PSP sends to the user and the vendor the receipt of the transaction, signed with his own private key.

*PayWord.* It is three-actors protocol proposed by Rivest and Shamir in 1996 [1]. It has been conceived to minimize the public key cryptographic operations required for each transaction. Instead of these operations, the protocol mostly uses some very simple hash functions with a much lower computational cost. In this protocol, the user initially contacts the PSP asking for an account and receives, as a result, a digital certificate. Then, when he is going to purchase a product or a service from a vendor, he signs a commitment and forges electronic coins, called paywords, based on a chained hash function. The PSP will redeem the paywords collected by the vendors periodically and charge the user for the same value.

In our implementation, if a client his going to make a transaction with a vendor for the first time, then he generates the payword and sends the commitment to the server. Otherwise, he will use the payword left from the last transaction made with that vendor. In any of these two cases, the payword remaining to the client after a transaction is stored using the secure locale storage facility provided by our framework.

## 3.4   Channel Adapters

One of the main goal of our framework is to make it possible for client applications to run a micropayment service seamlessly, independently from the communication channel used to interact with the micropayment server. In order to achieve this goal, we designed a standard interface defining all the communication functions needed to run these protocols. The implementation of this interface is delegated to some special-purpose communication channel adapters. It is up to these adapters to implement the generic communication function on a particular channel, including all the operations needed to prepare the data to be sent and to process the data being received. Currently, our framework supports the following adapters (as shown in Figure 2).

*SMS adapter.* This adapter makes it possible to run a micropayment protocol through the exchange of SMS messages. The main issue with SMS is that each message can only carry 140 bytes. We overcame this limitation by splitting the stream of data in batches of 140 bytes and using concatenated SMS to send them. Both the client side adapter has been implemented using the standard Java Wireless Messaging library [23].

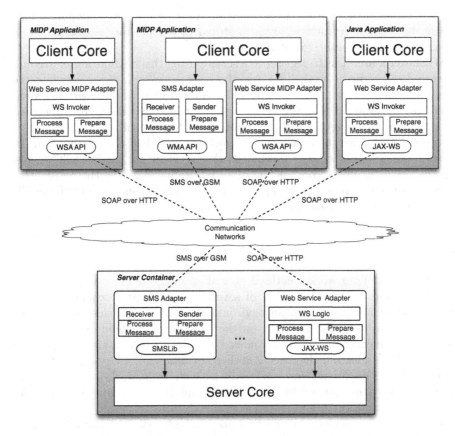

**Fig. 2.** Structure of the Channel Adapters available with our Framework

*Web Service adapter.* This adapter makes it possible to run a micropayment protocol on top of any transportation channel supporting the HTTP protocol. The interaction between client and server is modeled as a Web service and follows the Java API XML-Based Web Services and the J2ME Web Services standard specifications defined in [24,25]. The XML language is used to describe the format of data exchanged between client and server while the communication between the two endpoints uses an implementation of the SOAP protocol.

## 3.5  Registration Protocol

Many micropayment schemes require the use of personal digital certificates, released by a trusted Certification Authority (CA). Unfortunately, the operations needed for enrollment of a certificate are often very complex and slow, and their use could be impractical. On the other hand, the availability of a digital certificate is often a strong requirement for the implementation of many of these scheme.

In order to overcome this problem, our framework includes a light weight CA that can be used to release digital certificates, sign the the certificates with the key pairs generated by a service vendor and publish the corresponding public certificate. Vendor certificates are also stored in a repository accessible to all protocols implementations available on a server.

Whenever a user asks to register to a service using this module, a user account is created and returned to the user, together with a *nonce*. In the meanwhile, the user downloads the client core module and generates a pair of cryptographic keys. Then, the generated keys are used to sign the *nonce* that is, in turn, returned back to the server together with the public key of the client.

In order to reduce the number of interactions and then the relative communication costs, when the user downloads the payment application will receive, together with the client core, all the material produced during the registration phase or other information useful for future communications, such as the public key of the vendor involved in the current transaction.

## 4  Conclusion

The main goal of our work was the design of an integrated environment for the implementation and the execution of several micropayment schemes at once. Our expectation is that such an environment would, on a side, simplify the implementation of a scheme while, on the other side, it would allow a vendor to offer micropayment services customized according to the users' needs and to different communication channels. Another advantage of our system is that by putting all the micropayment services in a single framework it is possible to share some services that would be otherwise duplicated with a possible penalty on the overall performance of a system.

There are however several issues that need to be faced. First of all, the framework has been developed using a traditional client-server paradigm. This means that protocol requiring the interaction between three or more actors have to be simulated using multiple clients and servers at once. This solution may be difficult to cope with, especially when implementing very complex protocols. Instead, it would be desirable to have in the framework an explicit support for protocols dealing, at least, with three actors.

Another issue worth to be considered concerns with an exact estimation of the overhead added by our framework to the average execution cost of a transaction, both in terms of computational cost and time delay. This estimation would require an extensive performance analysis whose results should be compared with the cost to be paid for performing the same transaction in a traditional setting, without relying on our framework.

## References

1. Rivest, R.L., Shamir, A.: Payword and micromint: Two simple micropayment schemes. In: Lomas, M. (ed.) Security Protocols 1996. LNCS, vol. 1189, pp. 69–87. Springer, Heidelberg (1997)

2. Pedersen, T.P.: Electronic payments of small amounts. In: Lomas, M. (ed.) Security Protocols 1996. LNCS, vol. 1189, pp. 59–68. Springer, Heidelberg (1997)
3. Sirbu, M.A., Tygar, J.D.: Netbill: An internet commerce system optimized for network delivered services. In: COMPCON, pp. 20–25 (1995)
4. Glassman, S., Manasse, M., Abadi, M., Gauthier, P., Sobalvarro, P.: The millicent protocol for inexpensive electronic commerce. In: World Wide Web Journal, Fourth International World Wide Web Conference Proceedings, pp. 603–618 (1995)
5. Hauser, R., Hauser, R., Steiner, M., Steiner, M., Waidner, M., Waidner, M.: Micropayments based on ikp. Research Report 2791, IBM Research (1996)
6. Anderson, R.J., Manifavas, C., Sutherland, C.: Netcard - a practical electronic-cash system. In: Lomas, M. (ed.) Security Protocols 1996. LNCS, vol. 1189, pp. 49–57. Springer, Heidelberg (1997)
7. BitPass (online visited, March 2009), http://www.reg.net/bitpass/
8. PayStone Technologies (online visited, March 2009), http://www.paystone.com/
9. Digicash, http://www.digicash.com/
10. Pay2See (online visited, March 2009), http://www.pay2see.com/
11. ECash, http://www.ecash.com/
12. Furche, A., Wrightson, G.: Subscrip an efficient protocol for pay-per-view payments on. In: The Internet, The 5 th Annual International Conference on Computer Communications and Networks, pp. 16–19 (1996)
13. NetCash (online visited, March 2009), http://www.netcash.com/
14. van Someren, N., Odlyzko, A.M., Rivest, R., Jones, T., Goldie-Scot, D.: Does anyone really need microPayments? In: Wright, R.N. (ed.) FC 2003. LNCS, vol. 2742, pp. 69–76. Springer, Heidelberg (2003)
15. Geer, D.: E-micropayments sweat the small stuff. IEEE Computer 37(8), 19–22 (2004)
16. Tripunitara, M.V., Messerges, T.S.: Resolving the micropayment problem. IEEE Computer 40(2), 104–106 (2007)
17. PayPal (online visited, March 2009), http://www.paypal.com
18. TowerGroup (online visited, March 2009),
    http://www.towergroup.com/research/news/news.htm?newsId=820
19. JSR 229 Expert Group: Payment API, Maintenance Release (January 2006),
    http://jcp.org/en/jsr/detail?id=229
20. Java 2 Enterprise Edition, http://java.sun.com/javaee/
21. Sun Microsystems: Java Naming and Directory Interface (JNDI) .
    http://java.sun.com/products/jndi/ (online visited, March 2009)
22. Micali, S., Rivest, R.L.: Micropayments revisited. In: Preneel, B. (ed.) CT-RSA 2002. LNCS, vol. 2271, pp. 149–163. Springer, Heidelberg (2002)
23. JSR 205 Expert Group: Wireless Messaging API 2.0. (June 2004),
    http://jcp.org/en/jsr/detail?id=229
24. JSR 172 Expert Group: J2ME Web Services Specification (March 2004),
    http://jcp.org/en/jsr/detail?id=172
25. JSR 224 Expert Group: Java API for XML-Based Web Services (JAX-WS) 2.0, Maintenance Release 2 (May 2007), http://jcp.org/en/jsr/detail?id=224

# Secure Transaction Protocol for CEPS Compliant EPS in Limited Connectivity Environment

Satish Devane[1] and Deepak Phatak[2]

[1] Ramrao Adik Institute of Technology,
Dr D Y Patil Vidyanagar, Nerul, Navi Mumbai, India- 400706
satish@rait.ac.in
[2] Indian Institute of Technology Bombay
Powai, Mumbai, India-400076
dbp@it.iitb.ac.in

**Abstract.** Common Electronic Purse Specification (CEPS) used by European countries, elaborately defines the transaction between customer's CEP card and merchant's point of sales (POS) terminal. However it merely defines the specification to transfer the transactions between the Merchant and Merchant Acquirer (MA). This paper proposes a novel approach by introducing an entity, mobile merchant acquirer (MMA) which is a trusted agent of MA and principally works on man in middle concept, but facilitates remote two fold mutual authentication and secure transaction transfer between Merchant and MA through MMA. This approach removes the bottle-neck of connectivity issues between Merchant and MA in limited connectivity environment. The proposed protocol ensures the confidentiality, integrity and money atomicity of transaction batch. The proposed protocol has been verified for correctness by Spin, a model checker and security properties of the protocol have been verified by avispa.

**Keywords:** Electronic Payment system, E-commerce, Payment Protocol.

## 1 Introduction

Developed countries like USA, UK and European are far ahead in the implementation of electronic payment system whereas developing countries are yet to adopt the full fledged electronic payment system. Specially, in rural areas, use of electronic payment systems is hampered by the inadequate communication infrastructure. It is thus clear that if such countries have to adopt smart card based electronic payment system on large scale, it is necessary to introduce some very novel schemes, which can work in a limited networked environment. These schemes must permit offline transactions, and must have features that will carry such transaction information to back-end settlement servers either off-line or on-line.

Common Electronic Purse Specification (CEPS) has been developed by European countries with a facility to have cross border transaction and gives complete details of the protocol for transferring payment from Customer's smartcard (CEP) to the merchant's point of sales (POS) terminal. The transaction stored in the merchant's POS

T. Di Noia and F. Buccafurri (Eds.): EC-Web 2009, LNCS 5692, pp. 72–83, 2009.

need to be transferred for settlement to merchant acquirer(MA), usually a bank. CEPS has not defined the protocol and security for transactions to be transferred to MA and left its implementation on service provider. A good electronic payment system should satisfy the characteristics stated by Dennis Abrazhevich in [1], Gennadey Medvinsky and B. Clifford Neuman in [2], however the completeness of the protocol depend upon the transactions finally getting settled at back-end system. A protocol for implementing CEPS [3], where the merchant's transactions for a day are batched together and are to be transferred to the MA, is required to be defined and analyzed for its correctness and security.

The work reported in this paper defines a complete protocol compliant with CEPS for transfer of transaction batches from Merchant to MA and a novel approach is proposed for transferring transaction batch in limited or no connectivity environment. The proposed novel scheme introduces an entity called "Mobile Merchant Acquirer" (MMA) acting as a carrier of transaction batches to MA. Working of the MMA is principally based on the man in middle, where MMA behaves as MA and transfers transaction batches (TB) from many Merchant's POS terminals and at the end, it behaves like merchant's POS terminal and downloads all transaction batches to MA for settlement.

Introduction of MMA in this scheme raises many security issues, as MMA is an offline entity working on behalf of MA. Proposed scheme builds on existing standards and still provides an affordable solution that is as secure as the conventional scheme. A novel approach proposes two fold authentication mechanisms to authenticate merchant to MA through MMA and end to end security of transaction batch (TB). The proposed protocol is graphically specified and modeled for verifying various properties like correctness and reliability, by introducing the unreliable communication channel in SPIN, followed by the failure analysis of the protocol. The its security properties are verified by avispa.

## 2 CEPS Transactions

Normal purchase transactions are done through out the day between customer card and merchant POS device exactly as stipulated in CEPS section 10.1of [4] except that the batch data is stored on the merchant PSAM. This batch of transaction is transferred at the end of day to MA for settlement. This is where CEPS is silent on the protocol. CEPS only specifies the minimum data required to be transferred between merchant and MA for settlement. As CEPS make it mandatory to have mutual authentication and PKI based security for all transactions, hence it is mandatory for implementer to design the Transferring Transaction Batch (TTB) protocol to have mutual authentication and secure transaction batch transfer between Merchant and MA.

### 2.1 Novel Approach for TTB

As long as there is direct connectivity in between Merchant and MA, protocol TTB transfers transaction batch TB to MA, but in case of limited or no connectivity, we have proposed a novel approach by introducing a trusted agent of MA named as *Mobile Merchant Acquirer* (MMA) shown in Fig 1. This agent carries a small hand held

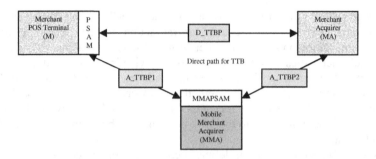

**Fig. 1.** Transaction flow between Merchant and Merchant Acquirer through MMA

terminal with two slots for smartcards; one is of his own MMAPSAM and other slot for merchants PSAM containing the TB. As stated earlier MMA works on principle of man-in-middle. Transfer of TB through this MMA is referred as alternate path; consisting of two protocols A_TTBP1 and A_TTBP2.

Transaction Batch can be transferred to MA through D_TTB or through MMA as shown in Fig 1. MMA behaves as MA and mutually authenticates to PSAM and transfers encrypted TB from all possible merchants, who don't have connectivity. Later at end of day MMA behaves as merchant and after mutual authentication transfers all encrypted TBs collected throughout day to MA. After transferring all batches, MMA collects acknowledgement with encrypted status and passes it on to Merchants on his subsequent visit.

## 3   Protocols for Transferring Transaction Batch

This section gives details of the TTB protocol in both paths.

### 3.1   Protocol D_TTB

The sequences of messages in the direct protocol are as follows

$1. MA \rightarrow PSAM : IAR, ID_{MA}$
$2. PSAM \rightarrow MA : R\_IAR, ID_{PSAM}$
$3. MA \rightarrow PSAM : TTB, ID_{MA}, \{\{ID_{MA}, SESSKey_{MA}\}_{SKMA}\}_{PKPSAM}$
$4. PSAM \rightarrow MA : R\_TTB, ETB, ID_{UB}, S7$
$5. MA \rightarrow PSAM : ACK, ID_{UB}, \{ID_{UB}, ST\} SESSKey_{MA}$

Where   $ETB = \{TB, ID_{UB}\}_{SESSKeyMA}, ID_{PSAM}, ID_{BATCH}, S7)$
        $ID_{UB} = ID_{PSAM}, ID_{BATCH}$

The first two steps of our proposed protocol TTB consist of initialization and certification verification.

**Initialization & Certificate Verification:** All purchase transactions are stored in PSAM which is a smartcard given to merchant POS terminal by Card Issuer, used to authenticate customer CEP card. PSAM is personalized to necessary keys and certificate by MA or by PSAM creator. The card initialization process is started by a terminal holding this card and consists of application selection, currency determination, checking the expiration date and, checking the card-blocking list. After initialization of card by terminal, MA sends request for transferring transaction batch, along with data giving information to the PSAM about the transaction date, currency in use and location, country & domain of MA. After this PSAM does verification and returns information to MA for version verification.

**Batch transfer & Authentication:** MA generates session key **SESSKey$_{MA}$** and in message 3, MA sends message to PSAM consisting of command for Transfer of Transaction Batch (TTB) and digitally signed and encrypted session key **SESSKey$_{MA}$**. The digital signature helps to authenticate MA to PSAM. In response with this command TTB, PSAM decrypts the message by his own secret key **SK$_{PSAM}$** and again decrypts with public key of MA to get Session key **SESSKey$_{MA}$**. PSAM prepares the transaction batch (**TB**) by appending each purchase transaction data with MAC as stated in section 10.1 of [4] and finally appends the batch summary record. In message 4, PSAM responds to the MA for TTB command by R_TTB message which contains ETB i.e. encrypted transaction batch along with ID of PSAM and BATCH by Session Key **SESSKey$_{MA}$** received from MA in TTB message and **S7** MAC which is generated from encrypted **TB**, **ID$_{PSAM}$**, **ID$_{BATCH}$**. After receiving encrypted Transaction Batch from PSAM, MA verifies **S7** MAC for correctness of the encrypted batch. MA then decrypts ETB by session key **SESSKey$_{MA}$** to get Transaction batch, thereby authenticating PSAM to MA. MA verifies batch summary record and each purchase transaction. It also checks if **ID$_{PSAM}$**, **ID$_{BATCH}$** is already received to identify duplicate or double transaction batch.

**Acknowledgement:** After verification, MA prepares the acknowledgment message 5, for the PSAM containing the acknowledgement of the current batch. **ST** is the status code indicating whether transaction batch has been received successfully or not. Upon receiving this acknowledgment, the batch in the merchant's PSAM can be deleted making space for more transactions. In case of an error, another attempt is made to transfer the TB.

## 3.2   Alternate Approach for Transferring Transaction Batch

The concept of adding the MMA is to split the protocol D_TTB in two parts giving an offline environment. MMA behaves as MA while transferring transaction batch from merchant and collects encrypted transaction batches (ETB) from various merchants. This same MMA will behave as merchant while transferring these collected transaction batches to MA. Thus the steps in the protocol A_TTBP1 used to transfer the transaction batch between Merchant's PSAM and MMA and in protocol A_TTBP2 used to transfer the collected transaction batches to MA from MMAPSAM, are similar except for the final acknowledgement. MMA gives temporary acknowledgement to each merchant after collecting transaction batch, and when MMA transfers all these batches to MA, he collects acknowledgement from MA and delivers these final acknowledgements to merchant on his subsequent visit. First two steps of the messages are same in both the protocol i.e. initialization and certificate verification are similar to the D_TTB.

**Batch transfer & authentication:** In message 3, MMA sends request for transfer of transaction batch along with the digitally signed message consisting of its ID and random number (#RND) and this is encrypted with PSAM's public key $PK_{PSAM}$. PSAM generate the session key **SESSKey$_{PSAM}$** and encrypt the transaction batch with this session key (ETB). In message 4, PSAM sends ETB, function of #RND received in message 3 and digitally signed session key encrypted with public key of MA and S8 MAC. f(#RND) is to authenticate PSAM to MMA. ETB transaction batch encrypted by session key **SESSKey$_{PSAM}$** is sent by PSAM to MMA only to be forwarded to MA. The digitally signed session key which is encrypted by $PK_{MA}$ later helps to authenticate PSAM to MA without direct communication between PSAM and MA. Thus a unique two fold authentication is used where MMA acts as man-in-middle. In message 5, MMA sends a temporary acknowledgement, batch and PSAM ID (**ID$_{UB}$**) along with status code and final acknowledgement of the earlier transaction batch transfer if any. The message flow is given below

```
1. MMA→PSAM  : IAR,ID_MMA
2. PSAM → MMA: R_IAR,ID_PSAM
3. MMA→PSAM  : TTB,ID_MMA,{{ID_MMA,#RND}_SKMMA}_PKPSAM)
4. PSAM → MMA: R_TTB,ETB,{SESSKey_PSAM}_SKPSAM}_PKMA,ID_UB,f(#RND),S8
5. MMA→PSAM  : ACK_MSG,ID_UB {ID_UB,ST}_SESSKeyPSAM
```

Similarly, the messages in protocol for A_TTBP2 are of same sequence as A_TTBP1 expect, here MMAPSAM transfer transaction batches to MA along with count of batches NNT in message no 2 and S9 MAC in message 4.

```
1. MA  → MMAPSAM: IAR,ID_MA
2. MMAPSAM → MA: R_IAR,ID_MMAPSAM, NNT
3. MA  → MMAPSAM: TTB,ID_MA,{{ID_MA,#RND}_SKMA}_PKMMAPSAM)
4. MMAPSAM→MA   : R_TTB,ETB,{SESSKey_PSAM}_SKPSAM}_PKMA,ID_UB,f(#RND),S9
5. MA  → MMAPSAM: ACK_MSG,ID_UB{ID_UB,ST}_SESSKeyPSAM
```

## 4  Formal Verification Using SPIN to Simulate and Verify Protocol

Model checkers can be used to obtain an assurance of desirable properties such as money atomicity, goods atomicity and validated receipt to be satisfied, even in the presence of a communication failure. Model checking is a completely automated technique and considerably faster than other approaches such as theorem proving [5]. Heintze et al [6] focus on the non-security aspects of e-commerce protocols and use the FDR model checker to verify the money and goods atomicity properties of two e-commerce protocols NetBill[7] and Digicash[8]. Indrakshi Ray[5] also uses the FDR model checker to analyze an e-commerce protocol.

Spin is a model-checker, a tool for analyzing the logical consistency of distributed systems, specifically of data communication protocols. The system is described in a modeling language called Promela (Process or Protocol Meta Language). The language allows for the dynamic creation of concurrent processes. Communication via message channels can be defined to be synchronous, or asynchronous. The purpose of applying SPIN to proposed protocol is to verify the resistance of the protocol to malicious manipulations like false message sequences or message sequences with false contents which could be accepted as genuine. The protocol entities are modeled using PROMELA.

### 4.1 Modeling the Protocol

Protocol D_TTBP, A_TTBP1 and A_TTBP2 have one common feature, as the batch (batches) is (are) always in smart card either PSAM or MMAPSAM. Henceforth we model senders as 'S', having transaction batch in smartcard and receivers as 'R', who is receiving the transaction batch, in these protocols. As the objective here is to verify the correctness and reliability of the transaction protocol, the cryptographic components of these protocols are eliminated while modeling to form a common theme described by a single common protocol which can then be independently modeled and verified. Security properties are separately verified using AVISPA.

1.    $R \rightarrow S$ : IAR, $ID_{MA/MMA}$
2.    $S \rightarrow R$ : R_IAR, $ID_{PSAM/MMAPSAM}$, NNT
3.    $R \rightarrow S$ : TTB, $ID_{MA/MMA}$
4.    $S \rightarrow R$ : R_TTB, ETB, $ID_{UB}$,
5.    $R \rightarrow S$ : ACK_MSG, $ID_{UB}$, ST

### 4.2 Implementation

State transition diagrams are used for describing the inside details of behavior. Oval boxes represent here the event that makes the transition happen and "/"B is an action that takes place when the transition is committed. State transition diagrams for sender and receiver are shown in Figure 2 and Figure 3.

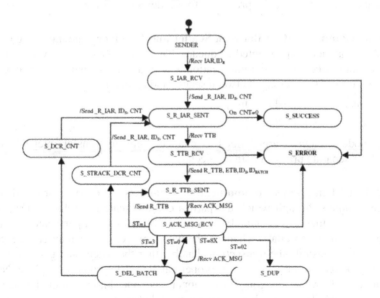

**Fig. 2.** State Transition diagram for Sender

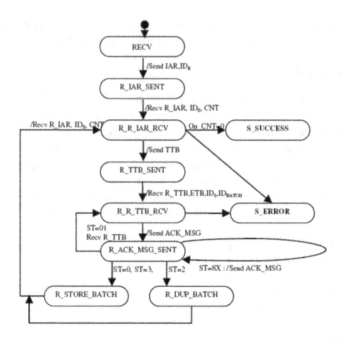

**Fig. 3.** State Transition diagram for Receiver

Sender is Merchant in D_TTBP and A_TTBP1 while it is MMA in A_TTBP2. Similarly receiver is MA in D_TTBP1and A_TTBP2 while it is MMAPSAM in A_TTBP1.This logical model is translated into a SPIN model. A process is built for each object. Thus we have the processes for sender and receiver.

**Modeling Communication Between Sender and Receiver:** The modeling is accomplished by channels implemented as queues. There is a channel for every pair of two processes and directions of communication. Communication channel 's_r' and 'r_s' are used here to send the message between sender and receiver.

> chan s_r[N]=[10] of { int };
>
> chan r_s[N]=[10] of { int };

In this model, channels are defined as channel array to transfer integers. Separate channel for separate protocol path are declared.

**Modeling of Unreliable Communication Channels:** The basic protocol assumes that the channels through which the parties communicate are reliable. Data sent by one party to another will eventually be received by the second party and is not lost in transmission. In an unreliable channel, the data may get lost or may change. So after the Merchant transmits the transactions batch either the batch may get lost, a corrupt batch may be received by receiver or proper batch transfer could take place. Note that the choice of what is going to happen is not known and happens non-deterministically. The unreliable channel is modeled as:

```
:: state==s_TTB_RCV ->
        if ::y1 == TTB ->
                s2r!R_TTB,etb,sa,id_batch;state = s_R_TTB_SENT
          ::else ->
                ec=EN_TTB;state = s_ERROR}
        fi
:: state==s_TTB_RCV ->
        if ::y1 == TTB ->
                s2r!R_TTB,ntb,sa,id_batch;state = s_R_TTB_SENT
          ::else ->
                ec=EN_TTB;state = s_ERROR}
        fi
```

It is possible in promela to write two parallel statements like ::state=s_TTB_RCV but one of these send correct encrypted batch 'etb' and the other sends incorrect encrypted transaction batch 'ntb'.

**Modeling Site Failure:** Site failure is one of the common problems in the countries where power failure is frequent. We need to model this failure to show how the properties get violated when one of the entities in the system fails or tends to failure in one of the processes. To model this, for example, if sender fails after receiving TTB message then sender will not communicate further to receiver, bringing receiver to time out state. This example can be modeled in promela as follows

```
:: state==s_TTB_RCV ->
        if ::y1 == TTB ->
                s2r!R_TTB,etb,sa,id_batch;
                state = s_R_TTB_SENT
          ::else ->
                ec=EN_TTB;state = s_ERROR
        fi
:: state==s_TTB_RCV ->
        abort;
```

**Modeling Channel Failure:** Communication channel failure is also modeled in same way shown below,

```
:: state==s_TTB_RCV ->
        if ::y1 == TTB ->
                s2r!R_TTB,etb,sa,id_batch;
                state = s_R_TTB_SENT
          ::else ->
ec=EN_TTB;state = s_ERROR
        fi
:: state==s_TTB_RCV ->
        if ::y1 == TTB ->
                state = s_R_TTB_SENT
          ::else ->
ec=EN_TTB;state = s_ERROR
        fi
```

**Modeling Money Atomicity Property:** This property is viewed here as the transaction batch atomicity property, i.e. the transaction batch should not get destroyed or duplicated while being transferred. To satisfy this property, the Merchant Acquirer process is modeled to check for duplicate transaction batch by verifying the $ID_{UB}$. Merchant won't delete the transaction batch until he gets ACK message from receiver either directly from MA or through MMA. Initially, MMA gives ACK with TEMP status code to Merchant, indicating the batch is under transfer state and when MMA finally transfers all transaction batches to MA, he collects acknowledgement of each transaction batch from MA containing the 'FINAL' status, which he delivers to Merchant on his subsequent visit.

### 4.3  Failure Analysis of Proposed Protocol

The proposed protocols being distributed in nature and having a large dependency on connectivity, failure of either the terminal or the communication link could lead to a discontinuity in the transaction process. The concept of MMA is itself a vulnerable concept, as this entity works in offline mode and may get lost or may try to tamper with the information contents. Following are the possible failure scenario.

**Failure of communication:** If at any point of time, failure occurs in the communication channel, it will result in the loss of message causing receiving process to wait indefinitely, ultimately resulting in a timeout state. These failures in communication link are analyzed during the execution of our proposed protocol and are discussed here.

**Failure in communication channel after step 1:** Sender receives IAR message and sends R_IAR message to receiver, in this case R_IAR fails to reach receiver process, receiver will wait for certain amount of time and raises the Error as timeout. Properties won't get violated as no transaction batch is transferred.

**Failure in communication channel after step 2:** Receiver receives the R_IAR message and sends TTB command to sender; in this case TTB message won't reach sender, process at sender waits for certain amount of time and raises Error as time out. The process at receiver side assumes that the message is sent and then waits for receipt of ETB, which he never gets. Receiver also waits for certain amount of time and discards the information. Sender or receiver only gets the information like ID's and certificate of each other, which they discard after timeout, here also properties won't get violated.

**Failure in communication channel after step 3:** If communication breaks or fails after execution of step 3, senders have the knowledge of session key in the path D_TTBP1 or encrypted digitally signed nonce in alternate path A_TTBP. In this case receiver is waiting for receiving the ETB, a encrypted transaction batch, which he won't get in time, and changes to error state and terminates the protocol. Property holds good for considering transaction batch atomicity but in case of cryptanalysis, reuse of the session key may happen by the malicious sender.

**Failure in communication channel after step 4:** In case of failure after step 4, receiver sends back ACK_MSG after receiving ETB but sender does not receive it. At this point of time sender has already closed the batch and transferred it, but does not receive any acknowledgement either TEMP or FINAL, after timeout he raises error and terminates the execution of protocol, but keeps transaction batch in closed state. Sender re-sends this closed transaction batch on next opportunity and waits for ACK_MSG. As receiver has a log of received batches along with details about identity of batch and sender, this is sufficient for the receiver to conclude that it is a duplicate batch and send ACK_MSG containing 'DUP' status code.

**Failure of process or site:** If for any reason, a site fails, or the process fails, the ultimate result is same as in the case of break in communication sequence. In such situation, the other entity will go into error state with timeout. Failure of site at any point of time is as good as failure in communication link; hence all above analysis is true in this case also.

### 4.4  Result of SPIN

```
(SPIN Version 4.2.9 -- 8 February 2007)
    + Partial Order Reduction

Full statespace search for:
    never claim     - (none specified)
    assertion violations  +
    acceptance cycles   - (not selected)
    invalid end states   +

State-vector 508 byte, depth reached 302, errors: 0
  448 states, stored
  22 states, matched
  470 transitions (= stored+matched)
  16 atomic steps
hash conflicts: 0 (resolved)

    2.827 memory usage (Mbyte)
```

By referring result we can conclude that more depth without error indicates the protocol correctness. As one of the features of the SPIN is rubber state vector technique, the depth first search requires only 2.827 Mbytes of memory. Since the protocol simulation itself produces the required sequence of operation, no accept cycles are specified. So its verification contains no states as accept states. As the protocol executed successfully, no invalid sates are encountered.

## 5  Verification Using AVISPA

The AVISPA is Automated Validation of Internet Security Protocol and Applications. It is a security protocol analyzer, supports the specification of security protocols and properties by means of a modular and expressive specification language HLPSL-High Level Protocol Specification Language. It integrates different back-ends implementing a variety of automatic analysis techniques for protocol falsification by finding an attack on the input protocol. The protocol D_TTB P has been modeled and verified in[11], the proposed goal for verification was

```
goal

    secrecy_of sec_m,sec_ma
    %MMA authenticates MA on na_nb1
    authentication_on na_nb1
    %MA authenticates M on na_nb2
    authentication_on na_nb2

end goal
```

**Verification Results**

The verification result consists of:

```
SUMMARY
 SAFE
DETAILS
 BOUNDED_NUMBER_OF_SESSIONS
 TYPED_MODEL
PROTOCOL
 /root/avispa-1.1/testsuite/results/pr_6.if
GOAL
 As Specified
BACKEND
 CL-AtSe
STATISTICS
 Analysed : 18412 states
 Reachable : 7364 states
 Translation: 0.03 seconds
 Computation: 9.41 seconds
```

By referring the result generated using AVISPA; we can conclude that the protocol is safe. It indicates that there is neither authentication attack nor secrecy attack on the protocol. There is no attack found on session key by the intruder. The secrecy of the session key and the transferred messages between the parties are also maintained. The backend itself is the attack searcher, which gives no information about any attack, indicating protocol is safe. As more number of states are analyzed and reachable, the protocol is safer. Thus three security properties are modeled and verified using AVISPA tool.

# 6  Conclusion

To overcome the limitation of the CEPS in limited connectivity environment we proposed two secure protocols for transferring transaction batches in CEPS compliant electronic payment system. One is a direct protocol for transferring batches from merchant to merchant acquirer and alternate approach is proposed with an additional entity Mobile Merchant Acquirer, which works in offline mode. This is the cost effective and secure solution for the rural part of the country where connectivity is limited. We have verified the correctness of the proposed protocol using model checker spin and modeling language Promela. Analysis shows that the properties of the protocol hold good in case of communication failure, site failure or terminal failure.

# References

1. Abrazhevich, D.: Classification and Characteristics of Electronic Payment Systems. In: Bauknecht, K., Madria, S.K., Pernul, G. (eds.) EC-Web 2001. LNCS, vol. 2115, pp. 81–90. Springer, Heidelberg (2001)
2. Medvinsky, G., Neuman, B.C.: NetCash-A design for practical electronic currency on internet. In: Proceedings of the first ACM conference on computer and communication security (November 1993)
3. Devane, S.R., Phatak, D.B.: Introducing MMA in CEPS for Indian business Scenario. In: Proceedings The Future of Smart Card, e-smart 2003, Sofia Antipolice, France (2003)
4. Common Electronic Purse Specifications, Technical Specification, Version 2.3 (March 2001) (Copyright CEPSCO 1999, 2000, 2001)
5. Ray, I., Ray, I.: Failure Analysis of an E-commerce Protocol Using Model Checking. In: Proceedings of the Second International Workshop on Advanced Issues of E-Commerce and Web-based Information Systems, Milpitas, CA, June 2000, pp. 176–183 (2000)
6. Heintze, N., Tygar, J., Wing, J., Wong, H.: Model Checking Electronic Commerce Protocols. In: Proceedings of the 2nd USENIX Workshop in Electronic Commerce, November 1996, pp. 146–164 (1996)
7. Cox, B., Tygar, J.D., Sirbu, M.: NetBill Security and Transaction Protocol. In: Proceedings of the 1st USENIX Workshop in Electronic Commerce, July 1995, pp. 77–88 (1995)
8. Chaum, A.F.D., Naor, M.: Untraceable electronic cash. In: Menezes, A., Vanstone, S.A. (eds.) CRYPTO 1990. LNCS, vol. 537, pp. 200–212. Springer, Heidelberg (1991)
9. Holzmann, G.J.: The Model Checker SPIN. IEEE Transactions On Software Engineering 23(5) (May 1997)
10. Jøsang, A.: Security protocol verification using SPIN. In: Gregoire, J.-C. (ed.) Proceedings of the First SPIN Workshop, INRS-Telecommunications, Montreal, Canada (1995); SPIN Manual, http://www.spinroot.com (downloaded, January 25 2006)
11. Shaikh, R., Devane, S.: Formal Verification of Protocol Using SPIN and AVISPA., M.E. Dissertation report, Mumbai University, Mumbai (2007)

# Trust Enhanced Authorization for Mobile Agents

Chun Ruan[1] and Vijay Varadharajan[1,2]

[1] School of Computing and Mathematics
University of Western Sydney, Penrith South DC, NSW 1797 Australia
chun@scm.uws.edu.au
[2] Department of Computing
Macquarie University, North Ryde, NSW 2109 Australia
vijay@ics.mq.edu.au

**Abstract.** Trust has been recognized as an important aspect for mobile agent security. In this paper, we develop a logic based trust model which enables the capturing of a comprehensive set of trust relationships to enhance the security of conventional access control mechanisms in a mobile based applications. We first discuss the notion of trust and its relevance to mobile agent security. Next we define a logic program based language to facilitate the modelling process. To enforce the security related trustworthy behaviours, we then define a set of general rules to capture the semantics. Finally, the language is applied in a mobile agent context to demonstrate how the trust can be explicitly modelled and reasoned about to support better security decisions for the mobile agent based systems.

**Keywords:** trust, authorization, mobile agent, logic programming.

## 1 Introduction

Mobile agent model is a promising paradigm for distributed computing which offers unique features such as reducing the network load, executing asynchronously and autonomously, and adapting dynamically. Mobile agents are autonomous programs and follow a route, migrate through a network of agent enabled sites to accomplish tasks on behalf of their owners. The mobile agent model has been considered as an attractive option to build the infrastructures of internet-based e-commerce applications, which have been growing increasingly popular in recent years. While mobile agent based e-commerce offers attractive features, security has been a big challenge. Mobile agent systems are vulnerable to a number of attacks in an open network. These include attacks on the host by malicious mobile agents and attacks on the mobile agent by the malicious hosts. This presents challenges to the mobile agent security in two aspects: protection of service provider hosts is difficult, due to the fact that the identity of a requesting party can no longer be determined with certainty and agents from a malicious host can attempt to do harms to a receiving host. On the other hand, clients requesting

T. Di Noia and F. Buccafurri (Eds.): EC-Web 2009, LNCS 5692, pp. 84–95, 2009.

goods and services now have the difficulties in protecting their agents while they roam around a series of hosts conducting itinerant mobile e-commerce transactions, such as conducting a complete travel plan for its human principal in terms of booking the airline tickets, hotel reservations and car rental etc. Most of existing security solutions for mobile agents are based on traditional security mechanisms, which can not guarantee how actually the authorized entities will behave. While these issues are difficult to solve within the context of security mechanisms, some researchers have pointed out that trust is an important notion for mobile agent security and have developed security solutions with trust. These trust based security models have shown the potential to overcome the drawbacks of traditional security models by ensuring a higher level of trustworthiness of authorized entities and thus raising the security levels.

In the past, considerable efforts have been spent on formalising security protocols and access control schemes for general distributed systems, which include the authentication logic and access control calculus by Abadi et al. [7,1], a logical language for authorisation specifications proposed by Jajodia et al. [10], an access control policy description language proposed by Kurkowski et al. [5], the PKI trust models by Maurer [8] and by Levien et al. [6] respectively. Perhaps one of the better-known systems is that of Blaze et al. [2], which can be thought of as an approach to distributed "trust" management from the perspective of combining authentication and authorisation services. However, those models did not approach trust directly, rather they dealt with trust in an indirect way in that they use it as an construct for identifying security flaws in the existing security protocols. Hence these models do not use trust as an independent device for security decision enhancement. In the mobile agent context, we have observed that only limited efforts in the usage of indirect trust in security decisions exist, such as using verification servers for trusted execution [11] and in mobile agent authentication [3].

Therefore, we need to set up a new trust model which not only offers the explicit modelling of trust, but also facilitates the specification and design of the trust based mechanisms. To achieve this, we draw inspirations from the above research literature and develop a logical language to help to capture the trust relationships explicitly. Within the language, we also introduce a set of general rules which form the basis for enforcing desirable security related trustworthy behaviours. These in turn can be used to support the new trust enhanced security solutions for mobile agents. To take advantage of strong expressive and reasoning power of logic programming, we will develop our framework based on extended logic programs [4], which supports both negation as failure and classical negation. As the incomplete information is a common issue in the trust world, many trust policies are easier to specify in extended logic programs. For example, if we want to express denial by default, such as Alice is denied to read a file $F$ if she is not specified as trusted, then the negation as failure is often the most direct way to express this intention. On the other hand, classical negation is useful to explicitly specify that something is forbidden.

In this paper, we study trust enhanced authorization model for mobil agents. We believe a logic based trust model will provide many benefits. We will explicitly model trust relationships which indicate one agent host's belief in another in terms of authentication of the relevant host's identity (i.e. *Authentication Trust*) and the belief in the benevolence and competence of another host (usually the owner host) in producing good code (i.e. *Code Trust*) and the belief in the honesty, and faithful and competent execution of the task requested by a visiting mobile agent (i.e. *Execution Trust*). In our framework, trust rules are specified in a Trust Program (TP) which is an extended logic program. The semantics of a TP is defined based on the well-known stable model semantics. The desirable trustworthy behaviours are achieved through a set of general rules. The basic idea is to combine these general rules with a set of domain-dependent rules defined by users to derive the trust relationships holding at any time in the system.

The paper is organised as follows. Section 2 introduces the mobile agent security models. Section 3 describes the syntax of the Trust program (TP). Section 4 discusses various aspects that are taken into account for the semantics of TP, while Section 5 formally defines the semantics of TP. Section 6 presents an application. Finally Section 7 concludes the paper with some remarks.

## 2   Mobile Agent Security Models

This section gives a brief introduction to practical aspects of mobile agent security models. Let us start with a simple model comprising two main components, namely an agent and an agent host. The agent consists of the code and state information needed to perform some computation. The agent can migrate from one host to another and the computation is mobile. We will refer to the host in which an agent is created and from where it originates as the *agent owner host*. When an agent moves to another host, it may be referred to as the foreign execution host. The agent migration involves the transfer of both program code and data.

There is a variety of ways of classifying security threats in such a mobile computation environment. We consider these broadly in terms of agents attacking hosts and host attacking agents[1]. In protecting hosts, it is required to authenticate both the foreign execution hosts and the owner host of the agent. Furthermore, in mobile agent systems, often programs are obtained from unknown or untrusted sources, hence mutual authentication is required in host-to-host transactions. In protecting a host, the host itself needs first to authenticate the mobile agent, then it needs to determine what actions the mobile agent is allowed to perform and whether it has the necessary privileges to carry them out. In general, the authorisation decision for a mobile agent to perform a certain action can be based on a combination of privileges such as the privileges of the owner of the mobile agent, the execution hosts of the mobile agent as well as

---

[1] Agents attacking each other in a host can be regarded as the problem of agent attacking host.

the function of the program code and the state of the agent. The authorisation mechanisms control the behaviour of the agent within the host thereby allowing protection of local resources. In protecting the agent, the migration of a mobile agent from one host to another over the network needs to be protected against unauthorised disclosure and unauthorised modification. Similarly any message that is sent by the mobile agent over an untrusted network needs to·be protected. In principle, this can be achieved using cryptographic techniques such as encryption and cryptographic checksums.

## 3   Syntax of Trust Programs

Our language $\mathcal{L}$ is a many-sorted first order language, with four disjoint *sorts* for principals, asymmetric cryptographic keys, mobile agents, and privileges respectively. Let $\mathcal{L}$ have the following vocabulary:

1. *Sort principal P*: with principal *constant* $P_{ttp}, P_1, P_2, ...$, and principal *variables* $p_1, p_2, p_3, ...$, where $P_{ttp}$ denotes the trusted third parties in the system.

2. *Sort asymmetric cryptographic keys K*: with key *constant* $K_1, K_2, ...$, and key *variables* $k_1, k_2, k_3, ...$

3. *Sort Object O*: with object *constant* $O_1, O_2, ...$ and agent *variables* $o_1, o_2, ...$

4. *Sort privileges R*: with privilege *constant* set $R = +K, -K, +R, -R, R_1, R_2,$ ..., and privilege *variables* $r_1, r_2, r_3, ....$ Here privileges mean the access rights to objects such as owning, reading, modifying, writing and executing files, directories and networks ports. Four special privileges are defined with the following meanings. $+K$ means the privilege to assign an asymmetric cryptographic key to a principal,$-K$ means the privilege to revoke an asymmetric cryptographic key from a principal, $+R$ means the privilege to assign a privilege to objects to a principal, and $-R$ means the privilege to revoke a privilege to objects from a principal.

5. *Sort time point T*: with time *constant* $T_1, T_2, ...$ and time variable $t_1, t_2, ...$

6. *Predicate Symbol* set *P*: $P$ consists of a set of ordinary predicates defined by users, and a set of built-in predicates. We will introduce the built-in predicates in the next subsection.

A *term* is either a variable or a constant. Note that we prohibit function symbols in our language. An *atom* is a construct of the form $p(t_1, ..., t_n)$, where $p$ is a predicate of arity $n$ in $P$ and $t_1, ..., t_n$ are terms. A *literal* is either an atom $p$ or the negation of the atom $\neg p$, where the negation sign $\neg$ represents classical negation. Two literals are *complementary* if they are of the form $p$ and $\neg p$, for some atom $p$. A *rule r* is a statement of the form:

$$b_0 \leftarrow b_1, ..., b_k, not\ b_{k+1}, ..., not\ b_m, m >= 0$$

where $b_0, b_1, ..., b_m$ are literals, and *not* is the negation as failure symbol. The $b_0$ is the *head* of $r$, while the conjunction of $b_1, ..., b_k, not\ b_{k+1}, ..., not\ b_m$ is the *body* of $r$. Obviously, the body of $r$ could be empty. We sometimes use $Head_r$ and $Body_r$ to denote the head and body of $r$ respectively.

A *Trust Program*, $TP$, consists of a finite set of rules.

A term, an atom, a literal, a rule or program is *ground* if no variable appears in it.

## 3.1  Built-In Predicates

In this section, we define a set of built-in predicates to facilitate modelling process of trust systems.

Predicates for trust:

There are four predicates about the trust operations which are $Trust*$, $TrustAuth, TrustCode, TrustExe$. They have the same type of $P \times K \times P \times K \times T$. Intuitively, $Trust * (P_i, K_i, P_j, K_j, T)$ means that the principal $P_i$ possessing an asymmetric key $K_i$ trusts "blindly" principal $P_j$ which is identified by an asymmetric key $K_j$ at time $T$. This is the highest form of trust as it implies that $P_i$ trusts whatever $P_j$ does or says (i.e. unconditional trust).

$TrustAuth(P_i, K_i, P_j, K_j, T_k)$ means that at time $T_k$, the principal $P_i$ possessing an asymmetric key $K_i$ trusts that the principal $P_j$ is identifiable by an asymmetric key $K_j$ and $K_j$ is authentic.

$TrustCode(P_i, K_i, P_j, K_j, T_k)$ means that at time $T_k$, the principal $P_i$ possessing an asymmetric key $K_i$ trusts that principal $P_j$ which is identified by an asymmetric key $K_j$ has the ability and the benevolent intentions of generating safe and competent code.

$TrustExe(P_i, K_i, P_j, K_j, T_k)$ means that at time $T_k$, the principal $P_i$ possessing an asymmetric key $K_i$ trusts that principal $P_j$ which is identified by an asymmetric key $K_j$ has the ability and the benevolent intentions of executing the agent deployed by $P_i$ faithfully and competently.

Predicates for key operations:

Predicates GiveKey and RevokeKey have the same type of $P \times K \times P \times K \times T$. $GiveKey(P_i, K_i, P_j, K_j, T_k)$ means that at time $T_k$, the principal $P_i$ possessing an asymmetric key $K_i$ gave the principal $P_j$ the key $K_j$ at time $T_k$. Here giving the key denotes issuing the key certificate[2] and the key is valid until it is revoked.

$RevokeKey(P_i, K_i, P_j, K_j, T_k)$ means that at time $T_k$, the principal $P_i$, possessing an asymmetric key $K_i$ revoked the key $K_j$ of the principal $P_j$ at time $T_k$. The key revocation means adding this key to the key revocation list of $P_i$.

Predicates for privilege operations:

Predicates GivePriv and RevokePriv have the same type of $P \times K \times P \times K \times R \times O \times T$. $GivePriv(P_i, K_i, P_j, K_j, R_k, O_k, T_k)$ means that, at time $T_k$ the principal $P_i$ possessing an asymmetric key $K_i$ has given the principal $P_j$ possessing an asymmetric key $K_j$ the right to use privilege $R_k$ on Object $O_k$. Here giving the

---

[2] A (public) key certificate binds a subject name to a public key value, along with information needed to perform certain cryptographic functions.

privilege represents issuing a certificate for the privilege and the certificate is valid until it is revoked.

$RevokePriv(P_i, K_i, P_j, K_j, R_k, O_k, T_k)$ means that, at time $T_k$ the principal $P_i$, possessing an asymmetric key $K_i$ has taken from the principal $P_j$ the right to use privilege $R_k$. Taking away the privilege means adding this privilege to the privilege revocation list of $P_i$.

A system state $\eta$ is a set consisting of the above trust, key and privilege predicates. A local state $\eta_i$ is a set of the above trust and privilege predicates performed by a principal $P_i$.

*Example 1.* Let $P = \{P_{ttp}, P_1, P_2, p_1, p_2\}$, $K = \{K_{ttp}, K_1, K_2, k_1, k_2\}$, $T = \{T_1, T_2, t_1, t_2, t_3\}$, then the following is a simple example of $TP$:

$r_1 : GiveKey(P_{ttp}, K_{ttp}, P_1, K_1, T_1) \leftarrow$
(The trusted third party $P_{ttp}$ possessing an asymmetric key $K_{ttp}$ gave principal $P_1$ the key $K_1$ at time $T_1$.)

$r_2 : GiveKey(P_{ttp}, K_{ttp}, P_2, K_2, T_2) \leftarrow$
(The trusted third party $P_{ttp}$ possessing an asymmetric key $K_{ttp}$ gave principal $P_2$ the key $K_2$ at time $T_2$.)

$r_3 : TrustAuth(p_1, k_1, p_2, k_2, t_1) \leftarrow GiveKey(P_{ttp}, K_{ttp}, p_2, k_2, t_2),$
$\qquad notRevokeKey(P_{ttp}, K_{ttp}, p_2, k_2, t_3), t_2 \leq t_3, t_3 \leq t_1$
(A principal $p_2$ is trusted to be identifiable by an asymmetric key $k_2$ and $k_2$ is authentic if $k_2$ is granted to $p_2$ by the trusted third party $P_{ttp}$.)

## 4 Semantic Considerations

To develop a formal semantics of a TP, three aspects should be taken into consideration: relationships between grant and revoke operations, relationships between trust operations, relationships between trust and grant/revoke operations.

*Relationships between grant and revoke operations*

1. If a principal wants to revoke a key $K$ from another principal, then it should have given $K$ to this principal before, and the key has not been cancelled. More formally, if $RevokeKey(P_i, K_i, P_j, K_j, T_k)$ is in the system state $\eta$, then the operation $GiveKey(P_i, K_i, P_j, K_j, T_l)$ should also be in $\eta$, and there is no operation $RevokeKey(P_i, K_i, P_j, K_j, T_m)$ in $\eta$, where $T_l < T_m < T_k$.
2. If a principal wants to revoke a Privilege $R$ from another principal, then it should have given $R$ before which has not been cancelled. More formally, if $RevokePriv(P_i, K_i, P_j, K_j, R_j, O_j, T_k)$ is in system state $\eta$, then the operation $GivePriv(P_i, K_i, P_j, K_j, R_j, O_j, T_l)$ should also be in $\eta$, and there is no operation $RevokePriv(P_i, K_i, P_j, K_j, R_j, O_j, T_m)$ in $\eta$, where $T_l < T_m < T_k$.

3. If a principal wants to give a key at time $T$, it should hold privilege $+K$ privilege at time $T$. More formally, if $\text{GiveKey}(P_i, K_i, P_j, K_j, T_l)$ is in the system state $\eta$, then the operation $\text{GivePriv}(P_n, K_n, P_i, K_i, +K, \_, T_m)$ should also be in the $\eta$, and the operation $\text{RevokePriv}(P_n, K_n, P_i, K_i, +K, \_, T_n)$ should not be in $\eta$, where $p_i \neq p_{ttp}, T_m < T_n < T_l$. Please note that $\_$ in the predicates means it has no meaning.

4. If a principal wants to give a privilege at time $T$, it should hold privilege $+R$ privilege at time $T$. More formally, if $\text{GivePriv}(P_i, K_i, P_j, K_j, R_j, O_j, T_k)$ is in the system state $\eta$, then the operation $\text{GivePriv}(P_n, K_n, P_i, K_i, +R, O_j, T_l)$ should also be in $\eta$, and there is no operation $\text{RevokePriv}(P_n, K_n, P_i, K_i, +R, O_j, T_m)$ in $\eta$, where $T_l < T_m < T_k$.

5. If a principal wants to revoke a key at time $T$, it should hold privilege $-K$ at time $T$. More formally, if $\text{RevokeKey}(P_i, K_i, P_j, K_j, T_k)$ is in the system state $\eta$, then the operation $\text{GivePriv}(P_n, K_n, P_i, K_i, -K, \_, T_l)$ should also be in $\eta$, and there is no operation $\text{RevokeKey}(P_n, K_n, P_i, K_i, -K, \_, T_m)$ in $\eta$, where $T_l < T_m < T_k$.

6. If a principal wants to revoke a privilege at time $T$, it should hold privilege $-R$ at time $T$. More formally, if $\text{RevokePriv}(P_i, K_i, P_j, K_j, R_j, O_j, T_l)$ is in the system state $\eta$, then the operation $\text{GivePriv}(P_n, K_n, P_i, K_i, -R, O_j, T_m)$ should also be in $\eta$, and there is no operation $\text{RevokePriv}(P_n, K_n, P_i, K_i, -R, O_j, T_n)$ in $\eta$, where $T_m < T_n < T_l$.

7. One cannot grant/revoke privileges/keys to himself/herself.

*Relationships between trust operations*

1. If a principal $P_i$ trusts that another principal $P_j$ has the ability and benevolent intentions of generating safe code, then $P_i$ should also trust that $P_j$ is identified by an asymmetric key $K_j$. More formally, if $\text{TrustCode}(P_i, K_i, P_j, K_j, T_k)$ is in the system state $\eta$, then the operation $\text{TrustAuth}(P_i, K_i, P_j, K_j, T_l)$ should also be in $\eta$, and there is no $\text{RevokeKey}(P_m, K_m, P_j, K_j, T_m)$ in $\eta$, where $T_m < T_n < T_l$.

2. If a principal $P_i$ trusts that another principal $P_j$ has the ability and benevolent intentions of executing the agent deployed by $P_i$, then $P_i$ should also trust that $P_j$ is identified by an asymmetric key $K_j$. More formally, if $\text{TrustExe}(P_i, K_i, P_j, K_j, T_k)$ is in the system state $\eta$, then $\text{TrustAuth}(P_i, K_i, P_j, K_j, T_l)$ should also be in $\eta$, and there is no $\text{RevokeKey}(P_m, K_m, P_j, K_j, T_m)$ in $\eta$, where $T_m < T_n < T_l$.

3. The trust predicate *trust* denotes the *unconditional trust* which implies all other forms of trust. This axiom formally captures the notion of *unconditional trust* or *blind trust* [9] in the mobile agent security context. This can be used for specifying the assumptions of maximum trustworthiness in a mobile agent system. More formally, if $\text{Trust}^*(P_i, K_i, P_j, K_j, T_k)$ is in $\eta$, then $\text{TrustAuth}(P_i, K_i, P_j, K_j, T_k)$, $\text{TrustCode}(P_i, K_i, P_j, K_j, T_k)$, and $\text{TrustExe}(P_i, K_i, P_j, K_j, T_k)$ will all be in $\eta$.

4. All principals trust themselves at any time.

*Relationships between trust and grant/revoke operations*

1. If a principal $P_i$ trusts that another principal $P_j$ is identified by an asymmetric key $K_j$, then $P_j$ should be given this key before which is not cancelled. More formally, if TrustAuth($P_i, K_i, P_j, K_j, T_k$) is in the system state $\eta$, GiveKey($P_m, K_m, P_j, K_j, T_l$) should also be in $\eta$, and there is no RevokeKey( $P_m, K_m, P_j, K_j, T_m$) in $\eta$, where $T_m < T_n < T_l$.
2. If a principal $P_i$ grants an exec privilege to another principal $P_j$, then $P_i$ should trust $P_j$ in terms of executing the code. More formally, if GivePriv($P_i$, $K_i, P_j, K_j, exe, O_j, T_k$) is in the system state $\eta$, then the operation TrustExe( $P_i, K_i, P_j, K_j, T_l$) should also be in $\eta$, where $T_l < T_k$.

A system state $\eta$ is trust consistent if it satisfies all the above conditions.

## *Stable model semantics*

In our approach, we will develop a stable model [4] based semantics for our TPs as stable model semantics provides a flexible manner to deal with defeasible and incomplete information, and hence suitable for our purpose of handling trust and authorization.

## 5  Formal Definition of Semantics

This section presents the formal semantics for TP which is based on the stable model. We will define a set of rules to make TP a trust consistent program. These rules are domain-independent, and will combine with any user defined program to calculate the answer set.

We first define the rules which are corresponding to relationship between grant and revoke operations given in Section 3.

The following two rules define two new predicates *HasKey* and *HasPriv*. $HasKey(P_i, K_i, T_k)$ means that principal $P_i$ holds the key $K_i$ at time $T_k$, while $HasPriv(P_i, K_i, R_i, O_i, T_k)$ means that principal $P_i$ holds the privilege $R_i$ at time $T_k$.

$s_1 : HasKey(p_i, k_i, t_k) \leftarrow GiveKey(p_j, k_j, p_i, k_i, t_j),$
  not $RevokeKey(p_m, k_m, p_i, k_i, t_m), t_m > t_j, t_m < t_k$
$s_2 : HasPriv(p_i, k_i, r_i, o_i, t_k) \leftarrow GivePriv(p_j, k_j, p_i, k_i, r_i, o_i, t_j),$
  not $RevokePriv(p_m, k_m, p_i, k_i, r_i, o_i, t_m), t_m > t_j, t_m < t_k$

The following two rules specify the constraints that one can only revoke the key/privilege when they hold the key/privilege.

$s_3 : \leftarrow RevokeKey(p_i, k_i, p_j, k_j, t_k),$ not $HasKey(p_j, k_j, t_K)$
$s_4 : \leftarrow RevokePriv(p_i, k_i, p_j, k_j, r_j, o_j, t_k),$ not $HasPriv(p_j, k_j, r_j, o_j, t_k)$

The following four rules specify that only the one who holds the privilege +K/+R can grant a key/privilege, and only the one who holds -K/-R can revoke a key/privilege.

$$s_5 : \leftarrow GiveKey(p_i, k_i, p_j, k_j, t_k), \; not \; HasPriv(p_i, k_i, +K,, t_k)$$
$$s_6 : \leftarrow GivePriv(p_i, k_i, p_j, r_j, t_k), \; not \; HasPriv(p_i, k_i, +R,, t_k)$$
$$s_7 : \leftarrow RevokeKey(p_i, k_i, p_j, k_j, t_k), \; not \; HasPriv(p_i, k_i, -K,, t_k)$$
$$s_8 : \leftarrow RevokePriv(p_i, k_i, p_j, r_j, t_k), \; not \; HasPriv(p_i, k_i, -R,, t_k)$$

The next rules specify that one cannot grant/revoke privileges/keys to himself/herself.

$$s_9 : \leftarrow GivePriv(p_i, k_i, p_i, k_i, r_j, o_j, t_k)$$
$$s_{10} : \leftarrow RevokePriv(p_i, k_i, p_i, k_i, r_j, o_j, t_k)$$
$$s_{11} : \leftarrow GiveKey(p_i, k_i, p_i, k_j, t_k)$$
$$s_{12} : \leftarrow RevokeKey(p_i, k_i, p_i, k_j, t_k)$$

We next define the rules corresponding to the relationships between trust operations. We first introduce a new predicate $HasTrustAuth(P_i, K_i, P_j, K_j, T_k)$ which means that principal $P_i$ has trusted $P_j$ being authenticated by $K_j$ until time $T_k$.

$$t_1 : HasTrustAuth(p_i, k_i, p_j, k_j, t_k) \leftarrow TrustAuth(p_i, k_i, p_j, k_j, t_l),$$
$$HasKey(p_j, k_j, t_k)$$

The following rules describe the relationship between the four trust predicates.

$$t_2 : TrustsAuth(p_i, k_i, p_j, k_j, t_k) \leftarrow Trust * (p_i, k_i, p_j, k_j, t_k)$$
$$t_3 : TrustsCode(p_i, k_i, p_j, k_j, t_k) \leftarrow Trust * (p_i, k_i, p_j, k_j, t_k)$$
$$t_4 : TrustsExe(p_i, k_i, p_j, k_j, t_k) \leftarrow Trust * (p_i, k_i, p_j, k_j, t_k)$$
$$t_5 : \leftarrow TrustExe(p_i, k_i, p_j, k_j, t_k), \; not \; HasTrustAuth(p_i, k_i, p_j, k_j, t_k)$$
$$t_6 : \leftarrow TrustCode(p_i, k_i, p_j, k_j, t_k), \; not \; HasTrustAuth(p_i, k_i, p_j, k_j, t_l)$$

The next rule states the natural system assumption that all principals trust themselves at any time.

$$t_7 : Trusts * (p_i, k_i, p_i, k_i, t_k) \leftarrow$$

We finally define the rules corresponding to the relationships between trust and grant/revoke operations.

$$ts_1 : \leftarrow TrustAuth(p_i, k_i, p_j, k_j, t_k), \; not \; HasKey(p_j, k_j, t_k)$$
$$ts_2 : \leftarrow GivePriv(p_i, k_i, p_j, k_j, Exe, code, t_k) \; not \; TrustExe(p_i, k_i, p_j, k_j, t_l),$$
$$t_l < t_k$$

Let X be the set of all the above rules, ie. $X = s_1, ..., s_{12}, t_1, ..., t_7, ts_1, ts_2$. Now we can define the answer set semantics for a trust program (TP). Let $\Pi$ be a TP, the *Base $B_\Pi$* of $\Pi$ is the set of all possible ground literals constructed from the system reserved predicates and predicates appearing in the rules of $\Pi$, the constants occurring in $P, K, R, O, T$ and function symbols in $\Pi$. A *ground* *instance* of $r$ is a rule obtained from $r$ by replacing every variable $x$ in $r$ by $\delta(x)$, where $\delta(x)$ is a mapping from the variables to the constants in the same sorts. Let $G(\Pi)$ denotes all ground instances of the rules occurring in $\Pi$. A subset of the Base of $B_\Pi$ is *consistent* if no pair of complementary is in it. An *interpretation* $I$ is any consistent subset of the Base of $B_\Pi$.

**Definition 1.** *Given a TP $\Pi$, an interpretation for $\Pi$ is any interpretation of $\Pi \cup X$.*

**Definition 2.** *Let $I$ be an interpretation for a TP $G(\Pi)$, the reduction of $\Pi$ w.r.t $I$, denoted by $\Pi^I$, is defined as the set of rules obtained from $G(\Pi \cup X)$ by deleting (1) each rule that has a formula not $L$ in its body with $L \in I$, and (2) all formulas of the form not $L$ in the bodies of the remaining rules.*

Given a set $R$ of ground rules, we denote by $pos(R)$ the positive version of $R$, obtained from $R$ by considering each negative literal $\neg p(t_1, ..., t_n)$ as a positive one with predicate symbol $\neg p$.

**Definition 3.** *Let $M$ be an interpretation for $\Pi$. We say that $M$ is an answer set for $\Pi$ if $M$ is a minimal model of the positive version $pos(\Pi^M)$.*

We can define our access control policy now. A query is a four-ary tuple $(p, k, r, o, t)$ in $P \times K \times R \times O \times T$, which denotes a principal $p$ identified by asymmetric key $k$ requests access $r$ over object $o$ at time $t$. The access control policy is a function $f$ from $P \times K \times R \times O \times T$ to $\{true, false\}$. Given a request $(p, k, r, o, t)$, if $f(p, k, r, o, t) = true$ then it is granted. If $f(p, k, r, o, t) = false$ then it is denied.

According to stable model semantics, there may exist several authorization answer sets for a given TP, and they may not consistent with each other in the sense that they may contain complementary literals. We will adopt optimistic approach to deal with this problem. Let $\Pi$ be a TP, $A_1, ..., A_m$ be its authorization answer sets. For any query $(p, k, r, o, t)$, $f(p, k, r, o,) = true$ if there exists $HasPriv(p, k, r, o, t)$ in some $A_i, 1 \le i \le m$. Otherwise, $f(p, k, r, o, t) = false$. On the other hand, there may exist no authorization answer set for a given TP $\Pi$. In this case, we say $\Pi$ is not well-defined.

# 6   Application

In this section, we apply our trust model to the secure mobile agent systems specified in Section 2. Our aim is to show how a trust model can be applied to the mobile agent security system and to demonstrate the features of trust specification for improving security decisions. Recall that we have proposed three trust relationships to facilitate the trust enhanced security approach, namely the authentication trust, execution trust and code trust. With our logical language, we can now specify policies to capture the trust requirements explicitly in the operations of a mobile agent security system.

*Policies for trust enhanced mobile agent security*

- *Authentication Trust Policy.* The following policy formally specifies the requirements for authentication trust evaluation, which states that in order for Host $P_i$ to have the authentication trust in host $P_j$, $P_i$ must satisfy that $P_j$ was given the public key $K_j$ by some trusted entity $P_{ttp}$, which has not been revoked.

$$P_1 : TrustAuth(p_i, k_i, p_j, k_j, t_1) \leftarrow GiveKey(P_{ttp}, K_{ttp}, p_j, k_j, t_2),$$
$$notRevokeKey(P_{ttp}, K_{ttp}, p_j, k_j, t_3), t_2 \leq t_3, t_3 \leq t_1$$

- *Code Trust Policy.* The following policy formally specifies the requirements for code trust evaluation, which states that in order for Host $P_i$ to have the code trust in host $P_j$, $P_i$ must satisfy that $P_j$ was code trusted by by some trusted entity $P_{ttp}$.

$$P_2 : TrustCode(p_i, k_i, p_j, k_j, t_1) \leftarrow TrustCode(P_{ttp}, K_{ttp}, p_j, k_j, t_2),$$
$$HasKey(p_j, k_j, t_1), t_2 \leq t_1$$

- *Execution Trust Policy.* The following policy formally specifies the requirements for execution trust evaluation. This policy is to be enforced by the owner host when determining whether an execution host can be included into the itinerary. The following policy captures the most common requirement used by most mobile agent systems that if the owner host can authenticate an execution host, then the owner host can add such host into the itineracy of its agent.

$$P_3 : TrustExe(p_i, k_i, p_j, k_j, t_1) \leftarrow TrustAuth(p_i, k_i, p_j, k_j, t_2),$$
$$HasKey(p_j, k_j, t_1), t_2 \leq t_1$$

- *Execution Privilege Policy.* The following policy formally specifies the requirements for execution privilege evaluation. This policy is to be enforced by the foreign execution host of the mobile agent. It states that to execute the code in a mobile agent generated by $p_i$, $p_j$ must be granted the exe privilege by $p_i$, and, on the other hand, $p_i$ must trust that $p_j$ has the ability and benevolent intentions of generating safe code.

$$P_4 : Exe(Code, p_i, k_i, t_1) \leftarrow TrustCode(p_j, k_j, p_i, k_i, t_2),$$
$$GivePriv(p_i, k_i, p_j, k_j, Exe, code, t_3), t_2 \leq t_1, t_3 \leq t_1$$

Here $Exe(Code, p_i, k_i, t_1)$ means the operation of executing the *Code* generated by $p_i$.

# 7   Conclusions

In this paper, we have developed a logic based model to reason about trusts and authorizations in a networked environment. A number of predicates are defined to describe different trust relationships, key operations and privilege operations. The security policies are represented by an extended logic program, and the answer set semantics is achieved through the evaluation of user defined rules together with a set of application independent rules.

The proposed model not only offers the explicit modelling of trust and secure authorization in systems, but also facilitates the specification and design of the trust based mechanisms. The logical language helps to reason and capture the trust relationships explicitly and directly from the underlying conventional security mechanisms. Within the language, we also introduced a set of domain independent rules which form the basis for enforcing desirable security related trustworthy behaviours. These in turn can be used to support the trust enhanced security solutions for mobile agents.

There are several interesting issues that worth further exploring. Firstly, we are considering to extend our current model by modelling soft trust which concerns about trust relationship built on observable evidence about the system entity's behaviour, either through direct experiences or indirect experiences or a combination of both. Secondly, we are extending the model to consider the trust delegations and various degrees of trust. We are in the process of implementing a prototype of our framework using logic programming.

# References

1. Abadi, M., Burrows, M., Lampson, B., Plotkin, G.: A calculus for access control in distributed systems. ACM Trans. on programming languages and systems 15(4), 706–734 (1993)
2. Blaze, M., Feigenhaum, J., Strauss, M.: Decentralized trust management. In: Proceedings of the 1996 IEEE Conference on Security and Privacy, pp. 164–173 (1996)
3. Berkovits, S., Guttman, J.D., Swarup, V.: Authentication for mobile agents. In: Vigna, G. (ed.) Mobile Agents and Security. LNCS, vol. 1419, p. 114. Springer, Heidelberg (1998)
4. Gelfond, M., Lifschitz, V.: Classical negation in logic programs and disjunctive databases. New Generation Computing 9, 365–385 (1991)
5. Kurkowski, M., Pejas, J.: A propositional logic for access control policy in distributed systems. In: Artificial Intelligence and Security in Computing Systems, pp. 175–189 (2003)
6. Levien, R., Aiken, A.: Attack-resistant trust metrics for public key certification. In: Proceedings of 7th USENIX Security Symposium (1998)
7. Lampson, B., Abadi, M., Burrows, M., Wobber, E.: Authentication in distributed systems: theory and practice. ACM Trans. on Computer Systems 10(4), 265–310 (1992)
8. Maurer, U.: Modelling a public-key infrasturcture. In: Martella, G., Kurth, H., Montolivo, E., Bertino, E. (eds.) ESORICS 1996. LNCS, vol. 1146. Springer, Heidelberg (1996)
9. McKnight, D.H., Chervany, N.L.: The meanings of trust. Tech- nical Report, MISRC Working Paper Series 96-04, University of Minnesota, Management Information Systems Reseach Center (1996), http://misrc.umn.edu/wpaper/
10. Jajodia, S., Samarati, P., Subrahmanian, V.S.: A logic language for expressing authorizations. In: Proc. IEEE Symp. on Research in Security and Privacy, pp. 31–42 (1997)
11. Tan, H.K., Moreau, L.: Trust relationships in a mobile agent system. In: Proc. of Fifth IEEE International Conference on Mobile Agents (2001)

# Towards Semantic Modelling of Business Processes for Networked Enterprises

Karol Furdík[1], Marián Mach[2], and Tomáš Sabol[3]

[1] InterSoft, a.s., Florianska 19, 040 01 Kosice, Slovakia
karol.furdik@intersoft.sk
[2] Department of Cybernetics and Artificial Intelligence, Technical University of Kosice,
Letna 9, 040 01 Kosice, Slovakia
marian.mach@tuke.sk
[3] Faculty of Economics, Technical University of Kosice,
Letna 9, 040 01 Kosice, Slovakia
tomas.sabol@tuke.sk

**Abstract.** The paper presents an approach to the semantic modelling and annotation of business processes and information resources, as it was designed
within the FP7 ICT EU project SPIKE to support creation and maintenance of
short-term business alliances and networked enterprises. A methodology for the
development of the resource ontology, as a shareable knowledge model for semantic description of business processes, is proposed. Systematically collected
user requirements, conceptual models implied by the selected implementation
platform as well as available ontology resources and standards are employed in
the ontology creation. The process of semantic annotation is described and illustrated using an example taken from a real application case.

**Keywords:** Business process modelling, semantic technologies, ontology development, semantic annotation.

## 1 Introduction

Effective collaboration of organizations cooperating in a flexible business network is
one of the critical success factors and competitive advantages on the global market [7]
and is especially important in today's challenging economy situation. Standardized
technologies as business modelling frameworks, service-oriented architecture, and
Semantic Web services enable to design solutions supporting the interoperability
between cooperating enterprises [8]. The business networking based on interoperable
services and shareable information resources was identified also by the European
Commission in 7th Framework Programme [5] as a progressive way of business collaboration and a promising answer to the challenges of global market pressures.

Development of a platform that will enable fast setup and maintenance of project-
oriented short-term alliances of collaborating business organizations is in the focus of
the FP7 ICT project *Secure Process-oriented Integrative Service Infrastructure for
Networked Enterprises* (SPIKE, www.spike-project.eu). The technological and research objectives of the SPIKE project are focused on design and implementation of a

T. Di Noia and F. Buccafurri (Eds.): EC-Web 2009, LNCS 5692, pp. 96–107, 2009.
© Springer-Verlag Berlin Heidelberg 2009

generic solution for inter-enterprise interoperability and business collaboration by employing technologies such as enterprise service bus, semantic business process modelling, and advanced security infrastructure. The system being developed using these technologies will provide a portal-based interface for users participating in collaboration processes, user-friendly administration of alliances, ad-hoc workflow modelling and process handling.

The research related to the SPIKE objectives includes a wide area of business process modelling supported by employing semantic technologies [7], [8]. The EU FP6 projects *TrustCoM* (www.eu-trustcom.com) and *SUPER* (www.ip-super.org) can be especially mentioned as the resources of ideas, software solutions and tools that are reused and enriched within the SPIKE project. The TrustCoM results were considered during the specification of system components, namely the Alliance Manager module (cf. sections 2 and 4). The semantic representation of business processes, which is not covered by the TrustCoM, was adopted from the SUPER project. The BPMO, sBPMN, sBPEL and related process ontologies [9] were used as a conceptual background for process modelling and for transformation of standardized BPMN [12] and BPEL [1] notations into an ontology-based representation. The SPIKE project extents this solution by providing a methodology and software support for systematic development and customization of a knowledge base focused on particular application case, namely for a creation of short-term project-oriented business alliances.

The semantic modelling of business processes, services, and exchanged information, as it was proposed in SPIKE platform, will be elaborated in this paper. Based on a brief description of system architecture, basic system modules and data types, the process of semantic annotation and mark-up of business process elements is described in section 2. An approach and methodology employed for the design of a knowledge base for semantic enhancement of the identified information resources is presented in section 3. Maintenance of designed semantic structures within the life cycle of the ontology evolution process is discussed in section 4. Finally, the methodology is illustrated on an example of a real application case.

## 2   Semantic Annotation and Modelling

The architecture of the SPIKE system [6] consists of three main component groups: 1) a core sub-system; 2) client applications; and 3) external services, which are remotely referenced and integrated by the software platform. The core sub-system is composed of inner functional modules - managers that expose a business logic of the system, maintain and process all the system data, and communicate internally via the system's enterprise service bus. The client applications include a graphical user interface acting as a front-end to the core sub-system, as well as an administration interface for monitoring, maintaining, and reporting functions on a day-to-day basis.

A structure of main data elements, identified in the information view of the SPIKE system architecture, is presented in Fig. 1. The *Process*, *Workflow*, and *Task* elements are basic building blocks for modelling an alliance of collaborative business processes. The *Task* element, representing particular workflow actions, is further specified by parameters as inputs, transformations, and outputs. These parameters, consumed and produced by a task in a workflow, are represented by a set of sub-types of the

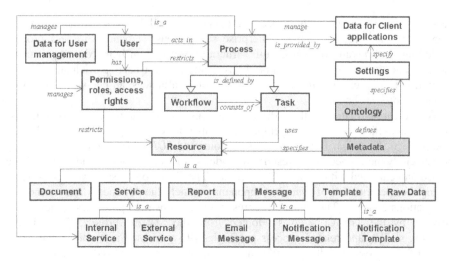

**Fig. 1.** A structure of basic data elements, designed for the SPIKE system

generic and abstract *Resource* data element. This element defines a common set of properties inherited by all its child data elements, in particular by the resource types as *Document*, *Service*, *Report*, *Message*, etc. Properties of these information resources are provided as semantic metadata, defined in an ontology schema. This solution enables to combine the standardized business process modelling with semantic descriptions created according to the Semantic Web principles [2].

The SPIKE platform employs semantic technologies to enable interoperability between services and information resources originating from heterogeneous environments of the collaboration participants – partners within a business alliance [8]. The ontology, as a common semantic knowledge base and a conceptual model of the given domain, provides a shareable vocabulary of terms that can be used for metadata specification of used data elements. A semantic enhancement of business process elements and resources gives an opportunity to manipulate with the data according to their meaning. It also enables data mediation, reasoning, and retrieval of the semantically described (i.e. annotated) elements and consequently ensures the desired service interoperability.

Semantic annotation can be defined as a process of associating raw digital data with some of the ontology concepts, where these associations (i.e. semantic descriptions, annotations) are persistently stored and are formally expressed in a machine-readable way. This process, schematically depicted in Fig. 2, includes identification of data portions being annotated (e.g. words or paragraphs in a text, tasks or activities in a process, etc.), selection of ontology concepts suitable to represent the meaning of the data, and creation of annotations – relationships between the data portions and the selected concepts.

Business processes, services, and information resources, i.e. artefacts of various types that are produced or consumed by the activities of the process workflow, are the objects that are to be semantically described within the platform. The means of the semantic annotation differ slightly for each of these objects, as it is described in the following paragraphs.

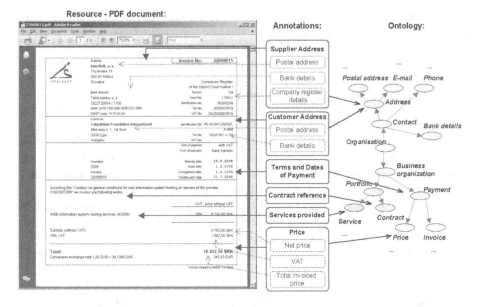

**Fig. 2.** Semantic annotation of a PDF document, as an information resource

*Business processes*, that is, dynamic series of actions performed in a business organization, can be described by an abstract or an executable process model [1]. Today's market-leading industry standards are BPMN [12] for visual design of abstract business processes and BPEL [1] for modelling executable processes. Despite the fact that neither BPMN nor BPEL are "true" semantic structures, they provide a set of predefined elements for describing the workflow structure and can serve as a common interpretation base for business processes. That is why these formalisms can be considered as a kind of formal annotation, which is a first step towards the fully featured semantic annotation.

The BPMN is a standard for graphical notation, while the BPEL is an XML-based format; the mapping between BPMN and BPEL is not so straightforward [11]. Nevertheless, it is supported by various algorithms that work on a sub-set of BPMN constructs. The modelling of business processes in the SPIKE platform can thus start with abstract BPMN, which will then be transformed (e.g. using the BPEL4WS formalization [1] and/or the semantic enhancements of business process elements) into an executable BPEL form.

A business process can be further semantically described by means of available (and customized) ontologies for modelling entire processes, services provided and consumed by these processes, or artefacts manipulated by the process services. The advanced BPMO, sBPMN, and sBPEL ontologies [9], provided as outcomes of the EU FP6 project SUPER [4], were proposed as basic semantic structures for representing the elements of business processes in SPIKE. It enables to integrate the ontology-based representation of business processes with the representation of services and other information resources exchanged in a process workflow, which will be semantically described by means of domain ontologies. A semantically annotated business process is then represented as an instantiated workflow of activities, containing references to the services that consume and/or produce various artefacts as their inputs or outputs. The business process itself can be registered within the SPIKE system as an internal service and can be reused (nested) as a partial activity in another business process (cf. Fig. 1).

*Services* are executable actions organized into a workflow and referenced by the business process activities. Several service types can be distinguished according to the accessibility, usability, and possibility of immediate execution, i.e. the *Web services*, *electronic services* (e.g. web forms, emails etc.; available on-line, but without a Web service interface), and *conventional asynchronous services* (not available on-line). The Web services were taken as a reference type for the semantic annotation, assuming that the services of other types will be transformed into this type before the annotation. A semantic wrapping, e.g. by providing some textual information that describes an asynchronous service for users or specifies inputs and outputs of an electronic service, is envisioned as a reasonable way of such a transformation.

The WSMO-Lite ontology [13] was identified as a suitable mechanism to annotate the Web services by means of a simple WSDL extension. The set of five WSMO-Lite top concepts is used as a simple vocabulary for basic semantic description of services in a workflow. Additional semantic specifications, applicable at all the service types, are handled by reference and transformation annotations that enhance the WSDL interface components for abstract definition as well as for implementation of services. Consequently, the WSMO-Lite ontology employed in the SPIKE platform enables to integrate an executable WSDL grounding with powerful semantic enhancements of WSMO (www.wsmo.org) to support the tasks as service discovery, mediation, composition, and invocation.

The *artefacts*, or *information resources*, are separate information units that can be required (as inputs or preconditions) or produced (as outputs or effects) by a service. The physical objects as textual documents, multimedia files, reports, messages, etc., are the resource types that will be supported by the SPIKE platform. The data elements that represent these types of artefacts are inherited from the generic *Resource* data element, as it is depicted in Fig. 1. Semantic annotation of the artefacts includes specification of concrete values for a set of common properties, given by the metadata defined in the ontology. A widely accepted standard, as e.g. Dublin Core (www.dublincore.org), can be employed for the metadata definition. In addition, the artefacts containing textual information may be annotated by identifying the content units and then describing them semantically (cf. Fig. 2), possibly using the support of semi-automatic text mining and information extraction methods.

## 3   Design of the Resource Ontologies

The semantic annotation requires a presence of a common knowledge base, i.e. an ontology that is capable to provide useful metadata specification for all the annotated information types. The structure of resource ontologies designed for the SPIKE platform is based on the identified data elements and information resources (see Fig. 1) and includes a separate ontology for business processes, services, and artefacts. Four additional ontologies were specified for modelling the domain- and system-specific information, namely the core, domain, system, and user ontologies. All the ontologies are represented as WSML files and are stored in a repository maintained by the core sub-system of the SPIKE platform.

Three resources were identified for the ontology creation, namely:

1. a *conceptual model*, which is determined by the selected ontology implementation platform (BPMO, sBPMN, sBPEL, WSMO-Lite);
2. *existing ontology resources*, reused and adapted from available ontology libraries and standards (e.g. Dublin Core, various domain-specific ontologies);
3. *requirements* formulated by targeted system users, systematically collected, processed, and formalized into the resulting ontology representation.

The first two ontology resources ensure a compliance with external standards and should make the SPIKE platform interoperable with other similar solutions. In addition, the ontology representation of business processes enables to mediate the semantically customized process elements by a common vocabulary and to employ the reasoning and semantic service discovery across ontologies in a uniform way.

As far as the third resource is concerned, the requirement-driven approach [10] can be employed to capture the information content and quality required by the users for the semantic modelling of a given application case. This approach, originally developed for the e-Government domain, defines a step-by-step procedure for systematic design and formalization of an ontology according to user requirements. We have customized it for the development of ontologies for the business process modelling, assuming the following participants – actors in this process:

- *User partners*, "owners" of the modelled application case that are able to formulate the user requirements and descriptions of a given domain;
- *Knowledge engineers*, responsible for analysis of the application case described by user partners, for identification of key semantic elements as concepts, attributes, relations, constraints, etc., and for creation of a knowledge base capable to model the application case;
- *System developers*, responsible for formalization of the resulting ontology structure and content into a proper representation, as well as for the implementation and integration of the ontology into the whole software platform.

The procedure of ontology design takes the *information architecture* and *information quality* as the key concepts that should be understood, captured, and modelled according to the user requirements. The information architecture covers an explicit formulation of users' information needs, including a selection of proper terminology, labeling of terms, and proper categorization of the extracted information. An adequate information quality of the resulting semantic structures can be supported by effective cooperation of actors during the design, as well as by reusing the existing ontology resources and standards. Particular steps of the ontology design, including the actors involved and outputs generated, are presented in Table 1.

**Table 1.** Steps of the ontology design and development procedure, defined according to the requirement-driven approach customized for the domain of business process modelling

| Step 1. Identify the information needs |
| --- |
| *Actors*: user partners<br>*Output*: Textual description of the application case. It includes a specification of the activity scenarios and use-cases. |
| **Step 2. Identify required information quality** |
| *Actors*: user partners, knowledge engineers<br>*Output*: Specification of relevant business processes and episodes, co-operating participants (process actors), activities (services), and artefacts. |
| **Step 3. Create a glossary of topics and terms** |
| *Actors*: user partners, knowledge engineers<br>*Output*: Glossary of relevant topics and terms in a table format. The table includes the term name in English, term translations to other languages used in the application case, a description, and notes. Concepts from available external ontologies can be reused to ensure a wider acceptance of the identified terms. |
| **Step 4. Create a controlled vocabulary** |
| *Actors*: knowledge engineers, user partners<br>*Output*: Controlled vocabulary – hierarchy of terms, created from the glossary by grouping the terms into the hierarchical subgroups. |
| **Step 5. Group and relate terms** |
| *Actors*: knowledge engineers, user partners<br>*Output*: Ontology-like structure that includes the relations and dependencies between the concepts. The hierarchy in the controlled vocabulary determines the *is_a* relations; other relation types are derived from the attributes and descriptions that accompany the terms in the vocabulary and glossary. |
| **Step 6. Design the resource ontology** |
| *Actors*: system developers, knowledge engineers<br>*Output*: A formally expressed ontology. In SPIKE, the ontology will be represented in the WSML notation. The meaning of terms and relations of the ontology-like structure is fixed and formalized in the WSML. The resulting expressions are reviewed to validate that their formal meaning reflects the corresponding informal description in the glossary. |
| **Step 7. Implementation of the semantics** |
| *Actors*: system developers, knowledge engineers<br>*Output*: Formal representation of ontology, enhanced by the workflow structures. The "business rules" as input and output specifications, conditional if-then-else expressions, loops, and workflow sequences are added as enhancements of the ontology elements. These enhancements are especially applied to describe a dynamic behavior of services, namely by their choreography, orchestration, and capability interfaces. |

After these seven steps, originally proposed in [10] for the requirement-driven approach towards ontology modelling, an additional step can be included for practical reasons, that is, to verify and tune the resulting ontology design on real data. Main aim of this verification is to ensure that the designed ontology formalism, created mostly on the user-defined scenarios, will be capable to model all the entities that are necessary for semantic modelling and annotation of the application case. To verify the resulting ontology, the user partners should provide a sample pattern of real data in a format suitable and understandable for all the actors, e.g. as a spreadsheet or a table.

Knowledge engineers then may apply the data to the implemented ontology to obtain the mapping between the ontology elements and the data, usually by creating the instances for particular data portions. System developers can then check the mapping and make the corrections. Knowledge engineers then distribute the resulting ontology with mapped data back to the user partners; they are asked to verify the correctness of the representation and to propose the necessary changes. The process iterates until all the actors accept the resulting ontology structure.

Finally, to review the overall quality, usability, and potential of wider acceptance of the resulting ontologies, some of a wide variety of ontology evaluation techniques [3] can be applied and used for further improvement in the next design cycle.

## 4  Ontology Life-Cycle Management

The development of the resource ontologies is usually a one-time effort, despite the fact that it is complex and may require several cycles of re-design. However, after final verification and validation, the resource ontologies should be more-less stable; no significant changes of the structure of concepts and relations are expected during the system run-time. This is especially applicable to the business process, core, and system ontologies, containing the most fundamental semantic descriptions and models of the domain. The changes and modifications of the remaining ontologies are allowed and may affect the instantiated metadata, the annotated services and service types, namely the updates of the service's capability interfaces.

Besides 1) the ontology development, the phases of 2) ontology maintenance and administration, as well as 3) actual usage of the ontologies for semantic annotation can be identified and described as parts of the overall ontology life cycle. These two phases are performed in parallel during the system run-time and enable to express the processes, services, and artefacts of the application case by means of an adequate semantic model.

The required maintenance functionality is supported on each of the ontology life cycle phases by a suite of proper tools and formalisms. Besides the tables, spreadsheets, taxonomy of categories, and ontology-like formalism used for steps 1-5 of the requirement-driven approach, the *WSMO Studio* (www.wsmostudio.org) is employed as a general toolkit for the ontology development, implementation, and administering. In addition to that, the Semantic Manager, Content Manager, and Alliance Manager modules are designed within the SPIKE core sub-system to provide the back-office functionality for the ontology maintenance. Finally, a specialized annotation tool that includes capability of visual business process modelling, semantic annotation of services and artefacts, as well as management of business alliances is proposed to support the third phase of the ontology life cycle.

The *ontology administration phase* includes customization of the ontology elements and adaptation of the semantic knowledge base to the newly raised requirements. Editing operations (i.e. create, update, and delete) over the ontology concepts on the class level enables to manipulate the types of alliances, business processes, services, artefacts, and user roles. It is also possible to edit the metadata instances, which can be considered as a supervision of the semantic annotation.

The *semantic annotation phase*, i.e. actual usage of the formalized ontologies, requires separate tools for process modelling and semantic description of process elements. The *Eclipse BPMN Modeler* (www.eclipse.org/bpmn/), compatible with the WSMO framework, can be used for visual process modelling and creation of the abstract process representation. Transformation to the executable BPEL and to the semantic representation of process elements by means of the BPMO, sBPMN, and sBPEL ontologies is performed automatically, by the core SPIKE components that employ the *BPMO-to-sBPEL* translation mechanism [4]. The visual process modeller is included into the specialized annotation tool, functionally integrated in the system administration interface, which also enables to semantically instantiate the process elements by specifying values for metadata of the services and artefacts.

Further annotation procedure includes identification and semantic description of the processes, services, and information resources for an application case. To accomplish it within the SPIKE, we have proposed the following steps:

1. Design of an abstract non-executable business process, using a visual tool for BPMN business process modelling. Specification of the pools and lanes corresponding to the business entities that interact in a collaborative process.
2. Specification of flow objects (events, activities, gateways), connecting objects (sequences, messages, associations), and artefacts (data objects, groups, textual annotations). Specification of the sub-processes for each of the complex activities.
3. Identification of services and their types (Semantic Web services, Web services, electronic services, asynchronous off-line or on-line services) for each of the activities specified in the abstract process.
4. Semantic annotation of services. Specification of the capability interface for services: inputs, outputs, preconditions, effects. Data flow between the services.
5. Identification and semantic description of the information resources (artefacts) produced or consumed by the services.
6. Automatic transformation of the modelled abstract process into an executable BPEL representation. Formalization and publishing of the process instance.
7. Automatic semantic annotation of the modelled executable process by means of the rule-based mapping to the concepts of the BPMO-based business process ontology.
8. Identification and semantic description of the actors that are participating as providers or consumers on the services and are manipulating with the artefacts.

Semantic modelling and annotation can be seen as a transformation or migration of internal processes and resources into semantically described publicly available and shareable entities in the sense of the Semantic Web [2]. This transformation, similarly as the above-mentioned ontology development, is a one-time effort, although it requires a constant follow-up to ensure and maintain the quality of the semantic descriptions. Therefore, the migration towards the Semantic Web can be organized as a project that starts with a cost-benefit analysis and continues by a sequence of activities as business process analysis, goals definition, and preparation of available resources, tools, and IT infrastructure. Import and adaptation of a suitable semantic model can follow the approaches and methods described in section 3. The consequent semantic annotation of business processes, services, and artefacts should be followed by a testing and fine-tuning phase. The migration finishes by publishing and information alignment of the semantically enhanced resources.

## 5   An Example of Applying the Methodology

The SPIKE system is expected to be tested in autumn 2009 on pilot applications in Finland (application case: Documentation Management) and Austria (two application cases: Business Alliances and Identity Federation). The *Business Alliances* case is focused on the creation and management of business alliances, including maintenance of service providers, location and configuration of services, integration into a work-flow, as well as the tracking, contracting, and ordering of services. The *Identity Federation* case will demonstrate the management of user identities in a networked enterprise, namely the maintenance of access rights, roles, and resources within a collaborative environment. The *Documentation Management* application case, focus-ing on intra-enterprise product development, will provide a support for documentation services by means of secure knowledge and content management.

The methodology described in the above sections has been developed for the se-mantic modelling of business processes of all the application cases. For example, the Identity Federation case will provide the functionality that can be conceptually mod-elled in four steps, as depicted in Fig. 3.

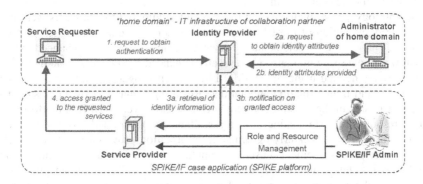

**Fig. 3.** A conceptual schema of the identity federation management

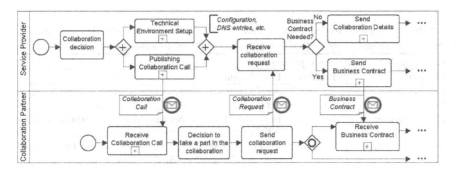

**Fig. 4.** Fragment of a BPMN representation of the collaboration setup sub-process

Business processes and activities were initially described for this application case by means of the *if-then-else* block diagram. This non-standardized formalization does not allow a direct transformation into a proper semantic or business process representation. To enable the integration into the SPIKE platform, the processes were re-designed using the BPMN notation. For example, the BPMN representation of an initial process of setting up a business collaboration between two actors, identified as a use-case of the identity federation, is depicted in Fig. 4. The abstract BPMN process is designed in the Eclipse BPMN modeler and then is automatically transformed into the semantic BPMO representation. The process elements are ready for further semantic annotation by the concepts of the customized resource ontology.

To design the resource ontology for this application case, the steps of the requirement-driven approach were applied. Activities, sub-processes, services, exchanged artefacts, and process actors were identified and textually described. Glossary and controlled vocabulary of hierarchically organized terms were created and were used to produce a core of the domain ontology. The designed ontology contains general class concepts as *Organization*, *Business Contract*, *Business Partner*, *Contact*, etc., as well as more specific concepts labeled with properties and relations to other concepts. An example of the *B2B collaboration prerequisites* concept, produced as a result of the step 4 of the requirement-driven approach and represented as an entry of the controlled vocabulary, is depicted in Table 2.

The ontology was implemented in the WSMO Studio and the concepts were used for semantic annotation of the BPMO process elements. The sub-processes were decomposed into particular elementary services, which were then enhanced by the workflow and data flow models. Semantically enhanced WSDL representation of the services was generated using the WSMO-Lite concepts together with the mechanism of reference and transformation annotations. Resulting semantic structures, stored as process instances in the resource ontology, can be employed in SPIKE platform as a generic resource for establishing a business alliance with defined process workflow and specified services. Underlying semantic information provided by the ontologies and annotated process elements ensures compatibility with standards (by adopting the BPMN/BPEL notation and reusing external ontologies), flexibility and adaptability to particular application case (by means of the requirement-driven approach), and consequently should provide facilities for semantic interoperability of cooperating organizations in a goal-oriented business alliance.

**Table 2.** Sample identified concept, represented as an item of the controlled vocabulary

| Concept: B2B collaboration prerequisites | | |
|---|---|---|
| **Property** | **Format** | **Description** |
| Organization | ID | A reference to the partner negotiating a collaboration. |
| Collaboration | ID | A reference to the collaboration negotiated. |
| Prior experience with B2B solutions | Boolean | Indication if the partner has already any experience with B2B solutions before starting a cooperation. |
| B2B/EDI standards used | ID list | Listing of references to the possible B2B/EDI standards used, e.g. RosettaNet, EDIFACT, EDIFICE, etc. |
| Description of a prior experience with B2B solutions | text (optional) | Describes the experience of the partners within the area of B2B, i.e. which solutions or standards have been already used by the partner within previous projects. |

# 6 Conclusions and Future Work

The presented approach to the creation of semantic structures for modelling the business processes has been successfully employed in three real application cases. It will be used for the development of the SPIKE resource ontologies in June 2009. At the time of writing the paper (May 2009), the architecture design and specification of functional components is finished and implementation of the platform components is ongoing. The first release of the implemented system should be ready in September 2009. After that, the platform will be tested on the pilot applications within the first trial. More information on the project can be found at www.spike-project.eu.

**Acknowledgments.** The SPIKE project is co-funded by the European Commission within the contract No. FP7-ICT-217098. The work presented in the paper was also supported by the Slovak Grant Agency of the Ministry of Education and Academy of Science of the Slovak Republic within the 1/4074/07 Project "Methods for annotation, search, creation, and accessing knowledge employing metadata for semantic description of knowledge".

# References

1. Andrews, T., et al.: Business Process Execution Language for Web Services. Ver. 1.1. IBM developers' library (2003)
2. Berners-Lee, T., Hendler, J., Lassila, O.: The Semantic Web. In: Scientific American (2001)
3. Brank, J., Grobelnik, M., Mladenic, D.: A survey of ontology evaluation techniques. In: Proc. of the Conference on Data Mining and Data Warehouses, Ljubljana, Slovenia (2005)
4. Deliverable 1.1: Business Process Ontology Framework. Project IST 026850 SUPER, Public Deliverable (2007)
5. Framework Programme 7, CORDIS ICT Work Programme 2009-2010, Challenge 1: Pervasive and Trusted Network and Service Infrastructures, http://cordis.europa.eu/fp7/ict/programme/challenge1_en.html
6. Furdik, K., Mach, M., Sabol, T.: Architecture of a system supporting business alliances. In: Proceedings of WIKT 2008, pp. 53–57. STU, Bratislava (2009)
7. Gong, R., et al.: Business Process Collaboration Using Semantic Interoperability: Review and Framework. In: Mizoguchi, R., Shi, Z.-Z., Giunchiglia, F. (eds.) ASWC 2006. LNCS, vol. 4185, pp. 191–204. Springer, Heidelberg (2006)
8. Hepp, M., et al.: Semantic Business Process Management: A Vision Towards Using Semantic Web Services for Business Process Management. In: Proc. of the IEEE ICEBE 2005, Beijing, China, October 18-20, 2005, pp. 535–540 (2005)
9. Hepp, M., Roman, D.: An Ontology Framework for Semantic Business Process Management. In: Proc. of Wirtschaftsinformatik 2007, Karlsruhe, pp. 423–440 (2007)
10. Klischewski, R., Ukena, S.: Designing Semantic e-Government Services Driven by user Requirements. In: Wimmer, M.A., Scholl, J., Grönlund, Å. (eds.) EGOV 2007. LNCS, vol. 4656, pp. 133–140. Springer, Heidelberg (2007)
11. Ouyang, C., et al.: From BPMN Process Models to BPEL Web Services. In: Proc. of International Conference on Web Services (ICWS 2006), Chicago, IL, pp. 285–292 (2006)
12. Roj, J., Owen, M.: BPMN and Business Process Management. PopkinSoftware (2003)
13. Vitvar, T., Kopecky, J., Fensel, D.: WSMO-Lite: Lightweight Semantic Descriptions for Services on the Web. WSMO Deliverable D11, Ver.0.2. DERI (2008)

# Metadata-Driven SOA-Based Application for Facilitation of Real-Time Data Warehousing

Damir Pintar, Mihaela Vranić, and Zoran Skočir

Faculty of Electrical Engineering and Computing
University of Zagreb
Croatia

**Abstract.** Service-oriented architecture (SOA) has already been widely recognized as an effective paradigm for achieving integration of diverse information systems. SOA-based applications can cross boundaries of platforms, operation systems and proprietary data standards, commonly through the usage of Web Services technology. On the other side, metadata is also commonly referred to as a potential integration tool given the fact that standardized metadata objects can provide useful information about specifics of unknown information systems with which one has interest in communicating with, using an approach commonly called "model-based integration". This paper presents the result of research regarding possible synergy between those two integration facilitators. This is accomplished with a vertical example of a metadata-driven SOA-based business process that provides ETL (Extraction, Transformation and Loading) and metadata services to a data warehousing system in need of a real-time ETL support.

**Keywords:** SOA, ETL, real-time data warehousing, Web Services, CWM.

## 1 Introduction

Model-based integration is a term describing automated or semi-automated integration of heterogeneous systems with the help of abstract models developed through a standardized language (most commonly UML or related standard). The basic idea is integration through a construction of a predefined interface for gathering metadata which describes systems involved in the integration and then using said data in such a manner to achieve the integration itself. The concept of *sharing* data is the driving force behind this approach, and for data to be successfully shared it has to adhere to a standard agreed upon between all the systems involved in the integration. A model for this "standard description" is provided by the chosen metadata standard.

The second integration approach, as stated in [1] and elaborated in [2], is done through the use of contemporary SOA which is a technology that fully leverages development of working integration architectures. SOA gives the ability to achieve cross-platform interoperability by "wrapping" business services implemented as stand-alone applications in SOA services, therefore facilitating their integration in an interconnected business system. Furthermore, with SOA it is possible to augment or

T. Di Noia and F. Buccafurri (Eds.): EC-Web 2009, LNCS 5692, pp. 108–119, 2009.

replace existing integration channels which can result in a system better suited to a modern dynamic e-business environment, one that involves the need to quickly respond to technical or business-related changes.

The goal of this paper is an evaluation of possible synergy between SOA-based systems and standardized metadata for realization of a real-time ETL support for a data warehousing system. This is done by exploiting the benefits of both approaches and devising a working, Web-service and metadata-based solution which would be put to use in a real-life business scenario. The conceptualization of the problem is accompanied with the actual working implementation that uses the proposed concepts. The implementation is enabled through the use of currently available standards and open technologies.

The paper is structured as follows: Chapter 2 will give description of basic premises and drivers behind this paper, and Chapter 3 will follow with a short description of the proposed modifications and extensions of CWM specification given the constructed metadata exchange pattern. In Chapter 4 a formal description of exchange messages is given. Chapter 5 describes the actual implementation and finally, a conclusion is given.

## 2 Motivation and Related Work

The ETL process for real-time data warehousing was chosen as a test bed for the synergy of an SOA-based business process and standardized metadata for various reasons which will be elaborated upon in the following paragraphs.

A similar idea as the one discussed in this paper is elaborated in [3]. Authors discuss the notion of real-time data warehousing implementation method with the help of SOA, more specifically with Web Services as a front-end for various source systems and real-time data updating. Paper doesn't delve with specifics about the concrete implementation and technologies used but offers various useful insights about message queueing and especially the problem of continual updates and cache-based repositories.

Issues concerning differences between real-time data warehousing as a theoretical concept and realistic needs, requirements and expectations – as discussed in [4] – were taken very seriously during the implementation discussed in this paper. Henceforth the emphasis was put on creating a solution applicable in an actual business environment as opposed to constructing an elaborate theoretical construct.

In [5], in his evaluation of real-time data warehousing and possible implementation scenarios Ralph Kimball acknowledges EAI (*Enterprise Application Integration*) as powerful enabling method for real-time data warehousing. Kimball's description of the EAI approach to real-time data warehousing using a real-time data partition was the main inspiration for the high-level architecture of the system (shown on Figure 1.), implementation of which is described in this paper.

In [6], the authors showcase Web Services as efficient wrappers of source-specific and target-specific parts of the ETL process. However, modeling the transformations via Web services is not discussed.

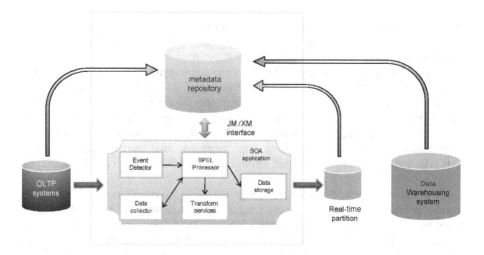

**Fig. 1.** A high-level view of the system architecture, inspired by Ralph Kimball's description of an EAI approach to real-time data warehousing using a real-time partition

Finally, in [7], the authors offer an approach for solving problems of *data programmability,* e.g. a model management engine which would facilitate the process of devising mappings between heterogeneous data models. Since one of the biggest aspects of ETL is the transformation of data between the data sources and the data warehouse, model management system offered an effective way to deal with specifications of mappings used in transformations as part of the ETL process.

Ultimately, with Web Services as today's leading SOA implementation technology it is viable to consider an SOA system providing real-time ETL support for a data warehousing environment. Since collection, transformation and storage of data is entirely executed in a service-oriented environment, providing additional functionality to the process is equivalent to the process integrating another service which uses the predefined protocols and messages. In a firm which already conducts business through the use of service-based business processes the real-time ETL process becomes yet another process which can be managed by the same software and same people in charge of managing other business processes. Therefore there is no need for a separate information system. Additionally, since movement of data is almost entirely based on transforming and managing XML documents, it's much easier to create audit trails and data checks on the entire ETL process.

However, due to its nature, data warehousing environment incorporates many different information systems, data standards and various other information which is used in its daily operation. Keeping track of all this information is often cumbersome, especially if software used for data warehousing doesn't implement a capable metadata registry and metadata management system (and if it does, there is also a question of the format the metadata is kept in and potential ways of its interpretation and usage).

One of the rare successful attempts of developing a standard metadata model for data warehousing was published by the OMG group [8], a consortium which deals with setting standards for distributed object-oriented systems, modeling and model-based system. CWM specification [9] offered a standardized way of keeping track of data warehousing environment via various modules, each focused on different aspect of the environment in question. This ambitious project was endorsed by many major software companies (such as Oracle, IBM and Microsoft) who extend many of their database and data warehousing products with a possibility of exporting certain meta-data information in CWM-based format.

Metadata can play an important role in system integration, especially in a diverse system such as a data warehousing environment. A well-constructed metadata management system can facilitate integration. *Dynamic* integration could present a further evolution of the concept of metadata as an integration tool – software components can learn the specifics of a system by gathering, interpreting and acting upon the received metadata. In this way, metadata represents an outsourced knowledge about the system as well as a mechanism to enable dynamic metadata-driven adaptation to their environment without the need of re-engineering their internal structure.

Other purposes of metadata shouldn't be ignored. At first and foremost, metadata exists to give accurate description of a specific information system which can be used by any external entity interested in the system. This information might be its origin, various characteristics of data itself, and the relationship between real-time data situated in a real-time partition and available data from regular, "static" data warehouse. This is especially important in scenarios where the integration of these two types of data is left to the responsibility of business intelligence applications and/or systems managing the real-time partition which then have to be provided with specific information channels on how this integration should be executed.

This paper deals with a scenario of upgrading a data warehousing environment with real-time support where the task of gathering and adapting the data for the real time partition is realized with an SOA-based system working closely with the metadata registry. This metadata will be CWM-based, although the CWM itself will only be used as a foundation and will be extended and modified in a significant extent. The SOA-based ETL application will be designed in such a way to use metadata in as large extent as possible, keeping in mind the restrictions given by the available technologies, performance ramifications as well as keeping the complexity of the system to a minimum to facilitate easier implementation.

To achieve this, certain restrictions on the data warehousing environment as well as real-time data warehousing requests were imposed. The real-time support is implemented with the use of a real time partition. It is expected that the data required to be collected in real-time is made of facts (or "cubes"), and that the SOA-based ETL system gathers facts on the lowest available granularity. The responsibility of aggregation and integration is largely left to the mechanisms residing in the real-time partition itself (which could be a database using JIM (*Just-in-time*) or RJIM (*Reverse Just-In-Time*) modules, as discussed in [10]) or business intelligence applications which use the available data in their analysis. However, it is very important to emphasize the implication that metadata plays an important role in this process (which is partly a reason why it's considered an essential part of the data warehousing environment). The metadata contains all the necessary information dealing with mapping the collected data to the underlying OLAP system ( an example of how this is done can be found in [11]). It is implied that software systems partaking in the data warehousing environment can also access the metadata registry and interpret the information collected within, greatly facilitating the integration process and actual usage of real-time data.

## 3  Extending, Modifying and Sampling the CWM Specification

CWM is defined as a metadata standard for data warehousing and business analysis consisting of a common metamodel defining shared metadata for data warehousing needs, a common metadata interchange format and a common programming interface for accessing shared metadata. It is split into 21 modules, each describing a different aspect of a data warehousing environment. These modules are organized into layers where each layer depends on certain number of lower-layered modules. Contents of each module closely resemble an UML Class diagram, with metadata defined as classes and their relationships (of which the most important is inheritance).

This paper uses CWM as a foundation for standardized metadata, but the actual modules are being heavily restricted and modified to suit the needs of the application. The reasoning for this follows the recommendations stated in [11]: even though the metadata registry can potentially implement the entire CWM specification, applications using CWM as integration tool always use the information in certain context, and this context may or may not include all the available elements. That's why those applications should map the context they use in a specific "metadata exchange pattern", used between application implementing CWM as an integration tool and agreed upon with aforementioned context  as the main source for defining said pattern. This way, applications can interpret metadata in deterministic and intentional manner, without encountering ambiguous or unknown situations.

One of the definitions of a metadata exchange pattern is that it's a subset of the metamodel partitioned or separated from the metamodel in the manner allowable by the metamodel definition. For the SOA-based ETL application metadata exchange patterns were constructed by developing appropriate XML Schemas which use sets of CWM elements sampled from the model, ordered in predefined combinations and formatted using XMI patterns. It is implied that documents based on these schemas can be extracted from metadata registry as long as metadata contained within is a superset of information the SOA application needs. The appropriate XSLT documents were also constructed which could be used to transform the standard CWM notation into the format used by the SOA application.

The first step was evaluating the CWM specification [9] against the needs of a SOA-based application for real-time ETL – choosing modules (or module elements) which are most useful for the application needs and defining modifications and extensions of module elements as needed. Also, since SOA application works mostly with XML elements, a standard way of encoding information should be devised (especially because CWM specification as yet does not provide XSD descriptions of its elements). Figure 2. presents a high-level view of a portion of extensions defined on CWM elements.

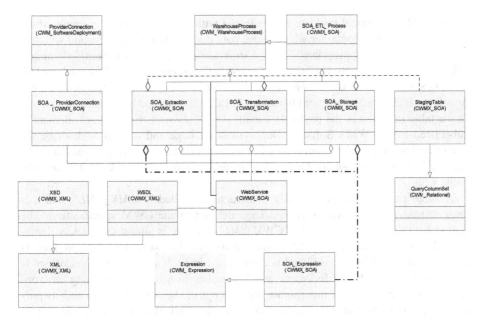

**Fig. 2.** A part of the metamodel depicting extensions to the CWM elements used by the SOA application. All the elements denoted with "CWMX_XML" and "CWMX_SOA" are newly created elements realized for this implementation. Triangles should be interpreted as "sub-class of" while deltoids denote the "elementOwnership" relationship. Different line patterns are only used to enable greater clarity of presentation. All the presented relationships are of type 1:1 (lines should only be traced from "owning" element to the "owned" element, not between two "owning" elements; same goes for the "subclass" relationships). Relationships between extended elements and other elements from the CWM specification are implied by the subclass relationships and can be inferred by using [9].

The entire scope of extensions as well as a formal description of the entire metadata exchange pattern is outside the scope of this paper, so an abridged description of the process will be given. The extensions will be described from top-level elements.

New package constructed for the purposes of a SOA-based real-time ETL scenario was named "*CWMX_SOA*", denoting its role as an extension of CWM and its implied connection to the SOA use-case scenario. Main element from this package is called "*SOA_ETL_Process*" and it is a placeholder for a single process which executes moving event data from operation sources to the real-time partition. "*SOA_ETL_Process*" owns three new elements, also newly defined, called "*SOA_Extraction*", "*SOA_Transformation*" and "*SOA_Storage*".

These elements split the process in logically defined coarse-grained segments and are expected to contain metadata elements describing important parts of each phase of the process. Another new element is simply called "*WebService*", and it describes a Web Service component partaking in the process (regardless of its actual functionality). Each part of the process is expected to be coupled with a specific Web Service, as well as some other elements described further on. A "*QueryColumnSet*" element from CWM's Relational package is subclassed with a "*StagingTable*" element which is used to describe a container which stores data during the ETL process and which is connected to the appropriate "*SOA_Extraction*", "*SOA_Transformation*" and/or "*SOA_Storage*" elements via "*elementOwnership*" association. A "*QueryColumnSet*" was chosen instead of the "*Table*" element to allow an optional inclusion of an expression which can be used both to extract but also to store the information contained in the table included in the payload). Finally, "*SOA_ProviderConnection*" element is subclassed from CWM's Software Deployment package and is used to describe the connection to the physical data source (or storage target). All these elements are subclassed from the "*WarehouseProcess*" element situated in the package it shares the name with.

Another package that was freshly constructed is called "*CWMX_XML*", and it is used instead of the "*CWM XML*" package defined in the CWM specification. The reason for this is the fact that the "*CWM XML*" package is almost completely deprecated by recent technologies and unsuitable for practical purposes. This package is almost completely DTD-based and is constructed in such a way that a breakdown is given on a certain XML document which partakes in a data warehousing environment. However, it doesn't incorporate the concept of the XML Schema and its purpose is found to be somewhat redundant, since an XML document coupled with an appropriate schema together contain the majority of important metadata dealing with the "XML"-related characteristic of a specific document.

The newly defined "*CWMX_XML*" package is similar to the black-box "*Expression*" element from the CWM's "*Expression*" package. Element simply called "*XML*" is subclassed from "*ModelElement*" – the core class of CWM specification – and it can contain its entire contents in its "value" attribute. Element called "*XSD*" is both subclassed and owned by the "*XML*" element. It can also contain its contents in the "value" attribute and this is in fact preferred, since logically a schema provides important metadata of an XML document itself.

Finally, the aforementioned "*Expression*" element is subclassed with a "*SOA_Expression*" element which is similar to the black-box expression but is extended with the possibility to hold parameters.

## 4   Defining the Messages Format

There are three *basic* messages used in the SOA ETL system:

1. *PopulatedStagingTables* – the main container for moving the information through the process. This format was chosen  because it was deemed convenient to recycle the existing format of staging tables used by the "regular" ETL process, if available, but also because a common exchange format is needed and the relational structure of a table represented in XML format is easy to construct and rather self-explanatory, especially if system involves auditing the process of moving and transforming data. This element is basically a set of relational tables described with the help of sampled elements from CWM Relational module coupled with instances of

"*RowSet*" elements which describe the "instances" of tables, e.g. the information contained within.[1]

2. *ExtractionDetails* – message detailing a way to connect to the data source and extract the data, as well as providing a container in which to put the collected information (the aforementioned *PopulatedStagingTable* element).

3. *TransformationDetails* – message containing data as well and instructions on how to transform it. Currently the instructions constitute of XSLT templates for schema matching. In the future, a more complex schema matching tool is planned for analysis and implementation.

4. *StorageDetails* – a counterpart of the "*ExtractionDetails*" element; a message containing data which passed the final transformation activities and is ready to be stored in the real-time partition.

The last two messages contain a *PopulatedStagingTables* as part of the payload.

As stated, these are only the "basic" messages which are expected to be used in every SOA ETL process and as such are the main building blocks of the communication exchange in the process. However, since the system is designed to be easily extendable, it is expected that various other message can be used to augment the functionality of the process. For instance, the reference implementation defines messages such as "*InitializationParameters*" and "*CallbackParameters*" which are used to facilitate the construction of the expression for gathering the data, as well as optimizing the execution of the process.

# 5 Implementation

The first order of business is evaluating the available information of the data warehousing system in question against the needs of the SOA ETL application. The following preconditions are supposed:

1) The data warehousing system needs a real-time data warehousing support for certain facts whose availability is mission-critical to BI applications

2) The real-time data warehousing support is being enabled through the use of a real-time partition

3) A business that requires the real-time data warehousing support has a defined metadata management strategy, which implements a metadata registry

4) This metadata registry supports the CWM specification and is reachable through appropriate protocols, as shown on Figure 1.

---

[1] It is important to emphasize that messages described here do not follow the usual format of CWM XMI messages. As stated in [8] CWM *can* be used to export relational data, but is not well suited to do so due to its verboseness. Therefore the chosen format was changed to a "shorthand version" which is compatible with CWM by using a simple XSLT transformation (even though it involves losing certain important data such as certain unique identifiers of the elements, but this is not a big issue because parts of the messages which carry information are in large extent only *based* on CWM standard, not strongly coupled with actual information residing in the metadata registry).

The metadata registry therefore contains:

a) metadata about data sources – most notably the address and protocol which may be used to reach them and the table structures contained within

b) metadata about data warehouse structures – dimensions and facts as well as physical tables that house them

c) metadata about the ETL process – formal or informal description of moving data from data sources towards the data warehouse, together with the structure and purpose of the staging tables

The next step is designing the Web Services which will be the backbone of the SOA-based ETL application . These Web Services were constructed adhering to the following arbitrary categorization:

- "**metadata driven**" Web Services – these services are utilitarian in nature, meaning that they are designed with flexibility and re-use in mind. These services need metadata about the system to execute their functionality. They can be re-used in every ETL process and do not require re-engineering when it comes to new changes in the system (if the change is properly reflected in the metadata the service uses)

- "**non-metadata driven**" Web Services – these services are especially designed for usage in the ETL process. This doesn't mean they cannot be re-used, but they will require re-engineering when changes appear in the system. Because of their specialized nature these services have much narrower functionality then metadata driven Web Services.

The ultimate solution would consist of mostly metadata driven services which would be reused by every SOA ETL process and could potentially be provided by outside sources. However in current stages of the project this is still a rather ambitious goal and the working implementation still heavily relies on non-metadata driven services whose function is still properly documented with relevant metadata stored in the metadata registry.

Business process is partially defined by the flow of data within. In this application the goal is to move the data from operational sources, transform it and then store it in the real-time partition. Data is moved from the source through components that have knowledge on how to process it, with the final result being data in the form expected by the real-time partition and usable by business intelligence systems. Figure 3. presents an UML sequence diagram of the simplest ETL process which the SOA ETL application can execute.

ETL process begins with the event that causes the appearance of new data in the operational source. This event - which will eventually be processed into a fact which will be stored in real-time partition - should trigger the initialization of the ETL process. The mechanism of event detection is outside of the scope of the process being implemented (a Web service-based Change-Data-Capture mechanism was used for the reference implementation). Process Manager receives the initialization request. The process then interacts with the Web service interfacing with the metadata registry ("*Registry Client*" Web Service), which provides all the outsourced information the process needs, mainly the connection details, the expression for data collection and details about staging XML tables which will be used as containers for the data throughout the transformation process.

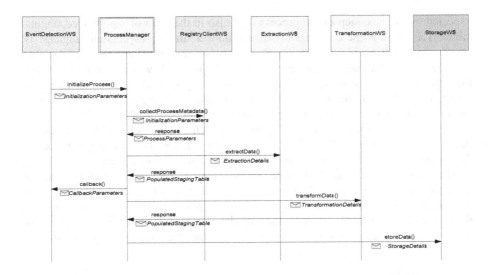

**Fig. 3.** Sequence diagram of the simplest ETL process model which showcases gathering data about a single business event, includes only one source and one simple transformation. Darker color indicates services communicating with external data sources (transactional data source, metadata registry and real-time partition respectively), while double-lined service presents a WS-BPEL execution module.

Extraction service done in a "metadata driven" way will accept the "*ExpressionDetails*" message which was populated with the help of gathered metadata from the previous step. If the extraction service is not done in an "metadata driven" way, the process can just query it for new data (optionally forwarding information which helps in its identification). In both cases, data is returned in the appropriate container, ready for the transformation sequence.

Reference implementation contains a metadata driven "*Extraction*" Web Service tailored to connect to a number of relational databases with the help of included JDBC drivers. This Web Service also uses JDBC to pull out the JDBC's *Database-MetaData* object[2] from gathered data which is then validated against the *Populated-StagingTables* element whose structure is collected from the metadata registry. If the collected set matches, the *PopulatedStagingTables* message is filled with the appropriate *RowSet* instances and forwarded back to the process.

In the initial implementation, Transformation services are designed either as XSLT transformation services (specialized services that transform an XML document with the help of an appropriate XSLT template) or specialized opaque Transformation services especially designed for use in a certain Transformation step. The former will accept the data enclosed in a "*TransformationDetails*" message which contains populated staging tables and a XSLT template which will transform them in the form

---

[2] This object can also be used for gathering initial metadata about tables in operational sources as well as those in the data warehouse. In the reference implementation parts of the metadata registry were populated with the help of JDBC *DatabaseMetaData* object which was then used to facilitate the construction of metadata pertaining to the staging tables.

expected by the next step of the process (and also in the form of a populated staging table). The latter is the current workaround until a suitable expression language is found which will enable description of diverse dynamic transformations in declaratory manner implementable with programming logic which will not severely impact the performance nor increase the complexity of the system. In future versions of the system it is expected that the Transformation Services will use approaches presented the *Model Management System* [7] to certain extent, because the MMS can potentially provide a way to express schema mappings in such a way they could be stored as metadata which would allow the transformation services to be entirely metadata driven. As such, modeling transformations will be a large focus of future work.

The final stop is storage of the data. Service does the opposite from the extraction services – it receives a special *"StorageDetails"* element which contains connection and expression details as well as payload data which has to be stored in the real-time data partition. The process is concluded with data residing in a real-time data partition where it can be used as-is or further processed by other data warehousing systems.

## 6  Conclusion

One of the main ideas behind constructing an SOA-based ETL application was evaluating the usefulness of standard metadata as a runtime integration tool. The ultimate solution would be an SOA ETL system which could largely operate in an autonomous manner, gathering and interpreting data warehousing system metadata and then using it as a "recipe" for the actual execution of the ETL process, while still keeping all the benefits offered by the SOA approach. This way modeling of the ETL system would essentially boil down to modeling the metadata in the appropriate way and merely setting up essential parameters for the real-time ETL execution. However, as powerful as today's technologies are they still operate under certain limitations which as yet don't make development of such a solution feasible. This paper presents a reference implementation which serves as an initial step towards achieving this goal.

Since the described process is SOA-based, it is perfectly reasonable to upgrade it with additional services. The reference  implementation for instance includes an optimization "identifier bootstrapping" technique which halts the event detector so it doesn't report new events until the data extraction is complete, upon which detector receives the identifier of the last row collected and only points out new events if their row identifier is even higher than the received one. Also, this process incorporates audit services which store XML documents containing data being moved through the process so outside auditing can be performed if necessary. Finally, since the entire system is Web Services-based, it can also benefit from the myriad of options offered by WS-Extensions. The system can  be augmented with the security or reliability services as deemed appropriate by the implementation developers. More detailed description of the system architecture with expanded functionality as well as a more significant shift towards a generic, re-usable SOA ETL application will all be accompanied in the future work.

Finally, it is important to emphasize that the described implemented application is not limited to real-time ETL in data warehousing environment which was only used as a convenient vertical scenario. It is expected that the application can serve as a provider of data moving services between different data repositories in any business scenario where such service is needed. In the current incarnation the application is oriented mainly towards the needs of a real-time data warehousing support, but in the future, a more generalized usage is expected.

# References

1. Erl, T.: Service-Oriented Architecture, Concepts, Technology, and Design. Prentice Hall, Englewood Cliffs (2006)
2. Erl, T.: Service-Oriented Architecture, a field guide to integrating XML and Web Services. Prentice-Hall, Englewood Cliffs (2004)
3. Zhu, Y., An, L., Liu, S.: Data Updating and Query in Real-Time Data Warehouse System. In: CSSE, International Conference on Computer Science and Software Engineering, vol. 5, pp. 1295–1297 (2008)
4. Langseth, J.: Real-Time Data Warehousing: Challenges and Solutions, DSSResources.COM, 02/08/2004
5. Kimball, R., Caserta, J.: The Data Warehouse ETL Toolkit. In: Practical Techniques for Extracting, Cleaning, Conforming and Delivering Data. Wiley, Chichester (2004)
6. Schlesinger, L., Irmert, F., Lehner, W.: Supporting the ETL process by Web Service technologies. International Journal of Web and Grid Services 1, 31–47 (2005)
7. Bernstein, P.A., Melnik, S.: Model Management 2.0: Manipulating Richer Mappings. In: SIGMOD 2007: Proceedings of the 2007 ACM SIGMOD international conference on Management of data, pp. 1–12 (2007)
8. http://www.omg.org – home site of the Object Management Group
9. Object Management Group, Inc: Common Warehouse Metamodel (CWM) Specification, vol. 1, formal/03-03-02 (March 2003)
10. Langseth, J.: Real-Time Data Warehousing: Challenges and Solutions, DSSResources.COM (02/08/2004)
11. Poole, J., Chang, D., Tolbert, D., Mellor, D.: Common Warehouse Metamodel: Developer's Guide. Wiley, Chichester (2003)

# Exploiting Domain Knowledge by Automated Taxonomy Generation in Recommender Systems

Tao Li and Sarabjot S. Anand

Department of Computer Science, University of Warwick
Coventry, United Kingdom
{li.tao,s.s.anand}@warwick.ac.uk

**Abstract.** The effectiveness of incorporating domain knowledge into recommender systems to address their sparseness problem and improve their prediction accuracy has been discussed in many research works. However, this technique is usually restrained in practice because of its high computational expense. Although cluster analysis can alleviate the computational complexity of the recommendation procedure, it is not satisfactory in preserving pair-wise item similarities, which would severely impair the recommendation quality. In this paper, we propose an efficient approach based on the technique of Automated Taxonomy Generation to exploit relational domain knowledge in recommender systems so as to achieve high system scalability and prediction accuracy. Based on the domain knowledge, a hierarchical data model is synthesized in an offline phase to preserve the original pairwise item similarities. The model is then used by online recommender systems to facilitate the similarity calculation and keep their recommendation quality comparable to those systems by means of real-time exploiting domain knowledge. Experiments were conducted upon real datasets to evaluate our approach.

## 1   Introduction

Recommender systems utilize content-based filtering or collaborative filtering techniques to select items (for example movies, music or books) that best match the interests of different users [1]. Traditionally all the items and users are represented as propositional vectors. Their pairwise similarities, which is the key to discover the neighborhood of items/users and thus generate the recommendations, can easily be calculated based on the vector model.

To improve the recommendation quality and address the problem of data sparseness, recent research focuses on exploiting domain knowledge about items [8][14][3]. However, dealing with semantic relational knowledge will greatly increase the complexity of similarity calculation and hence impair the scalability of recommender systems. To clarify our discussion, we consider an example of recommending movies here. Fig. 1 shows the ontology of a relational movie dataset, in which each concept may refer to other concepts as its features. Hence, a movie is described by propositional features (title, duration, etc) as well as relational features (the director and the cast of actors). Similarly, an actor is described by

T. Di Noia and F. Buccafurri (Eds.): EC-Web 2009, LNCS 5692, pp. 120–131, 2009.

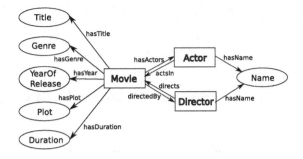

**Fig. 1.** Ontology of a movie dataset

his name and the list of movies he acted in. When calculating similarity between movies, it is obvious that the similarity between their casts should be considered in addition to other features. Determining the similarity between casts is based on the comparison of their included actors, which in turn depends on the similarities between movies these actors acted in.[1] Obviously such a recursive computation is too expensive for the time-critical recommendation services.

Various clustering techniques have been applied as an offline pre-processing step to improve the scalability of recommender systems [15]. The primary motivation behind these approaches is to group items or users and then employ traditional collaborative filtering algorithms upon the group profiles [15] or independently within each group rather than all items/users [16]. Nevertheless, these approaches are less helpful when the items are defined by sophisticated domain knowledge. As in the above example, calculating the pairwise similarities within a small set of items is still time-consuming. A better solution is to construct some data models for preserving the item similarities. Recommender systems can then retrieve these values directly instead of computing them in real-time when generating recommendations. Model-based approaches are more suitable for this purpose because the huge amount of candidate items often prevents the utilization of memory-based approaches in practice.

In this paper we propose an efficient approach based on the technique of Automated Taxonomy Generation (ATG) to incorporate relational domain knowledge into recommender systems so as to achieve high system scalability and predication accuracy. By analyzing domain knowledge about items in the offline phase, a hierarchical data model is synthesized to simulate the pair-wise item similarities. The derived data model is then used by online recommender systems to facilitate the similarity calculation and at the same time keep their recommendation quality comparable to the memory-based systems that exploit the domain knowledge in real-time.

The rest of our paper is organized as follows: In Section 2 the recommendation algorithm together with the adopted relational similarity measure are briefly introduced. In Section 3 we describe our method of automatically constructing

---

[1] The analysis for the directors is very similar, so we ignore here for brevity.

taxonomy based on the domain knowledge of items, and then incorporating the derived data model into the recommendation process. Section 4 provides our experimental results. Some related works are reviewed in Section 5. Finally, Section 6 summarizes our conclusions and future works.

## 2 Recommender System and Relational Similarity Measure

Recommender systems aim at finding a bundle of candidate items that best match the current user's interest, i.e. most similar to the items he likes and most dissimilar to those he dislikes [1]. Content-based filtering and user-based collaborative filtering are common techniques used in the recommender systems. Traditionally all the items are represented as numeric vectors, e.g. the keyword vectors (extracted from the textual description by Information Retrieval techniques) in content-based filtering or the user rating vectors (explicitly or implicitly collected by Web Usage Mining techniques) in collaborative filtering. The similarities between items or users, which is the key to discovering the neighborhood of items/users and thus generate the recommendations, can easily be calculated from these vector models by using standard metrics such as cosine similarity or Pearson's correlation coefficient.

Compared with content-based filtering, the user-based collaborative filtering algorithms are more utilized in practice and have achieved some commercial success. However, the effectiveness of this approach is severely impacted when the user-rating matrix is very sparse. In order to address the data sparseness problem and improve the prediction accuracy, recent research has focused on exploiting domain knowledge about items as the supplement of user-ratings. An effective method is to combine the pair-wise item similarities evaluated based on their relational features with the user similarities derived from user ratings to generate recommendations [3].

Given the item ontology denoted as the graph $G = (V, E)$, in which vertices $V$ stand for the concepts in the ontology and edges $E = \{e \mid \text{edge } e : c \rightarrow c'; c, c' \in V\}$ for the reference relationships between these concepts. To construct an object $\mathbf{x}$ of concept $c$, we find the feature list $MF(c)$ composed of all concepts referenced by $c$ and then link the corresponding objects $\{\mathbf{y}_i\}$ to $\mathbf{x}$ if $\mathbf{y}_i$ is an instance of concept $c'$ and $c' \in MF(c)$. For brevity, we say that $\mathbf{y}_i$ is appended into the relational feature $\mathbf{x}.c'$ of $\mathbf{x}$. The above procedure is launched iteratively for each $\mathbf{y}_i$ until $MF(c) = \emptyset$ or a depth bound is reached. Using the movie ontology (Fig.1) as an example, different ontological concepts have different data types: *Title*, *YearOfRelease*, *Certificate* and *Genre* are string, numeric, categorical and taxonomy-based respectively. According to the relationship structure, we have $MF(Actor) = MF(Director) = \{Name, Movie\}$ and $MF(Movie) = \{Title, Genre, YearOfRelease, Plot, Duration, Actor, Director\}$. Therefore, a relational data object representing an actor will link to all the movies he acted in, which in turn link to other actors and directors he cooperated with in those movies.

**Table 1.** Algorihm for Determining $S$

*CalculateS* (items $\mathbf{X}_a$, items $\mathbf{X}_b$, measure $fs_{item}(\cdot,\cdot)$)

1. For $\mathbf{x}_i^{(a)} \in \mathbf{X}_a$ and $\mathbf{x}_j^{(b)} \in \mathbf{X}_b$, create the set of triples $(\mathbf{x}_i^{(a)}, \mathbf{x}_j^{(b)}, fs_{item}(\mathbf{x}_i^{(a)}, \mathbf{x}_j^{(b)}))$.
2. Sort the resulting set of triples in descending order of similarity values, creating a new list of triples $(\mathbf{x}_v^{(a)}, \mathbf{x}_v^{(b)}, fs_{item}(\mathbf{x}_v^{(a)}, \mathbf{x}_v^{(b)}))$, where $1 \le v \le |\mathbf{X}_a||\mathbf{X}_b|$
3. Let $S = \emptyset$, $S_a = \emptyset$, $S_b = \emptyset$. For $1 \le v \le |\mathbf{X}_a||\mathbf{X}_b|$:
   If $\mathbf{x}_v^{(a)} \notin S_a$ and $\mathbf{x}_v^{(b)} \notin S_b$, then add $\mathbf{x}_v^{(a)} \to S_a$, $\mathbf{x}_v^{(b)} \to S_b$, and $(\mathbf{x}_v^{(a)}, \mathbf{x}_v^{(b)}) \to S$
4. Return $S$

If two relational data objects $\mathbf{x}_i$ and $\mathbf{x}_j$ of concept $c$ have been constructed, their similarity can be calculated by:

$$fs_{item}(\mathbf{x}_i, \mathbf{x}_j) = \sum_{c' \in MF(c)} w_{c,c'} \cdot fs_{set}(\mathbf{x}_i.c', \mathbf{x}_j.c') \tag{1}$$

where weight $w_{c,c'}$ ($w_{c,c'} \le 1$ and $\sum_{c'} w_{c,c'} = 1$) represent the importance of member concept $c'$ in the feature list $MF(c)$ and $fs_{set}(\mathbf{x}_i.c', \mathbf{x}_j.c')$ is defined as:

$$fs_{set}(\mathbf{x}_i.c', \mathbf{x}_j.c') = \begin{cases} \frac{1}{|\mathbf{x}_i.c'|} \sum_{y_l \in \mathbf{x}_j.c'} \max_{y_k \in \mathbf{x}_i.c'} fs(\mathbf{y}_k, \mathbf{y}_l), & \text{if } |\mathbf{x}_i.c'| \ge |\mathbf{x}_j.c'| > 0. \\ \frac{1}{|\mathbf{x}_j.c'|} \sum_{y_k \in \mathbf{x}_i.c'} \max_{y_l \in \mathbf{x}_j.c'} fs(\mathbf{y}_k, \mathbf{y}_l), & \text{if } |\mathbf{x}_j.c'| \ge |\mathbf{x}_i.c'| > 0. \\ 0, & \text{if } |\mathbf{x}_i.c'| = 0 \text{ or } |\mathbf{x}_j.c'| = 0. \end{cases} \tag{2}$$

If $MF(c') \neq \emptyset$, the value of $fs(\mathbf{y}_k, \mathbf{y}_l)$ in Eq. 2 is recursively calculated by Eq. 1. It means to replace $\mathbf{x}_i$ (resp. $\mathbf{x}_j$) by $\mathbf{y}_k$ (resp. $\mathbf{y}_l$) in Eq. 1 and then use Eq. 2 to compare all the associated objects that are referenced by $\mathbf{y}_k$ or $\mathbf{y}_l$. Such recursive procedure explores the linkage structure of the relational objects.

Given the above similarity measure between items, the pairwise similarities between users are computed using the Generalized Cosine Max (GCM) metric:

$$fs_{user}(\mathbf{u}_a, \mathbf{u}_b) = \sum_{(\mathbf{x}_i, \mathbf{x}_j) \in S} r_a(\mathbf{x}_i) \times r_b(\mathbf{x}_j) \times fs_{item}(\mathbf{x}_i, \mathbf{x}_j)$$

where users $\mathbf{u}_a$ and $\mathbf{u}_b$ visit sets of items $\mathbf{X}_a$ and $\mathbf{X}_b$ respectively. $r_a(\mathbf{x}_i)$ is the rating value that user $\mathbf{u}_a$ assigns to item $\mathbf{x}_i$, and so does $r_b(\mathbf{x}_j)$. The candidate set $S \subset \mathbf{X}_a \times \mathbf{X}_b$ is computed by algorithm *CalculateS* (shown in Table 1). Here we can see the similarity computation between items plays an important role in finding the neighbors of users. Generally speaking, exploiting more ontological information during the item similarity computation can bring benefit for the recommendation generation, but at the same time the recommendation algorithm becomes far more computationally expensive. To reduce the impact of exploiting domain knowledge on the system scalability, our solution is to preserve the item similarities in an offline phase so that the recommender systems can retrieve these values directly instead of computing them in real-time. However, the vast number of candidate items makes the exhaustive storage of item similarities infeasible, so we will build some data models to simulate the pair-wise item similarities.

# 3    Incorporating Taxonomy into Recommender Systems

A taxonomy organizes large amounts of information into a hierarchical structure to facilitate people's navigating and browsing actions [18][12]. Compared with the cluster analysis that divides the original dataset into independent clusters, the taxonomy describes the pairwise proximity of nodes via the taxonomic structure. Therefore, we develop a taxonomy-like structure to preserve the pairwise similarities between items and utilize the data model to accelerate the online recommendation procedure. Our ATG algorithm is composed of three steps (Table 2): *division*, *agglomeration* and *pruning*. First the whole dataset is divided into some micro-clusters, a hierarchical dendrogram is then built on these micro-clusters using the agglomerative approach, and finally a series of levels within the dendrogram are selected to prune the hierarchical structure.

To facilitate the procedure of taxonomy generation, we introduce the idea of Representative Objects, which are some maximum-spread objects in a given dataset $D$. With a random startpoint $\mathbf{x}_0$, the $i$-th RO is selected by:

$$\mathbf{ro}_i = \begin{cases} \underset{\mathbf{x} \in D}{\arg\min} \, fs_{item}(\mathbf{x}, \mathbf{x}_0) & \text{if } i = 1 \\ \underset{\mathbf{x} \in D}{\arg\min} \left( \underset{1 \leq j < i}{\max} \, fs_{item}(\mathbf{x}, \mathbf{ro}_j) \right) & \text{if } 2 \leq i \leq r \end{cases}$$

The variance of $D$ is defined as: $Var(D) = 1 - \min_{1 \leq i,j \leq r} fs_{item}(\mathbf{ro}_i, \mathbf{ro}_j)$. Generally speaking, smaller variance means items are more similar (homogeneous) to each other. The original dataset $D$ is recursively divided as follows: A cluster will be divided if its variance is greater than a threshold $v$. The least similar ROs are used as the absorbent objects of sub-clusters respectively, and the other objects are distributed according to their similarity the absorbent objects. Hence, the threshold $v$ controls the homogeneity of the derived clusters.

**Table 2.** Main Framework of ATG Algorithm

ATG (dataset $D$, number of ROs $r$, variance $v$)

1. cluster set $\{C_k\}$ ← call the *Divisive-Step*, given $D$, $r$ and $v$ as the parameters.
2. dendrogram $T$ ← call the *Agglomerative-Step*, given $\{C_k\}$ as the parameter.
3. taxonomy $T'$ ← determine a series of cutting levels in $T$ to prune the dendrogram and then weight edges to preserve the original item similarities.

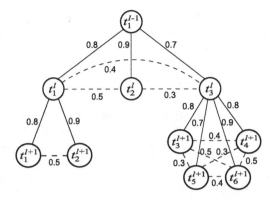

**Fig. 2.** Hierarchical taxonomy for preserving similarity values

In order to build the hierarchical dendrogram $T$ as well as remedy inaccurate partitioning in the divisive step, an agglomerative step is utilized to recursively merge the above derived clusters according to their pairwise similarity:

$$fs_{node}(t_l, t_{l'}) = \min_{i,j} fs_{item}(ro_i^{(t_l)}, ro_j^{(t_{l'})})$$

where $\{ro_i^{(t_l)}\}$ and $\{ro_j^{(t_{l'})}\}$ are the set of ROs for node $t_l$ and in node $t_{l'}$ respectively (the words "cluster" and "node" are used interchangeable in the paper).

The binary-split hierarchical dendrogram $T$ will be adjusted further, because: (i) Not all levels in $T$ are natural for reflecting the data distribution in $D$ [9]; (ii) Sibling nodes are only linked via their parent nodes, which is inconvenient for similarity retrieval and simulation. To solve the first issue, a series of cutting levels are heuristically determined to prune $T$, as discussed in [12]. We expect all the taxonomic nodes located at the same level are approximately of the same granularity and all the sibling nodes under the same parent node are as distinctive as possible, so we use the measure:

$$G(l) = \frac{g_{intra}(l) - g_{intra}(l-1)}{g_{inter}(l) - g_{inter}(l-1)}$$

where $l$ is the index of a certain level in $T$, being numbered from top to bottom. $g_{intra}(l)$ and $g_{inter}(l)$ compute the intra- and inter-node similarity of level $l$:

$$g_{intra}(l) = \frac{1}{K_l} \sum_{k=1}^{K_l} \left( \min_{i,j} fs_{item}(ro_i^{(t_k^l)}, ro_j^{(t_k^l)}) \right)$$

$$g_{inter}(l) = \frac{1}{K_{l-1}} \sum_{p=1}^{K_{l-1}} \left( \min_{\substack{k_1,k_2 \\ P(t_{k_1}^l)=P(t_{k_2}^l)=t_p^{l-1}}} fs_{node}(t_{k_1}^l, t_{k_2}^l) \right)$$

assuming there are $K_l$ nodes located at the $l$-th level of $T$, denoted as $\{t_k^l\}$ ($1 \leq k \leq K_l$). $P(t_k^l)$ is the parent node of $t_k^l$. Then the level $l$ is selected if $G(l) > 1$.

After determining all the cutting levels, dendrogram $T$ is pruned by merging each super-node and its sub-nodes if they are together located between two neighboring cutting levels or below the lowest cutting level. Additionally, we manually add edges between each pair of sibling nodes in the pruned hierarchy to solve the second issue mentioned above. Fig. 2 shows an example of the pruned taxonomy (with weighted edges).

Before introducing our strategy of weighting the taxonomic edges, we need to define the path-based similarity metric: Given a weighted taxonomy $T'$, a unique path connecting two leaf nodes $t_1$ and $t_Q$ in $T'$ is identified by $t_1 \rightarrow \ldots \rightarrow t_q \rightarrow t_{q+1} \rightarrow \ldots \rightarrow t_Q$, in which $t_q \rightarrow t_{q+1}$ is one and the only one edge between sibling nodes and all the others connect nodes and their parent. The path similarity is calculated by:

$$fs_{path}(t_1, t_Q) = \prod_{q=1}^{Q} w(t_q, t_{q+1}) \tag{3}$$

For example, assume two data objects $\mathbf{x}_1$ and $\mathbf{x}_2$ are contained in node $t_1^{l+1}$ and $t_4^{l+1}$ respectively in Fig. 2, the path connecting these two nodes is $t_1^{l+1} \rightarrow t_1^l \rightarrow t_3^l \rightarrow t_4^{l+1}$. Accordingly we can use all the edge weights along this path to estimate the original similarity value between $\mathbf{x}_1$ and $\mathbf{x}_2$: $fs_{path}(\mathbf{x}_1, \mathbf{x}_2) = 0.8 \times 0.4 \times 0.8 = 0.256$.

Now the question becomes: *How should we assign weights to the taxonomic edges so that the above path-based similarities effectively preserve the original item similarity values computed by Eqs. 1 and 2 ?* We utilize the average value of item similarities as the weight of edges between nodes, so:

- The weight of an edge connecting a parent node $t_p$ and its child node $t_c$ is:

$$w(t_p, t_c) = \frac{1}{|t_p| \cdot |t_c|} \sum_{i,j} fs_{item}(\mathbf{x}_i^{(t_p)}, \mathbf{x}_j^{(t_c)})$$

- The weight of an edge connecting two sibling nodes $t_c$ and $t_{c'}$ is:

$$w(t_c, t_{c'}) = \frac{1}{|t_c| \cdot |t_{c'}|} \sum_{i,j} fs_{item}(\mathbf{x}_i^{(t_c)}, \mathbf{x}_j^{(t_{c'})})$$

where $|t_p|$ and $|t_c|$ denote the amount of items in nodes $t_p$ and $t_{c'}$ respectively. By utilizing Eq. 3 based on the derived taxonomy in the recommender systems, the cost of computing item similarities in real-time will be reduced greatly.

It is worth noting that Yin et al. proposed another data structure, named *SimTree*, in [17] for preserving pair-wise similarities between items, but our method is more appealing because: First, in the SimTree each leaf node corresponds to an item and each non-leaf node has at most $c$ child nodes, where $c$ is a user-specified parameter, so "unnatural" data structures will be generated in practice if the parameter $c$ is inappropriately specified. Actually finding the optimal value of $c$ is not easy. In contrast, our approach can automatically generate the taxonomic structure without manually specified parameters and thus better reflects the real distribution of the data objects. Second, the initial SimTrees are built by using the frequent mining techniques, and then path-based similarities in one SimTree is used to adjust the structures and edge-weights of other SimTrees. Property features of the data objects are not exploited, which will definitely degrades the accuracy of the final result. Our approach is based on the relational similarity metric (Eqs. 1 and 2) that exploits the ontological information of items. Therefore, more ontological information and knowledge are preserved in the derived taxonomy.

## 4   Experimental Results

We compare the performance of our approach in the recommender systems with that of the following methods: (1) baseline (ORG) which purely uses the original similarity values in the procedure of recommendation generation; (2) cluster model based on real similarity values (CLUS), which uses the original similarity values between two items if they belong to the same cluster or otherwise uses 0 instead; (3) SimTree proposed in [17], which simulates the similarity values based on the synthesized SimTree structure. Finally, the word "RoATG" is used to represent our approach proposed in this paper. Two criteria were used to evaluate the effectiveness of different methods:

1. *Mean Absolute Error* (MAE): When the actual time spent by a user to visit a candidate item is known, the MAE between the predicted and the actual time spent reflects the predication accuracy of the recommendations.
2. *F-Score*: This is the harmonic mean of precision and recall that have been used widely in the field of Information Retrieval [9]. The higher value of F-Score means the high probabilities that the items returned by the recommender system will satisfy the user's interest and the potentially interesting items will be discovered by the system at the same time.

Our experiments were conducted on two real datasets:

### 4.1   MovieLens

This dataset contains 3,883 movies, 31,650 actors and 1,903 directors. All the movies are assigned into 18 genre categories. Additionally, there are 988,259

**Table 3.** Recommendations for MovieLens

|         | Time ($10^3$ sec) | MAE | F-Score |
|---------|-------------------|-----|---------|
| ORG     | –                 | 0.78 | 0.376  |
| CLUS    | 46.9              | 0.81 | 0.297  |
| SimTree | 53.0              | 0.79 | 0.326  |
| RoATG   | 55.5              | 0.72 | 0.364  |

**Table 4.** Recommendations for Movie Dataset ($NumRec = 100$)

| | Time (sec) | MAE | F-Score | | | Time (sec) | MAE | F-Score |
|---|---|---|---|---|---|---|---|---|
| ORG | $> 2.5 \times 10^5$ | 1.05 | 0.265 | | ORG | $> 2.5 \times 10^5$ | 1.02 | 0.416 |
| CLUS | 1378 | 1.11 | 0.171 | | CLUS | 1861 | 1.06 | 0.268 |
| SimTree | 1519 | 1.06 | 0.228 | | SimTree | 1895 | 1.01 | 0.367 |
| RoATG | 1422 | 1.04 | 0.263 | | RoATG | 1753 | 1.01 | 0.403 |

|      (a) User-based      |      (b) Visit-based      |

browsing records in 4,846 sessions. We used 80% of the browsing records as the training data and the other 20% as the test data.

The classic clustering method k-Medoid was adopted in CLUS, given the parameter $k = 50$. In SimTree, we set the parameter $c$, which controls the number of node's branches, as 15. In RoATG, the variance $v$ was set as 0.40. For each user, 100 candidate items were returned in total as the recommendations. The experimental results are shown in Table 3. The approach ORG needs a few days to finish the experiment, which is much slower than the other three methods. When evaluated by MAE, we find that RoATG is the best among the four approaches. For the criterion F-Score, RoATG and ORG achieve very close results, which means their recommendation best satisfied users' interests and many potentially interesting items could be found, but CLUS and SimTree have 26.6% and 15.3% loss respectively.

## 4.2   MovieRetailer

This dataset was provided by a movie retailer on the Web, containing 62,955 movies, 40,826 actors, 9,189 directors as well as a genre taxonomy of 186 genres. There are 923,987 ratings in 15,741 sessions from 10,151 users. Since this dataset is very sparse compared with the previous one, the proportions of training and test data were 85% and 15% respectively. The number of sessions made by different users ranges from 1 to 814. Based on the user visits, we select 10,000 most popular movies for our analysis. The parameters for different approaches were set the same as those in the first experiment.

Since the dataset contains multiple visits made by the same user, the recommendations could be generated on the basis of users or visits (sessions). The corresponding experimental results are reported in Tables 5a and 5b respectively. The first column is the time spent for generating recommendations, proving that all the model-based methods (CLUS, SimTree and RoATG) can effectively reduce a magnitude of time compared with that of computing the original similarity metric in real-time (ORG). For the criterion MAE that evaluates the recommendation quality, both SimTree and RoATG performance close to the baseline ORG, but CLUS has 5% loss compared with the other methods. When evaluated by the F-Score, we can see that ORG achieves the highest score. The F-Score of RoATG is almost the same as that of ORG, but SimTree has 16.8% and 13.4% loss in the user-based and visit-based cases respectively. Again, CLUS is the worst among the four approaches.

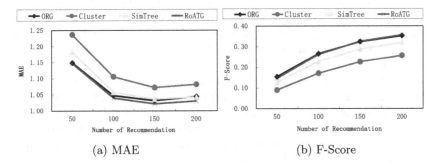

**Fig. 3.** Recommendations for Movie Dataset

Furthermore, we evaluate the approaches w.r.t different recommendation numbers. The conclusion is also suitable for the visit-based recommendation). The curves of MAE and F-Score are shown in Figs. 3a and 3b respectively. We can see the MAEs of different approaches drop as the increase of the recommendation numbers, but RoATG is always better than the others. When evaluated by F-Score, RoATG is very close to ORG under different values of recommendation numbers, while the approaches of SimTree and CLUS have about 34% and 13% loss respectively.

## 5   Related Work

Recommender systems utilize information filtering techniques to find new items that best match the interests of different users. Information filtering techniques can be categorized as *content-based filtering* and *collaborative filtering*. In content-based filtering, each item is represented as a set of textual or numeric attributes extracted from the item's content description. The profile of the current user, being composed of the above attributes, summarizes all the items he has viewed. Then new items are compared with this profile to generate the recommendations for the current user. In contrast, the collaborative filtering approaches does not deal with the content of items. The profiles of users, consisting of their rating upon items they have viewed, are used to find the nearest neighbors of the current user and produce recommendations accordingly. [1][2]

Exploiting domain knowledge about items is valuable for improving the recommendation quality, because the item characteristics as well as the user preferences will be better understood. Dai and Mobasher [8] presented a general framework of integrating domain knowledge within Web Usage Mining for user-based recommendation. Semantic attributes and relations about candidate items are first extracted from the web pages based on the ontology. Then "item-level" user profiles are transformed into ontology-enhanced "domain-level" aggregate profiles, which captures the common interests of user groups at the domain level. Finally, the aggregated profiles together with the current user profile are used as the input of the recommendation engine to produce domain-level recommendations, from which the real web objects are retrieved and recommended to the user. Middleton et al. [14] explored the use of an ontology in a recommender system to solve the cold-start problem and dynamically discover user interests. They applied the kNN algorithm to classify candidate papers as well as user interests, and then identified user communities by the ontology-based network analysis. Ziegler et al. [19] proposed a taxonomy-based recommender framework for exploiting relationships between super-concepts and sub-concepts in the domain taxonomy, which addresses the sparseness issue and diversifies the recommendation results to reflect the users specific interests, but their work assumed the existence of a taxonomy and hence limited in the context of simple Genre-based taxonomies while ignoring other item features.

Automated Taxonomy Generation (ATG) is used to organize a large dataset and discover knowledge within it so as to facilitate peoples navigation and browsing actions [18]. Traditional hierarchical (divisive or agglomerative) clustering algorithms can be used to construct a hierarchical taxonomy and some heuristic algorithms are applied to optimize the taxonomic structure [6][5]. Boley developed a divisive partitioning algorithm PDDP in [4], which iteratively performs binary divisions in each cluster when its scatter value is greater than a user-defined threshold. Clerkin et al. [7] applied the incremental conceptual clustering algorithm COBWEB to construct class hierarchies. Lawrie and Croft proposed the use of a set of topical summary terms for taxonomy construction. These topical terms are selected by maximizing the joint probability of their topicality and predictiveness [13]. Kummamuru et al. developed an incremental learning algorithm DisCover to maximize the coverage as well as the distinctiveness of the taxonomy [12]. A comprehensive survey can be found in [11].

## 6    Conclusion

By utilizing information filtering techniques, recommender systems can find items that best satisfy the interests of different users. Although exploiting domain knowledge can tackle the sparseness problem and improve the prediction accuracy, it is usually computationally expensive and hence impairs the scalability of online recommendation service. To address this difficulty, we propose to incorporate the technique of Automated Taxonomy Generation into the recommender systems. Domain knowledge about items is analyzed to automatically construct a hierarchical taxonomy. The derived taxonomy credibly approximates the pair-wise item similarities, which can then be used by the online recommender systems to accelerate the similarity calculation and at the same time keep their recommendation quality comparable to those systems that exploit domain knowledge within the process of recommendation generation.

In the future, we will continue to improve the algorithm of weighting taxonomic edges. Specifically, we aim at developing an approach for dynamically appending edges between sibling nodes only when the newly-added edges are helpful to estimate the pairwise similarity entries between data objects of the sibling nodes. More methods of generating optimal taxonomic structures that better reflect the internal data distribution are to be explored. The derived taxonomy will be used to expand the taxonomy-based recommender framework proposed in [19] as well as speed up the neighbourhood formulation in the recommendation process.

# References

1. Adomavicius, G., Tuzhilin, A.: Towards the next generation of recommendation systems: A survey of the state-of-the-art and possible extensions. IEEE Transaction on Knowledge and Data Engineering 17(6) (2005)
2. Anand, S.S., Mobasher, B.: Intelligent techniques for web personalization. In: Mobasher, B., Anand, S.S. (eds.) ITWP 2003. LNCS (LNAI), vol. 3169, pp. 1–36. Springer, Heidelberg (2005)
3. Anand, S.S., Kearney, P., Shapcott, M.: Generating semantically enriched user profiles for web personalization. ACM Transactions on Internet Technologies 7(3) (2007)
4. Boley, D.: Hierarchical taxonomies using divisive partitioning. Technical Report TR-98-012, Department of Computer Science, University of Minnesota (1998)
5. Cheng, P.-J., Chien, L.-F.: Auto-generation of topic hierarchies for web images from users' perspectives. In: Proceedings of ACM CIKM 2003 (2003)
6. Chuang, S.-L., Chien, L.-F.: Towards automatic generation of query taxonomy: A hierarchical query clustering approach. In: Proceedings of ICDM 2002 (2002)
7. Clerkin, P., Cunningham, P., Hayes, C.: Ontology discovery for the semantic web using hierarchical clustering. In: Proceedings of Semantic Web Mining Workshop co-located with ECML/PKDD (2001)
8. Dai, H., Mobasher, B.: A road map to more effective web personalization: Integrating domain knowledge with web usage mining. In: Proceedings of International Conference on Internet Computing (2003)
9. Duda, R.O., Hart, P.E., Stork, D.G.: Pattern Classification, 2nd edn (2001)
10. Džeroski, S., Lavrač, N.: Relational Data Mining (2001)
11. Krishnapuram, R., Kummamuru, K.: Automatic taxonomy generation: Issues and possibilities. In: De Baets, B., Kaynak, O., Bilgiç, T. (eds.) IFSA 2003. LNCS, vol. 2715, pp. 52–63. Springer, Heidelberg (2003)
12. Kummamuru, K., Lotlikar, R., Roy, S., Singal, K., Krishnapuram, R.: A hierarchical monothetic document clustering algorithm for summarization and browsing search results. In: Proceedings of WWW 2004 (2004)
13. Lawrie, D.J., Croft, W.B.: Generating hierarchical summaries for web searches. In: Proceedings of SIGIR 2003 (2003)
14. Middleton, S.E., Shadbolt, N.R., Roure, D.: Ontological user profiling in recommender systems. ACM Transactions on Information Systems 22(1) (2004)
15. Mobasher, B.: Data Mining for Personalization. The Adaptive Web (2007)
16. Suryavanshi, B., Shiri, N., Mudur, S.P.: A Fuzzy Hybrid Collaborative Filtering Technique for Web Personalization. In: Proceedings of Intelligent Techniques for Web Personalization (ITWP) Workshop co-located with IJCAI (2005)
17. Yin, X., Han, J., Yu, P.S.: LinkClus: efficient clustering via heterogeneous semantic links. In: Proceedings of VLDB 2006 (2006)
18. Zhao, Y., Karypis, G.: Evaluation of hierarchical clustering algorithms for document datasets. In: Proceedings of ACM CIKM 2002 (2002)
19. Ziegler, C.-N., Simon, K., Lausen, G., Schmidt-Thieme, L.: Taxonomy-driven computation of product recommendations. In: Proceedings of ACM CIKM 2004 (2006)

# Automatic Generation of Mashups for Personalized Commerce in Digital TV by Semantic Reasoning

Yolanda Blanco-Fernández, Martín López-Nores, José J. Pazos-Arias,
and Manuela I. Martín-Vicente*

Department of Telematics Engineering, University of Vigo,
ETSE Telecomunicación, Campus Universitario s/n, 36310 Vigo, Spain
{yolanda,mlnores,jose,mvicente}@det.uvigo.es
http://idtv.det.uvigo.es

**Abstract.** The evolution of information technologies is consolidating *recommender systems* as essential tools in e-commerce. To date, these systems have focused on discovering the items that best match the preferences, interests and needs of individual users, to end up listing those items by decreasing relevance in some menus. In this paper, we propose extending the current scope of recommender systems to better support trading activities, by automatically generating interactive applications that provide the users with personalized commercial functionalities related to the selected items. We explore this idea in the context of Digital TV advertising, with a system that brings together semantic reasoning techniques and new architectural solutions for web services and mashups.

## 1   Introduction

The advent of new devices (e.g., Digital TV receivers, mobile phones or media players) and usage habits (e.g., social networking) is progressively rendering the classical search engines of the Internet insufficient to support users in their grasp of an ever-expanding information space. Basically, it is no longer realistic to think that the users will always bother to visit a site and enter queries describing what they are looking for. This fact has brought about a new paradigm of *recommender systems*, which aim at proactively discovering the items that best match the preferences, interests and needs of each individual at any time. Such systems are already working behind the scenes in many e-commerce sites [1,2], as well as in personalized TV programming guides [3,4], news systems [5], web navigation assistants [6] and so on.

The problem we address in this paper is that recommender systems have hitherto limited themselves to providing the users with lists of items they may appreciate. This approach works well when the user's aims and attention are

---

* Work supported by the Ministerio de Educación y Ciencia (Gobierno de España) research project TSI2007-61599, and by the Consellería de Educación e Ordenación Universitaria (Xunta de Galicia) incentives file 2007/000016-0.

T. Di Noia and F. Buccafurri (Eds.): EC-Web 2009, LNCS 5692, pp. 132–143, 2009.

sufficiently close to the recommended items. For instance, if the user has finished watching a TV program, he may welcome a list of the most interesting forthcoming contents over the different channels available; likewise, when he has just entered an online bookshop, it makes perfect sense to face him with a list of potentially interesting books. In such contexts, which we classify under the metaphor *"the user inside the shop"*, the actions triggered by the user selecting one item from the list are either straightforward (zap to the new channel) or given by the provider in question (the bookshop), so the recommender system has completed its task. However, in settings where the user is not focused on the kind of items that may be recommended to him (e.g. in delivering publicity while he watches TV programs), one could expect the recommender to select the best offers from among various providers, to look for the pieces of information that describe each item in the most complete or accessible way, to arrange the most suitable interfaces to place an order, etc. In other words, with *"the user around the marketplace"*, we believe the recommender should be responsible for building the shop in which the user will feel most comfortable to browse the suggested items. Obviously, this is not a task for human developers, because no workforce would suffice to provide specific applications for all the different users, items and devices in all possible contexts.

We have realized the aforementioned vision by enhancing the recommender system of MiSPOT [7], originally designed to identify the best items to advertise within TV programs. The new version unleashes the possibilities of the Digital TV technologies for e-commerce, by automatically generating interactive applications (henceforth, *i-spots*) that provide the users with personalized commercial functionalities related to the selected items. To contextualize this work, Sect. 2 includes an overview of previous research the provision of interactive applications through the TV. Then, Sect. 3 describes the procedure behind the generation of i-spots, which involves solutions from the field of *web services* and the development of *web mashups*. Section 4 provides an example drawn from a system prototype, while Sect. 5 devotes a few words to the architectural challenges and opportunities raised by the specifics of Digital TV. Finally, Sect. 6 summarizes the conclusions from this research.

## 2   Context

During the development of the Digital TV technologies, stakeholders were enthusiastic about the possibility of broadcasting data and interactive applications jointly with the audiovisual contents, which would enable advanced opportunities for entertainment, education, electronic commerce, and so on [8]. However, even though standards like the *Multimedia Home Platform* (MHP) and various supporting tools have made things easier and easier for development and deployment, interactive applications are still the exception rather than the rule, and there are no systematic approaches to exploiting the new capabilities of the medium. *Electronic Programming Guides* are still the most common application, often linked to a recommender of TV programs that may either run entirely in the user's receiver (as in [3]) or act as a proxy to a server-side reasoning engine (as in [4]). There are also several systems that aim to personalize TV advertising, by means of simple heuristics [9], syntactic matching techniques [10,11] or semantic reasoning [7]. Unfortunately, none of these systems has generalized the possibility of linking the advertisements with interactive applications —no matter how simple— that would let the users browse details of the corresponding items, purchase online, subscribe to the notification of novelties, etc. At the most, they could link the advertisements to one from among a set of manually-developed applications, which is certainly insufficient.

A solution for the automatic generation of interactive applications can be inspired by the extensive literature of web services composition, that builds upon a set of standards (e.g. WSDL or OWL-S) to characterize web services in terms of inputs and outputs, some conceptualization of their internal processing or purpose, etc. There already exist various engines that can automatically provide the back-end logic of many e-commerce services on the Internet [12,13,14,15]. As regards the front-end, there have been various attempts to automate the generation of user interfaces from web service descriptions (e.g. WSUI, WSXL or WSGUI) but they have been discontinued. The important point for this paper, though, is that all of this research has implicitly targeted the World Wide Web as accessed from personal computers, therefore paying no attention to the specifics of the TV. Thus, there is nearly nothing in literature about (i) providing specialized user interfaces, (ii) assembling deferred/local interaction services when there is no return channel available for bidirectional communication, or (iii) harnessing the bandwidth and multicasting possibilities of the broadcast networks. In general, research is also scarce in considering user preferences during the composition process, to drive the decision of what providers to link, what types and pieces of information to display, etc.

## 3   I-Spot Generation

We conceive the i-spots as a sort of specialized mashups for Digital TV receivers, that bring together multimedia contents (e.g. pictures, videos or maps) from various sources and deliver functionality through web services. All the material is selected by considering the interests, preferences and needs of the target user.

### 3.1   Ingredients for an I-Spot

Next, we shall describe the multiple elements that come into play in the i-spot generation process, prior to explaining the process itself in Sect. 3.2.

**Domain ontology.** The personalization features of our system are enabled by semantic reasoning techniques, which depend on an ontology to formally represent the concepts and relationships of the e-commerce domain. A core part of the ontology we use is a hierarchy that classifies the items and their attributes as shown in the excerpt of Fig. 1, which includes a documentary about the *Bergamo Alps*, vinegar and wine brands from the Italian city of *Modena*, and a *sports car* also manufactured in Modena.

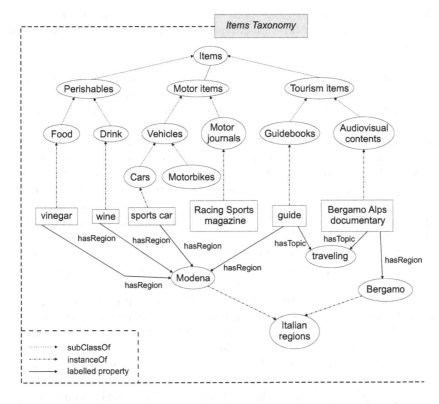

**Fig. 1.** A micro-excerpt from the items taxonomy of our domain ontology

**User profiles.** We capture the preferences of each user in a data structure that stores demographic information (e.g. gender, age, marital status, income, etc) plus *consumption* and *viewing histories* to keep track of items purchased and TV programs watched in the past. Items and programs are linked to a number between 0 and 1 that represents the level of interest of the user in them; this number may be explicitly provided by the user, or inferred from ratings given to other related concepts in the domain ontology (see [7] for the details).

**Item recommendation logic.** The selection of potentially interesting items is carried out by the recommendation logic of MiSPOT, that combines traditional recommendation strategies (content-based and collaborative filtering) with semantic reasoning techniques. In order to decide whether a given item might be appealing to a user, the system computes a *matching level* between his preferences and the semantic annotations of the item in the domain ontology, measuring similarity in terms of common ancestors in the items taxonomy, common attributes and sibling attributes (again, details can be found in [7]). For example, in Fig. 1, the *Racing Sports* magazine and a *sports car* are related through the ancestor *Motor items*; a given *guidebook* and *Bergamo Alps* *documentary* are similar because both share the attribute *traveling*, and also because they are bound to two *Italian regions* (*Modena* and *Bergamo* are sibling attributes).

**Functional services.** The functionality of the i-spots is assembled by combining three types of services, that may provide *real interactivity* (requiring access to the Internet for information retrieval), *local interactivity* (dealing exclusively with contents delivered in the broadcast stream) or *deferred interactivity* (halfway between the others, storing and forwarding information when a return channel is available). We characterize all of them as *semantic web services* using OWL-S annotations, which involve three interrelated subontologies: *Profile* ("*what the service does*" for purposes of discovery), *Process Model* ("*how the service works*" for invocation and composition) and *Grounding* (a realization of the process model into detailed specifications of message formats and protocols, commonly expressed in WSDL).

OWL-S provides an extensive ontology of functions where each class corresponds to a class of homogeneous functionalities (see [16]). Leaning on that ontology, we built a *services taxonomy* that represents the capabilities of the services that may be included in an i-spot. Our domain ontology merges the items and services taxonomy so that the semantic reasoning features can relate the available functionalities to the items stored in the user profiles. A micro-excerpt from the services taxonomy is depicted in Fig. 2, with each item linked to different types of services by *hasTypeofService* properties. For example, the guidebook about Modena is associated to a type of service (denoted by *OWL-S Service #1* ) that may be used to buy one copy while browsing information about the main tourist attractions of Modena; it is also linked to a service (*OWL-S Service #2*) that may be used to purchase a travel to this Italian region with possibilities to book accommodation and flight. Similarly, the sports car is linked to a service (*OWL-S Service #3*) that may be used to simply describe its features, and to a second one (*OWL-S Service #4*) that may offer the chance to arrange an appointment with a dealer.

**Templates.** The i-spots are realized over templates that provide the Java code (as per the MHP standard) that glues together different functional services and pieces of content. This includes the programming of the user interfaces and the SOAP logic needed to interact with web services. Actually, a same type service as described above can be offered through multiple templates, which differ from each other in the interactive elements shown to the user. This fact is represented in Fig. 2, where the elements of each template are identified by semantic concepts formalized in our ontology (e.g. *Map*, *Dealer* or *Calendar*).

**Semantics-enhanced UDDI registry.** To enable discovery of the functional services to include in a given template, we use a semantics-enhanced *registry* that combines the OWL-S and UDDI standards: the former provides the information needed to match the capabilities offered against the requested ones, whereas the latter provides the architecture for a worldwide distributed registry. Our registry

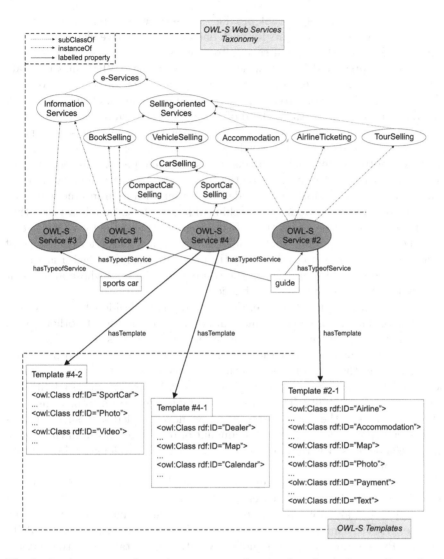

**Fig. 2.** A micro-excerpt from the taxonomy of semantic web services and templates

works just like the one introduced in [17], which allows to differentiate services that have different names and equivalent functionalities, and also services with identical names and totally unrelated operations.

## 3.2   Workflow of the Generation Process

The generation of an i-spot is triggered when the user shows interest in one of the items recommended to him. Then, it is necessary to decide which type of service best matches the user preferences, and which is the most convenient template to create one i-spot that provides the service. The template is finally populated by retrieving contents for each one of its interactive elements.

In order to select the type of service to provide, we adopt an approach similar to the one presented in [18], which consists of using SWRL rules to relate user preferences and context information in a personalization system. We have defined a set of SWRL rules to associate personal information of the users (such as hobbies and income) with the kind of services classified into the services taxonomy. The user preferences are antecedents in the rules, while the service types appear in their consequents. These rules enable to infer, for example, that a user who is fond of traveling may appreciate services that permit to book a tour, instead of services that only describe the tourist attractions of a given destination. Likewise, it is possible to conclude that a user with high income will more likely be interested in services for the selling of luxury items than in services that only provide information about them. Such inferences are made by a *Description Logic* (DL) reasoner module that computes a relevance factor for each type of service associated to the item chosen by the user. Obviously, the factor is greater when the type of service appears in the consequent of a rule whose antecedent is highly rated among the user's preferences.

Having selected a type of service, the next step is to decide which one of the templates associated to it may be most interesting for the user. In other words, the goal is to identify the most suitable interactive elements to assemble an i-spot about the item selected by the user. This decision is driven by both the user preferences (e.g. the kind of elements the user has accessed in previous i-spots) and parameters such as the computational power, input/output capabilities or return channel availability. Therefore, for example, we refrain from using templates with maps in the case of users who have never fiddled with such artifacts in previous i-spots, while we limit the amount of text to be shown in the case of small screen devices or with users who have never fully read lengthy descriptions of other items.

Following the selection of a template to shape the i-spot, it is time to look in the UDDI registry for services categorized in the taxonomy under the selected service type, and also for contents to place in all the elements of the selected template. With this information, an OWL-S/UDDI matchmaker maps the OWL-S Service Profile into the corresponding WSDL representations of the services offered in our semantic registry. As a result, the registry provides a set of services to retrieve the contents to be lodged in the template. For example, assembling an i-spot via *Template #2-1* shown in Fig. 2 requires to discover selling services that offer information about airlines and hotels providers, as well as maps and photos of rooms.

To conclude, it is necessary to invoke the OWL-S services discovered in the preceding step, by exploiting the WSDL descriptions of message formats and in/out arguments provided by the Service Groundings. This way, our i-spot composition logic retrieves contents that are pre-filtered considering the user preferences, which are finally put into the template.

## 4   Example

This section contains a brief example of the whole personalization process carried out by the new version of the MiSPOT system, to show that different users can be faced with totally different services even when they are watching the same TV program. We shall consider two users: Mary and Paul. Mary is a 30-year-old woman with two children and a middle-income economy (demographic data), who has recently enjoyed watching a documentary about the Italian region of Bergamo (viewing history) and has recently purchased some camping equipment (consumption history). Paul is a childless man in his early 20s with significant income (demographic data), who is subscribed to the *Racing Sports* magazine (consumption history).

Mary and Paul are currently watching a documentary about the Italian city of Modena, using high-end Digital TV receivers permanently connected to a cable network. At this moment, the item recommendation logic computes the level of matching between the four items related to the semantic concept *Modena* in the ontology of Fig. 1 and their respective preferences. Apparently, the tourist guide is the most appealing item for Mary, because her profile suggests some fondness for traveling with Italy as a destination.[1] On the other hand, the magazine included in Paul's consumption history reveals an interest in automotive technologies and racing, so the *sports car* manufactured in Modena comes up as the most suitable item, also bearing in mind his purchasing power.[2] Vinegar and wine are not recommended to either user, because there is no knowledge about their culinary preferences.

As the first step towards the generation of i-spots, some SWRL rules lead the DL reasoner to select a tour selling service (*OWL-S Service* #2 in Fig. 2) for Mary, basically due to her interest in traveling documentaries. Regarding Paul, the best option seems to be that of a car selling service (*OWL-S Service* #4) instead of one that simply provides information about the sports car (again, due to his high incomes). The computing and communication capabilities of the high-end receivers allow to choose templates with demanding interactive elements, namely $#2 - 1$ and $#4 - 2$ from Fig. 2.

Asking the UDDI semantic registry, we obtain the OWL-S services necessary for retrieving the contents of the template selected for each user, and the last step consists of filtering those contents considering their preferences. For instance, the template chosen for Mary's i-spot includes information for accommodation booking; from among the possible accommodation options given by the site easycamping.it, we end up with a selection of affordable camps with facilities for children. As shown in Fig. 3, the final i-spot mashes up a Google Maps widget showing the location of the selected camps (minimized to the top-left corner in the picture), photos of the premises retrieved from Flickr or from each camp's

---

[1] The *Bergamo Alps* documentary and the *guide* share the attribute *traveling* and have *Bergamo* and *Modena* as sibling attributes.

[2] The *sports car* and the *Racing Sports* magazine share the ancestor *Motor items*. The reasoning about demographic features is not described here for reasons of space.

**Fig. 3.** The i-spot assembled for Mary

**Fig. 4.** The i-spot assembled for Paul

web site, a calendar for availability checking and a button to access booking and payment (via Paypal).

On the other hand, as shown in Fig. 4, the i-spot assembled for Paul includes an interactive map to locate dealers of the sports car brand (Maserati) around the region where he lives, plus a calendar to arrange an appointment for a test drive. Other tabs, not displayed in the picture, provide information about the car specifications retrieved from Wikipedia and a collection of pictures from Flicker and videos from Youtube.

## 5   Architectural Questions

We have re-designed the MiSPOT system so that it is possible to arrange the logic explained in the previous sections in many different ways, in order to accommodate a range of scenarios defined by the continuous, intermittent or null availability of a return channel, the greater or lower bandwidth of the broadcast networks, the computational power of the receivers, privacy requirements and various other factors. To this aim, we have extended the architectural solutions presented in [7] for the recommendation of items, to embrace also the generation of i-spots. The supported possibilities match either of the following schemes:

– The *server-side scheme* is intended for scenarios with permanently-enabled return channels (e.g. with cable networks) and when service-level agreements ensure the legal conditions to store the users' profiles in a centralized repository. The personalization tasks are entirely carried out by dedicated servers, which may be powerful enough to apply complex reasoning processes (with content-based and collaborative strategies) over huge amounts of data about items, functional elements, service providers and so on. The receiver simply downloads a full-fledged application when the user decides to launch an i-spot for a given item.
– The *receiver-side scheme* enables personalization whenever the user's preferences can only be stored locally, so it is the receiver that must take charge of both the recommendation of items and the generation of i-spots. This is facilitated by a pre-filtering that takes place in servers, driven by a set of *stereotypes* that characterize the interests and needs of the potential audience of the TV programs being broadcast. The pre-selected material (corresponding to the items that may be most interesting in average) is delivered to all the receivers through broadcast, containing functional elements, pieces of content to populate templates and excerpts from the domain ontology, that will be matched against the profile of each user. The matching uses the same content-based and collaborative metrics as above, though the latter considers stereotypes rather than the profiles of other users (which are kept private). In this scheme, we have introduced a module that acts as a proxy to the semantic UDDI registry, in order to provide a unique interface to retrieve functional elements regardless of whether they are received through broadcast or through the return channel. This module prioritizes the material received one way or the other depending on the speed of the return channel and the latency times of the broadcast networks.

We had shown in [7] that the item recommendations provided by the client-side scheme are less accurate than the ones provided by the server-side scheme, because the latter can involve much more knowledge about users and items. Likewise, concerning the enhancements presented in this paper, the i-spots assembled by the client-side scheme may not bring into play functional elements and pieces of content that would appear otherwise. The quality of the semantic metrics employed in the pre-filtering phase and in the final filtering is therefore crucial for a suitable user experience, thus ruling out heuristic or syntactic approaches.

# 6   Conclusions

Traditional recommender systems do not fully meet the needs of e-commerce settings in which the users are not focused on the kind of items that may be offered to them. Instead of merely providing a list of potentially interesting items, the enhanced version of the MiSPOT recommender presented in this paper takes advantage of its internal reasoning about items and user profiles to automatically compose interactive applications offering personalized commercial functionalities. Applied to the specific domain of Digital TV, this proposal paves the road to generalizing the provision of interactive applications, which have been noticeable for their absence despite being one of the major assets of the new technologies. The general contributions from this work have to do with introducing semantic reasoning in the composition logic, and with fostering the convergence of web services and TV contents and networks.

As part of our ongoing work, we plan to continue the experiments initiated in [7] to assess the interest and viability of the MiSPOT innovations in practice. In those trials, we had evaluated the quality of the item recommendations in terms of precision, recall and subjective perception, but we could not fully assess the concept of personalized i-spots because, in the absence of automatic composition mechanisms, we could only work with a reduced set of applications developed manually by ourselves. The technical settings for the final stage of evaluation are ready, and we are almost done recruiting a sufficiently diverse and representative audience among our graduate/undergraduate students and their relatives or friends.

# References

1. Hung, L.: A personalized recommendation system based on product taxonomy for one-to-one marketing online. Expert Systems with Applications 29, 383–392 (2005)
2. Cho, Y., Kim, J.: Application of Web usage mining and product taxonomy to collaborative recommendations in e-commerce. Expert Systems with Applications 26, 233–246 (2004)
3. Zhang, H., Zheng, S., Yuan, J.: A personalized TV guide system compliant with MHP. IEEE Transactions on Consumer Electronics 51(2), 731–737 (2005)
4. Blanco-Fernández, Y., Pazos-Arias, J., López-Nores, M., Gil-Solla, A., Ramos-Cabrer, M.: AVATAR: An improved solution for personalized TV based on semantic inference. IEEE Transactions on Consumer Electronics 52(1), 223–231 (2006)
5. Maybury, M., Greiff, W., Boykin, S., Ponte, J., McHenry, C., Ferro, L.: Personalcasting: Tailored broadcast news. In: Personalized Digital Television. Targeting programs to individual users. Kluwer Academic Publishers, Dordrecht (2004)
6. Zhu, T., Greiner, R., Häubl, G.: An effective complete-web recommender system. In: Proceedings of the 12th International World Wide Web conference, Budapest, Hungary (May 2003)
7. López-Nores, M., Pazos-Arias, J.J., García-Duque, J., Blanco-Fernández, Y., Martín-Vicente, M.I., Fernández-Vilas, A., Ramos-Cabrer, M., Gil-Solla, A.: MiSPOT: Dynamic product placement for digital TV through MPEG-4 processing and semantic reasoning. In: Knowledge and Information Systems (in press) doi:10.1007/s10115-009-0200-8

8. Morris, S., Smith-Chaigneau, A.: Interactive TV standards. Focal Press (2005)
9. Thawani, A., Gopalan, S., Sridhar, V.: Context-aware personalized ad insertion in an Interactive TV environment. In: Proceedings of the 4th Workshop on Personalization in Future TV, Eindhoven, The Netherlands (August 2004)
10. Kastidou, G., Cohen, R.: An approach for delivering personalized ads in interactive TV customized to both users and advertisers. In: Proceedings of the 4th European Conference on Interactive Television, Athens, Greece (May 2006)
11. Lekakos, G., Giaglis, G.M.: A lifestyle-based approach for delivering personalised advertisements in digital interactive television. Journal of Computer-Mediated Communications 9(2) (2004)
12. Sirin, E., Parsia, B., Wu, D., Hendler, J.A., Nau, D.S.: HTN planning for Web Service composition using SHOP2. Journal of Web Semantics 1(4), 377–396 (2004)
13. Kvaloy, T.A., Rongen, E., Tirado-Ramos, A., Sloot, P.: Automatic composition and selection of semantic Web Services. In: Sloot, P.M.A., Hoekstra, A.G., Priol, T., Reinefeld, A., Bubak, M. (eds.) EGC 2005. LNCS, vol. 3470, pp. 184–192. Springer, Heidelberg (2005)
14. Lin, N., Kuter, U., Hendler, J.: Web Service composition via problem decomposition across multiple ontologies. In: Proceedings of the IEEE Congress on Services, Salt Lake City, USA (July 2007)
15. Hu, S., Muthusamy, V., Li, G., Jacobsen, H.A.: Distributed automatic service composition in large-scale systems. In: Proceedings of the 2nd International Conference on Distributed Event-Based Systems, Rome, Italy (July 2008)
16. Martin, D.L., Paolucci, M., McIlraith, S.A., Burstein, M.H., McDermott, D.V., McGuinness, D.L., Parsia, B., Payne, T.R., Sabou, M., Solanki, M., Srinivasan, N., Sycara, K.P.: Bringing semantics to Web Services: The OWL-S approach. In: Cardoso, J., Sheth, A.P. (eds.) SWSWPC 2004. LNCS, vol. 3387, pp. 26–42. Springer, Heidelberg (2005)
17. Kawamura, T., de Blasio, J.-A., Hasegawa, T., Paolucci, M., Sycara, K.P.: Public deployment of semantic service matchmaker with UDDI business registry. In: McIlraith, S.A., Plexousakis, D., van Harmelen, F. (eds.) ISWC 2004. LNCS, vol. 3298, pp. 752–766. Springer, Heidelberg (2004)
18. Plas, D., Verheijen, M., Zwaal, H., Hutschemaekers, M.: Manipulating context information with SWRL. Report of A-MUSE project (2006)

# Product Variety, Consumer Preferences, and Web Technology: Can the Web of Data Reduce Price Competition and Increase Customer Satisfaction?

Martin Hepp

E-Business and Web Science Research Group
Universität der Bundeswehr
Germany
mhepp@computer.org

**Abstract.** E-Commerce on the basis of current Web technology has created fierce competition with a strong focus on price. Despite a huge variety of offerings and diversity in the individual preferences of consumers, current Web search fosters a very early reduction of the search space to just a few commodity makes and models. As soon as this reduction has taken place, search is reduced to flat price comparison. This is unfortunate for the manufacturers and vendors, because their individual value proposition for a particular customer may get lost in the course of communication over the Web, and it is unfortunate for the customer, because he/she may not get the most utility for the money based on her/his preference function. A key limitation is that consumers cannot search using a consolidated view on all alternative offers across the Web. In this talk, I will (1) analyze the technical effects of products and services search on the Web that cause this mismatch between supply and demand, (2) evaluate how the GoodRelations vocabulary and the current Web of Data movement can improve the situation, (3) give a brief hands-on demonstration, and (4) sketch business models for the various market participants.

T. Di Noia and F. Buccafurri (Eds.): EC-Web 2009, LNCS 5692, p. 144, 2009.

# Perspectives for Web Service Intermediaries: How Influence on Quality Makes the Difference

Ulrich Scholten, Robin Fischer, and Christian Zirpins

Universität Karlsruhe (TH), Karlsruhe Services Research Institute (KSRI),
Englerstraße 11, 76131 Karlsruhe, Germany
{Ulrich.Scholten,Robin.Fischer,
Christian.Zirpins}@ksri.uni-karlsruhe.de

**Abstract.** In the service-oriented computing paradigm and the Web service architecture, the broker role is a key facilitator to leverage technical capabilities of loose coupling to achieve organizational capabilities of dynamic customer-provider-relationships. In practice, this role has quickly evolved into a variety of intermediary concepts that refine and extend the basic functionality of service brokerage with respect to various forms of added value like platform or market mechanisms. While this has initially led to a rich variety of Web service intermediaries, many of these are now going through a phase of stagnation or even decline in customer acceptance. In this paper we present a comparative study on insufficient service quality that is arguably one of the key reasons for this phenomenon. In search of a differentiation with respect to quality monitoring and management patterns, we categorize intermediaries into Infomediaries, e-Hubs, e-Markets and Integrators. A mapping of quality factors and control mechanisms to these categories depicts their respective strengths and weaknesses. The results show that Integrators have the highest overall performance, followed by e-Markets, e-Hubs and lastly Infomediaries. A comparative market survey confirms the conceptual findings.

**Keywords:** Web Service Intermediaries, Web Service Quality, QoS-Management, Monitoring Power, Stakeholder Power.

## 1 Introduction

According to Goldman Sachs the market for Software-as-a-Service (SaaS) will reach $21.4B in 2011. Gartner forecasts that by 2012, one-third of software revenue will be generated through SaaS [1]. While SaaS is enabled by a wide variety of Web technologies, it arguably builds on the service-oriented computing paradigm and one of its key facilitators is Web service architecture. Web services support the interaction between distributed software components of inter-organizational application systems based on Web-enabled middleware mechanisms. In particular, the growth of SaaS can be expected to go in sync with an increased requirement for Web service intermediaries that provide necessary platform and market mechanisms as value-added services.

Antipodal to this expectation, we observe the shrinkage of leading Web service directories like Xmethods (www.xmethods.com) and the discontinuation of the

T. Di Noia and F. Buccafurri (Eds.): EC-Web 2009, LNCS 5692, pp. 145–156, 2009.

Universal Business Registry (UBR) in 2005. In spite of more than 50,000 entries of individual Web services [2] UBR's failure is commonly explained by the unsatisfactory quality and relevance of the presented Web services [2, 3, 4]. Correspondingly, it can be observed that current practices of service utilization mainly concentrate on secondary business processes, where failures are less critical (e.g., weather service, SMS, address collection, sales & marketing support etc.). Safety-critical Web services like credit checks are usually the domain of specialist providers and rarely covered by all-purpose intermediaries.

For an initial indication of Web service quality, we conceived a comparison of the availability of 100 Web services based on the raw data of Seekda's daily-performed availability test (www.seekda.com). We applied raw data that was gathered in periods between six months and two years and found that 23 out of the 100 analyzed Web services were stated to be below 90% availability. A total of 22 Web services had an availability of between 90% and 97.99%. While 25 Web services were available between 99% and 99.99% of the time, only 14 of 100 Web services showed constant, i.e. 100% availability. For our sample of 100 Web services, we calculated an average availability of 91.22%. For comparison, Siemens describes the meantime between failures (MTBF) of a typical panel in industrial automation as 5.8-6.1 years at a 24/7 utilization (source: www.automation.siemens.com). This means that during these 6 years the component has 100% availability. In highly safety-relevant areas like air traffic management, 100% availability of software and components is expected for more than 10 years (source: Deutsche Flugsicherung). For an even higher quality, three redundant systems need to be deployed in parallel.

While this discrepancy in industrial practices might be due to a variety of reasons, it is an existential problem for Web service intermediaries to amend the situation. Part of the problem is to exactly understand, how different types of intermediaries might influence the quality of Web services and which general strategies of quality management they might apply to guarantee the quality of their Web service portfolio.

In this paper we present a study about significant quality factors for Web service intermediaries. In particular, we aim to contribute a conceptual framework to assist the discussion of intermediation strategies with respect to quality concerns. As to achieve this goal, we have conducted a comparative analysis of Web service intermediaries. Based on state-of-the art and aiming at a differentiation of quality management, we have refined a specific taxonomy for Web service intermediaries and selected a set of 21 quality factors as well as respective control mechanisms. These have been verified by means of actual observations from six Web service intermediaries. To the best of our knowledge, there is currently no other work addressing fundamental factors of Web service quality management for different groups of intermediaries.

In the next section, we present the basics of our taxonomy for intermediaries and Web services. In section three, we outline quality aspects for Web services and further present our mapping of quality factors to Web service intermediaries. The results of our market study of Web service intermediaries are presented in section four. Our work closes with conclusions and outlook in section five.

## 2  Working Taxonomy for Web Service Intermediaries

As our examination requires a specific perspective on Web service intermediaries, we have refined common classifications into a respective working taxonomy that differentiates significant factors of Web service quality management.

### 2.1  Working Taxonomy for Intermediaries

Tapscott [5] classified distributed networks in accordance to their level of integration and control into agora, aggregator, alliance and value chain. Agora stands for self-organized electronic marketplaces with negotiable pricings in contrast to the more hierarchically organized aggregator. For business models of higher integration, Tapscott positioned the alliance as a self-organized value creating community while the value chain is the most hierarchical and highly integrated form of a distributed network. In [6] Meier built on this taxonomy, dividing the value chain into integrator and distributor. Zooming further into the terminology of Web service intermediaries, Legner [2] provides a rather functional, tripartite taxonomy consisting of electronic Market (e-Market), electronic Hub (e-Hub) and Infomediaries. In her taxonomy, the functions that are analyzed for differentiation are information provision, customization, matching, transaction, assurance, logistics, collaboration, integration and standardization. Legner's definition of electronic markets unifies agora and aggregator into one single type. The emerging role of e-Hubs describes an intermediary that facilitates supply chain collaboration within a vertical industry.

In order to categorize intermediaries with respect to quality assurance and opportunities of improvement, we suggest further elaborating on Legner's taxonomy towards a more technical orientation that comprises the intermediaries' mechanisms and levels of integration and supply. Therefore, we add Meier's category of Integrators. The definition of the Integrator does not interleave with the existing classes, as it is the only category, where Web services are hosted within the intermediary's infrastructure and where he has detailed insight into and direct influence on the Web service and its environment. Table 1 summarizes our working taxonomy.

As an additional aspect, Fig. 1 outlines areas of influence for intermediaries in the supply infrastructure. Influence Area 1 is limited to the traffic between client and web service provider. Influence area 2 includes Area 1. Additionally it comprises the supply infrastructure as a whole. Infomediary and e-Hub do not influence any data traffic

**Table 1.** Technically oriented Taxonomy of Intermediaries

| Intermediary groups | Infomediary | e-Hubs | e-Market | Integrator |
|---|---|---|---|---|
| Goal | actively collecting, pre-processing and providing information | enabling supply chain collaboration, no sales | marketplace for web services | optimized, highly integrated supply chain |
| Characteristics | - web services off-site<br>- traffic off-site | - web services off-site<br>- traffic off-site | - web services off-site<br>- traffic routed through | - web service residence and integration on-site |
| Intermediary's stakeholding power | none | exclusion mandate for web services | influence on portfolio | influence of web service design and portfolio.<br>Owns supply infrastructure |
| Examples of Web service intermediaries | SeekDa | Xmethods, Remote Methods, WebServiceList | eSigma | StrikeIron |

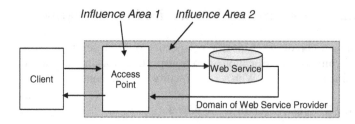

**Fig. 1.** Influences Areas on Quality of Web Services

while using a Web service. Thus, they cannot manipulate any of the Influence Areas. The e-Market serves as access point to the entirety of all offered Web services. Positioned in the *Influence Area 1*, e-Markets control all traffic between the client and the Web service provider(s). The Integrator is omniscient to all traffic coming from and going to the client (apart from network communication between client and Integrator). Thus he is in control of *Influence Area 2*, which includes Influence Area 1.

### 2.2 Taxonomy for Web Services with Respect to Intermediation

We understand a Web service as a software component that is identified by a URI. Its interfaces and bindings are capable of being defined, described and identified as XML artifacts. A Web service supports interactions with other software components using XML messages exchanged via Internet protocols [7, 8]. We have intentionally narrowed our study to this kind Web services and do not consider further connotations that include web application services or human-based Web services [9].

Following our refined taxonomy for intermediaries and in support of our goal to analyze their quality aspects, Web services can be further categorized according to their storage and execution location as off-site or on-site with respect to the intermediary. On-site Web services are hosted on an intermediary's own physical or virtual infrastructure and can be further sub-grouped into native (meaning produced by the intermediary or in accordance with the intermediary's design directives), and non-native Web services. For this study, we exclude quality effects that are specific to Web service composition. Therefore, we do not distinguish common categories such as atomic and composite Web services [7, 10].

## 3   Quality Factors of Web Service Intermediaries

Quality, like beauty, is in the eye of the beholder. It depends on the individual and on subjective requirements on non-functional Web service characteristics like response time, reliability or security [11, 12]. In contrast to functional characteristics that deal with the structural façade (e.g., service types, messages, interfaces and operations), non-functional attributes describe a set of constraints over the functionality of a Web service [13, 14]. In our understanding, this set of constraints defines the QoWS.

The need for a general QoWS concept is not new. Concerns on Quality of Service (QoS) have long-lasting roots in business fields such as marketing where research mainly focused on the viewpoint of the requestor. Seen generally, QoS relates to differences between expected and actual service provision [14]. In the more closely related field of distributed systems, QoS is not a novel problem either. However, SOC poses a number of additional issues [10]. Service-oriented systems consist of distributed components that are loosely coupled over public networks such as the Internet. Circumstances that are outside of the control of provider and consumer obviously influence a consumer's Web service experience. Thus, e.g. response times as a quality factor of Web services relate to additional network properties than those of locally distributed systems. This kind of distributed setting demands a definition of clear responsibilities in the process of measuring QoWS, e.g. what to measure, how to measure, who does the measuring and where measures are to be taken [10, 15].

For our analysis, we aim at a QoWS model that considers all stakeholders, i.e. consumer, intermediary and provider or, when put into a technical context, service environment (e.g., underlying hardware and network infrastructure), application services and end-users [16].

### 3.1 Applied Concept of Web Services Quality

For the purpose of our comparative study of Web services intermediaries, we took the Web Services Quality Model (WSQM) as starting point. This upcoming standard is still under development but published in consecutive draft versions by OASIS [17]. It incorporates quality attributes, so-called quality factors, for almost all aforementioned non-functional parameters of QoWS and is more suitable to assess the QoWS than generic quality of software standards such as ISO 9126 or ISO 25000. In our quality-driven, domain neutral analysis of Web services intermediaries, WSQM shortcomings such as missing abilities to consider emerging QoS parameters (e.g., adaptability, context-awareness) or the limits of semantic description [16] can be ignored.

WSQM is a conceptual model that defines the roles, activities and factors to assess Web service quality in the lifecycle of Web services. In WSQM, quality factors are categorized into three groups: *Business Value*, *Service Measurement* and *System Information*. Each group has up to four quality factors and many more sub-quality factors. In the current version of WSQM, we counted a total of six quality factors, 23 sub-quality factors and many lower level factors. The vast amount might be explained by OASIS's intention to provide a common ground for the definition of service level agreements for Web services.

Following our research goal to correlate influence mechanisms on QoWS with specific types of intermediaries, we can limit our analysis on WSQM's sub-quality factors. We only have to deviate from this coarse grained consideration in those specific cases, where the underlying lower level quality factors demand for differing influence mechanisms. In these cases, we integrated those lower level factors into the scope of our analysis. For the sake of clarity, we further merged the fine grained security sub-quality factors into *authorization management*, *trace management* and *distributed authorization*. In the following, we outline our relevant set of 21 quality factors for the evaluation of Web service intermediaries (see Table 2).

**Table 2.** Mapping Table of Quality Factors and Intermediaries (implications of "observe", "inquire", "negotiate", "adjust", and "define" are discussed in section 3.2)

| | Quality Factor | Intermediaries | | | |
|---|---|---|---|---|---|
| | | Infomediary | e-Hub | e-Market | Integrator |
| Business Value Quality | Service Cost | observe | inquire | inquire / negotiate | inquire / negotiate |
| | Service Sustainability | - | - | observe | adjust |
| | Service Aftereffect | - | - | observe | adjust |
| | Service Recognition | observe | observe | observe | observe |
| | Service Reputation | inquire | inquire | inquire | inquire |
| Service Level Measurement Quality | Response Time | observe | observe | observe | adjust |
| | Maximum Throughput | - | - | observe | adjust |
| | Availablitity | observe | observe | observe | adjust |
| | Accessibility | - | - | observe | adjust |
| | Sucessability | - | - | observe | adjust |
| Business Process Quality | Reliable Messaging | observe | observe | negotiate / define | define |
| | Transaction Processing Capability | observe | observe | negotiate / define | define |
| | Collaborability | observe | observe | negotiate / define | define |
| Suitability for Standards | Conformability | observe | observe | negotiate / define | define |
| | Interoperability | observe | observe | negotiate / define | define |
| Security Quality | Authorization Management | observe | observe | negotiate / define | define |
| | Trace Management | observe | observe | negotiate / define | define |
| | Distributed Authorization | - | - | define | define |
| Manageability Quality | Mangement Information Offerability | observe | observe | negotiate / define | define |
| | Observability | - | - | negotiate / define | define |
| | Controllability | - | - | negotiate / define | define |

To assess the quality factor *business value quality*, we analyze the sub-quality factors service cost, service sustainability, service after-effect, service recognition, and service reputation. Service cost summarizes the availability of qualitative information on pricing, billing and compensation that a provider of a Web service publishes to consumers or intermediaries. Service sustainability, qualitatively describing the business value that is brought into the company of the consumer, cannot be observed directly by intermediaries. However, we argue that intermediaries may infer positive service sustainability from recurring Web service requests by the same consumer. Similarly, service after-effects, describing rather quantitative effects of service consumptions such as Return-on-Investment, can only be inferred from recurring Web service invocations. Intermediaries can easily survey Service recognition, assessing a consumer's attitude towards a Web service before invocation, and Service reputation, being the counterpart of service recognition after invocation.

Sub-quality factors of *service level measurement quality* cannot only be observed qualitatively but can be measured quantitatively. Both, response time and maximum throughput can be revealed through monitoring network traffic. For both sub-quality factors, however, considerations based on the intermediary's positioning with respect to Influence Areas (see Fig. 1) need to be taken into account (e.g., additional network latency between client and access point is only measurable by clients but not intermediaries). Indicators of stability like availability, accessibility, and successability describe ratios of uptime against downtime. A similar measure is the number of Web service invocations compared to the number of acknowledgements and successful replies. Again, the ability of intermediaries to observe these quality factors will depend on the influence position of the individual Web service intermediary.

We assess *business process quality*, representing a Web service's available functionality for collaborating among other Web services, qualitatively by means of a Web service's support for reliable messaging, transactional processing quality and collaborability. The parameters of the quality factors *suitability for standards are* assessed by the sub-quality factors conformability and interoperability. We introduce the quality factors *authorization* and *trace management* to analyze capabilities of Web service intermediaries with respect to the quality factor service quality by aggregating all sub-quality factors that required authorization into the quality factor *authorization management* and all sub-quality factors requiring tracing capabilities into the factor *trace management*. Of particular interest in this respect are the stakeholder powers of intermediaries for influencing these quality factors, which is why we specifically looked for capabilities for the management of distributed authorization.

Finally, we assess manageability quality, defined as the ability to consistently manage Web services, by means of *management information offerability, observability* and *controllability*. While the sub-quality factor management information offerability represents the availability of Web service information that is not changed by the environment (e.g., relationship to other resources), observability and controllability refer to features that allow the user to monitor and control operational properties (e.g., operational status of a Web service and related resources).

### 3.2 Mapping Quality Factors to Intermediary Classes

In this section, we focus on the question of how quality factors can be observed in the individual business models of intermediaries. We are particularly interested in identifying differences among intermediaries. The resulting mapping of quality factors to potential levels of influence per type of intermediary is illustrated in Table 2 above.

For our analysis, we initially introduce the categories *observe, inquire, negotiate, define,* and *adjust* that indicate to the level of tangibility of quality factors for individual intermediaries. We consider intermediaries to have the ability to *observe* a certain quality factor, if they are able to identify the existence of a quality factor through analyzing Web service descriptions like WSDL or related resources. An intermediary has *inquire* capabilities assigned, if we see potential means to poll additional quality information through interviews or surveys. More powerful than pure observation is the co-determination of quality factors. We refer to this aspect as the ability to *negotiate* on the existence or level of quality factors. If an intermediary has abilities assigned that surpass co-determination such as the role of a dominator, we conceive that he exerts abilities to *define* values of quality factors. As soon as intermediaries not only define but also quickly respond to changes in value of quality factors, we assign the ability to *adjust* quality by regulating a Web service environment.

Furthermore, we identified two major types of influences that intermediaries may bring into effect. Firstly, intermediaries may exert *monitoring power*. Monitoring power may be applied to internal or external sources of quality. Thus, the category inquiry clearly relates to applying monitoring power of external sources of quality (e.g., inquire about service reputation among consumers), while the observe category may be applied to both internal and external resources (e.g., observe security quality as defined in WS Policy documents or observe a Web service's availability through active testing). Secondly, intermediaries may exert *stakeholder power*. By bringing stakeholder power into effect, Web service intermediaries may negotiate, define or adjust quality parameters according to the described levels of quality co-determination. Since the capability of quality adjustment closely relates to our concept of native and non-native Web services, we only identified adjustment capabilities for Integrators. Furthermore, we can conclude that monitoring powers are a prerequisite for stakeholder powers, since intermediaries cannot negotiate, define or adjust quality that they cannot observe or inquire.

The conceptual analysis leads us to the following hypothesis that we want to verify in the course of the following market analysis: (i) Infomediary's and e-Hub's levels of influence may only reach out as far as monitoring power is concerned. (ii) E-Markets and Integrators are equally powerful with respects to monitoring power but differ in their respective levels of stakeholder power. (iii) Integrators possess stronger stakeholder powers as they successfully apply their concept of native Web services.

## 4 Market Analysis

Based on Legner's sample set [2] we compared a number of active Web service intermediaries to underpin our hypothesis. We complemented the original set with the Infomediary *Seekda* due to its complementary concept (see Fig. 1) and its outstanding portfolio of Web services (>27000). The results were accomplished through explorative analysis of the intermediaries. We present our findings categorized into monitoring and stakeholder power according the powers of influence that we identified above. In the following only quality criteria are listed that were applied by at least one intermediary.

### 4.1 Communication of Quality

As shown in Table 3, all providers apart from the Infomediary offer possibilities of a trial. However, with regard to the many options, customers need pre-selection support from intermediaries before entering the phase of Web service selection.

In terms of business value quality, most intermediaries provide pricing information. Whereas e-Markets and Integrators have this information available based on their transaction mechanisms, e-Hubs depend on community cooperation. The Infomediary depends on the ability to correlate discovered WSDLs and price documents.

None of the analyzed intermediaries provides information on the quantity of invocations. Whereas this information is unavailable for Infomediaries and e-Hubs, e-Markets and Integrators have this information available and withhold this important information on sustainability from potential customers.

**Table 3.** Comparative Analysis on Monitored and Communicated Quality Factors

<table>
<tr><th colspan="2">Quality Factor</th><th>SeekDa!</th><th>WebServiceList</th><th>Xmethods</th><th>RemoteMethods</th><th>eSigma</th><th>StrikeIron<br>Market Place</th></tr>
<tr><td colspan="2">Business model</td><td>Infomediary</td><td>e-Hub</td><td>e-Hub</td><td>e-Hub</td><td>e-Market</td><td>Integrator</td></tr>
<tr><td colspan="2">Residence</td><td>off-site</td><td>off-site</td><td>off-site</td><td>off-site</td><td>off-site</td><td>on-site / native</td></tr>
<tr><td rowspan="5">Business<br>Value<br>Quality</td><td>Service Cost</td><td>yes</td><td>no</td><td>no</td><td>yes</td><td>yes</td><td>yes</td></tr>
<tr><td>Service Sustainability</td><td>no</td><td>no</td><td>no</td><td>no</td><td>no</td><td>no</td></tr>
<tr><td>Service Recognition</td><td>yes</td><td>no</td><td>no</td><td>no</td><td>no</td><td>no</td></tr>
<tr><td>Reputation (score)</td><td>yes</td><td>yes</td><td>no</td><td>yes</td><td>no</td><td>no</td></tr>
<tr><td>Reputation (Descriptive)</td><td>yes</td><td>no</td><td>no</td><td>yes</td><td>no</td><td>no</td></tr>
<tr><td rowspan="3">Service Level<br>Measurement<br>Quality</td><td>Response Time</td><td>yes</td><td>no</td><td>no</td><td>no</td><td>yes</td><td>yes</td></tr>
<tr><td>Availability</td><td>daily avail-<br>ability check</td><td>no</td><td>no</td><td>no</td><td>hourly avail-<br>ability check</td><td>minute-by-minute<br>availability check</td></tr>
<tr><td>General information<br>through trial</td><td>no</td><td>yes</td><td>yes</td><td>yes</td><td>yes</td><td>yes</td></tr>
</table>

As with commodity retailers like Amazon or Ebay, most of the intermediaries make use of reputation mechanisms. This qualitative reviewing system is valid in the commodity segment and certainly makes sense for safety- or security-irrelevant applications. However, for important business applications, the results are too vague and too easily influenced. We encountered multiple cases of descriptive reputations, where Web service providers themselves had entered the descriptions.

Only the crawler-based Infomediary makes use of Internet-traffic to indicate service recognition. Often utilized for this is the Google PageRank [18], which calculates the relevance of URLs. We see this as an indicator for service recognition. The analyzed e-Markets and Integrators frequently verify response time and availability. Further, the Infomediary verifies this information through daily testing routines. Being neither part of the process, nor actively searching for data, e-Hubs have no access to this kind of quality information.

### 4.2 Mechanisms to Ensure Web Service Quality

As important as decision support for the customer are pre-selection and maintenance of high quality standards. In this context, stakeholder power is decisive. Whereas Infomediaries and e-Hubs are limited on passing user-feedback to the Web service providers, e-Markets and Integrators can apply the whole catalog of portfolio management mechanisms. Table 4, gives a respective overview.

The analyzed e-Market fits this role with a precise and comprehensive initial quality revision process and a limitation of Web services according to specific standards insuring an initial level of quality. However, an obvious lack of quality maintenance procedures leads to the fact that eSigma's overall performance based on the quality factor is poor. Availability is only marginally differentiable from the average market performance. Being placed in Influence Area 1 (see Fig. 1), e-Markets only have basic portfolio management possibilities such as portfolio cleansing through eliminating low-performers. Further, they can apply motivational or assertive influence onto their ecosystem. This could comprise the completion of missing Web services or the improvement of underperforming Web services. Although no information was made available, the high quantity of non-available Web services in the e-Market suggests that no or at maximum only minor portfolio management mechanisms are exerted.

**Table 4.** Comparative Analysis on Exerted Stakeholder Power to Ensure Web Service Quality

| | Quality Factor | SeekDa! | WebServiceList | Xmethods | RemoteMethods | eSigma | StrikeIron Market Place |
|---|---|---|---|---|---|---|---|
| | Business model | Infomediary | e-Hub | e-Hub | e-Hub | e-Market | Integrator |
| | Residence | off-site | off-site | off-site | off-site | off-site | on-site / native |
| Portfolio Management at Intermediary level | Selective display of services based on quality | no | no | no | no | yes | yes |
| | entrance assessment per web service | no | no | no | no | yes | yes |
| | Continuous web service assessment / escalation routines | no | no | no | no | no | yes |
| | Portfolio optimisation | no | no | no | no | no | yes |
| | Portfolio cleansing | no | no | no | no | no | yes |
| Feedback to WS provider | Statistics | no | no | no | no | no | yes |
| | User-based error feedback | no | no | no | yes | no | yes |

Being equally powerful in terms of stakeholder force towards Web service providers, the Integrator wins a clear lead against the e-Market in terms of quality observation and exercisable control. With the services being hosted in the Integrator's domain, he has significantly better possibilities to monitor the quality of infrastructure and the performance of Web services. His insight even becomes omniscient if the Web services are of native nature. Secondly, being the owner of the domain and servers, many of the quality-deciding criteria depend directly on the Integrator's infrastructure. He decides upon levels of server utilization, concepts of replication etc.

The results of a comparative analysis of the quality factor *availability* for Integrator-hosted and not Integrator-hosted Web services supports this statement (see Fig. 2). The overall availability of the latter mentioned Web services is significantly lower than the availability of Integrator-hosted Web services. No difference in availability

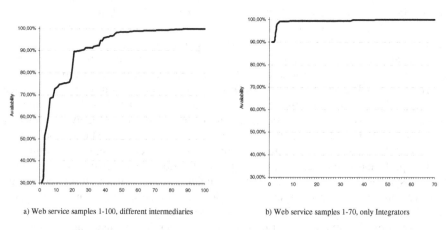

a) Web service samples 1-100, different intermediaries        b) Web service samples 1-70, only Integrators

**Fig. 2.** Comparison of Long-Time Availability of Web Services

of Web services was measurable between e-Hubs and e-Markets. When we compared 76 samples from StrikeIron's marketplace, we calculated an average availability of 99.37%. We therefore assume that the analyzed Integrator performs major factors of centralized portfolio management on the one hand, and decentralized optimization through escalation routines and statistics on the other hand.

## 5  Conclusions and Outlook

In this paper, we have presented the results of our comparative analysis of quality management for Web service intermediaries. Out of multiple sources, we refined a working taxonomy of Web service intermediaries and further identified a set of 21 quality factors. Based on the mapping of Web service quality factors to types of Web service intermediaries, we examined the Web service portfolio of existing intermediaries. In the performed comparison of potential and implemented mechanisms for quality assessment and publication to the customers, we found that none of the analyzed intermediaries exhausted their potential for improvement. A better monitoring of quality could reduce the customer's pre-selection time and support his choice of quality. Furthermore, the increased competitiveness in the market of intermediaries calls for more focus on quality factors.

Clearly, perspectives for Web service intermediaries will depend on their potential to maintain and improve quality and thus on the type of stakeholder power they possess. Control over Web service design or even control over the supply environment, i.e. platform ownership, will be increasingly required to stay competitive. Lacking both, neither Infomediaries nor e-Hubs are in a position to exercise sufficient quality monitoring or quality management. Accordingly, we expect a trend towards e-Markets and Integrators that is already observable. StrikeIron, originating from an e-Hub operates now as Integrator. eSigma just repositioned itself from an e-Hub to an e-Market. Also Seekda recently announced its upcoming e-Market.

But are there possibilities for e-Markets to balance their backlog against Integrators? Further research is recommended to investigate whether a transformation of the native Web service concept to a distributed context of e-Market and suppliers could reproduce the concept's inherent advantages coupled with the dynamism and emergence of the e-Markets' self-organized ecosystem. To shed light on this crucial question for the prospective shape of the market of intermediaries, an analysis needs to be conducted on collaboration, observation and control patterns from a managerial and a technical point of view.

## References

[1] Jetter, M., Satzger, G., Neus, A.: Technologische Innovation und die Auswirkung auf Geschäftsmodell, Organisation und Unternehmenskultur - Die Transformation der IBM zum global integrierten, dienstleistungsorientierten Unternehmen. Wirtschaftsinformatik (2009-01), 37–45 (2009)

[2] Legner, C.: Do web services foster specialization? – an analysis of commercial web services directories. In: Hansen, H.R., Karagiannis, D., Fill, H.G. (eds.) Business Services: Konzepte, Technologien, Anwendungen - 9. Internationale Tagung Wirtschaftsinformatik Wien, 25– 27 February 2009, vol. 1, pp. 67–76 (2009)

[3] CBDI: Ibm, microsoft and sap close down uddi business registry (December 2005),
    http://www.cbdiforum.com/public/news/index.php3?id=1494
    (visited, 30/03/2009)

[4] Hummel, O., Atkinson, C.: Using the web as a reuse repository. In: Morisio, M. (ed.)
    ICSR 2006. LNCS, vol. 4039, pp. 298–311. Springer, Heidelberg (2006)

[5] Tapscott, D., Ticoll, D., Lowy, A.: Digital capital. Harvard Business School Press (2000)

[6] Meier, A., Hofmann, J.: Zur Klassifikation von Geschäftsmodellen im Market Space.
    HMD - Praxis der Wirtschaftsinformatik 261, 7–19 (2008)

[7] Alonso, G., Casati, F., Kuno, H., Machiraju, V.: Web Services - Concepts, Architectures
    and Applications. Springer, Heidelberg (2004)

[8] Austin, D., Barbir, A., Ferris, C., Garg, S.: Web services architecture requirements. W3C
    Working Group Note, World Wide Web Consortium, Web Services Architecture Work-
    ing Group (February 11, 2004),
    http://www.w3.org/TR/2004/NOTE-wsa-reqs-20040211

[9] Kern, R., Zirpins, C., Agarwal, S.: Managing quality of human-based eservices. In: Inter-
    national Workshop on Enabling Service Business Ecosystems (ESBE 2008), Service-
    Oriented Computing ICSOC 2008 Workshop Proceedings. Springer, Heidelberg (to ap-
    pear, 2009)

[10] Ludwig, H.: Web services qos: External slas and internal policies or: How do we deliver
    what we promise? In: Proceedings Fourth International Conference on Web Information
    Systems Engineering Workshops (WISEW 2003), pp. 115–120. IEEE Computer Society,
    Los Alamitos (2003)

[11] Zeng, L., Benatallah, B., Dumas, M., Kalagnanam, J., Sheng, Q.Z.: Quality driven web
    services composition. In: WWW 2003: Proceedings of the 12th international conference
    on World Wide Web, pp. 411–421. ACM, New York (2003)

[12] Menascé, D.A.: Qos issues in web services. IEEE Internet Computing 6(6), 72–75 (2002)

[13] Papazoglou, M.P.: What's in a service? In: Oquendo, F. (ed.) ECSA 2007. LNCS,
    vol. 4758, pp. 11–28. Springer, Heidelberg (2007)

[14] O'Sullivan, J., Edmond, D., ter Hofstede, A.: What's in a service? towards accurate de-
    scription of non-functional service properties. Distributed and Parallel Databases 12(2-3),
    117–133 (2002)

[15] Menascé, D.A.: Composing web services: A qos view. IEEE Internet Computing 8(6),
    88–90 (2004)

[16] Mabrouk, N.B., Georgantas, N., Issarny, V.: A semantic qos model for dynamic service
    oriented environments. In: Proceedings International Workshop on Principles of Engi-
    neering Service Oriented Systems (PESOS 2009), Vancouver, Canada, May 18-19 (2009)
    (to appear)

[17] Kim, E., Lee, Y.: Web Service Quality Model v1.0. Committee Draft, The Organization
    for the Advancement of Structured Information Standards, OASIS (2008)

[18] Brin, S., Page, L.: The anatomy of a large-scale hypertextual web search engine. Com-
    puter Networks and ISDN Systems 30, 107–117 (1998)

# Aligning Risk Management and Compliance Considerations with Business Process Development

Martijn Zoet[1], Richard Welke[2], Johan Versendaal[1], and Pascal Ravesteyn[1]

[1] Institute of Information and Computing Science, Utrecht University,
Padualaan 14, 3584 CH Utrecht, The Netherlands
mmzoet@students.cs.uu.nl, {jversend,pascalr}@cs.uu.nl
[2] J. Mack Robinson College of Business, Georgia State University,
PO Box 5029, Atlanta, GA 30302, USA
rwelke@ceprin.org

**Abstract.** The improvement of business processes, to date, primarily focuses on effectiveness and efficiency, thereby creating additional value for the organization and its stakeholders. The design of processes should also ensure that its result and the value obtained compensates for the risks affecting this value. In this paper the different kinds of risk affecting a business process are introduced, after which solutions to the problem of risk mitigation are discussed, resulting in a proposed framework to mollify these risks by incorporating a class of risk-mitigation rules into business process development.

**Keywords:** Business Processes, Governance, Risk Management, Business Rules, Regulatory Compliance.

## 1 Introduction

Business processes are used by organizations to manage and execute their coordinated, value-adding activities and are thereby among an organization's most important assets [1]. A business process realizes business objectives or goals, thereby creating value for the organization [2]. To maintain and improve the value of business processes companies implement business process management [3][4]. From an historical perspective, the focus of business process management has been on improving business processes by making them more effective and efficient; thereby delivering increased value to the organization and its clients [2].

However, the way in which activities are performed within a business process can bring risks with them. This risk, in turn, can reduce the value that is created by the processes, and/or create negative returns by for example regulatory non-compliance. When the risk-adjusted value of a business process, as-is or to-be, is instead considered, the overall perceived value of the process to the organization [1][5][6] is changed. To preserve value, the process needs to be governed, with the identified risk(s) managed in an effective way. In order to do this companies implement compliance and risk management solutions [7][8].

Although organizations increasingly see the linkage between business process execution [1] and risk management, the two are often considered and performed as

T. Di Noia and F. Buccafurri (Eds.): EC-Web 2009, LNCS 5692, pp. 157–168, 2009.
© Springer-Verlag Berlin Heidelberg 2009

independent functions within a company [2], just as the communities of business process design and risk management are themselves more or less separated in the scientific field [5]. In research conducted by the Open Compliance and Ethics Group, nearly two-thirds of the 250 respondents indicated having redundancy or inconsistency in their governance, risk management and compliance program resulting from the fact these were treated as individual silos, separate and distinct from (business process) execution considerations. An additional result was that this silo thinking led to higher cost and, paradoxically, increased risk [9].

A tenet of this paper is that risk management considerations and business process development are closely related -- there needs to be more attention to risk-averse process design [1]. Where historically the (re-)design of business processes was about creating extra value through efficiency and effectiveness we posit that it should also focus on the preservation of this value potential that a process adds to the company by more adequately identifying and controlling for the risk that is affecting proper execution of the process [2].

The research question addressed by this paper is how to integrate risk management and compliance into the (re-)design and execution of business processes?

The paper is structured as follows. Section 2 discusses the relationship between operational and compliance risk and its influence on business processes. Section 3 contains a proposed solution to the direct integration of compliance and risk management consideration into business processes. Section 4 demonstrates an application of the framework to that of a real-world regulatory compliance problem. In Section 5, a high-level overview of related research is presented. Finally, in Section 6 conclusions and suggestions for further research are discussed.

## 2 The Influence of Risk

In scientific research two main sources of risk can be distinguished, namely compliance risk and operational risk. Compliance (management) is defined as: "acting in accordance with established laws, regulations, protocols, standards and specifications [7]." The risk related to compliance is caused by the failure to act in accordance with these regulatory documents. Operational risk is a form of risk caused by the failure of internal controls over people, process, technology and external events [7] to prevent "injury" to the organization [5][7]. In the existing literature these two areas of risk are discussed separately and are therefore seen as two different disciplines [5] [10].

Beside the mentioned difference Carroll [10] identified three differences between operational and compliance risk. First, compliance is established by external parties through the creation of regulations stating which rules a company needs to comply while with operational risk, the company itself decides which rules it wants enforce [7]. With compliance risk companies have to prove, based on externally imposed criteria, that they have established a sufficient system to control the different kinds of risk. For operational risk there is no externally applied criteria or need to prove sufficient control over risk; in this case companies can implement their own criteria and create a system for measuring this [11][12]. The third distinction Carroll makes is that there can be severe consequences when the compliance program with regards to regulatory rules is ineffective or not correctly managed. The consequences with regards to operational risk are also recognized but it is believed to be not as severe. While agreeing with the first two points of difference between compliance and operational risk management given above, an argument can be made against the last. Using an example provided by [5] the materialization of an operational risk caused the depleting of the cash reserves of a university. Another example is from the French bank Societe Generale where the materialization of an internal risk, in term of fraud by an employee, resulting in the loss of $7 billion dollar [26]. Both examples can be seen as severe consequences from ineffective risk management on an operational level. Although the examples come from different sources, the definition of risk used in both cases is the same, i.e., as "an uncertainty, that is, as the deviation from an expected outcome [11]" whereas the state from which to deviate is either set by sources outside (regulatory) or inside (operational) the company. Below we explore the 'business rules'-concept in order to address risk management.

To prevent activities or processes in the company significantly deviating from desired behaviors, companies create rules [13] [14]. Rules are intended to constrain the possibilities one has to execute a task. This is achieved by stating what must be done or what cannot be done [13], thereby establishing a higher degree of certainty on how a task is being performed. The rule constrains business behavior so we call it a *business* rule. A business rule is defined as: "a statement that defines or constrains some aspect of the business with the intention to assert business structure, or to control (influence) the behavior of the business [13]." If one changes the rules on a task performed, or decision made, the consequence can be that there will be altered behavior by the individuals performing the task and/or a different outcome of the activity they are performing [14]. Examples of different business rules are: (1) before opening a bank account, a person must be registered as a customer [15], (2) to be in compliance, you must segregate custodial and record-keeping functions [16] , (3) it is required to pre-number documents [16], or (4) all financial transaction records should be retained for at least five years after the transaction has taken place [15].

Business rules are thus used to constrain business activities. Business processes are used to execute and control business activity. Firstly, business rules can be used as a technique within the implementation phase of a business process management design/development lifecycle supporting the execution of the business processes [13][14]. In this relationship a business rules engine (BRE) can be used to support a decision within a business process where the rules define the 'how' and 'what,' and the business process defines the 'when' and 'who' [13][14]. The business process defines when a task or decision needs to be made and who is performing the task or making the decision, whereas the business rule restricts or decides what is going to happen in particular situation. The advantage, mostly expressed by the business rules discipline, is that the distinction in when and how something is going to happen makes processes more readable and flexible [13][14]. And, by having them all in one place, they can also be checked for consistency.

Secondly business rules can affect the design of the business process by affecting it at the structural level [17], the construction level [7] and runtime level [13][14].

At the structural level, business rules can influence business processes in two ways [17]. First, to conform to a rule, activities, events and/or decisions may need to be added, removed or reordered within the process. Secondly there might be a need to include or remove an actor, or re-assign tasks to different actors. At the construction level business rules influences the organizational, functional and technology elements needed for a proper execution of the process [3][4][18]. Whereas the structural level focuses on the process design the constructional level focuses on the structure to support it. An example is the '(re-) construction' of human resources: appointing people to perform roles within the process.

Business rules influence the business processes at the runtime level by affecting the process execution path taken by an individual instance, also called "effect inclusion" [17]. By effect is meant the specific instance of an event that results in the change of the task/decision that needs to be performed. For example where the task is to register the data of the customer, the effect can be that the customer is a married female in which case different steps need to be taken. An effect may cause an action/decision to be permitted, mandatory or prohibited.

To comply with rules and thereby increase the risk-adjusted value of a business process, the implementation of controls that counteract risks should be put in place while implementing the process [7][19]. The controls used to reduce or eliminate these risks are called internal controls, which in this case are implemented on the level of business process [7][19]. The main distinction in internal controls is preventive and detective controls [7][8][17]. Preventive controls are controls that prevent events and errors that can occur where detective controls identify events and errors that already occurred. Examples of preventive controls are controls that realize proper recording and authorization of data within the process [7][8]. Examples of detective controls are the monitoring and review of results from tasks performed in the process [19].

To summarize the influence of risk on business processes an overview of the relationship between the different concepts is shown in Figure 1, which is based on [1]. As stated a business process adds value to a company. To protect this value risk management is performed on the business processes activities. One result of these risk management activities are internal controls which are created to make the business process activities more risk averse. The internal controls and risk management activities are based on two kinds of risk namely operational and compliance risk.

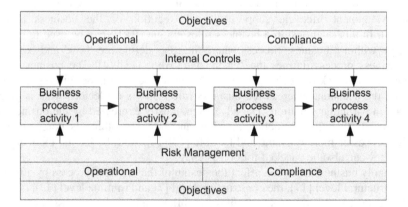

**Fig. 1.** Relationship between operational risk, compliance risk, internal controls and business processes

# 3  An Integrated Framework

In the preceding section, the relation between operational risk, compliance risk, internal control and business processes was established. In this section, an integrated framework to deal with this integration from a business process perspective is proposed. We proceed in two stages.

First, the categories of risk are defined from a business process perspective. Then, the integration with the business process life-cycle is provided in a framework where the risk categories are associated with the different phases of a business process life-cycle resulting in an overall process-framed, risk-management framework.

## 3.1  Categories of Risk Management and Compliance Rules

In Section 2 we discussed that rules set by law versus management can influence perspectives of a business process. In examining a diversity of operational and compliance risk and statements contained in existing literature, notably [7][8][13][14] [17][19] we were able to derive five generic categories of rules and categorize them in a way meaningful to business process developers. These are:

*Category 1: Task Sequencing*. This category contains rules that have an influence on the positioning of one or multiple task/events/decision [5] (hence process elements) within a business process. To make the process compliant with the defined rules, process elements need to be added, re-ordered or removed [17].

*Category 2: Actor Inclusion/Interaction*. This category contains rules that have an influence on the assignment of tasks or decision to specific actors. To make the process compliant with rules defined actors needs to be removed/added or appointed to different elements inside the process [17].

*Category 3: Effect Sequencing*. This category contains rules that have an influence on the paths chosen inside the process [12]. The path chosen is based on the values associated with individual transaction, in contrast with category 1 which influences the arrangement of the paths. An example is an insurance policy process where, depending on the age of the insured person, different process elements need to be executed. To make the process compliant, business rules need to be enforced during runtime. [13][14].

*Category 4: Data / Information Registration*. This category contains rules that have an influence on recording [19][20] and viewing data/information, and the authorizations related to this [19][20]. To make the process compliant, internal controls need to be implemented that deal with (1) timing: how long must the recorded data be kept [1][19][20], (2) accuracy: the registered data must be in predefined format [19][20], (3): completeness, the data registered must contain the following information [1][20] and (4) authorization, restricting access to predefined user and roles [20].

*Category 5: Detection Control.* This category contains rules that have an influence on how results from events (undesirable or desired) occurring in business processes are identified [7][12][19]. Examples include the results of two (in) dependent tasks that are compared to each other (reconciliation) [7][12][19]; results of a task or processes that are monitored for a certain value and audited [7][12][19]. To make a process compliant a multiple solutions can be used: (1) process elements can be added, re-ordered or removed [17], (2) internal control can be added to the process [7][19] or, (3) a new business process can be created to perform the control [7].

## 3.2   Situating the Rule Categories in Business Process Development

As stated in Section 2, and developed further in the five categories enumerated above, risk mitigation, when converted to business rules, will influence different aspects of a business processes design, configuration, and execution life-cycle. Likewise a business process management development method deals with different perspectives of designing and configuring a process at different stages [3][4][18]. The key then is to tie risk-mitigation rules to their appropriate stage of application in a business process development life cycle. Table 1 below outlines this association.

The first BPM-Phase identified in Table 1 is the (re-) design phase. Within the (re-) design phase in a BPM lifecycle, the business process is designed by assigning process elements [3][4][13][18] and roles to it [3][13][18]. The rule categories identified to which the assign of these elements are seen as solutions are task sequencing, actor inclusion/interaction and detection controls. Morgan [13] assessed the possibilities of implementing rules that affect the sequencing of the process and assignment of actors concluding that both can better be done in the design phase with regards to implementing a Business Rules Engine that controls this at runtime.

The second BPM-Phase identified in table 2 is the Construction Phase that in a BPM lifecycle occurs during the creation of the infrastructure and controls to support the process [3]. This generally means the implementation of some type of information system or business process management platform or "suite." For example, Debevoise [14] assessed the possibilities of implementing rules that affect the registration of data, and concluded that this is better arranged by the business processes and the way it controls the data created by it. The two categories identified that perform control on the process or the data it produces are data / information registration and detection control.

**Table 1.** A Rule Mapping Framework

| Rule Category | BPM-Phase |
|---|---|
| Task Sequencing | (Re-) Design |
| Actor Inclusion/Interaction | |
| Detection Control | |
| Data / Information Registration | Construction |
| Detection Control | |
| Effect Sequencing | Runtime |
| Detection Control | |

The runtime phase in a BPM lifecycle is when the process has gone live and is executed within the company [3][4]. In this phase, the activities and decisions made within the processes need to be monitored and controlled for proper execution [3][4]. To control and monitor the process, risk-related decisions need to be monitored at execution so that the execution of a related activity is can guided at that moment in time. The two rule categories identified that must be deferred to this stage in order to maintain risk control over the proper execution of activities within a process are effect sequencing and detection control.

## 4 Application

Generally speaking, risk control and regulatory compliance rules are first stated in some form of natural language, coming from sources internal or external to the organization. These serve as the starting point for the proposed method of application. The first step in the application of the framework, then, starts with this set of a priori rules.

We illustrate the hypothesized application (i.e. based upon the actual regulation but not a real-life organizational interpretation of it) of the framework by using rules that were taken from two different sources; namely, Basel II [15] and COSO [16]. Basel II is a proposed framework for regulation in the banking sector and serves as an example of externally imposed regulatory compliance. The COSO framework, at this moment, is adopted by organizations as a de_facto standard for the implementation of internal controls [19]. The COSO framework has been accepted by the US Securities and Exchange Commission [19] as well as the The Public Company Accounting Oversight Board [19] to realize and prove compliance with SOX.

From the Basel II documentation [15] a paragraph is derived stating part of the rules that should be complied to when a customer is opening a bank account: "For natural persons the following information should be obtained, where applicable: "legal name and any other names used (such as maiden name); correct permanent address (the full address should be obtained; a Post Office box number is not sufficient); telephone number, fax number, and e-mail address; date and place of birth; nationality...."

The second step is to categorize the text using the five rule categories. With regards to the Basel II text two categories can be recognized firstly a task sequencing patterns stated by the text as: "information should be obtained" indicating a task sequencing pattern. Secondly there is an enumeration of the different kinds of data that need to be recorded, indicating a data registration pattern.

With the rules identified and classified according to one the rule categories one can use the framework introduced to determine the most appropriate BPM-Phase in which to apply these derived rules. For the task-sequencing pattern the framework indicates that this is best dealt with in the BPM-phase (re-) design, refer to Table 2.

**Table 2.** Rules translation from the Basel II text

| Input | Pattern | BPM-Phase |
|---|---|---|
| The following information should be obtained | Task Sequencing | (Re-) Design phase |
| legal name and any other names used (such as maiden name); correct permanent address | Data Registration | Construction |

As a second example of how the framework can be used -this time applied to risk-mitigation associated with internal controls- a subset of recommended internal controls from the COSO documentation [16] were analyzed using the same steps outlined above (As shown in Table 3). The difference with the first table is that the second input has three BPM-phases as output. The reason for this is that detection controls can be solved within multiple phases and do not have one preferred phase.

**Table 3.** Rules translation from internal controls states by COSO framework

| Input | Pattern | BPM-Phase |
|---|---|---|
| Access to HR records is restricted to authorized personnel | Data registration | Implementation |
| Reconcile accounts payable subsidiary ledger with purchase and cash disbursement transactions | Detection Control | Design / Construction / / Runtime |
| Segregate custodial and record-keeping functions | Actor Inclusion/Interaction | (Re)Design Phase |

The preceding examples indicate that it is feasible to use a set of rule-categories to analyze existing internal and external controls, to convert them into business rules, and to include their implementation along the business process development life-cycle. That, in turn, achieves an usable approach to the integration between risk-management and business process management design and development considerations.

A sustainable approach towards operational and compliance risk should fundamentally have a preventative focus [24]. Applying rules focused on mitigating risk and achieving compliance should therefore be incorporated in the early stages of business process (re) design. The framework adheres to this by addressing rules in a stratified manner based on the phases of the business process life-cycle.

The application of the framework is twofold as it can be used to aid design and critique business processes. The framework aids process designers to integrate rules, and thereby mitigates risk, in their design by indicating the influence of the rules on different stages within the business process life-cycle. Therefore risk avoiding measures can be implemented during the design and do not have to be added after the process has been designed. In the latter situation the process designer might need to change the process after it has been designed, just to comply with regulations whereas in the first situation this is part of the design process.

Secondly the framework can be used to critique existing business processes with regard to where and how business rules are currently implemented.

## 5  Reflections on Related Prior Research

Research on integrating risk and compliance management into business processes can be divided into: architectures [21][22], techniques [5] and methods [23] all of which deal with one or more aspects concerning risk and compliance management. Architectures describe how rules can be enforced onto business process in the design and runtime phase [21][22]. Techniques [5] mostly focus on deriving and measuring the risk of certain activities [21][22], whereas methods [23] deal with making a processes compliant or risk-averse.

In Namiri et al. [22], an architecture for business process compliance is proposed. The authors argue that an automated architecture is needed to properly deal with compliance management. The input for the architecture are existing regulations that are formalized into semantic policies. From the semantic policies business rules are derived and applied to the business processes in design and runtime. The architecture describes, at a high level, how these policies are transformed but does not provide a framework or translation scheme for the rules, to deal with in the different phases. Our research adds to this research by providing a proposal on how to translate and assign different rules to the business process development phases and recommends solutions on how to integrate the different rules.

Namiri & Stojanovich [21] argue that the creation of a semantic layer is needed to implement compliance control on business processes. In their approach they build a semantic layer, called the "semantic mirror," on top of business processes to enforce the created rules. To do the compliance checking, the rules and business processes are translated to logical statements so that they can be compared to each other. The difference in their approach compared to that of Kharbili et al. [22] is that it concentrates more on the design of internal controls, which are then mapped to the business processes. The mapping is done by translating the internal controls and business processes into logical statements. Our research adds value to this research in the same way as it does to the research of Kharbili et al. [22], i.e., it provides a development framework against which the placement of the controls can be based.

In [23] a six-step, process-based approach to SOX compliance has been proposed. The author's second step, "Risk Assessment and Scoping," contains the identification of risk and design of internal controls to cope with these risks. As stated in Section 2 (above) different types of risk will lead to rules that cannot be enforced by design or during execution in which case the rules need to be enforced/controlled by monitoring. Our research can be an added value in this step to translate the rules to controls in a structured way.

## 6 Conclusions

In this paper we set out to find an answer to the following question: how to integrate risk management and compliance into the (re-)design and execution of business processes? In order to answer this question first we identified the difference between operational and compliance risk. Resulting to the answer that the difference lies in who states the rules, the company itself or external parties, and secondly the burden of proof to the external party related to compliance risk.

To deal with risk caused by operational execution and regulatory rules companies create rules to prevent activities or processes in the company to significantly deviate from desired behavior. The rules implemented affect business process at the structural level, the implementation level or through the fact that new business processes need to be created to comply with the rules (the design level).

We elaborated on the relationship between operational risk, compliance risk, internal controls and business processes resulting in the proposal of a framework to deal with the integration of the different areas from a business process perspective. The framework ties five identified categories of risk management and compliance rules to their appropriate stage of application in a business process development life-cycle. The application of the framework has been demonstrated by applying it to two different sources, Basel II [15] and COSO [16], of rules.

## 7 Discussion / Further Research

The suggested framework has its limitation. The framework is a suggested solution derived from the existing knowledge base in the area of business processes, governance, risk management and compliance and thereby the result of a 'generate design alternative' phase [25]. However, we believe that the proposed framework reached a level of maturity such that it can enter a detailed validation phase. At this moment we are conducting a survey to validate if the rule categories are exhaustive and mutually exclusive. The same validation also focus on the relationship between the different rule categories and the stages within the business process life-cycle.

In future work the framework proposed will be validated through the execution of a case study to demonstrate its usefulness. Secondly a pattern language needs to be developed that can be used to parse natural text and appoint rules to the specified category. We also want to develop standard rule extractions from regulations like Basel II, HIPAA and SOX.

# References

1. Rikhardsson, P., Best, P., Green, P., Rosemann, M.: Business Process Risk Management and Internal Control: A proposed Research Agenda in the context of Compliance and ERP Systems. In: Second Asia/Pacific Research Symposium on Accounting Information Systems, Melbourne (2006)
2. Sienou, A., Lamine, E., Pingaud, H.: A Method for Integrated Management of Process-risk. In: Sadiq, S., Indulska, M., Zur Muehlen, M., Franch, X., Hunt, E., Coletta, R. (eds.) GRCIS 2008, vol. 339, pp. 16–30 (2008)
3. Kettinger, W.J., Teng, J.T.C., Guha, S.: Business Process Change: A Study of Methodologies, Techniques, and Tools. MIS Quarterly 21, 55–80 (1997)
4. Jeston, J., Nelis, J.: Business Process Manaement - Practical Guidelines to Successful Implementations. Butterworth-Heinemann, Oxford (2006)
5. Zur Muehlen, M., Rosemann, M.: Integrating Risks in Business Process Models. In: 16th Australasian Conference on Information Systems, Sydney (2005)
6. Jallow, A., Majeed, B., Vergidis, K., Tiwari, A., Roy, R.: Operational risk analysis in business processes. BT Technology 25, 168–177 (2007)
7. Tarantino, A.: Governance, Risk, and Compliance Handbook. Wiley, New Jersey (2008)
8. Cobit 4.1: Framework Control Objectives Management Guidelines Maturity Models. IT Governance Institute, Rolling Meadows (2007)
9. Open Compliance Group (2008), http://www.oceg.org/
10. Carroll, R.: Risk Management Handbook for Health Care Organisations. Chicago Jossey Bass, San Francisco (2001)
11. Schroeck, G.: Risk Management and Value Creation in financial institutions. Wiley, New Jersey (2002)
12. Standard Australia.: Handbook: Risk Management Guidelines, Companion to AS/NZS 4360:2004. Standards Australia Internal Ltd, Sydney (2004)
13. Morgan, T.: Business Rules and Information Systems. Pearson Education, Indianapolis (2002)
14. Debevoise, T.: Business Process Management with a Business Rules Approach: Implementing the Service Oriented Architecture. Business Knowledge Architects, Canada (2005)
15. Basel Committee: General Guide to Account Opening and Customer Identification (2003)
16. Committee of Sponsoring Organizations of the Treadway Commission: Internal Control, Integrated Framework. Committee of Sponsoring Organizations of the Treadway Commission, New York (1991)
17. Ghose, A., Koliadist, G.: Auditing Business Process Compliance. In: Krämer, B.J., Lin, K.-J., Narasimhan, P. (eds.) ICSOC 2007. LNCS, vol. 4749, pp. 169–180. Springer, Heidelberg (2007)

18. Weske, M.: Business Process Management - Concepts, Languages, Architectures. Springer, New York (2007)
19. Marchetti, A.: Beyond Sarbanes-Oxly Compliance: Effective Enterprise Risk Management. Wiley, New Jersey (2005)
20. Lientz, B., Larssen, L.: Risk Management for IT Projects: How to Deal with over 150 Issues and Risks. Butterworth-Heinemann, Burlington (2006)
21. Namiri, K., Stojanovic, N.: A Formal Approach for Internal Controls Compliance in Business Processes. In: 8th Workshop on Business Process Modeling, Development, and Support (BPMDS 2007), Trondheim, pp. 1–9 (2007)
22. Kharbili, M.E., Stein, S., Markovic, I., Pulvermüller, E.: Towards a Framework for Semantic Business Process Compliance Management. In: Bellahsène, Z., Léonard, M. (eds.) CAiSE 2008. LNCS, vol. 5074, pp. 1–15. Springer, Heidelberg (2008)
23. Karagiannis, D., Mylopoulos, J., Schwab, M.: Business Process-Based Regulation Compliance: The Case of the Sarbanes-Oxley Act. In: 15th IEEE International Requirements Engineering Conference, pp. 315–321. Institute of Electrical and Electronics Engineers, New Delhi (2007)
24. Sadiq, S., Governatori, G., Naimiri, K.: Modeling Control Objectives for Business Process Compliance. In: Alonso, G., Dadam, P., Rosemann, M. (eds.) BPM 2007. LNCS, vol. 4714, pp. 149–164. Springer, Heidelberg (2007)
25. Hevner, A., March, S., Park, J., Ram, S.: Design Science in Information Systems Research. Management Information Systems Quarterly 28, 75–105 (2004)
26. Societe Generale - Corporate & Investment Banking (2008), http://www.sgcib.com/

# Using Knowledge Base for Event-Driven Scheduling of Web Monitoring Systems

Yang Sok Kim[1,2], Sung Won Kang[2], Byeong Ho Kang[2], and Paul Compton[1]

[1] School of Computer Science and Engineering, The University of New South Wales,
Sydney, 2001, New South Wales, Australia
{yskim,compton}@cse.unsw.edu.au
[2] School of Computing and Information Systems, University of Tasmania, Hobart,
7001 Tasmania, Australia
{swkang,bhkang}@utas.edu.au

**Abstract.** Web monitoring systems report any changes to their target web pages by revisiting them frequently. As they operate under significant resource constraints, it is essential to minimize revisits while ensuring minimal delay and maximum coverage. Various statistical scheduling methods have been proposed to resolve this problem; however, they are static and cannot easily cope with events in the real world. This paper proposes a new scheduling method that manages unpredictable events. An MCRDR (Multiple Classification Ripple-Down Rules) document classification knowledge base was reused to detect events and to initiate a prompt web monitoring process independent of a static monitoring schedule. Our experiment demonstrates that the approach improves monitoring efficiency significantly.

**Keywords:** web monitoring, scheduling, MCRDR.

## 1 Introduction

Nowadays a large amount of new and valuable information is posted on the web daily and people wish to access this in a timely and complete fashion. This may be done manually, in that, people go to specific web pages and check whether information is new. However, this approach has limitations. For example, it can be very difficult to identify which objects have been changed on the web page since the last visit. Various web monitoring systems, sometimes called continuous query (CQ) systems, have been proposed by many researchers, including CONQUER [1], Niagara [2], OpenCQ [3] and WebCQ [4]. Even though they were proposed in the different contexts, they were designed to help users to keep track of continually changing web pages and identified changed information on the specific web pages by revisiting them frequently and comparing objects. Web monitoring systems may focus on different objects on the web pages, including hyperlinks, images, and texts.

There are two main goals in web morning systems. On the one hand, they should find changed objects on the target web pages without missing any information. The problem here is that they may miss information when the revisit interval for a specific

T. Di Noia and F. Buccafurri (Eds.): EC-Web 2009, LNCS 5692, pp. 169–180, 2009.

web page is longer than its change interval. On the other hand, they should find changed objects without significant delay that is the gaps between publishing and collecting time. These two main goals may be achieved by very frequent revisits to the target web pages. However, there are significant restrictions to the revisit frequency as web monitoring systems operate under resource constraints related to computing power and network capacity, and there may be restrictions on access to specific web pages by the web servers. The goal then is a scheduling algorithm that minimizes delay and maximizes coverage given the resource constraints.

Various statistical approaches have been proposed to improve web monitoring efficiency. CAM [5] proposes web monitoring with a goal of capturing as many updates as possible. CAM estimates the probability of updates by probing sources at frequent intervals during a tracking phase, and using these statistics to determine the change frequency of each page. However, CAM does not explicitly model time-varying update frequencies to sources and cannot easily adapt to bursts. The WIC algorithm [6] converts pull-based data sources to push-based streams by periodically checking sources for updates. The algorithm is parameterized to allow users to control the trade-off between timeliness and completeness when bandwidth is limited. The algorithm chooses the objects to refresh based on both user preferences and the probability of updates to an object. However, the algorithm does not consider how to determine the probability of an object update, which is an important aspect of any pull-based scheduling. Bright et. al [7] proposed adaptive pull-based policies in the context of wide area data delivery, which is similar to web monitoring. They explicitly aim to reduce the overhead of contacting remote servers while meeting freshness requirements. They model updates information on data sources using update histories and proposes two history-based policies to estimate when updates occur. In addition, they also presented a set of adaptive policies to cope with update bursts or to estimate the behaviour of objects with insufficient histories available. The experimental evaluation of their policies using trace data from two very different wide area applications shows that their policies can indeed reduce communication overhead with servers while providing comparable data freshness to existing pull-based policies.

Although these approaches provide sophisticated scheduling policies, these have the following limitations: Firstly, the statistical approaches ignore how the user uses the monitored information or how different users value it. The users are often interested in specific topics such as sports or financial news. Furthermore, the user may try use further processes related to their own personal knowledge management, such as filtering and/or classification of the collected information, to overcome information overload problems. Users do not give equal importance to the all collected information. For example, if a user is a fund manager, he will probably be interested in financial news. If the user is interested in specific topics, the system should give information about these topics greater priority and the schedules should satisfy this requirement. Secondly, the statistical approaches underestimate the fact that the volume of information published may be affected by specific events. For example, when the investment company, Lehman Brothers, collapsed, many online newspapers published articles related to this specific event. The previous methods which used statistic or mathematically-based schedules for web monitoring systems cannot properly react to these kinds of event-based publication volatiles. Whereas the first issue is related to the information demand factor, this second issue is closely related to information supply.

This paper focuses on these two issues and tries to suggest solutions for them. Our research, however, does not deny the importance of the previous research efforts. Instead, our research aims to improve statistical scheduling approaches by complementing them with an event-driven scheduling approach. Our event-driven scheduler detects new events on the Web using document classification knowledge and then initiates new monitoring process. Section 2 explains our document classification method which was employed to construct a knowledge base for our study. Section 3 proposes our event driven scheduling method. The experimental design employed for our scheduling method evaluation is discussed in Section 4 and experimental results are summarized in Section 5. Conclusions and further study is in Section 6.

## 2 MCRDR Document Classification System

We base our approach on document classification. Multiple Classification Ripple-Down Rules (MCRDR)[8], an incremental knowledge acquisition method, was employed to develop a document classification system, called an MCRDR classifier. The system acquires classification knowledge incrementally, because documents are provided continually and classification knowledge changes over time. Figure 1 illustrates an example of the knowledge base structure of the MCRDR classifier. As illustrated in the right tree of Figure 1, the user's domain knowledge is managed by a category tree, which is similar to a common folder structure and represents hierarchical relationships among categories. It can be easily maintained by domain experts for managing a conceptual domain model through simple folder manipulation.

The user's heuristic classification knowledge is maintained by an n-ary rule tree. The left tree of Figure 1 represents a rule tree, which has hierarchical relationships. A child rule refines its parent rule and is added as an exception of its parent rule. For example, Rule 3 is an exception rule of Rule 1. One special exception rule is the stopping rule, which has no indicating category (null), in the conclusion part. Rule 5 is an example of a stopping rule. In the inference process, the MCRDR classifier evaluates each rule node of the knowledge base (KB). For example, suppose that a document that has a set of keywords with $T = \{a, b, d, k\}$ and $B = \{f, s, q, r\}$ is given to the MCRDR classifier whose knowledge base is the same as in Figure 1. The inference takes places as follows. The MCRDR classifier evaluates all of the rules (Rule 1 and Rule 4) in the first level of the rule tree for the given case. Then, it evaluates the rules at the next level which are refinements of the rule satisfied at the top level and so on. The process stops when there are no more children rules to evaluate or when none of these rules can be satisfied by the given case in hand. In this instance, there exist two satisfied rule paths (Path 1: Rule 0 – Rule 1 – Rule 3, Path 2: Rule 0 – Rule 4 – Rule 5), but there is only one classification folder (C5), because Rule 3 is a stopping rule (see below). The MCRDR classifier recommends C5 as a destination folder for the current case.

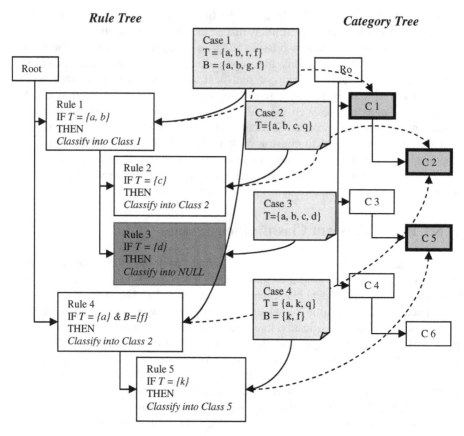

**Fig. 1.** Knowledge Base of MCRDR Classifier

The knowledge acquisition (KA) and inference processes are inextricably linked in an MCRDR classifier, so some KA steps depend on the inference structure and vice versa. Hereafter, Figure 1 will be used as an example to show how a knowledge base is constructed by the user. At the beginning, there is no rule in the knowledge base. The KA process begins when a case has been classified incorrectly or has no classification. If Case 1 is given to the MCRDR classifier, the system does not suggest any recommendation, because there is no rule in the knowledge base. The user creates two rules – Rule 1 and Rule 4 – using the current case. Therefore, the current case is classified into *C1* by Rule 1 and *C2* by Rule 2. This type of rule is called a refining rule in MCRDR, because it refines the default rule (Rule 0). This is a special type of refining rule because there is no recommendation. A general refining rule is exemplified by Case 2. If Case 2 is given to the system, the MCRDR-classifier suggests Class 1 as a recommendation according to Rule 1. Suppose the user does not satisfy this result and he/she wishes to classify this case into *C2*. After the user initiates the knowledge acquisition process, a new refining rule creation process is summarised in Figure 2:

Step 1: The user selects a destination folder from the category tree and the MCRDR classifier generates case attributes;

Step 2: The user selects keywords from the case attributes, for example 'c' in Title;

Step 3: The system generates document lists satisfying rules in this new rule path (Rule0 – Rule 1 – Rule 3 (new rule));

Step 4: If the user selects one or more of the documents in these lists to exclude them, the MCRDR–Classifier presents the difference lists instead of the case attributes; and

The user performs Step 2 ~ 4 iteratively until the remaining document lists do not include any irrelevant documents.

**Fig. 2.** Rule Creation Process

A stopping rule is exemplified by Case 3. If Case 3 is given to the MCRDR classifier, it suggests *C1* as a recommendation. Suppose the user does not classify this current case into this folder, but also does not want to classify it into any other folders, as a result, a stopping rule is created under the current firing rule (Rule 1). The stopping rule creation process is the same as the refining rule creation process, except that a stopping rule has no recommending folder. Prior studies show that this guarantees low cost knowledge maintenance[8]. The MCRDR classifier has been successfully used in various situations. Domain users can construct classification knowledge within a very short time and without any help from the knowledge engineer. Several papers have been written on performance evaluation of an MCRDR classifier [9-13].

## 3   Method

The MCRDR classifier was used to determine the similarity of web pages and identify the occurrence of particular events. The similarity between web pages can be defined by comparing the number of articles which have been classified into the same categories. For example, assume there is a monitoring system which has implemented an MCRDR classifier to classify collected articles and web pages, identified as A, B and C, are registered to be monitored. While the system is running, the classifier classify 17 articles from web pages A, 15 articles from web pages B and 4 articles from web page C into the same folder D. Clearly web pages A and B can be considered more likely to provide more similar information than web page C. Although web page C provides a few articles similar to web pages A and B, only a few articles have been classified into the same category.

We should be able to identify whether an event has been occurred by analysing the classification history. That is, an event can be defined as an occurrence of an abnormal pattern in the classification history of a particular web page. In this research, *average publication frequency per hour per day* was used to detect events, because publication patterns change according daily and even hourly basis[14]. For example, assume that normally an average of three articles from a web page are classified to a

- Register monitoring web pages of interest
- Set a schedule for monitoring each web page using naïve or statistical policies.
- Generates a day-hour average classification tables for each web page as 7 days × 24 hours matrices for each category.
- $A(K)_{ij}$ means web page K's average classifications at $j$ hour on $i$ day of week (e.g., 14:00 on Monday)
- Get the current classifications of each web page ($C(K)_{ij}$) (e.g., web page K's classification at 14:00 on Monday)
- If $C(K)_{ij} > A(K)_{ij} + \theta$ (classification threshold), then the system finds other monitoring web pages that provide similar contents and executes web monitoring regardless of original schedules.

**Fig. 3.** Event-Driven Scheduling Algorithm

particular category between 12:00pm and 2:00pm on Monday. However, if seven articles from the same web page are classified to the folder in the same time period and day, it can be considered that the some events may have occurred in the real world. To make this judgement, we need to set up a reasonable threshold for each web page to determine whether or not the web page is referring to a significant event. The event-driven scheduling algorithm is summarized in Figure 3.

There are three decision factors in the above algorithm. Firstly, it is necessary to determine how to generate a day-hour average classification tables. Each average value ($A(K)_{ij}$) can be calculated for an overall period or specific time span (e.g. the last five week). In this study, we used the overall experiment period to calculate this average. Secondly, it is necessary to determine the threshold value ($\theta$) that is used for event detection. This value may be determined by experience and in this study this value was set at $0.2 \times A(K)_{ij}$. Lastly, it is necessary to determine which web pages are related to a specific web page. This research uses the classification history of web pages to determine similarity between web pages. That is, web page similarity is decided by the classification frequency for a specific category.

# 4   Experiment Design

## 4.1   System Development

The Java programming language and MySQL database were used to develop our event-driven monitoring system. Figure 4 illustrates the system architecture of the event-based web monitoring system, which consists of five modules. The static scheduler initiates each static monitoring process. There are many previous researches on static scheduling methods, but they are not included in this research, because this research mainly focuses on the event-driven scheduling. In this system the user can specify fixed revisit intervals such as every 2 hours. This simple static scheduling may be replaced by more sophisticated methods, and the methods proposed here would go on top of these more sophisticated methods. As computing resources are generally limited, it is necessary to manage system resources efficiently and a thread pool may be used for this purpose. In our system, a Java thread pool was implemented

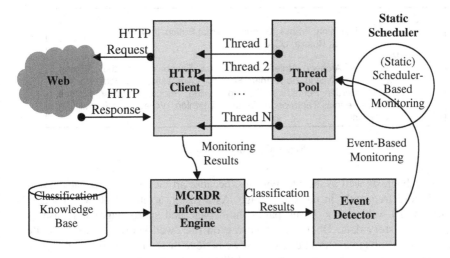

**Fig. 4.** Event-Based Web Monitoring System Architecture

to manage large scale HTTP requests, which protects against running out of resources. The Apache httpclient (http://hc.apache.org/httpclient-3.x/) library was used
in this project because this is stable and commonly used in the HTTP network programming. A HTML parser, called htmlparser (http://htmlparser.sourceforge.net/),
library was used to manipulate HTML/XHTML documents. The MCRDR (Multiple
Classification Ripple-Down Rules) inference engine automatically classified the collected documents. The event detector finds anomalous document classification results
from each monitoring session and initiates additional event-driven monitoring
processes when an abnormal increase of the publications occurs.

### 4.2  Data Collection

In order to collect web history data, 60 web pages were monitored every two hours
for about a month, from 8th August to 3rd September, 2008. This data collection period
corresponds with the Beijing Olympic period. The Olympic period provides an excel-
lent opportunity to examine event-driven scheduling performance compared with the
normal web environment as the Games sporting events are exactly the type of events
that event-driven scheduling should pick up. Web pages to be monitored are selected
as follows: First of all, we attempted to choose the countries which more tend to be
interested in Olympic Games, because web pages from those countries may publish
more articles which are related to Olympic Game than others. We selected Australia,
the United States and Great Britain as the countries to monitor. They were in the top
10 countries from the medal table for the 2004 Olympics in Athens and would be
expected to have a keen interest in the 2008 Olympics. In addition, articles published
in these countries will be in English. This is important because with the MCRDR
classifier we used a user can create rules for the MCRDR classifier only in English.
After selecting these countries, ten generally "well-known" news web sites were chosen from three different countries. We decided to monitor the sports page of each

Countries
    Australia, China, France, Germany, Great Britain, Italy, Japan,
    South Korea, Russia, USA
Sports
    Aquatics, Archery, Athletics, Badminton, Baseball, Basketball, Boxing,
    Canoeing, Cycling, Equestrian, Fencing, Gymnastics, Handball, Hockey,
    Judo, Morden Pentathlon, Rowing, Sailing, Shooting, Soccer, Softball,
    Table Tennis, Taekwondo, Tennis, Triathlon, Volleyball, Weightlifting,
    Wrestling

**Fig. 5.** Category Structure

selected web site as well as their homepages, because articles about Olympics may be updated more frequently in the sports page. As a result, a total of 60 web pages (3 countries × 10 web sites × 2 web pages (homepage and sports page) were used to collect web history data. Obviously, focusing on the "well-known" news web sites may bias our results to a certain degree, but we believe these sites are popular sites for many people. During this period, a total 131,831 web pages; 46,724 pages from Australia, 43,613 pages from United States and 41,494 pages from Great Britain were downloaded and stored into the database. The size of all collected data was around 580MB. Each data includes the information about its link (stored in the form of absolute URL), the link name (title), data origin (to indicate which Web site it was published from), its contents (HTML source associated with absolute URL) and the time it was captured by the system.

### 4.3   Classification with MCRDR Classifier

After collecting documents from the above web pages, a master's degree student classified the collected documents with the MCRDR classifier for about one month (between 5th September 2008 and 13th October 2008). We decided to define two major categories first, *Countries* and *Sports*, because these two concepts are the main subjects in Olympic Games. Under *Countries* category, the name of the top ten countries in the previous Olympic 2004 were created and 28 categories of summer sports, referred to on the official Web site of the Beijing 2008, were created as sub-categories of *Sports* category. Figure 5 summaries the category structure used in this experiment. A total 3,707 rules were manually created using 7,747 condition words. Each rule generally contains an average 2 condition words. The number of rules for the conclusion categories was 1,413 and the number of stop rules was 2,294. There are more of these as initially we made rules which were not specific enough and many articles that were not really related to a particular category were assigned to it, so the participants inevitably had to create many stop rules to correct errors. A total of 29,714 articles, about 22% of the entire articles from the dataset, were classified into the each classification category.

### 4.4   Simulated Web Monitoring

Simulated web monitoring was conducted to evaluate our event-driven scheduling method using the above data set. Our simulation system periodically retrieves the collected web pages with given intervals and calculates each article's delay time between the capturing time and the retrieving time. For example, if the system starts to retrieve the collected articles every four hours from 8th August 2008 00:00:00 and there was an article collected at 8th August 2008 02:10:00, its delay is 110 minutes. The top five sub-categories of *Countries*, in respect to the amount of the classified documents, were chosen for this experiment. Then the top five monitoring web pages of each category were selected according to their classified article count. Two types of simulated web monitoring were conducted with these five categories and their five web pages. Firstly, a static simulation was conducted to calculate a default delay with given intervals (2, 4, 8, 12, and 24 hours). Then three types of event-driven monitoring simulations were conducted with different **scheduling interval assignment strategies**. There are three possible ways to assign intervals based on the number of classified documents in a category and it is necessary to examine whether or not these assignment strategies affect on the performance of the event driven scheduling methods. Suppose that there are five web pages, called $P_1$ (100), $P_2$ (90), $P_3$ (80), $P_4$ (70), and $P_5$ (60), where the numbers show the classified documents in a category. Firstly, the shorter interval can be assigned to the web page that has higher number of documents. This is called the "top-down" strategy in this research. According to this strategy, each web page has the following intervals: $P_1$ (2 hours), $P_2$ (4 hours), $P_3$ (8 hours), $P_4$ (12 hours), and $P_5$ (24 hours). Secondly, the intervals may be assigned to the inverse order of the "top-down" strategy, which is called the "bottom-up" strategy. In this strategy, each web page has the following intervals: $P_1$ (24 hours), $P_2$ (12 hours), $P_3$ (8 hours), $P_4$ (4 hours), and $P_5$ (2 hours). Lastly, the intervals may be assigned randomly, which is called the "random" strategy.

## 5   Experimental Results

Figure 7 illustrates simulated web monitoring results with static scheduling method, where the horizontal axis represents simulated monitoring intervals in hours scale, the vertical axis represents each category's average delay time of five web pages by minute scale, and each bar represents the selected category number.

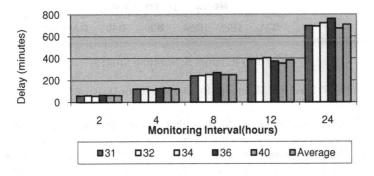

**Fig. 6.** Simulated Monitoring Results with Static Scheduling

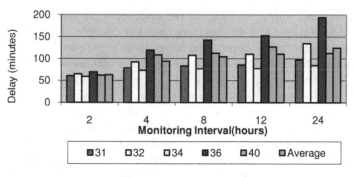

(a) Top-down Scheduling Strategy

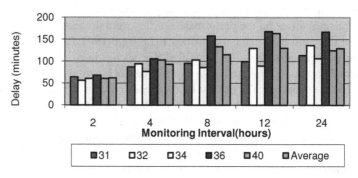

(b) Bottom-down Scheduling Strategy

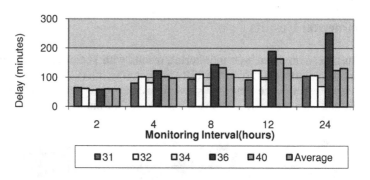

(c) Random Scheduling Strategy

**Fig. 7.** Simulated Monitoring Results with Event-Driven Scheduling

The static scheduling based results show that average delay time of each category's five web pages increase as the monitoring intervals increase and shows similar levels of delay for the same monitoring intervals. For example, whereas there is about 60 minutes delay when the monitoring interval is set two hours, there is about 700 minutes delay when the monitoring interval is set 24 hours. These results were used as default delay time for each category in the following discussion.

**Table 1.** Experimental Results

| Monitoring Methods | | Monitoring Intervals | | | | | |
|---|---|---|---|---|---|---|---|
| | | 2 | 4 | 8 | 12 | 24 | Average |
| Static Monitoring | | 60.8 | 122.6 | 251.3 | 384.2 | 708.8 | 305.5 |
| Event-Driven Monitoring | Top-down | 63.1 | 94.5 | 104.6 | 110.7 | 124.8 | 99.5 |
| | Bottom-up | 61.8 | 93.4 | 115.2 | 130.1 | 129.4 | 106.0 |
| | Random | 60.0 | 97.9 | 110.7 | 132.7 | 131.6 | 106.6 |
| | Average | 61.6 | 95.3 | 110.2 | 124.5 | 128.6 | 104.0 |
| | Improvements | 101% | 78% | 44% | 32% | 18% | 34% |

Three event-driven simulated web monitoring results with different scheduling interval assignment strategy are illustrated in Figure 7(a), Figure 7(b), and Figure 7 (c).The main findings are as follows: Firstly, the results show that the event driven scheduling significantly improves monitoring performance compared to the static scheduling method. Table 1 summaries average delays of all categories and it demonstrates that the delay time significantly improves as the event-driven scheduling methods applied to the monitoring. Secondly, the results show that the event-driven monitoring system improves more when the monitoring intervals are longer. For example, when the monitoring interval is four hours, the event-driven monitoring delay is 78% of the static monitoring delay, but when the monitoring interval is 24 hours, it is only 18%. Lastly, the results show that there is no significant difference between different event-driven monitoring strategies. Although overall performance of the top-down strategy is slightly better than those of other strategies, it is not so significant.

## 6   Conclusions and Further Work

In this paper, we pointed out the limitation of existing scheduling approaches in capturing event-based changes on the Web and introduced a possible scheduling algorithm to cover those changes for the monitoring system. A knowledge base scheduling algorithm is able to trigger the scheduler for other web pages, if an abnormal pattern has been detected on a particular web page. Our experiment was perform with 60 selected news web pages from three different countries; Australia, the United States and Great Britain. The results show that the monitoring system can significantly reduce the delay time, by implementing an event-driven scheduling algorithm. However, several issues still need to be addressed. First of all, the experiments were done by simulation; and the system has not yet been tested in a real situation. Secondly, we have not attempted to find the most appropriate threshold to define an event and the time span between the time when an event is detected and the time the system activates an event-based scheduler. Lastly, our rules were written specifically to classify information about the Olympics. We believe that for any specialist or even general monitoring system enough knowledge will gradually be entered to pick up all important events related to either general or particular specialist interests. A further interesting question is whether it would be useful to use such an approach not just for scheduling but providing alerts (e.g., flagging a user that many web pages were publishing a lot of new information about a particular topic).

# References

1. Liu, L., Pu, C., Han, W.: CONQUER: a continual query system for update monitoring in the WWW. Computer Systems Science and Engineering 14(2), 99–112 (1999)
2. Naughton, J., et al.: The Niagara internet query system. IEEE Data Engineering Bulletin 24(2), 27–33 (2001)
3. Liu, L., Pu, C., Tang, W.: Continual Queries for Internet Scale Event-Driven Information Delivery. IEEE Transactions on Knowledge and Data Engineering 11(4), 610–628 (1999)
4. Liu, L., Pu, C., Tang, W.: WebCQ: Detecting and delivering information changes on the Web. In: CIKM 2000. ACM Press, Washington D.C (2000)
5. Pandey, S., Ramamritham, K., Chakrabarti, S.: Monitoring the dynamic web to respond to continuous queries. In: WWW 2003, Budapest, Hungary (2003)
6. Pandey, S., Dhamdhere, K., Olston, C.: WIC: A General-Purpose Algorithm for Monitoring Web Information Sources. In: 30th VLDB Conference, Toronto, Canada (2004)
7. Bright, L., Gal, A., Raschid, L.: Adaptive pull-based policies for wide area data delivery. ACM Transactions on Database Systems (TODS) 31(2), 631–671 (2006)
8. Kang, B., Compton, P., Preston, P.: Multiple Classification Ripple Down Rules: Evaluation and Possibilities. In: 9th AAAI-Sponsored Banff Knowledge Acquisition for Knowledge-Based Systems Workshop, Banff, Canada, University of Calgary (1995)
9. Kim, Y.S., et al.: Adaptive Web Document Classification with MCRDR. In: International Conference on Information Technology: Coding and Computing ITCC 2004, Orleans, Las Vegas, Nevada, USA (2004)
10. Park, S.S., Kim, Y.S., Kang, B.H.: Web Document Classification: Managing Context Change. In: IADIS International Conference WWW/Internet 2004, Madrid, Spain (2004)
11. Kim, Y.S., et al.: Incremental Knowledge Management of Web Community Groups on Web Portals. In: 5th International Conference on Practical Aspects of Knowledge Management, Vienna, Austria (2004)
12. Kim, Y.S., et al.: Knowledge Acquisition Behavior Anaysis in the Open-ended Document Classification. In: 19th ACS Australian Joint Conference on Artificial Intelligence, Hobart, Australia (2006)
13. Kang, B.-h., Kim, Y.S., Choi, Y.J.: Does multi-user document classification really help knowledge management? In: Orgun, M.A., Thornton, J. (eds.) AI 2007. LNCS, vol. 4830, pp. 327–336. Springer, Heidelberg (2007)
14. Brewington, B.E., Cybenko, G.: Keeping Up with the Changing Web. Computer 33(5), 52–58 (2000)

# RCQ-GA: RDF Chain Query Optimization Using Genetic Algorithms

Alexander Hogenboom, Viorel Milea, Flavius Frasincar, and Uzay Kaymak

Erasmus School of Economics, Erasmus University Rotterdam
P.O. Box 1738, 3000 DR Rotterdam, The Netherlands
alexander.hogenboom@gmail.com,
{milea,frasincar,kaymak}@ese.eur.nl

**Abstract.** The application of Semantic Web technologies in an Electronic Commerce environment implies a need for good support tools. Fast query engines are needed for efficient querying of large amounts of data, usually represented using RDF. We focus on optimizing a special class of SPARQL queries, the so-called RDF chain queries. For this purpose, we devise a genetic algorithm called RCQ-GA that determines the order in which joins need to be performed for an efficient evaluation of RDF chain queries. The approach is benchmarked against a two-phase optimization algorithm, previously proposed in literature. The more complex a query is, the more RCQ-GA outperforms the benchmark in solution quality, execution time needed, and consistency of solution quality. When the algorithms are constrained by a time limit, the overall performance of RCQ-GA compared to the benchmark further improves.

## 1 Introduction

Semantic Web [1] technologies have more and more viable applications in today's Electronic Commerce environments. Compared to the current Web, the Semantic Web offers the possibility to query significant heaps of data from multiple heterogeneous sources more efficiently, returning more relevant results. In the context of the Semantic Web, the keyword is meta-data: describing the context of data and enabling a machine to interpret it. Semantic data is commonly represented using the Resource Description Framework (RDF), a World Wide Web Consortium (W3C) framework for describing and interchanging meta-data [2]. RDF sources can be queried using SPARQL [3]. When implemented in an Electronic Commerce environment, Semantic Web technologies can facilitate a personalized shopping experience for customers through, e.g., recommender systems. For instance, when product data in a webshop is represented using RDF, complex queries can be executed in order to find products of interest to a customer. In a real-time environment with many products per website and many products that need to be compared from different sources, fast RDF query engines are needed.

A successful implementation of an application that is able to query multiple heterogenous sources still seems far away, as several aspects of such an application are subject to ongoing research. An interesting research field in this context

T. Di Noia and F. Buccafurri (Eds.): EC-Web 2009, LNCS 5692, pp. 181–192, 2009.

is the determination of query paths: the order in which the different parts of a specified query are evaluated. The execution time of a query depends on this order. A good algorithm for determining the optimal query path can thus contribute to efficient querying. In the context of the Semantic Web, some research has already been done: an iterative improvement (II) algorithm followed by simulated annealing (SA), also referred to as the two-phase optimization (2PO) algorithm, addresses the optimal determination of query paths [4]. This implementation aims at optimizing the query path in an RDF query engine.

However, other algorithms have not yet been used for RDF query path determination, while genetic algorithms (GA) have proven to be more effective than SA in cases with some similar characteristics. For example, a GA performed better than SA in solving the circuit partitioning problem, where components have to be placed on a chip in such a way, that the number of interconnections is optimized [5]. The query path determination problem is somewhat similar to this problem, since the distinctive parts of the query have to be ordered in such a way, that the execution time is minimized. Furthermore, genetic algorithms have proven to generate good results in traditional query execution environments [6].

Therefore, we seek to apply this knowledge from traditional fields to an RDF query execution environment, which differs from traditional ones in that the RDF environment is generally more demanding when it comes to response time; entirely new queries should be optimized and resolved in real-time. In the traditional field of query optimization for relational databases, queries considered for optimization tend to be queries which are used (more) frequently. Such queries can hence be optimized and cached a priori, implying that the duration of the optimization process of such queries is less important. The main goal we pursue consists of investigating whether an approach based on GAs performs better than a 2PO algorithm in determining RDF query paths. As a first step, the current focus is on the performance of such algorithms when optimizing a special class of SPARQL queries, the so-called RDF chain queries, on a single source.

The outline of this paper is as follows. In Section 2 we provide a discussion on RDF and query paths, the optimization of which is discussed in Section 3. Section 4 introduces the genetic algorithm employed for the current purpose. The experimental setup and obtained results are detailed in Section 5. Finally, we conclude in Section 6.

## 2    RDF and Query Paths

Essentially, an RDF model is a collection of facts declared using RDF. The underlying structure of these facts is a collection of triples, each of which consists of a subject, a predicate and an object. These triples can be visualized using an RDF graph, which can be described as a node and directed-arc diagram, in which each triple is represented as a node-arc-node link [2]. The relationship between a subject node and an object node in an RDF graph is defined using an arc which denotes a predicate. This predicate indicates that the subject has got a certain property, which refers to the object.

An RDF query can be visualized using a tree. The leaf nodes of such a query tree represent inputs (sources), whereas the internal nodes represent algebra operations, which enable a user to specify basic retrieval requests on these sources [7]. The nodes in a query tree can be ordered in many different ways, which all produce the same result. These solutions all depict an order in which operations are executed in order to retrieve the requested data and are referred to as query plans or query paths.

The RDF queries considered in this paper are a specific subset of SPARQL queries, where the WHERE statement only contains a set of node-arc-node patterns, which are chained together. Each arc is to be interpreted as a predicate. Each node represents a concept and is to be interpreted as a subject associated with the predicate leaving this node and as an object associated with the predicate entering this node. When querying RDF sources is regarded as querying relational databases, computing results for paths from partial results resembles computing the results of a chain query. In a chain query, a path is followed by performing joins between its sub paths of length 1 [4]. The join condition used in joining the node-arc-node patterns considered here is that the object of the former pattern equals the subject of the latter pattern.

In order to illustrate chain queries in an RDF environment, let us consider an RDF model of the CIA World Factbook [8] containing data about 250 countries, defined in over $100,000$ statements, generated using QMap [9]. Suppose a company, currently located in South Africa, wants to expand its activities to a country already in a trading relationship (in this example an import partnership) with South Africa. In order to assess the risks involved, the board wants to identify the candidates that have one or more neighbours involved in an international dispute. This query can be expressed in SPARQL as follows:

```
1. PREFIX c: <http://www.daml.org/2001/09/countries/fips#>
2. PREFIX o: <http://www.daml.org/2003/09/factbook/factbook-ont#>
3. SELECT ?partner
4. WHERE { c:SouthAfrica o:importPartner ?impPartner .
5.         ?impPartner o:country ?partner .
6.         ?partner o:border ?border .
7.         ?border o:country ?neighbour .
8.         ?neighbour o:internationalDispute ?dispute .
9.       }
```

This query is a simple example of a chain query and can be subdivided into five parts: the query for information on the import partners of South Africa (line 4), the query for countries actually associated with other countries as import partners (line 5), the query for the borders of the latter countries (line 6), the query for countries associated with a country border as neighbours (line 7), and finally the query for the international disputes the neighbouring countries are involved in (line 8). The results of these sub queries can be joined in order to resolve the complete query. Here, the number of statements resulting from a join is equal to the number of statements compliant with both operands' constraints.

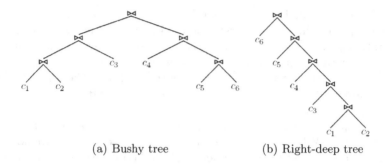

(a) Bushy tree                    (b) Right-deep tree

**Fig. 1.** Examples of possible query trees for a chain query with six concepts

In an RDF context, bushy and right-deep query trees can be considered [4]. In bushy trees, base relations (containing information from one source) as well as results of earlier joins can be joined. Right-deep trees, which are a subset of bushy trees, require the left-hand join operands to be base relations. Figure 1 depicts examples of a bushy tree and a right-deep tree, where concepts $(c_1, c_2, c_3, c_4, c_5, c_6)$ are joined and a $\bowtie$ represents a join. These concepts represent (c:SouthAfrica, ?impPartner, ?partner, ?border, ?neighbour, ?dispute).

## 3   RDF Query Path Optimization

The order of joins of sub paths in a query path is variable and affects the time needed for executing the query. In this context, the join-order problem arises. The challenge is to determine the right order in which the joins should be computed, hereby optimizing the overall response time. A solution space can be considered, in which each solution $s$ represents a query path and is associated with execution costs $C_s$, which are mainly realized by the cost of data transmission from the source to the processor and the cost of processing these data [4]. As we focus on a single source, we omit data transmission costs for now and only consider data processing costs: the sum of costs associated with all joins within solution $s$.

Join costs are influenced by the cardinalities of each operand and the join method used. Several methods can be used for implementing (two-way) joins, as discussed in [10]. We consider only nested-loop joins, as no index or hash key exists a priori for the source used here (making single-loop and hash joins impossible) and the source data are unsorted (requiring the sort-merge join algorithm to sort the data first, which would take up precious running time). When joining operands $c_1$ and $c_2$ using a nested-loop join, the processing costs $C_j^{nest}$ associated with this join $j$ are

$$C_j^{nest} = |c_1| \cdot |c_2|, \tag{1}$$

where the cardinalities of operand $c_1$ and $c_2$ are represented by $|c_1|$ and $|c_2|$, respectively.

In an RDF environment, cardinalities of results from joins could be estimated, as actually performing the joins in order to retrieve the number of elements resulting from each join of sub paths would imply the execution time of the optimization process to be very likely to exceed the execution time of a random query path. These estimations could be initialized as the number of elements in the Cartesian product of the operands and be updated after a query has been evaluated; computed join costs can be saved for possible re-use in order to reduce the time needed for evaluating joins.

In the solution space containing all possible query paths for an arbitrary query to be optimized, similar solutions are regarded as neighbours. Solutions are considered to be neighbouring solutions of a solution if they can be transformed into the latter solution by applying one of the following transformation rules once to one part of the query tree they represent [11]:

- Join commutativity: $c_1 \bowtie c_2 \Rightarrow c_2 \bowtie c_1$.
- Join associativity: $(c_1 \bowtie c_2) \bowtie c_3 \Leftrightarrow c_1 \bowtie (c_2 \bowtie c_3)$.
- Left join exchange: $(c_1 \bowtie c_2) \bowtie c_3 \Rightarrow (c_1 \bowtie c_3) \bowtie c_2$.
- Right join exchange: $c_1 \bowtie (c_2 \bowtie c_3) \Rightarrow c_2 \bowtie (c_1 \bowtie c_3)$.

Since not every query path is as efficient as others, the challenge in query path determination is to optimize query execution costs. When utilizing a relational view on RDF sources, queries on these sources could be translated into algebraic expressions. Using transformation rules for relational algebraic expressions, several algebraic query optimization heuristics have been developed [10, 7]. However, in complex solution spaces, these heuristics are not sufficient; randomized algorithms (e.g., II and SA) and GAs generate better results in traditional query execution environments [6]. Applying these algorithms in determining the order of SELECT operations in RDF chain queries would not be very interesting due to the lack of complexity in the associated solution spaces and due to the sufficiency of the heuristics mentioned above. The real challenge lies in optimizing the order and nature of the joins specified in the WHERE statement, whereby randomized algorithms and/or GAs are identified as promising approaches.

In the context of the Semantic Web, the query path determination problem has already been addressed using an II algorithm followed by SA, also referred to as the two-phase optimization (2PO) algorithm [4]. The II algorithm randomly generates a set of initial solutions, which are used as starting points for a walk in the solution space. Each step in such a walk is a step to a neighbouring solution in the solution space that yields improvement. At some point in a walk, a solution is reached for which no better neighbour can be found in a specified number of tries, in which case the current solution is assumed to be a local optimum. The number of times the algorithm tries to find a better neighbour (i.e., randomly selects a neighbour) is limited to the number of neighbours of that solution. The described process is repeated for all starting points.

The best local optimum thus found is subsequently used as a starting point for a SA algorithm, which tends to accept (with a declining probability) moves not yielding improvement. The latter algorithm thus searches the proximity of possibly sub-optimal solutions, hereby reducing the risk for a local optimum.

Inspired by the natural process of annealing of crystals from liquid solutions, SA simulates a continuous temperature reduction, enabling the system to cool down completely from a specified starting temperature to a state in which the system is considered to be frozen.

Just like II, the SA algorithm accepts moves in the solution space yielding lower costs. However, SA can also accept moves leading to higher costs, hereby reducing the chances for the algorithm to get stuck in a local optimum. The probability for accepting such moves depends on the system's temperature: the higher the temperature, the more likely the system is to accept moves leading to higher costs. However, for every state of the algorithm it applies that the more the costs associated with a solution exceed the current costs, the less likely the system is to accept such a move [12].

## 4   A Genetic RDF Query Path Determination Algorithm

As discussed in Section 1, GAs tend to perform better in query optimization, but have not been assessed in an RDF environment yet. In this paper, we propose to optimize RDF Chain Queries using a Genetic Algorithm: RCQ-GA.

A GA is an optimization algorithm simulating biological evolution according to the principle of survival of the fittest. A population (a set of chromosomes, representing solutions) is exposed to evolution, consisting of selection (where individual chromosomes are chosen to be part of the next generation), crossovers (creating offspring by combining some chromosomes) and mutations (randomly altering some chromosomes). Evolution is simulated until the maximum number of iterations is reached or several generations have not yielded any improvement. The fitness $F_s$ of a chromosome (expressing the quality of solution $s$) determines the chances of survival and depends on the associated solution costs $C_s$. The probability of a solution to be selected must be inversely proportional to its associated costs [6]. This can be accomplished by defining the fitness $F_s$ of solution $s$ as shown in (2), hereby assuming that the population contains $n$ solutions. The fitness-based selection probability can then be defined as shown in (3).

$$F_s = 1 - \frac{C_s}{\sum_{i=1}^{n} C_i}, \tag{2}$$

$$\Pr(s) = \frac{F_s}{\sum_{i=1}^{n} F_i}. \tag{3}$$

Since a GA utilizes a randomized search method rather than moving smoothly from one solution to another, a GA can move through the solution space more abruptly than for example II or SA, by replacing parent solutions with offsprings that may be radically different from their parents. Therefore, a GA is less likely to get stuck in local optima than for example II or SA. However, a GA can experience another problem: crowding [13]. An individual with a relatively high fitness compared to others could reproduce quickly due to its relatively high selection probability, hereby taking over a large part of the population. This reduces the population's diversity, which slows further progress of the GA.

Crowding can be reduced by using different selection criteria, sharing a solution's fitness amongst similar solutions or controlling the generation of offspring. Another option is using a hybrid GA (HGA), which essentially is a GA with some additional, embedded heuristics. However, high quality solutions are not guaranteed to be found within a reasonable running time, as the implemented heuristics often are time-consuming [14]. Ranking-based selection [6] can also reduce crowding. Here, the selection probability of a solution $s$ depends on its rank $R_s$ (the fittest solution is ranked best) in relation to the sum of all $n$ ranks:

$$\Pr(s) = \frac{R_s}{\sum_{c=1}^{n} R_c}. \tag{4}$$

## 4.1  Settings

In order for a GA to be applicable in RDF query path determination, several parameters must be set. Due to the time constraint associated with executing queries in an RDF environment, using an HGA is not an option. It would be best to opt for a basic GA, adopting the settings best performing in [6]. The algorithm, BushyGenetic (BG), considers a solution space containing bushy query processing trees. A crowding prevention attempt is made by implementing ranking-based selection. Furthermore, the population consists of 128 chromosomes. The crossover rate is 65%, while the mutation rate equals 5%. The stopping condition is 50 generations without improvement. However, long executing times are not desirable for a GA in an RDF query execution environment. Therefore, the stopping condition is complemented with a time limit.

In literature, a GA has been proven to generate better results than a 2PO algorithm in many cases. However, in order to accomplish these results, a GA needs more execution time than 2PO to accomplish this. On the other hand, a GA is aware of good solutions faster than 2PO [6]. Hence, the algorithm spends a lot of time optimizing good results before it terminates. This is an interesting property to exploit in RCQ-GA; since in a real-time environment like the Semantic Web queries need to be resolved as quickly as possible, preliminary and/or quicker convergence of the model might not be such a bad idea after all. If the algorithm could be configured such that it converges quickly when optimizing relatively good solutions, the execution time could be reduced remarkably and the sub-optimal result would not be too far from the global optimum. The challenge is to find a balance between execution time and solution quality.

The BG algorithm could be adapted in order to improve its performance in an RDF query execution environment. The algorithm could be forced to select the best solution for proliferation in the next generation at least once (elitist selection), hereby avoiding losing a good solution. Ranking-based selection could also be replaced with fitness-based selection, as this increases the probability of relatively fit solutions to be selected, which could result in quicker convergence of the model due to increased crowding. Furthermore, evolution could be considered to have stopped after, e.g., 30 generations without improvement instead of 50; long enough in order for the algorithm to be able to determine with sufficient certainty that the best known solution is either a very good local optimum or a global optimum. Finally, the population size could be reduced to for example 64 solutions, which would noticeably reduce the time needed for computing the costs of all solutions in the population and would provide just enough room for diversity in the population, hereby also enforcing quicker model convergence.

## 4.2   Query Path Encoding

Encoding of query processing trees is done using an ordinal number encoding scheme for bushy trees, proposed in [6], which not only efficiently represents bushy trees (including the subset of right-deep trees), but enables relatively easy and efficient crossover operations as well. This encoding algorithm iteratively joins two concepts in an ordered list of concepts, the result of which is saved in the position of the first appearing concept. In each iteration, the positions of the selected concepts are saved into the encoded solution.

For example, consider the following ordered list of concepts: $(c_1, c_2, c_3, c_4)$. An initial join between the third and fourth concept yields the list $(c_1, c_2, c_3 c_4)$. Another join between the first and second concept in this new list yields $(c_1 c_2, c_3 c_4)$. A final join between the first and second concept in this list results in $(c_1 c_2 c_3 c_4)$. A possible encoded notation of these joins is $((3,4), (1,2), (1,2))$. Additional information, such as the applied join method, can also be stored in this encoded notation. For details on the crossover and mutation methodology applied for the current goal, we refer to [6].

# 5    Experimental Setup and Results

## 5.1   Experimental Setup

All experiments performed for the current purpose are run in a Microsoft Windows XP environment, on a $2,400$ MHz Intel Pentium 4 system with $1,534$ MB physical memory (DDR SDRAM). Tests are conducted on a single source: an RDF version of the CIA World Factbook [8], generated using QMap [9]. The first algorithm to be tested is the 2PO algorithm as proposed in [4]. The performance of the BG algorithm [6] and its improved version (RCQ-GA) as proposed in Section 4.1 are benchmarked as well. Finally, the performance of time-constrained 2PO and RCQ-GA (respectively 2POT and RCQ-GAT, in which the T denotes the time-constrained nature of these algorithms) is evaluated.

Several experiments are conducted in order to determine the performance of the considered algorithms; each algorithm is tested on chain queries varying in length from 2 to 20 predicates (see Section 2 for a 6-predicate example). Each experiment is iterated 100 times. The algorithms are configured according to the settings proposed in their sources and thus all consider the entire solution space containing bushy query trees. The time limit for 2POT and RCQ-GAT is set to 1000 milliseconds, as this allows the algorithms to perform at least a couple of iterations and we assume that a maximum waiting time of 1 second for efficiently executing a complex query, would be acceptable in a real-time environment.

**Table 1.** Parameters of considered optimization algorithms

| Parameter | 2PO | 2POT | Parameter | BG | RCQ-GA | RCQ-GAT |
|---|---|---|---|---|---|---|
| maxSol | 10 | 10 | popSize | 128 | 64 | 64 |
| startTempFactor | 0.1 | 0.1 | crossoverRate | 0.65 | 0.65 | 0.65 |
| tempRed | 0.05 | 0.05 | mutationRate | 0.05 | 0.05 | 0.05 |
| frozenTemp | 1 | 1 | stableFitnessGens | 50 | 30 | 30 |
| maxConsRedNoImpr | 4 | 4 | rankingBased | true | false | false |
| neighbourExpFactor | 16 | 16 | elitist | false | true | true |
| timeLimit (ms) | - | 1000 | timeLimit (ms) | - | - | 1000 |

Table 1 presents an overview of the algorithms' configurations. For the considered 2PO algorithms, the *maxSol* parameter sets the maximum number of starting solutions analyzed in the II part of 2PO. The fraction of the optimal cost resulting from II to be used as starting temperature in SA is specified in *startTempFactor*, whereas *tempRed* is the factor with which the temperature of the system is to be reduced every iteration of SA. The *frozenTemp* parameter defines the temperature below which the system is considered to be frozen. The maximum number of consecutive temperature reductions not yielding improvement is defined in *maxConsRedNoImpr*. For each visited solution, SA tries to move to neighbouring solutions for a limited number of times, which equals the number of joins in the query, multiplied by *neighbourExpFactor* [12]. The maximum running time in milliseconds is configured using the *timeLimit* parameter.

As for the considered GAs, the number of chromosomes is defined using the *popSize* parameter. The *crossoverRate* parameter represents the fraction of each new generation to be filled with offspring resulting from crossover operations between pairs of selected chromosomes. The rest of the new generation is filled with direct selections from the current generation; the fitter the chromosome, the higher the selection probability. The fraction of the new population to be mutated is defined using the *mutationRate* parameter. Furthermore, *stableFitnessGens* is the number of consecutive generations not showing improvement in optimal fitness needed for the fitness of the population to be considered stable. The *rankingBased* parameter is used to define whether ranking-based selection should be applied rather than fitness-based selection. The *elitist* parameter states whether the best chromosome should always be selected for the next generation. The time limit in milliseconds is defined in *timeLimit*.

## 5.2   Results

For each algorithm tested, Fig. 2(a) visualizes the extent to which the average time needed for optimizing chain queries deviates from the average time the 2PO algorithm needs for this optimization, divided by the latter average. This is done in order to directly provide insight into the performance of the tested approaches, with respect to the 2PO benchmark. The results are based on 100 iterations of the query optimization process per experiment.

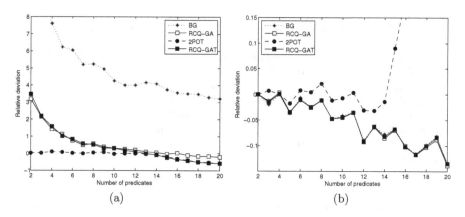

**Fig. 2.** Relative deviation of average execution times and optimal costs from 2PO average, depicted in (a) and (b), respectively

For all considered query lengths, on average, the BG algorithm needs the most execution time of all algorithms considered as alternative to 2PO. Furthermore, 2PO turns out to be the fastest performing optimization algorithm for relatively small chain queries containing up to about 10 predicates. For bigger chain queries, RCQ-GA is the fastest performing algorithm. The time-constrained variants of the 2PO and RCQ-GA algorithms obviously take the lead over the RCQ-GA algorithm for even bigger queries, where the execution time needed by the RCQ-GA algorithm exceeds the time limit.

Without a time limit, BG and RCQ-GA tend to find better solutions than 2PO with respect to the average costs associated with optimized chain query paths, especially for larger queries. When a time limit is set, a GA tends to generate even better results compared to 2PO (see Fig. 2(b)). The known behaviour of both algorithms supports this observation, as a GA tends to generate better results in less time, although it needs more time to converge than a 2PO algorithm (as discussed in Section 4.1). Therefore, the earlier in the optimization process both algorithms are forced to stop, the better the optimal solution found by a GA will be compared to the optimal solution generated by 2PO.

The consistency in performance is shown in Fig. 3, using coefficients of variation (standard deviation, divided by the mean) of the execution times and optimal solution costs, respectively, of chain queries of varying lengths. These statistics are based on 100 iterations of the query optimization process per experiment. For each considered algorithm, the deviation of these coefficients of the coefficient of variation of the 2PO algorithm is divided by the latter coefficient. A coefficient of variation close to 0 indicates all observed values are closely clustered around the average. Hence, a positive relative coefficient of variation indicates less consistency of performance of the algorithm, compared to 2PO.

The relative coefficients of variation indicate that compared to 2PO, time-constrained algorithms tend to perform more and more consistently in execution time needed for bigger chain queries. The latter observation can be explained

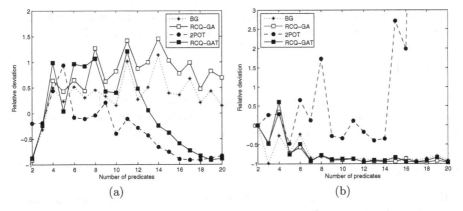

**Fig. 3.** Relative deviation of coefficients of variation of execution times and optimal costs from 2PO average, depicted in (a) and (b), respectively

by realizing that bigger chain queries require longer execution times, which are increasingly likely to exceed the time limit. Hence, increasing parts of iterations of bigger queries execute exactly as long as allowed, hereby reducing the variance in execution times. As for the algorithms not constrained by a time limit, the GAs appear to be less consistent in execution time needed than 2PO, especially for more complex queries.

Regarding the costs associated with found optimal solutions, BG and RCQ-GA tend to perform more consistently than 2PO. Also, the more predicates a chain query consists of, the more GAs outperform 2PO when it comes to consistency in solution quality. When a time limit is set, the relative coefficient of variation of the 2PO algorithm increases rapidly with the number of predicates in the chain queries. The consistency in solution quality of RCQ-GA on the other hand is not clearly affected by a time limit.

## 6    Conclusions

Semantic Web technologies are promising enablers for large-scale knowledge-based systems in an Electronic Commerce environment; they facilitate machine-interpretability of data through effective data representation. Fast query engines are needed in order to efficiently query large amounts of data, usually represented using RDF. The results detailed in this paper lead to the conclusion that in determining the (optimal) query path for chain queries in a single-source RDF query execution environment, the performance of a genetic algorithm compared to two-phase optimization is positively correlated with the complexity of the solution space and the restrictiveness of the environment (in this case a time limit). An appropriately configured genetic algorithm can outperform the two-phase optimization algorithm in solution quality, execution time needed, and consistency of solution quality. As future work, we would like to optimize the parameters of our algorithm, for instance using meta-algorithms [15] and try our algorithm in a distributed setting. Also, we plan to experiment with other algorithms, such as ant colony optimization or particle swarm optimization.

## Acknowledgement

The authors are partially supported by the EU funded IST STREP Project FP6 - 26896: Time-determined ontology-based information system for realtime stock market analysis. More information is available on http://www.towl.org.

## References

[1] Berners-Lee, T., Hendler, J., Lassila, O.: The Semantic Web. Scientific American 284(5), 34–43 (2001)
[2] Klyne, G., Carroll, J.J.: Resource Description Framework (RDF): Concepts and Abstract Syntax – W3C Recommendation, February 10 (2004)
[3] Prud'hommeaux, E., Seaborne, A.: SPARQL Query Language for RDF – W3C Recommendation, January 15 (2008)
[4] Stuckenschmidt, H., Vdovjak, R., Broekstra, J., Houben, G.-J.: Towards Distributed Processing of RDF Path Queries. International Journal of Web Engineering and Technology (IJWET) 2(2-3), 207–230 (2005)
[5] Manikas, T.W., Cain, J.T.: Genetic Algorithms vs. Simulated Annealing: A Comparison of Approaches for Solving the Circuit Partitioning Problem. Technical report, University of Pittsburgh (1996)
[6] Steinbrunn, M., Moerkotte, G., Kemper, A.: Heuristic and Randomized Optimization for the Join Ordering Problem. The VLDB Journal 6(3), 191–208 (1997)
[7] Frasincar, F., Houben, G.-J., Vdovjak, R., Barna, P.: RAL: An Algebra for Querying RDF. World Wide Web Journal 7(1), 83–109 (2004)
[8] Central Intelligence Agency: The CIA World Factbook (2008), https://www.cia.gov/cia/publications/factbook/ (last visited April 2008)
[9] Hogenboom, F., Hogenboom, A., van Gelder, R., Milea, V., Frasincar, F., Kaymak, U.: QMap: An RDF-Based Queryable World Map. In: Third International Conference on Knowledge Management in Organizations (KMO 2008), Vaasa, Finland, pp. 99–110 (2008)
[10] Elmasri, R., Navathe, S.B.: Fundamentals of Database Systems, 4th edn. Addison-Wesley, Reading (2004)
[11] Ioannidis, Y.E., Kang, Y.C.: Randomized Algorithms for Optimizing Large Join Queries. In: The 1990 ACM SIGMOD International Conference on Management of Data (SIGMOD 1990), pp. 312–321. ACM Press, New York (1990)
[12] Swami, A., Gupta, A.: Optimization of Large Join Queries. In: The 1988 ACM SIGMOD International Conference on Management of Data (SIGMOD 1988), pp. 8–17. ACM Press, New York (1988)
[13] Mitchell, T.M.: Machine Learning. McGraw-Hill Series in Computer Science. McGraw-Hill, New York (1997)
[14] Misevicius, A.: A Fast Hybrid Genetic Algorithm for the Quadratic Assignment Problem. In: The 8th Annual Conference on Genetic and Evolutionary Computation (GECCO 2006), pp. 1257–1264. ACM Press, New York (2006)
[15] de Landgraaf, W.A., Eiben, A.E., Nannen, V.: Parameter Calibration using Meta-Algorithms. In: IEEE Congress on Evolutionary Computation, pp. 71–78 (2007)

# Integrating Markets to Bridge Supply and Demand for Knowledge Intensive Tasks

Sietse Overbeek[1], Marijn Janssen[1], and Patrick van Bommel[2]

[1] Faculty of Technology, Policy and Management, Delft University of Technology,
Jaffalaan 5, 2600 GA Delft, The Netherlands
{S.J.Overbeek,M.F.W.H.A.Janssen}@tudelft.nl
[2] Institute for Computing and Information Sciences, Radboud University Nijmegen,
Toernooiveld 1, 6525 ED Nijmegen, The Netherlands
P.vanBommel@cs.ru.nl

**Abstract.** The advent of the knowledge-based economy has underlined the importance of intellectual capital that is possessed by knowledge intensive organizations. Three general observations of knowledge intensive work produced by actors working in such organizations served as the basis for the initiation of this research. First, knowledge intensive tasks become increasingly complex. Second, actors that perform such tasks experience an increase in cognitive load. Third, the desired quality of task performance and the produced task results are at stake due to the aforementioned two developments. In this research we investigate how supply and demand of intangible assets such as knowledge, cognitive characteristics, and quality factors can be matched based on market mechanisms.

**Keywords:** cognitive matchmaking, knowledge market, task quality.

## 1 Introduction

It has become obvious that the knowledge-based economy is becoming the main driver of international society in the 21st century [4]. Human lifestyles and economic structures have been influenced by continuously innovating computer technologies, which have enabled new possibilities to discover and retrieve data, information, and knowledge. Yet, knowledge is fragmented and bringing supply and demand of knowledge together is a difficult task. Knowledge is formed by accumulating a large number of pieces of information over a long period of time [5]. The pieces of information involved must be related somehow. Therefore, knowledge is a selective combination of related pieces of information. Knowledge can be regarded as 'wrapped' in information, whilst information is 'carried' by data (expressions in a symbol language) [5]. In a knowledge-based economy, the value of contemporary organizations contains not only financial capital but also intellectual capital. Intellectual capital consists of assets created through intellectual activities ranging from acquiring new knowledge (learning) and inventions leading to the creation of valuable relationships [4]. An asset can be defined as an entity that can be traded in a market. Organizations that derive their

T. Di Noia and F. Buccafurri (Eds.): EC-Web 2009, LNCS 5692, pp. 193–204, 2009.

*raison d'être* to a large extent from intellectual capital can be referred to as *knowledge intensive organizations.*

Knowledge exchange is a necessity to improve core competencies of actors working in such knowledge intensive organizations. An actor can be defined as an entity (such as a human or a computer) that is able to perform a task. Actors utilize knowledge or are able to supply knowledge. The tasks that can be performed by an actor can be differentiated into *qualifying* tasks and knowledge intensive *execution* tasks, where a qualifying task can be defined as a task executed by an actor if knowledge is required to improve competencies that have already been gained in the past or to gain new competencies. An actor working in a knowledge intensive organization possesses competencies to perform knowledge intensive *execution* tasks. These are tasks for which acquisition, application, or testing of knowledge is necessary in order to successfully fulfill the task [7]. However, the complexity of these tasks increases because of, e.g., organizational growth, increased globalization, growing product complexity, an increasing customer power, outsourcing, and inter-organizational alliances. Actors that are responsible to fulfill knowledge intensive tasks in organizations may experience an increased cognitive load if task complexity increases. Cognitive load, increased by growing task complexity, can influence the frequency of errors by affecting the strength of procedural and sensory cues [3,6]. Eventually, the quality of fulfilled tasks may be negatively influenced. Stakeholder requirements may not be met if the results are too low, where a stakeholder is defined as an entity that may be highly concerned about, or have interests in, the quality factors of a fulfilled knowledge intensive task. Examples of stakeholders are, amongst many others, a supplier, an employee, and a customer. It is assumed that a stakeholder has a *goal* related to the fulfillment of a task that leads to quality expectations.

Considering the aforementioned motivation it can be noticed that the study presented in this paper is related with *supply and demand* of *knowledge, cognition,* and *quality.* Three theoretical models and applications of those models have been developed in our previous work to seize on the observations of *growing task complexity, increasing cognitive load,* and *decreasing task quality* [7]. The aim of this paper is to integrate these models and their applications to bridge supply and demand for knowledge intensive tasks by discussing and relating our current theoretical results together with conducted validation of the theory and the used research strategy. First, an overall picture of the research that has been conducted is presented in section 2 in terms of a reasoning framework. Section 3 crystallizes the strategy. The theoretical results are mapped out in section 4 and validation of these results is discussed in section 5. Section 6 concludes this paper and gives an overview of future work.

## 2   Reasoning Framework

Figure 1 shows a reasoning framework for this research consisting of three market models and the main concepts by which the models are connected. It is an integration of three separate models in which supply and demand of intangible assets are matched. The reasoning framework integrates the knowledge market, the knowledge workers market, and the knowledge quality market [2,7].

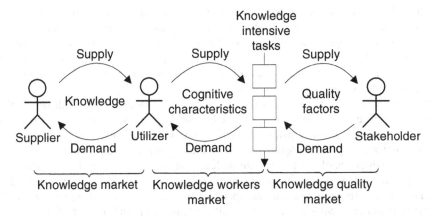

**Fig. 1.** Three market models combined in a reasoning framework

Figure 1 can be explained as follows. First, the knowledge market paradigm can be introduced, which can be identified in the most left-hand part of the figure. This paradigm provides insights on how to improve the matchmaking of supply and demand of knowledge involving actors working in knowledge intensive organizations. Adopting the knowledge market paradigm may lead to a more successful increase in core competencies compared to more traditional knowledge exchange approaches [2].

Actors participating in the knowledge market can enact several roles. Two basic roles are shown in figure 1. The supplier role is depicted in the most left-hand part of the figure. The supplier delivers knowledge, which requires a 'client' who would like to utilize the knowledge. This client is materialized by the utilizer role. The potential knowledge utilizer is searching for knowledge, but does not know if that knowledge can be found. Often, a utilizer does also often not know which knowledge is necessary to fulfill the need. Knowledge is eventually acquired by the utilizer by exchanging knowledge with other actors in the market. It is assumed that an increase in core competencies may lead to more successful task fulfillment and improved task quality. A thorough understanding of knowledge exchange in the knowledge market has been realized by studying the foundations of knowledge exchange [7]. These foundations contain a formal notation for knowledge exchange events, the inclusion of a question and answer mechanism in a knowledge exchange event, knowledge input and output, knowledge carriers, and knowledge similarities. By formally defining parts of the theory we are able to prevent preliminary flaws during the process of theory building. This is related with the required research effort to think very hard and precise about the theory that is developed when using formalisms.

In a knowledge exchange event, an actor may ask a question (or write a query) and receive an answer. Note that in case a question is not immediately answered in some knowledge exchange event, but in a later stage, an answer can be considered empty for that event. It may also be possible that a knowledge exchange event contains an answer but not a question. An example of such a case occurs if knowledge is transferred to an actor if a request for that knowledge has been uttered in an earlier exchange event. When knowledge is exchanged between actors, an actor may experience knowledge input and may produce knowledge output. Similarities between these inputs and outputs can be measured by similarity functions. Such functions can be used to indicate if an answer indeed contains knowledge that can serve as a solution for an actor that requires knowledge and has expressed this in terms of a question. Subsequently, knowledge in a knowledge exchange event is 'carried' by knowledge carriers, such as a human brain, a database, a Web page, and so on. The knowledge market is further elaborated in section 4.1.

Second, the knowledge workers market can be introduced, which is shown in the middle of figure 1. Actors in the knowledge workers market utilize the cognitive characteristics they possess when performing knowledge intensive tasks. Cognitive characteristics are specific cognitive parts of the cognitive system that are possessed by an actor which enable an actor to think, learn, and make decisions [6]. Because the primary ability of actors in the knowledge workers market is to perform knowledge intensive tasks, these actors can be specifically coined as *knowledge workers*. A knowledge worker is an actor that has significant autonomy in how to perform a task, has a high level of education in a certain area of expertise, performs a substantial amount of tasks in which knowledge is acquired, applied, or tested, is informed by or learns from the knowledge processed, and performs tasks which are not just clerical, communicative nor purely concentrated on information [3]. Subsequently, the knowledge workers market is specifically aimed at matching supply and demand of cognitive characteristics. Adopting this market provides more insight in which knowledge intensive tasks can be allocated to which actors from a cognitive point of view. Task allocation based on matching supply and demand of cognitive characteristics may reduce cognitive load while performing complex knowledge intensive tasks. The knowledge workers market is materialized by a framework for cognitive matchmaking and a prototype of the cognitive matchmaker system. This system is in fact a software implementation of the formal matchmaking framework. The knowledge workers market is further elaborated in section 4.2.

Third, the knowledge quality market is depicted in the most right-hand side of figure 1. If an actor fulfills a task, it is possible to conceive the quality of the process that has led to the fulfillment as well as the quality of the task result [4]. Quality factors are considered as the tradeable assets in the knowledge quality market. A quality factor is an abstract term denoting a specific part of task quality that can be measured. Quality factors boil down to one or more quality metrics. A quality metric can concretely measure a quality factor, i.e., a specific quality part. For example, the quality factor called *complexity* can be measured by a quality metric that measures the complexity of the process that has led to a task's fulfillment. In the knowledge quality market, the supplied task quality is matched with the quality requirements of stakeholders. Adopting the knowledge quality market provides more insight in quality expectations for knowledge intensive tasks.

In brief, it can be concluded that the notions of cognition, knowledge, and quality are utilized to bridge the gap between supply and demand for knowledge intensive tasks. This implies that other possible factors that lead to more successful performance of knowledge intensive tasks are considered out of scope. Bridging supply and demand of cognitive characteristics, knowledge assets, and quality factors for knowledge intensive tasks is considered to improve core competencies, decrease cognitive load, and improve task quality.

# 3  Research Strategy

A research strategy can be viewed as an overall approach that indicates how to carry out a research project. A suitable research approach for this study is probably more qualitative, exploratory, and inductive than quantitative, confirmatory, and deductive in nature. This is because the emphasis is on realism of context in a natural situation, but precision in control of variables and behavior measurement cannot be achieved. For instance, if the market models are to be validated and evaluated, then this will be done in practical situations with variables that have a certain state and exist at that point in time when the models are tested. Also, there is a huge diversity of variables in those models and the focus is on what things exist instead of determining how many there are. For example, it is interesting to know what can help us to match actors and tasks based on cognition. Therefore, it is suggested that a suitable approach for the research that we are concerned with should be relatively soft in nature. The *inductive-hypothetical research strategy* [8] fits the needs related to the aforementioned observations. This research strategy consists of the following phases and is visualized in figure 2:

1. Initiation, in which empirical knowledge of the problem domain is elicited.
2. Abstraction, in which the elicited knowledge is applied in a descriptive conceptual model.
3. Theory formulation, in which the descriptive conceptual model is made prescriptive.
4. Implementation, in which the prescriptive conceptual model is empirically tested.
5. Evaluation, a comparison of the elicited knowledge (1) with the prescriptive empirical model (4).

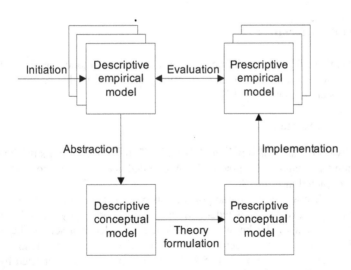

**Fig. 2.** The inductive-hypothetical research strategy, adapted from [8]

An application of the strategy for this study can be derived from this structure and results in the following steps:

1.  Identification of the problem area. This is outlined in the introduction of this paper and has resulted in empirical knowledge showing developments with respect to increasing task complexity, increasing cognitive load, and concerns about task quality.
2.  Positioning and foundation of elicited knowledge about the problem area in current literature, including suggestions to extend the current state of art. These suggestions have been presented in the reasoning framework of section 2.
3.  Development of the three markets to understand how supply and demand of knowledge, cognition, and quality for knowledge intensive tasks can be bridged. The results of this phase are outlined in section 4.
4.  Applications of the three market models to validate them and to determine practical relevance. The conducted attempts to validate the theoretical results are discussed in section 5. A case study has also been part of phase 4. This case study has been classified as a multiple-case study design, because two cases have been distinguished that were based on the same design [9]. In addition, the case study design is a multiple-case embedded design as multiple units of analysis, in this case individual employees and information systems engineering projects, are included. Various sources of evidence were used to collect the data for the research. Data was gathered from documentation, Web pages, interviews, and e-mail correspondence. The case study provides insights in how task allocation can be improved in practice based on cognitive matchmaking and how a prototype of the cognitive matchmaker system can provide assistance in such processes.
5.  Evaluation of the overall research, which can be found in the remaining sections.

## 4   Theoretical Results

The theoretical results can be divided in the three market models as depicted in the reasoning framework of figure 1 and are briefly discussed in this section. The three market models are elaborated in [7].

### 4.1  Knowledge Market

A market always consists of supply and demand of an asset and actors participating in markets intend to match such assets [2]. A detailed view of the knowledge market paradigm is depicted in figure 3.

The merchandize within this paradigm consists of knowledge assets. These *assets* are tradeable forms of revealed knowledge, which are transported physically by the transporter. In the context of the knowledge market, a knowledge asset can be explicitly defined to be an entity that is accessible for the supplier and can provide knowledge to the utilizer in the knowledge market [5,7]. If the transporter role is enacted by a computerized actor, this actor may equal an intelligent Web application that is able to

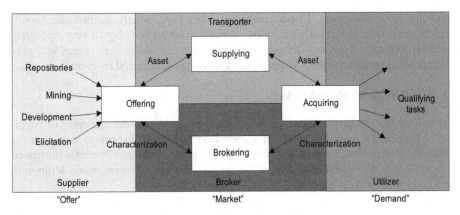

**Fig. 3.** A knowledge market paradigm

mediate between the supplier and the broker about the merchandize. The transporter not only delivers the knowledge assets but can also check whether or not these assets match the demand of the utilizer. This is typically the case if the knowledge that is supplied is *paraphrased*. Suppose that the utilizer has acquired images from the transporter showing business process models. The transporter asks if the images indeed contain the models that the utilizer had in mind. Subsequently, the utilizer may answer with, for example, 'Yes, those images depict the models I was looking for', or, 'No, I meant low-level process models that are more detailed'. Knowledge assets are not necessarily *explicit* knowledge assets, though. Implicit knowledge inside people's heads is also tradeable, because one can take its implicit knowledge to a certain situation where that implicit knowledge is wanted. This is what, e.g., physicians do when explaining a patient's status to a colleague.

An actor successfully plays the role of supplier if that actor is able to deliver knowledge, which requires a 'client' who would like to utilize the knowledge. This is only possible if the supplier is able to make clear what is on offer, hence it is vital that the knowledge is correctly *characterized*. Such a characterization comprises the formulation of a description of the knowledge needed by a potential utilizer in terms of a question (which contains the description but which is not directed to someone), or a query (which communicates the question to a machine). This is not always an easy job because semantic terminology issues can throw a spanner in the works and characterizing an intangible asset like knowledge needs a shared understanding between a buyer and a seller. Poor characterizations inevitably lead to supplying irrelevant knowledge, or omitting to supply relevant knowledge.

On the supply side of the knowledge market various resources can be accessed: Repositories, data collections and warehouses, knowledge that is actively developed, or experts that can be questioned (elicitation). A reliable supplier offers *revealed knowledge* which is localizable and available. It is possible to offer implicit knowledge, e.g., by means of a reliable expert, as long as is assured that the implicit knowledge can be applied by the utilizer (albeit a certain competence). The potential utilizer is searching for knowledge, but does not know if that knowledge can be found. Often, a utilizer does not even know which knowledge is necessary to fulfill the need. The knowledge is concealed for the potential utilizer, but does certainly not have to be concealed for the supplier. Characterization is key here, which matches the knowledge demand with the knowledge to be supplied. The broker plays a very important role in matching supply and demand. It can be said that the broker comes into play when potential utilisers do not know which knowledge is required by them.

## 4.2  Knowledge Workers Market

The knowledge workers market is specifically concerned with the *matching* of cognitive characteristics required to fulfill a knowledge intensive execution task with the cognitive characteristics actually *possessed* by an actor. The main concepts illustrated in figure 4 provide a first overview of the aspects that are taken into consideration in the knowledge workers market.

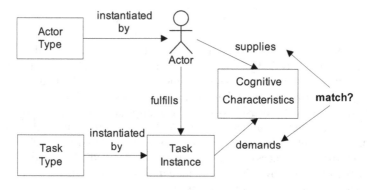

**Fig. 4.** Main concepts of the knowledge workers market

Figure 4 shows that an actor type and a task type can be instantiated by an actor respectively a task instance. Several types of actors that can work in knowledge intensive organizations have been characterized by the cognitive characteristics such types can supply to perform execution tasks [7]. An example of such an actor type is the *expert* type. Suppose that John is an assistant professor working at a university and he would like to solve a difficult mathematical problem. As an expert he can use his knowledge about mathematics to solve it. John is also able to combine and modify his own knowledge while solving the problem and he can also learn from that. Types of execution tasks have also been characterized based on the characteristics that are demanded to fulfill such tasks [7].

The following knowledge intensive task types have been distinguished: The acquisition task type, the synthesis task type, and the testing task type [7]. The acquisition type is related with the acquisition of knowledge. This can be illustrated by a student reading a book in order to prepare himself for an exam. The synthesis type is related with the actual utilization of the acquired knowledge. An example is a student who utilizes knowledge (acquired by reading a book) while performing an exam. The testing task type is related with the identification and application of knowledge in practice inducing an improvement of the specific knowledge applied. E.g., a student who failed an exam studies a teacher's feedback on his exam. Then, a re-examination attempt follows to improve his previously acquired and utilized knowledge. While fulfilling a task, an actor supplies cognitive characteristics. Figure 4 shows that the task instance that is fulfilled by the actor demands cognitive characteristics for successful fulfillment. The match of supply and demand can then be studied. A cognitive match is determined based on the total amount of characteristics supplied and demanded in a combination of an actor and a task. This implies that all the characteristics involved in the characterization of the actor type as well as the task type need to be taken into account when determining a match.

We have developed a *framework for cognitive matchmaking* to determine if an actor of a specific type is suitable to fulfill a task of a specific type based on a cognitive match [7]. Several steps have to be completed before a match is determined. First, it is determined on what *levels* an actor supplies cognitive characteristics and a task demands cognitive characteristics. More specifically, the way how an actor supplies a cognitive characteristic can range from very bad to very good. In the same way, the levels on which a task demands a cognitive characteristic can range from very low to very high. These levels can be denoted by numerical values or linguistic values indicating how well an actor can supply a characteristic or to what extent a task demands it. Next, the levels are matched to determine how well supply and demand of each characteristic match. These results are used as input for the next step, in which each cognitive characteristic can be weighed to determine if one characteristic is more important than another when determining a cognitive match. Finally, the weighed characteristic match results are summated to generate a final match value.

## 4.3  Knowledge Quality Market

The level on which cognitive characteristics are supplied by actors may influence the quality of fulfilled knowledge intensive tasks [6]. If an actor fulfills a task, it is possible to conceive the quality of the *process* that has led to the fulfillment as well as the quality of the task *result* [1]. Quality of the task result refers to product factors and the extent to which they meet stakeholder demands. When viewing process quality from a cognitive standpoint, the quality factors of the application of cognitive characteristics during task execution can be considered. This can be dubbed as *cognitive process quality*. Simply put, an actor applies several cognitive characteristics during task execution. This application may vary in quality dependent of how well an actor is able to supply them. It can now be observed that quality factors are 'supplied' by means of the task result and the cognitive process. These factors are demanded by stakeholders of fulfilled knowledge intensive tasks. Supply and demand of quality can be *matched* to let product and process quality increase [6].

Our theoretical model of the knowledge quality market consists of three parts. First, it contains a *framework for qualitative matchmaking*, which is an adaptation of the framework for cognitive matchmaking in such way that it matches quality factors instead of cognitive characteristics [7]. Second, relations between the main concepts that are involved in influencing the quality of knowledge intensive task fulfillment and the roles that these concepts play in knowledge intensive work are clarified. This has been done by developing a conceptual model of quality factors and relating it with a conceptual model of cognitive characteristics. The five main concepts in the knowledge quality market that may influence the quality of task fulfillment are the actor type, the cognitive characteristic, the task type, the quality factor, and the stakeholder.

Third, the knowledge quality market model contributes to an understanding of the effects of changes to cognitive characteristics and quality factors during knowledge intensive work and the dependencies between the main concepts.

## 5  Validation

Phase 4 of the research strategy shown in section 3 includes several steps in which the theory has been validated. Each market model has been validated in different ways to concentrate on different aspects of the market models. The knowledge market model has been implemented in a Web-based application called 'Dexar', which is an abbreviation for Discovery and eXchange of Revealed knowledge [7]. This illustrates that a computer-based actor can enact one or more roles in the knowledge market. For example, if Dexar plays the role of broker it can assist the utilizer by matching supply and demand of knowledge assets. Dexar can also act as a transporter by interacting with the supplier and the utilizer. In the latter case, the utilizer can interact with Dexar to actually receive knowledge assets and to determine if the utilizer is satisfied with the received assets. Furthermore, knowledge exchange between the roles in the knowledge market has been studied by applying the knowledge market in a scenario for which a math teacher wishes to acquire knowledge on how to improve his knowledge collection capabilities on the Web about a specific mathematical topic.

The knowledge workers market model has been tested by means of a case study and the framework for cognitive matchmaking has been implemented in the cognitive matchmaker system. This system is a prototype Web-based application to match actors and tasks based on the supplied and demanded cognitive characteristics [7]. This validates that a working prototype can be realized that is founded on the framework for cognitive matchmaking. The knowledge workers market and the prototype system have been validated and evaluated in two real information systems engineering (ISE) projects as part of the case study. The first case is related with a completed ISE project at the company 'e-office'. This is a company specialized in providing computer-aided support for human actors to support them in their office work. The ISE project has been concerned with the development of an 'Action Reporting Tool' (ART for short) for an international provider of banking and insurance services to customers. The action reporting tool is a Web-based application that can generate risk reports for the user. This tool should assist risk management to better monitor and control insurance risks. This includes monitoring and controlling the risks themselves and also the actions of the actors involved in providing insurance services. The second case as part of the case study is related with an ISE project at 'Everest'. This is a company specialized in the modeling and automation of business processes. The customers of Everest can be found for a large part in the mortgage and insurance domain. The studied ISE project is concerned with the renewal of an 'international Automated Mortgage System' (iAMS for short) for an international provider of mortgage services. The upgrade of iAMS should enable a fully electronic workflow process that services the monetary transactions and the required securitization when enacting mortgage business processes. The case study indicated that allocation of tasks to the project members that were part of the studied projects could be improved by utilizing the prototype based on the framework for cognitive matchmaking. For instance, the ART project included software testing tasks that were performed by actors playing a software developer role. Introducing specific software tester roles in the project improved the match of testing tasks and actors that enacted a specific *software tester* role. In practice, the cognitive matchmaker system can be used to allocate tasks based on cognitive matchmaking before a project starts, to allocate additional (newly introduced) tasks during runtime of a project or after the project has finished to evaluate the match results.

The knowledge quality market contains quality factors to verbalize the quality of 'knowledge products' as the result of knowledge intensive execution task fulfillment and to verbalize the quality of the supplied cognitive characteristics during the process of task execution. Specific quality metrics are part of the knowledge quality market to actually measure these quality factors. For instance, the *completeness* factor can be measured by a metric that divides the knowledge assets that are deemed applicable for a specific task by the total amount of knowledge assets that are the result of task fulfillment. For a full list of task quality factors and metrics see [7]. In the application of the knowledge quality market we have measured the product and process quality of a task that involved the design of a *use case* in which a Web-based application creates a risk report for the user [7].

# 6   Conclusions and Future Work

Three developments served as the basis for the initiation of this research. First, knowledge intensive tasks in organizations thriving on knowledge become increasingly complex. Second, actors that perform such tasks experience an increase in cognitive load. Third, the desired quality of task performance and the produced task results are at stake due to the aforementioned two developments. Following from these observations it has been stated that the notions of knowledge, cognition, and quality are interwoven with knowledge intensive task fulfillment. The field of knowledge management indicated that knowledge exchange within and across organizations can be powered by mechanisms that are also displayed by markets that exchange tangible goods. This principle has inspired us to study how supply and demand of intangible assets such as knowledge, cognitive characteristics, and quality factors can be matched based on markets. Bridging the gap between supply and demand of the three aforementioned core notions can improve the match between required and offered assets in the process of task fulfillment. The knowledge need of a potential utilizer in the knowledge market can be diminished in a better way due to the broker and transporter roles that mediate between a supplier and a utilizer. Organizational task allocation is improved by applying the knowledge workers market in organizations. The knowledge quality market enables that stakeholder demands for knowledge intensive tasks are met by understanding their quality requirements. Eventually, the application of the three markets may decrease cognitive load, and improve core competencies and quality.

There are various suggestions that can be made for future research which have not been studied yet. Some suggestions for future work related to *static* and *dynamic* learning can be mentioned here. By implementing static learning in a market model the intention is to indicate what is necessary to learn by an actor to reach a goal. If static learning is implemented in the knowledge market, suggestions can be provided to an actor that enacts the utilizer role. These suggestions can indicate what that actor should learn to successfully fulfill a qualifying task that is performed by the actor. If static learning is implemented in the knowledge workers market, suggestions can be provided to an actor that supplies cognitive characteristics while performing a task. These suggestions can indicate what that actor should learn to successfully fulfill that task. If static learning is implemented in the knowledge quality market, suggestions can be provided how certain quality levels should be reached to satisfy a stakeholder's requirements. These suggestions can indicate what an actor should learn to reach the required quality levels while performing a knowledge intensive task. An actor can be led through a personal learning process dependent of, e.g., an actor's function profile or the goals of an actor by taking the notion of *dynamic learning* into account. Translated to the specific markets, dynamic learning can provide suggestions for an actor to indicate what an actor should learn in each market to reach the actor's ambitions or goals possibly described in a function profile.

# References

1. Allison, I., Merali, Y.: Software process improvement as emergent change: A structurational analysis. Information and Software Technology 49, 668–681 (2007)
2. Desouza, K.C.: Strategic contributions of game rooms to knowledge management: Some prelimenary insights. Information and Management 41, 63–74 (2003)
3. Hayman, A., Elliman, T.: Human elements in information system design for knowledge workers. International Journal of Information Management 20, 297–309 (2000)
4. Hsu, G.J.Y., Lin, Y.-H., Wei, Z.-Y.: Competition policy for technological innovation in an era of knowledge-based economy. Knowledge-Based Systems 21, 826–832 (2008)
5. Liang, T.Y.: The basic entity model: A fundamental theoretical model of information and information processing. Information Processing & Management 30, 647–661 (1994)
6. Meiran, N.: Modeling cognitive control in task-switching. Psychological Research 63, 234–249 (2000)
7. Overbeek, S.J.: Bridging Supply and Demand for Knowledge Intensive Tasks – Based on Knowledge, Cognition, and Quality. PhD thesis, Radboud University Nijmegen, The Netherlands (2009)
8. Sol, H.G.: Simulation in Information Systems. PhD thesis, University of Groningen, The Netherlands (1982)
9. Yin, R.K.: Case Study Research: Design and Methods, 3rd edn. Sage Publications, Thousand Oaks (2003)

# Real-Time Robust Adaptive Modeling and Scheduling for an Electronic Commerce Server

Bing Du[1] and Chun Ruan[2]

[1] School of Electrical and Information Engineering, University of Sydney, Australia
bing@ee.usyd.edu.au
[2] School of Computing and Mathematics, University of Western Sydney, Australia
c.ruan@uws.edu.au

**Abstract.** With the increasing importance and pervasiveness of Internet services, it is becoming a challenge for the proliferation of electronic commerce services to provide performance guarantees under extreme overload. This paper describes a real-time optimization modeling and scheduling approach for performance guarantee of electronic commerce servers. We show that an electronic commerce server may be simulated as a multi-tank system. A robust adaptive server model is subject to unknown additive load disturbances and uncertain model matching. Overload control techniques are based on adaptive admission control to achieve timing guarantees. We evaluate the performance of the model using a complex simulation that is subjected to varying model parameters and massive overload.

**Keywords:** robust adaptive control, modeling, real-time scheduling.

## 1 Introduction

The electronic commerce servers have become a complex and vital resource for many critical business applications, such as stock-trading, banking, and business transactions, in which the resource requirements and server load are very difficult to predict. These businesses rely on these servers and its performance management. They typically combine of an HTTP server and a database server. For many Electronic Commerce Systems-based mission-critical applications, the services are required to achieve robust performance guarantees and overload management on a wide range of services, in which load is subjected to huge variations and unpredictability. More important requests should be served more promptly. Unfortunately, the traditional approach for achieving performance guarantees in computing systems works well only when workload and resource knowledge are previously known. A common approach that applies fixed resource limits to overload control often leads to underutilised resources or overload under widely fluctuating loads. When the amount of requests for content exceeds the capacity for serving them, this results in overload and can render the website unusable. Many concurrency models and operating systems do not focus on overload management that provide responsive service to clients when

T. Di Noia and F. Buccafurri (Eds.): EC-Web 2009, LNCS 5692, pp. 205–216, 2009.

users make unpredictable web requests or when demand outstrips the capacity of the web servers. We focus on the server system itself. When the server is overloaded, the server's response times may lead to unacceptable delays, and exhaustion of resources may cause connection failures. The performance of traditional systems relies on worst-case estimates of workload and resource availability. It is infeasible to handle serious overload by overprovision of the server resources demanded. Furthermore, services themselves are becoming more complex; service logic tends to change rapidly; and services are increasingly hosted on general-purpose facilities. We must apply new design techniques to manage this load as the demand for electronic commerce grows.

In recent years, control theories have been increasingly applied to Internet servers [25] as a foundation for providing performance guarantees. The main motivation has been to develop robust techniques for controlling different resources, different metrics and types of QoS guarantees. In [27], the control theoretical approach was used to deal with web-server resource management. Both memory and CPU utilisation in web servers can achieve absolute convergence guarantees by multi-input, multi-output (MIMO) control [28]. Feedback control and fuzzy control were applied to input queue length control with admission control in [23, 24]. A double queue structure is applied to performance admission control in a web analytical model [26].

Disadvantages of these approaches are that they cannot guarantee more prompt response times for more important requests. The main obstacle that prevents control theories from being applied effectively in computing systems is how to construct a computing model that works in open and unpredictable environments. Existing feedback scheduling approaches are difficult to guarantee robust performance properties, as they only use a simplistic maximum constant model and "classical" control theory to design a complex real-time scheduling system. However, when the electronic commerce server dynamics are complex and poorly modeled, or when the performance specifications are particularly stringent, no solution is forthcoming. High-performance electronic commerce server should undergo drastic changes in their application. It cannot be modelled as a constant and handled by constant-gain feedback control.

In this paper, we extended our prior work [1,15,18,21,22] and propose a new robust model reference adaptive control (RMRAC) [16, 17] design framework for modelling, detecting and responding overload conditions, and achieving performance guarantees. This sophisticated controller can learn and accommodate changes in the server environment. Robust adaptive control scheme combination of an online parameter estimator, which provides estimates of the unknown parameters at each instant of time, with indirect adaptive control that is motivated from the known parameter. The electronic commerce server parameters are estimated online and used to calculate the controller parameters at each time t. The main contribution of this paper can be summarized as follows: 1.Integrate queuing theory, robust adaptive control, and performance control strategies to provide robust QoS performance and response-time delay guarantees. Parameter estimator generates parameter estimates online and combines with a control law, in order to control classes of electronic commerce servers whose parameters are completely unknown and /or could change with time in an unpredictable manner. 2.Analyzing how to model a electronic commerce server with the multi liquid tank model and demonstrating that the dynamics characteristics of web server's queuing structures are similar with multi-tank liquid system. 3.An adaptive architecture included utilization controlling and delay controlling virtual servers.

The rest of this paper is organized as follows. In Section 2, we briefly describe background about the operation of a typical electronic commerce server, present its simulation model of dynamic two-tank system. In section 3, we apply modern control theories to systematically design controllers to satisfy the desired performance of the electronic commerce server. The simulation experimental evaluations are presented in section 4. The chapter concludes and remaining challenges in section 5.

## 2  Electronic Commerce Service Architecture

Electronic commerce server usually adopts a multithreaded model. The client requests aggregate at a server across a communication network. The difference between the arrival and served requests is the number of requests queued in client request queue. The requests are further queued up in different queues by the server. In a multithreaded server, each thread processes incoming requests, executes according to arriving sequence of client requests and generates responses. A kernel entity reads client requests from an input queue and hands them to different worker threads that are independent schedulable entities. Worker threads are queued for CPU and get the CPU to execute when the CPU schedules them. The CPU scheduling policy determines the order that threads get the CPU to execute. Each thread processes incoming requests and generates responses. The thread at the top of a ready queue executes for a particular time quantum or until it is blocked. A worker thread enable request processing to access server resource. Each resource has a queue and is available to the thread at the top of the queue. The corresponding thread re-enter the CPU ready queue and run again. The worker thread sends a response back into outgoing network queue for transmission to the client when request processing is done.

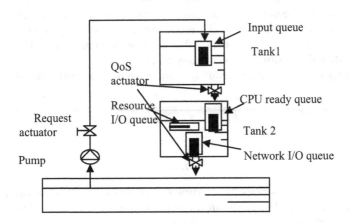

**Fig. 1.** Two-tank System Model of a Web Server

When control theory is applied to analyse and design an electronic commerce server, a server model is required. It is very difficult to analyse and model a service precisely, as there are no physical relationships between the system input and output. However, time-related performance metrics in software systems such as delay, response time and latency are related to the queue, which can be simulated as liquid flowing into a tank. A lower level of liquid implies shorter delays. The progress of client requests into the server queues is similar to a fluid flow into a two-tank system, as illustrated in Figure 1. They have the same dynamics due to their intrinsic queuing structure.

The client requests aggregate at a server across a communication network. A succession of client requests arrives at a server can be mapped to fluid that is conveyed from a basin into input queue by a pump. The difference between the arrivaland served requests is the number of requests queued in the input queue. The input queue is viewed as the upper-level tank 1 that receives the requests waiting to be processed. When the server operates at a nontrivial load, the input queue cannot accept all client requests. The request actuator simulates to decide which requests are allowed or rejected into the input queue.

The requests are further queued up in different queues by the server. In a multi-threaded server, each thread processes incoming requests, executes them according to the arriving sequence of client requests and generates responses. A kernel entity reads client requests from an input queue and hands them to different worker threads that are independent schedulable entities. Worker threads are queued for the CPU and obtain the CPU's execution when the CPU schedules them. The CPU scheduling policy determines the order in which the threads obtain the CPU's execution. Each thread processes incoming requests and generates responses. The thread at the top of a ready queue executes for a particular time quantum or until it is blocked. A worker thread enables request-processing to access the server resources. Each resource has a queue and is available to the thread at the top of the queue. The corresponding thread re-enters the CPU ready queue and runs again. The worker thread sends a response back into the outgoing network queue for transmission to the client when the request processing has been completed. The process can be mapped to dequeued requests flowing into a liquid tank. The CPU's ready queue and outgoing network queue are modelled as a lower-level liquid tank 2 that needs to be controlled. The resource I/O queue is modelled as a structure uncertainty block.

The transfer function of the scheduling system can be now written as follows:

$$\frac{U(s)}{R(s)} = \frac{K^*}{(T_1 s + 1)(T_2 s + 1)} \tag{1}$$

Where:

$$K^* = \frac{1}{L}\sqrt{\frac{2U_0}{g}}$$

The two-tank system describes the dynamics of requests, but does not make assumptions on how individual requests are prioritised. The queuing theory and real-time scheduling theory have well-explained foundations such as queue length, total workload, utilisation and delay. Development of control loops has combined with real-time scheduling and queuing analysis to produce the desired client delay.

The bottleneck resource limits the capacity of the server. The utilization of the bottleneck resource is $U = \sum_i C_i / D_i$ , where $D_i$ is the deadline of i th request or the maximum tolerable server response times, $C_i$ is the amount of the bottleneck resource consumed by i th request and U is the summation of all current requests. Deadline monotonic scheduling theory [7] has been recently proved that a group of aperiodic tasks with individual arrival times, computation times, and relative deadlines or maximum response times will always meet their deadline constraints as long as U < 0.58 [14]. This result can be used as a reference value to guarantee a server to meet all request deadlines if utilization does not exceed the upper bound.

Another important performance metric for time-critical web-based applications is delay control problem. Delay of a request includes connection delay that denotes the time interval for establishing a TCP connection with a server process, the processing delay which the server complete local computations, and the network delays that transmit these requests and response over an established TCP connection. The connection delay may be significant even when the server is not in overload conditions and all processes are tied up with existing connections

A electronic commerce server can be separated to multiple virtual servers, which associate with hosted independent sites. An advantage of grouping virtual servers is better reusing extra server capacity than physically separated servers. The reference utilization $= aR_{max\ i} + bW_{max\ i}$ will guarantee virtual server i to meet its throughput [13]. The utilization U of the server is the utilization sum of all virtual server residing on the same machine, $U = \sum_i u_i$ . To meet service response time of individual requests, the reference utilization sum of all virtual servers should be less than 0.58.

The performance attributes of QoS-aware web servers depend on the class of the requests. The virtual server supports different client's priorities. The more important requests receive higher priority and better service. These requests have QoS guaranteed first. The lower priority requests are degraded first.

## 3 RMRAC Control Framework for Web Server

In this section, we present robust electronic commerce server architecture (as shown in Figure 2) to provide the above performance guarantees. Figure 3 shows the basic structure of RMRAC. The plant transfer function is Gp(k, $\theta_p^*$ ), where $\theta_p^*$ is a vector with all the coefficients of Gp. The controller transfer function is C(z, $\theta_c^*$ ) , where $\theta_c^*$ is a vector with the coefficients of C(z). We design the transfer function C(z, $\theta_c^*$ ), and $\theta_c^*$ so that the closed-loop transfer function of the plant from the reference input r to y$_p$ is equal to W$_m$(z); i.e.,

F is a function of the plant parameter $\theta_p^*$ to satisfy the matching equation (2).

$$\frac{y_p(z)}{r(z)} = W_m(z) = \frac{y_m(z)}{r(z)} \qquad (2)$$

The goal of our architecture is to maintain all client requests' performance metrics around their targets. The overload management has a variety of performance metrics. We combine CPU utilisation and delay as a realistic system performance. CPU utilisation performance can be used to model a robust stability web-service system. However, the relationship between the total requested utilisation and the controlled utilisation U is saturation nonlinear when the requested utilisation is larger than 0.58. When the server is severely overloaded, the utilisation controller cannot provide utilisation adjustment for all requests. We have to reject some clients unless the web server limits the maximum client number that can be served by a single server concurrently. Delay metrics comprise an intuitive measure of the perceived system performance. Clients should be provided with delay service guarantees. The delay is easily captured by the experience of the service performance. When the utilisation is at saturation, the service differentiation controller will provide delay guarantees to high-priority classes. The system administrator can specify a target value for the delay time based on the request type or user classification. Controllers implement both the robust performance of the transient-state response and the steady-state error for delay and utilisation. The architecture is composed of two RMRAC, a adaptive observer, an admission actuator, a QoS actuator, two performance monitors, a capacity allocator, a comparator, a queuing model predictor, a connection scheduler, a delay reference allocator, n virtual servers, and n fixed pool of virtual server processes. We describe the design of the components as follows.

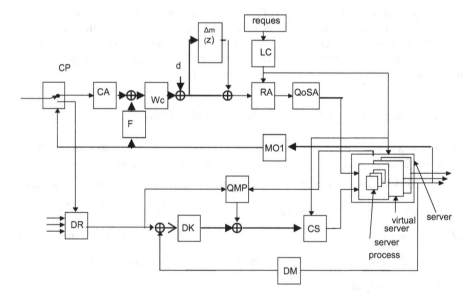

**Fig. 2.** The utilization and delay RMRAC control architecture

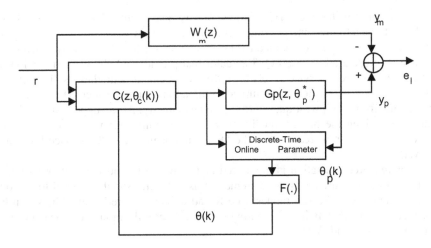

**Fig. 3.** RMRAC control architecture

The comparator (CP) compares the sampled connection delay of the highest priority class with the desired delay and dynamically switches between the performance controller and delay controller. If the delay guarantee of the highest priority class is violated, the server switches to the delay controller by CP; otherwise, the CP switches from the delay controller to the performance controller.

The RMRAC controllers Wc is responsible for maintaining the machine server QoS reference that provides guarantees for all request deadlines. Virtual capacity is requested utilisation for each virtual server. If there are n virtual servers, the initial target capacity of each virtual server is 0.58/n. The capacity adjustor (CA) allocates the appropriate QoS balance between virtual servers by a new reference, so that the excess resources available when a virtual server does not consume all its allotted resources are made available to other virtual servers. This allows them to exceed their initial target capacity allocation to avoid client degradation.

Input requests can be classified based on the requested content, the site name embedded in the URL string, or other information. A load classifier (LC) identifies and puts the requests to the virtual server that is responsible for serving requests.

Suppose there are N priority classes within a virtual server and every request belongs to a class j ($1 \leq j \leq m$). The priority 0 is highest, and priority m is lowest. Each class j is assigned a desired delay $D_j(k)$ by the delay reference classifier (DRC). The connection delay $C_j(k)$ at the sampling instant k is defined as the average connection delay of all established connections of class j in time ((k-1)T, kT) seconds, where T is a sampling period. A delay guarantee requires that $C_j(k) \leq D_j(k)$.

The request actuator (RA) is used to prevent web servers from being overwhelmed by overload. It will reduce the amount of work when overloaded. Request control decides which clients may access the server and which clients are denied service concurrently, and whether a service should be admitted or a request rejected, depending on request utilisation. If the client is rejected, the server will return a message to the client, informing it that the service is temporarily unavailable. The actuators choose the clients to be admitted and provide performance guarantees.

In a web server, the QoS actuator (QoSA) can also offer further service level adjustment. We use a table-based QoS actuator that provides an abbreviated version of content. The different service levels have different content degradations. The level 0 denotes all requests rejected and returned to the admission controller. The level 1,…, k represents from the lowest quality to the highest quality. At the upper extreme k, all requests are given the highest quality service. Server utilisation and the amount of load on a server will increase when the QoS actuator increases the service level and vice versa.

Server resource utilisation is monitored and provided by most operating systems. But utilisation measurements are extremely noisy. A filter should be used to smooth these measurements. Served request rate R and delivered byte bandwidth W can be measured very accurately in a computing server. Server utilisation U can be expressed as a function of R and W [19]:

$$U = a\,Rs\, +\, b\,Ws \tag{3}$$

where a and b are constants. a = 830us, and b = 33us/kB can be computed by a linear regression.

Server response time relates to service rate and server capacity. Queuing theory offers a model that is used to determine a specified average delay by computing the current service rate. The service rate that is given by the queuing model can meet a particular response time. To achieve the desired service rate, we can allocate a fraction of CPU capacity to the server or change the dynamic voltage scaling (DVS). Dynamic voltage scaling (DVS) is a promising method for embedded systems to exploit multiple voltage and frequency levels and a standard technique for managing the power consumption of a system [151]. For an M/M/1 queue with arrival rate $\lambda$ and service rate $\mu_s$, connection delay D for the clients is computed by queuing theory. This model is called a queuing predictor.

$$D = \frac{\lambda}{\mu_s(\mu_s - \lambda)} \tag{4}$$

where $\lambda < \mu_s$.

The queuing actuator controls the delays in different client request classes by listening to the well-known port and computing the outputs from the queuing predictor and H∞ controller. In the sampling period (kT, (k+1)T), the process budget Bk(k) is the number of server processes allocated to class k. Adjusting the process budget can control the connection delay of a server class. The connection delay of a server class becomes shorter when the process budget of this class is increased. The actuator allocates server processes for different classes by using an adaptive proportional share policy. Every class j (0 ≤ j ≤ N) is assigned at most server process budgets Bk(k) in the kth sampling period. The process budgets are satisfied in the priority order. High-priority classes always satisfy the process budgets before low-priority classes and achieve guarantee violations. For each class k, the actuator maintains a (FIFO) connection queue Qk that holds the connections of class k before they are allocated server processes, and a process counter Rk that is the number of processes allocated to class k. The queuing actuator classifies the newly accepted connection and inserts the connection to the scheduling queue corresponding to its class. If class k has the highest priority and a server process becomes available, a connection at the front of a scheduling queue Qk will be dispatched. The H controller dynamically adjusts the process budgets with the non-pre-emptive scheduling to maintain the desired delays. The server process in a fixed pool of server processes reads the connection descriptors from the queuing actuator. A server process reports the queuing actuator and is available to process new connections if a server process closes a TCP connection.

At each sampling instant, the delay monitor (DM) is invoked to compute the average connection delay of all classes at a virtual server. The delay controller uses them to compute new process proportions.

The delay controller (DK) that inputs error between reference delay and measured delay corrects the actuator input until the error is eliminated. The controller computes new process budgets, which are used by the queuing actuator to reallocate server processes and to adjust the server delay of each class to the desired set value.

For each virtual server with N service classes, there are n delay controllers to implement delay guarantees. A separate delay controller controls the delay of every class k. The controller should increase the process budget to allocate more processes to class k if the measured server delay is larger than the reference delay in overload conditions. However, delay controllers cannot control the delay of every class if the sum of the computed process budgets of all classes exceeds the total number of server processes. This is called queuing delay control saturation. The lower-priority requests will be rejected to guarantee the request delay of the highest priority classes.

When the server is not severely overloaded, the RMRAC controller Wc control architecture, depicted in Figure 7.3, can keep the server utilisation at 0.58. The server can be approximated by a two-tank model. The utilisation control loop measures server utilisation and determines which requests may receive service at the current time. The amount of the subset can be adjusted to maintain the utilisation at the desired value.

## 4  Design of the Controller

In this section, we apply the RMRAC framework to design the controller. The system controller design can be separated two parts. When the highest priority request class satisfies the service delay, RMRAC are used to keep most service requests to satisfy their performance guarantees. Otherwise, the queuing delay controller keeps the most important or highest priority requests to satisfy the service delay.

### 4.1  MRAC Controller

We apply MRAC controller to design the utilization controller for a electronic server. The server is separated n virtual servers and reference utilization of virtual server is 0.58/n. The capacity adjustor can reassign virtual reference utilizations for each virtual server as following.

$$\text{If } \sum_i u_i > 0.58$$

$$u_i = 0.58/n;$$

else if $0.58/n - u_i$ (measured) $> 0$ && $0.58/n - u_k$ (measured)$<0$

$$u_k = 1.16/n - u_i \text{ (measured) ;}$$

MRAC controller of scheduling systems can be described as following [20]:

$$Q(z) = \frac{\Lambda(z)c_0^*}{\Lambda(z) - \theta_1^{*T} \partial(z),} \;;\; F(z) = -\frac{\theta_2^{*T} \partial(z) + \theta_3^* \Lambda(z)}{c_0^* \Lambda(z),} \tag{5}$$

## 4.2 Queuing Delay Controller

When the server is overload, the utilization for each virtual server is assigned to higher priority classes. We can still use tanks model for the classes in each virtual server. The desired average reference delay $D_r$ and the estimated arrival rate $\lambda$ can be used to compute the corresponding service rate $\mu_s$

$$\mu_s = \frac{\lambda}{2} + \sqrt{\frac{\lambda^2}{4} + \frac{\lambda}{D_r}} \tag{6}$$

Then, the queuing delay controller applies RMRAC robust feedback controller that uses actual delay measurements and reference delay to adjust this feed-forward signal. The objective of the delay control is to keep the service delay of high priority classes as close as possible to a desired reference delay. Class utilization sensors monitor utilizations of all classes in virtual servers. Class admission actuators accept the highest priority class and the classes that add requested utilizations not more than 0.58/n in order of priority.

## 5 Simulation Evaluation

The computational tools available in MATLAB were utilized in the controller design. The maximum number of server processes is configured to 128. The sampling period is set to 1 second. In this simulation, we use a step function as a sudden load change that is more difficult to control than small incremental changes. The request rate on the server was increased suddenly from zero to a rate that overloads the server. The reference utilization is set to 0.56. The server works as two virtual servers. The reference utilization of each virtual server is 0.28. In the beginning of the run, 100 users from class 0, 200 users from class 1 and 200 from class 2 generate requests to the server. This can be used to simulate that 50 users from class 0, 100 users from class 1 and 100 users from class 2 generate requests to each virtual server. Another 50 users from class 0 generate requests that are simulated as 50 users request to virtual server 1 at time 20. The requests of class 1 reduce to 175, which are simulated as 75 users request to virtual server 2 at time 25. The reference delays for class 0, 1 and 2 to the delay controller are 2, 4, and 6 second. The results of the simulations shown that the performances was successful around their target. The isolation mechanism allows two virtual servers with individual rate and bandwidth guarantees.

If only considered delay control, the delay of class 2 on virtual server 1 will increase to 47 sec that is almost 6.4 times delay time of our controllers. It fails to provide delay guarantee for lower priority class because the total budgets of all classes exceed the total number of server processes. The delay control can not adjust processes control saturation.

## 6  Conclusions

In this chapter, we apply the RMRAC framework to develop a robust model and adaptive architecture for electronic commerce server performance control and service delay guarantees. Server model approximates server components with a two tank system that includes many uncertainly components. The contribution of this work is the architecture based on robust adaptive control and queuing model predictor that enforce server utilization and delay guarantees for different classes on virtual servers. In contrast with electronic commerce server delay control that only control delay, our mechanism integrates queuing theory and robust control theory to avoid delay control saturation, and gives a systematically platform to investigate electronic commerce server model. A performance evaluation using simulation demonstrates that RMRAC robust adaptive control can provide robust request utilization and request response time for electronic commerce servers.

## References

1. Du, B., Levy, D.C.: A Robust Modelling and Overload Control for Web Servers. In: Proceedings of The Seventh International Conference on Information Integration and Web-based Applications & Services, Kuala Lumpur, pp. 965–975 (2005)
2. Lu. C., Stankovic. J.A., Abdelzaher. T.F., Tao. G., Son. S.H., Marley. M.,: Performance specifications and metrics for adaptive real-time systems. In: Proceedings of the 21th IEEE Real-Time Systems Symposium,Orlando, FL (December 2000)
3. Lu, C., Stankovic, J.A., Tao, G., Son, S.H.: Feedback Control Real-Time Scheduling: Framework, Modeling, and Algorithms. Real-Time Systems Journal 23(1/2), 85–126 (2002)
4. Lu, C., Abdelzaher, T., Stankovic, J., Son, S.: A feedback control approach for guaranteeing relative delays in web servers. In: IEEE Real-Time Technology and Applications Symposium, TaiPei, Taiwain (June 2001)
5. Steere, D., Goel, A., Gruenberg, J., McNamee, D., Pu, C., Walpole, J.: A feedbackdriven proportion allocator for real-time scheduling. In: Proceedings of the Third usenix-osdi. Pub-usenix (February 1999)
6. Chetto, H., Chetto, M.: Some results of the earliest deadline scheduling algorithm. IEEE Transactions on Software Engineering 15(10), 1261–1269 (1989)
7. Duda, K., Cheriton, D.: Borrowed-Virtual-Time (BVT) Scheduling: Supporting Latency-Sensitive Threads in a General-Purpose Scheduler. In: Proceedings of the Seventeenth ACM Symposium on Operating Systems Principles, Kiawah Island Resort, SC, pp. 261–276 (1999)
8. Li, B., Nahrstedt, K.A.: Control theoretic model for quality of service adaptations. In: Proceedings of Sixth International Workshop on Quality of Service, pp. 145–153 (1998)

9. Bianchi, L., Campbell, A., Liao, R.: On Utility-Fair Adaptive Services in Wireless Networks. In: Proceedings of Sixth International Workshop on Quality of Service, May 1998, pp. 256–267 (1998)
10. Open Management Group, in: Real-Time CORBA Specification (Version 1.1) (August 2002)
11. Abdelzaher, T.T., Shin, K.G., Bhatti, N.: Performance guarantees for web server end-systems: A control-theoretical approach. IEEE Transactions on Parallel and Distributed Systems (January 2002)
12. Nakajima, T.: Resource reservation for adaptive qos mapping in real-time mach. In: Sixth International Workshop on Parallel and Distributed Real-Time Systems (WPDRTS) (April 1998)
13. Abdelzaher, T., Shin, K.G.: QoS provisioning with qcontracts in web and multimedia servers. In: IEEE Real-Time Systems Symposium, Phoenix, jArizona (December 1999)
14. Abdelzaher, T.F., Lu, C.: Schedulability analysis and utilization bounds for highly scalable real-time services. In: Real-Time Technology and Applications Symposium, Phoenix, Arizona (June 2001)
15. Du, B., Ruan, C.: FEL-H Robust Control Real-Time Scheduling. Journal of Software Engineering and Applications (JSEA) 2(1), 60–65 (2009)
16. Athans, M., Fekri, S., Pascoal, A.: Issues on robust adaptive feedback control. In: Proceedings of the 16th IFAC World Congress, Prague (2005)
17. Wang, R., Safonov, M.G.: Stability of unfalsified adaptive control using multiple controllers. In: Proceedings of the American Control Conference, pp. 3162–3167 (2005)
18. Du, B., Ruan, C.: Robust Feedback Scheduling in Distributed Embedded Real-Time Systems. In: The Proceedings of the 6th IEEE/IFIP International Conference On Embedded and Ubiquitous Computing (EUC 2008), Shanghai, China, pp. 90–96 (2008)
19. Abdelzaher, T.F.: QoS-Adaptation in Real-Time Systems. PhD thesis, University of Michigan, Ann Arbor, Michigan (August 1999)
20. Loannou, P., Fidan, B.: Adaptive Control Tutorial. SIAM, Philadelphia (2006)
21. Du, B., Levy, D.: H∞ Robust Scheduling Design Methodology in Real-Time Systems. In: The Proceedings of the 2003 International Conferenceon Embedded Systems and Applications, USA, pp. 285–291 (2003)
22. Du, B., Levy, D.: A Robust Control Real-Time Scheduling Design. Special issue: Advanced Control and Real-Time Systems of DCEMP journal 13(3-4), 335–340 (2005)
23. Diao, Y., Hellerstein, J.L., Parekh, S.: Using fuzzy control to maximize profits in service level management. IBM Syst. J. 41(3), 403–420 (2002)
24. Parekh, S., Gandhi, N., Hellerstein, J., Tilbury, D., Jayram, T., Bigus, J.: Using control theory to achieve service level objectives in performance management. In: IFIP/IEEE International Symposium on Integrated Network Management, Seattle, WA, pp. 127–141 (2001)
25. Chen, H., Mohapatra, P.: Session-based overload control in QoS-aware Web servers. In: Proceedings of IEEE INFOCOM 2002, New York, June 2002, pp. 98–203 (2002)
26. Chen, X., Chen, H., Mohapatra, P.: An admission control scheme for predictable server response time for Web accesses. In: Proceeding of the 10th World Wide Web Conference, Hong Kong, May 2001, pp. 545–554 (2001)
27. Abdelzaher, T., Shin, K.G., Bhatti, N.: Performance guarantees for web server end-systems: A control-theoretical approach. IEEE Transactions on Parallel and Distributed Systems, 121–130 (January 2002)
28. Diao, Y., Gandhi, N., Hellerstein, S., Parekh, D., Tilbury, M.: MIMO control of an Apache Web server: Modeling and controller design. In: Proceedings of American Control Conference, Anchorage, AK, May 2002, pp. 4922–4927 (2002)

# Content-Based Personalization Services Integrating Folksonomies

Cataldo Musto, Fedelucio Narducci, Pasquale Lops,
Marco de Gemmis, and Giovanni Semeraro

Department of Computer Science,
University of Bari "Aldo Moro", Italy
{musto,narducci,lops,degemmis,semeraro}@di.uniba.it
http://www.di.uniba.it/

**Abstract.** Basic content-based personalization consists in matching up the attributes of a user profile, in which preferences and interests are stored, with the attributes of a content object. The Web 2.0 (r)evolution has changed the game for personalization, from 'elitary' Web 1.0, written by few and read by many, to web content generated by everyone (*user-generated content* - UGC), since the role of people has evolved from passive consumers of information to that of active contributors.

One of the forms of UGC that has drawn most attention of the research community is folksonomy, a taxonomy generated by users who collaboratively annotate and categorize resources of interests with freely chosen keywords called tags.

FIRSt (<u>F</u>olksonomy-based <u>I</u>tem <u>R</u>ecommender sy<u>St</u>em) is a content-based recommender system developed at the University of Bari which integrates UGC (through social tagging) in a classic content-based model, letting users express their preferences for items by entering a numerical rating as well as to annotate rated items with free tags. FIRSt is capable of providing recommendations for items in several domains (e.g., movies, music, books), provided that descriptions of items are available as text documents (e.g. plot summaries, reviews, short abstracts). This paper describes the system general architecture and user modeling approach, showing how this recommendation model has been applied to recommend the artworks located at the Vatican Picture Gallery (Pinacoteca Vaticana), providing users with a personalized museum tour tailored on their tastes.

**Keywords:** Content-based Recommender Systems, Web 2.0, Folksonomy, Machine Learning, Semantics.

## 1 Introduction

The amount of information available on the Web and in Digital Libraries is increasing over time. In this context, the role of user modeling and personalized information access is becoming crucial: users need a personalized support in sifting through large amount of retrieved information according to their interests.

T. Di Noia and F. Buccafurri (Eds.): EC-Web 2009, LNCS 5692, pp. 217–228, 2009.

Information filtering systems, relying on this idea, adapt their behavior to individual users by learning their preferences during the interaction in order to construct a profile of the user that can be later exploited in selecting relevant items. Indeed, content personalization basically consists in matching up the attributes of a user profile, in which preferences and interests are stored, against the attributes of a content object.

Recently, Web 2.0 (r)evolution has changed the game for personalization, from 'elitary' Web 1.0, written by few and read by many, to web content generated by everyone (*user-generated content* - UGC), since the role of people has evolved from passive consumers of information to that of active contributors.

UGC refers to various kinds of media content, publicly available, that are produced by end-users. For example, on Amazon.com the majority of content is prepared by administrators, but numerous user reviews of the products being sold are submitted by regular visitors to the site. Similarly, collaborative platforms like YouTube, Wikipedia, Flickr, Del.icio.us, Photobucket, although supplying heterogeneous content, are completely founded on data freely created by users.

In [3] we began an analysis of UGC impact (namely, tags impact) in recommender systems. The main outcome of that work was that UGC integration in a content-based recommender system causes an increase of the predictive accuracy in the process of filtering relevant items for users.

In this work we will continue this analysis proving how this higher accuracy showed by recommender systems can be exploited for personalization goals in a real-world application. FIRSt (First Item Recommender SysTem) is a content-based recommender system developed at the University of Bari which integrates UGC (through social tagging) in a classic content-based model, letting users to express their preferences for items by entering a numerical rating as well as to annotate rated items with free tags. FIRSt is capable of providing recommendations for items in several domains (e.g., movies, music, books), provided that descriptions of items are available as text documents (e.g. plot summaries, reviews, short abstracts). We exposed FIRSt basic features through a set of web services, and we exploited them in a museum personalization scenario, letting Vatican Picture Gallery visitors receive suggestions about artworks they could be interested in and tailoring museum tours on their tastes.

This research has been conducted within the CHAT project (Cultural Heritage fruition and e-learning applications of new Advanced multimodal Technologies), that aims at developing new systems and services for multimodal fruition of cultural heritage content. Data has been gathered from the collections of the Vatican Picture Gallery, for which both images and detailed textual information of paintings are available, and letting users involved in the study both rate and annotate them with tags.

The paper is organized as follows. Section 2 introduces the general problem of information filtering and recommender systems; the architecture of FIRSt is described in Section 3 whereas Section 4 focuses the attention on design and development of web services to expose FIRSt functionalities. The experimental session carried out to evaluate the effectiveness of implemented web services is presented in Section 5. Related work are briefly analyzed in Section 6, while conclusions and directions for future work are drawn in the last section.

## 2  Information Filtering and Recommender Systems

As proved by the continuous growth of web sites which embody recommender systems as a way of personalizing their content for users, nowadays these systems represent the main field of application of principles and techniques coming from Information Filtering (IF) [9].

As IF techniques usually perform a progressive removal of non-relevant content according to the information stored in a user profile, recommendation algorithms process information about customer interests - acquired in an explicit (e.g., letting users express their opinion about items) or implicit (e.g., studying some behavioural features) way - and exploit this data to generate a list of recommended items, guiding users in a personalized way to interesting or useful objects in a large space of possible options [4].

Among different recommendation techniques that have already been put forward in studies on this matter, the collaborative and content-based filtering approaches are the most widely adopted to date.

Content-based systems analyze a set of documents, usually textual descriptions of the items previously rated by an individual user, and build a model or profile of user interests based on the features of the objects rated by that user [8]. In this approach static content associated to items (the plot of a film, the description of an artwork, etc.) is usually exploited. The profile is then used to recommend new relevant items.

Collaborative recommender systems differ from content-based ones in that user opinions are used, instead of content. User ratings about objects are gathered and stored in a centralized or distributed database. To provide recommendations to user X, the system firstly computes the neighborhood of that user (i.e. the subset of users that have a taste similar to X). Similarity in taste is measured by computing the closeness of ratings for objects that were rated by both users. The system then recommends objects that users in X's neighborhood indicated to like, provided that they have not yet been rated by X.

Although each type of filtering method has its own weaknesses and strengths [1,12], in this work we focused our attention only on a single class of recommenders, introducing in the next section the general architecture of FIRSt, which represents the core of personalization mechanisms designed for Vatican Picture Gallery scenario.

## 3  FIRSt: Folksonomy-Based Item Recommender syStem

FIRSt is a semantic content-based recommender system capable of providing recommendations for items in several domains (e.g., movies, music, books), provided

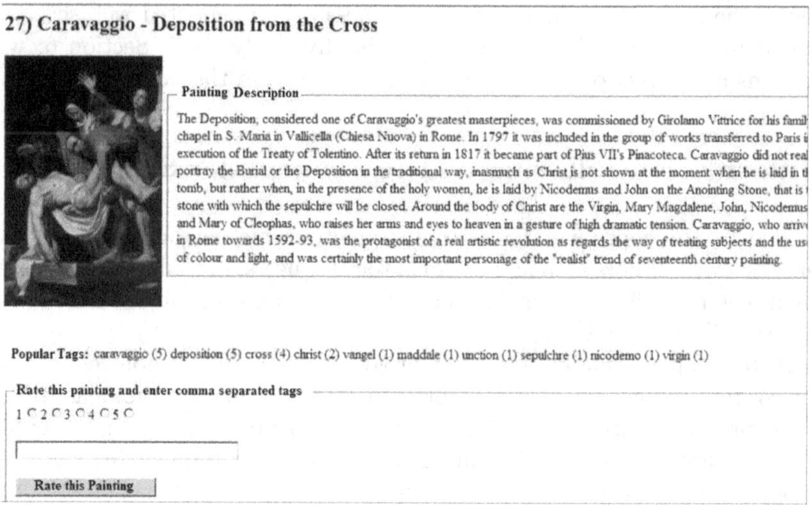

**27) Caravaggio - Deposition from the Cross**

Painting Description

The Deposition, considered one of Caravaggio's greatest masterpieces, was commissioned by Girolamo Vittrice for his family chapel in S. Maria in Vallicella (Chiesa Nuova) in Rome. In 1797 it was included in the group of works transferred to Paris in execution of the Treaty of Tolentino. After its return in 1817 it became part of Pius VII's Pinacoteca. Caravaggio did not real portray the Burial or the Deposition in the traditional way, inasmuch as Christ is not shown at the moment when he is laid in tomb, but rather when, in the presence of the holy women, he is laid by Nicodemus and John on the Anointing Stone, that is stone with which the sepulchre will be closed. Around the body of Christ are the Virgin, Mary Magdalene, John, Nicodemus and Mary of Cleophas, who raises her arms and eyes to heaven in a gesture of high dramatic tension. Caravaggio, who arrive in Rome towards 1592-93, was the protagonist of a real artistic revolution as regards the way of treating subjects and the us of colour and light, and was certainly the most important personage of the "realist" trend of seventeenth century painting.

Popular Tags: caravaggio (5) deposition (5) cross (4) christ (2) vangel (1) maddale (1) unction (1) sepulchre (1) nicodemo (1) virgin (1)

Rate this painting and enter comma separated tags

1 ○ 2 ○ 3 ○ 4 ○ 5 ○

Rate this Painting

**Fig. 1.** Screenshot of Learning Platform

that descriptions of items are available as text documents (e.g. plot summaries, reviews, short abstracts) [6].

In the context of cultural heritage personalization, for example, an artwork can be represented by at least three textual components (called slots), namely *artist*, *title*, and *description*.

The inceptive idea behind FIRSt is to include folksonomies in a classic content-based recommendation model, integrating *static* content describing items with *dynamic* user-generated content (namely tags, through social tagging of items to be recommended) in the process of learning user profiles.

Tags are collected during the training step (Figure 1) by letting users:

1. express their preferences for items through a numerical rating
2. annotate rated items with free tags.

Tags are then stored into an additional slot, different from those containing static content, and are exploited in the profile learning phase in order to include them in the user profiles.

The general architecture of FIRSt is depicted in Figure 2. The recommendation process is performed in three steps, each of which is handled by a separate component:

– CONTENT ANALYZER – it allows introducing semantics in the recommendation process by analyzing documents and tags in order to identify relevant concepts representing the content. This process selects, among all the possible meanings (senses) of each polysemous word, the correct one according to the context in which the word occurs. In this way, documents and tags are represented using concepts instead of keywords, in an attempt to overcome

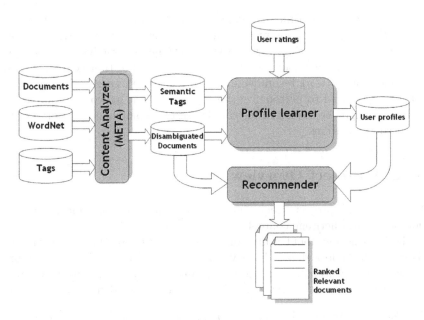

**Fig. 2.** FIRSt General Architecture

the problems due to the natural language ambiguity. The final outcome of
the preprocessing step is a repository of disambiguated documents. This semantic indexing is strongly based on natural language processing techniques,
such as Word Sense Disambiguation (WSD), and heavily relies on linguistic
knowledge stored in the WORDNET [7] lexical ontology. Semantic indexing
of contents is performed by the Content Analyzer, which relies on META
(Multi Language Text Analyzer), a natural language processing tool developed at the University of Bari, able to deal with documents in English or
Italian [2].
The complete description of the adopted WSD strategy is not described here,
because already published in [11].

- PROFILE LEARNER – it implements a supervised learning technique for learning a probabilistic model of user interests from disambiguated documents rated
  according to her interests. This model represents the semantic profile, which
  includes those concepts that turn out to be the most indicative of the user preferences. In FIRSt the problem of learning user profiles is casted as a binary Text
  Categorization task [10] since each document has to be classified as interesting or not with respect to the user preferences. The algorithm for inferring user
  profiles is naïve Bayes text learning, widely adopted in content-based recommenders. Details about implemented algorithm are provided in [5].
- RECOMMENDER – it exploits the user profile to suggest relevant documents
  by matching concepts contained in the semantic profile against those contained in documents to be recommended.

The outcome of the experiments conducted in [3] demonstrated that tag integration in the recommendation process causes an increase of predictive accuracy of the recommender. In this work we will continue this analysis, by showing how this higher accuracy can be exploited for personalization goals in a real-world application: artwork recommendation in Vatican Picture Gallery scenario. The strategy adopted to personalize the services for the artwork recommendation scenario might be exploited for the design of recommendation services for e-commerce applications.

## 4    CHAT Project Overview

CHAT is a research project which aims to developing a platform for multimodal fruition of cultural heritage content.

All the information about a museum is contained in specific data structures and is stored in Fedora digital library[1]. The contents in the Fedora are represented by digital objects. In our data modeling (Figure 3) we have three main digital objects: *opus*, *room*, and *author*. Some relations are defined among them:

- *hasCollectionMember* that relates a *room* with an *opus* (the inverse relation is *hasLocation*);
- *isAuthorOf* that relates an *author* with an *opus* (the inverse relation is *hasAuthor*);

Every digital object in Fedora can have one or more datastreams (image, audio, video, text). For each *opus* (painting) we have the following datastreams: *description* (txt or html), *image* (jpg format), *audio* (wav or mp3), *video* (mpeg); *author* and *room* have only textual contents.

All this data are static and not personalized: thus, starting from the same request (for example, a more detailed textual description of an artworks), all users obtain the same answer.

*How can we improve the quality of information showed to the visitors?*

In the expected scenario every visitor entering the museum is provided with a device (PDA/smart phone) with a specific application installed. Thanks to some localization sensors, it is possible to know in which room of the museum the user is, while coming trough the doorway, the visitor can acquire detailed information on each painting in that room.

The core of the CHAT system architecture is the Adaptive Dialog Manager (Figure 4), whose purpose is to manage personalization mechanisms in order to let visitors receive suggestions about artworks they could be interested in.

The Adaptive Dialog Manager embeds many components, called *reasoners*, each of which manages different types of information (about the environment, such as the noise and brightness, about the user, such as the age and interaction speed, and about user tastes) coming from different input channels and localization sensors.

---

[1] http://www.fedora-commons.org/

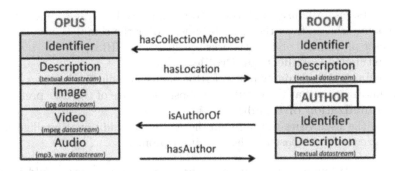

**Fig. 3.** Data modeling in Fedora Digital Library

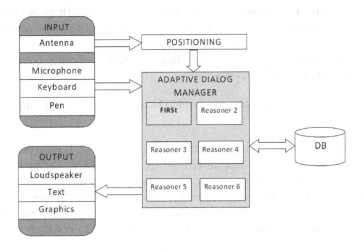

**Fig. 4.** CHAT Adaptive Dialog Manager for multimodal and personalized fruition

All the data gathered from each reasoner are merged by the Adaptive Dialog Manager, which exploits the *user profile* to find the most interesting items and the most appropriate way to present them, such as just audio or audio and text, video, etc.

## 4.1 FIRSt@Work in CHAT

FIRSt manages the *content-based profile*, which contains all the information about user preferences on artworks (data that cannot be omitted for personalization goals). The typical steps in a scenario for creating content-based profiles are:

1. **Registration to the Museum Portal**
   In a preliminary phase a user has to subscribe to a dedicated portal. After entering typical demographic data, such as age, sex, instruction, explicit

interests, etc., the user performs a training phase by voting some artworks, randomly chosen from the available ones. After the completion of this step, all user preferences about artworks are stored by FIRSt;

2. **Construction of the User Profile**

   Once finished the training phase, FIRSt builds a profile for each user containing information that turns out to be most indicative of the user preferences;

3. **Personalization of Results**

   When the user visits the museum, he will enjoy additional intelligent personalized services, based on her own user profile.

Specifically, we found two situations where personalized access could improve user experience:

– When data about user interests are gathered, splitting paintings in two disjoint sets, *interesting*, and *not interesting* could be useful to build a personalized tour.

– When the user enters into a room, providing suggestions about paintings she can be interested in can be useful.

To fulfil these specific requirements, we develop two Web Services exposing these functionalities:

– **Tour**: the main idea behind this service is to provide the target user with the subset of items she could be interested in (according to her profile). It is possible to return the first $n$ items for a single user, for example to have the most significant paintings for her. In this service there is not a room-based partition. *This service has been used in CHAT to build a personalized museum tour showing visitors a list of paintings ordered according to their interests.*

– **Room**: it provides the target user with content related to items located in a specific room of the museum. This service takes as input the room identifier (provided by environment sensors) and returns all the artworks in that location.

   *Room* can be adapted to a specific user by exploiting the FIRSt system, that, according to the information stored in the user profile, is able to rank the paintings according to the user interests.

   This service has been used in CHAT to discover the most interesting rooms in the museum. This could be very useful when the visitor has no much time to visit the entire museum. In that case, the visitor could plan her visit by starting from the first $n$ locations of interest suggested by the system.

## 5   Experimental Evaluation

The goal of the experimental evaluation was to understand whether the use of FIRSt in this scenario brings to a substantial improvement of user experience in museum collection fruition. The test has been carried out by using an online platform which allows registered users to train the system by rating some paintings belonging to the art gallery. The rating scale varies from 1 (dislikes) to 5 (likes). A group of 30 users has been recruited for the test. The task has been divided in three phases:

1. Registration and login;
2. Rating the artworks;
3. Tagging the artworks.

After the registration, each user rated 45 artworks taken from the Vatican Picture Gallery web site and annotated them with a set of free tags. In order to evaluate the effectiveness of the services, we adopted the Normalized Distance-based Performance Measure (NDPM) [16] in order to compare the ranking imposed by the user ratings, with that computed by FIRSt. More specifically, NDPM is used to measure the distance between votes given by a single user $u$ and votes predicted by the system $s$ for a set of items. Given a couple of items $t_i, t_j$ in the Test Set T of an user, the distance between them is calculated through the following schema:

$$\delta_{>u,>s}(t_i, t_j) = \begin{cases} 2 \iff (t_i >_u t_j \wedge t_j >_s t_i) \vee (t_i >_s t_j \wedge t_j >_u t_i) \\ 1 \iff (t_i >_s t_j \vee t_j >_s t_i) \wedge t_i \approx_u t_j \\ 0 \iff otherwise \end{cases} \qquad (1)$$

The value of NDPM on the Test Set T is calculated through the following equation, where $n$ is the number of couple of items:

$$NDPM_{>u,>s}(T) = \frac{\sum_{i \neq j} \delta_{>u,>s}(t_i, t_j)}{2 \cdot n} \qquad (2)$$

For the *Room* service, a single room was set as test set, in order to measure the distance between the ranking imposed on paintings in a room by the user ratings and the ranking predicted by FIRSt.

The methodology of the experiment was as follows:

1. the Training Set $(TS_i)$ for user $u_i, i = 1..30$ is built, by including 50% of all ratings given by $u_i$ (randomly selected);
2. the profile for $u_i$ is built by FIRSt, by exploiting ratings in $TS_i$;
3. the profile is used for the computation of the classification scores for the class *likes* for the paintings not included in $TS_i$;
4. scores computed by FIRSt and ratings given by users on paintings not included in $TS_i$ are compared.

The test was carried out for 3 rooms in which paintings are located. Generally, NDPM values lower than 0.5 reveal acceptable agreement between the two rankings.

From results reported in Table 1, it can be noticed that the average NDPM is lower than 0.5. In particular, values are lower than 0.5 for 19 users out of 30

**Table 1.** NDPM for each user (averaged on 3 rooms

| User | NDPM | User | NDPM | User | NDPM | User | NDPM | User | NDPM |
|------|------|------|------|------|------|------|------|------|------|
| $u_1$ | 0.56 | $u_2$ | **0.48** | $u_3$ | 0.53 | $u_4$ | 0.65 | $u_5$ | 0.57 |
| $u_6$ | 0.52 | $u_7$ | **0.38** | $u_8$ | 0.54 | $u_9$ | **0.39** | $u_{10}$ | **0.39** |
| $u_{11}$ | **0.46** | $u_{12}$ | 0.51 | $u_{13}$ | **0.49** | $u_{14}$ | **0.46** | $u_{15}$ | **0.35** |
| $u_{16}$ | **0.43** | $u_{17}$ | **0.45** | $u_{18}$ | **0.36** | $u_{19}$ | **0.46** | $u_{20}$ | **0.35** |
| $u_{21}$ | 0.51 | $u_{22}$ | **0.47** | $u_{23}$ | **0.39** | $u_{24}$ | 0.55 | $u_{25}$ | **0.36** |
| $u_{26}$ | **0.46** | $u_{27}$ | **0.39** | $u_{28}$ | **0.42** | $u_{29}$ | 0.60 | $u_{30}$ | 0.55 |
| | | | | | | | | *Avg* | *0.47* |

(63%), highlighted in bold in the table. Among these users, NDPM for 9 of them is even lower than 0.4, thus revealing that the ranking of paintings proposed by FIRSt is very effective for 30% of the population involved in the test. The main conclusion which can be drawn from the experiment is that the service is capable of providing a quite effective user experience in museum fruition.

# 6 Related Work

Museums have already recognized the importance of providing visitors with personalized access to artifacts. PEACH (Personal Experience with Active Cultural Heritage) [13] and CHIP (Cultural Heritage Information Personalization) [15] projects are only two examples of the research efforts devoted to support visitors in fulfilling a personalized experience and tour when visiting artwork collections. In particular, the recommender system developed within CHIP aims to provide personalized access to the collections of the Rijksmuseum in Amsterdam. It combines Semantic Web technologies and content-based algorithms for inferring visitors' preference from a set of scored artifacts and then, recommending other artworks and related content topics.

The Steve.museum consortium [14] has begun to explore the use of social tagging and folksonomy in cultural heritage personalization scenarios, to increase audience engagement with museums' collections. Supporting social tagging of artifacts and providing access based on the resulting folksonomy, open museum collections to new interpretations, which reflect visitors' perspectives rather than curators' ones, and help to bridge the gap between the professional language of the curator and the popular language of the museum visitors. Preliminary explorations conducted at the Metropolitan Museum of Art of New York have shown that professional perspectives differ significantly from those of naïve visitors. Hence, if tags are associated to artworks, the resulting folksonomy can be used as a different and valuable source of information to be carefully taken into account when providing recommendations to museum visitors. As in the above mentioned works, we have proposed a solution to the challenging task of identifying user interests from tags. Since the main problem lies in the fact that tags are freely chosen by users and their actual meaning is usually not very clear, the distinguishing feature of our approach is a strategy for the "semantic" interpretation of tags by means of WordNet.

# 7   Conclusions and Future Work

In this paper we investigated about the design of recommendation services based on folksonomies and their concrete exploitation in real-world applications. We evaluated the FIRSt recommender system in the cultural heritage domain, by integrating the system in an adaptive platform for multimodal and personalized access to museum collections. Each visitor, equipped with a mobile terminal, enjoys an intelligent guide service which helps her to find the most interesting artworks according to her profile and contextual information (such as her current location in the museum, noise level, brightness, etc.). Experimental evaluations showed that FIRSt is capable of improving user museum experience, by ranking artworks according to visitor tastes, included in user profiles. The profiles are automatically inferred from both static content describing the artworks and tags chosen by visitors to freely annotate preferred artworks. The personalized ranking allows building services for adaptive museum tours. Since FIRSt is capable of providing recommendations for items in several domains, provided that descriptions of items are available as text documents (e.g. plot summaries, reviews, short abstracts), we will try to investigate its application in different scenarios such as book or movie recommendation.

# Acknowledgments

This research was partially funded by MIUR (Ministero dell'Universita' e della Ricerca) under the contract Legge 297/99, Prot.691 CHAT "Cultural Heritage fruition & e-Learning applications of new Advanced (multimodal) Technologies" (2006-08). The authors are grateful to Massimo Bux for his effort in developing the services and performing the experimental evaluation.

# References

1. Balabanovic, M., Shoham, Y.: Fab: Content-based, Collaborative Recommendation. Communications of the ACM 40(3), 66–72 (1997)
2. Basile, P., de Gemmis, M., Gentile, A.L., Iaquinta, L., Lops, P., Semeraro, G.: META - MultilanguagE Text Analyzer. In: Proceedings of the Language and Speech Technnology Conference - LangTech 2008, Rome, Italy, February 28-29, 2008, pp. 137–140 (2008)
3. Basile, P., de Gemmis, M., Lops, P., Semeraro, G., Bux, M., Musto, C., Narducci, F.: FIRSt: a Content-based Recommender System Integrating Tags for Cultural Heritage Personalization. In: Nesi, P., Ng, K., Delgado, J. (eds.) Proceedings of the 4th International Conference on Automated Solutions for Cross Media Content and Multi-channel Distribution (AXMEDIS 2008) - Workshop Panels and Industrial Applications, Florence, Italy, November 17-19, 2008, pp. 103–106. Firenze University Press (2008)

4. Burke, R.: Hybrid Recommender Systems: Survey and Experiments. User Modeling and User-Adapted Interaction 12(4), 331–370 (2002)
5. de Gemmis, M., Lops, P., Semeraro, G., Basile, P.: Integrating Tags in a Semantic Content-based Recommender. In: Proceedings of the 2008 ACM Conference on Recommender Systems, RecSys 2008, Lausanne, Switzerland, October 23-25, 2008, pp. 163–170 (2008)
6. Lops, P., Degemmis, M., Semeraro, G.: Improving Social Filtering Techniques Through WordNet-Based User Profiles. In: Conati, C., McCoy, K., Paliouras, G. (eds.) UM 2007. LNCS, vol. 4511, pp. 268–277. Springer, Heidelberg (2007)
7. Miller, G.: WordNet: An On-Line Lexical Database. International Journal of Lexicography 3(4) (1990); Special Issue
8. Mladenic, D.: Text-learning and related intelligent agents: a survey. IEEE Intelligent Systems 14(4), 44–54 (1999)
9. Resnick, P., Varian, H.: Recommender Systems. Communications of the ACM 40(3), 56–58 (1997)
10. Sebastiani, F.: Machine Learning in Automated Text Categorization. ACM Computing Surveys 34(1) (2002)
11. Semeraro, G., Degemmis, M., Lops, P., Basile, P.: Combining Learning and Word Sense Disambiguation for Intelligent User Profiling. In: Veloso, M.M. (ed.) Proceedings of the 20th International Joint Conference on Artificial Intelligence, pp. 2856–2861 (2007) ISBN 978-I-57735-298-3
12. Shardanand, U., Maes, P.: Social Information Filtering: Algorithms for Automating "Word of Mouth". In: Proceedings of ACM CHI 1995 Conference on Human Factors in Computing Systems, vol. 1, pp. 210–217 (1995)
13. Stock, O., Zancanaro, M., Busetta, P., Callaway, C.B., Krüger, A., Kruppa, M., Kuflik, T., Not, E., Rocchi, C.: Adaptive, intelligent presentation of information for the museum visitor in peach. User Model. User-Adapt. Interact. 17(3), 257–304 (2007)
14. Trant, J., Wyman, B.: Investigating social tagging and folksonomy in art museums with steve.museum. In: Collaborative Web Tagging Workshop at WWW 2006, Edinburgh, Scotland (May 2006)
15. Wang, Y., Aroyo, L.M., Stash, N., Rutledge, L.: Interactive user modeling for personalized access to museum collections: The rijksmuseum case study. In: Conati, C., McCoy, K., Paliouras, G. (eds.) UM 2007. LNCS, vol. 4511, pp. 385–389. Springer, Heidelberg (2007)
16. Yao, Y.Y.: Measuring retrieval effectiveness based on user preference of documents. Journal of the American Society for Information Science 46(2), 133–145 (1995)

# Computational Complexity Reduction for Factorization-Based Collaborative Filtering Algorithms

István Pilászy* and Domonkos Tikk**

Budapest University of Technology and Economics
Magyar Tudósok krt. 2.
Budapest, Hungary * * *
info@gravitrd.com

**Abstract.** Alternating least squares (ALS) is a powerful matrix factorization (MF) algorithm for both implicit and explicit feedback based recommender systems. We show that by using the Sherman-Morrison formula (SMF), we can reduce the computational complexity of several ALS based algorithms. It also reduces the complexity of greedy forward and backward feature selection algorithms by an order of magnitude. We propose linear kernel ridge regression (KRR) for users with few ratings. We show that both SMF and KRR can efficiently handle new ratings.

**Keywords:** matrix factorization, collaborative filtering, alternating least squares, Sherman-Morrison formula, kernel ridge regression, greedy feature selection.

## 1 Introduction

The goal of recommender systems is to give personalized recommendation on items to users. Typically the recommendation is based on the former and current activity of the users, and metadata about users and items, if available. Collaborative filtering (CF) methods are based only on the activity of users, while content-based filtering (CBF) methods use only metadata. Hybrid methods try to benefit from both information sources.

Users can express their opinion on items in different ways. They give explicit or implicit feedback on their preferences. The former mainly includes opinion expression via *ratings* of items on a predefined scale, while the latter consists of other user activities, such as purchasing, viewing, renting or searching of items.

A good recommender system recommends such items that meets the users' need. Measuring the effectiveness of real a recommender system is difficult, since

---

* István Pilászy was supported by National Office for Research and Technology (NKTH), Hungary.
** Domonkos Tikk was supported by the Alexander von Humboldt Foundation.
* * * Both authors are also affiliated with Gravity Research & Development Ltd., H-1092 Budapest, Kinizsi u. 11., Hungary.

T. Di Noia and F. Buccafurri (Eds.): EC-Web 2009, LNCS 5692, pp. 229–239, 2009.

the goal may be for example to maximize the profit of an online DVD-rental company, but in scientific context performance measures evaluate the recommendation systems offline, e.g. by measuring the error of prediction with RMSE (root mean square error) or MAE (mean absolute error).

The importance of a good recommender system was recognized by Netflix, an online DVD-rental company, who announced the Netflix Prize (NP) competition in October 2006. Netflix generously published a part of their rating dataset, which consists of 100 480 507 ratings of 480 189 customers on 17 770 movies. Ratings are integer numbers on a 1-to-5 scale. In addition to that, the date of the ratings and the title and release year of the movies are also provided. This is currently the largest available CF dataset and it fits onto a compact disc.

The NP competition motivated the development of new CF methods that are able to handle datasets of such a size. Typical running times of algorithms varies between few minutes and a couple of days. The NP competition focuses only on the good prediction performance: the competitors have to minimize the error of predicted ratings measured on a hold-out set. However, real recommender systems also have to address some other problems beside the good predictive performance. In this paper, we will focus on some practical issues of alternating least squares as a matrix factorization (MF) algorithm.

This paper is organized as follows. Section 2 includes the notation, related works and introduces alternating least squares as a MF algorithm. In Section 3 we describe how the Sherman-Morrison formula (SMF) can be applied to speed up the solution of least squares problems in recommender systems. Section 4 shows when and how kernel ridge regression (KRR) can be applied to address the same problems.

## 2   Related Works

### 2.1   Notation

In this paper we use the following notations:

$N$: number of users
$M$: number of movies or items.
$u \in \{1, \ldots, N\}$: index for users.
$i, j \in \{1, \ldots, M\}$: indexes for movies or items.
$r_{ui}$: the rating of user $u$ on item $i$.
$\hat{r}_{ui}$: the prediction of $r_{ui}$. In general, superscript "hat" denotes the prediction of the given quantity, that is, $\hat{x}$ is the prediction of $x$.
$\mathbf{R}$: the matrix of $r_{ui}$ values (for both explicit and implicit ratings).
$\mathcal{R}$: for explicit feedback, the set of $(u, i)$ indexes of $\mathbf{R}$ where a rating is provided; for implicit feedback: the set of all indexes of $\mathbf{R}$.
$\mathcal{R}^+$: only for implicit feedback, the set of $(u, i)$ indexes of $\mathbf{R}$ where the feedback is non-zero (user $u$ watched item $i$).
$n_u$: number of ratings of user $u$, i.e. $n_u = |\{i : (u, i) \in \mathcal{R}\}|$.

$\mathbf{A}_u$: used for ridge regression, denoting the covariance matrix of input (considering user $u$ in context).

$\mathbf{B}_u$: like $\mathbf{A}_u$, but contains also the regularization term (increased diagonal).

$\mathbf{d}_u$: used for ridge regression, denoting the input-output covariance vector.

$\mathbf{I}$: denotes the identity matrix of the appropriate size.

$\lambda$: regularization parameter.

We assume that CF methods strive to minimize the prediction error in terms of RMSE $= \sqrt{\sum_{(u,i)\in\mathcal{V}}(r_{ui} - \hat{r}_{ui})^2/|\mathcal{V}|}$, where $\mathcal{V}$ is a validation set.

Matrix factorization approaches have been applied successfully for both rating-based and implicit feedback-based CF problems [1,2,3,4,5,6,7]. The goal of MF methods is to approximate the matrix $\mathbf{R}$ as a product of two lower rank matrices: $\mathbf{R} \approx \mathbf{P}\mathbf{Q}^T$, where $\mathbf{P} \in \mathbb{R}^{N \times K}$ is the user feature matrix, $\mathbf{Q} \in \mathbb{R}^{M \times K}$ is the item (or movie) feature matrix, $K$ is the number of features that is a predefined constant, and the approximation is only performed at $(u, i) \in \mathcal{R}$ positions. The $r_{ui}$ element of $\mathbf{R}$ is approximated by

$$\hat{r}_{ui} = \mathbf{p}_u^T\mathbf{q}_i.$$

Here $\mathbf{p}_u \in \mathbb{R}^{K \times 1}$ is the user feature vector, the $u$-th row of $\mathbf{P}$, and $\mathbf{q}_i \in \mathbb{R}^{K \times 1}$ is the movie feature vector, the $i$-th row of $\mathbf{Q}$. The approximation aims to minimize the error of prediction, $e_{ui} = r_{ui} - \hat{r}_{ui}$ while keeping the Euclidean norm of the user and movie feature vectors small:

$$(\mathbf{P}^*, \mathbf{Q}^*) = \arg\min_{\mathbf{P},\mathbf{Q}} \sum_{(u,i)\in\mathcal{R}} \left(e_{ui}^2 + \lambda\mathbf{p}_u^T\mathbf{p}_u + \lambda\mathbf{q}_i^T\mathbf{q}_i\right).$$

The predefined regularization parameter $\lambda$ trades off between small training error and small model weights.

In the NP competition alternating least squares (ALS) was found a good MF algorithm, first proposed by team BellKor [1].

BellKor's alternating least squares approach alternates between two steps: step 1 fixes $\mathbf{P}$ and recomputes $\mathbf{Q}$, step 2 fixes $\mathbf{Q}$ and recomputes $\mathbf{P}$. The recomputation of $\mathbf{P}$ is performed by solving a separate least squares problem for each user: for the $u$-th user it takes the feature vector ($\mathbf{q}_i$) of movies rated by the user as input variables, and the value of the ratings ($r_{ui}$) as output variable, and finds the optimal $\mathbf{p}_u$ by ridge regression (RR). BellKor proposed non-negative RR, however, in this paper, ALS and RR refer to the general variants, where negative values are allowed.

Borrowing the notations from [1], let the matrix $\mathbf{Q}[u] \in \mathbb{R}^{n_u \times K}$ denote the restriction of $\mathbf{Q}$ to the movies rated by user $u$, the vector $\mathbf{r}_u \in \mathbb{R}^{n_u \times 1}$ denote the ratings given by the $u$-th user to the corresponding movies, and let

$$\mathbf{A}_u = \mathbf{Q}[u]^T\mathbf{Q}[u] = \sum_{i:(u,i)\in\mathcal{R}} \mathbf{q}_i\mathbf{q}_i^T, \quad \mathbf{d}_u = \mathbf{Q}[u]^T\mathbf{r}_u = \sum_{i:(u,i)\in\mathcal{R}} r_{ui}\cdot\mathbf{q}_i. \quad (1)$$

Then RR recomputes $\mathbf{p}_u$ as

$$\mathbf{p}_u = (\lambda n_u\mathbf{I} + \mathbf{A}_u)^{-1}\mathbf{d}_u. \quad (2)$$

Here two operations are dominant: (1) the computation of $\mathbf{A}_u$ that requires $O(K^2 \cdot n_u)$ time, and (2) the inversion that requires $O(K^3)$ time.

Thus, the recomputation of $\mathbf{P}$ requires $O(\sum_{u=1}^{N}(K^2 \cdot n_u + K^3))$, which is equal to $O(K^2 \cdot |\mathcal{R}| + N \cdot K^3)$, as it has been noted in [2,4]. Similarly, the recomputation of $\mathbf{Q}$ requires $O(K^2 \cdot |\mathcal{R}| + M \cdot K^3)$. According to [1,2], the number of recomputations needed ranges between 10 and a "few tens".

It has been pointed out that larger $K$ yields more accurate predictions [2,3,4].

In the next two sections we show how to apply the Sherman-Morrison formula and kernel ridge regression in order to reduce the computational complexity of ALS for large $K$ values.

# 3    Applications of the Sherman-Morrison Formula

**Definition 1.** *Sherman-Morrison formula (SMF)* [8]*: suppose that* $\mathbf{A} \in \mathbb{R}^{n \times n}$ *is an invertible matrix,* $\mathbf{u}, \mathbf{v} \in \mathbb{R}^n$ *are column vectors, and* $1 + \mathbf{v}^T \mathbf{A}^{-1} \mathbf{u} \neq 0$*. Then the inverse of* $\mathbf{A} + \mathbf{u}\mathbf{v}^T$ *can be computed as:*

$$(\mathbf{A} + \mathbf{u}\mathbf{v}^T)^{-1} = \mathbf{A}^{-1} - \frac{(\mathbf{A}^{-1}\mathbf{u})(\mathbf{v}^T\mathbf{A}^{-1})}{1 + \mathbf{v}^T\mathbf{A}^{-1}\mathbf{u}}$$

This formula allows us to compute the inverse of a modified matrix in $O(n^2)$, when the modification is an addition of a dyadic product ($\mathbf{u}\mathbf{v}^T$) and the inverse of the original matrix is precomputed.

Note that when we extend $\mathbf{A}$ with a new row and a new column, the inverse of the new $(n+1) \times (n+1)$ matrix can be computed in $O(n^2)$ time using the SMF (assuming that the above conditions are met): first we extend $\mathbf{A}$ and $\mathbf{A}^{-1}$ with the last row and last column of the $(n + 1) \times (n + 1)$ identity matrix, and then change the $n + 1$-th column of the new $\mathbf{A}$ and update the inverse with the SMF. Then we change the $n + 1$-th row. Deleting a row and column can be treated similarly. In the followings we investigate some recommender algorithms where the Sherman-Morrison formula is applicable.

## 3.1    ALS on Explicit Feedback Datasets

It has been noted in Section 2, that the recomputation of $\mathbf{p}_u$ requires $O(K^2 \cdot n_u + K^3)$ time. When $n_u \leq K$, then $O(K^3)$ is dominant. Now we show how to eliminate it. Recall that from eq. (1), we have $\mathbf{A}_u = \sum_{i:(u,i)\in\mathcal{R}} \mathbf{q}_i\mathbf{q}_i^T$. Algorithm 1 computes the inverse of $(\lambda n_u \mathbf{I} + \mathbf{A}_u)$ in $O(K^2 \cdot n_u)$ time, starting with the regularization term $\lambda n_u \mathbf{I}$, and then successively adding the $\mathbf{q}_i\mathbf{q}_i^T$ dyadic products.

For users with $n_u \geq K$ ratings, the application of Sherman-Morrison formula does not increase the running time (in the $O(\cdot)$ sense), while for users with $n_u < K$, it can greatly speed it up. To recompute $\mathbf{P}$, the time complexity is reduced from $O(K^2 \cdot |\mathcal{R}| + N \cdot K^3)$ to $O(K^2 \cdot |\mathcal{R}|)$, yielding exactly the same $\mathbf{P}$ as the original ALS. $\mathbf{Q}$ can be treated similarly.

**Input**: $\mathbf{R}$: matrix of ratings, $\mathcal{R}$: the set of indexes of ratings.
$K$: number of features, $\mathbf{Q} \in \mathbb{R}^{M \times K}$: the movie feature matrix,
$\lambda$: regularization parameter, $u$: user id, $n_u$: number of ratings of $u$.
**Output**: $\mathbf{p}_u$: the recomputed user feature vector
    Let $\mathbf{I} \in \mathbb{R}^{K \times K}$ be the identity matrix
    Let $\mathbf{B}_u \in \mathbb{R}^{K \times K} = \lambda n_u \mathbf{I}$ // The covariance matrix and regularization term

    Let $\mathbf{W}_u \in \mathbb{R}^{K \times K} = \begin{cases} 0 \cdot \mathbf{I}, & \text{if } \lambda = 0 \\ \frac{1}{\lambda \cdot n_u} \cdot \mathbf{I}, & \text{otherwise} \end{cases}$ // The inverse of $\mathbf{B}_u$

    Let $\mathbf{d}_u \in \mathbb{R}^{K \times 1} = \mathbf{0}$ // The input-output covariance vector
    **for each** $i : (u, i) \in \mathcal{R}$
        Let $\mathbf{B}_u = \mathbf{B}_u + \mathbf{q}_i \mathbf{q}_i^{\mathsf{T}}$
        Let $\mathbf{W}_u = \mathbf{W}_u - \frac{(\mathbf{W}_u \mathbf{q}_i)(\mathbf{q}_i^{\mathsf{T}} \mathbf{W}_u)}{1 + \mathbf{q}_i^{\mathsf{T}} \mathbf{W}_u \mathbf{q}_i}$ // Applying the Sherman-Morrison formula
        Let $\mathbf{d}_u = \mathbf{d}_u + \mathbf{q}_i \cdot r_{ui}$
    **end**
    Let $\mathbf{p}_u = \mathbf{W}_u \mathbf{d}_u$
**end**

**Algorithm 1.** Algorithm to recompute $\mathbf{p}_u$ in $O(K^2 \cdot n_u)$ time for explicit feedback datasets.

### 3.2 ALS on Implicit Feedback Datasets

In the case of the implicit feedback, $\mathbf{R}$ is fully filled, as opposed to the explicit case, where only a small subset of its values is known. In the case of NP competition, an average user rates only each 85th movie. If we consider the NP dataset as implicit feedback—substituting known ratings with 1 and unknown ratings with 0, indicating which movies users rated and which not—then a recommendation algorithm has to deal with 85 times more data than at explicit feedback, i.e. $|\mathcal{R}|/|\mathcal{R}^+| = 85$.

Hu et al. [2] suggested an elegant method to handle implicit feedback datasets, more specifically, for recommending IPTV movies for users based on their watching habits. The key idea behind their approach is to assign a preference (here: $r_{ui}$) and a confidence level $c_{ui}$ for each element of $\mathbf{R}$. Preference typically takes values 0 and 1, indicating whether a user watched a particular movie or not. Confidence level is related to the amount of time the user spent watching a particular movie. They define the optimal model as:

$$(\mathbf{P}^*, \mathbf{Q}^*) = \underset{\mathbf{P}, \mathbf{Q}}{\arg\min} \sum_{(u,i) \in \mathcal{R}} c_{ui} \cdot e_{ui}^2 + \lambda \sum_u \mathbf{p}_u^{\mathsf{T}} \mathbf{p}_u + \lambda \sum_i \mathbf{q}_i^{\mathsf{T}} \mathbf{q}_i,$$

where $e_{ui} = r_{ui} - \mathbf{p}_u^{\mathsf{T}} \mathbf{q}_i$ is the prediction error. Note that $\mathcal{R}$ contains all $(u, i)$ pairs regardless of whether user $u$ has watched movie $i$ or not. The authors use one restriction, namely if $u$ has not watched $i$, then $r_{ui} = r_0 = 0$ and $c_{ui} = c_0 = 1$, where $r_0$ and $c_0$ are predefined constants. Similarly to the rating-based case, the authors used ALS to solve the problem, but with the following two differences:

- handling confidence levels: the covariance matrix $\mathbf{A}_u$ and covariance vector $\mathbf{d}_u$ contains now a confidence-weighted sum.
- the sums are taken over all items (since all user rated all items).

The authors propose an efficient solution to the second issue: when recomputing $\mathbf{P}$, they calculate an initial covariance matrix $\mathbf{A}_0$ and a vector $\mathbf{d}_0$ for a virtual user who watched no movies:

$$\mathbf{A}_0 = \sum_i c_0 \cdot \mathbf{q}_i \mathbf{q}_i^{\mathrm{T}}, \quad \mathbf{d}_0 = \sum_i c_0 \cdot r_0 \cdot \mathbf{q}_i.$$

Recall that $\mathcal{R}^+$ denotes the set of $(u, i)$ values of positive feedback. In this case, let $\mathcal{R}^+ = \{(u, i) : r_{ui} \neq r_0 \vee c_{ui} \neq c_0\}$. For user $u$, they start with that precomputed covariance matrix, and for each movie watched by the user, they replace the did-not-watch-assumption. Then it yields:

$$\mathbf{A}_u = \mathbf{A}_0 + \sum_{i:\ (u,i)\in\mathcal{R}^+} (-c_0 + c_{ui}) \cdot \mathbf{q}_i^{\mathrm{T}} \mathbf{q}_i, \quad \mathbf{d}_u = \mathbf{d}_0 + \sum_{i:\ (u,i)\in\mathcal{R}^+} (-c_0 \cdot r_0 + c_{ui} \cdot r_{ui}) \cdot \mathbf{q}_i.$$

Then $\mathbf{p}_u$ is computed by RR:

$$\mathbf{p}_u = (\lambda\mathbf{I} + \mathbf{A}_u)^{-1}\mathbf{d}_u. \tag{3}$$

The authors note that the running time of recomputing $\mathbf{P}$ or $\mathbf{Q}$ are $O(K^2 \cdot |\mathcal{R}^+| + K^3 \cdot N)$ and $O(K^2 \cdot |\mathcal{R}^+| + K^3 \cdot M)$, resp. They show experimentally that larger $K$ values yield better prediction performance.

We will show that the Sherman-Morrison formula can be used here to speed up the recomputations of both $\mathbf{P}$ and $\mathbf{Q}$ to $O(K^2 \cdot |\mathcal{R}^+|)$. Here we present the solution for $\mathbf{P}$. For $\mathbf{Q}$, it can be derived analogously.

Note that $(\lambda\mathbf{I} + \mathbf{A}_0)$, $\mathbf{d}_0$ and $(\lambda\mathbf{I} + \mathbf{A}_0)^{-1}$ can be computed in $O(K^2 \cdot M)$: we initialize a $K \times K$ matrix with $\lambda\mathbf{I}$ and then add $c_0 \mathbf{q}_i \mathbf{q}_i^{\mathrm{T}}$ values for each $i$, and also initialize the inverse of that (diagonal) matrix, and keep maintained by the Sherman-Morrison formula. Note that the regularization term is added at the beginning, not at the end, since the Sherman-Morrison formula cannot be applied for such modification; and the regularization term is the same for all users, as opposed to the explicit feedback case, where it is $\lambda n_u \mathbf{I}$.

When we are at user $u$, we start with $\mathbf{A}_u := (\lambda\mathbf{I} + \mathbf{A}_0)$, $\mathbf{d}_u := \mathbf{d}_0$ and $\mathbf{W}_u := (\lambda\mathbf{I} + \mathbf{A}_0)^{-1}$. We iterate over $i : (u, i) \in \mathcal{R}^+$, and update $\mathbf{A}_u$ and $\mathbf{d}_u$ as

$$\mathbf{A}_u := \mathbf{A}_u + (-c_0 + c_{ui}) \cdot \mathbf{q}_i \mathbf{q}_i^{\mathrm{T}}, \quad \mathbf{d}_u := \mathbf{d}_u + (-c_0 \cdot r_0 + c_{ui} \cdot r_{ui}) \cdot \mathbf{q}_i.$$

$\mathbf{W}_u$ can be maintained with the SMF, since $\mathbf{A}_u$ is modified by the dyadic product $(-c_0 + c_{ui}) \cdot \mathbf{q}_i \mathbf{q}_i^{\mathrm{T}}$. After the iteration, $\mathbf{p}_u$ can be computed: $\mathbf{p}_u = \mathbf{W}_u \mathbf{d}_u$. Thus, the time to recompute $\mathbf{P}$ is $O(K^2 \cdot M + K^2 \cdot |\mathcal{R}^+|)$. Assuming that each movie has at least one non-zero rating, then $M < |\mathcal{R}^+|$, and the time complexity reduces to $O(K^2 \cdot |\mathcal{R}^+|)$.

Note that the confidence-weighted ALS allows to evaluate it on implicit feedback datasets: for $r_{ui}$-s in the test set, we set $c_{ui} = 0$ in the training set, thus no information about those ratings will be contained in the model. Note that SMF can be used here to speed up cross-validation: assuming $\mathbf{Q}$ is fixed, moving one example from the training set to the test set (or vice versa), the new $\mathbf{p}_u$ can be computed in $O(K^2)$.

## 3.3   Handling New Ratings of Users with ALS

In real recommender systems users can rate items, and expect to be provided with instant recommendations based on all available information.

The Sherman-Morrison formula can be used to efficiently handle this for ALS-based recommender algorithms. Let us assume that the sets of users and items do not change. Furthermore, we may assume that there are more users than items. When user $u$ signs in to the service that uses the recommender system, we calculate $\mathbf{A}_u$, $\mathbf{W}_u$, $\mathbf{d}_u$ and $\mathbf{p}_u$ based on her ratings. When $u$ rates a new item (or cancels a rating), we can update these variables and get the new $\mathbf{p}_u$ value in $O(K^2)$ time. We can do the same for $\mathbf{q}_i$ variables, however, for items with many ratings the benefit of instant recomputation of features may be negligible. Note that recomputing $\mathbf{p}_u$ using the traditional way (i.e. inverting $\lambda \mathbf{I} + \mathbf{A}_u$, not using the SMF) requires $O(K^3)$ time.

Note that when a user changes one of its ratings, neither $\mathbf{A}_u$ nor $\mathbf{W}_u$ changes (recall eqs. (1)–(2)), only $\mathbf{d}_u$. However, computing $\mathbf{W}_u\mathbf{d}_u$ requires $O(K^2)$ time in this case as well, unless we store the precomputed value of $\mathbf{W}_u\mathbf{Q}[u]^{\mathrm{T}}$ (recall that $\mathbf{d}_u = \mathbf{Q}[u]^{\mathrm{T}}\mathbf{r}_u$), in which case it is reduces to $O(K)$ at the cost of increased memory requirement. A good trade-off may be to store $\mathbf{W}_u\mathbf{Q}[u]^{\mathrm{T}}$ restricted to the last few ratings of the user, i.e. restricted to those ratings that are likely to be changed.

We remark that the Sherman-Morrison formula has already been proposed for recommendation systems to handle new data in a web recommendation system [9], where a square matrix of probabilities gets updated.

## 3.4   Backward and Forward Feature Selection

The ridge regression of many predictors may improve the performance measured by RMSE. For example, team BellKor combined 107 predictors in [5]. When we have many predictors, it is crucial to be able to select the best performing ones. A straightforward way is to apply the greedy forward or backward feature selection. Suppose that we have $F$ different predictors (in the above example $F = 107$), and for notational simplicity we assume that RR with regularization parameter $\lambda$ is optimized on $\mathcal{R}$, not on a separate validation set. Let $\hat{r}_{ui}(f)$ denote the prediction of the $f$-th predictor ($f \in \{1, \ldots, F\}$) for the $(u, i)$-th rating, and $\hat{\mathbf{r}}_{ui} = (\hat{r}_{ui}(1), \ldots, \hat{r}_{ui}(f))^{\mathrm{T}} \in \mathbb{R}^{F \times 1}$ denote the prediction vector for the $(u, i)$-th rating. Assume that the variables $\mathbf{B} = \lambda \mathbf{I} + \sum_{(u,i) \in \mathcal{R}} \hat{\mathbf{r}}_{ui}\hat{\mathbf{r}}_{ui}^{\mathrm{T}}$ and $\mathbf{d} = \sum_{(u,i) \in \mathcal{R}} \hat{\mathbf{r}}_{ui}r_{ui}$ are precomputed.

The greedy forward feature selection (GFFS) works as follows: suppose we have selected $n$ out of the $F$ predictors. Now we examine, how each one of the rest $F - n$ predictors can further improve RMSE. We select the best predictor from these $F - n$ predictors, and extend the set of already selected $n$ predictors with the new one. Then the process is repeated with the $n + 1$ predictors, until the difference of the actual RMSE and the RMSE of using all predictors goes below a threshold. We begin with $n = 0$.

The greedy backward feature selection (GBFS) works in the opposite way: we begin with $n = F$, and exclude those predictions the removal of which minimally increases RMSE.

Both GFFS and GBFS requires to run linear regression for $1+\ldots+F = O(F^2)$ times. Since RR requires $O(n^3)$ time for $n$ variables, a complete GFFS or GBFS requires $O(F^5)$ time. Now we show how the Sherman-Morrison formula can be applied to speed up the process to $O(F^4)$.

For GFFS, suppose that we have selected $n$ out of the $F$ predictors. Let $\mathbf{B}[n] \in \mathbb{R}^{n \times n}$ and $\mathbf{d}[n] \in \mathbb{R}^{n \times 1}$ denote the restriction of $\mathbf{B}$ and $\mathbf{d}$ to the selected predictors resp. Assume that $\mathbf{B}[n]^{-1}$ is precomputed. To include a new predictor, we extend $\mathbf{B}[n]$ to $\mathbf{B}[n + 1]$ by adding a new row and a new column. Thus, the inverse of $\mathbf{B}[n + 1]$ can be computed in $O(F^2)$ using the SMF, instead of $O(F^3)$.

For GBFS, the same applies, except that $\mathbf{B}[n]$ is not extended by a row and a column, but deleted. Thus, applying the Sherman-Morrison formula we can reduce the time complexity of the greedy backward or forward feature selection algorithms from $O(F^5)$ to $O(F^4)$, with the RMSE as performance measure.

## 4    Applications of Kernel Ridge Regression

Kernel ridge regression (KRR) has been applied for the NP dataset first by Paterek [7]. He used KRR to post-process the results of an MF: after determining $\mathbf{P}$ and $\mathbf{Q}$ with an MF algorithm, he applied KRR with a Gaussian kernel variant to recompute $\mathbf{p}_u$-s. Now $\mathbf{p}_u$ is not in $\mathbb{R}^{K \times 1}$, but it is in the feature space of the applied kernel function. However, for linear kernel, these two spaces coincide.

In this section we propose the usage of KRR for users with less than $K$ ratings, using linear kernel function: $K(\mathbf{q}_1, \mathbf{q}_2) := \mathbf{q}_1^T \mathbf{q}_2$.

Recall that in eqs. (1)–(2), ALS recalculates $\mathbf{p}_u$ in the following way:

$$\mathbf{p}_u = \left(\lambda n_u \mathbf{I} + \mathbf{Q}[u]^T \mathbf{Q}[u]\right)^{-1} \left(\mathbf{Q}[u]^T \mathbf{r}_u\right).$$

The equivalent dual formulation involving the Gram matrix $\mathbf{Q}[u]\mathbf{Q}[u]^T$ is the following [7]:

$$\mathbf{p}_u = \mathbf{Q}[u]^T \left(\lambda n_u \mathbf{I} + \mathbf{Q}[u]\mathbf{Q}[u]^T\right)^{-1} \mathbf{r}_u. \tag{4}$$

## 4.1    KRR on Explicit Feedback Datasets

Note that the size of the Gram matrix is $n_u \times n_u$, as opposed to $K \times K$ of $\mathbf{Q}[u]^T\mathbf{Q}[u]$. To recalculate $\mathbf{p}_u$, we following operations are needed:

- calculate $\lambda n_u \mathbf{I} + \mathbf{Q}[u]\mathbf{Q}[u]^T$, which is $O(K \cdot n_u^2)$.
- invert that matrix, which is $O(n_u^3)$.
- multiply by $\mathbf{r}_u$ from right, which is $O(n_u^2)$.
- multiply by $\mathbf{Q}[u]^T$ from left, which is $O(K \cdot n_u)$.

Thus, $\mathbf{p}_u$ can be recomputed in $O(K \cdot n_u^2 + n_u^3)$ time. Assuming $n_u \leq K$, it is $O(K \cdot n_u^2)$. Thus, we have two new algorithms to recompute $\mathbf{p}_u$ (or $\mathbf{q}_i$), which outperform in terms of computational complexity the original algorithm that has $O(K^2 \cdot n_u + K^3)$:

1. if $n_u \leq K$: KRR, with $O(K \cdot n_u^2)$
2. if $n_u \geq K$: Sherman-Morrison formula, with $O(K^2 \cdot n_u)$

Note that for users with very few ratings, the ratio $K/n_u$ can be huge, which means that the application of KRR can greatly speed up the learning process in such a case. This allows us to increase $K$ while not worrying too much about the running time.

Note that the proposed method is not usable for implicit feedback datasets, where for all $u$: $n_u = M$ (unless $K > M$, which would be unusual).

**Evaluation.** We compared the running time of using KRR and using the formula of eq. (2) on the Netflix Prize dataset. The experiments were performed on a Intel Core2 Quad Q9300 cpu on 3.3GHz, using only 1 core. We refer to the first method as KRR, and to the second method as RR.

First, we compared whether the two methods provide the same result or not. Although theoretically the two results should be the same, they could differ due

**Table 1.** Average running time of recomputing a $K$-dimensional user feature vector, when the number of ratings of the user is in an interval. First we report the running time of RR (ridge regression), then the running time of KRR, in $10^{-4}$ seconds.

| K | 10 | | 20 | | 50 | | 100 | |
|---|---|---|---|---|---|---|---|---|
| $n_u$ | RR | KRR | RR | KRR | RR | KRR | RR | KRR |
| 0-10 | 0.360 | 0.272 | 0.833 | 0.284 | 4.065 | 0.343 | 24.027 | 0.461 |
| 10-20 | 0.511 | 0.706 | 1.235 | 0.985 | 4.470 | 1.123 | 24.800 | 1.344 |
| 20-30 | 0.547 | 1.191 | 1.627 | 1.835 | 5.819 | 2.615 | 26.955 | 2.961 |
| 30-40 | 0.582 | 1.977 | 1.760 | 2.747 | 7.274 | 4.800 | 29.682 | 5.661 |
| 40-50 | | | | | 8.953 | 7.673 | 33.014 | 9.349 |
| 50-60 | | | | | 10.269 | 10.756 | 36.603 | 14.100 |
| 60-70 | | | | | 10.976 | 14.615 | 40.628 | 20.682 |
| 70-80 | | | | | | | 45.038 | 28.791 |
| 80-90 | | | | | | | 49.359 | 37.323 |
| 90-100 | | | | | | | 53.700 | 47.358 |
| 100-110 | | | | | | | 57.419 | 57.198 |
| 130-140 | | | | | | | 63.947 | 127.678 |

to floating point computations. The experiments showed, that RMSE values are equal (up to 5 digits, we used floating point numbers with 32 bit precision).

Next, we partitioned the dataset based on the number of ratings of the users. We created one partition for users with $0 < n_u < 10$, $10 \leq n_u < 20$, and so on. We evaluated the running time of recomputing the user feature vectors in each partition. Since the number of users in each partition differs, the average time per user is of interest.

Table 1 summarizes the results: when the number of features is 100 (i.e. $K = 100$), then to recompute the feature vector of a user, whose number of ratings are between 30 and 40, it takes $29.682 \cdot 10^{-4}$ seconds with RR, while KRR needs only $5.661 \cdot 10^{-4}$ seconds.

One can verify, that when $n_u$ is close to $K$, then the running time of RR and KRR are roughly equal. When $n_u < K$, KRR is much faster than RR.

## 4.2   Handling New Ratings of Users with KRR

The Sherman-Morrison formula can be applied when we extend a matrix with one row or column. When we apply KRR, the regularized Gram matrix $\lambda n_u \mathbf{I} + \mathbf{Q}[u]\mathbf{Q}[u]^{\mathrm{T}}$ is extended by one row and one column, thus, the SMF is applicable. The following steps are required to compute the new $\mathbf{p}_u$, according to (4):

- Compute the new row and column of the matrix: $O(K \cdot n_u)$.
- Update the inverse of the Gram matrix: $O(n_u^2)$.
- multiply by $\mathbf{r}_u$ from right: $O(n_u^2)$.
- multiply by $\mathbf{Q}[u]^{\mathrm{T}}$ from left: $O(K \cdot n_u)$.

Total: $O(K \cdot n_u + n_u^2)$.

Let us compare the time complexity of adding or removing one rating for users with $n_u < K$ using the Sherman-Morrison formula (as proposed in Section 3.3) and KRR:

- Sherman-Morrison formula: $O(K^2)$.
- KRR: $O(K \cdot n_u + n_u^2)$, which reduces to $O(K \cdot n_u)$, since $n_u < K$.

Clearly, KRR is better if $n_u < O(K)$.

# 5   Conclusion

In this work we focused on reducing the time complexity of alternating least squares based matrix-factorization algorithms. We showed that by using the Sherman-Morrison formula ALS based algorithms can be speeded up both on explicit and implicit feedback datasets. For explicit feedback, we improved from $O(K^2 \cdot |\mathcal{R}| + K^3 \cdot N)$ to $O(K^2 \cdot |\mathcal{R}|)$ the time complexity of the recomputation of the user feature matrix ($\mathbf{P}$). For implicit feedback $O(K^2 \cdot |\mathcal{R}^+| + K^3 \cdot N)$ is reduced to $O(K^2 \cdot |\mathcal{R}^+|)$. For the item feature matrix $\mathbf{Q}$ analog results hold. We proved that SMF can also be applied to reduce the complexity of greedy feature selection algorithms on $F$ predictors from $O(F^5)$ to $O(F^4)$. Then we showed, how linear kernel ridge regression can speed up ALS for users with $n_u < K$ ratings: the original $O(K^2 \cdot n_u + K^3)$ is reduced with SMF to $O(K^2 \cdot n_u)$, and with KRR it reduces to $O(K \cdot n_u^2)$. We performed experiments to show how much computational performance gain can be brought by KRR.

We pointed out that the addition or deletion of ratings can be handled in $O(K^2)$ by SMF, and if $n_u < K$, then in $O(K \cdot n_u)$ with KRR, while the traditional way requires $O(K^3)$ operations. These proposed methods allows ALS to be used in practical recommender systems, where the recommender system must respond instantly, when a new user rating arrives.

# References

1. Bell, R.M., Koren, Y.: Scalable collaborative filtering with jointly derived neighborhood interpolation weights. In: Proc of. ICDM 2007, 7th IEEE Int. Conf. on Data Mining, Omaha, Nebraska, USA, pp. 43–52 (2007)
2. Hu, Y., Koren, Y., Volinsky, C.: Collaborative filtering for implicit feedback datasets. In: Proc. of ICDM 2008, 8th IEEE Int. Conf. on Data Mining, Pisa, Italy, pp. 263–272 (2008)
3. Takács, G., Pilászy, I., Németh, B., Tikk, D.: On the Gravity recommendation system. In: Proc. of KDD Cup Workshop at SIGKDD 2007, 13th ACM Int. Conf. on Knowledge Discovery and Data Mining, San Jose, California, USA, pp. 22–30 (2007)
4. Takács, G., Pilászy, I., Németh, B., Tikk, D.: Investigation of various matrix factorization methods for large recommender systems. In: 2nd Netflix-KDD Workshop, Las Vegas, NV, USA, August 24 (2008)
5. Bell, R.M., Koren, Y., Volinsky, C.: The BellKor solution to the Netflix Prize. Technical Report, AT&T Labs Research (2007),
   http://www.netflixprize.com/assets/ProgressPrize2007_KorBell.pdf
6. Takács, G., Pilászy, I., Németh, B., Tikk, D.: A unified approach of factor models and neighbor based methods for large recommender systems. In: Proc. of ICADIWT 2008, 1st IEEE Workshop on Recommender Systems and Personalized Retrieval, August 2008, pp. 186–191 (2008)
7. Paterek, A.: Improving regularized singular value decomposition for collaborative filtering. In: Proc. of KDD Cup Workshop at SIGKDD-07, 13th ACM Int. Conf. on Knowledge Discovery and Data Mining, San Jose, California, USA, pp. 39–42 (2007)
8. Bernstein, D.S.: Matrix Mathematics: Theory, Facts, and Formulas with Application to Linear Systems Theory. Princeton University Press, Princeton (2005)
9. Sutjandra, Y., Budalakoti, S.: A web recommendation system with online updates. Ee380l: Data mining class project technical report, The University of Texas at Austin (2007)

# Sequence-Based Trust for Document Recommendation

Hsuan Chiu, Duen-Ren Liu, and Chin-Hui Lai

Institute of Information Management
National Chiao Tung University, Taiwan
cherylautumn.iim96g@g2.nctu.edu.tw,
{dliu,chlai}@iim.nctu.edu.tw

**Abstract.** Collaborative Filtering (CF) recommender systems have emerged in various applications to support item recommendation, which solve the information-overload problem by suggesting items of interests to users. Recently, trust-based recommender systems have incorporated the trustworthiness of users into the CF techniques to improve the quality of recommendation. They propose trust computation models to derive the trust value based on users' past ratings on items. A user is more trustworthy if he has contributed more accurate predictions than other users. Nevertheless, none of them derive the trust value based on a sequence of user's ratings on items. We propose a sequence-based trust model to derive the trust value based on users' sequences of ratings on documents. In knowledge-intensive environments, users normally have various information needs to access required documents over time, which forms a sequence of documents ordered according to their access time. The model considers two factors - time factor and document similarity in computing the trustworthiness of users. The proposed model is incorporated into standard collaborative filtering method to discover trustworthy neighbors for making predictions. The experiment result shows that the proposed model can improve the prediction accuracy of CF method comparing to other trust-based recommender systems.

**Keywords:** Sequence-based Trust, Collaborative Filtering, Recommender System.

## 1 Introduction

Recommender systems have emerged in various applications to support item recommendation[1, 2], solving the information-overload problem by suggesting items of interest to users. Various recommendation methods have been proposed. The collaborative filtering (CF) method [3] has been successfully used in various applications. It predicts user preferences for items in a word-of-mouth manner. User preferences are predicted by considering the opinions (in the form of preference ratings) of other "like-minded" users.

Recently, trust-based recommender systems [4] have incorporated the trustworthiness of users into the CF techniques to improve the quality of recommendation. According to [5], trust can be defined as how much a trustor believes that a trustee is willing and able to perform under a given situation. Massa et al. [6-9] proposed a trust

T. Di Noia and F. Buccafurri (Eds.): EC-Web 2009, LNCS 5692, pp. 240–251, 2009.
© Springer-Verlag Berlin Heidelberg 2009

recommender system based on a user's web of trust, which explicitly specifies the friends s/he trusts. For instance, in Epinions.com, users are allowed to assign their personal trust value to the review writers. Through trust propagation from the web of trust, the trust value between two users can be predicted even though there is no direct trust value specified (connection) between them. Their work, however, relies on the user's explicit assignment of trust value that is not easy to collect and may create a heavy burden on users.

Some researches [10-12] have proposed trust computation models to derive the trust value based on users' past ratings of items. O'Donovan et al. [11] suggest that if a user has usually delivered accurate predictions in the past, s/he merits being called reliable and trustworthy. A prediction on an item contributed from a given user (producer) is accurate to a target user (consumer) if the difference between their ratings on the item is within a predefined error bound. Generally, a user is more trustworthy if s/he has contributed more accurate predictions than other users. Their proposed trust metrics is a global trust, which basically accumulates the given user's accurate predictions made to other users or a group of users. Their trust model includes the item level and profile level. The item-level / profile-level trust metric of a given user is derived by computing the ratio of accurate predictions that s/he has made to other users over a particular item / all items that s/he has rated in the past. In addition, Hwang and Chen [12] propose a local trust metric to derive the trust value between two users by calculating the ratio of accurate predictions over all co-rated items, i.e., those items that have been rated by both of them. The proposed local trust metric is more personalized than the global trust metric. Their proposed trust metrics are combined with the standard CF technique to improve prediction quality for a MovieLens dataset.

Nevertheless, no one has derived trust value based on a sequence of user's ratings of items. In knowledge-intensive environments, users normally have various information needs in accessing required documents over time, producing a sequence of documents ordered according to their access time. For such environments, the ordering of documents required by a user may be important. For example, a user may need to access documents with prerequisite and basic knowledge first and then documents with advanced knowledge.

In this work, we propose a sequence-based trust model to derive trust value based on users' sequences of document ratings. The proposed model considers time factor, and document similarity in computing the trustworthiness of users. Generally, an accurate prediction made in the recent past contributes more trustworthiness than one made earlier. Moreover, conventional trust computational models use the ratings on the same item to derive the accuracy of prediction and compute the trust value. In knowledge-intensive environments, users often have the information needs to access documents with similar contents. A user's rating of a document generally reflects the user's perception of the relevance of the document content to his/her information needs. Thus, the ratings on different documents with similar contents should also help to derive the trustworthiness of users. Accordingly, we consider the time factor and the ratings on similar documents to derive a sequence-based trust computation model. The proposed model is incorporated into the standard CF method to effectively discover trustworthy neighbors for making predictions. The experiment result shows that the proposed model can improve the prediction accuracy of the CF method compared with other trust-based recommender systems.

The paper is organized as follows. We present related work of the trust-based recommendation methods in Section 2 and overview of sequence-based trust in Section 3. Section 4 describes our proposed trust computation model and the CF method. The experiment evaluations and results are presented in Section 5. Conclusions are finally made in Section 6.

## 2 Related Work

The collaborative filtering (CF) method [3] has been successfully used in various applications to support item recommendation [1, 2]. Trust-based recommender systems [4] have incorporated the trustworthiness of users into the CF techniques to improve the quality of recommendation. Some researches [10-12] have proposed trust computation models to derive the trust value based on users' past ratings of items.

O'Donovan and Smyth [11] propose profile-level trust and item-level trust derived from user rating data. They use a simple version of Resnick's prediction formula [3] to calculate a target user $c$'s predicted rating on an item $i_k$ from a recommender $p$'s rating on $i_k$, as defined in Eq. 1.

$$\hat{P}^p_{c,i_k} = \bar{r}_c + (r_{p,i_k} - \bar{r}_p)$$ (1)

where $\hat{P}^p_{c,i_k}$ is a predicted rating of the target user $c$ on item $i_k$; $\bar{r}_c$ and $\bar{r}_p$ refer to the mean ratings of target user $c$ and recommender $p$; and $r_{p,i_k}$ is $p$'s rating on $i_k$. They claim that accurate recommendation in the past is important and reliable and a user is viewed as trustworthy if s/he always contributes a precise prediction, as shown in Eq. 2.

$$Correct(i_k, p, c) \Leftrightarrow |\hat{P}^p_{c,i_k} - r_{c,i_k}| < \varepsilon$$ (2)

where $r_{c,d_k}$ is a real rating of the item $i_k$ given by the target user $c$; and $\varepsilon$ is an error bound measuring the closeness. According to this equation, recommender $p$ is regarded as trustworthy if his/her prediction on item $i_k$ in target user $c$'s view is close to $c$'s real rating $r_{c,i_k}$. The profile-level trust, $Trust^p(p)$, is calculated in the percentage of correct prediction that the recommender $p$ has made; while the concept of item-level trust, $Trust^I(p,i_k)$, is similar but focuses on a specific item $i_k$.

$$Trust^P(p) = \frac{|CorrSet(p)|}{RecSet(P)} \; ; \quad Trust^I(p,i_k) = \frac{|\{(c_k,i_k) \in CorrSet(p)\}|}{|\{(c_k,i_k) \in RecSet(p)\}|}$$ (3)

The neighbors of target users are selected by filtering out users whose profile-level trust values are lower than a specified threshold (Eq. 4). The weight between user $p$ and the target user $c$ is derived by combining the value of profile-level trust with user similarity in a harmonic mean (Eq. 5). Then, these user weights are applied in a modified version of Resnick's formula for prediction, as illustrated in Eq. 6. The item-level trust can be applied similarly in the recommendation phase.

$$NS = \{Trust^P(p) > threshold\}$$ (4)

$$w_{c,p}^{Trust^p} = \frac{2(sim(c,p))(Trust^p(p))}{sim(c,p)+Trust^p(p)} \tag{5}$$

$$p_{c,i_j} = \bar{r}_c + \frac{\sum_{p \in NS} w_{c,p}^{Trust^p} (r_{p,i_j} - \bar{r}_p)}{\sum_{p \in NS} w_{c,p}^{Trust^p}} \tag{6}$$

Hwang and Chen [12] consider the trustor's subjective opinions to obtain more personalization effects when predicting the trust value which s/he placed on the trustee. Similarly to [11], they calculate personal trust degree based on the user's past rating data, as shown in Eq. 7.

$$T_{c \to p} = \frac{1}{|(I_c \cap I_p)|} \sum_{i_k \in (I_c \cap I_p)} (1 - \frac{|\hat{p}_{c,i_k}^p - r_{c,i_k}|}{M}) \tag{7}$$

Recommender $p$ predicting item $i_k$ in target user $c$'s view is denoted as $\hat{p}_{c,i_k}^p$. Instead of filtering with an error bound, however, they use all items that are co-rated by $p$ and $c$ to compute personal trust. $M$ is the range of the rating score between maximum and minimum rating scores.

## 3 The Sequence-Based Trust for Recommendation

In knowledge-intensive environments, users normally have various information needs in accessing required documents over time. To proactively and accurately provide required documents to users, a sequence-based trust recommendation method is proposed. A document sequence of a given user denotes the sequence of documents accessed by the user, while a user's rating sequence represents his ratings on the documents he had accessed over time. Most trust computation models consider accurate predictions derived from past rating records to derive the trust value. We consider the time factor and the ratings on similar documents to derive a sequence-based trust computation model.

As illustrated in Fig. 1, our method consists of several steps. First, documents are pre-processed by the *tf-idf* approach to generate document profiles describing the key contents of documents. In addition, the system records the accessing time of documents, the accessing behavior or user's and ratings of documents. Because each user has various information needs at different times, his/ her documents are arranged as a document sequence by their access time. In addition, the similarities among document profiles are derived in the similarity computation step. Next, these document similarities and document ratings in users' document sequences are incorporated into our trust model to obtain the sequenced-based trust values which denote the trustworthiness among users. We propose three sorts of trust models which consider time factor, document similarity and both time factor and document similarity, respectively. These trust values of users are used to discover highly trustworthy users as neighbors for a target user. Notably, the neighbors selected by use of different trust computation models for the same target user may vary. Based on the trust values and the document ratings of these neighbors, the proposed CF methods can predict required documents and generate a recommendation list for the target user.

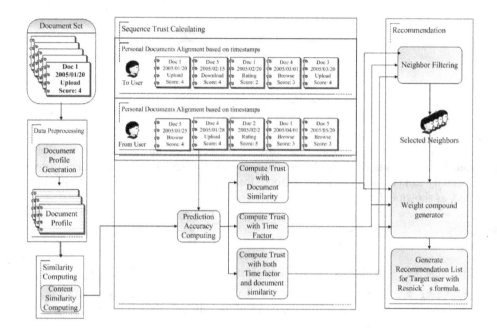

**Fig. 1.** An overview of the sequence-based trust recommendation method

## 4  Sequence-Based Trust Models and CF Methods

In the following, we will describe the proposed sequenced-based trust models from Sections 4.1 to Section 4.3 respectively. Then, in Section 4.4, we will introduce the sequence-based recommendation methods and illustrate their details.

### 4.1  Sequence-Based Trust with Time Factor

In this section, we illustrate the trust computation model considering the time factor. Each user has a document sequence and corresponding rating sequence, where the ratings of documents are ordered by a time index. The documents / ratings of users are aligned according to their relative time index in corresponding sequences.

The conventional trust model calculates the ratio of accurate predictions made according to past ratings without considering the time factor. Our proposed trust model derives the trust value of a given user not only based on the ratio of accurate predictions but also on the time that the accurate predictions were made.

Similarly to the conventional trust computation models [11, 12], we also use a simple version of Resnick's prediction formula [3] to calculate a target user $c$'s predicted rating of a document $d_k$, $\hat{p}_{c,d}^{p}$, which is derived from a recommender $p$'s rating of $d_k$, as defined in Eq. 8.

$$\hat{P}_{c,d_k}^{p} = \bar{r}_c + (r_{p,d_k} - \bar{r}_p) \tag{8}$$

where $\bar{r}_c$ and $\bar{r}_p$ refer to the mean ratings of target user $c$ and recommender $p$; and $r_{p,d_k}$ is $p$'s rating of document $d_k$. If $\hat{P}^p_{c,d_k}$ is close to the real rating score of user $c$ on $d_k$, i.e., $r_{c,d_k}$, we conclude that both the target user $c$ and the recommender $p$ have a similar perspective on document $d_k$. The more similar the perspective, the more trust they have, as illustrated in Eq. 9.

$$T^{pure}_{c,p,d_k} = 1 - \frac{\left| \hat{P}^p_{c,d_k} - r_{c,d_k} \right|}{M} \tag{9}$$

where $T^{pure}_{c,p,d_k}$ is the pure trust value between target user $c$ and recommender $p$ pertaining to document $d_k$ that is derived from the rating data without considering the time factor; and $M$ is the range of the rating score, which equals the difference of the maximum and minimum rating scores.

Generally, the latest documents accessed by a given user more precisely reflect his/her current information needs. Similarly, an accurate prediction made in the recent past contributes more trustworthiness than the one made some time ago.

A document sequence of a user $c$ is a time-ordered sequence arranged by the access times of the documents. Let $S^D_p$ and $S^R_p$ be the document sequence and rating sequence of a recommender $p$ respectively. The document sequence is defined as $S^D_c = <d^{t_{c1}}_{k1,c}, ..., d^{t_{cj}}_{kj,c}, ..., d^{t_{cf}}_{kf,c}>$ and $t_{c1} < t_{c2} < \cdots < t_{cf}$, where $d^{t_{cj}}_{k,c}$ denotes the document $d_k$ that the user $c$ accessed at time $t_{cj}$; $t_{c1}$ is the starting time index of the first document accessed in his/her sequence; and $t_{cf}$ is the index of the time the user accessed the most recent document in his/her sequence. The rating sequence of user $c$, $S^R_c$, can be similarly defined. Assume that a document $d_k$ is accessed by user $c$ at time $t_{cj}$ and accessed by recommender $p$ at time $t_{pi}$. The time factor $TF^{p,t_{pi}}_{c,t_{cj}}$ of a prediction, which is made based on the ratings $r^{t_{cj}}_{c,d_k}$ and $r^{t_{pi}}_{p,d_k}$, is defined as Eq. 10. The time factor considers the time weights of user $c$'s rating and user $p$'s rating..

$$TF^{p,t_{pi}}_{c,tcj} = \frac{2 \times tw^{cj}_c \times tw^{pi}_p}{tw^{cj}_c + tw^{pi}_p} \tag{10}$$

The two time weights are calculated from the time index $t_{cj}$ of user $c$'s sequence and the time index $t_{pi}$ of user $p$'s sequence respectively. Higher time weights are given to ratings with more recent time indices. The time weight of a rating made at time $t_{pi}$ by user $p$ is defined as $tw^{pi}_p = \frac{t_{pi} - t_{p1}}{t_{pf} - t_{p1}}$, where $t_{p1} / t_{pf}$ is the starting / latest time index in user $p$'s sequence. The time weight of a rating made at time $t_{cj}$ by user $c$ is defined similarly. The time factor uses the harmonic mean of the two time weights; thus the time factor of a prediction will be high if both the time weights of the ratings are high, i.e., both the ratings are made in more recent time.

Eq. 9 derives the pure trust value of a prediction without considering the time factor. We further use the time factor of a prediction to denote the importance (weight) of the prediction contributing to the trustworthiness. The trust value of user $c$ with respect to recommender $p$ is then derived by taking the weighted average of the pure trust values of predictions made on co-rated documents between them. Consequently, $T_{c,p}^{TF}$, the sequence-based trust metric considering time factor is defined as in Eq. 11.

$$
T_{c,p}^{TF} = \frac{\displaystyle\sum_{d_{k,c}^{t_{cj}} \text{in } S_c^D} \sum_{d_{k,p}^{t_{pi}} \text{in } S_p^D} (1 - \frac{\left| \hat{P}_{c,d_k}^{p,t_{pi}} - r_{c,d_k}^{t_{cj}} \right|}{M}) \times TF_{c,t_{cj}}^{p,t_{pi}}}{\displaystyle\sum_{d_{k,c}^{t_{cj}} \text{in } S_c^D} \sum_{d_{k,p}^{t_{pi}} \text{in } S_p^D} TF_{c,t_{cj}}^{p,t_{pi}}}
\tag{11}
$$

where $\hat{P}_{c,d_k}^{p,t_{pi}}$ is the target user $c$'s predicted rating on a document $d_k$, which is derived from a recommender $p$'s rating on $d_k$ at time $t_{pi}$, as defined similarly in Eq. 8; $S_c^D$ and $S_p^D$ are document sequences of the target user $c$ and recommender $p$ respectively; and $M$ is the range of the rating score, which equals the difference of the maximum and minimum rating scores.

## 4.2 Sequence-Based Trust with Document Similarity

In this section, we consider the ratings of similar documents to derive a sequence-based trust computation model. Even though two users do not access the same documents, their ratings of different documents with similar contents should also help to derive the trustworthiness of users. The cosine similarity is used to derive the similarity of documents based on their document profiles which are represented as term vectors by the *tf-idf* approach [13]. The reason for using content similarity is that the trust still exists if users have similar views on documents with similar contents.

Eq. 9 derives the pure trust value of a prediction for an identical document without considering the document similarity. Eq. 12 is used to predict a trust value, $T_{c,p}^{DS}$, based on documents with similar contents.

$$
T_{c,p}^{DS} = \frac{\displaystyle\sum_{d_{k,c}^{t_{cj}} \text{in } S_c^D} \sum_{\substack{d_{l,p}^{t_{pi}} \text{in } S_p^D \text{ and } DS_{c,d_k}^{p,d_l} \geq \theta}} (1 - \frac{\left| \hat{P}_{c,d_k}^{p,t_{pi},d_l} - r_{c,d_k}^{t_{cj}} \right|}{M}) \times DS_{c,d_k}^{p,d_l}}{\displaystyle\sum_{d_{k,c}^{t_{cj}} \text{in } S_c^D} \sum_{\substack{d_{l,p}^{t_{pi}} \text{in } S_p^D \text{ and } DS_{c,d_k}^{p,d_l} \geq \theta}} DS_{c,d_k}^{p,d_l}}
\tag{12}
$$

$\hat{P}_{c,d_k}^{p,t_{pi},d_l}$ is the target user $c$'s predicted rating of a document $d_k$, which is derived from a recommender $p$'s rating of document $d_l$ at time $t_{pi}$, as defined similarly in Eq. 8; $DS_{c,d_k}^{p,d_l}$ is the document similarity between documents $d_k$ and $d_l$ that is derived by use of the cosine similarity.

### 4.3  Sequence-Based Trust with Time Factor and Document Similarity

In order to gain the advantage of both time factor and document similarity, we combine them to derive a sequence-based trust metric, $T_{c,p}^H$, as defined in Eq. 13. The trust metric in this method is a hybrid of time factor and document similarity. The trust value of target user $c$ on recommender $p$ will be higher if $p$ has contributed more recent and accurate predictions on documents more similar to user $c$'s documents.

$$
T_{c,p}^H = \frac{\displaystyle\sum_{d_{k,c}^{t_{cj}} \text{ in } S_c^D} \sum_{d_{l,p}^{t_{pi}} \text{ in } S_p^D \text{ and } DS_{c,d_k}^{p,d_l} \geq \theta} (1 - \frac{\left|\hat{P}_{c,d_k}^{p,t_{pi},d_l} - r_{c,d_k}^{t_{cj}}\right|}{M}) \times TF_{c,t_{cj}}^{p,t_{pi}} \times DS_{c,d_k}^{p,d_l}}{\displaystyle\sum_{d_{k,c}^{t_{cj}} \text{ in } S_c^D} \sum_{d_{l,p}^{t_{pi}} \text{ in } S_p^D \text{ and } DS_{c,d_k}^{p,d_l} \geq \theta} TF_{c,t_{cj}}^{p,t_{pi}} \times DS_{c,d_k}^{p,d_l}} \tag{13}
$$

### 4.4  Sequence-Based Trust for Recommendation

In the recommendation phase, the trust value is used as a filtering mechanism to select neighbors with high trust degrees for a target user. Such trust values and the item ratings of neighbors are incorporated into our recommendation methods to make document predictions for the target user. The following section describes the details.

#### 4.4.1  Recommendation with Sequence-Based Trust Filtering
According to the trust relationship between users as illustrated in Section 4.1-4.3, users whose trust values are higher than a pre-specified threshold are selected as neighbors for a target user. Let $NS$ be a neighbor set; $T_{c,p}^{Factor}$ be the sequence-based trust degree between a target user $c$ and other user $p$; and *Factor* may be *TF*, *DS* or *H* which represents one of our proposed trust models, as described in Section 4.1-4.3. *TF* which denotes the sequence-based trust model with time factor utilizes users' time-ordered sequences arranged according to the access times of the documents to derive trust values. *DS* which denotes the sequence-based trust model with document similarity obtains the trust value of a prediction on users' different documents with similar content. *H* which denotes the sequence-based trust model with both time factor and document similarity derives the trust value by combing the effects of time factor and document similarity. To choose the trustworthy users as neighbors for a target user, we define Eq. 14 as the principle of the neighbor selection. That is, the neighbors of a target user have to fulfill this requirement.

$$
NS = \{T_{c,p}^{Factor} > threshold\} \tag{14}
$$

#### 4.4.2  Recommendation with Sequence-Based Trust Weighting
To predict documents that may interest a target user, we propose a recommendation method based on our sequence-based trust models. Such method utilizes the sequence-based trusts as weightings and the document ratings of the selected neighbors to make recommendations. The predicted rating of a document $d$ for a target user $c$, $\hat{P}_{c,d}$, is calculated by Eq. 15.

$$\hat{P}_{c,d} = \overline{r}_c + \frac{\sum_{p \in NS} T_{c,p}^{Factor}(r_{p,d} - \overline{r}_p)}{\sum_{p \in NS} T_{c,p}^{Factor}}, \tag{15}$$

where $NS$ is a neighbor set of the target user $c$; $p$ is a neighbor of user $c$; $\overline{r}_c / \overline{r}_p$ is the average rating of documents given by the target user $c$/ user $p$; $r_{p,d}$ is the rating of a document $d$ given by user $p$; $T_{c,p}^{Factor}$ is the sequence-based trust degree between a target user $c$ and user $p$; and *Factor* may be *TF*, *DS* or *H* which represents one of our proposed trust models, as described in Section 4.1-4.3. According to the Eq. 15, documents with high predicted ratings are used to compile a recommendation list, from which the top-*N* documents are chosen and recommended to the target user.

## 5   Experiments and Evaluations

In this section, we conduct experiments to evaluate the recommendation quality for our proposed methods and compare them with other trust-based recommendation methods. We describe the experiment setup in Section 5.1 and demonstrate the experimental results in Section 5.2.

### 5.1   Experiment Setup

In our experiment, we collect a data set from the laboratory of a research institute. There are over 500 research-related documents and about 50 users in the data set. We extract knowledge from these documents to derive the document profiles. Generally, each document profile consists of 800 distinct terms after information extraction and document pre-processing, i.e., case folding, stemming and stop words removal. Besides the documents, other information such as user information and user behaviors is necessary to implement our methods. Since the information needs may change over time, users will access and rate documents to fulfill their research work. Such user behavior is recorded in a log. Each user may access 45 documents on average according to the log data. In addition, each behavior except rate is given a default score (three for browsing behavior and four for uploading or downloading behavior) to represent how much a user may be interested in a document. For the rating behavior, the user may give a document a rating score on a scale of 1 to 5 to indicate whether the document is perceived as useful and relevant. A high rating, i.e., 4 or 5, indicates that the document is perceived as useful and relevant; while a low rating, i.e., 1 or 2, suggests that the document is deemed not useful. Since it is difficult to obtain such a data set, using the real application domain restricts the sample size of the data in our experiments.

In our experiment, the data set is divided as follows: 70% for training and 30% for testing. The training set is used to generate recommendation lists, while the test set is used to verify the quality of the recommendations. Accordingly, we evaluate the performances of our proposed methods and compare them with the traditional CF method and other trust-based recommendation methods.

To measure the quality of recommendations, the Mean Absolute Error (MAE) which evaluates the average absolute deviation between a predicted rating and the user's true rating is used to measure the sequence-based trust methods, as shown in Eq. 16. The lower the MAE, the more accurate the method will be.

$$MAE = \frac{\sum_{i=1}^{N}\left|\hat{P}_{d_i} - r_{d_i}\right|}{N} \tag{16}$$

Here $N$ is the amount of testing data, $\hat{P}_{d_i}$ is the predicted rating of document $d_i$ and $r_{d_i}$ is the real rating of document $d_i$.

### 5.2 Experiment Results

In the trust-based recommendation methods, the trust degree is obtained by the use of different trust computation models for selecting neighbors for a target user. Thus, we use different strategies based on these models to make recommendations and then analyze ·their recommendation performances. These recommendation strategies are defined as follows.

- **CF:** The standard Resnick model in GroupLens [3]. The Pearson correlation co-efficient is used in filtering and making predictions.
- **Profile-TrustCF (Profile-TCF):** The profile-level trust is used in filtering and the weight which combines both profile-level trust and user similarity derived by Pearson correlation coefficient is used to make predictions [11].
- **Item-TrustCF (Item-TCF):** The item-level trust is used in filtering and the weight which combines both item-level trust with user similarity derived by Pearson correlation coefficient is used to make predictions [11].
- **Personal-TrustCF (Personal-TCF):** Personal trust between two users is calculated by averaging the prediction error of their co-rated items [12].
- **Time-SeqTrustCF (T-STCF):** Recommendation with sequence-based trust with time factor, derived by using Eq. 11.
- **DocSim-SeqTrustCF (DS-STCF):** Recommendation with sequence-based trust with document similarity, derived by using Eq. 12.
- **Time-DocSim-SeqTrustCF (T-DS-STCF):** Recommendation with sequence-based trust with both time factor and document similarity, derived by using Eq. 13.

**Table 1.** Comparing the MAE values of all methods under different number of neighbors

| Number of Neighbors | CF | Profile-TCF | Item-TCF | Personal-TCF | Time-STCF | DS-STCF | T-DS-STCF |
|---|---|---|---|---|---|---|---|
| 2 | 0.7450 | 0.7430 | 0.7318 | 0.7181 | 0.7004 | 0.7043 | 0.7043 |
| 4 | 0.7843 | 0.7909 | 0.7221 | 0.6902 | 0.6645 | 0.6809 | 0.6558 |
| 6 | 0.8378 | 0.8033 | 0.7273 | 0.7024 | 0.6622 | 0.6990 | 0.6665 |
| 8 | 0.8652 | 0.8236 | 0.7168 | 0.7154 | 0.6937 | 0.6960 | 0.6854 |
| 10 | 0.8301 | 0.7014 | 0.6897 | 0.7432 | 0.6897 | 0.6964 | 0.6833 |

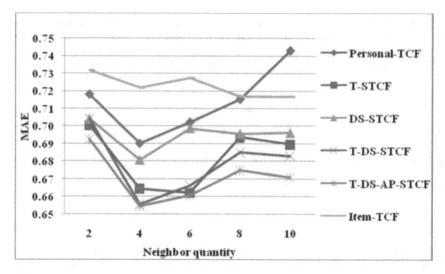

**Fig. 2.** The performances of the compared methods under different number of neighbors

In the experiment, we compare various recommendation methods under different number of neighbors, as shown in Fig. 2. Their MAE values are listed in Table 1. The proposed sequence-based trust method, T-DS-STCF, performs better than the other methods. This indicates that considering the time factor and the similarity of document content in our methods indeed improve the recommendation quality. For the trust-based recommendation methods, the effectiveness of both profile-level trust and item-level trust are not affected much by the number of neighbors. We also observe that the item-level trust outperforms the profile-level trust. Such observation is consistent with the research result of O'Donovan [11]. Additionally, the performances of these recommendation methods depend on the number of selected neighborhood. Generally these methods have the lowest MAE value when using four neighbors to make recommendations. In brief, our proposed methods outperform other methods and contribute to improve the prediction accuracy of recommendations.

## 6   Conclusions and Future Work

In this research, we propose sequence-based trust recommendation methods to derive the degree of trust based on user's sequences of ratings of documents. Such methods involve two main factors, time factor and document similarity, in computing the trustworthiness of users in the recommendation phase. The rationale behind using the time factor is that the predictions generated close to the current time provide more trustworthiness than those far away from the current time. In addition, the ratings of different documents with similar contents should also help to derive the trustworthiness of users. Accordingly, we employ the time factor and the ratings of similar documents to derive a sequence-based trust computation model. Eventually, the proposed model is incorporated into the standard CF method effectively to discover trustworthy neighbors for making recommendations. From the experimental results, we discover that the prediction accuracy of recommendation is indeed improved by using these two factors and our trust metric performs satisfactorily when both factors are combined and incorporated with user's interest over time. In future work, we will investigate how to infer user's reputation with respect to profile level and item level from our basic concept. We also expect that our methods will be applied in various domains and further applications will be developed.

## Acknowledgement

This research was supported in part by the National Science Council of the Taiwan under the grant NSC 96-2416-H-009-007-MY3.

## References

1. Resnick, P., Varian, H.R.: Recommender Systems. Communication of the ACM 40, 56–58 (1997)
2. Schafer, J.B., Frankowski, D., Herlocker, J., Sen, S.: Collaborative Filtering Recommender Systems. In: Brusilovsky, P., Kobsa, A., Nejdl, W. (eds.) Adaptive Web 2007. LNCS, vol. 4321, pp. 291–324. Springer, Heidelberg (2007)
3. Resnick, P., Iacovou, N., Suchak, M., Bergstrom, P., Riedl, J.: GroupLens: an open architecture for collaborative filtering of netnews. In: Proceedings of the 1994 ACM conference on Computer supported cooperative work, pp. 175–186. ACM/Chapel Hill, North Carolina/United States (1994)
4. Wang, Y., Lin, K.J.: Reputation-Oriented Trustworthy Computing in E-Commerce Environments. IEEE Internet Computing 12, 55–59 (2008)
5. Audun, J., Roslan, I., Colin, B.: A survey of trust and reputation systems for online service provision. Decis. Support Syst. 43, 618–644 (2007)
6. Massa, P., Avesani, P.: Trust-aware recommender systems. In: Proceedings of the 2007 ACM conference on Recommender systems, pp. 17–24. ACM, Minneapolis (2007)
7. Massa, P., Avesani, P.: Trust Metrics on Controversial Users: Balancing Between Tyranny of the Majority. International Journal on Semantic Web & Information Systems 3, 39–64 (2007)
8. Massa, P., Avesani, P.: Trust-aware collaborative filtering for recommender systems. In: Meersman, R., Tari, Z. (eds.) OTM 2004. LNCS, vol. 3291, pp. 492–508. Springer, Heidelberg (2004)
9. Massa, P., Bhattacharjee, B.: Using trust in recommender systems: an experimental analysis. In: Jensen, C., Poslad, S., Dimitrakos, T. (eds.) iTrust 2004. LNCS, vol. 2995, pp. 221–235. Springer, Heidelberg (2004)
10. Kim, Y.A., Le, M.-T., Lauw, H.W., Lim, E.-P., Liu, H., Srivastava, J.: Building a web of trust without explicit trust ratings. In: IEEE 24th International Conference on Data Engineering Workshop (ICDEW 2008), pp. 531–536 (2008)
11. O'Donovan, J., Smyth, B.: Trust in recommender systems. In: Proceedings of the 10th international conference on Intelligent user interfaces, pp. 167–174. ACM Press, San Diego (2005)
12. Hwang, C.-S., Chen, Y.-P.: Using Trust in Collaborative Filtering Recommendation. In: Okuno, H.G., Ali, M. (eds.) IEA/AIE 2007. LNCS, vol. 4570, pp. 1052–1060. Springer, Heidelberg (2007)
13. Baeza-Yates, R., Ribeiro-Neto, B.: Modern information retrieval. ACM Press, New York (1999)

# Recommender Systems on the Web: A Model-Driven Approach

Gonzalo Rojas, Francisco Domínguez, and Stefano Salvatori

Department of Computer Science, University of Concepción
Edmundo Larenas 215, Concepción, Chile
{gonzalorojas,fdominguez,ssalvatori}@udec.cl

**Abstract.** Recommendation techniques have been increasingly incorporated in e-commerce applications, supporting clients in identifying those items that best fit their needs. Unfortunately, little effort has been made to integrate these techniques into methodological proposals of Web development, discouraging the adoption of engineering approaches to face the complexity of recommender systems. This paper introduces a proposal to develop Web-based recommender systems from a model-driven perspective, specifying the elements of recommendation algorithms from a high abstraction level. Adopting the item-to-item approach, this proposal adopts the conceptual models of an existing Web development process to represent the preferences of users for different items, the similarity between obtained from different algorithms, and the selection and ordering of the recommended items according to a predicted rating value. Along with systematizing the development of these systems, this approach permits to evaluate different algorithms with minor changes at conceptual level, simplifying their mapping to final implementations.

**Keywords:** recommender systems, model-driven development, item-to-item recommendations.

## 1 Introduction

E-commerce is a natural field for the implementation of recommender systems. From large databases of different products, these systems select a subset of items that are likely to be preferred by a given user, and sort them according to the predicted interest that this user would have for each of them. Fruit of an intensive research activity, multiple recommendation techniques have been developed, facing the challenge of providing high-quality recommendations in demanding interaction scenarios. However, although increasing, the low number of success recommender e-commerce systems shows that the integration of this rationale into Web environment is still an unsolved problem.

Along with the intrinsic complexity of the development process of Web applications, the implementation of recommendation techniques considers some additional aspects like: the election of the recommender algorithms that best fulfil specific application goals; the specification of user characteristics and interactions on which the recommendations are based; or the implementation of

T. Di Noia and F. Buccafurri (Eds.): EC-Web 2009, LNCS 5692, pp. 252–263, 2009.

algorithms through different adaptive techniques. In front of this scenario, Web developers may easily feel discouraged about adopting recommendation techniques if they are not provided with the proper methods and tools that help them to deal with this complexity. Indeed, research efforts have been mostly oriented to improve the efficiency and scalability of recommendation algorithms and, in the side of Web development, to enhance conceptual models to specify adaptive interfaces. However, there is a lack of model-driven proposals that facilitate the integration of these efforts, through high-level proposals that support the specification of: (a) the elements on which recommendation algorithms are based; (b) the functionality of these algorithms in terms of domain-independent structures; and (c) the interface elements that can be adapted according to this functionality.

In [1], we introduce a model-driven method to develop Adaptive Web Applications, based on the OOWS development process [2], which supports the conceptual specification of well-known adaptive methods and techniques [3]. In this paper, we complement that work by defining a modelling proposal that integrates recommendation algorithms into the specification of e-commerce applications. Adopting the Item-to-Item recommendation approach, it is possible to specify the three main aspects of such algorithms: the preferences of users for different catalogue items, the estimated similarity between these items, and the selection and ordering of the recommended items according to a predicted rating value. From the obtained conceptual schemas, it is possible to implement different recommendation algorithms with minor changes at conceptual level. This proposal permits to systematize the development of recommender systems on the Web, combining the solid knowledge on recommendation technologies with the best practices of software engineering.

The rest of this paper has the following structure: Section 2 presents a summary of related research; Section 3 describes the OOWS Navigational Model that is used to specify the different aspects of recommender algorithms; Section 4 introduces the three main phases of the proposal: domain modelling, functional specification and navigational modelling; Section 5 describes the application of this proposal in two case studies. Finally, conclusions and description of future works are presented.

## 2   Related Research

Three major approaches have ruled the design of recommender systems [4]: Content-Based Recommendations, Collaborative Filtering and Item-to-Item Recommendations. *Content-based recommendation systems* [5] select the recommended items based on descriptions of their content. For this purpose, developers need to define a proper representation of the items, and to choose the recommendation algorithms that are suited for the defined representation. *Collaborative Filtering* is the process of filtering or evaluating items using the opinions of other people [6]. A collaborative filtering system computes a similarity value between each pair of users, and recommends items to the active user by selecting those preferred by her most similar users. In this kind of systems, a costumer is defined as an $n$-dimensional vector, where $n$ is the number of the distinct catalog items, and which is composed of the rating values that the costumer has given to each item. *Item-to-Item Recommendation systems* [7] recommends those items that are more similar to those preferred by the active user, but unlike the content-based approach, in this case the similarity is calculated from the rating values that users give to these items. Each item is represented through a $m$-dimensional vector, where $m$ is the number of the application's users, and which contains the ratings that each costumer has given to the item.

The computation of similarities between pairs of users (in the case of collaborative filtering) and between pairs of items (for item-to-item recommendations) is performed through recommendation algorithms. The vectorial representation of users and items allows adopting techniques of vector similarity to obtain these values. One of the most used techniques is the *cosine-based similarity* [8], represented in the following expression. Vectors $A$ and $B$ may represent users or items, according to the adopted recommendation approach.

$$sim(A, B) = cos(\overrightarrow{A}, \overrightarrow{B}) = \frac{\overrightarrow{A} \cdot \overrightarrow{B}}{||\overrightarrow{A}|| * ||\overrightarrow{B}||} . \tag{1}$$

A more accurate technique of similarity is achieved through the *Pearson-r correlation* [8], where co-rated cases are isolated, i.e., only items that have been rated by both users $A$ and $B$ (collaborative filtering), and only users that have rated both items $A$ and $B$ (item-to-item recommendations), are considered. The following expression corresponds to the Pearson-r correlation for the item-to-item approach:

$$sim(A, B) = corr_{A,B} = \frac{\Sigma_{u \varepsilon U}(R_{u,A} - \bar{R}_A)(R_{u,B} - \bar{R}_B)}{\sqrt{\Sigma_{u \varepsilon U}(R_{u,A} - \bar{R}_A)^2}\sqrt{\Sigma_{u \varepsilon U}(R_{u,B} - \bar{R}_B)^2}} . \tag{2}$$

As stated in [7], content-based systems provide recommendations with a relatively poor quality, being often either too general or too narrow, due to the difficulty in describing items whose content is hardly to be parsed, like multimedia items. More accurate recommendations are provided through collaborative filtering; however, this technique presents some problems of scalability and performance for large data sets, along with low quality recommendations for users with unusual tastes [9]. Although presenting some of these problems as well, the item-to-item recommendation approach has been increasingly recognized as one of the most suitable technique to deal with the exigencies of a recommendation-based e-commerce application, in terms of quality of recommendations and scalability [10,11]. The successful experience of the recommendation functionalities of Amazon.com is a visible proof of the advantages of this technology. This is the recommendation strategy that the present work adopts.

Facing the increasing demand for adaptive Web applications, Model-Driven proposals have augmented the expressiveness of their conceptual models to incorporate adaptive functionality in their resulting applications. Proposals for adaptive hypermedia development, like the introduced by WebML [12], OO-HDM [13], WSDM [14], Hera [15], etc., share several characteristics, such as the definition of a User Model as part of the domain specification (except Hera, which does it into the navigational modelling phase); or the conceptual modelling of adaptive characteristics in their respective Navigational Models. Although most of them provide conceptual primitives that represent the selection and ordering of a list of items according to user-based criteria, none of the proposals provides explicit support to the most referred recommendation algorithms. The present work introduces concepts and modelling strategies that can be easily adapted to these model-driven proposals.

## 3   The OOWS Navigational Model

*OOWS (Object-Oriented Web Solution)* [2] is a Model-Driven development process of Web applications which proposes an automatic code generation strategy from a set of highly descriptive, UML-compliant conceptual models. The *OOWS Navigational Model* provides developers with conceptual primitives to model the navigational characteristics of a Web application. This is made from two perspectives: (a) the modelling of the global structure of the application, by means of a set of navigational maps that describe the navigational topology of the application in terms of its nodes (*navigational contexts*) and links; and (b) the modelling of the inner navigational structure, in terms of the data, operations and hyperlinks that can be accessed in each context, which are defined as views of the domain description (a UML Class Diagram).

Navigational Contexts represent interaction points that provide users with access to data and operations, through the aggregation of one or more navigational views of the Class Diagram. These views are called *Abstract Information Units (AIU)*. Each AIU is composed of one or more *Navigational Classes* which are related through *Navigational Relationships*. Both structures are navigational views of classes and associations from the Class Diagram of the application, respectively. The navigational class that provides the main information of the AIU is called *manager class*, while those that provide complementary information are called *complementary classes*. When a navigational relationship is crossed, the information of the selected object is carried to a target context. According to their dependence of this information, OOWS distinguishes two types of AIUs: (a) *Contextual AIU* (labelled with a circled "C" tag), which instantiates its manager class to the object received as contextual information; and (b) *Non-Contextual AIU* (labelled with a circled "NC" tag), which does not depend on the contextual information received by its containing context. Finally, two structures can be defined in any navigational class: *Population Filter*, which constrains the objects that are shown to users; and *Ordering Pattern*, which defines an order of presentation of the retrieved objects. Both filter constraints and ordering criteria are specified through OCL expressions.

# 4    Modelling Web-Based Recommender Systems

The present proposal describes a basic but frequent scenario of implementation of recommendation techniques in e-commerce applications. This scenario considers the presentation of a list of recommended items, which are selected and ordered according to the predicted relevance that each of them has for the active user. Each item of this list contains a link that leads to a page that provides detailed information about the selected item, along with a list of similar items that may be of interest for the active user. Additionally, this page provides mechanisms that allow users to rate the presented item. In order to answer these requirements, the system must consider the following aspects: (a) means to measure the interest or preference of users for the different catalog items of the application; (b) an algorithm that calculates the similarity between the catalog items, based on the ratings submitted by users; and (c) an algorithm that predicts the rating that a given customer would give to a candidate item, based on the obtained similarity of this item with those preferred by this user.

## 4.1    Requisites of Recommender Systems

In order to develop a Web application that fulfil all these requirements, and adopting a traditional three-layered architecture, we need to consider the following requisites for each of the layers:

1. Persistence Layer: along with the data that describe the catalog items from the application domain perspective, the application needs to maintain data of the registered customers and the ratings that they give to the items. Optionally, and according to the strategy of execution adopted, data about similarity between items may be stored as well.
2. Business Logic Layer: the basic functionality of the recommender system must consider at least: methods to capture and update the (explicit and/or implicit) ratings provided by customers; methods that compute the similarity between two items according to such ratings; and methods that calculate the predicted rating for different (customer,item) pairs.
3. Interface Layer: the interaction requirements of the application demand the provision of dynamic pages, which must identify the current user from the set of registered customers, and be flexible enough to provide different customers with different navigational alternatives. Furthermore, mechanisms that filter the presentation of a set of candidate items and organize their displaying according to their predicted rating are also needed.

## 4.2    Conceptual Modelling Proposal

Unlike many data-intensive e-commerce applications, in which business logic layer is mainly focused on the management of database queries, recommender systems demand a special consideration of this layer, due to the incorporation of rating mechanisms and recommendation techniques. This complexity makes the

Object-Oriented paradigm a suitable approach to develop this kind of systems, due to its natural management of data and methods, along with the decomposition mechanisms that help to break such complex algorithms into small, more manageable pieces. The specification of the aspects of each layer is performed by using the following models from the OOWS method:

1. Class Diagram (Persistence Layer): by means of classes from a traditional UML Class Diagram, the developer can describe the different *catalogues* of the store and their respective *items*, along with their registered *users*. Furthermore, the *rating* values provided by customers and the obtained *similarity* values between items can also be expressed through classes and associations.
2. Interaction Diagram (Business Logic Layer): a UML Communication Diagram allows splitting complex recommendation algorithms into small units, reducing the problem of computing the similarity between items to the management of the messages between objects and the construction of one single-method that calculates that similarity.
3. OOWS Navigational Diagram (Interface Layer): this schema, which specifies the navigational structure of a Web application from both *in-the-large* and *in-the-small* perspectives, also provides developers with conceptual structures to represent indexed lists, by means of *population filters* and *ordering patterns* that allow selecting and sorting the top-n candidate items according to the fulfilment of user-based OCL constraints.

### 4.3   Class Diagram

The main concepts involved in the process of recommendation are specified through the Class Diagram shown in Fig. 1. The modelled concepts are domain-independent, and its classes may be renamed and complemented according to the requirements of specific application domains. The defined classes are:

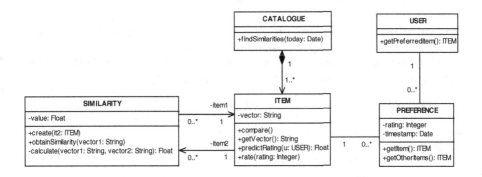

**Fig. 1.** Class diagram of a generic recommender system

- **CATALOGUE**: it represents a catalogue of information items. One application can provide users with different catalogues (e.g., a store that offers one catalogue of books and other of CD's);
- **ITEM**: it models the information items to be evaluated by and recommended to different users. Each object of this class contains a *preference vector*, which is a string of length $m$, that represents the preferences of each of the $m$ registered users for the corresponding item. This vector may contain unary values (representing only positive preferences), binary values (positive and negative preferences), or integer values (rating of an item).
- **USER**: it represents the registered users of the application, which receive recommendations from the system.
- **PREFERENCE**: it describes the explicit of implicit action of marking an item as preferred by a registered user. For instance, it may describe the purchase of a product, the rating of an article (explicit actions), or the visit of the page that give details about a product (implicit action). It includes an optional *rating* attribute, which represents the evaluation of the item by the associated user; and a *timestamp* attribute, which describes the time in which the preference has been marked.
- **SIMILARITY**: it represents the similarity between two information items. Its private method *calculate* implements a similarity algorithm, which compares the rating vectors of the two item objects, obtaining a *similarity value* that is used to select and sort the recommended items.

### 4.4 Communication Diagram

From the classes and associations included in the Class Diagram of Fig. 1, different recommender algorithms can be represented in terms of the interactions between the objects of the application domain, through UML communication (or collaboration) diagrams. Two diagrams are defined: one that represents the offline calculus of similarity between items of a given catalogue, based on the ratings marked by registered users; and other representing the prediction of the ranking value that a user would give to a given item.

**Computation of Item-to-Item Similarity.** The communication diagram that specifies the computation of similarity between different pairs of catalogue items is based on the iterative algorithm proposed by Amazon.com in the context of its item-to-item collaborative filtering technique [7].

*Amazon Item-to-Item Recommendation Algorithm*

```
For each item in product catalog, I1
    For each costumer C who purchased I1
        For each item I2 purchased by customer C
            Record that a customer purchased I1 and I2
    For each item I2
        Compute the similarity between I1 and I2
```

This algorithm gives developers the freedom to choose the method that computes the similarity. For our proposal, this means a great advantage, because we can easily adopt different similarity techniques according to the specific needs of the application, with minor changes at conceptual level. Figure 2 shows the Communication Diagram that represents this algorithm. This diagram is valid for any recommender algorithm that calculates the similarity between two items from a vectorial representation of the rating values submitted by different users, e.g., the cosine-based similarity and the Pearson-r correlation. One remarkable aspect of this approach is that the complexity of this algorithm is distributed among different objects, and the calculation of the similarity is finally performed in one single operation (*calculate*, invoked by message 2.5.2 in Fig. 2). The rest of invoked operations are mainly dedicated to search and select the proper items to be compared.

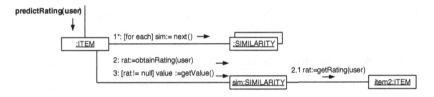

**Fig. 2.** Communication diagram of the computation of item similarity

**Computation of Predicted Preference.** Once the similarity values between pairs of items are calculated, the recommender system obtains the top-n recommended items for a given user. From the database of candidate items, the system uses these similarity values to predict how close is a given item to the preferences of the active user. One of the most used techniques to make this prediction is the *weighted sum*, where the predicted rating value $P_{u,i}$ that a user $u$ gives on an item $i$ is given by

$$P_{u,i} = \frac{\sum_{allsimilaritems,n} (s_{i,j} * R_{u,j})}{\sum_{allsimilaritems,n} |(s_{i,j})|} . \tag{3}$$

where each rating value given by $u$ on the $n$ items similar to $i$ ($R_{u,j}$) is weighted by the corresponding similarity $s_{i,j}$ between $i$ and the rated item $j$. The communication diagram of Fig. 3 describes this process. The operation *predictRating()* is executed by the object that represents the candidate item $i$, receiving as a parameter the object corresponding to the active user $u$. This operation calculates the prediction value once all the needed values of similarity and ratings are retrieved from the corresponding objects.

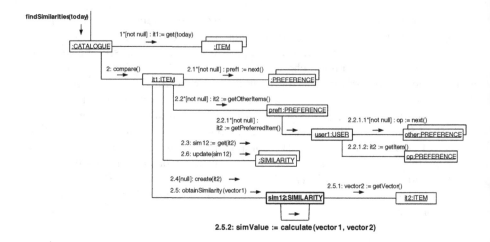

**Fig. 3.** Communication diagram of the computation of predicted preferences

## 4.5   OOWS Navigational Schema

Finally, the navigational schema of the two pages from the described scenario is defined. Figure 4 shows the inner structure of both pages, through respective OOWS navigational contexts. The left context shows a navigational class, which is a view of the ITEM class, including the attributes and operations that are visible to the user. A navigational relationship leads users to another page that shows detailed information on the selected item. Furthermore, it contains a population filter (bottom of the class) and an ordering pattern (top tag), which filter and order the recommended items according to the fulfilment of OCL constraints, respectively. For readability purposes, these constraints are detailed next.

The following OCL expression corresponds to *Adaptive Population Filter 1* from Fig. 4. The invariant of this filter uses the *predictRating()* operation described through the communication diagram of Fig. 3, and specifies the condition to be fulfilled by self object to be included into the top-n recommended items.

*OCL constraint to select the Top-n Recommended Items*

```
context ITEM
    let currentUser:USER = system.currentUser() in
        inv: self.predictRating(currentUser) >= x
```

The OCL expression of *Ordering Pattern 1* is a query that returns the predicted rating value obtained from the *predictRating()* operation. In this way, the list of recommended items is ordered according to their respective predicted rating.

*OCL constraint to order the Top-n Recommended Items*

```
context ITEM::query_order(): Real
    let currentUser: USER = system.currentUser()
        in self.predictRating(currentUser)
```

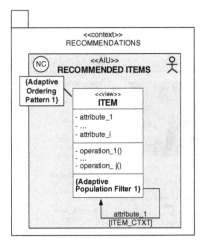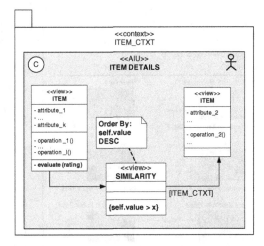

**Fig. 4.** OOWS navigational schema of a typical recommender system: a list of recommended items (*left*) and details of a selected item, with a list of similar items (*right*)

The right context of Fig. 4 represents the page of a selected item, which also includes another list of recommended items that are similar to the currently displayed. It contains a contextual AIU that uses the information selected in the previous context (page) to determine the object whose information is shown. To display the recommended related items, the system retrieves a subset of comparisons whose similarity values are bigger than an x, which is represented by a SIMILARITY complementary class whose objects are constrained by a population filter and sorted by a ordering pattern. Associated to each similarity object, the recommended items are displayed, through the ITEM complementary class.

## 5  Case Study

This modelling proposal has been successfully applied in different case studies of e-commerce applications. One of them is an online travel agency, which recommends different trips and tours based on the explicit rating values that users submit. Figure 5 shows two pages of this application: the left page shows the list of recommended trips, while the right page shows the details of a selected trip. Both are implementations of corresponding navigational contexts of Fig. 4, where ITEM class corresponds to a TRIP class. As seen in Fig. 5, left, cosine-based and Pearson-r correlation were used and, for illustration purposes only, the predicted values of preference were included for each recommended trip. The right page shows the details of a selected trip, including a rating mechanism and a list of similar trips of interest to the active user. This system was implemented in a MySQL/PHP platform, and the methods of similarity calculation and rating prediction were easily mapped from conceptual schemas to concise pieces of code. Similarity values are periodically calculated offline, for performance purposes,

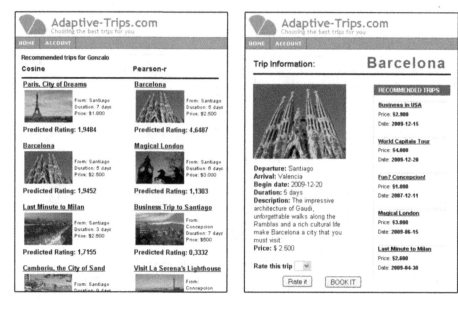

**Fig. 5.** Implemented pages of a recommender system (travel agency)

and stored in a database table. From these values, predictions are calculated online when the active user accesses the corresponding page.

The development of this case study took about half the time of the development time of an alternative content-based recommender system, which implements a simpler and less accurate recommendation strategy. In other example, an existing non-adaptive bookstore system was enhanced, by introducing the described recommendation functionality. This integration took only about 24 man-hours. These results show that this approach may be successfully integrated into existing e-commerce applications, with little investment in time and effort.[1]

## 6   Conclusions

The present work shows a Model-Driven proposal to incorporate recommender techniques into the development of e-commerce applications. By using conceptual structures from an existing approach of development of adaptive Web applications, the main aspects of recommender algorithms can be fully described at a high abstraction level, following a systematic and traceable process. The application of this proposal in different case studies has shown the advantages of an engineering approach to develop this kind of systems, saving time and effort in a scenario where new algorithms are constantly introduced and improved. Future works are oriented to support this modelling approach with development tools that permit to automatize this process and incorporate a broader set of

---

[1] Both applications and their code are available in http://www.inf.udec.cl/adweb

recommender algorithms, considering strategies that improve their scalability and performance. Furthermore, we are working on the specification of a CASE tool that permits to obtain rapid prototypes of recommender systems.

## Acknowledgments

This research is sponsored by the National Council for Scientific and Technological Research (FONDECYT, Chile) under Grant No.11080277.

## References

1. Rojas, G.: Modelling Adaptive Web Applications in OOWS. PhD thesis, Technical University of Valencia, Spain (2008)
2. Pastor, O., Pelechano, V., Fons, J., Abrahão, S.: Conceptual Modelling of Web Applications: the OOWS Approach. In: Mendes, E., Mosley, N. (eds.) Web Engineering, pp. 277–301. Springer, Heidelberg (2005)
3. Brusilovsky, P.: Methods and Techniques of Adaptive Hypermedia. User Modeling and User-Adapted Interaction 6(2-3), 87–129 (1996)
4. Balabanović, M., Shoham, Y.: Content-Based, Collaborative Recommendation. Commun. ACM. 40(3), 66–72 (1997)
5. Pazzani, M.J., Billsus, D.: Content-Based Recommendation Systems. In: Brusilovsky, P., Kobsa, A., Nejdl, W. (eds.) Adaptive Web 2007. LNCS, vol. 4321, pp. 325–341. Springer, Heidelberg (2007)
6. Schafer, J.B., Frankowski, D., Herlocker, J.L., Sen, S.: Collaborative Filtering Recommender Systems. In: Brusilovsky, P., Kobsa, A., Nejdl, W. (eds.) Adaptive Web 2007. LNCS, vol. 4321, pp. 291–324. Springer, Heidelberg (2007)
7. Linden, G., Smith, B., York, J.: Amazon.com Recommendations: Item-to-Item Collaborative Filtering. IEEE Internet Computing 7(1), 76–80 (2003)
8. Sarwar, B., Karypis, G., Konstan, J., Riedl, J.: Analysis of Recommendation Algorithms for E-commerce. In: EC 2000: Proceedings of the 2nd ACM Conference on Electronic Commerce, pp. 158–167. ACM, New York (2000)
9. Linden, G.D., Jacobi, J.A., Benson, E.A.: Collaborative Recommendations using Item-to-item Similarity Mappings. Patent No. US 6.266.649 (2001)
10. Deshpande, M., Karypis, G.: Item-based Top-n Recommendation Algorithms. ACM Trans. Inf. Syst. 22(1), 143–177 (2004)
11. Sarwar, B., Karypis, G., Konstan, J., Reidl, J.: Item-based Collaborative Filtering Recommendation Algorithms. In: 10th International Conference on World Wide Web, pp. 285–295. ACM, New York (2001)
12. Ceri, S., Daniel, F., Matera, M., Facca, F.M.: Model-Driven Development of Context-Aware Web Applications. ACM Trans. Inter. Tech. 7(1) (2007)
13. Schwabe, D., Guimarães, R., Rossi, G.: Cohesive Design of Personalized Web Applications. IEEE Internet Computing 6(2), 34–43 (2002)
14. Casteleyn, S.: Designer Specified Self Re-organizing Websites. PhD thesis, Vrije Universiteit Brussel, Belgium (2005)
15. Barna, P., Houben, G.J., Frasincar, F.: Specification of Adaptive Behavior using a General-Purpose Design Methodology for Dynamic Web Applications. In: De Bra, P.M.E., Nejdl, W. (eds.) AH 2004. LNCS, vol. 3137, pp. 283–286. Springer, Heidelberg (2004)

# Designing a Metamodel-Based Recommender System

Sven Radde[1], Bettina Zach[2], and Burkhard Freitag[1]

[1] Institute for Information Systems and Software Technology
University of Passau
D-94030 Passau, Germany
sven.radde@uni-passau.de, burkhard.freitag@uni-passau.de
http://www.ifis.uni-passau.de/
[2] :a:k:t: Informationssysteme AG
Dr.-Emil-Brichta-Straße 7
D-94036 Passau, Germany
bettina.zach@akt-infosys.de
http://www.akt-infosys.de/

**Abstract.** Current recommender systems have to cope with a certain reservation because they are considered to be hard to maintain and to give rather schematic advice. This paper presents an approach to increase maintainability by generating essential parts of the recommender system based on thorough metamodeling. Moreover, preferences are elicited on the basis of user needs rather than product features thus leading to a more user-oriented behavior. The metamodel-based design allows to efficiently adapt all domain-dependent parts of the system.

**Keywords:** conversational recommender system, metamodelling, industrial application.

## 1 Introduction

High quality assistance in complex product domains requires recommender systems to move away from strictly feature-centric recommendation approaches towards customer-oriented models. Good salespersons try to elicit the customer's needs and expectations about a product rather than asking overly technical questions. The matching of the customer's preferences with the technical attributes of a product is then left to the salesperson's experience and technical expertise.

Furthermore, e-commerce activities gain more and more importance but, on the other hand, cannot be mediated by human sales experts. Particularly if the product domain is highly complex or changes frequently, however, customers expect a quality of recommendation when shopping online that is comparable to visiting a store. Hence, digital recommender systems must surpass the common simple "configurators" in functionality to increase acceptance of online sales.

The main contribution of this paper is an industrial-strength architecture for a conversational recommender system based on an elaborate customer- and product-metamodel. The metamodel is coupled with a Bayesian inference engine which is

T. Di Noia and F. Buccafurri (Eds.): EC-Web 2009, LNCS 5692, pp. 264–275, 2009.

automatically derived from an instance of the customer model. This approach allows the recommender system to classify users with respect to different stereotypes, to assess their needs and, finally, to obtain information about the most recommendable products by inferring likelihoods for the different possible technical characteristics of the matching products. Based on the inferred results, the recommender system adapts its dialogue dynamically and obtains product recommendations by querying a ranking-enabled database that contains the product catalogue.

The solution presented in this paper is the result of a joint R&D effort with contributions from both science and business. This ensures that the developed metamodel closely resembles the natural recommendation procedures in the target market of mobile telecommunications. In addition, we found that a wide range of business domains share the basic assumptions of our metamodel, thus enabling the re-use of our approach by simply re-instantiating the metamodel. The latter effectively hides the mathematical complexity of the backend and therefore allows for a less involved, intuitive maintenance process. Business people have often argued that this could be a crucial point for recommender systems, particulary in fast changing domains.

In summary, we present:

- a metamodel-based approach for the efficient maintenance of a recommender system;
- an innovative industrial application of recommendation technology based on this approach;
- some experiences from a real-life implementation of the described principles;

The rest of the paper is organized as follows: In section 2 we describe our use case in the mobile telecommunications domain, identifying the need for support by recommender systems. Section 3 introduces the metamodel, while section 4 gives an overview of the proposed architecture. We detail experiences from our prototypical implementation in section 5, with particular attention on question selection, generation of recommendations and model maintenance. In section 6 we review some related work, before concluding with an outlook in section 7.

# 2   Use Case and Market Situation

Today's market for mobile phones is characterized by a huge number of choices. It is not uncommon to see more than 100 different items in shops, many of them differing only in details. The technology itself progresses rather fast, with permanently increasing computing power, new hardware options like GPS receivers, or integration of online services. Customers need qualified consultation to match their (often vague) preferences with these complex product models. However, when visiting the web sites of major mobile service providers, one finds most of them lacking sophisticated recommendation functionality. Commonly, these websites merely allow customers to restrict the catalogue of available cellphones by specifying purely technical constraints.

The course of action of specialized dealers is notably different: Initially the customer is classified according to a set of broad stereotypes, such as "young", "business customer", or the anticipated amount of money he or she would be willing to spend. This classification determines the broad course of the further dialogue. Based on their professional experience, sales people then try to assess the customer's needs and expectations which are finally mapped onto suggestions for technical features and, consequently, available products. We argue that emphasising *soft criteria* like "elegant phone" is one of the key differences between a natural sales dialogue and the common technology-oriented online phone configurators.

In addition to its complexity, the product domain changes frequently and often radically. Updates of the product domain may stem from a temporary marketing campaign, the introduction of new mobile phone variants, or technical innovations. In particular the latter often requires significant adjustments to a recommendation dialogue to accommodate previously unknown functionality. It is commonly not sufficient to change some parameters and therefore necessary to involve programmers thus leading to correspondingly high delays and costs.

Also, the constant requirement to train shop assistants for these adaptations or to modify online recommender applications, however, is counteracted by the need to cut costs, because average monthly revenues per customer decline, forcing retailers to deal with smaller profit margins. In this context, particularly when looking at retail chains with their even smaller margins, providing salespersons with a suitably powerful electronic recommender system is a way to keep costs low. For retail chains and e-commerce use in general, such a system will allow for a high quality recommendation process, while independent retailers and specialized dealers will be able to keep up their high standards of recommendation quality with a significantly reduced training overhead.

## 3 Metamodel Design

The use-case described in the previous section has been investigated in a joint R&D project conducted in cooperation of academic researchers and an industry partner having long-term expertise in the field. One of the primary goals is to achieve a separation between domain-dependent parts of the system which have to be adapted to changes on the one hand and a domain-neutral core that can remain stable even in face of significant changes within the domain on the other hand. To this end, we propose a domain metamodel basically expressing our assumption that stereotypes, needs and technical attributes form a network of mutual influences (see Fig. 1 for a UML representation). Instances of the metamodel must be created by a suitably experienced domain expert.

For presentation reasons, the product model has been simplified by not including those parts that enable the representation of "bundled" articles (i.e., the combination of two distinct articles to form the eventually sold item as is the case, e.g., with mobile phones and the corresponding contracts). It is noteworthy that the presented metamodel is not capable to capture configurable products with implicit relations (e.g., "Chosen AC adapter must be able to power all other components.") without further ado. Explicit relations, such as "allowed bundles", can be modelled and used to construct valid recommendations.

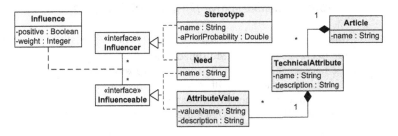

**Fig. 1.** UML diagram of the domain metamodel

First of all, *Stereotypes* are broad categories used to classify customers into classes that are considered representative for the particular application domain. They can be seen as a set of labels, a subset of which applies to any particular customer, forming his/her "composite" stereotype. *Stereotypes* have an *a priori probability* assigned that models statistical demographic knowledge about the prospective customers. Whenever the recommender system does not have positive knowledge about a *Stereotype* (e.g., the customer refuses to answer a corresponding question), it may use the modelled probability (in order to avoid "stalling" the dialogue). Obviously, this modelling is ideally suited to our use of Bayesian networks (cf. section 4), but other formalisms may also choose to exploit this information appropriately. Some *Stereotypes* will be independent of each other, while others may exclude or imply another *Stereotype*.

*Example 1.* As a brief example within our telecommunications domain, assume that the following *Stereotypes* are defined: "Age below 21", "Age between 21 and 55", "Age greater than 55", "Business customer" and "Fun-oriented user". Obviously, a customer would be assigned one of the "Age" *Stereotypes* and one, both or neither of the other two *Stereotypes*.

The customer's composite stereotype influences the *Needs* that he or she is likely to have. As opposed to *Stereotypes*, having or not having certain *Needs* is rarely a purely boolean decision. Rather, customers are able to choose from a set of values ranging from "Not at all." to "Yes, absolutely." when answering inquiries about *Needs*. *Influences* between *Needs* and *Stereotypes* represent the fact that being of a certain *Stereotype* changes the likelihood of having certain *Needs*.

Accordingly, *Influences* have a type (positive/negative) indicating the kind, i.e., strengthening or weakening, of their effect and a numerical weight expressing their relative importance. The semantic of *Influences* is dependent on their type: Positive *Influences* increase the likelihood that a customer will feel a *Need* when he or she belongs to the corresponding *Stereotype* and decrease it when this is not the case. Negative *Influences* have the opposite meaning. It is worth noting that a *Need* is both an *Influencer* and an *Influenceable* in our metamodel, thus enabling "recursion" to model more complex hierarchies of *Needs*.

*Example 2.* Extending the set of *Stereotypes* from example 1, assume that a domain expert defines the *Needs* "Office use" and "Multimedia use". To integrate them with the *Stereotypes*, some representative *Influences* as shown in Table 1 are defined.

**Table 1.** Representative *Influences* for example 2

| Stereotype | Need | Type | Weight |
|---|---|---|---|
| Age below 21 | Multimedia use | positive | 1 |
| Age between 21 and 55 | Office use | positive | 1 |
| Business customer | Office use | positive | 3 |
| Fun-oriented customer | Multimedia use | positive | 2 |
| Age below 21 | Office use | negative | 1 |

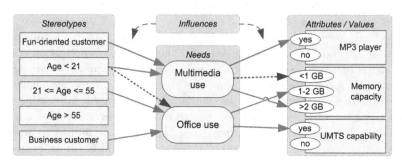

**Fig. 2.** Exemplary domain model. Solid lines denote positive *Influences*, dotted lines negative ones.

In the domain metamodel, an *Article* is seen as having a number of *Technical-Attributes* which, in turn, have discrete ranges of possible *AttributeValues*, modelled as a hierarchy of compositions in Fig. 1. Often, a *TechnicalAttribute* will have a boolean value range, indicating the presence or absence of a certain property. Domain experts may also use this feature to extend technical information with subjective annotations, such as "fancy casing", "trendy" or similar.

It is important to establish the notion that the product part of the domain model for our sample domain does not contain information about concrete products, i.e., concrete cellphones. Rather, it abstracts from this point of view by providing a more general description of how "cellphones as a whole" may look like by enumerating the characteristics of their technical properties. Finally, product catalogues or databases can be seen as instances of our domain model, i.e., they form the domain itself. The concrete cellphones available for sale are represented at this level, described by the terms defined in the domain model.

We note that restricting our domain metamodel to cover only discrete value ranges is not a significant loss: Even attributes that would normally be considered to have continuous value ranges often follow quite regular patterns, e.g., "price" is usually defined in terms of discrete "price bands" anyway. If there are too many discrete values, one can define buckets and classify the actual values accordingly.

Again, *Influences* link *AttributeValues* to *Stereotypes* and *Needs*, based on the notion that, given a certain *TechnicalAttribute*, some of its *AttributeValues* are more likely so satisfy the customer's *Needs* than others. See Fig. 2 for a simplified instance of the domain metamodel, extending examples 1 and 2.

While aiming primarily at the telecommunications market, the underlying assumptions of the metamodel apply to a wide range of similarly structured business domains. A technology prototype of our system was used in a completely different context where it was used to recommend a program of study to potential beginners, thus demonstrating the general adaptability of the metamodel.

## 4   Preference Elicitation and Domain Model Usage

All domain-dependent parts of the recommender system described in this paper can be generated from instances of the metamodel shown in section 3 and are combined with a domain-independent system core. In [1], we presented a dialogue structuring method, which acts as the underlying controller component for the course of the dialogue. [2] presents the Bayesian inference engine and particularly its generation-method in more detail. Fig. 3 illustrates how these components are integrated with a ranking-enabled database [3] and the metamodel instance for a given domain to form our recommender system architecture.

As illustrated by Fig. 3, the recommendation dialogue is generated automatically from the current domain model after a maintenance iteration has been finished. The dialogue itself consists of a series of steps, each of which contains a variable number of questions. The generation step creates one question for each stereotype and need defined in the domain model. Another set of questions to cover the technical attributes of the domain model is generated as well, so that the dialogue may transition to this fine-grained level of detail if necessary.

A question is designed in a way that its answer expresses the customer's preferences with respect to the corresponding model element, e.g., the need "Office use". The *Dialogue Manager* component, which uses statecharts (see [4,5]) as its internal dialogue structuring model, is responsible for the selection of the most appropriate question and its presentation.

The initial strategy of the dialogue is to attempt to obtain evidences for the stereotype nodes by asking the corresponding questions first, thus providing a quick personalization of the network's state. Afterwards, the customer's needs are elicited, leading to further individualization. Answers are passed to the *Inference Engine*, which treats them as evidences for its internal Bayesian network (see,

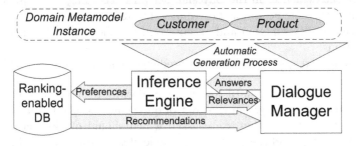

**Fig. 3.** System architecture overview

**Table 2.** Generated system elements

| Domain metamodel element | Generated element(s) |
|---|---|
| Stereotype | Question & Boolean node in the Bayes net |
| Need | Question & "Graded" node in the Bayes net |
| Technical attribute | Question |
| Attribute value | Boolean node in the Bayes net |
| Influence | Edge in the Bayes net & Defines the CPTs |

e.g., chapter 14 of [6]). The latter is also based on the domain model and is constructed during the generation step.

Table 2 gives a summary of the system elements that are generated from the domain model. Stereotypes are represented as chance nodes with a boolean value range (and a-priori probabilities are set according to the domain model), whereas needs are modeled as chance nodes with a value range to reflect the possible "graded" answers mentioned in section 3. Product attributes are included in the network by creating one boolean node for each element of their respective ranges of attribute values. Finally, the modeled influences are represented as edges between the corresponding nodes. The conditional probability tables (CPTs) of the influenced nodes are designed to reflect the causal effects implied by the influences of the domain model (cf. [2] for details): 1) Belonging to certain stereotypes implies that some needs are more likely than others; 2) Having a certain need implies that a product with appropriate technical properties will be more useful than another.

As discussed in subsection 5.1 below, the *Inference Engine* computes estimations of the importance of each question which the *Dialogue Manager*, in turn, uses to select the most relevant question to ask next. By tracking the causal influences mentioned above, the *Inference Engine* also provides estimations of the usefulness of technical attributes. Based on the results, a personalized multi-attribute utility function is constructed which is then used by the *Ranking Database* to sort the products in the catalogue and to determine the current, personalized recommendation. Conceptionally, the whole product catalogue is ranked, but Top-K operators may be used to limit the size of the recommendation (e.g., to match the capabilities of the user interfaces at hand).

To summarize, a complete dialogue step contains the following actions:

1. Present the current questions to the customer and receive answers;
2. Update the evidences in the Bayesian network according to the answers;
3. Calculate the new posteriori probability distributions;
4. Construct utility function and execute ranking query to create new recommendations;
5. Determine next questions based on predicted answers;

Dialogue steps are iterated until the customer decides to buy one of the recommended products or the system runs out of questions. For the latter case, questions about technical attributes are asked which should quickly narrow down the available choices and therefore eventually lead to the purchasing decision. In addition, customers are *always* able to supply technical requirements which are taken into account for ranking purposes. Alternatively these requirements may be treated as *hard* constraints. Having hard constraints in the system, however, leads to the possibility of empty recommendations and therefore may require constraint relaxation, whereas representing technical requirements as soft constraints implicitly ensures that always at least one recommendation is available. Hence, hard constraints are only enabled at the explicit request of the customer.

The current recommendation is displayed in parallel to the questions of the current dialogue step and the customer is of course free to end the dialogue at any time (either by buying or by leaving the website).

## 5    Experiences

A recommender system based on the approach described above has been implemented as an ASP.net web application (cf. Fig. 4). Our prototype exhibited reasonable performance and will be integrated into an established order management system. The system has been demonstrated to selected customers and will continue to be presented to interested parties. We have already gathered valuable feedback from these initial evaluations. In addition, we are planning to conduct a large-scale field-test to obtain statistical results about the quality of recommendations and intuitiveness of dialogue management.

### 5.1    Selecting the Next Question

The dialogue manager selects questions based on the probabilities that the Bayesian network predicts for the possible answers (cf. [2]). In our current prototype, the most relevant questions are those with particularly confident predictions. The basic assumption is that the customer has a clear opinion about these questions and that, because of this, they should be asked first. Also, our prototype can display "empathic" behaviour by pre-selecting the most probable answer option for these questions in the GUI. Our experiences with the prototype show that customers generally agree that the questions shown this way are very relevant for the recommendation process and that the preselected answers resembled more or less exactly the choice the user would have made.

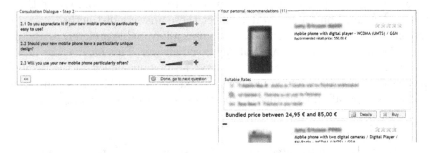

**Fig. 4.** Application screenshots showing questions (*left*) and recommendations (*right*)

However, the approach also exhibited a few shortcomings during our tests. Due to the described way of choosing questions, the early phases of the dialogue mostly consist of confirming the predictions of the inference engine predictions. As a consequence, the Bayesian network does not acquire much "new" knowledge quickly, meaning that its calculated a posteriori probabilities do not change much. As the latter are also used to obtain the recommended products, this leads to the following observed behaviour:

1. Defining the stereotypes at the beginning of the dialogue has a significant influence on the generated recommendations;
2. Confirming the confidently predicted questions during the early dialogue does not change the recommendations significantly;
3. Only later on, when other questions are answered, do the recommendations stabilize towards the eventually preferred products;

To improve this behaviour, the dialogue manager will be modified to prefer exactly those questions that have a particularly uncertain answer prediction. Initial evaluations show that this leads to more significant early changes within the Bayesian network that tend to stabilize later on. In other words, the Bayesian network obtains the most important knowledge earlier and only confirms its predictions afterwards. We will enter our field-test with both variants to investigate the user-friendliness of the approaches but we expect that the tendency towards shorter, more "efficient" dialogues will prove superior to our previous strategy.

Also, it is desirable to exploit possible semantic connections between individual needs and their corresponding questions. A question might, for instance, be a logical successor of another, or answering a given question in a certain way may mean that some other questions are useless to ask. Therefore, the dialogue manager will be extended to infer these relationships from the structure of the Bayesian network as far as possible. The goal is to form sensible chains of dialogue steps without having to extend the metamodel with capabilities to explicitly define "cliques" of questions.

## 5.2   Recommendations

During our evaluations we observed that users commonly assign a higher subjective importance to their most recent answers. Consequently, products satisfying the corresponding needs were expected to be displayed as a recommendation in the next dialogue step. Recommendations were regarded as incomplete if the top products displayed on screen do not reflect these answers distinctly.

In contrast, our ranking method always uses all available preferences and does not specifically consider the "age" of any given answer. This means that in some cases the most recent questions do not have an obvious effect on the displayed recommendations. Researching measures to extend the ranking mechanism by a notion of "temporal" importance of questions is part of our ongoing work.

## 5.3   Model Maintenance

To qualify for being integrated into the industrial sales/distribution processes, any approach must minimize the required maintenance overheads. The mere existence of a model already reduces maintenance efforts for the most common case: Adding new products is fully transparent, as long as they can be described in terms of the established domain model. Conventional approaches would require adaptation to integrate the new products. The product model itself needs adaptation only if technical innovations cause the addition of new *TechnicalAttributes* or an extension of the value ranges of existing attributes.

Considering the maintainability of the customer model, the *Stereotypes* exhibited reasonable stability over time, and, to a certain extent, even across different business domains. This is obviously due to the fact that they represent sociodemographic knowledge about the customers. Domain experts primarily have to define the *Needs* and *Influences* of the domain model. As the *Influences* are defined with respect to *AttributeValues* of the domain model (as compared to concrete products), these associations remain stable when new products are added. Once changes have been applied to the model, the system backend is re-generated automatically (see section 4), completely hiding the mathematical and informatical complexities from the model designer.

In addition, integrating the maintenance of the domain model into the existing business processes of catalogue creation and maintenance provides potential for even further optimizations. As the model contains a significant amount of marketing knowledge, it can be re-used, e.g., to simplify the creation of printed marketing materials by automatically annotating products with information about which needs they satisfy particularly well.

# 6  Related Work

Our recommendation approach is notably different from collaborative filtering methods (cf., e.g., [7,8]) by not requiring item ratings. Assuming that the same user will not interact with the system very frequently (typically, in our domain, a user will buy a single new cellphone about every two years), we cannot rely on buying histories to build our model of the user. While eliciting explicit ratings may be acceptable in an online context, it is not an adequate form of interaction between salespersons and customers. Hence, our user-model builds on information that can be elicited during the course of a natural sales dialogue.

Ardissono et al. [9,10] present a personalized recommender system for configurable products. Their approach involves preference elicitation techniques that employ reasoning about customer profiles to tailor the dialogue to a particular customer by providing explanations and smartly chosen default values wherever possible. The customer preferences learned this way are then used as constraints in the configuration problem at hand to generate the recommended product configuration, which might result in empty recommendations (i.e., the specified constraints are not satisfyable), requiring repair actions. Our approach does not directly exploit the elicited preferences as constraints but rather uses them as an input to ranking database queries which return a list of product recommendations ordered according to the customer's preferences. To suggest personalized default answers to questions, our approach does not need to rely on a set of business rules as appears to be the case in [9].

In [11], the dialogue-oriented recommender suite CWAdvisor is presented. Their knowledge-base is similar to ours but it includes an explicit representation of the "recommender process definition", i.e. all possible dialogue paths in a tree-like structure. While obviously able to specify a fine-grained dialogue, the achievable level of detail is limited by the complexity of the dialogue specification. Our approach generates the (equally complex) dialogue specification from a much more compact model and is more flexible by incorporating mixed-initiative selection of questions, easy belief revision and adaptive personalization.

An adaptive approach to select technical questions is presented in [12] that is able to suggest "tightenings" (i.e. further questions) to reduce recommendation size based on a previously learned probability model. Their approach includes the possibility to re-learn the model when more dialogue histories are available. In contrast, our approach does not include a learning step but delegates that task to a domain expert. Also, our model is not concerned with direct connections between dialogue elements as is the case in [12] but rather specifies a more abstract view on the product domain from which the dialogue structure is inferred.

An approach similar to ours is presented in [13]. However, the utility estimations (the "value tree") of Jameson et al. do not seem to be built on an explicit model of the currently served customer but rather on an average user of their system. Hence, the recommendations are not personalized as strongly as in our approach which allows an adaption even to atypical customers by setting the appropriate stereotypes. Also, as the value tree is a strictly hierarchical structure, it cannot capture the fact that a technical attribute may be influenced by more than a single need. Furthermore, it is not completely clear how informal statements (e.g., "I am a law student.") can be interpreted as relevant knowledge (e.g., an increased interest in politics) by the system apart from the possibility that a domain expert models this association directly within the Bayesian network.

A domain model based on dynamic logic programming was introduced by Leite and Babini in [14]. Both customer and user model are represented using a massive set of declarative rules which allows a detailed and powerful specification of the business domain – possibly even extended by user-supplied rules. However, the complex formal models appear expensive to maintain when confronted with domain changes. Furthermore, it seems unlikely that domain experts, much less customers, are able to express their knowledge by logic rules, whereas intuitiveness and maintainability of the model are two key points of our approach.

# 7   Conclusion

This paper presents an approach for a dialogue-based recommender system, taking industrial maintainability requirements into consideration. The focus of our prototypical implementation is the telecommunications market, but the system has been designed with domain-independence in mind and therefore establishes a strict separation of domain-dependent and domain-independent parts. This is achieved by using a domain metamodel explicitly designed to allow efficient maintenance. All domain-specific parts of the system are generated from instances of the metamodel. The overall architecture comprises a dynamic dialogue management, a preference elicitation component based on Bayesian networks, and a ranking-based retrieval from the product database.

The evaluation of a prototypical implementation proved the general usability of our approach and also yielded valuable lessons for further technical improvements: Determining questions' relevances and aligning the recommendations with the customers' expectations are the crucial points for our ongoing research. We will refine our approach based on the first evaluation and a thorough field-test relating the computed outcome of the recommender system with the experience and expectations of users and sales experts.

# References

1. Radde, S., Beck, M., Freitag, B.: Generating recommendation dialogues from product models. In: Proc. of the AAAI 2007 Workshop on Recommender Systems in E-Commerce. AAAI Press, Menlo Park (2007)
2. Radde, S., Kaiser, A., Freitag, B.: A model-based customer inference engine. In: Proc. of the ECAI 2008 Workshop on Recommender Systems (2008)
3. Beck, M., Freitag, B.: Weighted boolean conditions for ranking. In: Proc. of the IEEE 24th International Conference on Data Engineering (ICDE 2008) – 2nd International Workshop on Ranking in Databases, DBRank 2008 (2008)
4. Harel, D.: Statecharts: A Visual Formalism for Complex Systems. Science of Computer Programming 8(3), 231–274 (1987)
5. Wieringa, R.: Design Methods for Reactive Systems. Morgan Kaufmann, San Francisco (2003)
6. Russel, S., Norvig, P.: Artificial Intelligence: A Modern Approach. Prentice Hall International Editions (1995)
7. Jin, R., Si, L., Zhang, C.: A study of mixture models for collaborative filtering. Information Retrieval 9(3), 357–382 (2006)
8. Herlocker, J., Konstan, J., Terveen, L., Riedl, J.: Evaluating Collaborative Filtering Recommender Systems. ACM Trans. on Information Systems 22(1), 5–53 (2004)
9. Ardissono, L., Felfernig, A., Friedrich, G., Goy, A., Jannach, D., Meyer, M., Petrone, G., Schaefer, R., Schuetz, W., Zanker, M.: Personalizing online configuration of products and services. In: Proc. of the 15th European Conference on Artificial Intelligence, ECAI 2002 (2002)
10. Ardissono, L., Felfernig, A., Friedrich, G., Goy, A., Jannach, D., Petrone, G., Schaefer, R., Zanker, M.: A framework for the development of personalized, distributed web-based configuration systems. AI Magazine 24(3), 93–110 (2003)
11. Felfernig, A., Friedrich, G., Jannach, D., Zanker, M.: An integrated environment for the development of knowledge-based recommender applications. Intl. Journal of Electronic Commerce 11(2), 11–34 (2006)
12. Mahmood, T., Ricci, F.: Learning and adaptivity in interactive recommender systems. In: Proc. of the 9th Intl. Conference on Electronic Commerce. ACM Press, New York (2007)
13. Jameson, A., Schaefer, R., Simons, J., Weis, T.: Adaptive provision of evaluation-oriented information: Tasks and techniques. In: Proc. of the 14th Intl. Joint Conference on Artificial Intelligence, IJCAI 1995 (1995)
14. Leite, J., Babini, M.: Dynamic knowledge based user modeling for recommender systems. In: Proc. of the ECAI 2006 Workshop on Recommender Systems (2006)

# Towards Privacy Compliant and Anytime Recommender Systems

Armelle Brun and Anne Boyer

LORIA, Université Nancy2,
615, rue du Jardin Botanique, 54506 Vandoeuvre-lès-Nancy,
{brun,boyer}@loria.fr
http://kiwi.loria.fr

**Abstract.** Recommendation technologies have traditionally been used in domains such as E-commerce and Web navigation to recommend resources to customers so as to help them to get the pertinent resources. Among the possible
approaches is collaborative filtering that does not take into account the content of
the resources: only the traces of usage of the resources are considered. State of
the art models, such as sequential association-rules and Markov models, that can
be used in the frame of privacy concerns, are usually studied in terms of performance, state space complexity and time complexity. Many of them have a large
time complexity and require a long time to compute recommendations. However,
there are domains of application of the models where recommendations may be
required quickly. This paper focuses on the study of how these state of the art
models can be adapted so as to be anytime. In that case recommendations can be
proposed to the user whatever is the computation time available, the quality of
the recommendations increases according to the computation time. We show that
such models can be adapted so as to be anytime and we propose several strategies
to compute recommendations iteratively. We also show that the computation time
needed by these new models is not increased compared to classical ones; even so,
it sometimes decreases.

## 1 Introduction

Web personalization alleviates the burden of information overload by tailoring the information presented to users based on their needs and preferences. In recent years, personalized search has attracted interest in the research community as to provide more effective and efficient information access. Web personalization has applications in various
domains such as E-commerce to recommend products to customers or Web navigation
to recommend resources to a particular user, named active user.

Recommender systems are a means to perform Web personalization, they generally
fall into three categories of content-based systems [1] which make recommendations
based on semantic content of data, knowledge-based systems [2] which make recommendations based on knowledge about the active user and pre-established heuristics and
collaborative-filtering systems [3] which make recommendations by examining past interactions of the active user with the system, called traces of *usage*.

T. Di Noia and F. Buccafurri (Eds.): EC-Web 2009, LNCS 5692, pp. 276–287, 2009.

In this paper, we are especially interested in Web navigation and E-commerce. In that case, collaborative filtering (and usage analysis) seems to be the most appropriate approach for several reasons. First, resources do not have to be tagged: only the id of each resource has to be known, that is an advantage when the set of resources is large and evolves over time, which is the case on the Web. Second, no *a priori* information has to be known about users (no demographic information, no predefined preferences, etc.). The only information available is the trace of usage of users for the resources. In that case recommender systems perform Web log or usage traces, analysis.

Nowadays, privacy concerns have to be considered by recommender systems [4]. To face this problem, we propose here to store the traces of usage without any information about the corresponding users. More specifically, these traces are stored under the form of anonymous sequences of navigation, privacy is thus respected. The set of sequences of navigation stored is named *training dataset*. Let us notice that there several ways to store navigation sequences so as they are anonymous (on multiple databases for example), the way we choose to store them is the simpler one.

To perform recommendations by using collaborative filtering, data mining techniques are classically used to discover usage patterns that will be exploited to compute predictions. Techniques such as similarity between users or resources [5], Markov models of sequential navigation [6], or sequential association mining [7] have been proposed in the literature.

All these approaches have an off-line part that computes a model/representation of the training dataset that aims at discovering usage (navigation) patterns.

In the on-line part, the algorithm exploits the usage patterns from the off-line part and the information available about the active user is used to compute the interest of each resource for him/her.

In our case, the only information available about the active user is reduced to his/her active session of navigation, as his/her past navigations are stored anonymously in the training dataset.

Among the possible approaches, as the past navigations of each user are stored anonymously, no similarity between users can be computed, thus the approach based on such information cannot be investigated. In the same way, the popular item-based approach that exploits similarities between resources [5] cannot be exploited neither. Indeed, in such an approach the set of resources cannot evolve and votes or ratings on the resources have to be given by users, which is not our case.

However, Markov models and association mining approaches can deal with anonymous navigations and do not require any votes, they can thus be used to compute recommendations.

In the frame of E-commerce or Web navigation, a few amount of time may be available to compute predictions. Indeed, when a user goes on a web page, the recommender has to present him/her the list of recommendations right away, when the page he/she wants to consult appears (the recommendations can then be changed).

Most of recommendation algorithms either run to completion or provide no solution at all. However, computing the optimal recommendation set may require a large amount of computation time and an answer may be required at any moment. Anytime algorithms have the advantage to provide an answer (here a recommendation) whenever the algorithm is stopped and the quality of results improves regularly as computation time increases. The answer generated by anytime algorithms is an approximation of the optimal answer.

In this article, we are thus interested in anytime privacy-compliant recommendation algorithms in order to match specificities of E-commerce or Web navigation. More specifically, we focus on classical recommendation algorithms that are originally not anytime, and we study how they can be adapted so as to be anytime and thus recommend resources whatever computation time is available.

The second section presents the way recommender systems compute the recommendations. In the third and fourth sections, the two recommendation algorithms we are interested in (sequential association-rules and Markov models) are presented and strategies to make such systems being anytime are put forward. In the fifth section, conclusion and perspectives are detailed.

## 2   Recommender Systems

The recommendation problem is typically formulated as a prediction task in which a prediction model is built according to the prior training dataset and then the model is used in conjunction with the active user dynamic profile to predict the level of interest (score) of the active user for each resource.

The profile of the active user is made up of the resources he/she has consulted in the active session (as no additional information is known about the user). However, as a session may be long and as the resources that have been consulted early in the session may be less useful than the resources consulted recently, most of the models use a sliding time window that contains the last $n$ resources the active user has consulted. These last $n$ resources approximate his/her dynamic profile. From now on, the dynamic profile of the active user will be called *active profile*.

The recommendation problem can be viewed as follows: given the past consultations of the user, his/her active profile $ap$, what is/are the most pertinent resource(s) $r_m$ to recommend? The resource(s) to be recommended are the ones with the highest score that maximize the following equation:

$$r_m^* = argmax_{r_m} \ S(r_m|ap) \tag{1}$$

Where $(S(r_m|ap))$ is the score of the resource $r_m$ given the active profile $ap$.

The literature is usually interested in the way to estimate $S(r_m|ap)$. In this article, we focus on the way classical approaches can be adapted so as to be anytime. The approaches we are interested in are sequential association-rules and Markov models as they are the most popular data mining approaches and they can be used on anonymous data. Moreover, these algorithms can be used to compute recommendations without requiring the active user is identified.

# 3  Sequential Association-Rules Based Recommenders

## 3.1  Sequential Association-Rules

The framework of association rules (AR) was introduced into the data mining community by Agrawal et al [8]. Association rules were used to capture relationships among items based on patterns of co-occurrence across transactions.

Sequential Association-Rules (SAR) are an evolution of AR, in which the order of the items is considered. The framework of SAR mining was introduced by Agrawal et al [7] to capture ordered relationships between items.

A SAR is an expression of the form $X \Rightarrow Y$, where $X$ (called the antecedent) and $Y$ (the consequent) are sequences of resources. Usually $X \Rightarrow Y$ is considered as a SAR if both its support and confidence are above two thresholds that have to be fixed. Support is defined as the number of transactions that contain both $X$ and $Y$ and confidence is the number transactions that contain both $X$ and $Y$ divided by the number of transactions that contain $X$ (confidence can be viewed as the conditional probability of $Y$ given $X$).

In the frame of usage mining [9], SAR refer to resource associations and capture resource dependencies in sessions of navigation. A SAR means that, when users have consulted the sequence of all resources in $X$, they usually consult $Y$. Here, as the goal is to predict the next resource to be seen, $Y$ is made up of a single resource. In SAR, resources can be either contiguous or non-contiguous [10,11,12].

The off-line part of SAR based recommender systems searches all the SAR according to their support and confidence. A large variety of algorithms for mining SAR have been published in the literature, as Apriori [13] and DIS [14] algorithms. These algorithms are incremental and SAR made up of $k + 1$ resources are deduced from the SAR of $k$ resources.

## 3.2  Score Computation

To compute predictions in the on-line part, a score has to be assigned to each resource $r_m$. SAR based recommender systems exploit the sequence of resources in the active profile of the user, and compare it to the antecedents of the SAR from the off-line part. The rules that match the active profile of the user are then used to compute the score of each resource.

A rule that matches the active profile (called a matching rule) is a rule with an antecedent that is a subsequence of the active profile $(ap)$. Let $SubSeq$ be the function mapping $ap$ to the list of sub-sequences of $ap$. The resources $(r_m)$ that are consequence of the matching rules are then candidates to be recommended.

To compute the score of each resource $S(r_m|ap)$, the confidence of each matching rule (confidence($X \Rightarrow r_m$)) is used. In the case that several matching rules have the same consequence, several policies are used in the literature:

- The max_policy: given a resource $r_m$, the recommendation algorithm searches the SAR that have $r_m$ as consequence, with an antecedent $X$ that matches the active profile of the user ($X \in SubSeq(ap)$). Among these SAR, the one with the highest confidence for resource $r_m$ is retained and the confidence of this SAR is assigned to the score of $r_m$ [15,16]:

$$S(r_m|ap) = \underset{X \in SubSeq(ap)}{max} \text{confidence}(X \Rightarrow r_m) \tag{2}$$

- The sum_policy: as for max_policy, all the SAR with consequent $r_m$ and that have an antecedent that matches the active profile, are retained. The sum of the confidence values over these SAR is computed and then assigned to the score of the resource $r_m$. This strategy enables to give more weight to the resources that are associated with more rules [17].

$$S(r_m|ap) = \underset{X \in SubSeq(ap)}{sum} \text{confidence}(X \Rightarrow r_m) \tag{3}$$

These works mainly focused on the way to evaluate the "final" score of each resource, by using matching rules. However, they do not focus on the exact way to integrate these rules so as to make the recommender anytime.

Some other works have been interested in anytime recommenders, however they only focus on the off-line part, for example [18] has been interested in anytime SAR mining in peer-to-peer systems.

### 3.3 Anytime SAR Based Recommenders

A SAR-based recommender is basically not anytime: the recommender searches all the matching rules $(X \Rightarrow r_m)$ with $X \in SubSeq(ap)$, then it computes the score for each resource $r_m$ according to these matching rules and the policy chosen (max_policy or sum_policy).

Some works have been interested in the way to store rules to improve the access and computation time to construct the recommendation list. For example [19] proposes to store rules in a navigational pattern tree; even so the computation of the recommendation list may take time. To reduce this time, we propose to implement anytime SAR-based recommender systems.

Let us notice that when anytime algorithms run to completion, recommendations are similar to the ones computed by classical approaches.

We propose here three strategies for one anytime rule-based recommender.

**Small Antecedent First Strategy (SAF)**
The SAF strategy is based on the following hypothesis:
**Hypothesis 1**: The probability that a resource is the consequence of a SAR with an antecedent made up of only few resources is higher than the probability that a resource is the consequence of a SAR that has an antecedent with a larger number of resources. In other words, given a resource $r_m$ and $X_1, X_2$ two sequences of resources (with cardinals $|X_1|$ and $|X_2|$) with $X_1 \in SubSeq(ap)$, $X_2 \in SubSeq(ap)$ and $|X_1| \ll |X_2|$. Then, the probability that the rule $(X_1 \Rightarrow r_m)$ exists is greater than the probability that the rule $(X_2 \Rightarrow r_m)$ exists.

An anytime algorithm has to assign a score to each resource early in the process and then refines these scores if time is available. The SAF strategy we propose first assigns to each resource its confidence *a priori*. Let us recall that the confidence of a SAR can be viewed as the conditional probability of the consequence given the antecedent.

Thus, in the case the antecedent is empty, the confidence is the probability *a priori* of the consequence. If the algorithm has to stop at this step, recommendations can be presented as a score is assigned to each resource, the probability *a priori* of a resource is a first approximation of the "final" score of each resource.

Second, based on the hypothesis 1, the algorithm uses SAR in the list of matching rules with antecedents of size $k = 1$ so as to refine the score of each resource. The probability of finding a corresponding SAR is still relatively high and the score of each resource is a better approximation of the "final" score than at the end of the preceding step.

The algorithm then iterates on the value of $k$, by increasing $k$. At each step $k$, SAR with an antecedent of size $k$ are used and scores are updated.

Based once more on hypothesis 1, we can notice that the probability that a SAR matches the active profile decreases as the value of $k$ increases. Thus, if there is no time left to compute iterations with high values of $k$, the score of each resource may be even so a good approximation of the "final" score.

Whenever the algorithm stops, a score is assigned to each resource, and recommendations can be performed, by using Equation (1).

With the SAF strategy, the SAR have to be accessed both via the consequence-resource and the size of the antecedent. We thus propose to store the whole list of SAR in several lists of SAR: one list for each consequence-resource and for each size of antecedent, as presented in Figure 1.

During the score estimation, given the consequence-resource $r_m$ and the size of the antecedent $k$, the system traverses the corresponding SAR list $L_{r_m,k}$ to find the SAR that match the active profile.

In the literature, some works store the set of rules in a tree that requires less storage space. Such trees are not optimal for the SAF strategy. Indeed, the access has to be made on the consequence of the rules. We can thus imagine to store rules so as the consequence of the rules are stored at depth 1 in the tree, the last element of the antecedents is stored at depth 2, etc. However, as the algorithms have to perform breadth-first traversal, a classical tree cannot be used as traversal will take time.

| List name | Antec. size | Conseq.-Resource | SAR list |
|---|---|---|---|
| $L_{1,1}$ | 1 | $R_1$ | $((R_x, S(R_x => R_1)), (R_y, S(R_y => R_1)) \dots )$ |
| $L_{1,2}$ | 2 | $R_1$ | $((R_x, R_y, S((R_x, R_y) => R_1)), (R_y, R_z, S((R_y, R_z) => R_1)) \dots )$ |
| $L_{1,3}$ | 3 | $R_1$ | $((R_x, R_y, R_t, S((R_x, R_y, R_t) => R_1)), (R_y, R_z, R_m, S((R_y, R_z, R_m) => R_1)) \dots )$ |
| $\vdots$ | | | |
| $L_{2,1}$ | 1 | $R_2$ | $((R_x, S(R_x => R_1)), (R_y, S(R_y => R_1)) \dots )$ |
| $L_{2,2}$ | 2 | $R_2$ | $((R_x, R_y, S((R_x, R_y) => R_1)), (R_y, R_z, S((R_y, R_z) => R_1)) \dots )$ |
| $L_{2,3}$ | 3 | $R_2$ | $((R_x, R_y, R_t, S((R_x, R_y, R_t) => R_1)), (R_y, R_z, R_m, S((R_y, R_z, R_m) => R_1)) \dots )$ |
| $\vdots$ | | | |

**Fig. 1.** Lists of SAR stored so as to be managed by the SAF strategy

The advantage of the SAF strategy is that a score is assigned to each resource early in the process (hypothesis 1). However, this score may not be a reliable approximation of the "final" score, whatever is the policy used (max_policy or sum_policy).

What about the computation time of such an anytime recommender? Usual rule-based recommenders systematically traverse once the whole set of SAR. Concerning the anytime SAF version, if a pointer is placed on each list, that memorize the last SAR used; then if time is available, this algorithm also traverses the whole set of rules (all the lists) once, thus computation time is similar to the classical one.

**Highest Confidence First Strategy (HCF)**

The HCF strategy is based on the following hypothesis:

**Hypothesis 2**: The SAR with the highest confidence for a given consequence-resource is a good approximation of the "final" score of a given resource.

With the HCF strategy, the SAR with the highest confidence have to be accessed first to have a good approximation of the final score as early as possible.

SAR have thus to be accessed according to the consequence-resource and their confidence value, the storage has to be different from the one of the SAF strategy (Figure 1). We propose to create one SAR list for each consequence-resource, the elements of a list being ordered according to their confidence value, whatever is the size of the antecedent, as presented in Figure 2.

When the max_policy is chosen, the algorithm considers one list after the other (each list corresponds to one resource). When a SAR in a given list matches the active profile, the algorithm stops the evaluation of the score of the resource and evaluates the score of another resource. In that case, the algorithm cannot be considered as anytime as the "final" score of each resource is directly found. Indeed, when a matching SAR is found, it is the one that maximizes the confidence, thus it is the one that will be retained by the policy.

However, in the case the sum_policy is chosen, in the first step the algorithm searches the first SAR that matches the active profile, for each resource (as for the max_policy). Then, the score of each resource can be refined step by step while traversing the rest of the lists.

This strategy has the advantage of having a good estimation of the "final" score once a matching rule is found. However, as the highest confidence usually corresponds to

| List name | Conseq.-Resource | SAR lists ordered by confidence values |
|-----------|------------------|----------------------------------------|
| $L_1$ | $R_1$ | $((R_y,R_z,S((R_y,R_z)=>R_1))$, $(R_x,S(R_x=>R_1))$, $(R_y,R_z,R_m,S((R_y,R_z,R_m)=>R_1))$, $(R_y,S(R_y=>R_1))$  ...  ) |
| $L_2$ | $R_2$ | $((R_x,R_y,S((R_x,R_y)=>R_2))$, $(R_x,R_y,R_z,S((R_x,R_y,R_z)=>R_2))$, $(R_x,S(R_x=>R_2))$  ... ) |
| $L_3$ | $R_3$ | $((R_t,S(R_t=>R_3))$, $(R_y,R_z,R_m,S((R_y,R_z,R_m)=>R_3))$, $(R_y,R_z,R_m,R_t,R_x,S((R_y,R_z,R_m,R_t,R_x)=>R_3))$  ... ) |
| ⋮ | ⋮ | ⋮ |

**Fig. 2.** Lists of SAR stored so as to be managed by the HCF strategy

a SAR with a large antecedent (see Hypothesis 3 below), and as the probability the active profile matches a SAR with a large antecedent is low (Hypothesis 1), then the computation time required to assign a score to a resource may be large.

In the case the max_policy is used, the algorithm traverses at worst all the lists once (if pointers on lists are stored), thus computation time is similar. However, in many cases a matching rule will be found before the list is completely traversed, thus computation time is lower.

In the case of the sum_policy, the lists are at worst entirely traversed once. Computation time is thus similar to classical ways to compute scores.

**Small Antecedent and Highest Confidence First Strategy (SAHCF)**

The SAHCF strategy is based on an additional hypothesis:

**Hypothesis 3**: The highest confidence of a resource $r_m$ is usually provided by a SAR with a large antecedent.

This hypothesis 3 is mixed with the two previous strategies: the SAHCF strategy tends to assign a score to a resource as early as possible in the process (SAF strategy) while using SAR with the highest confidence first.

One list is thus constructed for each resource and for each size of antecedent (as in Figure 1) and the elements of each list are ordered according to their confidence value (as in Figure 2).

If the max_policy is chosen: in the first step the confidence value of the first matching SAR with an antecedent of size 1 (lists $L_{*1}$ in Figure 1) is assigned to the score of the resource. These lists are no more considered when a matching SAR is found. In the second step, the lists $L_{*2}$ are traversed and the step ends when one SAR matches, etc. The hypothesis 3 is not used with the max_policy as the traversal of a list is stopped when a matching SAR is found.

When the sum_policy is chosen, the hypothesis 3 is used: at the end of the first step, a matching SAR is found for each resource (on lists $L_{*1}$). The question is then: does the second step focus on the rest of lists $L_{*1}$ or does it first search a matching rule in lists $L_{*2}$ ? Following the hypothesis 3, matching SAR are first searched in lists $L_{*2}$, $L_{*3}$, etc. then, traversal of lists $L_{*1}$ are ended.

Compared to the SAF strategy, SAHCF runs more quickly in the case of max_policy as the maximal confidence is found early in the process for each list with antecedents of size $k$. In the case of sum_policy, the process has similar computation time (still in the case of the use of pointers) and has a better estimation of the "final" score earlier in the process as high confidence values are integrated first in the score.

# 4 Markov Models

We focus now on the well-known Markov-based recommender systems and study how they can be adapted to provide recommendations whatever is the time allowed to the recommender.

## 4.1 k Order Markov Models

A $k$-order Markov model (KMM) assumes that the consultation of a resource by the active user is influenced by only and exactly the last $k$ resources he/she has accessed, the resources he/she has consulted before these $k$ resources are considered as non-informative.

A Markov Model is a set of conditional probabilities $P(r_m|X)$, where $X$ is a sequence of resources and $X$ will be called the antecedent, as in the SAR framework. A KMM is thus a set of conditional probabilities where the size of the antecedents is exactly $k$. These probabilities are learnt during the off-line part, on the training dataset.

On the on-line part, a KMM-based recommender computes the score of a resource to be consulted by the active user given the sequence of his/her exactly $k$ previously accessed resources. The active profile of the user is in that case approximated by the sequence of these $k$ resources. The score of a resource is in that case its conditional probability. Given the set of conditional probabilities, the probability of a resource $r_m$ is the one among the conditional probabilities that has an antecedent equal to the active profile of the user.

The resources that are recommended are the ones that have the highest probability. Obviously, the higher the value of $k$ is, the most accurate the probabilities are (in the case of no sparse data problem), and it has been shown [20] that, when applied to recommender systems, the accuracy of KMM increases with the value of $k$.

However, the higher the value of $k$ is, the larger the number of states to be stored is and the lower the coverage is (cf hypothesis 1: the probability that the active profile of size $k$ perfectly matches one antecedent in the model is low in the case of high values of $k$).

Markov models are a popular approach used in recommenders, due to their accuracy. A recommender based on Markov models of order $k$ cannot be adapted so as to be anytime as the probability of a resource is directly known: either the sequence of the $k$ last resources the active user has consulted matches the antecedent of one of the conditional probabilities, or it does not. In the case it matches, the probability of each resource is known right away.

## 4.2   All kth Order Markov Models

To cope with the coverage problem of KMM, All-$kth$-order Markov Models (AKMM) have been proposed in [6]. In AKMM, various KMM of different order $k$ are trained and used to make predictions.

The AKMM are based on the following hypothesis:
**Hypothesis 4**: The larger the sequence of navigation used to compute prediction is, the more accurate the probability is.
It has been shown that this hypothesis is true in the case of KMM (see section 4.1.

Following hypothesis 4, predictions are thus first computed by using a $k$-order MM. This step leads to an accurate recommendation as predictions are made by using a large sequence of navigation. If no prediction can be performed (as the coverage in that case is low), a $k - 1$ order KMM is used, etc. The value of $k$ is iteratively decreased until a recommendation can be made. The coverage of AKMM is thus highly increased. In AKMM, all sequences of navigation (with their corresponding conditional probability) are stored, whatever is their size (in the limit of $k$).

The drawback of AKMM is their state space complexity: the number of states dramatically increases with the value of $k$. However, some works have been interested in the way to store this model to decrease the space complexity. [21] for example stores navigational patterns in a suffix tree and at each node, the conditional probability of this node given its parent node is stored.

AKMM also suffer from time complexity: predictions are first computed with a KMM of order $k$ (hypothesis 4). Due to the coverage problem of high values of $k$ (hypothesis 1), the order of the model is frequently decreased, and of course it takes time. Consequently, if a small time is available to compute predictions, in some cases, no recommendation can be proposed to the user.

In the frame of the storage of navigation patterns in a tree, [22] proposes a real-time recommender algorithm: all navigation patterns are stored in the tree (the tree evolves as new user navigations arrive), confidence and support are computed when traversing the tree to find candidate patterns to compute predictions, that takes time. Moreover, the "final" score of a resource is computed before computing the one of the following resource, the recommendation is thus not anytime.

### 4.3 Anytime All kth Order Markov Model

We propose to adapt the AKMM so as it is anytime. This strategy is based on a hypothesis 1: the probability that the active profile of size $k$ perfectly matches one antecedent in the model is high in the case of low values of $k$)

Given this hypothesis, we thus propose to inverse the way to use $k$ (the order of the models) by increasing its value instead of decreasing it step by step. Recommendations are first computed with a low order KMM (a 0-order KMM for example, that corresponds to the probability *a priori* of the resources). The use of such a model guarantees a high coverage value. Then if time is available, predictions are refined by using higher-order KMM. At an iteration value $k$, the recommender searches, in the set of conditional probabilities, the antecedents of size $k$ that match the active profile of size $k$. If a match is found, the recommender replaces the score of each resource (computed during iteration step $k - 1$) by the new scores (from iteration step $k$).

Let us notice that at a step value $k$. The replacement of the score values between two steps guarantees that recommendations will be similar to the ones made with classical AKMM.

Such an approach makes the recommendation process anytime: in the first iteration step, an *a priori* probability is assigned to each resource, recommendations can be made at this step. Then these probabilities are refined if time is available.

Let us notice that the HCF strategy proposed in section 3.3 cannot be applied on AKMM. Indeed, with AKMM the iterations have to be done on the size of the antecedent, thus matching cannot be dependent on the conditional probability.

The computation time of this anytime model is similar to the one of the classical AKMM. Furthermore, the time required to run to completion may be lower than for classical AKMM. In the case of a high value of $k$, the probability that the active profile matches an antecedent of size $k$ is low, then classical AKMM may have to iterate many times until recommendations can be performed (with a low value of $k$).

At the opposite, the anytime recommender may run more quickly: at a step $k$, if no antecedent matches the active profile, the recommender can stop. Indeed, if the active profile of size $k$ does not match any antecedent, thus no antecedent of size greater than

$k$ can match the active profile of size greater than $k$. Thus, the highest value $k$ with a matching antecedent can be reached in a lower number of iterations than with classical AKMM.

## 5  Conclusion and Perspectives

Data mining approaches are classically used in recommender systems based on collaborative filtering. This article studies the way recommender systems, that use data mining techniques, can be adapted to be anytime. To this end, the frame of this article is first presented: Web recommender systems that deal with privacy concerns. After having presented classical recommender systems, we present why they cannot guarantee to provide recommendations in the case few computation time is available.

We propose several strategies, based on various hypothesis, to compute iteratively recommendations, thus they can be presented to the user, whatever is the time allowed to the recommender. We show that these strategies and these anytime recommenders, have a computation time similar to the one of classical approaches and the computation time until completion is even decreased in some cases.

As a future work, we intend to evaluate the evolution of the quality of recommendations according to the number of iterations, and the strategy used. In addition, we will study how such recommenders can also be incremental and take advantage of the recommendations made at the preceding step to compute recommendations to make in one step.

## References

1. Pazzani, M.J., Billsus, D.: Content-Based Recommendation Systems. In: Brusilovsky, P., Kobsa, A., Nejdl, W. (eds.) Adaptive Web 2007. LNCS, vol. 4321, pp. 325–341. Springer, Heidelberg (2007)
2. Burke, R., Hammond, K., Cooper, E.: Knowledge-based navigation of complex information spaces. In: Proceedings of the 13th National Conference on Artificial Intelligence, Menlo Park, Canada, pp. 462–468 (1996)
3. Goldberg, D., Nichols, D., Oki, B., Terry, D.: Using collaborative filtering to weave an information tapestry. Communications of the ACM 35(12), 61–70 (1992)
4. Aïmeur, E., Brassard, G., Fernandez, J., Mani, A.: Alambic: a privacy-preserving recommender system for electronic commerce. International Journal of Information Security 7(5), 307–334 (2008)
5. Sarwar, B.M., Karypis, G., Konstan, J.A., Reidl, J.: Item-based collaborative filtering recommendation algorithms. In: World Wide Web, pp. 285–295 (2001)
6. Pitkow, J., Pirolli, P.: Mining longest repeating subsequences to predict world wide web surfing. In: USITS 1999: Proceedings of the 2nd conference on USENIX Symposium on Internet Technologies and Systems (1999)
7. Srikant, R., Agrawal, R.: Mining sequential patterns: Generalizations and performance improvements. In: Proceedings of the 5th International Conference on Extending Database Technology, pp. 3–17 (1996)
8. Agrawal, R., Imielinski, T., Swami, A.: Mining association rules between sets of items in large databases. In: Proceedings of the ACM SIGMOD Conference on Management od Data, pp. 207–216 (1993)

9. Fu, X., Budzik, J., Hammond, K.: Mining navigation history for recommendation. In: Proceedings of the 5th International Conference on Intelligent User Interfaces, pp. 106–112 (2000)
10. Mobasher, B.: Data mining for web personalization. In: Brusilovsky, P., Kobsa, A., Nejdl, W. (eds.) Adaptive Web 2007. LNCS, vol. 4321, pp. 90–135. Springer, Heidelberg (2007)
11. Lu, L., Dunham, M.H., Meng, Y.: Mining significant usage patterns from clickstream data. In: Nasraoui, O., Zaïane, O.R., Spiliopoulou, M., Mobasher, B., Masand, B., Yu, P.S. (eds.) WebKDD 2005. LNCS, vol. 4198, pp. 1–17. Springer, Heidelberg (2006)
12. Shyu, M., Haruechaiyasak, C., Chen, S., Zhao, N.: Collaborative filtering by mining association rules from user access sequences. In: International Workshop on Challenges in Web Information Retrieval and Integration (2005)
13. Agrawal, R., Srikant, R.: Mining sequential patterns. In: Proceedings of the International Conference on Data Engineering (ICDE 1995), pp. 3–14 (1995)
14. Brin, S., Motwani, R., Ullman, J., Tsur, S.: Dynamic itemset counting and implication rules for market basket data. In: Proceedings of the ACM SIGMOD International Conference on Management of Data, May 1997, pp. 255–264 (1997)
15. Sarwar, B., Karypis, G., Konstan, J., Riedl, J.: Analysis of recommendation algorithms for e-commerce. In: ACM Conference on Electronic Commerce (2000)
16. Yong, W., Zhanhuai, L., Yang, Z.: Mining sequential association-rule for improving web document prediction. In: Proceedings of the Sixth International Conference on Computational Intelligence and Multimedia Applications, ICCIMA 2005 (2005)
17. Kim, C., Kim, J.: A recommendation algorithm using multi-level association rules. In: Proceedings of the IEEE/WIC International Conference on Web Intelligence, WI 2003 (2003)
18. Wolff, R., Schuster, A.: Association rule mining in peer-to-peer systems. IEEE Transactions on Systems, Man and Cybernetics (2004)
19. Tan, X., Yao, M., Xu, M.: An effective technique for personalization recommendation based on access sequential patterns. In: Proceedings of the IEEE Asia-Pacific Conference on Services Computing, APSCC 2006 (2006)
20. Deshpande, M., Karypis, G.: Selective markov models for predicting web-page accesses. In: First SIAM International Conference on Data Mining (2001)
21. Xiao, Y., Dunham, M.: Efficient mining of traversal patterns. Data and Knwoledge Engineering 39(2), 191–214 (2001)
22. Huang, Y., Kuo, Y., Chen, J., Jeng, Y.: Np-miner: A real time recommendation algorithm by using web usage mining. Knowledge-Based Systems 19, 272–286 (2006)

# Assessing Robustness of Reputation Systems Regarding Interdependent Manipulations

Ivo Reitzenstein and Ralf Peters

Chair of E-Business, Martin-Luther-University Halle-Wittenberg
06099 Halle (Saale), Germany
{Ivo.Reitzenstein,Ralf.Peters}@wiwi.uni-halle.de

**Abstract.** Reputation systems are subject to several types of manipulations, often in context of fraud. The current literature offers mainly partial solutions for specific manipulations. However, in practice a reputation system should be robust against all relevant threats. This paper explores the combination of several partial solutions in an evolutionary simulation model. The analysis shows that some partial solutions interfere with each other. In particular, it turns out that there is a crucial tradeoff between sanctioning and rehabilitation of bad behaviour that can be solved by a minimal transaction fee.

## 1 Introduction

The emergence of the so-called "Web 2.0" noticeably changed the way of using the internet in recent years. On several websites like eBay, youtube and facebook users now actively take part in platform events. On those sites, interaction typically occurs between anonymous, unknown users. As a result, uncertainty arises, because a user may not know the abilities or intentions of his possible partner [1, pp. 48 - 49]. As this may prevent users to interact, uncertainty or lacking trust may compromise site events and could even lead to platform failure like Akerlof [2] shows. Therefore, trust is becoming an important element for successfully running a platform.

Reputation systems offer a solution to the described trust problem by collecting, aggregating and distributing feedback about the past behaviour of a user [3, p. 46]. Therefore, it is possible to inform others about the trustworthiness of the possible partner and to avoid untrustworthy ones. Trust is induced by the *dual function* of a reputation system. First, the system *signals* the past behaviour of the rated user and may reveal those who behaved untrustworthy in the past. Second, the *sanctioning*-function causes untrustworthy users to be avoided by others. Because bad behaviour influences future interactions negatively, this so-called "shadow of the future" [4, pp. 126 - 133] creates an incentive to behave trustworthy.

Practice shows that manipulation and strategic behaviour interfere with a reputation system's trust building dual function. Though various publications [5 - 8] suggest improvements for reputation systems, proposed solutions hitherto address problems separately. To gain robustness against various manipulations, some approaches combine several solutions against known problems. An interesting example is the Sporas reputation system proposed by Zacharia et al. [9]. Due to possible interdependencies

T. Di Noia and F. Buccafurri (Eds.): EC-Web 2009, LNCS 5692, pp. 288–299, 2009.
© Springer-Verlag Berlin Heidelberg 2009

between manipulations and solutions, the efficiency of such approaches may therefore be questionable. Thus if a solution could solve a specific manipulation it may simply promote another manipulation. This question has not been investigated yet and its missing examination has been criticised by other authors [7] as a gap in the approach of Zacharia et al..

This paper examines possible interdependencies between manipulations and solutions. The analysis is based on a multi-agent-simulation, which applies concepts of evolutionary game theory. The proposed evolutionary approach examines whether a strategy could penetrate a population successfully. This allows evaluating if a reputation system could successfully prevent manipulation strategies. As an example, the paper assesses the Sporas-algorithm and hence closes the above mentioned gap.

The paper is organized as follows. The next section gives a review of known strategic behaviour and manipulations of reputation systems. Section 3 shows how the Sporas reputation function combines solutions against manipulations. Section 4 introduces the underlying evolutionary game theoretic model of the multi-agent-simulation. Section 5 presents experimental results by applying the multi-agent-simulation to the Sporas reputation system. The final section discusses the main findings of this paper and points out possible directions for future research.

## 2 Manipulation of Reputation Systems

Manipulations and strategic behaviour generally tend to take advantage of the, economic value of a good reputation, which has been analysed in several studies [10, pp. 1411 – 1413, 11, pp. 83 – 87, 12]. Practice shows various types of such manipulations and strategic behaviour.

The rest-on-the-laurels (ROTL)-strategy builds up a good reputation in order to milk its value in future transactions by negative, untrustworthy behaviour [10, p. 1419]. Other strategies base on fake transactions between several players [7]. Within the ballot-stuffing (BS)-strategy a group of players colludes by giving each other unfair positive ratings to improve their own reputation. Besides gaining direct competitive advantages, e.g. higher prices or improved chances to sell, this strategy may also be used to prepare a ROTL-exploit or to compensate for previously negative-rated untrustworthy behaviour. In opposition to this, the bad mouthing (BM)-strategy aims for damaging a competitors reputation with unfair negative ratings that may cause competitive disadvantages or even drive the competitor out of the market.

Other manipulations exploit the easy obtaining of identities in the internet. The sibyl attack implies the obtaining of several fake-identities [13], which allows a single player to accomplish a BS- or BM-attack. Furthermore, a player could whitewash his bad reputation by changing his identity and restart with a clean reputation profile [14].

Beyond this, free riding problems [8, p. 1359] and the fear of retaliatory bad ratings [12, p. 24] may prevent users to give feedback and can lead to incomplete reputation profiles.

The described problems reveal that manipulation and strategic behaviour interfere with the dual function of a reputation system and its applicability for building trust may therefore be questionable.

## 3 Improving Reputation Systems

Plenty of contributions suggest improvements to gain higher robustness of reputation systems against the variety of manipulations. To prevent a ROTL-strategy, authors suggest putting more weight on recent ratings, e.g. by publishing only recent feedback [10, p. 1419]. This creates an incentive to behave trustworthy, because current actions now have stronger influence on reputation. To avoid whitewashing, users may start with the lowest possible reputation value [15]. Because a user's reputation does then not fall below a new user's reputation, this eliminates the incentive to change identity. Entry-fees or the use of "once-in-a-lifetime" pseudonyms may prevent identity change alternatively [14]. The latter is also suitable to avoid sybil attacks.

Other approaches target on preventing collusion-based attacks. Therefore, consequences of a BM- or BS-attack may be confined by revealing suspicious ratings using cluster-analysis [7]. Other approaches allow for collecting feedback in turn for collected ratings to avoid such strategies [10, p. 1408]. Various other approaches provide for letting users rate each other only once, minimizing a single person's influence on reputation values [9]. Mostly this is achieved by keeping the newest value if users rate each other more than once. Another idea is to weight ratings based on the rater's reputation [16]. This may increase reliability of collected ratings because it is assumed that trustworthy users rate honestly more likely. Furthermore, this minimizes influence of new user's identities on reputation values and therefore may be qualified to prevent sybil attacks [9].

The sporas reputation function [9] combines some of the described approaches to achieve a wider robustness against manipulations. Based on the rating $W$ and the rater's reputation $R^{other}$ the sporas formula updates the reputation value by:

$$R_{t+1} = \frac{1}{\theta} \sum_{1}^{t} \Phi(R_i) \bullet R_i^{other} \bullet (W_{i+1} - E(R_{i+1}))$$

$$\text{with } \Phi(R) = 1 - \frac{1}{1 + e^{\frac{-(R-D)}{\sigma}}} \quad \text{and} \quad E(R_{t+1}) = {R_t}/{D} \tag{1}$$

The parameter $D$ specifies the maximum reputation value and yields range $R \in [0, D]$ of the sporas function. The parameter $\theta$ yields a weighting of given ratings and is therefore capable to prevent a ROTL-strategy. Additionally, rating is weighted by $R^{other}$ so new identities that are possibly obtained by a sybil attack couldn't exert much influence on reputation values which prevents BM- or BS-attacks. The latter should further be avoided by keeping the newest rating, if users rate each other more than once. However, if "real" users accomplish these attacks, the suitability of this solution may be questionable. To avoid whitewashing, a reputation value $R = 0$ is assigned to new users. Furthermore, the Sporas formula contains a damping function $\Phi$. While Zacharia et al. do not explain its purpose; $\Phi$ may be capable to prevent a BM because influence of ratings on high reputation values is decreased. In this regard, the parameter $\sigma$ controls the steepness of $\Phi$. Increasing $\sigma$ reduces steepness of $\Phi$. Therefore, the influence of ratings on lower reputation values decreases, which strengthens the damping of $\Phi$. However, one may ask if this might interfere with the weighting parameter $\theta$, which then may favour a ROTL-strategy.

## 4 Evaluating Robustness of Reputation Systems

### 4.1 Basic Model

To analyze the robustness of a reputation system, consider a hypothetical market for a certain homogeneous good. The good is traded between a set of buyers $B$ and sellers $S$. Assume that buyers and sellers are each allocated on a single market side, and therefore $B \cap S = \emptyset$. Further, assume that market actions repeatedly take place in periods $t \in \aleph$. In each period $t=1, 2 \ldots$ buyers and sellers are paired together by random matching [17, p. 84]. Each pair $(b_i^t, s_j^t) \in B \times S$ plays the simple trust game, shown in figure 1.

The simple trust game models a decision problem typically occurring on electronic marketplaces. Assume a reservation price $r > 0$, reflecting the value of the good to the seller. In each period the seller offers the good to the buyer and for that he chooses a price $p_t > r$. Further, assume that the buyer's willingness to pay is $w_i > r$.[1] In each period $t$, the buyer decides to either accept or reject the sellers offer. In case of accepting, the seller afterwards has the option to behave trustworthy by delivering the good or to betray by refusing delivery and keeping the buyers payment. This creates a moral hazard because in each period the seller may increase his own profit by $p - (p - r) = r$ due to untrustworthy behaviour.

To solve the described trust problem a reputation system $R$ is introduced, which collects ratings $r = \{-1; 1\}$ from buyers. Assume that buyers rate a sellers untrustworthy behaviour by $r = -1$ and $r = 1$ otherwise. For every seller $j$ a reputation profile $R_j = \{r_1, r_2, r_3 \ldots \}$ exists, where all obtained ratings $r_t$ are collected. For simplicity this paper does not allow for buy side reputation as the simple trust game induces a sell-side trust problem only and players are not allowed to change market side. Introducing buy-side reputation could yet be an interesting enhancement of our model.

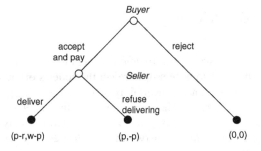

**Fig. 1.** Simple trust game

---

[1] This is a necessary condition to achieve trading. Otherwise, if $w < r$ the seller would not offer the good and therefore consumes it for himself.

Finally the seller's aggregated reputation value $f(R_j)$ is published on the marketplace. An important feature of the reputation system is the design of the function $f()$. This paper analyzes the previously described sporas reputation function (1).

## 4.2  Imitation of Strategies

As the simple trust game in figure 1 shows simple basic options the player could take in $t$, a strategy $s$ defines the actual action taken in a specific period in the repeated trust game. For buyers $B$ and sellers $S$ assume different sets $S_B$; $S_S$ of strategies from which every player chooses exactly one single strategy $s$. According to this, actual interaction in period $t$ respectively results from the pairing $(b_i^t, s_j^t)$ and yields the payoffs shown in figure 1, based on chosen strategy. The success of a strategy is measured by the fitness [18, pp. 934 - 935], which is calculated as the average payoff a player obtained so far.

Consider that a player's strategy choice must not be final. Assume that players review their strategy from time to time and change it, if another strategy is more successful. We achieve this by adopting an imitation behaviour, which comprises that a player compares his fitness to a randomly selected partner and imitates his strategy if higher payoff is achieved [19, pp. 152 - 161]. As a result a selection of strategies occurs, because if fitness is below average a strategy may extinct from population and otherwise superior strategies may be able to spread in population. Finally, the described process possibly may evolve equilibriums where fractions of strategies remain stable in population [18, pp. 948ff.].

## 4.3  Robustness

We propose the analysis of these equilibriums as an approach to evaluate the robustness of a reputation system. A reputation system is robust if it is capable to crowd out all possible manipulation strategies and leads to an equilibrium of cooperating strategies. This also implies that a robust reputation system has to provide for stability of this cooperating strategy yielding equilibrium in case of possible appearance of new strategies.

## 4.4  Modelling Agent Behaviour

### Buyers
According our previously made simplification, buyers have to solve the following decision problem by choosing to accept or to reject the seller's offer. As figure 1 shows, this turns out to be a choice under uncertainty [20, pp. 220 - 227], because sellers behaviour is unknown in advance. Therefore, rejecting the seller's offer yields the determined zero outcome. On accepting, two possible outcomes may arise as the buyer could gain $(w_i - p_j^t)$ if the seller is trustworthy and looses $p_j^t$ otherwise. Thereby the buyer bases his decision on the expected transaction outcome:

$$E(a) = (p_j^t - w_i)p_{succ} - p_j^t(1 - p_{succ}) \qquad (2)$$

Thus, $p_{succ}$ specifies the probability for a successful transaction and combines two elements. First, based on $R_j$, the reputation system itself yields a probability for success by $p_{rep} = f(R_j)$. Second, as findings like [21, pp. 17-21] show, buyers irrespectively gain experience about transaction success on the marketplace for themselves. Accounting for this, assume, that a buyer additionally estimates a subjective probability for success by $p_{sub}$ = |*number of successful transactions*| / |*total transactions*|. Finally, $p_{succ}$ results from the weighted average:

$$P_{succ} = g \cdot P_{rep} + (1 - g) \cdot P_{sub}, \ 0 \leq g \leq 1, \ g \in \Re \qquad (3)$$

Notice that $g$ specifies the amount of "trust" a buyer places in the market's reputation system. Therefore, let $g = 1$ if buyers perfectly trust in reputation systems proper function. Otherwise, if a seller betrays despite his good reputation, this may indicate an exploitation of the reputation system. The buyer then decreases $g$ and thereby reduces the reputation systems influence on his decision. Likewise, $g$ would be increased in case of observing sellers trustworthy behaviour.

Finally, (2) allows for deriving a simple rule for buyer's decision. Therefore, a buyer accepts an offer in case $E(a) > 0$ and rejects it otherwise. Besides its simplicity, this rule has some appealing other properties. Firstly, on increasing reputation buyers accept higher prices, which therefore accounts for the concept of reputation rents [22, pp. 122 – 123]. On the contrary, a lower reputation value indicates a possibly risky transaction and may therefore reduce the buyer's willingness to pay. Furthermore, a buyer's willingness to pay also reduces on decreasing trust in reputation system. Additionally, a buyer may even exclude the reputation system from his decision.

**Sellers**
According to his chosen and subsequently depicted strategy $s_j$, in each period $t$ a seller may decide to cooperate, to betray or to manipulate the reputation system as well. Additionally, at the beginning of period $t$, the seller also decides to choose a price $p_j^t$ to offer the good to the randomly assigned buyer.

To maximise his profit, assume that the seller adapts his chosen price to the actual buyer's willingness to pay. Therefore, seller test demand by performing a "derivative follower (DF) strategy" [23, pp. 89-90] and adjust prices according to the transactions success. Thus in case a buyer accepted a seller's last offer, price will be increased by $p_j^{t+1} = p_j^t + b$, while $b$ is chosen randomly from $[0, s]$, $s << p$. Likewise, if the last offer was rejected, the seller decreases $p_j^t$ by step $b$.

Besides cooperating, the seller also has the possibility to manipulate the reputation system in order to prepare a fraud. Currently, our simulation model allows for the implementation of a ROTL-, BM-, BS- and a whitewashing-strategy.

With the intention of skimming the value of a good reputation, we introduce a ROTL-strategy which cooperates $n$ periods and then chooses option "refuse deliver" and afterwards cooperates $n$ periods again. While this strategy may gain higher payoff on betraying, a player executing this strategy also collects negative ratings in $R_j$ during the simulation run.

According to this, a player may have an incentive to whitewash from a possibly negatively rated transaction. To account for such a whitewashing-strategy we enhance the ROTL-strategy as a player may change his identity by reregistering on the marketplace after betraying. As a result, the player gains a new "fresh" reputation profile $R_j$ and may therefore be able to elude possibly negative consequences of a bad rating.

Furthermore, if we enhance the ROTL-strategy in another way, we are able to implement a BS-strategy, which tries to improve reputation by unfairly collecting $m$ additional positive ratings. Our version of a BS-strategy therefore aims to compensate for a negative rating, caused by the underlying ROTL-behaviour.

Finally, we introduce a BM-strategy, which aims for manipulating other player's reputation profiles. Therefore, in each period $t$ the BM-strategy randomly chooses a number of $m$ sellers and rates them negative. As a result, other player's reputation will be damaged during the simulation run.

## 5   Simulation

In order to use our approach on examining the robustness of the Sporas formula (2) we developed a multi-agent-simulation (MAS), based on the *JADE Framework*. The MAS consists of buyer and seller agents, acting according to the strategies, which we defined in section 4. Additionally a marketplace-agent represents the market mechanism and controls simulation flow.

According to Zacharia et al. we use the following version of Sporas which allows iterative calculation of reputation values during the simulation run.

$$R_{t+1} = \frac{1}{\theta}\Phi(R_i)R_{i+1}^{other}\left(W_{i+1} - \frac{R_t}{D}\right) + R_t \tag{4}$$

Zacharia et al. [9] specified a range $R \in [0; 3000]$ for reputation values. In order to apply the Sporas-reputation system to our decision rule, we map $R$ to the interval $p_{rep} = [0; 1] \in \mathfrak{R}$. Therefore, we assigned $p_{rep} = 1$ for $max(R) = 3000$ and $p_{rep} = 0$ for $min(R) = 0$. Corresponding to Zacharia et al. we also set $\theta = 10$. While its impact is not explained, we initially chose $\sigma = 1.0$ and therefore attain a minimal damping of $\Phi$.

Below we examine simple reputation scenarios yielding a population of $n = 100$ agents. For buyer-agents we chose $w_i = 1$ so that the market price ranges in the interval $p \in [r, 1]$. Initially all agents play a "cooperating" strategy. In period $t = 150$ we destabilize the cooperating equilibrium by a small sized mutation, as single agents switch to a certain manipulation strategy.

*Initial scenario*
Initially we analyzed population dynamics on letting mutate a ROTL, BS, BM and a whitewashing-strategy simultaneously. Fig. 2 shows that the BS-strategy is then able to successful invade the hitherto cooperating population. This indicates that Sporas may be exploitable to a part of possible manipulation strategies. For a more detailed analysis, we examine the underlying dynamics of the selection process in the following. Therefore, we account for mutation of one single manipulation strategy only.

*Population dynamics on mutating single manipulation strategies*
Likewise the basic scenario, we observed it's swiftly crowding out on mutating a single whitewashing strategy. Thus, by switching his identity, the whitewashing agent successfully can elude possible negative consequences caused by a bad rating after a fraud. Though, the agent then is not able to perform further transactions due to the fact that his reputation is reduced to zero afterwards.

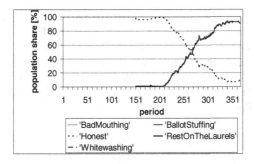

**Fig. 2.** Population dynamics in initial scenario

Furthermore, Sporas shows robustness against the mutation of a single BM-strategy in that way, that this strategy is not able to spread in population. Due to damping of high reputation values, the BM-agent is not able to sufficiently damage the other seller's reputation and therefore could not gain competitive advantage by bad mouthing his competitors. Notice that some simulation runs of the basic scenario showed a temporary spread of the BM-strategy which turned out to be favored by BS and the ROTL-strategy. As BS and ROTL damage their reputation, ratings then have more impact on their decreased reputation due to the low acceleration factor $\sigma$ of the damping function $\Phi$. Thus a BM-Strategy could temporarily gain success by bad mouthing a ROTL or BS-Strategy and therefore additionally decreasing their reputation value. This may indicate that adjusting $\sigma$ could be required to achieve higher robustness of Sporas. We discuss the consequences of such an adjustment below.

In addition, the successful mutation of a single BS-Strategy points out a possible need for adjusting $\sigma$ as the low acceleration factor yields a quick adaption of reputation values. Figure 3 reveals the underlying dynamics. We observed that in period $t=171$ the BS-agent chooses "refuse deliver". As his reputation decreases afterwards due to the negative rating, the buyer then rejects the BS-agents offer in the next period. The BS-agent afterwards decreases his offer and is therefore able to accomplish another transaction in the next period. As a result, the BS-agent's reputation increases again on collecting positive ratings from the buyer and himself as well. Due to the low acceleration factor, the reputation increases fast enough so that the BS-agent is able to betray after 10 rounds again, which he could shortly outweigh as well. Likewise, we also observed this process on a successful mutation of the ROTL-strategy.

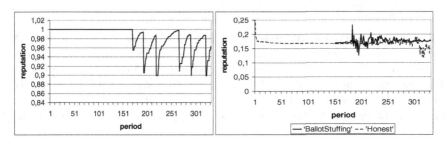

**Fig. 3.** Development of reputation of a BS-Agent (a) and average fitness of the BS-Strategy (b)

*Establishing robustness of the Sporas reputation system*
It turns out that low $\sigma$ reduces robustness of the sporas reputation system by favouring spreading of a BS- and ROTL-strategy as it interferes the weighing parameter $\theta$ by making a short outweighing of bad ratings possible. Thus, $\sigma$ also favours temporary spreading of the BM-attack, as values could easily be damaged if reputation values slightly decrease. Therefore, we examine if we could establish robustness Sporas by adjusting $\sigma$ in the following.

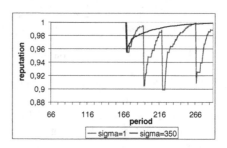

**Fig. 4.** Reputation of a BS-Agent on varying $\sigma$

We observed that $\sigma = 350$ prevents BS and ROTL from successfully invading the population. As $\Phi$ now covers lower reputation values, it turns out that sporas yields a delayed adjustment of the reputation system on new ratings[2], which is shown by figure 4. This decreases fitness of BS and ROTL attacks as now more periods are necessary to recover from a bad rating.

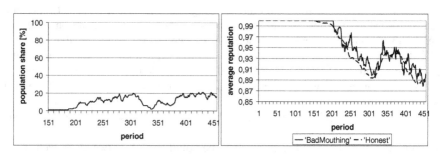

**Fig. 5.** Development of population share (a) and average reputation (b) by mutation a BM-strategy and $\sigma = 550$

We further observed a spreading of the BM-Attack if $\sigma=550$. Due to their DF-behaviour, agents now very slowly recover from an unfair bad rating, which increases the fitness of BM-strategy for the time. As shown in figure 5 (b), agents playing a co-operating-strategy now imitate the BM-strategy as their reputation is damaged. This afterwards decreases the average reputation of the BM-strategy. As the overall number of bad ratings in the market increases, average reputation of the BM strategy

---

[2] Dellarocas [24] discusses similar findings, as he shows that on lowering the frequency a reputation value is updated, such a delayed adjustment could increase the efficiency of a reputation system.

further decreases as BM-agents also collect unfair bad ratings from other agents. Since this causes an additional loss of fitness, some agents switch back to the cooperating strategy. Finally, figure 5 (a) shows that population share of the BM-strategy stabilizes at about 18 percent. It reveals that Sporas is exploitable to a BM-attack. It also turns out that preventing a BS or ROTL attack by increasing $\sigma$ simply promotes another manipulation. To sum it up, our experiments indicate that $\sigma$ may only be partially suitable to improve robustness of the Sporas reputation system.

Therefore, we further examined if adjusting the weighting parameter $\theta$ has an effect on the robustness of the reputation system. Figure 6 shows the results of several simulation runs on varying $\theta$. We observed that both BS and BM are crowded out by the cooperating strategy if $\theta = 5$. It reveals that higher weight decreases reputation so much, that profits gained by fraud are compensated by the DF-behaviour. This decreases the fitness of the BS strategy as well and the market returns to cooperating equilibrium. In addition, the reputation system is also robust against the BM as it allows unfair bad rated agents to swiftly restore their damaged reputation due to the low acceleration factor of the damping function $\Phi$.

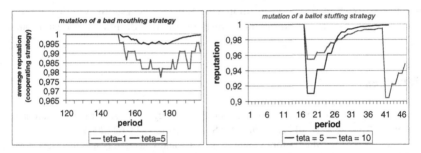

**Fig. 6.** Consequences of adjusting $\theta$ on robustness of the sporas reputation system

Our experiments further indicate that $\theta$ should be well balanced in order to achieve robustness of the Sporas reputation system. Figure 6 clarifies this finding. If $\theta < 5$, we observed that the cooperating strategy could not recover sufficiently from an unfair bad rating due to the high weighting of ratings and then the BM-Strategy successfully invades the population. Otherwise, if $\theta > 5$, BM is crowded out but now ROTL is able to compensate for a bad rating and crowds out the cooperating strategy.

Furthermore, our experiments reveal that BS spreads in population again as it successfully outweighs a bad rating if $m \geq 2$ and therefore overrides the higher weighting $\theta = 5$. Additionally adjusting the damping function $\Phi$ to $\sigma = 350$ turns out to be a limited solution as BS overrides the decelerated adaption of the reputation values, if $m \geq 3$. Hence, our results show that BS overrides possible solutions on increasing the number of ballots $m$. Thus, solutions contemplated so far establish robustness only partially. We therefore examined the impact of an additional transaction fee $tf$ as percentage of sales. Assuming that each ballot is charged with a transaction fee, it turned out that BS could be crowded out if $tf \geq 1\%$ off $p_j^t$. This points out, that complementary solutions are needed for enhancing robustness of the examined reputation system.

# 6  Conclusions

In this paper, we presented an approach for evaluating the robustness of reputation systems by applying concepts of evolutionary game theory. On transferring our model to a multi-agent-simulation, we were able to test Zacharia et al.'s [9] experimental Sporas reputation system. We observed that depending on a proper choice of its parameters, Sporas shows robustness against manipulations. Therefore, the presented results confirm that it is possible to construct robust reputation systems by combining different solutions against manipulations. Additionally, our approach also reveals interactions between solutions and manipulations. We were able to show that a solution could promote another manipulation. Particularly, the presented results indicate that well balanced sanctioning and rehabilitation may be of importance for the robustness of a reputation system.

Future studies will address this issue. On applying our approach to other reputation systems, we will examine if the principle of an optimal weighting is also valid in other settings. We therefore aim for including additional and even more complex manipulation strategies to our analysis. Summarizing, it turns out that our approach complements existing research on improving reputation systems. On developing our approach, we aim for revealing more insights on the design of robust reputation systems.

# References

1. Bierhoff, H.W., Vornefeld, B.: The Social Psychology of Trust with Applications in the Internet. Analyse & Kritik. Zeitschrift für Sozialtheorie 1, 48–62 (2004)
2. Akerlof, G.A.: The Market for "Lemons": Quality and Uncertainty and the Market Mechanism. The Quaterly Journal of Economics 84, 488–500 (1970)
3. Resnick, P., Zeckhauser, R., Friedmann, E., Kuwabara, K.: Reputation Systems. Communications of the ACM 43, 45–48 (2000)
4. Axelrodt, R.: The Evolution of Cooperation. Penguin Books, London (1990)
5. Friedmann, E., Resnick, P.: The Social Cost of Cheap Pseudonyms. Journal of Economics and Management Strategy 10, 173–199 (2001)
6. Dellarocas, C.: Efficiency through feedback-contingent fees and rewards in auction marketplaces with adverse selection and moral hazard. In: 3rd ACM Conference on Electronic Commerce (EC 2003), pp. 11–18. ACM, New York (2003)
7. Dellarocas, C.: Immunizing online reputation reporting systems against unfair ratings and discriminating behavior. In: Proceedings of the 2nd ACM conference on electronic commerce, pp. 150–157. ACM, New York (2000)
8. Miller, N., Resnick, P., Zeckhauser, R.: Eliciting Honest Feedback: The Peer-Prediction Method. Management Science 51, 1359–1373 (2005)
9. Zacharia, G., Moukas, A., Maes, P.: Collaborative reputation mechanisms for electronic marketplaces. Decision Support Systems 29, 371–388 (2000)
10. Dellarocas, C.: The Digitization of Word of Mouth: Promise and Challenges of Online Feedback Mechanisms. Management Science 49, 1407–1424 (2003)
11. Resnick, P., Zeckhauser, R., Swanson, J., Lockwood, K.: The value of reputation on eBay: a controlled experiment. Experimental Economics 9, 79–101 (2006)

12. Kennes, J., Schiff, A.: The Value of a Reputation System. Working Paper, University of Auckland (2003)
13. Douceur, J.R.: The Sybil Attack. In: Druschel, P., Kaashoek, M.F., Rowstron, A. (eds.) IPTPS 2002, vol. 2429, p. 251. Springer, Heidelberg (2002)
14. Friedman, E., Resnick, P.: The Social Cost of Cheap Pseudonyms. Journal of Economics and Management Strategy 10, 173–199 (2001)
15. Dellarocas, C.: Efficiency and robustness of binary feedback: mechanisms in trading environments with moral hazard. Workin Paper, MIT Sloan School of Management, Cambridge Mass (2003)
16. Mui, L., Halberstadt, A., Mohtashemi, M.: Notions of Reputation in Multi-Agents Systems: A Review. In: Falcone, R., Barber, S.K., Korba, L., Singh, M.P. (eds.) AAMAS 2002. LNCS, vol. 2631, pp. 280–287. Springer, Heidelberg (2003)
17. Samuelson, L.: Evolutionary Games and Equilibrium Selection. MIT Press, Cambridge (1997)
18. Hammerstein, P., Selten, R.: Game Theory and Evolutionary Biology. In: Aumann, R., Hart, S. (eds.) Handbook of Game Theory, 2nd edn., vol. 2, pp. 929–993. Elsevier, Amsterdam (2003)
19. Weibull, J.W.: Evolutionary Game Theory, 5th edn. The MIT Press, Cambridge (2002)
20. Varian, H.R.: Intermediate microeconomics: a modern approach, 6th edn. Norton, New York (2006)
21. Bolton, G., Katok, E., Ockenfels, A.: How Effective are Online Reputation Mechanisms? Discussion Papers on Strategic Interaction No. 2002-25, Max Planck Institute of Economics (2002)
22. Tirole, J.: The theory of industrial organization. The MIT Press, Cambridge (2003)
23. Zacharia, et al.: Economics of Dynamic Pricing in a Reputation Brokered Agent Mediated Marketplace. Electronic Commerce Research 1, 85–100 (2001)
24. Dellarocas, C.: How Often Should Reputation Mechanisms Update a Trader's Reputation Profile? Information Systems Research 17, 271–285 (2006)

# Fraud Detection by Human Agents: A Pilot Study

Vinicius Almendra and Daniel Schwabe

Departamento de Informática, Pontifícia Universidade Católica do Rio de Janeiro,
Rio de Janeiro, Brazil
vinicius.almendra@gmail.com, dschwabe@inf.puc-rio.br

**Abstract.** Fraud is a constant problem for online auction sites. Besides failures in detecting fraudsters, the currently employed methods yield many false positives: bona fide sellers that end up harassed by the auction site as suspects. We advocate the use of human computation (also called crowdsourcing) to improve precision and recall of current fraud detection techniques. To examine the feasibility of our proposal, we did a pilot study with a set of human subjects, testing whether they could distinguish fraudsters from common sellers before negative feedback arrived and looking just at a snapshot of seller profiles. Here we present the methodology used and the obtained results, in terms of precision and recall of human classifiers, showing positive evidence that detecting fraudsters with human computation is viable.

**Keywords:** fraud, human computation, e-commerce, classification.

## 1 Introduction

In the last years we have witnessed a tremendous growth in electronic markets, of which online auction sites have an important share. Fraud levels have been increasing at a similar pace [8,12,15]. Online auction sites actively try to reduce fraud levels, through internal controls that filter out suspicious users or limit the amount of negotiations they can be involved in, for example. These restrictions reduce losses with frauds and reduce the perceived risk, as less people end up being swindled.

However, these controls are far from perfect, as fraudsters actively try to disguise themselves as honest users. This means that many honest sellers will be erroneously treated as suspicious. When treated as fraudsters, hitherto honest sellers might abandon the market, go to a competitor or at least slow down their sales. As online auction sites' primary source of revenue is the amount of commissions charged to sellers, such mistakes must be kept at a minimum. The investigations spawned by fraud detection mechanisms also bear some cost, so the number of users that have to be examined also impacts negatively on profit.

We do not have access to the online auction sites' controls, but we can regard them as classifiers that categorize users to support risk analysis: users with a higher risk of fraudulent behavior have more operational restrictions. The challenge is to balance the benefits of fraud reduction with the losses due to misclassification. In other terms, online auction sites need to balance the precision and the recall of their classifiers, as both influence the net profit from fraud detection activities. We advocate a new

T. Di Noia and F. Buccafurri (Eds.): EC-Web 2009, LNCS 5692, pp. 300–311, 2009.
© Springer-Verlag Berlin Heidelberg 2009

approach to improve this balance. Instead of relying solely on automatic classifiers to find suspects, we propose an ulterior analysis of their results with *human computation* [1,9]: "outsourcing" this refinement task to people recruited on Internet, who would check suspicious seller profiles in order to confirm suspicion or reject it. Given the previous classification done by current mechanisms, the number of seller profiles to be analyzed would be manageable. The paradigm of human computation has been successfully applied by the site Mechanical Turk[1], where thousands of tasks are distributed each day to virtually anonymous users. This has also been called "crowd-sourcing" [5].

In order to check the viability of this proposal, we have done a pilot study with a group of unskilled people. The task we assigned to them was to predict non-delivery fraud, the most common complaint in online auction sites [8,11,12]. Given a group of active sellers from MercadoLivre[2], the biggest Brazilian auction site, we wanted to check whether those people could predict which sellers would commit fraud in the near future; we also wanted to know how precise this prediction would be. In other words, looking at humans as classifiers, we wanted to know their precision and recall.

### 1.1 Why Use Human Computation?

There are several reported uses of human computation in the literature: labeling images from the web [1], conducting user studies [14], credit analysis [7], collection of human-reviewed data [18], moderation of textual comments in discussion forums [13]. All these studies confirm the usefulness of this new paradigm.

In the domain of fraud detection, we argue that human computation provides a scalable solution, as the use of human agents can be adjusted to match current needs: if fraud increases, one can employ more agents; less fraud, fewer agents can be used. This is much harder to accomplish with traditional organizational structures, as hiring and dismissing people are expensive operations.

The performance of human agents recruited arbitrarily on the Internet is certainly lower than those who an enterprise could hire through traditional focused methods (interviews, resume analysis etc.). However, this can be counterbalanced by the use of multiple agents to solve the same problem, a strategy already employed by Mechanical Turk.

### 1.2 Related Work

There is an ongoing research on finding fraudsters through data mining in social networks [6,16,19]. The basic idea is to uncover one of the strategies used by fraudsters in online auction sites, which leads to the formation of a bipartite negotiation graph: "honest" identities on one side and fraudulent identities on the other. The "honest" identities are used to boost the reputation of fraudulent identities, through false trades. Then the reputation obtained is used to commit fraud. The "honest" identities are also used in normal negotiations, making it difficult to link them with fraudulent activity. These identities can be "reused" many times by fraudsters, reducing the total cost to carry out deceptive activities.

---

[1] www.mturk.com
[2] www.mercadolivre.com.br

While offering an interesting solution, they target a very specific fraudulent strategy. Our work complements theirs and gives a more general and long-lasting solution: fraudsters change strategy, but are always fraudsters, which implies in using some sort of lying detectable by humans [15].

On the side of human computation, the best known work is the ESP game [1], which is a computer game were people generate textual labels for arbitrary images. Players are matched in pairs and on each round both are exposed to an image. They have some time to type words, knowing that they gain points when one of them writes a word that the other has already typed. As the only means of communication between them is the image, it turns out that when a match occurs, there is a high probability the matching word is a good descriptive label for the image. The game is based on the fact the problem of describing images is very easy for people, but extremely difficult for computers. If one can make lots of people solve those problems for a low-cost reward, then we have some sort of viable "human computer".

A notable difference between our work and the preceding one is the complexity of the task. Detecting fraudsters is certainly more difficult than giving descriptive labels for images. This raises two important questions: whether this task is viable, i.e. the results are good enough, and whether the amount spent with rewards does not exceed what the online auction site recovers with aborted frauds. One may argue that Mechanical Turk "crowdsources" tasks that are not easy. However, we should first check if people are really capable of detecting fraudsters, at least in a reasonable time; this is the objective of our work.

Gentry et al. [9] proposed a framework for human computation, deriving some theoretical results but without empirical ones. Belenkiy et al. [4] present an incentive mechanism for outsourced computation in a strategic setting, where "contractors" solve computational problems to a "boss". They focus on computational tasks solvable through some known deterministic algorithm, which is not our case.

## 2   Problem Statement

In order to use human computation, we need to model the problem we are going to solve. Let $VE$ be set of sellers with active listings at a certain moment of time. We have the following subsets of interest:

- $VE_F$: the subset of $VE$ containing sellers whose listings are fraudulent, that is, who will commit non-delivery fraud.
- $VE_N$: the subset of $VE$ containing bona fide users (hereafter called *normal users*), that is, those who will deliver the merchandise currently advertised in their listings. This set is the complement of the previous one.

Obviously the auction site does not know beforehand which sellers belong to each category. The true class of fraudsters is revealed when buyers start complaining of non-delivery fraud; this happens several days after sales have been made. When this condition *does not* happen for a specific seller, then his/her true class is the other one, of the normal sellers.

The problem in question is to *predict* the correct classification of each seller. This prediction yields two new subsets of $VE$:

- $VE_{CF}$: the subset of sellers classified as fraudsters.
- $VE_{CN}$: the subset of sellers classified as normal.

The problem of interest for the auction site is to find a binary classifier that better approximates the true nature of sellers. We can measure this approximation using information retrieval metrics – *precision, recall, fall-out* and *F-measure* [17] –, adapted to our scenario. Precision is the fraction of true fraudsters classified as such among all sellers classified as fraudsters:

$$PREC = \frac{|VE_{CF} \cap VE_F|}{|VE_{CF}|}$$

Recall is the fraction of true fraudsters classified as such among all fraudsters:

$$REC = \frac{|VE_{CF} \cap VE_F|}{|VE_F|}$$

To obtain a joint value of these two metrics, we can use the F-measure:

$$F = 2 \cdot \frac{PREC \cdot REC}{PREC + REC}$$

Another relevant metric is the fall-out, which is the fraction of false positives:

$$FO = \frac{|VE_{CF} \cap VE_N|}{|VE_N|}$$

This last measure is important, as it quantifies the impact of fraud detection on normal sellers. A big fall-out means more harassed (and dissatisfied) sellers.

We will say that a human classifier *contributes* if s/he does better than a random classifier, that is, his precision is greater than $|VE_F|/|VE|$. To order human classifiers, we will use the F-measure.

# 3  Pilot Test Design

We designed a pilot test to evaluate the performance of human agents in the classification task outlined in the previous section. We selected a sample of people and, for each subject, followed this procedure:

1. We presented a written training material about fraud in auction sites. We suggested them to study that material for a maximum of 30 minutes;
2. We presented a written explanation of what s/he was expected to do in the pilot test, how to fill the questionnaire, what they could not do etc.;
3. We provided a link to a worksheet where answers and some personal data should be recorded: age, profession, and if had already used MercadoLivre (hereafter referred to as ML);
4. We presented a list of links to seller profiles, where each one pointed to an offline snapshot of the profile of a seller in ML;
5. We instructed them to fill the worksheet, recording their opinion about each seller (whether or not s/he would commit fraud); the moment they started

analyzing the seller; the moment they gave the answer; and the certainty degree of his/her answer (more certainty or less certainty). We also instructed them to do the test sequentially, in order to better capture time spent on each seller and to prevent influence of posterior experiences on previous answers.

After all subjects had done the test, we compared the answers supplied with the real outcome and we computed the metrics presented in the previous section for each one. In the next sections we will give a more detailed account of some aspects.

## 3.1  Sample Selection

We used a convenience sample of 26 people, recruited by the authors. None of them had earlier background on fraud detection, although seven had already done a simplified version of the pilot study, gaining some experience. We highlight the demographics of the sample in Table 1.

**Table 1.** Demographics of pilot study sample

| | | | | | |
|---|---|---|---|---|---|
| | **Age** | From 14 to 56 years old<br>Mean: 28,3 years / median: 25,5 years | | | |
| | | IT professionals | 5 | Engineers | 1 |
| | **Occupation** | Physicians | 3 | High school teacher | 1 |
| | | Economists | 3 | Undergraduate students | 11 |
| | | Lawyers | 1 | High school student | 1 |
| **Experience with ML** | | 13 have already used ML before | | | |
| **Earlier experience with pilot study?** | | 7 did a previous version of the pilot study | | | |

## 3.2  Seller Profiles

Subjects were asked to evaluate 20 profiles of real sellers from ML, containing seven fraudsters and 13 normal sellers. Instead of evaluating the current profile of the seller, they were allowed to view only a *snapshot* of it. This snapshot contained a local copy of the following web pages, crawled from the online auction site:

- The seller profile, containing received qualifications (positive, negative or neutral), along with textual comments;
- Profiles of users who qualified the seller;
- Seller's current listings;
- Seller's past listings.

Those pages are interlinked, mirroring the actual user experience of a buyer while examining a seller profile in the real live site. Links to web pages not contained in the snapshot were removed.

This approach was adopted for two reasons: (i) to guarantee that all members of the sample analyzed the same information; (ii) to guarantee a minimum number of fraudsters. The latter one deserves some explanation.

In order to build a set of profiles containing normal sellers and fraudsters, we could not choose sellers randomly, as the probability to find a fraudster would be very small. Besides that, we could not ask the human agents to evaluate a huge number of profiles. It was necessary to build a set of profiles in a more controlled manner. For that, we chose a set of active sellers, took snapshots of their profiles, and started monitoring their evolution over time, i.e. the outcome of their sales. When some of them displayed signals of fraudulent activity, we labeled their past snapshots as belonging to a fraudster. When they did not display any signs of fraudulent activity after some weeks, we labeled them as belonging to normal sellers. Dubious cases were excluded from analysis.

Auction sites do not give an official confirmation that a seller has committed non-delivery fraud. So, we used the following set of indicators, validated in a previous work [3]:

- The seller received several negative feedbacks over a short period of time;
- His/her account was suspended by the auction site and was not reinstated;
- Textual comments explicitly mention non-delivery fraud.

When none of those criteria were satisfied, we considered the seller to be a normal one. When just one or two of them were satisfied, we treated it as a dubious case.

The selection of sellers to be monitored and the moment chosen to take the snapshot of their profiles also obeyed some criteria, in order to increase the probability of finding fraudsters and, at the same time, avoiding profiles that already displayed some signs of fraud, as we wanted to test the ability of *predicting fraud occurrence when there are no clear signs indicating that* (e.g. recent negative qualifications). The chosen criteria to decide the moment to take a snapshot were based on the temporal model of non-delivery fraud shown in Figure 1.

Many cases of non-delivery fraud fit in this model. First, the fraudster obtains an account with enough reputation. Then, s/he lists many good selling products with attractive prices, becoming part of the set of sellers with *fraud potential*. After a short time, people start buying from the fraudster, as his/her listings are very attractive. When some buyers realize the fraudulent scheme, they complain to the auction site, besides giving negative qualifications to the seller. In a short period of time after that the auction site suspends the account and the fraudster disappears with buyer's money. We called *fraud window* the time interval between first sales and account suspension. This is the "latency" period of the swindle. Of course many normal sellers also "fit" in this model, except for the final part, as they usually deliver merchandise sold.

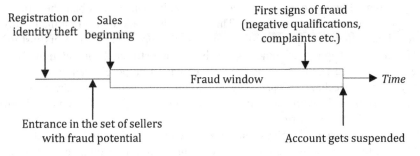

**Fig. 1.** Temporal model of non-delivery fraud

Our intention was to take the snapshot after the occurrence of the first three events: account acquisition, becoming part of the set of sellers with fraud potential and beginning of sales. We devised the following criteria to guarantee this:

- Seller was active: suspended sellers were ignored.
- Seller had no negative qualifications in the previous 30 days: recent negative qualifications trigger suspicion and a fraudster would avoid them.
- Seller had received less than 400 positive qualifications: we had evidence that most fraudsters use identities with fewer positive qualifications.
- Active listings were posted no earlier than 16 days: in many cases, complaints about the seller appear earlier than this.
- Seller has negotiated fewer than 100 products in the last six months (excluding the current one): again, we have evidence that fraudsters display this behavior.
- Four or more products from current listings were already sold: we focus on attractive listings, i.e. those that end up in sales.
- Value at stake (sum of listed products' price) is more than US$ 1,500.00: a bigger value at stake means more profit to the fraudster.
- At least one of the listed products belonged to a category known to attract fraudsters (cell phones, laptops, digital cameras etc.).

We did a daily inspection of thousands of seller profiles along several weeks. When one of them satisfied the conditions above, we took the snapshot and started monitoring it. When we finished this process, we had snapshots of profiles from 7 fraudsters and 59 normal sellers. The average fraud window was of five days, that is, in average sellers were suspended five days after we had taken the snapshot.

We took 13 normal seller profiles and mixed randomly with the 7 fraudster profiles. As we predicted people doing the test would be insecure in the first answers, we added 3 more normal sellers on the beginning of the list. Those three first answers were ignored in the data analysis. We informed subjects that the number of fraudsters among sellers was random: there could be many, but there could be none.

## 3.3  Training Material

The paradigm of human computation demands that human agents obtain benefits from their collaboration to solve problems. These benefits should depend on the quality of the job done; otherwise opportunistic agents would supply bogus answers just to get the benefits, as it happens in some systems based on distributed computation [4]. The benefits may range from fun, as in the "games with a purpose" scenario [1], to real money, like in Mechanical Turk. The important point here is that the presence of benefits creates an *incentive* to solve the problem well: agents will end up learning how to improve their performance.

Capturing this aspect involves long-running experiments, which we could not afford to, due to practical limitations. However, putting it aside would be a hindrance to our test, as the phenomenon we wish to observe is not the fraud detection abilities of a random Internet user; we are focusing on unspecialized users *with incentive and means to improve their results*. The simplest way to improve fraud detection skills is to search the Internet, as there are many sites discussing this issue, presenting famous cases, giving hints on how to avoid fraudsters etc.

In order to take into account the presence of incentive, we opted to give people from the sample a 10-page *training material*, containing information about fraud in online auction sites. Following is a more detailed description of this material's content:

- Links to ML help pages, for those who were not familiarized with the site;
- An explanation of non-delivery fraud. This explanation presented some common strategies to obtain reputation: selling items of small value; identity theft of good sellers; simulating negotiations through the use of other identities; building up reputation through buying instead of selling, since ML does not make a distinction when earning points;
- Hints about common misunderstandings on the meaning of some features that may unduly increase trust in sellers (e.g. "Safe User" label, posting tracking numbers of delivered merchandise);
- Text excerpts from fraud information sites, three detailed descriptions of alleged frauds, and an explanation of non-delivery fraud, all of them with links to their sources;
- Links to five seller profiles that fit into our description of non-delivery fraud. For each profile, we pointed out some signals that could raise suspicion on the seller. These signals were based on the preceding information and on the fraud strategies depicted in a research paper [15]. The links pointed to the real seller profiles, that is, *after* the alleged fraud has been committed.

We also urged those who would do the test to be as precise as possible, as their performance would depend on their recall *and* precision: classifying many sellers as fraudsters to "guarantee" a good recall would be of no help.

To avoid bias in this training material, the author did not examine the seven profiles of fraudsters used in the pilot study.

## 4  Data Collected

In Table 2 we display the metrics associated with each person in the sample. Notice that *true positives* is the number of fraudsters correctly pointed as such and *false positives* is the number of normal sellers wrongly pointed as fraudsters. Some outstanding numbers of precision, recall and fall-out are highlighted.

In Table 3 we show the number of "votes" received by each seller. A participant "voted" on a seller when s/he pointed him/her as a fraudster. In the fourth line we indicate with an "X" whether the seller was really a fraudster.

**Table 2.** Metrics of participant performance (ordered by F-measure)

| Person | True positives (out of 7) | False positives (out of 13) | Precision | Recall | Fall-out | F-measure |
|--------|---------------------------|------------------------------|-----------|--------|----------|-----------|
| 1 | 7 | 2 | 78% | 100% | 15% | 88% |
| 10 | 6 | 2 | 75% | 86% | 15% | 80% |
| 4 | 5 | 1 | 83% | 71% | 8% | 77% |
| 23 | 4 | 0 | 100% | 57% | 0% | 73% |
| 9 | 4 | 0 | 100% | 57% | 0% | 73% |
| 7 | 4 | 0 | 100% | 57% | 0% | 73% |
| 12 | 4 | 0 | 100% | 57% | 0% | 73% |
| 18 | 6 | 4 | 60% | 86% | 31% | 71% |
| 11 | 5 | 3 | 63% | 71% | 23% | 67% |
| 5 | 4 | 1 | 80% | 57% | 8% | 67% |
| 13 | 6 | 6 | 50% | 86% | 46% | 63% |
| 26 | 6 | 7 | 46% | 86% | 54% | 60% |
| 20 | 6 | 7 | 46% | 86% | 54% | 60% |
| 2 | 5 | 5 | 50% | 71% | 38% | 59% |
| 21 | 5 | 5 | 50% | 71% | 38% | 59% |
| 15 | 5 | 6 | 45% | 71% | 46% | 56% |
| 14 | 3 | 1 | 75% | 43% | 8% | 55% |
| 6 | 5 | 7 | 42% | 71% | 54% | 53% |
| 25 | 5 | 7 | 42% | 71% | 54% | 53% |
| 22 | 5 | 8 | 38% | 71% | 62% | 50% |
| 8 | 3 | 2 | 60% | 43% | 15% | 50% |
| 19 | 4 | 6 | 40% | 57% | 46% | 47% |
| 17 | 2 | 0 | 100% | 29% | 0% | 44% |
| 3 | 2 | 0 | 100% | 29% | 0% | 44% |
| 16 | 2 | 2 | 50% | 29% | 15% | 36% |
| 24 | 1 | 2 | 33% | 14% | 15% | 20% |
| **Averages** | **4,4** | **3,2** | **66%** | **63%** | **25%** | **60%** |

**Table 3.** Results by seller (ordered by the number of votes, from left to right)

| Rank | 1st | 2nd | 3rd | 4th | 5th | 6th | 7th | 8th | 9th | 10th | 11th | 12th | 13th | 14th | 15th | 16th | 17th | 18th | 19th | 20th |
|------|-----|-----|-----|-----|-----|-----|-----|-----|-----|------|------|------|------|------|------|------|------|------|------|------|
| Seller | 16 | 15 | 7 | 12 | 19 | 21 | 8 | 9 | 10 | 17 | 18 | 4 | 13 | 11 | 14 | 20 | 6 | 5 | 23 | 22 |
| Votes | 22 | 21 | 19 | 19 | 17 | 13 | 11 | 9 | 8 | 7 | 7 | 7 | 6 | 6 | 5 | 5 | 5 | 5 | 3 | 3 |
| Fraudster? | X | X | X | X | X | X | - | - | - | - | - | - | - | - | - | - | - | - | - | X |

## 5   Results Analysis

The results obtained are encouraging: only one person (no. 24) did not contribute, i.e., had a precision below 35%, which is the proportion of fraudsters in the set of seller profiles. There were 10 subjects with precision *and* recall greater than 50%. It is worth of noticing that five subjects achieved a precision of 100%, i.e., did not have false positives; those subjects also had a recall greater than 25%: they were able to catch more than a quarter of fraudsters without harassing normal sellers.

Observing Table 2, we notice that almost 70% of the subjects (18) classified *correctly* a number of fraudsters equal or greater than the number of normal sellers *incorrectly* classified as fraudsters. That is remarkable, given that there are almost twice more normal sellers then fraudsters.

The relevance of these results shows up in Table 3. If we count each answer as a vote, all fraudsters except one received more votes than normal sellers. This result is important, as it supports the use of human computation to find fraudsters using a voting schema. Gentry et al. [9] discussed the theoretical viability of majority voting on human computation; in our case, majority voting (more than 13 votes) would uncover 5 of 7 fraudsters without penalizing any normal seller, a relevant result.

Another interesting fact is the time spent by subjects. We told them to avoid spending more than ten minutes analyzing each seller. This time limit was chosen based on Mechanical Turk: most tasks with small payment have a time allotted around ten minutes. In fact, only 1% of the analyses took more than ten minutes to be completed and the average time spent on each seller profile was 3,72 minutes.

Nevertheless, we must look at these results with caution, due to methodological limitations. A convenience sample was used, preventing the use of average values as estimators of population mean. The small number of fraudsters and normal sellers analyzed also reduces the utility of precision and recall values as estimators, as their variances will be high. It should be noted, however, that average measures of precision and recall were high (66% and 63%, respectively), giving more confidence on results.

The representativeness of the set of sellers examined in the pilot test is limited, especially of fraudsters; perhaps those ones were much easier to detect. It would be necessary to choose fraudsters from a greater sample. We also analyzed one type of fraud (non-delivery), although it is the most common one, according to the literature.

The fraction of fraudsters (35%) present in the set of sellers is also significantly higher than what is observed in online auction sites (reportedly between 0,01% to 0,2% [3,10]). Even though we count on the existence of a previous automatic classification to increase the proportion of fraudsters, we did not find any published results about of how well this automatic classification could perform.

## 6 Conclusions and Future Work

We presented a pilot study on fraudster identification by non-specialized people, where each one was asked to analyze serially snapshots of seller profiles from an online auction site, pointing out the ones they believed were fraudsters. Those snapshots were taken prior to first signs of fraudulent behavior, in many cases several days before, mimicking what a common buyer would see.

Results were positive: more than a third of the subjects had a precision and recall greater than 50% and several of them achieved a precision of 100% with recall greater than 25%, indicating the viability of the approach and encouraging further research. Nonetheless, these results cannot be easily generalized, due to methodological limitations. A full-fledged experiment would be necessary to confirm our findings.

This pilot study is part of a larger research on fraudster identification in electronic markets through human computation [2], also comprising an empirical model for assessing fraud occurrence in online auction sites using publically available data; an empirical evaluation of fraud occurrence at MercadoLivre; and a fraudster identification mechanism using human computation with incentives, dealing with strategic issues like remuneration and fraudsters attempts to manipulate results.

The next step of this research is to strengthen empirical results through a more refined methodology. The pilot study with human subjects can be improved through a prototype implementation of a game with the purpose of predicting fraudulent behavior, rewarding "players" just with points, as ESP game does. The challenge would be to motivate enough people to use the system in order to obtain a good sample.

**Acknowledgments.** This research was sponsored by UOL (www.uol.com.br), through its UOL Bolsa Pesquisa program, process number 20060601215400a, and by CNPq, process number 140768/2004-1. Daniel Schwabe was partially supported by a grant from CNPq.

# References

1. Ahn, L.V., Dabbish, L.: Labeling images with a computer game. In: Conference on Human factors in computing systems. ACM Press, New York (2004)
2. Almendra, V.: A study on fraudster identification in electronic markets through human computation. PhD thesis. PUC-Rio (2008)
3. Almendra, V., Schwabe, D.: Analysis of Fraudulent Activity in a Brazilian Auction Site. In: Latin American Alternate Track of 18th International World Wide Web Conference (2009)
4. Belenkiy, M., Chase, M., Erway, C.C., Jannotti, J., Küpçü, A., Lysyanskaya, A.: Incentivizing outsourced computation. In: Third International Workshop on Economics of Networked Systems. ACM Press, New York (2008)
5. Brabham, D.C.: Crowdsourcing as a Model for Problem Solving: An Introduction and Cases. Convergence 14(1), 75–90 (2008)
6. Chau, D.H., Faloutsos, C.: Fraud Detection in Electronic Auction. In: European Web Mining Forum (2005),
   http://www.cs.cmu.edu/~dchau/papers/chau_fraud_detection.pdf
7. Duarte, J., Siegel, S., Young, L.A.: Trust and Credit. SSRN eLibrary (2009),
   http://papers.ssrn.com/sol3/papers.cfm?abstract_id=1343275
8. Gavish, B., Tucci, C.: Fraudulent auctions on the Internet. Electronic Commerce Research 6(2), 127–140 (2006)
9. Gentry, C., Ramzan, Z., Stubblebine, S.: Secure distributed human computation. In: 6th ACM conference on Electronic commerce. ACM Press, New York (2005)
10. Gregg, D.G., Scott, J.E.: The Role of Reputation Systems in Reducing On-Line Auction Fraud. International Journal of Electronic Commerce 10(3), 95–120 (2006)
11. Gregg, D.G., Scott, J.E.: A typology of complaints about ebay sellers. Communications of the ACM 51(4), 69–74 (2008)
12. Internet Crime Complaint Center: 2007 Internet Crime Report,
    http://www.ic3.gov/media/annualreport/2007_IC3Report.pdf
    (Accessed, June 10 2008)
13. Jøsang, A., Ismail, R., Boyd, C.: A survey of trust and reputation systems for online service provision. Decis. Support Syst. 43(2), 618–644 (2007)

14. Kittur, A., Chi, E.H., Suh, B.: Crowdsourcing user studies with Mechanical Turk. In: 26th annual SIGCHI conference on Human factors in computing systems. ACM Press, New York (2008)

15. Nikitkov, A., Stone, D.: Towards a Model of Online Auction Deception. In: ECAIS - European Conference on Accounting Information Systems (2006),
   http://www.fdewb.unimaas.nl/marc/ecais_new/files/2006/
   Paper5.pdf

16. Pandit, S., Chau, D.H., Wang, S., Faloutsos, C.: NetProbe: A Fast and Scalable System for Fraud Detection in Online Auction Networks. In: International World Wide Web Conference. ACM Press, New York (2007)

17. Rijsbergen, C.J.V.: Information Retrieval. Butterworth-Heinemann (1979)

18. Su, Q., Pavlov, D., Chow, J., Baker, W.C.: Internet-scale collection of human-reviewed data. In: 16th International Conference on World Wide Web. ACM Press, New York (2007)

19. Zhang, B., Zhou, Y., Faloutsos, C.: Toward a Comprehensive Model in Internet Auction Fraud Detection. In: 41st Annual Hawaii International Conference on System Sciences. IEEE Computer Society Press, Los Alamitos (2008)

# Finding *My* Needle in the Haystack: Effective Personalized Re-ranking of Search Results in Prospector*

Florian König[1], Lex van Velsen[2], and Alexandros Paramythis[1]

[1] Johannes Kepler University
Institute for Information Processing and Microprocessor Technology (FIM)
Altenbergerstraße 69, A-4040 Linz, Austria
{alpar,koenig}@fim.uni-linz.ac.at
[2] University of Twente, Dpt. of Technical and Professional Communication
P.O. Box 217, 7500 AE Enschede, The Netherlands
l.s.vanvelsen@utwente.nl

**Abstract.** This paper provides an overview of Prospector, a personalized Internet meta-search engine, which utilizes a combination of ontological information, ratings-based models of user interests, and complementary theme-oriented group models to recommend (through re-ranking) search results obtained from an underlying search engine. Re-ranking brings "closer to the top" those items that are of particular interest to a user or have high relevance to a given theme. A user-based, real-world evaluation has shown that the system is effective in promoting results of interest, but lags behind Google in user acceptance, possibly due to the absence of features popularized by said search engine. Overall, users would consider employing a personalized search engine to perform searches with terms that require disambiguation and / or contextualization.

**Keywords:** personalized web search, Open Directory Project (ODP), collaborative search, user evaluation, scrutability, adaptive search result re-ranking.

## 1 Introduction

The continuously increasing rate at which information gets generated and accumulated on the Internet constitute a strong motivator for devising approaches that support the personalized retrieval and delivery of information items to users. Personalization in this context is intended to tailor the information- or result- spaces to individuals, in order to improve the relevance of retrieved items to their information needs. Prospector [1, 2] is a system that applies a range of techniques towards this end.

Specifically, Prospector is an adaptive meta-search engine / front-end that retrieves results from a user-selected, underlying search engine (e.g., Google, MS Live Search, Yahoo!) and personalizes their order (through re-ranking) to better match its users' interests. The later are modeled according to the users' ratings of results. The ontology of the Open Directory Project (ODP)[1] categorizes more than 4 million web sites in over 700.000 topics, and provides the semantic meta-data for classifying results, recording ratings in the model(s) and calculating the relevance probabilities for

---

[1] For information on the Open Directory Project please refer to: http://www.dmoz.org

T. Di Noia and F. Buccafurri (Eds.): EC-Web 2009, LNCS 5692, pp. 312–323, 2009.

re-ranking. This meta-data also allows the system to disambiguate homonymous interests and queries. Furthermore, Prospector makes use of group models (in the form of collective models for individuals with similar search interests) which are used for "bootstrapping" individual user models, and for predicting the user's search intentions using the preferences of like-minded users as a guide. Overall, Prospector implements a hybrid web search support layer, using concepts and techniques both from collaborative web searching, and from semantically enriched result filtering / re-ordering, to achieve high levels of search result personalization.

In this paper we first briefly relate the system to existing implementations of personalized search engines in section 2. In section 3 we present the main features of the third generation of the Prospector system, which has been preceded by two other versions, described in [1, 2]. We discuss several new features that are based on an evaluation of the second version, reported in [3]. The most important modifications implemented include better use of existing meta-data (see 3.1), usability enhancements (see 3.2), and a more stable re-ranking algorithm (see 3.3). In section 4 we report on a user-based, real-world evaluation of this version of the system, which has shown it to be effective in promoting results of interest to individual users. Section 5 discusses these and other results obtained, as well as their significance in the context of personalized search. Finally, directions for future work are also outlined.

## 2  Related Work

Prospector can be broadly categorized as an adaptive search engine. The literature on this type of system is quite extensive (see [4] for an overview of work on personalized web search) and there are a number of personalized search systems that are related to Prospector in one or more characteristics. To start with, users in Prospector have a personal model of interests like in [5, 6, 7], the OBIWAN [8] and Persona [9] systems, and the first [10] and second [4] attempts at personalized search by Google. This sets it apart from purely collaborative engines like I-SPY [10] and makes it more similar to the Quickstep [11] system and its follow-up development Foxtrot [12]. In the current incarnation[2] of Google's personalized search, a similar approach is pursued, allowing users for example to move results up and down in the list and view other users' aggregated ratings and the corresponding ranking.

Whereas other systems rely on implicit feedback like search/click history [4, 5, 9, 10, 11, 12], general web surf history [8] or the current work context (documents, emails) [6], Prospector elicits explicit relevance feedback from its users. This approach has also been implemented in Persona [9], Quickstep [11], Foxtrot [12] and Google's current personalization features; this approach, although arguably more demanding for users, has the benefit of precision.

Similar to Chirita et al. [7] and Google's first search personalization engine, Prospector allows users to manually set high-level interests. However, in contrast to the aforementioned systems, these settings are not the only indications but merely act as a starting point for bootstrapping the user model and facilitating early personalization.

---

[2] A prototype is described at http://www.google.com/experimental/a840e102.html

Quite a number of personalized search engines base the structure of their models on an ontology like the one from the Open Directory Project. Mostly they use just a few top levels and corresponding nodes of the mainly hierarchical topic categorizations [5, 6, 7, 10, 11, 12]. Prospector allows its models to be as fine grained as the full ODP ontology, similar to the OBIWAN [8] and the Persona [9] system. Specific measures to handle the resulting large size and possible sparsity of the model had to be employed as described in section 3.1.

In order to map query terms or search results to topics in the ontology, so that they can be related to the relevance information in the models, most of the systems mentioned up to now employ classification methods from machine learning. Prospector, like Persona [9] and the system by Chirita et al. [7] relies on the web resources already classified in the ontology. While this approach can only map a fraction of the total number of sites on the Internet, it avoids ambiguities and, as will be seen in the evaluation section (4.3), can still assign ontological meta-data to a high number of search results encountered in real-life searches.

Most of the systems mentioned so far don't allow users to view or edit their user model. Notable exceptions are Google's first and second personalized search engine as well as the Foxtrot system [12]. Allowing users to give direct profile feedback was found beneficial for the latter and has been implemented in Prospector as well.

## 3   The Prospector System

The operation of Prospector can be summarized as follows: first, the underlying search engine is used to retrieve (non-personalized) results for the user's query. These results are classified into thematic topics using the ODP meta-data. Classifications and corresponding interest information stored in the system-maintained user- and group- models are then used to determine an appropriate (personalized) ranking of the results. Users are presented with the re-ranked results, which they can rate on a per-result-item basis. The system uses these ratings and the classifications to update the individual and group models. The rest of this section elaborates on the operation of the system, explaining the modeling and re-ranking algorithms and focusing on new and modified features in the current third version of the system. A full account of the technical details including all the necessary internal calculations can be found in [2].

### 3.1   Ontology-Based Modeling of User Interests

Prospector uses taxonomies as overlay [13] over the ODP ontology for modeling user and group interests. The structure of the models follows the mainly hierarchical layout of topics in the ODP ontology. Topics are identified by their path (e.g., "Arts > Music > DJs"), which provides the structural information for the taxonomy in the models. The overlay is formed by storing probabilities of interest in specific topics, for later use in personalizing result rankings (e.g., Arts*[0.66]* > Music*[0.79]* > DJs*[0.34]*).

In addition to each user's personal model there exist a fixed number of thematic group models. They are named after 13 top-level ODP topics (e.g., "Arts", "Sports") and represent high-level interests that users may share. Users have a certain degree of affinity from 0 ("no interest") to 5 ("high interest") to each of those groups. This determines the impact of a user's ratings on the group models, as well as the level of influence of group models on the personalization of search results. User and group models each have separate taxonomies, and for both types all of the ODP ontology can be used in the overlay (i.e., group models are not constrained to the sub-topics of the their corresponding top-level topic). To counteract the cold start problem [14], group models are initialized with the maximum probability of 1.0 for the top-level topic corresponding to the name of the group (i.e., in the group model "Arts" the probability of top-level topic "Arts" is set to 1.0). The following description of the modeling algorithm outlines additional aspects of the utilization of the ODP ontology.

To start with, each result item returned from the underlying search engine is classified in the ODP ontology. The system first looks for the whole URL in the ODP data and, if no match is found, searches for the host and domain part only. Classification returns zero or more topics (i.e., a web resource may be referenced in more than one place in the ODP ontology), all of which are taken into account in the new modeling and personalization algorithms. Although simplifying subsequent calculations, it proved problematic to limit the classification to a single, "best matching" topic [3].

Successfully classified result items can then be rated by the user, thus recording the interest feedback for the topic(s) in which they were classified. This operation involves several steps for each of the topics: First, the path of topics and sub-topics (in whole or parts) is created in the model without interest probabilities if it does not exist yet (e.g., Sports[0.72] > Soccer[] > Coaching[]). Second, probabilities are derived for newly created topics either from topics higher-up in the hierarchy, group models or (as a weighted sum) from both if possible. If no probability can be derived, the neutral default probability of 0.5 (i.e., neither interested nor not interested) is used.

The first method (deriving from parent topics) implements inter-topic interest propagation [13] and addresses the problem of sparsity [14]. It ensures that probabilities are available for a large number of topics, even if only few receive ratings. To model the increasing uncertainty as the distance to the "source" topic grows, derived values progressively tends towards the neutral probability (e.g., Sports[0.72] > Soccer[0.61] > Coaching[0.57]). Probabilities of corresponding topics in group models are derived by weighting them with the user's affinity to the respective group and taking the average of these probabilities. The values are again calculated to tend towards 0.5, only this time with decreasing affinity. This second derivation method addresses the latency problem [14] and bootstraps model parts that have not yet received a rating.

The final step after deriving probabilities is recording the actual rating by increasing or decreasing the values in the user model and (weighted by the affinity) the group models. This affects the entire path, scaled to the distance from the target topic, which receives the largest change (e.g., a negative rating of a result in 'Coaching' causes Sports[0.72] > Soccer[0.61] > Coaching[0.57] to become Sports[0.67] > Soccer[0.50] > Coaching[0.41]). The amount of change is non-linearly dependent on the original probability: ratings around the neutral probability 0.5 show more effect than those near the bounds of 0 and 1. This allows topics with low interest specificity to quickly converge to a certain bias and at the same time keeps unambiguous interests stable.

## 3.2  Interactive Features

In order to get personalized search results users first have to register. At the first login they are asked to specify their interest in the 13 top-level ODP topics. It is explained to the users that this way they will benefit from result ratings by users with similar interests. In the evaluation of the preceding version of the system [3], people had difficulty judging the meaning and scope of the topics by just their name. Therefore, the topics are now described in more detail by also listing representative sub-topics.

For each search, users may choose the underlying search engine to be used by selecting the corresponding tab above the query text field (see Fig. 1). When issuing a query, this engine is accessed, and its results are retrieved and classified as described above. The classification paths are displayed for each result, and the tree control on the left side of the results page lets users filter results by these topical categories.

By rating individual results positively (thumbs up) or negatively (thumbs down) users implicitly express their preference for certain topics. In its previous version, Prospector displayed a rating frame at the top of the page of a clicked result. This approach was abandoned as it created both technical and usability problems [3]: some sites employ "frame breakout" mechanisms that cause the frame to disappear, and users were observed overlooking or disregarding the possibility to rate. Quickly evaluating a result is now possible by toggling an embedded preview below the result with the magnification glass icon; opening a result in a new window is facilitated by the arrow icon. When previewing or returning from an opened result, the user is notified / reminded of the possibility to rate that result, by pulsating its thumbs a few times.

Each rating modifies the appropriate user- and group- models, thus affecting the calculation of relevance probabilities of classified results in subsequent searches. A combination of these probabilities with each result's original rank is used for

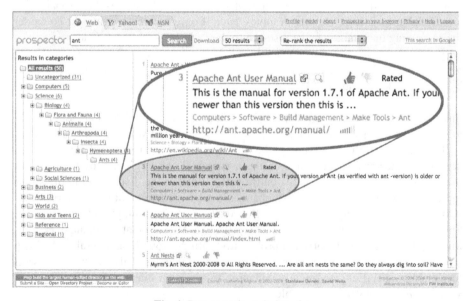

**Fig. 1.** Prospector's main interface

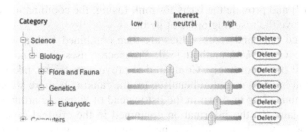

**Fig. 2.** Prospector's user model view

re-ranking (explained further in the next section). To give users a way to quickly assess the system-calculated relevance of a result, its probability is visualized next to the URL by means of a "connection quality" indicator, as used in mobile phones. Hovering over the bars with the mouse shows the exact relevance percentage in a tool-tip. This graphical representation was chosen because it better caters to users' preferences over (long) textual relevance information, as suggested by Coyle and Smyth [15].

For logged in users the ranking is by default personalized with respect to their user model and the models of associated groups. In addition, users can request that results be re-ranked using a particular group model (e.g., "re-rank for people interested in arts"). This feature is intended to let users focus on the specific high-level topic represented by the group, and is also available for anonymous, not logged in users.

The user models in Prospector are scrutable [16], allowing users to inspect, correct and fine-tune them, while at the same time strengthening their confidence in the system. Affinities to groups, as set when registering, can be changed at any time. The interests inferred from the ratings can be viewed and changed as well (see Fig. 2): They are presented by means of a tree summarization of the user model taxonomy and show the paths to the topics for which a result has been rated. The interest probability of each topic is visualized by a stepless slider, ranging from low to high. Users can change the probabilities via these sliders. Topics can also be removed from the model, which gives users the means to purge old or invalid interest information.

### 3.3  Personalized Re-ranking of Search Results

For re-ranking the relevance probability of each result item needs to be calculated. This value is composed from the interest probability of each topic in which the result has been classified and its original rank. If the user model does not contain an interest probability for a topic, the value is derived as described in section 3.1. If a value cannot be established by any of these methods, the neutral probability 0.5 is used. The calculated relevance probabilities of each topic are combined to a weighted average. The affinity of the user to the group with the same name as the top-level topic in the full classification path of the topic at hand is used as the respective weight.

Finally, each result's relevance probability is combined with its rank as returned by the underlying search engine (as suggested also by Teevan et al. [8]). The rank is normalized into the interval [0..1] (e.g., with 50 results: first result's rank becomes 1, the 25th one 0.5 and the last one 0). The relevance probabilities are normalized as well, in the same value space. These methods for rank and score normalization are described by [17] and provide the basis for rank fusing: the combination of individual rankings to improve the resulting order of items.

The normalized rank and score values are then combined with a weighted extension [17] of the *CombSUM* method [18]. Prospector uses this final value for re-ranking the result list accordingly. Compared to previous versions, taking the original rank into account has two essential benefits: (a) the ranking is more stable and results are only gently nudged up or down in the list instead of "jumping around" after rating and searching again; (b) the information contained in the original ranking, which is based on the query itself rather than on the interests of the user, is not lost and helps better represent the search needs of the user.

## 4  Evaluating Prospector

The current (third) version of Prospector underwent a longitudinal evaluation in which the participants were free to use the system as they liked for a longer period of time. This evaluation followed a task-based experimental evaluation of the system, reported in [3]. Where the first evaluation provided us with information on how Prospector functions in a controlled setting and how this can be improved upon, the evaluation reported here assesses the usefulness and usability of Prospector in a real-life setting, comprising a great diversity in search tasks per person, and changing interests. In other words, this approach ensures high ecological validity. The rest of this section describes the evaluation setup and our findings. A more detailed account of the evaluation with a stronger focus on the evaluation design, user-centered qualitative findings elicited by questionnaires and system-centered quantitative results from the data logs can be found in [19].

### 4.1  Evaluation Setup

The evaluation involved 21 volunteers (out of 130 contacted) who agreed to use Prospector as their primary search engine for 12 days, to have their use with the system logged and, finally, to complete questionnaires. Specifically, users responded to three questionnaires, one before starting to use the system, one after five days of use, and one after the total 12 days of use. These questionnaires covered the following issues, primarily by means of open-ended questions: (a) demographics, internet use, experience with personalized systems and use of search engines; (b) expectations of using Prospector and the usefulness of a scrutable user model; (c) perceived usefulness of Google and of Prospector; (d) comparisons between Prospector and Google; (e) important (satisfactory or dissatisfactory) incidents the users experienced; (f) the clarity and correctness of the system's scrutable user model; and, finally, (g) different dimensions of usability (such as predictability, controllability and privacy) which have been shown to be of particular relevance to adaptive systems (see [20]).

### 4.2  Findings from Questionnaire Responses

Nineteen men and two women participated in the study, with an average age of 25.8 years (SD = 2.8). Most of them were students in the Johannes Kepler University in

Linz, Austria. They rated their computer skills as high and used the Internet on a daily basis. All participants used Google as their primary search engine, and approximately two thirds performed at least five searches a day (up to more than 15).

Most participants expected Prospector to outperform Google, by reducing search times (six participants) and giving better results (six participants). However, end results showed that the users perceived Google as more useful than Prospector. They also indicated that they preferred Google for searching; interestingly, some of the participants stated that their preference depended on the nature of the search task. They liked Google better for searching for simple facts, but thought Prospector had an added value when conducting searches related to their personal interests or study. Furthermore, several participants appeared to prefer Google because Prospector did not offer results in German (the mother tongue of all participants). As one person stated: "I prefer Google, because it provides the possibility to search nationally. With Prospector one doesn't find regional results. The program doesn't like German words."

The analysis of noteworthy incidents reported by the users revealed two causes that led to dissatisfaction with Prospector: irrelevant search results (mentioned 9 times) and illogical re-ranking of search results (mentioned 6 times). On the positive side, participants mentioned more than once Prospector's particular helpfulness when submitting a query containing words with ambiguous meanings, and specific searches for which Prospector was useful, like product reviews or scientific articles.

As far as Prospector's scrutable user models are concerned, participants almost uniformly stated that they understood the user model visualization. The majority of the participants also found their user model to be a mostly accurate reflection of their search interests, with several of the remaining participants stating that they had not provided the system with enough feedback to generate a correct user model. However, the data logs cast doubts over the participants' answers. Even though all participants gave their opinion about the user model, the data logs show that only 16 of them inspected their user model during their use of the system, and only 11 had done so before answering about the understandability of the user model's visualization. Therefore, the results regarding user modeling remain inconclusive.

Regarding the usability issues predictability, comprehensibility, unobtrusiveness and breadth of experience: most participants stated they thought they were fully or for a larger part in control over the system; privacy was not thought of as a barrier to use Prospector; the majority of the participants believed that Prospector could deliver the results they desired (interestingly, six participants commented that the system had the potential to deliver relevant search results, but conditionally – e.g., if results in the German language were to be taken into account).

### 4.3  Data Log Analyses

Recording of ratings and the calculation of a personalized score require a search result item to be classified in the ODP. Even though the size of the ontology is small compared to the total number of pages on the Internet, approximately 35% of the results returned from the underlying search engine could be classified by Prospector.

The average number of searches performed daily by all users over the 12 days of the study was 54.33 ($SD = 27.97$). The average total number of positive and negative ratings was 19.75 ($SD = 18.20$). The trend was declining in all cases. Of note is the fact that there is no significant difference between the number of positive and negative ratings, also over time [19].

To determine whether personalization has positively affected the ranking of search results, we examined whether the results participants clicked on were ranked higher than in the original set. Specifically, for all days, we calculated the distance between the personalized and original ranks of viewed results. This distance was positive if the result had been promoted, negative if it had been demoted, and 0 if it had retained its rank. Fig. 3 displays the average distance between these ranks for each day. For most days, the difference was positive for the personalized rank. For all 12 days, the viewed pages had been promoted by, on average, 4.75 ranks ($SD = 11.52$). To test the re-ranking effect, we compared the average rank distance for each viewed result to 0. This difference is significant ($t = 9.14$; $df = 490$; $p<.01$): Search results that participants viewed were, on average, placed higher up in the list, due to personalization.

To ascertain that participants did not consult search results simply because they were ranked highly, regardless of their relevance, we examined whether the first 12 results contained a disproportionately high percentage of items brought there by Prospector. We chose 12, as on an average-sized screen a user would see 6 results in one screen-full and most people do not look beyond the first 10 [21] – we rounded that number up to two screen-fulls. Fig. 3 displays the daily average percentage of results among the first 12 that were originally there. Over 12 days, the mean percentage is 65.10%. This implies that although the majority of "visible" results would have been there anyway, users chose the re-ranked results on purpose and not because they were conveniently placed at the top of the list. In addition, the improved ranking algorithm (see 3.3) allows re-ranked results to stay interspersed with the not re-ranked ones.

Furthermore, the two metrics "Rank scoring" [22] and "Average Rank" [23] were employed. Rank scoring shows how close to the optimal ranking a set of search results is, whereby 'optimal' denotes a situation in which all the consulted results appear at the top of the list. The importance of the ranks decreases exponentially (e.g., a correct rank 1 creates a better score than a correct rank 10). We performed a paired samples t-test between the original rank score average ($M = 5.05$, $SD = .59$) and the

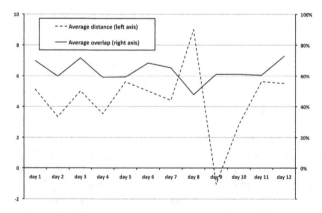

**Fig. 3.** Average distance between original and re-ranked results, and average percentage of original results still ranked between 1 and 12 after re-ranking ("overlap") per day

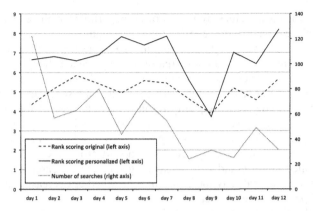

**Fig. 4.** Rank scoring of the personalized and original ranks of viewed results. Higher scores mean, that the ranking is closer to the optimal ranking (i.e., all user-clicked results at the top).

personalized rank score average ($M = 6.75$, $SD = 1.19$). The averages were calculated from the rank score values of the 12 days. This difference is significant ($t = -6.92$; df = 11; p<.01): Personalized rank scores were higher than the original ones, which means that the personalized rankings were closer to the optimal ranking (see Fig. 4).

The average rank measure was calculated for the original and the personalized ranking of consulted results on a per day basis. The personalized results had a lower average rank in all cases, except on day 9. A lower average rank means that the consulted results appeared higher up in the result list. These results reinforce the findings derived through the average distance measure (see also [19]).

## 5   Conclusions and Future Work

In this paper we have discussed the Prospector system and a real-life, user based evaluation. This study has shown that Prospector effectively brings up search results with relevant informational value in a list of search results. However, user perceptions on the usefulness of the system were not in favor of Prospector: the participants thought their primary search engine (Google) was more useful. The comments they provided throughout the evaluation led us to think that this opinion was partly due to missing features popularized by the Google search engine (specifically, localized search, spelling suggestion). As has been shown, people attribute high value to the appearance and features their primary search engine offers [21]. Prospector offered a different interface with different features and this may have biased the participants' perception of its usefulness, regardless of the system's actual value for searching. One way to design for this implication is to replicate the features and 'look and feel' people expect of a search engine – the 'look and feel' has been shown to have a major impact on users' perception of performance, independently of the search results themselves [24]. A different solution would be to offer Prospector as a browser plug-in that personalizes the results page of an existing search engine "in place".

The Prospector algorithm can currently be adjusted via two weight values: one gearing user models and group models unto each other, the other concerned with balancing personalized ranking against original ranking. It will be crucial to acquire optimal ranges for these values by means of an experiment with several versions of Prospector, each set to a different configuration of weight values.

The participants had very high expectations of Prospector, and expected it to out-perform Google. This meant that the search result they needed should be listed first or second, but not lower. These expectations are apparently hard to meet, especially as users will want to see an added value fast and it may take some time for a personal-ized search engine to deliver top-quality results. This emphasizes the fact that intro-ducing a new personalized search engine in a market dominated by Google is a very hard challenge. In addition, the slight decrease in perceived usefulness over time sug-gests that the system's measures against the cold start problem can still be improved. A more controlled study could help in keeping the usage (searching, rating) at an equal level throughout and may therefore indicate whether decreasing usage was the reason for bad performance and perception.

In closing, the evaluation has suggested some circumstances in which personalized search might be more rewarding for users. These are the searches which our partici-pants described as 'personal' or searches without a clear-cut answer. Typical for these searches are, as Marchionini terms it, relatively low answer specificity, high volume and high timeliness [25]: the answer to the search is not easily recognized as being correct (e.g., a suitable hotel in Amsterdam), it has to be found in a large body of in-formation and, finally, the user has to invest some time in finding the right answer. This implies that personalized search may have more success in specialized areas of search (e.g., digital libraries) than it has for finding general information.

**Acknowledgements.** The work reported in this paper has been supported in part by: (a) the EU-funded "Adaptive Learning Spaces" (ALS) project (229714-CP-1-2006-1-NL-MPP); and (b) the "Adaptive Support for Collaborative E-Learning" (ASCOLLA) project, supported by the Austrian Science Fund (FWF; project number P20260-N15).

# References

1. Schwendtner, C., König, F., Paramythis, A.: Prospector: an adaptive front-end to the Google search engine. In: LWA 2006: 14th Workshop on Adaptivity and User Modeling in Interactive System, pp. 56–61. University of Hildesheim, Institute of Computer Science, Hildesheim (2006)
2. Paramythis, A., König, F., Schwendtner, C., Van Velsen, L.: Using thematic ontologies for user- and group-based adaptive personalization in web searching. Paper presented at the 6th International Workshop on Adaptive Multimedia Retrieval, Berlin (2008)
3. Van Velsen, L., Paramythis, A., Van der Geest, T.: User-centered formative evaluation of a personalized internet meta-search engine (in review)
4. Micarelli, A., Gasparetti, F., Sciarrone, F., Gauch, S.: Personalized Search on the World Wide Web. In: Brusilovsky, P., Kobsa, A., Nejdl, W. (eds.) The Adaptive Web 2007. LNCS, vol. 4321, pp. 195–230. Springer, Heidelberg (2007)
5. Pretschner, A., Gauch, S.: Ontology based personalized search. In: 11th IEEE International Con-ference on Tools with Artificial Intelligence, pp. 391–398. IEEE Computer Society Press, Los Alamitos (1999)
6. Liu, F., Yu, C., Meng, W.: Personalized web search by mapping user queries to categories. In: 11th international conference on Information and knowledge management, pp. 558–565. ACM, New York (2002)

7. Chirita, P.A., Nejdl, W., Paiu, R., Kohlschütter, C.: Using ODP Metadata to Personalize Search. In: 28th ACM International SIGIR Conference on Research and Development in Information Retrieval, pp. 178–185. ACM, New York (2005)
8. Teevan, J., Dumais, S.T., Horvitz, E.: Personalizing search via automated analysis of interests and activities. In: 28th annual international ACM SIGIR conference on Research and development in information retrieval, pp. 449–456. ACM, New York (2005)
9. Tanudjaja, F., Mui, L.: Persona: A contextualized and personalized web search. In: 35th Annual Hawaii International Conference on System Sciences, pp. 67–75. IEEE Computer Society Press, Los Alamitos (2002)
10. Smyth, B., Balfe, E.: Anonymous personalization in collaborative web search. Information Retrieval 9, 165–190 (2006)
11. Middleton, S.E., De Roure, D.C., Shadbolt, N.R.: Capturing Knowledge of User Preferences: on-tologies on recommender systems. In: 1st International Conference on Knowledge Capture, pp. 100–107. ACM, New York (2001)
12. Middleton, S.E., Shadbolt, N.R., De Roure, D.C.: Ontological User Profiling in Recommender Systems. ACM Transactions on Information Systems 22, 54–88 (2004)
13. Brusilovsky, P., Millán, E.: User Models for Adaptive Hypermedia and Adaptive Educational Systems. In: Brusilovsky, P., Kobsa, A., Nejdl, W. (eds.) The Adaptive Web 2007. LNCS, vol. 4321, pp. 3–53. Springer, Heidelberg (2007)
14. Anand, S., Mobasher, B.: Intelligent Techniques for Web Personalization. In: Mobasher, B., Anand, S.S. (eds.) ITWP 2003. LNCS, vol. 3169, pp. 1–36. Springer, Heidelberg (2005)
15. Coyle, M., Smyth, B.: Supporting intelligent web search. ACM Transactions on Internet Technology 7, 20 (2007)
16. Kay, J.: Stereotypes, student models and scrutability. In: Gauthier, G., Frasson, C., VanLehn, K. (eds.) ITS 2000. LNCS, vol. 1839, pp. 19–30. Springer, Heidelberg (2000)
17. Renda, M.E., Umberto, S.: Web metasearch: rank vs. score based rank aggregation methods. In: 2003 ACM symposium on Applied computing, pp. 841–846. ACM, New York (2003)
18. Shaw, J., Fox, E.: Combination of Multiple Searches. Paper presented at the Text REtrieval Conference, Gaithersburg, USA (1993)
19. Van Velsen, L., König, F., Paramythis, A.: Assessing the Effectiveness and Usability of Personalized Internet Search through a Longitudinal Evaluation. In: 6th Workshop on User-Centred Design and Evaluation of Adaptive Systems, held in conjunction with the International Conference on User Modeling, Adaptation, and Personalization, pp. 44–53 (2009) CEUR-WS.org
20. Paramythis, A., Weibelzahl, S.: A decomposition model for the layered evaluation of interactive adaptive systems. In: Ardissono, L., Brna, P., Mitrović, A. (eds.) UM 2005. LNCS, vol. 3538, pp. 438–442. Springer, Heidelberg (2005)
21. Keane, M.T., O'Brien, M., Smyth, B.: Are people biased in their use of search engines? Communications of the ACM 51, 49–52 (2008)
22. Breese, J.S., Heckerman, D., Kadie, C.: Empirical analysis of predictive algorithms for collabora-tive filtering. In: 14th Annual Conference on Uncertainty in Artificial Intelligence, pp. 43–52. Morgan Kaufman, San Francisco (1998)
23. Dou, Z., Song, R., Wen, J.: A large-scale evaluation and analysis of personalized search strategies. In: 16th international conference on WWW, pp. 581–590. ACM, New York (2007)
24. Jansen, B.J., Zhang, M., Zhang, Y.: The effect of brand awareness on the evaluation of search engine results. In: CHI 2007 Extended Abstracts on Human Factors in Computing Systems, pp. 2471–2476. ACM, New York (2007)
25. Marchionini, G.: Information seeking in electronic environments. Cambridge University Press, New York (1995)

# RATC: A Robust Automated Tag Clustering Technique

Ludovico Boratto[1], Salvatore Carta[1], and Eloisa Vargiu[2]

[1] Dip.to di Matematica e Informatica, Università di Cagliari, Italy
boratto@sc.unica.it, salvatore@unica.it
[2] Dip.to di Ingegneria Elettrica ed Elettronica, Università di Cagliari, Italy
vargiu@diee.unica.it

**Abstract.** Nowadays, the most dominant and noteworthy web information sources are developed according to the collaborative-web paradigm, also known as Web 2.0. In particular, it represents a novel paradigm in the way users interact with the web. Users (also called prosumers) are no longer passive consumers of published content, but become involved, implicitly and explicitly, as they cooperate by providing their own resources in an "architecture of participation". In this scenario, collaborative tagging, i.e., the process of classifying shared resources by using keywords, becomes more and more popular. The main problem in such task is related to well-known linguistic phenomena, such as polysemy and synonymy, making effective content retrieval harder. In this paper, an approach that monitors users activity in a tagging system and dynamically quantifies associations among tags is presented. The associations are then used to create tags clusters. Experiments are performed comparing the proposed approach with a state-of-the-art tag clustering technique. Results –given in terms of classical precision and recall– show that the approach is quite effective in the presence of strongly related tags in a cluster.

## 1 Introduction

The developement of Web 2.0 applications, like blogs and wikis, led to a continuous growth of information sources, with daily uploaded resources shared by many users [1]. Besides traditional techniques to categorize and index data, new approaches based on collaborative tagging have been effectively proposed and adopted. The success of those approaches is due to the fact that tagging does not require specific skills and seems a natural way for people to classify any kind of resource.

A set of tags (*tagspace*) can be explored in several ways and many tagging systems usually define sets of related tags, called *tag clouds*, that help the tagspace visualization. However, as highlighted in [2], there are some well-known linguistic limitations that can inhibit information retrieval in those systems. In particular, the meaning or semantics of a tag is usually unknown. For instance, tag "orange" might refer either to a fruit or a color. Moreover, people use several tags

T. Di Noia and F. Buccafurri (Eds.): EC-Web 2009, LNCS 5692, pp. 324–335, 2009.

to select the same resources. For example, a resource related to a pasta dish could be tagged as "Italian food", "spaghetti", "first course", etc. On the one hand, user can freely choose which tags classify resources in a useful way; on the other hand, the searching activity of other users within the tagspace could be limited. In fact, to find a resource it might be necessary to search several times using different keywords, and people must evaluate the relevance of the retrieved documents.

Grouping related tags together would avoid such limitations and simplify the exploration of a tagging system [3]. In fact, the definition of sets of related tags would help the identification of a context that would avoid polysemy and synononymy and make resources retrieval easier.

In this paper, we propose RATC (Robust Automated Tag Clustering), a technique that monitors users activity in the search engine of a tagging system in order to exploit implicit feedbacks provided by users. A feedback is collected each time a user finds a relevant resource during a search in a tagging system. The algorithm uses the feedback to dynamically strengthen associations between the resource indicated by the user and the tags used in the search string. Tag-resource associations are then used to infer tag-tag associations by adopting a standard correlation measure. Tag-tag associations allow to cluster tags in order to find strongly related tag sets. Results have been compared with the ones obtained by adopting the state-of-the-art approach proposed in [4] showing an improvement in the presence of strongly related tags in a cluster.

The main contribution of the proposed approach is that, by supervising users activity in a tagging system and monitoring their searches, we can progressively create and update tag-resource associations and tag-tag associations, rewarding the real semantic relations among tags and penalizing the misleading ones.

The rest of the paper is organized as follows: section 2 presents state-of-the-art in tag clustering; section 3 contains a detailed description of the steps we followed to build our technique; section 4 describes the performed experiments and outlines main results; section 5 discusses conclusions and future work.

## 2 Related Work

In the literature, several techniques, aimed at grouping tags by adopting different clustering algorithms and heuristics, have been presented.

In [5], an approach that tries to infer the semantics behind a tag space is proposed. The corresponding collaborative tagging can help in finding groups of concepts and partial ontologies. This is achieved by using a combination of shallow pre-processing strategies and statistical techniques together with knowledge provided by ontologies available on the semantic web. This technique starts pre-processing the data and cleaning up the tag space, then, evaluating co-occurrences, it finds tag-tag associations and clusters them. Semantic relations are extracted from the clusters and the results consist of groups of highly related tags that conceptualize specific facets of knowledge and correspond to elements in ontologies. This approach differs from the one proposed in this paper since our technique does not pre-process the tagspace. Our approach, in fact, is able to adaptively remove noisy tags by monitoring user interactions.

In [6], being aimed at extracting ontologies, authors proposed a way to integrate a social network with collaborative tagging. The usual tripartite models of ontologies based on users, tags and instances, are integrated with user-user relations. Concepts in each community (called *p-concepts*) are considered different and this model was used to resolve the polysemy/homonymy problem. This technique aims to group p-concepts and find keywords associations by using an algorithm that considers the interactions among users and p-concepts. Our approach differs in the sense that we consider users interaction just to link resources to tags, without creating explicit associations among users and resources.

In [7], an approach aimed at generating groups of semantically related tags through a probabilistic model is presented. The technique is based on evaluating co-occurrence of tags, resources, and users. The approach proposed in this paper differs because it does not rely on a probabilistic model and it does not consider users.

In [8], a co-clustering approach, based on the one proposed in [9], is employed. In this approach, tags and resources belonging to different datasets are clustered together. The clustering activity is based on a similarity metric that uses tag co-occurrences and semantic knowledge about the tags. The relations among the elements are used to enrich ontologies and to train multimedia processing algorithms. On the contrary, in our approach, the clustering activity is based just on tags and new knowledge is inferred by clustering elements of the same dataset.

In [10], a technique to exploit information from queries is presented. Associations between the keywords used in a query and the relevant resources retrieved by a search engine are exploited in order to rank search results based on the past users activity. The technique proposed in this paper creates associations also between a resource and the tags used to classify it when uploaded.

In [11], an approach to create clusters of queries is presented. Related queries are clustered together, in order to recommend a better query to users. This is achieved by finding the most descriptive words in a cluster and recommending better queries to users. In our approach, queries are used in a different way. We do not infer associations among tags clustering queries themselves, but tags associations are derived considering the resources that they classify.

In [4], a technique to cluster strongly related tags is presented. The algorithm is based on counting the number of co-occurrences (tags that are used for the same resource) of any pair of tags and a cut-off point is determined to decide if the co-occurrence count is significant enough to be used. Tags are clustered with an algorithm that is based on the spectral bisection and uses the modularity function to measure the quality of a partitioning. Related tags are then automatically discovered by incrementing a counter for each pair of tags that belong to the same cluster. Although the approach presented in this paper is quite similar, the main difference is that tag-resource associations are continuously updated during the use of the system.

# 3   RATC: Robust Automated Tag Clustering

RATC, which stands for Robust Automated Tag Clustering, monitors users activity in the search engine of a tagging system. The technique has been defined "robust" to put into evidence its ability to overwhelm the misleading resource classification problem.

## 3.1   Top Level View of the Approach

RATC encompasses four main steps:

***Tag-resource* associations creation.** As in any tagging system, each time a new resource is put into the system, a *tag-resource* association is created among that resource and the tags used to describe it.

**Dynamic *tag-resource* associations evaluation.** Users activity in the tagging system search engine is monitored and exploited in order to update existing *tag-resource* associations and to create new ones.

***Tag-tag* associations creation and quantification** Dynamic    *tag-resource* associations are exploited to create associations among tags (*tag-tag* associations). A standard cosine similarity measure [12] is used to evaluate the similarity among tags. The result of this process is a weighted graph (*tag similarity graph*) in which each node represents a tag and each weighted arc represents the similarity value of the tags it connects.

**Clustering.** The community detection algorithm proposed by [13] is applied to the tag similarity graph in order to identify the intrinsic communities of tags.

## 3.2   Representation of a Tagging System

A tagging system is a community driven tool that allows users to classify resources by using tags. It can be represented as a bipartite graph that contains:

- a set $T$ of tags $t$;
- a set $R$ of resources $r$;
- a set $A : (T \times R)$ of weighted arcs $t-r$, representing tag-resource associations. The weight of the tag-resource associations represents the number of times that a tag has been associated to a resource by users.

As depicted in Fig.1, a tagging system is composed by a set of tags (rectangular nodes) linked by a weighted arc to a subset of resources (round nodes). In the example in figure there are three resources concerning with "goal actions" in a soccer game [1]. All of those resources has been classified with the tags *soccer* and *goal* and the weight of each arc represents the strength of the association between a tag and a resource. Each tag has some outgoing dotted arcs, which indicate that there are other resources linked to those tags, not depicted in the example.

---

[1] Resources represent multimedia documents, like videos or pictures.

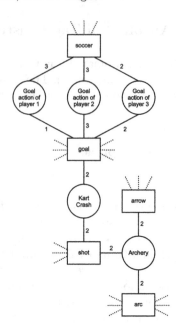

**Fig. 1.** A tagging system example

As a final remark, let us note that our approach does not take into account different meaning referring to a same word (i.e. polysemy). For instance, in the example in Fig.1, tag *goal* is used either as a successful attempt at scoring in a soccer game or as the place designed at the end of a race.

### 3.3    Tag-Resource Associations Quantification

The standard search paradigm provided by tagging services is based on query strings containing one (or more) tag. The search returns a list of resources associated to these tags. To provide such list, a ranking of the results is derived according to the tag-resource associations available in the tagging system that can be considered as the strength of the association between a resource and each tag used to describe it. While tagging systems usually associate tags and resources at upload time, implicit user feedback, coming from its search activity, can be exploited to improve *tag-resource* associations.

To represent the strength of *tag-resource* associations we adopted an algorithm based on counters. The algorithm exploits users feedback to discover and emphasize correct associations strength, while making negligible the contribution of "noisy" associations. The strength of each association evolves according to an extremely simple and effective mechanism. A *tag-resource* association is created each time a resource is added to the system by a user. After a search operation based on a tag, each time the user selects a resource, the counter of the tag-resource association is increased (an example of tag-resource associations is shown in Fig.1). Although a huge number of resources may be related to a single tag, their relevance will depend on the feedbacks provided by the community of users. In such a way the association of a misleading tag to a resource will give a negligible contribution.

In order to contain the counters relative to tag-resource associations, a matrix $W = \{w_{rt}\}$ is defined, where $w_{rt}$ is the association between resource $r$ and tag $t$ (an example is depicted in Fig.2).

Initial values are assigned when a new resource is uploaded and values are updated either when a user adds a tag already in the database or when a feedback is given [2]. When a new resource is uploaded to the tagging system together with some tags, the corresponding *tag-resource* counter is set to 1. If such association is already oin the system, the corresponding $w_{ij}$ is incremented. The matrix is also updated when a user performs a search in the tagging system and selects one of the results as relevant. At this stage, after the user selection took place, the counters between the selected resource and all the tags in the query list are incremented, namely $w_{rt} = w_{rt} + 1$.

The tagging system shown in Fig.1 has been built using the tag-resource counters described above. Let us stress the fact that the strength of the relation between a tag and a resource in our tagging system is based on the feedbacks left by the users during the use of the system. For example, tag *soccer* has been used three times to classify and search the second resource concerning with the goal action of a player.

### 3.4 Tag-Tag Associations Quantification

Let $v_i$ be the vector of associations among a tag $i$ and its related resources and $v_j$ be the vector of associations among a tag $j$ and its releated resources. The association $a_{ij}$ between tag $i$ and tag $j$ can be measured by the cosine similarity between the vectors as follows:

$$a_{ij} = cos(v_i, v_j) = \frac{v_i \cdot v_j}{\|v_i\|_2 \times \|v_j\|_2} = \frac{v_{i1} \cdot v_{j1} + ... + v_{ik} \cdot v_{jk}}{\|v_i\|_2 \times \|v_j\|_2}$$

These associations can be represented in a graph, call *tag similarity graph*, which links each couple of associated tags with a weighted arc. An example, built using the associations among tags and the resources shown in Fig.1, is represented in Fig.2.

### 3.5 Clustering

To perform clustering we adopted MCL (Markov Clustering Algorithm) [13]. MCL is a Community Detection [14] algorithm, built to find cluster structure in simple graphs, considering the similarity between vertexes. The MCL algorithm tries to simulate the flow within a graph, considering just the part where the flow is strong and removing weak connections. If natural groups are in the graph, the links between the groups disappear, leaving the cluster structure.

---

[2] The initial values are just a starting point that evolve as the feedbacks are collected.

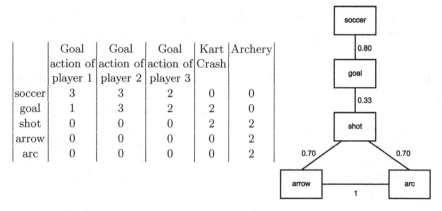

| | Goal action of player 1 | Goal action of player 2 | Goal action of player 3 | Kart Crash | Archery |
|---|---|---|---|---|---|
| soccer | 3 | 3 | 2 | 0 | 0 |
| goal | 1 | 3 | 2 | 2 | 0 |
| shot | 0 | 0 | 0 | 2 | 2 |
| arrow | 0 | 0 | 0 | 0 | 2 |
| arc | 0 | 0 | 0 | 0 | 2 |

**Fig. 2.** Similarities graph

The flow is simulated by a transformation of the graph into a Markov graph (a graph where for all nodes the sum of the weights of outgoing arcs is 1) and is expanded by computing powers of the associated stochastic (Markov) matrix.

Since these operations are not enough and do not reveal the clusters in the graph, a new operator (inflation) is inserted. Flow inflation [13] is the entry-wise HadamardSchur product of the matrix combined with a diagonal scaling, while flow expansion is represented by the usual matrix product. The inflation operator has been introduced to strengthen and weaken the flow, and the expansion operator is responsible for allowing flow to connect different regions of the graph.

As the MCL algorithm basically consists of alternation of two different operators on matrices, followed by interpretation of the resulting limit, its formulation is quite simple. It is also possible to find clusters of different granularities, by varying its parameters.

A more detailed description of this algorithm is beyond the scope of this paper. The interested reader could refer to [13] for further details.

## 4   Experiments and Results

To evaluate the proposed approach, first, we adopted a tagging system with an internal experimental search engine [15], and then, we compared the performances with a state-of-the-art approach [4].

Several aspects have been taken into account while performing comparisons regarding the robustness of the two approaches. In particular, to analyze the impact of noise in the performances, we suitably added noisy tags to the tagging system. The quality of the obtained clusters have been evaluated comparing results with the ones provided by a domain engineer in terms of precision and recall. The adaptive capability of our approach (i.e., the users activity monitoring and their feedback) has been evaluated measuring the temporal evolution of clusters quality.

## 4.1  Setting Up the Experiments

To conduct the experiments 10 volunteers populated a tagging system [15] (*resource acquisition* step). They were asked to select as many videos as they wanted from YouTube [3] and add them to the tagging system. The application domain was limited to "sport" as specific topic, which can be considered a concept domain. Each video was classified with four tags related to the resource and two tags (the noisy tags) not related to the resource. Noisy tags were added to simulate the noise that typically occurs in practice.

Once the tagging systems was populated, volunteers were asked to perform normal searches in the tagging system (*feedback collection* step). During this step, RATC improves its performances monitoring users search activity. Videos are chosen based on a preview shown to the user and their original description. This step started as soon as the resource acquisition step was completed. The reason was to neatly separate the initial values of the correlations from their evolutions caused by the feedbacks of the users.

**Resources Acquisition.** Each time a volunteer added a new video to the application, she/he had to create two sets of tags. The former is devoted to contain (at least) four characteristic tags, strongly related to the video; the latter is devoted to contain two tags not related to the video but in the same domain (in this experiments, "sport"). This tag set is required to create some verifiable noise and it has been used to monitor the progressive decreasing of their correlation with the video they had been initially introduced with. Such noise is useful to evelute the clustering algorithm. In particular, in this way we are able to monitor how the clusters structure changes and to evaluate the quality of the clusters.

The tagging system was populated with a total of 406 videos, 1021 tags, 2597 video-tag correlations. Although in [2] authors show that tags that identify qualities or characteristics can be effective in recommendation systems, being interested in clustering tags according to their meaning, we disregarded such kind of tags (i.e., those that express emotions or feelings). At the end of this step, the system involves 964 tags.

**Feedback Collection.** During this step, each volunteer performed 300 searches in the tagging systems. For each search, each volunteer: (i) entered a list of tags as query for the search; and (ii) selected, from the videos in the results list, the video most related with the query.

A feedback is then collected each time a user performed a search and consequently tag-resource counters are incremented. After entering a list of tags, she/he was free to analyze the videos resulting from the search (during this phase the user could also play all the videos to help her/his choice). At the end of this activity, the user had to pick a video from the output list providing a feedback. This emulates a real world scenario in which a user, after the result of a search is displayed, selects the resources she/he is interested in.

---

[3] http://www.youtube.com

## 4.2  Benchmark Algorithm Description

The technique selected for comparison with RATC is ATC (which stands for Automated Tag Clustering) [4].

ATC is aimed at clustering tags to improve user experience in the use of a tagging system and minimize the classical linguistic limitations. The approach defines an algorithm to find strongly related tags counting the number of tag co-occurrences used for a page. A cut-off point is determined to evaluate when a counter is useful. A spars matrix is produced and its elements are the similarities among tags.

A graph representation of the similarities is defined and the tags are grouped with a graph clustering algorithm based on the spectral bisection. The quality of the partitioning is measured with the "modularity function" $Q$ [16]. ATC performs the following steps: (i) it uses spectral bisection to split the graph into two clusters; (ii) it compares the value of the modularity function $Q_0$ of the original unpartitioned graph to the value of the modularity function $Q_1$ of the partitioned graph, if $Q_1 > Q_0$ accepts the partitioning, otherwise rejects the partitioning; and (iii) it proceeds recursively on each accepted partition.

A similarity counter is increased for each pair of tags that belong to the same cluster and the top similar pairs of tags are extracted.

The choice to compare RATC with this approach is motivated by the fact that both approaches use tag-resource counters to define associations among tags. Let us also note that the main difference is on the way the counter is incremented. In fact, as previously explained, RATC counter is incremented also during the search activity.

## 4.3  Evaluation Measures

To assess the ability of RATC to learn from users activity monitoring, the state of the tagging system (i.e., the current values of each tag-resource association) has been saved and used to evaluate clusters quality every 50 feedbacks. In this way, 6 tagging system sessions, which can be used to compare the two tag clustering approaches, are available. As already pointed out, a subset of known tags was added to the tagging system to create some verifiable noise. To evaluate the quality of the clusters created by each algorithm in presence of noise we conducted experiments considering both the original dataset and a dataset in which we removed the noisy tags. The only parameter that had to be set is the inflation value in the clustering step (set to 3.0).

To make fair comparisons, first, a domain engineer clustered the involved tags. Each cluster was created considering tags that refer to the same *concept*, i.e., a particular event or a clear topic that groups tags. Subsequently, the tag clustering obtained by the domain engineer is compared with the clusters automatically generated by using RATC and the ones obtained by applying ATC. Each cluster produced by both RATC and ATC was evaluated considering the most related cluster generated by the domain engineer and producing the following sets:

- *true positive tags* (TP): tags that appear both in a cluster generated by RATC (ATC) and in the cluster of the domain engineer partition.
- *true negative tags* (TN): tags that do not appear both in a cluster generated by RATC (ATC) and in the cluster of the domain engineer partition.
- *false positive tags* (FP): tags that appear in a cluster generated by RATC (ATC) and do not appear in the cluster of the domain engineer partition.
- *false negative tags* (FN): tags that do not appear in a cluster generated by RATC (ATC), but appear in the cluster of the domain engineer partition.

To validate the approach, we resort to classical information retrieval measures, such as micro- and macro-averaging of precision and recall [17]. Let us recall here that micro- and macro-averaging are aimed at obtaining estimates of $\pi$ and $\rho$ relative to the whole category set. In particular, micro-averaging evaluates the overall $\pi$ and $\rho$ by globally summing over all individual decisions. In symbols:

$$\pi^{\mu} = \frac{TP}{TP + FP}; \quad \rho^{\mu} = \frac{TP}{TP + FN} = \frac{\sum_{i=1}^{m} TP_i}{\sum_{i=1}^{m}(TP_i + FN_i)} \quad (1)$$

where the "$\mu$" superscript stands for microaveraging. On the other hand, macro-averaging first evaluates $\pi$ and $\rho$ "locally" for each category, and then "globally" by averaging over the results of the different categories. In symbols:

$$\pi^{M} = \frac{\sum_{i=1} mP_i}{m}; \quad rho^{M} = \frac{\sum_{i=1} mP_i}{m} \quad (2)$$

where the "M" superscript stands for macroaveraging.

## 4.4   Results

Fig. 3 compares the results in terms of macro-averaging precision (Fig. 3-a) and recall (Fig. 3-b) obtained by adopting RATC and ATC with and without noisy tags. Fig. 4 compares the results in terms of micro-averaging precision (Fig. 4-a) and recall (Fig. 4-b) obtained by adopting RATC and ATC with and without noisy tags. Results show that RATC performs always better than ATC, and that

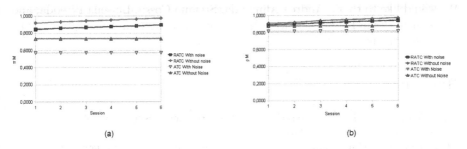

**Fig. 3.** Macro-averaging precision (a) and recall (b)

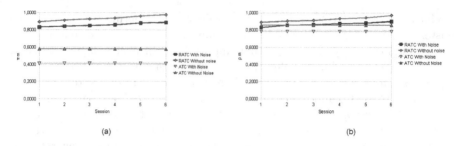

**Fig. 4.** Micro-averaging precision (a) and recall (b)

such performances improve session by session, due to the fact that tag-resource associations and tag-tag associations get better with the use of the system (i.e., by applying the feedback mechanism).

Let us put into evidence that, in the first session, the tag-resource associations have the same values for both algorithms, as no search activity was done in the system. Considering that RATC achieves better results even in this session, we can state that cosine similarity represents a better way to measure associations among tags.

## 5    Conclusions and Future Work

In this paper we proposed a technique able to cluster tags in a tagging system, with the ability to dynamically improve its performances while the tagging system is being used. The algorithm monitors users activity and exploits implicit feedbacks left by users. Experimental results highlight the effectiveness of the approach in the presence of strongly related tags in a cluster.

As for future work, we are currently studying how to improve the proposed approach by adopting a multi-layered clustering algorithm that, for each tag, takes into account the different contexts in which a tag is used.

## Acknowledgments

We would like to thank Andrea Alimonda, Stefano Cossu, Luisella Piredda, and G. Michele Pinna for participating in the definition and implementation of the proposed system.

## References

1. O'Reilly, T.: What is web 2.0? Design patterns and business models for the next generation of software (2005)
2. Golder, S.A., Huberman, B.A.: Usage patterns of collaborative tagging systems. J. Inf. Sci. 32, 198–208 (2006)

3. Bielenberg, K., Zacher, M.: Groups in Social Software: Utilizing Tagging to Integrate Individual Contexts for Social Navigation. PhD thesis, Media Universität Breme (2005)
4. Begelman, G., Keller, P., Smadja, F.: Automated tag clustering: Improving search and exploration in the tag space. In: Proceedings of the WWW Collaborative Web Tagging Workshop, Edinburgh, Scotland (2006)
5. Specia, L., Motta, E.: Integrating folksonomies with the semantic web. In: Franconi, E., Kifer, M., May, W. (eds.) ESWC 2007. LNCS, vol. 4519, pp. 624–639. Springer, Heidelberg (2007)
6. Hamasaki, M., Matsuo, Y., Nishimura, T., Takeda, H.: Ontology extraction by collaborative tagging with social networking. In: Proceedings of the WWW 2008 (2008)
7. Wu, X., Zhang, L., Yu, Y.: Exploring social annotations for the semantic web. In: WWW 2006: Proceedings of the 15th international conference on World Wide Web, pp. 417–426. ACM, New York (2006)
8. Giannakidou, E., Koutsonikola, V., Vakali, A., Kompatsiaris, Y.: Co-clustering tags and social data sources. In: The Ninth International Conference on Web-Age Information Management, 2008. WAIM 2008, pp. 317–324 (2008)
9. Dhillon, I.S.: Co-clustering documents and words using bipartite spectral graph partitioning. In: KDD 2001: Proceedings of the seventh ACM SIGKDD international conference on Knowledge discovery and data mining, pp. 269–274. ACM, New York (2001)
10. Smyth, B., Freyne, J., Coyle, M., Briggs, P., Balfe, E.: I-SPY: Anonymous, Community-Based Personalization by Collaborative Web Search. In: Proceedings of the 23rd SGAI International Conference on Innovative Techniques, pp. 367–380. Springer, Heidelberg (2003)
11. Baeza-Yates, R.: Applications of Web Query Mining. In: Losada, D.E., Fernández-Luna, J.M. (eds.) ECIR 2005. LNCS, vol. 3408, pp. 7–22. Springer, Heidelberg (2005)
12. Baeza-Yates, R., Ribeiro-Neto, B.: Modern Information Retrieval. Addison-Wesley, Reading (1999)
13. van Dongen, S.: Graph Clustering by Flow Simulation. PhD thesis, University of Utrecht (2000)
14. Porter, M.A., Onnela, J.P., Mucha, P.J.: Communities in networks (2009)
15. Carta, S., Alimonda, A., Clemente, M., Agelli, M.: Glue: Improving tag-based contents retrieval exploiting implicit user feedback. In: Hoenkamp, E., de Cock, M., Hoste, V. (eds.) Proceedings Of The 8th Dutch-Belgian Information Retrieval Workshop (DIR 2008), pp. 29–35 (2008)
16. Newman, M.E.J., Girvan, M.: Finding and evaluating community structure in networks. Phys. Rev. E 69 (2004)
17. Sebastiani, F.: Machine learning in automated text categorization. ACM Computing Surveys (CSUR) 34, 1–55 (2002)

# ISeller: A Flexible Personalization Infrastructure for e-Commerce Applications

Markus Jessenitschnig and Markus Zanker

University Klagenfurt
9020 Klagenfurt, Austria
{markus.jessenitschnig,markus.zanker}@uni-klu.ac.at

**Abstract.** We present *ISeller*, an industrial-strength recommendation system for a diverse range of commercial application domains. The system supports several recommendation paradigms such as collaborative, content-based and knowledge-based filtering, as well as one-shot and conversational interaction modes out of the box. A generic user modeling component allows different forms of hybrid personalization and enables the system to support process-oriented interactive selling in various product domains. This paper contributes a detailed discussion of a domain independent and flexible recommendation system from a software architecture viewpoint and illustrates it with different usage scenarios.

## 1 Introduction

Recommender systems (RS) are designed to help users when they are confronted with large choices presenting them with items likely to be of interest. Nowadays, many large online shopping platforms like *amazon.com* employ RS as a convenient service feature as well as a means to increase buying conversion rates. Despite the fact that these systems are appreciated by online shoppers, most small and medium sized e-commerce presences are unable to provide personalized recommendation services to their users. Having founded a company for interactive selling applications in 2002 and having deployed more than 30 commercial recommendation applications since then, we have experienced rather similar challenges with most prospective clients. For instance, besides budget and time constraints in general, the recommendation approach needs to be flexibly adapted to the application domain, e.g. financial service recommendations face legal hurdles with respect to liability for the advice, the consumer electronics domain has to cope with large product assortments and high online competition and bundled items in e-tourism become immensely complex when users are interested in not only accommodation and flights but also in including leisure activities and cultural experiences. As a result, the development of a domain independent RS that is interoperable with diverse technical host environments and legacy applications is a major challenge. For instance Adomavicius and Tuzhilin mention the *flexibility* of recommendation methods as opposed to "hard-wired" strategies in their discussion of capability extensions to RS [1]. From the viewpoint of user experience, more flexible RS could enable their users to specify the

T. Di Noia and F. Buccafurri (Eds.): EC-Web 2009, LNCS 5692, pp. 336–347, 2009.

type of recommendation required at runtime, e.g. *"Propose a movie in a nearby theater tonight"* vs. *"Propose three movies I haven't seen yet"*, as discussed by [2]. Furthermore, flexibility with respect to the application domain is especially of interest from an economic viewpoint. It enables providers to gain *economies of scale* and provide RS to small and medium-sized etailers. In addition, Berkovsky et al. [3] demonstrated the potential benefits in terms of improving recommendation quality obtained by integrating several data representation models and recommendation strategies.

This paper discusses the development of the commercial *ISeller* RS that achieves the goals of domain independence and flexibility. Thus, the contribution of this paper lies in its detailed discussion of the development of a generic RS from an architectural and engineering perspective. We relate architectural decisions to the requirements derived from the system's domain and describe two commercially innovative usage scenarios for RS.

The paper is organized as follows: first, we start by discussing related work. Afterwards, a detailed discussion on the system architecture is presented in Section 3. Finally, we outline two usage scenarios that demonstrate the generic applicability of the system in Section 4.

# 2   Related Work

User modeling and personalization in e-commerce have been active research areas since the early nineties. Over the past two decades, the focus of personalization has changed from personalized greetings to product recommendations. Goy et al. give a comprehensive overview of personalization techniques in the e-commerce domain both on the research level as well as in terms of commercial applications [4]. Regardless of the recommendation technique, all systems require a certain amount of information about users in order to compute personalized recommendations. Fink and Kobsa compared selected user modeling servers against real-world requirements and found a centralized user modeling approach to be promising especially for e-commerce applications [5]. Berkovsky et al. focus on the development of a generic mediation mechanism for integrating user modeling data into distributed environments to facilitate interoperability between recommendation systems [3].

According to Burke [6], five basic recommendation techniques exist, namely collaborative, content-based, demographic, utility-based and knowledge-based.

Among these, collaborative and content-based filtering are the most important techniques. In the field of recommender systems, the GroupLens research group from the University of Minnesota can be considered as one of its pioneers [7]. Starting with news and website recommendations, the movie domain quickly became the most attractive application area for research [8]. The worldwide online bookseller *amazon.com* was one the first companies to adopt collaborative filtering commercially and became the most prominent example of the application of recommendation technology in e-commerce. Since then, recommendation techniques have been applied in many different domains, such as music [9], restaurant

[6] and tourism recommendations [10], TV-guides [11], and financial services [12] to name a few.

Although most system claim to be domain independent with respect to algorithm implementation, few platforms can easily switch recommendation strategies. Therefore, the *ISeller* system presented here is innovative due to the considerable engineering effort exerted in implementing a pluggable modular system architecture with a generic user modeling component as outlined in the next section.

## 3     ISeller

This section discusses the engineering aspects of building a flexible and domain independent RS. It describes the architecture of *ISeller* and relates the applied technologies to the requirements of a flexible personalization infrastructure. Starting from abstract key requirements, an overview of the system architecture is given followed by a detailed description of the anatomy of particular modules.

### 3.1     Requirements

In addition to general system requirements such as usability, maintainability and scalability that are obvious for most software engineering projects, the following aspects were addressed throughout the project and are subsequently discussed in greater detail:

**Flexibility and Domain Independence:** As previously indicated, domain independence requires the system to support different recommendation strategies together with hybrid variants thereof. One approach is to implement a generic user modeling component supporting a generic representation of user data as proposed by [3]. For instance, knowledge-based methods may be used to collect abstract user requirements and map them to item characteristics [13] or collaborative filtering processes user ratings [7]. In order to be able to flexibly hybridize different recommendation strategies according to Burke's taxonomy [6], all recommendation strategies need to support the same API description. The requirements for developing hybrid variants lead us to the next aspect.

**Modularity and Extensibility:** Different recommendation approaches are applicable depending on the business domain and the amount and type of knowledge available. While collaborative techniques need a relatively large community of active users to disclose their assessment of different product items to the system, knowledge-based techniques require means-end knowledge and structured product information in order to compute sensible recommendations. A modular system, such as that of ISeller, must be able to be modified to fit the requirements of the business client. Obviously the heterogeneous nature of potential target domains means that not all circumstances can be considered during system design. A flexible extension mechanism ensures that existing components can be customized and extended with new functionality. The following section examines these aspects in more detail.

**Interoperability:** Interoperability is a fundamental requirement from a data integration viewpoint as well as from the perspective of integrating personalization mechanisms into legacy platforms. Different types of knowledge from existing legacy applications such as product data, transaction records or customer records are required to bootstrap recommendation techniques and need to be continuously updated. In addition, recommendations from the *ISeller* system need to be communicated to target platforms that may have been developed using a multitude of web development languages and environments such as .Net, php or Ruby.

## 3.2  System Architecture

From a software engineering perspective, the major challenge laid in conceptualizing the incorporated service orientation, extension mechanisms and pluggable component structure.

Most recommender systems follow a monolithic architecture in terms of strongly interweaved functionality and can therefore not be reused in different domains and hybrid algorithm designs. As a consequence, the architecture of the *ISeller* was conceptualized as a component-based plug-in system architecture following the principles of extensibility and modularity and is purely implemented in Java. From a software engineering perspective the development of a consistent pluggable and modular architecture from the data access level to the user interfaces of the maintenance editors is a contribution in itself that can be reused in different application domains and is not specific to recommendation systems. In conjunction with the modularization of the recommendation process and the modeling of different extension points a novel piece of work on the interface between software engineering and recommender systems is contributed.

At the base of our personalization infrastructure is a *Core Library* that implements common service components. These are small reusable functional units or abstract implementations which may be refined in concrete implementations. It integrates third party libraries and also specifies the principle anatomy of modules within the application by providing standardized interfaces. Importantly, other modules which wish to be integrated into *ISeller* and thus reside on top of the *Core Library* must only implement this small set of interfaces to conform to the architecture.

One of the most time consuming tasks when fielding recommendation applications within existing commercial infrastructures is the integration of existing legacy data like product catalogues, user transaction logs or other customer databases needed for computing personalized recommendations. In order to make legacy data accessible to other modules, the *Data Integration Service* implements various adapters for different types of data stores such as relational databases and XML-based data stores. The *Data Integration Service* normalizes legacy data to an internal representation and performs necessary pre-processing steps so that other modules can access and use this data in a uniform fashion.

The *User Modeling Service* and a *Recommendation Service* are located on top of the *Data Integration Service*. The *User Modeling Service* uses the *Data Integration Service* to bootstrap user models from existing user and usage data and warehouses all additional profiling and interaction data. Depending on the recommendation strategy, the *Recommendation Service* uses the *Data Integration Service* as well as the *User Modeling Service* to obtain the required input data for the recommendation algorithms.

### 3.3   Core Library

The *Core Library* is the basis for all other modules within *ISeller*. It offers common functionality to module implementations and defines the system's architecture in the form of interfaces. In order to be seamlessly integrated into the system, modules must implement these interfaces.

A very essential requirement is the composition of the system from loosely coupled modules. Modules may be implemented by different developers in parallel, third party modules may be integrated or components of *ISeller* itself may be used within other systems as third party software. To stay abreast of these requirements, *ISeller* follows an service-oriented architecture (SOA) by implementing a central *Module and Service Management* unit as well as an *Extension Management* unit which allow the implementation of loosely coupled extensible applications [14,15,16].

In additional, a number of smaller components provide low-level but very reusable functionality to other modules. These include a component for unified configuration data access, a data store access component to standardize data management concerns across the application and other components which are responsible for transaction handling, logging and tracing as well as a component for handling security issues. The following presents a more detailed description of the most important components.

**Module and Service Management:** The *Module and Service Management* unit is a central component of the *Core Library* and can be seen as the micro-kernel of the application. It utilizes a variety of third party libraries, including Hive-Mind[1], a light weight service container, to build an extensible infrastructure for loosely coupled components following principles of service-oriented architectures. During application startup this unit analyzes the deployment of the application and tries to find additional modules. In order to be able to do this, each module includes a XML module description file holding information about the module itself and the services it provides. Furthermore, this file contains information which instructs the framework on how to create services. The *Interceptor Pattern* is used to enrich services with additional generic functionality and the *Dependency Injection* design pattern allows the system to connect services in a declarative way comparable to AOP[17]. After the initialization phase, the central *Service Registry* can be consulted to obtain references about the services available.

---

[1] See http://hivemind.apache.org for details

**Extension Management:** One of the primary goals of *ISeller* is to be extensible as requirements change or new requirements arise. An extension mechanism was implemented that allows the basic functionality of modules to be extended without actually changing existing code. Within *ISeller*, both the user interface as well as business logic components (e.g. recommendation algorithms) may be extended. The Eclipse Rich Client Platform (RCP)[2] provides both the system's administrative user interfaces and user interface extension methods. A simplified version of extension mechanism of RCP was developed for server side components which is able to cope with our requirements. Modules, which serve as hosts for new extensions, define extension points to which other modules can contribute their functionality.

The following subsection describes the business modules responsible for implementing the flexible personalization infrastructure in more detail. These build upon the low-level infrastructure services .

### 3.4 Data Integration Service

The *Data Integration Service* provides access to various types of data sources such as relational databases and XML or MS Excel files. Figure 1(a) depicts the architecture of the *Data Integration Service*. The *Data Source Adapter Extension Point* serves as a host for data source adapters and is responsible for locating adapter implementations during the application's startup sequence. Out of the box, the system includes implementations for XML data stores, relational databases as well as for other popular file formats. Within the e-commerce domain many different database management systems are in use.Typically, these range from open-source solutions like MySQL or PostgreSQL to high-end commercial products such as Oracle, depending on the size of the business. Each database system typically extends the standard query language with database dependent features. To cope with these differences the standard relational database adapter utilizes Hibernate.

In addition to existing implementations, new adapters can be easily plugged into the extension point. Providers are only required to implement an interface and to give a description of the adapter (e.g. what parameters have to be specified for accessing the data source) as part of deployment descriptor following the rules of the adapter extension point. After the physical access rules are realized in the form of an adapter implementation, logical data source access can be modeled using the *Data Source Definition* unit. Once developers have specified the parameters required for access, the domain objects and their attributes can be selected. After this step, the *Data Integration Service* is able to access legacy domain data.

The *Data Object Construction* unit utilizes a domain ontology and a data source definition to construct an appropriate data structure, allowing data structure definitions to be externalized from application code. Based on the description of how domain data can be accessed, additional data structures can be defined to model more complex structures using the *Data Object Definition* unit.

---

[2] See http://www.eclipse.org/rcp for details

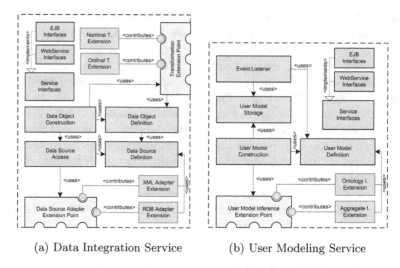

(a) Data Integration Service        (b) User Modeling Service

**Fig. 1.** Architecture of core components

In most cases recommendation strategies require additional data transformation and pre-processing steps (e.g. relations, transposing rows to columns, de-normalization or value mappings) to be performed. Therefore, after the first construction phase several pre-processing steps can be applied. In a similar fashion to data source adapters, new transformation and pre-processing algorithms can be introduced using the extension mechanisms provided by the *Core Library*.

## 3.5   User Modeling Service

Recommendation strategies differentiate themselves in terms of the type of user data they require. As a result the ISeller system utilizes a generic user model representation to ensure that the system is not limited to a specific recommendation technique.

According to Kobsa [18] the purpose of the *User Modeling Service* is generally to collect and warehouse all forms of user preferences and transaction data to enable means-end oriented personalization and user interaction. Using a query interface recommender services can evaluate arbitrary expressions on the user model for a single user as well as to retrieve a set users satisfying a given expression.

Following the proposal of a generic user modeling approach from Kobsa [18], the *User Modeling Service* supports assumptions on system's beliefs about users' beliefs, where system as well as user beliefs are represented by probability values. Domain experts can define structured user profiles as well as transaction series on a graphical level. Based on the data objects identified in the underlying *Data Integration* component, user models may be initialized from existing legacy data. Beside data collection and warehousing functionality, the implemented *User Modeling Service* also owns strong inferential capabilities. They range from simple aggregation and explicit personalization rules to forms of ontological reasoning [19].

Figure 1(b) illustrates the architecture of the *User Modeling Service*. The *User Model Definition* defines and implements the structure of the user models used within the system. These models are then bootstrapped with existing data by the *User Model Construction* component. The *User Model Storage* unit is responsible for physical organization and storage as well as for ensuring that other components have efficient access to user data. The *Event Listener* framework offers general functionality to other components allowing them to add or update user data as well as to be notified when user models are modified. See [20] for a more detailed technical description of the *User Modeling Service*.

## 3.6   Recommendation Service

As previously noted, a particular recommendation technique may be more suitable for a given application depending on contextual factors such as the types of knowledge available. For this reason, the *Recommendation Service* provides extensibility infrastructure such that the personalization framework is not limited to one specific technique. More specifically, the recommendation core component utilizes the *User Modeling Service* to access information on the current user and the community as well as the *Data Integration Service* to obtain domain data.

Implementations of specific recommendation techniques use this core functionality on an individual level and are integrated into the *Recommendation Service*. As depicted in Figure 2, the core component offers three extension points to algorithm implementations. As recommendation algorithms and in particular model-based approaches may have to perform time-intensive batch computations generic data structures are usually inappropriate for this task. Therefore specific algorithm implementations can expose user model adapters to the *User Model Adaption* extension point in order to facilitate the conversion process. An additional model-building step utilizes the transformed data, before final recommendations are produced. Both model-building algorithms as well as algorithms which actually compute recommendations can be contributed via extension points.

By now, all recommendation approaches according to Burke's taxonomy [6] have been implemented within *ISeller*. In addition *weighted, mixed, feature-augmentation* and *combination, cascaded, switching* and *meta-level* hybridization strategies have been explored. See [21,22] for comparative evaluation studies and [23,24] for detailed descriptions on implemented and evaluated hybrid recommendation strategies.

The evaluation of algorithms is crucial for analysis and algorithm selection. For this purpose the recommendation module also contains an evaluation component for automatically evaluating and replaying recommendation strategies using historical transaction datasets. The attained information is then used to optimize hybrid algorithm designs and tune algorithm parameters.

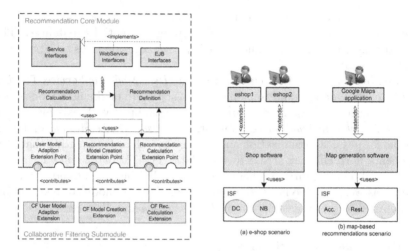

**Fig. 2.** Recommendation
Service Architecture

**Fig. 3.** Usage scenarios

# 4 Usage Scenarios

*ISeller*'s generic architecture allows it to support a wide range of usage scenarios. We present the *e-shop scenario* and the *map-based recommendations* scenario here as they are innovative in terms of community syndication and the presentation context.

In the **e-shop scenario**, *ISeller* serves as the personalization infrastructure for commercial shop software. Recommendation applications have been fielded in diverse domains such as tourism, luxury goods or consumer electronics.

Making personalized recommendations in the electronics and hardware domain for instance is challenging for several reasons. First, many online shoppers are interested only in the lowest price, using price comparison platforms as their entry point. Thus, they spend only a relatively short amount of time in the online shop itself resulting in shallow user models and the new user problem. Second, the product domain is characterized by the fast pace of technological advancements which leads to frequently changing product portfolios and the new item problem. Third, none of the shop operators have a large customer base (compared with *amazon.com*) and thus collaborative methods suffer from sparse rating data and a small community.

The new user and new item problems can however be addressed by exploiting explicit customer requirements and hybridizing knowledge-based and collaborative techniques [22]. Furthermore, the service-oriented design allows different shop operators to syndicate their anonymous user communities to a common and thus larger rating base.

As depicted in Figure 3(a) ISeller provides different recommendation applications such as recommenders for digital cameras (DC) or notebooks (NB) to the shop environment that can be accessed by customers of different etailers.

Users may enter abstract domain requirements such as the proposed use of the product item (e.g. *gaming* or solely *word processing* and *Internet* in the notebook domain) or technical product parameters like *memory size* and *processor type*. The user models consist therefore of these explicit user requirements and of binary ratings on items that have been actually put into a shopping basket. Internally, the system utilizes a hybrid recommendation approach that cascades a knowledge-based and a collaborative algorithm. The knowledge-based algorithm implementation exploits means-end knowledge in the form of personalization constraints that remove inappropriate items from the recommendation list, e.g. *Propose only notebooks with 1 GB of main memory if the customer wants to run computer games or graphical applications.* The collaborative algorithm builds on rating matrices that relate users' explicit requirements to actually bought items as described in [22]. For each application domain, i.e. notebooks, digital cameras, video projectors or display devices, a central user model scheme for all online shops is installed that collects explicit requirements and ratings from the anonymous online customers. This way, the syndicated ratings table is obviously larger than that obtained from a single online shop, thus enabling the collaborative algorithm to derive more accurate recommendations. Due to the cascaded hybrid algorithm design, the knowledge-based method ensures that the list of potential recommendations includes only items that are in the product portfolio of the respective e-shop, while the collaborative method is responsible for the sorting scheme.

Another usage scenario for *ISeller* is for providing personalized recommendations about geospatial objects in the e-tourism domain, thus exploiting the geographic information systems (GIS) have become commonplace on many e-tourism sites. Due to the intangible nature of tourism goods and services, most potential guests expect to find high-quality content on the web. Consequently, exploring the location of tourism objects such as the surrounding hotels, restaurants and other points of interest via map-based navigation can help users to evaluate different travel destinations. However, in comparison with traditional web interaction models, web-based GIS can also lead to information overload for users. Subsequently, the development of adaptation and context-aware personalization mechanisms for map-based interactions was for instance investigated in [25]. ISeller is currently being used in an ongoing research project with a GIS provider and a tourism destination platform to deliver adaptive Google Maps services (see Figure 3(b)). Given a specific geographical context the recommendation service delivers accommodation (Acc.), restaurants (Rest.) and sights within the area that will presumably be of interest to the current user [26].

## 5   Conclusions

This paper presented the architecture and design of the *ISeller* recommendation system, a modular system for providing personalization mechanisms to small- and medium-sized etailers in diverse product domains. The system architecture supports the requirements of the target market by incorporating service orientation, extension mechanisms and a pluggable component structure which collectively allow it to customize its recommendation strategies to diverse application domains. The paper also contributed a detailed discussion of the engineering aspects surrounding flexible recommendation systems and illustrated the success of the system with two commercially innovative usage scenarios.

# References

1. Adomavicius, G., Tuzhilin, A.: Towards the next generation of recommender systems: A survey of the state-of-the-art and possible extensions. IEEE Transactions on Knowledge and Data Engineering 17(6) (2005)
2. Adomavicius, G., Tuzhilin, A.: Multidimensional recommender systems: A data warehousing approach. In: Fiege, L., Mühl, G., Wilhelm, U.G. (eds.) WELCOM 2001. LNCS, vol. 2232, pp. 180–192. Springer, Heidelberg (2001)
3. Berkovsky, S., Kuflik, T., Ricci, F.: Mediation of user models for enhanced personalization in recommender systems. User Modeling and User-Adapted Interaction 18(3), 245–286 (2008)
4. Goy, A., Ardissono, L., Petrone, G.: Personalization in e-commerce applications. In: The Adaptive Web. LNCS, vol. 4321, pp. 485–520. Springer, Heidelberg (2007)
5. Fink, J., Kobsa, A.: A review and analysis of commercial user modeling servers for personalization on the world wide web. User Modeling and User-Adapted Interaction 10(2-3), 209–249 (2000)
6. Burke, R.: Hybrid recommender systems: Survey and experiments. User Modeling and User-Adapted Interaction 12(4), 331–370 (2002)
7. Resnick, P., Iacovou, N., Suchak, N., Bergstrom, P., Riedl, J.: Grouplens: An open architecture for collaborative filtering of netnews. In: Computer Supported Collaborative Work (CSCW). Chapel Hill, NC (1994)
8. Herlocker, J.L., Konstan, J.A., Borchers, A., Riedl, J.: An algorithmic framework for performing collaborative filtering. In: International ACM SIGIR Conference on Research and Development in Information Retrieval, pp. 230–237. ACM, New York (1999)
9. Shardanand, U., Maes, P.: Social information filtering: Algorithms for automating word of mouth. In: Conference on Human Factors in Computing Systems (CHI), pp. 210–217 (1995)
10. Ricci, F., Werthner, H.: Case base querying for travel planning recommendation. Information Technology and Tourism 3, 215–266 (2002)
11. Cotter, P., Smyth, B.: Ptv: Intelligent personalized tv guides. In: 12th Innovative Applications of Artificial Intelligence (IAAI). AAAI Press, Menlo Park (2000)
12. Felfernig, A., Friedrich, G., Jannach, D., Zanker, M.: An integrated environment for the development of knowledge-based recommender applications. International Journal of Electronic Commerce 11(2), 11–34 (2007)
13. Burke, R.: Knowledge-based recommender systems. Encyclopedia of Library and Information Systems 69(2) (2000)
14. Huhns, M.N., Singh, M.P.: Service-oriented computing: Key concepts and principles. IEEE Internet Computing 9(1), 75–81 (2005)
15. Papazoglou, M.P.: Service-oriented computing: Concepts, characteristics and directions. In: Proceedings of the 4th International Conference on Web Information Systems Engineering (WISE), pp. 3–12 (2003)

16. Stal, M.: Using architectural patterns and blueprints for service-oriented architecture. IEEE Software 23(2), 54–61 (2006)
17. Kiczales, G., Lamping, J., Menhdhekar, A., Maeda, C., Lopes, C., Loingtier, J.M., Irwin, J.: Aspect-oriented programming. In: Akşit, M., Matsuoka, S. (eds.) ECOOP 1997. LNCS, vol. 1241, pp. 220–242. Springer, Heidelberg (1997)
18. Kobsa, A.: Generic user modeling systems. User Modeling and User-Adapted Interaction 11(1-2), 49–63 (2001)
19. Middleton, S.E., Shadbolt, N.R., Roure, D.C.D.: Ontological user profiling in recommender systems. ACM Trans. Inf. Syst. 22(1), 54–88 (2004)
20. Jessenitschnig, M., Zanker, M.: A generic user modeling component for hybrid recommendation strategies. In: 11th IEEE Conference on Commerce and Enterprise Computing (CEC), Vienna, Austria. IEEE Press, Los Alamitos (2009)
21. Zanker, M., Jessenitschnig, M., Jannach, D., Gordea, S.: Comparing recommendation strategies in a commercial context. IEEE Intelligent Systems 22(3), 69–73 (2007)
22. Markus, Z., Markus, J.: Case-studies on exploiting explicit customer requirements in recommender systems. User Modeling and User-Adapted Interaction 19(1-2), 133–166 (2009)
23. Zanker, M.: A Collaborative Constraint-Based Meta-Level Recommender. In: 2nd ACM International Conference on Recommender Systems (ACM RecSys), Lausanne, Switzerland, pp. 139–146. ACM Press, New York (2008)
24. Zanker, M., Jessenitschnig, M.: Collaborative feature-combination recommender exploiting explicit and implicit user feedback. In: 11th IEEE Conference on Commerce and Enterprise Computing (CEC), Vienna, Austria. IEEE Computer Society Press, Los Alamitos (2009)
25. Zipf, A.: User-adaptive maps for location-based services (lbs) for tourism. In: Information and Communication Technologies in Tourism (ENTER 2002). Springer, Heidelberg (2002)
26. Zanker, M., Fuchs, M., Seebacher, A., Jessenitschnig, M., Stromberger, M.: An Automated Approach for Deriving Semantic Annotations of Tourism Products based on Geospatial Information. In: Proceedings of the Conference on Information and Communication Technologies in Tourism (ENTER), pp. 211–221 (2009)

# Comparing Pre-filtering and Post-filtering Approach in a Collaborative Contextual Recommender System: An Application to E-Commerce

Umberto Panniello[1], Michele Gorgoglione[1], and Cosimo Palmisano[2]

[1] Polytechnic of Bari, Department of mechanical and business engineering,
Bari, Italy
{u.panniello,m.gorgoglione}@poliba.it
[2] Aizoon consulting, Senior consultant at Fiat Group Automobiles,
Turin, Italy
{cosimo.palmisano}@aizoon.it

**Abstract.** Recent literature predicts that including context in a recommender system may improve its performance. The context-based recommendation approaches are classified as pre-filtering, post-filtering and contextual modeling. Little research has been done on studying whether including context in a recommender system improves the recommendation performance and no research has compared yet the different approaches to contextual RS. The research contribution of this work lies in studying the effect of the context on the recommendation performance and comparing a pre-filtering approach to a post-filtering using a collaborative filtering recommender system.

**Keywords:** recommender system, e-commerce, pre-filtering, post-filtering, context, collaborative filtering.

## 1 Introduction

Recommender systems (RS) are useful to companies in e-commerce because by personalizing the suggestions of products to buy, they can enhance sales, intensify the cross-selling effect, and improve the customer satisfaction. Various classifications of RS have been proposed [1], [2], [3]. The recommendation engines are usually based on collaborative filtering [4], [5], content-based filtering [6], [7], [8] or a combination of these two methods [9], [10].

Several studies [11] demonstrated that context induces important changes in a customer purchasing behavior. Experimental research on customer modeling suggests that including context in a customer behavior model improves the ability of predicting a his/her behavior in some conditions [12]. Capturing contextual information, such as the intent of a purchase, allows the analyst to identify more homogeneous patterns in the data describing the purchasing history of a customer [12].

In the field of RSs, several scholars have maintained that including context is expected to improve the recommendation performance. Some studies focus on the way context should be included in a RS [13]. [14] described an approach to including more

T. Di Noia and F. Buccafurri (Eds.): EC-Web 2009, LNCS 5692, pp. 348–359, 2009.

information using a multidimensional approach to recommendations where the traditional two-dimensional user/item paradigm was extended to support additional dimensions capturing the context in which recommendations are made. However, very few experimental studies have been done so far to prove how a contextual approach may outperforms a traditional. For instance, [15] showed that including the context in which a transaction takes place in a RS, improves the ability of recommending items to users.

A classification of various context-based recommendation approaches is presented in [16]. In particular, the contextual information can be used as follows (Fig. 1):

1. To filter out irrelevant ratings before they are used for computing recommendations (contextual pre-filtering).
2. After the classical (2 dimensional) recommendation methods are applied to the standard recommendation data (contextual post-filtering).
3. Inside the recommendation-generating algorithms (contextual modeling).

A collaborative recommender system predicts the way a customer would rate an item, based on ratings previously given by users to other items. Literature suggests that ratings may be either explicit or implicit and that it is possible to obtain implicit ratings by customers purchasing behavior [17]. In real situations (e.g., an e-commerce portal) it is more likely to work with purchasing information, such as purchasing frequencies or time spent on a web page, than ratings explicitly given by customers [18].

This research aims at studying whether including context in a collaborative RS improves the recommendation performance and at comparing a pre-filtering approach to a post-filtering. We used a database coming from an e-commerce portal, including transactional data. We built two RSs (one including context, one which does not), measured three types of predictive performance, used two approaches to include the contextual variable in the contextual RS (pre-filtering and post-filtering), used two ways of evaluating the performance and compared the RSs to each other in several experimental settings. We show that the post-filtering approach reaches better performance than the pre-filtering approach and that the contextual post-filtering RS increases its performance more than the un-contextual RS if we try to generate less obvious recommendations.

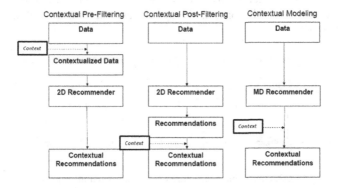

**Fig. 1.** How to use context in the recommendation process

## 2 Problem Formulation

Traditionally, recommender systems deal with two types of entities, users (e.g., customers) and items (e.g., products, Web pages). First, each user rates the items that he/she has seen in the past, indicating how much he/she liked these items. Ratings may be either explicit or implicit. Based on these ratings an RS tries to estimate the ratings of the yet unseen items for each user. In other words, a RS can be viewed as the rating function R that maps each user/item pair to a particular rating value [15]:

$$R: \text{Users x Items} \rightarrow \text{Ratings} . \tag{1}$$

As it was mentioned above, in our study we used implicit ratings drawn from transactional data, collected in a matrix $X$ (Users x Items) in which each cell $x_{ij}$ contains the purchasing frequency of product $j$ purchased by user $i$ (quantity of product $j$ purchased by user $i$).

In our study, context is defined as "the period of the year" in which a customer makes a purchase on an e-commerce portal. The same customer may show a different behavior in different periods of the year: for instance, he/she can spend more in Winter during Christmas and less during the rest of the year or change the product categories and the frequency of purchase. The contextual information is hierarchically structured as shown in Figure 2. At the first level ($K_1$) we distinguish whether the purchased is made in Winter or Summer, at the second level ($K_2$) whether it is made during holidays or not. Although this contextual information is not very rich, compared to other definitions of context (e.g., intent of a purchase, state of mind), it is always available in any business application. Some comments on the limits of this definition are reported in the last section.

We used the collaborative filtering approach to develop the RSs [4], [19]. The reason is that collaborative filtering is the recommender system technology to date, used in most real applications on the Web. It recommends products to a target customer, based on the ratings of other customers [20]. Collaborative filtering recommender systems employ statistical techniques to find a set of customers known as neighbors, that are similar to the target user (i.e., they tend to buy similar sets of products). Once a neighborhood of users is formed, the system uses several algorithms to produce recommendations.

**Fig. 2.** Hierarchical structure of the contextual information

We distinguish between un-contextual and contextual recommender system (CRS). The un-contextual RS was built by using all the transactional data, while the CRS uses context by pre-filtering data or post-filtering. The next section describes the way context is included according to the two approaches.

Two degrees of contextual information were considered. In the first ($K_1$) a coarse knowledge of context is included in the RS, the contextual variable can take two values. In the second ($K_2$) a finer knowledge of context is included in the RS, the contextual variable can take four values.

## 2.1 The Pre-filtering Approach

According to the pre-filtering approach (Fig. 1), the contextual information is used as a label for filtering out those ratings that do not correspond to the specified contextual information. The CRS selects from the initial set of all the ratings only those referring to a specific context $k$ and it generates a *Users x Items* matrix containing only the data related to context $k$. After that, the collaborative filtering is launched on this reduced dataset in order to obtain the recommendations related to context $k$.

## 2.2 The Post-filtering Approach

According to the post-filtering approach (Fig. 1), we have used the contextual information after the main recommendation method is launched. Once unknown ratings are estimated, the system analyzes data for a given user in a given context to find specific item usage patterns and uses these patterns to "contextualize" the recommendations obtained from the collaborative filtering [16]. There exist various methods for contextualizing the 2D recommendations. In our case, the system analyze data for a given user in a given context to calculate a contextual probability with which the user chooses a certain type of item in the given context; the contextual probability $P_k(i,j)$, with which the $i$-th customer purchases the $j$-th item in context $k$, is computed as the number of neighbors (customers similar to $i$) who purchased the same item in the same context divided by the total number of neighbors. After that, the recommendations obtained using the 2D method are "contextualized" by filtering the 2D ratings out based on a threshold value of $P_k(i,j)$. In particular, the rating for the $i$-th customer and $j$-th item in context $k$ is:

$$Rating_k(i,j) = \begin{cases} Rating\ (i,j) & if \quad P_k(i,j) \geq P^* \\ 0 & if \quad P_k(i,j) < P^* \end{cases} \tag{2}$$

where *Rating (i, j)* is the rating for user $i$-th and item $j$-th obtained using the 2D method and $P^*$ is the threshold value.

## 2.3 Performance Measure

In the literature [21], the most common two approaches for evaluating recommender systems via retrospective data seem to be:

1.  The use of a cross-validation approach (including the leave-one-out approach).
2.  Selecting training and validation set on a temporal basis.

In the first case, leave-one-out cross-validation involves using a single observation from the original sample as the validation data, and the remaining observations as the training data. This is repeated such that each observation in the sample is used once as the validation data. In particular, if the system predicts a rating higher than two (it means that an item will be purchased more than two times), we consider that as a positive rating (recommendable item), otherwise, if the system predicts a rating lower than two (it means that an item will be purchased less than two times), we consider that as a negative rating (not recommendable item).

In the second case, we divide the database in $t_1$ (training set) and $t_2$ (validation set) by a temporal splitting. In our case, we use data related to the years 2004 and 2005 as $t_1$ and data related to the year 2006 as $t_2$. The RS estimates the unknown ratings by using the data related to $t_1$ and validates them using the data related to $t_2$. The performance are measured as for the previous case (an item is recommendable if it has a rating higher than two). The second method is particularly useful because it mirrors the way a recommender system works in real applications [22].

## 3  Experimental Setup

The experiments were performed on a database coming from an e-commerce portal which sells electronic products to approximately 120.000 users and includes about 220.000 transactions. We considered product categories instead of single items because of the high specialization of the item database; in particular, we had 24 product categories.

According to the collaborative filtering approach, the neighborhood was formed using the cosine similarity [23], which is given by:

$$sim(x, y) = \cos(\vec{x}, \vec{y}) = \frac{\vec{x} \bullet \vec{y}}{\|\vec{x}\|_2 \times \|\vec{y}\|_2} = \frac{\sum\limits_{s \in S_{xy}} r_{x,s} r_{y,s}}{\sqrt{\sum\limits_{s \in S_{xy}} r_{x,s}^2} \sqrt{\sum\limits_{s \in S_{xy}} r_{y,s}^2}} \quad (3)$$

where $r_{x,s}$ and $r_{y,s}$ are the ratings of item $s$ assigned by users $x$ and $y$ respectively, $S_{xy} = \{s \in Items \mid r_{x,s} \neq \emptyset \wedge r_{y,s} \neq \emptyset\}$ is the set of all items co-rated by both customers $x$ and $y$, and $\vec{x} \bullet \vec{y}$ denotes the dot-product between the vectors $\vec{x}$ and $\vec{y}$. The neighborhood size was set to 80 users, which turned out to be the optimal size after a series of experiments.

We used two ways of including the contextual information (as it was mentioned previously, using pre-filtering and post-filtering approaches).

The experiments were done for all the degrees of contextual knowledge (uncontextual, $K_1$ and $K_2$).

We varied the similarity threshold used to find users similar to the active customer. The choice of this similarity threshold is important because it affects the quality and the refinement of recommendations. In particular, we used two values of similarity threshold, respectively 1 and 0.9. When the threshold is 1, the RS finds neighbors which are almost identical to the active customer (the customer for whom we want to recommend items), while when the threshold is 0.9, the RS finds neighbors which present some differences with respect to the active customer. These values represent the trade-off between making recommendations which have a high probability to fit the active customer's preferences (neighbors are identical) and making non-obvious recommendations (they are built upon the preferences of neighbors slightly different from the active customer). Using lower similarity threshold values would be counter-productive because if neighbors are too different from the active customer the recommendations made may be wrong.

The performance measured are Precision (P), Recall (R) and F-Measure as suggested by [21]. Precision represents the probability that a recommended item is relevant (for the user). Recall represents the probability that the RS recommends a relevant item. The F-Measure combines both metrics into a single given by:

$$F_1 = \frac{2PR}{P+R} \qquad (4)$$

Since in our prior work [24] we have showed that there is a relation between sparsity and performance when pre-filtering is used, we measured sparsity. It was measured as:

$$Sparsity = 1 - \frac{NonZeroEntries}{TotalEntries} \qquad (5)$$

which represents the share of missing ratings. Sparsity is expected to affect the performance of a pre-filtering contextual recommender, while a post-filtering approach is not affected by an increase in sparsity. In fact, the pre-filtering approach works on less data compared to the un-contextual because only a subset of data is used to build the contextual "User x Item" matrix. On the contrary, post-filtering generates recommendations based on the complete "User x Item" matrix, and context is used only to adjust the recommendations afterwards.

## 4  Results

In order to evaluating the CRS on historical data, we have used two evaluation strategies as mentioned above. The first sub-section presents the results obtained by evaluating the RSs by using the leave-one-out approach. The second sub-section presents those obtained by using a "training – validation set" approach.

### 4.1  Results Obtained Using the Leave-One-Out Approach

In this case we compare the three recommenders (un-contextual, pre-filtering, post-filtering) by measuring their ability to predict the whole "User x Item" matrix based on all the transactions. Figure 3 reports the F-measure of the un-contextual RS (it is a straight line because it doesn't change with the context degree) with the two contextual approaches (the two continuous lines) in each contextual degree (moving right on the x-axis), and the sparsity (the dashed line) related to the pre-filtering RS and to

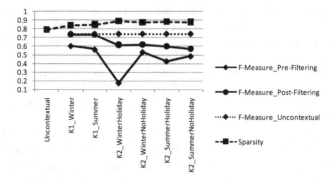

**Fig. 3.** F-Measure related to the un-contextual and contextual RSs, using a pre-filtering and a post-filtering approach, and sparsity level

each contextual degree of the CRS (moving right on the x-axis). The sparsity is related to the matrix used to generate the recommendations using the pre-filtering approach. Although bar chart would be more appropriate, we used graph with continuous lines in order to improve the results visualization.

The results obtained by the pre-filtering approach show that:

1.  The un-contextual RS outperforms the CRS. In particular, the un-contextual outperforms the contextual degree $K_1$ of almost 15% while it outperforms the degree $K_2$ of almost 25% on average. The finer the contextual information the more the un-contextual model outperforms the contextual.
2.  Including context increases sparsity. The more we use contextual information for implementing the collaborative filtering the more the sparsity increases. For the degree $K_2$ we have that the sparsity level increases of almost 10% respect to the un-contextual model. In particular the spike corresponding to "winter holiday" is due to the fact that in this context we have the higher level of sparsity.
3.  Sparsity increases as finer degrees of contextual information are used. The results are due to the fact that when the dataset is pre-filtered by labeling data with context, we filter out more data from the initial database thus decreasing the quantity of information. Therefore, a slight increase in sparsity induces a large decrease in performance.

The results obtained by the post-filtering approach show that:

1.  The performance of the un-contextual RS is almost identical to that of the contextual RS at the degree $K_1$.
2.  If we increase the degree of context (finer contextual information) there is a difference of 15% between them.
3.  The post-filtering approach does not generate any change in sparsity level.

We have varied the similarity threshold used to find the neighbors, and we have found that the performance decrease for both the RSs, un-contextual and contextual (Fig. 4). We report only the results related to the pre-filtering approach because these are the same using the post-filtering approach or the un-contextual RS; moreover, we have not enough space to show these all. The results are due to the fact that in this case the aim is to replicate the actual matrix, then finding not identical neighbors decreases the performance.

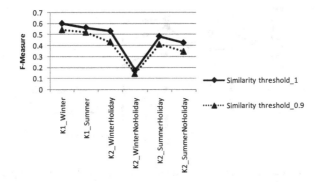

**Fig. 4.** F-Measure related to the RSs moving from 1 to 0.9 as similarity threshold using a pre-filtering approach.

In conclusion, we can assume that the post-filtering achieves better performance than the pre-filtering. The contextual variable introduces a certain degree of homogeneity in the User x Item matrix but increases the sparsity. The sparsity effect dominates the homogeneity effect in the pre-filtering approach.

The post-filtering approach does not suffer from the sparsity effect because it includes the contextual variable after the recommendation engine generates the recommendations. However, the performance does not increase.

### 4.2 Results Obtained Using Training and Validation Set on a Temporal Basis

In this case, we divide the database in $t_1$ and $t_2$ by a temporal splitting, and we use $t_1$ to predict the unknown ratings while $t_2$ to validate the results. This method mirrors the way a RS would work on real applications [22]. Figure 5 reports the F-measure of the un-contextual RS with the two contextual approaches in each contextual degree (moving right on the x-axis), and the sparsity (the dashed line) related to the pre-filtering RS and to each contextual degree of the CRS (moving right on the x-axis). The sparsity is related to the matrix used to generate the recommendations, that in this case is the matrix obtained by $t_1$ (one for each contextual level).

The results obtained by using the pre-filtering approach show that:

1. The un-contextual RS outperforms the CRS (Fig. 5). In particular, the difference of performance between un-contextual RS and CRS is lower in this case than in the case described in the previous sub-section, but it confirms the same results.
2. If the similarity threshold for identifying the neighbors is reduced (as seen in Section 3 of this work) the performance of the CRS increases, while the performance of the un-contextual RS slightly decreases (Fig. 6). In particular, moving from 1 to 0.9 (similarity threshold), the performance of the un-contextual does not change while the performance gain of the CRS ranges from 1% to 7% (depending on the contextual degree).
3. If the similarity threshold is reduced, the finer the contextual degree, the higher the improvement in performance (we have higher increase for the finest degree of context, $K_2$) (Fig. 6)

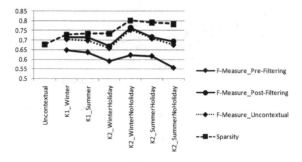

**Fig. 5.** F-Measure related to the un-contextual and contextual RSs, using a pre-filtering and a post-filtering approach

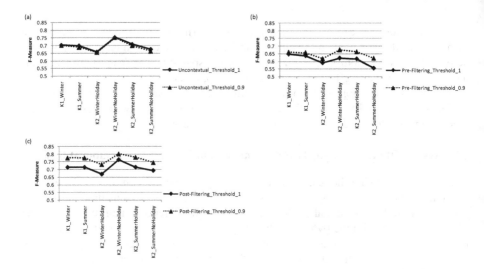

**Fig. 6.** F-Measure related to (a) un-contextual RS, (b) CRS with pre-filtering approach and (c) CRS with post-filtering approach moving from 1 to 0.9 as similarity threshold used to generate the neighborhood

The experiments with a post-filtering approach, show that:

1. The CRS outperforms the un-contextual RS in all the degrees of context (Fig. 5). There is a little difference between the two RSs, but in all the degrees of context we have that the CRS outperforms the un-contextual for almost 1%.
2. If the similarity threshold is reduced, the performance for the CRS increases and the difference of performance between it and the un-contextual RS becomes higher (Fig. 6).

The post-filtering CRS outperforms the un-contextual RS as in the previous subsection. Moreover, as the results obtained by varying the similarity threshold show, if one tries to generate less obvious recommendations, by varying the threshold, the post-filtering CRS increases its performance more than the un-contextual RS. These results contradict the results of the previous section because of the different evaluation strategy used (selecting of training and validation set instead of leave-one-out approach). In particular, when we use the post-filtering with the leave-one-out approach, the systems takes the predicted ratings of the un-contextual method (which predicts the unknown ratings using the whole dataset), contextualizes those ratings using the contextual variable and verifies the results. Since the data set used to predict the unknown ratings and the dataset used to verify the recommendations are the same, the post-filtering approach could reach the same results of the un-contextual method but could not improve it.

## 5  Conclusions and Future Work

This research aims at studying the performance of a collaborative recommender system when context is included in the recommendation process. Moreover, the pre-filtering and post-filtering approaches to including context are compared. The systems are experimented with by using real transactional data coming from an e-commerce portal.

The experimental results show that the post-filtering approach always reaches better performance than the pre-filtering approach. The reason is that the latter suffers from a sparsity-homogeneity trade-off, where the effect of the sparsity increase when labeling data with context dominates the homogeneity increase of using data (transactions) related to a specific context.

The contextual post-filtering RS outperforms the un-contextual RS when the performance is measured by comparing the recommendations generated based on a set of data related to a certain period $t_1$ are compared to the actual behavior of customers in a future period $t_2$; moreover, if one tries to generate less obvious recommendations, the contextual post-filtering RS increases its performance more than the un-contextual RS. While, if the performance is measured using the leave-one-out approach, the un-contextual RS performs better than the contextual RSs. We believe that the first way of evaluating the systems performance may mirror more closely the actual way recommender systems work in real e-commerce applications, however future research is required in order to understand the different results obtained using the different evaluation strategies.

Although we used only one definition of context and only one database, there are some strengths. First of all, an implicit contextual information such as the one used in this research ("season", "day of the week", "time in a day") is almost always available in business applications, while richer contextual variables should be explicitly asked to users and moreover, the same experiments can be done by using other databases and contextual variables.

Further research is required in order to better understand the use of context in RS. In particular, we are doing experiments using different contextual variables (such as, the intent of a purchase), different databases and other approaches (e.g., contextual modeling and different post-filtering methods).

# References

1. Adomavicius, G., Tuzhilin, A.: Toward the next generation of recommender systems: a survey of the state-of-the-art and possible extensions. Transactions on Knowledge and Data Engineering 17, 734–749 (2005)
2. Anand, S.S., Mobasher, B.: Intelligent techniques in web personalization. Springer, Heidelberg (2005)
3. Burke, R.: Hybrid recommender systems: Survey and experiments. In: User Modeling and User Adapted Interaction, vol. 12, pp. 331–370. ACM, New York (2002)
4. Resnick, P., Iacovou, N., Suchak, M., Bergstrom, P., Riedl, J.: GroupLens: An Open Architecture for Collaborative Filtering of Netnews. In: Proceedings of CSCW 1994, pp. 175–186. ACM, New York (1994)
5. Hill, W., Stead, L., Rosenstein, M., Furnas, G.: Recommending and evaluating choices in a virtual community of use. In: Proceedings of CHI 1995 Conference, pp. 194–201. ACM, New York (1995)
6. Lang, K.: Newsweeder: Learning to filter netnews. In: Proceedings of the 12th International Conference on Machine Learning, pp. 331–339. Morgan Kaufmann, San Francisco (1995)
7. Pazzani, M., Muramatsu, J., Billus, D.: Syskill & Webert: Identifying interesting web sites. In: Proceeedings of the National Conference on Artificial Intelligence, pp. 54–61. AAAI Press, Portland (1996)
8. Mooney, R.J., Bennett, P.N., Roy, L.: Book recommending using text categorization with extracted information. In: Recommender Systems. Papers from 1998 Workshop. Technical Report WS-98-08, pp. 70–74. AAAI Press, Menlo Park (1998)
9. Balabanovic, M., Shoham, Y.: Fab: Content-based, collaborative recommendation. Communications of the ACM 40, 66–72 (1997)
10. Pazzani, M.: A framework for collaborative, content-based and demographic filtering. Artificial Intelligence Review 13, 393–408 (1999)
11. Bettman, J.R., Luce, M.F., Payne, J.W.: Constructive consumer choice processes. Journal of consumer research 25, 187–217 (1998)
12. Tuzhilin, A., Gorgoglione, M., Palmisano, C.: Using Context to Improve Predictive Models of Customers in Personalization Applications. IEEE Transactions on Knowledge and Data Engineering, 1535–1549 (2008)
13. Anand, A., Mobasher, B.: Contextual Recommendation. In: From Web to Social Web: Discovering and Deploying User and Content Profiles. Springer, Heidelberg (2007)
14. Adomavicius, G., Tuzhilin, A.: Multidimensional recommender systems: a data warehousing approach. In: Fiege, L., Mühl, G., Wilhelm, U.G. (eds.) WELCOM 2001. LNCS, vol. 2232, pp. 180–192. Springer, Heidelberg (2001)
15. Adomavicius, G., Sankaranarayanan, R., Sen, S., Tuzhilin, A.: Incorporating contextual information in recommender systems using a multidimensional approach. Transactions on Information Systems 23, 103–145 (2005)
16. Tuzhilin, A., Adomavicius, G.: Context-Aware Recommender Systems. In: Proceedings of the 2008 ACM conference on Recommender systems, pp. 335–336. ACM, New York (2008)
17. Nichols, D.M.: Implicit rating and filtering. In: Proceedings of the fifth DELOS Workshop on Filtering and Collaborative Filtering, ERCIM, Budapest, pp. 31–36 (1998)
18. Chen, L.S., Hsu, F.H., Chen, M.C., Hsu, Y.C.: Developing recommender systems with the consideration of product profitability for sellers. In: Information Science, vol. 178, pp. 1032–1048. ACM, New York (2008)

19. Konstan, J., Miller, B., Maltz, D., Herlocker, J., Gordon, L., Riedl, J.: GroupLens: Applying Collaborative Filtering to Usenet News. Communications of the ACM 40, 77–87 (1997)
20. Sarwar, B.M., Karypis, G., Konstan, J.A., Riedl, J.: Analysis of Recommendation Algorithms for E-Commerce. In: Proceedings of the ACM EC 2000 Conference, pp. 158–167. ACM, New York (2000)
21. Herlocker, J.L., Konstan, J.A., Terveen, L.G., Riedl, J.T.: Evaluating collaborative filtering recommender systems. ACM Transactions on Information Systems 22, 5–53 (2004)
22. Sordo-Garcia, C.M., Dias, M.B., Li, M., El-Deredy, W., Lisboa, P.J.G.: Evaluating Retail Recommender Systems via Retrospective Data: Lessons Learnt from a Live-Intervention Study. Transaction on Information Systems 22, 5–53 (2007)
23. Breese, J.S., Heckerman, D., Kadie, C.: Empirical analysis of predictive algorithms for collaborative filtering. In: Proceedings of the 14th Conference on Uncertainty in Artificial Intelligence, Madison, WI, pp. 43–52 (1998)
24. Panniello, U., Gorgoglione, M.: Including Context in a Transactional Recommender System Using a Pre-Filtering Approach: Two Real E-Commerce Applications. Accepted for presentation: The IEEE 23rd International Conference on Advanced Information Networking and Applications (May 2009)

# Providing Relevant Background Information in Smart Environments

Berardina De Carolis and Sebastiano Pizzutilo

Intelligent Interfaces, Department of Computer Science
University of Bari, Italy
{decarolis,pizzutilo}@di.uniba.it

**Abstract.** In this paper we describe a system, called GAIN (Group Adapted Interaction for News), which selects background information to be displayed in public shared environments according to preferences of the group of people present in there. In ambient intelligence contexts, we cannot assume that the system will be able to know every users physically present in the environment and therefore to access to their profiles in order to compute the preferences of the entire group. For this reason, we assume that group members may be i) totally unknown, ii) completely or iii) partially known by the system. As we describe in the paper, in the first case, the system uses a group profile that is built statistically according to the results of a preliminary study. In the second case, the model of the group is created from the profiles of known users. In the third situation the group interests are modeled by integrating preferences of known members with a statistical prediction of the interests of unknown ones. Evaluation results proved that adapting news display to the group was more effective in matching the members' interests in all the three cases than the in the non-adaptive modality.

## 1 Introduction

Communal and shared spaces are typically inhabited by groups of people that are there for a particular reason, for the will of a person, or even accidentally. Today, many public places are provided with large-screen, digital displays or other output devices typical of the particular environment: examples are cardio-fitness machines in a fitness center, displays of a food dispensers, bus/train/plane notice-boards, etc..

In opposite to on-line information seeking, such displays promote the experience of "encountering" the information while carrying on another activity [5]. We denote with "background information" contents and news that are secondary to the main reason or tasks which led users to that particular environment. Background information is different from "peripheral" information, though not being central for the current task enables the person who is performing it to learn better or to keep track of less important tasks [11].

Examples of background information are those that may be provided when people are in a queue at an automatic coffee dispenser, at a bus stop, or in some social places, like fitness or commercial centres, where people go for reasons different from receiving and reading news. In these places, people might be interested in receiving some

T. Di Noia and F. Buccafurri (Eds.): EC-Web 2009, LNCS 5692, pp. 360–371, 2009.

information. The information system of the environment may, in turn, be interested in recommending (promoting) items or in entertaining users with some specific news.

Considering the importance that casually acquired information has in the construction of our knowledge, than it might be important for the environment to tailor information and news to the need of the target audience.

In this case, adaptation to the presumed preferences of the group seems indispensable for satisfying the information needs of the target population present in the environment. Adapting content and news to be provided requires knowledge of the interests and information needs of the group of people that is usually present at a particular time in that place.

Providing a solution to this problem, in our opinion, requires a different approach from the one used by web-based systems that recommend, for instance, movies to groups of users [12] or that adapt music in a fitness center according to preferences of people present in there [13]. In these cases the system identifies those who are logged into it, recognizes their interest when explicitly stated, or builds incrementally their profile as a consequence of the feedback or rating they provide [2].

This approach is not always applicable in a physical place where the system may be not aware of all the nearby people. In fact, even if we assume that, with the evolution of technology, mobile personal devices will be used to interact with an active environment and therefore the system will be able to understand who is in the place, we cannot assume that everybody will use this technology or will give the permission to use their data or to detect their presence in the environment. So, it is reasonable to assume that, while modelling the group of people present in a given location, a part or even all of them will be unknown to the environment.

In this paper we propose an approach to group modelling that aims at providing background information adapted to the presumed information needs of people present in a communal space and to some context features such as the particular activity zone in which information is displayed, the time of the day and so on.

The system adopts an approach in computing the profile of the group present in a particular activity zone of the overall environment that considers the fact that people to which information is addressed may be totally **unknown**, or may be **known** in full or in part, if the profiles of all or some of the users may be transferred to the environment [3,8].

In order to test the system we selected as active environment a Fitness Center[1]. This type of environment is interesting for the main purpose of this research since:

i)      people subscribe a contract with the center and, contextually, it is possible to ask them to fill a questionnaire about their interests;

ii)     users are often provided with magnetic badges that allows identifying their entrance in the environment;

iii)    users are heterogeneous and have different interests, furthermore for certain period of time their presence is quite stable with some turn-over periods;

iv)     the overall environment can be divided in different activity zones in which it is plausible that people have different information needs;

---

[1] A.S.D. BodyEnergy, Mola di Bari, Italy.

v)     it is possible to make a statistical forecast of how many and which categories of users are present in an activity zone in a given time slice and
therefore to combine this information with the profiles accessible by the
system.

For testing the system behaviour we conducted an evaluation study whose results
indicate first of all that people like receiving background information, then that adapting news to the group of people being in a public place is promising and may improve
the efficacy of information provided in daily life. In particular, users expressed more
satisfaction in watching group adapted than not adapted news.

The paper is structured as follows: Section 2 briefly describes the system architecture, then Section 3 describes the group modelling strategy used in GAIN. Section 4
describes the study that we performed for evaluating the system. Finally, in Section 5,
conclusions and future work directions are discussed.

## 2   The GAIN System

The approach presented in this paper is an evolution of GAIN (Group Adapted Interaction for News) [15].

In this phase of the project first of all we have installed and tested the system in a
new environment in which time-slices and activity zones play a important role in
determining the distribution of people in the environment; then, we have implemented
the updating functionality both for the non-interactive and interactive conditions.

The system (Figure 1) has been designed using a Service Oriented Architecture
(SOA,[6]) and exploits the features of the *web services* (WS) technology to enable
flexibility and interoperability.

The main component of the system is the GAIN Web Application (WA) that is intended to be used by people at-
tending the target space.

Adaptation to the group and
context is realized by) the Group
Modeling WS, responsible for
computing the preferences and
interests of the group, and the RSS
News Reader WS, responsible for
searching news on the Internet.

In presence of people whose
profile can be accessed by the
system (*known group*), the Group
Modeling WS, starting from information about their interests,
computes the profile of the group
by combining these data with a
statistical forecast of the unknown
group composition, as described
in the next Section.

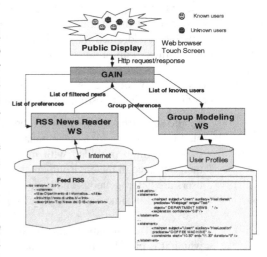

**Fig. 1.** GAIN Architecture

The profile of each known user is supposed to be accessible by the environment (i.e. stored in a personal device) according to its type and privacy settings.

The user profiles in GAIN are formalized using a common representation language. We decided to use the situational statement language UserML from Ubis-World [8], since we use it in other user modeling components that we developed for other projects.

UserML provides a language that allows representing the user model in a very detailed way by introducing information useful for the contextualization; furthermore it seems to be appropriate for this kind of system.

The following set of statements describes, for instance, the situation in which a female user is highly interested in reading news about "wellness" when is in the locker room:

```
<situation id="101">
<statement>
  <mainpart  subject="User1"  auxiliary="HasInterest"  predicate="Webpage"
  range="Text" object="WELLNESS NEWS" />
  <explanation confidence="0.8" />
</statement>
<statement>
  <mainpart subject="User1" auxiliary="HasLocation" predicate="fitness room" />
</statement>
</situation>
```

Starting from this profile, the system extracts the set of features necessary for filtering the news as a vector of items and their score or confidence, selected according to relevant contextual tags (i.e. time slice, activity zone).

The RSS News Reader WS allows to browse the Internet looking for news about a given topic, by using the RSS (Really Simple Syndication) Feed technology. In this way, updated information about several topics can be provided to the group.

Each RSS feed follows a standard syntax and consists of a set of news, each with a title, a description (which is an abstract of the news item), and a link to a web page where the news is located. A further tag describes the category of the news: this tag is important to filter news according to group preferences (for more details see [15]).

The list of filtered news is sorted according to the interest score that the group-modelling component calculated for every news item, and it is used to update periodically the public display.

As far as interaction is concerned, we developed different interfaces to be used in different situations: a non interactive wall display (Fig. 2a), an interactive kiosk display and a personal interface for mobile systems (Fig. 2b).

The described architecture is general enough to be adapted to domains different from the one considered in this paper. The system has been developed using standard protocols and languages. In addition, GAIN web services can be used as part of other systems or applications that need that particular service.

**Fig. 2. a.** A screenshot of the wall display. **b.** A screenshot of the mobile application.

## 3  Group Modeling Strategy

In ambient intelligence contexts modelling a group may result more complicated than for other types of application domains since the group may be constitute by heterogeneous people that randomly enter in the place without necessarily sharing a specific goal. Moreover, we have to consider that the system might have access only to the personal profiles of some group members. For this reason, to model the group we suppose that it can be split in two subgroups:

- the **known subgroup** that includes the set of users (and their profiles) that surely are nearby the display for a certain period of time: for instance, they have a personal device that allows them to log transparently into the system;

- the **unknown subgroup** that includes users that cannot be recognized by the system but that statistically are supposed to be there.

We made the hypothesis that, in order to improve the **level of effectiveness** of the adaptation process, a mixed approach to group modelling could be adopted, combining the statistical distribution of preferences of people that usually attend that place, with those of a subgroup that is known by the environment.

In order to collect these statistical data, we conducted a study concerning the people distribution and the interests about news in each activity zone of a Fitness Center. In particular, as activity zones we considered: the reception hall, the male and female locker rooms and the fitness rooms.

Groups in these places are made up of people that spend there a *limited* period of time (short or long) and their formation is *accidental* however it is implicitly regulated by the type of activity that people performs there (i.e. a collective course, a individual training, and so on).

The study involved 170 subjects (typical representation of the target users of our application during a day) that usually spend some time in the selected public space. Subjects were requested to fill a questionnaire that was divided in three sections aiming at:

- collecting some *demographic data* about the subjects (gender, age, category);

- understanding the *frequency of attendance* (at *what time*, for *how long* and *how many days* during the week subjects were attending the place) and in which activity zone subjects are supposed to stay in each time slice according to the habitual activity performed in the place. In particular, we identified 10 time slices, from 9.00 in the morning to 13.00 p.m. and from 16.00 to 22.00 in the evening.
- understanding which were the possible *topics* of interests by asking subjects to score hem in a list using a 1-5 Likert scale (from 1: *I really hate it* to 5: *I really like it*) for each activity zone.

For space reasons we do not show in details the results of this study. From this data we derived some information about the habits of every user, in term of average number of minutes spent in each activity zone during a day, and about their distribution in every time slice and about their flow in the smart environment according to their activity program. Figure 3 shows, in particular, the distribution of subjects' interests when being in the Fitness room around 10.00 a.m. and 18.00 p.m..

The two time slices were selected as being quite relevant: in the morning the fitness room is attended mainly by women while in the early evening there are mainly male students. From this example, one might infer that the user's gender is the triggering feature of a stereotypical profile of group interests, however it cannot be considered in this phase of the system development for two main reasons: i) the preliminary study showed that in another time slice (late in the evening)

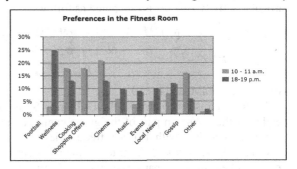

**Fig. 3.** Comparison of the average interests in two time slices

women have different interests (maybe because they have a different cultural background); ii) in our application domain users do not always connect to the system through their personal device, badge etc. and therefore the system might not have access to information about their gender.

Therefore, we used these data to build the *statistical dataset* of our group modelling module. From this set of data we have understood that the triggering factors were related mainly to the time slice and to the activity zone in which users were located. Then for each zone and time slice we derive the default confidences for a list of possible topics independently from personal data.

Then, the definition of the group model is made by combining the profiles of the known users with the statistical profile of the unknown group. In the method we propose, different weights may be assigned to the two groups, according to the relative importance one wants to give to the known group with respect to the unknown one, how many people are logged in, and the percentage of known users over the presumed total ones. In particular we denote as:

- $P_{SURE}$, the weight given to the preferences of known user group. This value varies in an interval between 0 and 1.
- $P_{PROBABLE}[2]$ , the weight given to the preferences of the unknown user group; again, this value varies in an interval between 0 and 1.
- $K$, the number of topics;
- $UM^i_j$ the score for *topic j* in the activity zone A from *user i;*
- $b$ the base of the votes; can be 1, 5, 10, 100, etc..
- $N$ , the number of known users;
- $M$ the number of users whose profiles constitute the statistical dataset;
- $f_i$ , the frequency of the attendance for every user of the selected public space, calculated as the number of days attended by *user i* divided by number of working days;
- $t_i$ , the average number of minutes in which the *user i* is queuing in the public space in the considered time slice;
- $F_m = \sum_{m=N+1}^{N+M} (f_m * t_m)$ , the frequency in which people attend the place in the statistical dataset;

Then, $C_j$, indicating the confidence value for a *topic j* to be shown to the group in a particular activity zone A, is computed as follows:

$$\forall j \in \{1,...K\}: C_j = \frac{\sum_{i=1}^{N}\left[\frac{UM_i^j}{b}*\frac{P_{SURE}}{N}\right] + \sum_{i=N+1}^{N+M}\left[\frac{UM_i^j}{b}*\left(\frac{f_i*t_i}{F_m}*P_{PROBABLE}\right)\right]}{P_{SURE}+P_{PROBABLE}} \quad (1)$$

with  N>0 and M>0 and b <>0.

This formula is a variation of the Utilitarian Strategy – Additive [12] in which the weight for the unknown part of the group cannot be uniformly distributed, as people are present in a place with different frequencies.

We introduced $(f_i*t_i)/F_m$ for filtering the news according to the fact that some users are more likely to be in that place at a certain time than others. The problem is therefore how to determine this frequency.

To this aim, the approximation of the presence of users is based on the time of the day and from a statistic derived from a questionnaire, as well as in other systems [7] in which uncertainty is considered.

In particular, we used this data for calculating $f_i$ and $t_i$ as the average number of minutes that a *user i* spends in each activity zone, during the week, in the time slice in which the group modelling function is activated.

For instance, if the user attends the fitness room for forty minutes three days in a week then his/her weight in the group model is *3/6 * 40*, where 6 is the number of working days in a week.

Obviously, when N=0 and M>0 we have to set $P_{SURE}$ =0 and $P_{PROBABLE}$ =1. In this case nobody is logged and known by the system and the statistical group profile is computed starting from the user profiles of the population distribution in the current time slice. When N>0 and  M=0: in this case we have to set $P_{PROBABLE}$=0, and $P_{SURE}$=1.

---

[2] We were interested in having the confidence of each topic expressed as a percentage. For this reason we set $P_{PROBABLE}$ = $f(P_{SURE})$, being f a function that relates these two values.

Once the group modeling web service computes the list of preferences with their confidence values, (UMij = {item$_j$, confidence$_j$}), this is used to filter the news by the GAIN web application (see [15] for more details).

## 3.1  Updating the Group Model

In the context in which GAIN is applied, the group model can be updated in different situations:

- in a **non-interactive** context in which users passively look at news on a wall display,
- in an **"collective" interactive context** in which news are display on a public interactive kiosk,
- in a **personal interactive** context in which the user may receive a personalized selection of news on his/her device.

In all cases, we believe it would be impracticable to update the model by asking people to explicitly rate the relevance of background news, especially if they are in that place for a different purpose [1].

In GAIN, group model updating occurs when **new users** come into the activity zone or when the **next time** slice is reached, according to the statistical distribution explained previously. The system re-applies the formula (1) to calculate the new confidence of all news categories. To avoid sudden changes of the topics list, scanning of known users is done every **n(A)** minutes. This time interval corresponds to the average time that subjects involved in the preliminary survey declared to spend in each activity zone **A** calculated for all the time slices.

However, in the second situation, unknown users may interact with the system by simply clicking on the proposed news. This is considered as a kind of implicit feedback, since we may assume that users do not click on news at random, but rather on news whose titles are interesting to them [10]. Therefore, the clicked links may be referred as positive samples, which match the user preferences from a statistical point of view. However, in our application domain we do not know who is the member of the group that made the selection. For this reason, we created a temporary profile for each time slice and for each activity zone (**GIP(A)**)$_t$: Group Interaction Profile for the activity zone **A** in time slice t).

This profile has the same structure of UM(A)$_i$ and contains a list of the news categories of the considered domain, but with an initial confidence value equal to 0. The only difference regards the lack of information about the average time spent in the shared place (**f$_i$*t$_i$**), because we consider it constant for the actual time slice. Every time a user selects a news belonging to a category **x**, this is denoted as a positive feedback and the relative counter is incremented. At the end of the time slice the confidence of each category is updated by dividing the relative counter by the total number of selected news.

For example if N is the number of all the news selected by the users, and we consider Kj as the counter of the selected news for each category, the confidence Cj in the **GIP(A)$_t$** for the category j, will be calculated as Kj/N. The temporary profile **GIP(A)$_t$** is then used to update the group preferences for the activity zone A in the given time slice, since it is added to the statistical dataset and used in the next computation according to the formula (1). In this case the number of profiles M, used to build the statistical dataset, is incremented.

This approach enables us to tune the statistical profile, in order to reach a situation that is closer to the real usage model of the system. However, a possible problem may regards the number of collected profiles (M) since they enrich the statistical dataset and are never discarded.

To solve this problem the idea is to stop with this way of gathering information about the user when we will have a quite large number of usage profiles (around 1000) and to use machine learning techniques to extract information for building stereotypes relative to activity zones and time slices. With this new approach the temporary profiles will be considered new examples for updating stereotypes.

The third situation regards the interaction through a personal device. A user, whose personal profile has been previously transferred to the system, is considered part of the known subgroup and the group model is updated as in the previous case, taking the selection of one of the news as a positive feedback and incrementing the relative confidence counter. The only difference is that with direct interaction through the personal device, we can identify the user, and we may use feedback to update his/her personal profile, as in a single user application.

## 4   Evaluation of GAIN

In order to validate our approach we tested the impact of the adaptation strategy first through a subjective evaluation study [4]. This study aimed at assessing whether users prefer the system **with** or **without adaptation** (to the group) of the news presentation.

The study involved 80 people that usually attend the Fitness Center. The test was carried out around 10.30 a.m. of two different days in the fitness room.

We formed two groups of 40 subjects each. Each group was composed of 15 males and 25 females chosen among people that attend the fitness center in that time slice (this distribution mirrored the one coming out from the preliminary study).

Both groups were provided for 30 minutes with a set of news selected by GAIN. According to the preliminary study, this was the average time people are staying in that activity zone in that time slice.

The interface used in the experiment was a non-interactive wall display and both user groups could look at the news on three displays positioned at the center of each wall of the room but all displaying the same set of news.

Before the experiment both groups received a short explanation describing the purpose of the experiment. Then, the first group was provided with news selected randomly, without adaptation to the group profile. For the second group, the experiment was conducted in the same conditions and with the same procedure except for the news selection method. In this case, news categories were filtered and ordered according to the group interest profile triggered by the activity zone and daytime (see the distribution of interests in Figure 3). The group was considered as totally unknown and therefore we used only the statistical dataset for modeling the interests of the group.

At the end of the experiment, both groups were asked to fill a post-test questionnaire as accurately and honestly as they could. The questionnaire took no more than 5 minutes to be completed, after which participants were fully debriefed.

**Table 3.** Analysis of results of the most relevant questions for evaluating the effectiveness of group adaptation (scores expressed in a scale from 1 to 5)

|  | No adaptation | Adaptation | p-value |
|---|---|---|---|
| *Q1: Interest* | 3,0 | 3,9 | 0,01 |
| *Q2: Appropriateness* | 3,3 | 4,3 | 0,004 |
| *Q3: Adequacy* | 2,7 | 3,3 | 0,01 |
| *Q4: Need for more categories* | 4,1 | 3,7 | 0,078 |
| *Q5: Liking* | 3,4 | 3,9 | 0,176 |
| *Q6: Need for interaction* | 4,5 | 4,7 | 0,388 |

Table 3 summarizes the results of this study and shows that subjects in the 'adaptation' modality gave, on average, a better evaluation score to first three questions. These questions, in fact, were aimed at assessing the impact of adaptation on individual satisfaction: the results indicate that adaptation seems to increase **appropriateness**, **adequacy** and **interest** of information provided.

Answers to the fourth question indicate that there was no need for different news categories in the adapted condition.

The table shows that, at least for these four questions, the p-value of the t-test is less or equal than 0.01, showing that the difference between the two conditions can be considered significant.

Results about question 5 show that in both cases people liked the service of background information provision and that they would have liked to have a personal interaction with the news, since the average score to question 6 is between 4 and 5.

## 5   Conclusions and Future Work

In this paper we presented an approach to group modeling for adapting background information provision in smart environments. To this aim, we studied the different strategies proposed in literature and implemented a group modeling service that is able to compute the group model in situations where members are totally unknown or partially or completely known.

This is an interesting situation in ubiquitous computing contexts in which a potential use of personal devices, storing relevant information about the user can be foreseen, in combination with environment computing facilities. The system combines the features of a news aggregator with those of a recommender system, mixing contents provided by a smart environment with information and news adapted to the users preferences.

By combining the statistical profile of people that is supposed to be in the environment with the profiles of known users it is possible to deal with situation typical of ambient intelligence contexts. In particular, the use of weights in the proposed formula allows modifying the strategy according to the situation. Indeed, the use of different weights for the known and unknown part of the group may enforce the position of some categories in the list that the environment, for some reasons, may want to favour (i.e. special guests, special categories, etc.).

Results obtained so far seem to show that the group that received news adapted to the group profile was in average more satisfied than the other group.

However, since this experiment was aiming only at assessing whether adaptation was preferred over randomly selected news and since results were self-reported, we have implemented a simulation system based on the idea of using a personal agent for representing every user present in the environment.

In this way it will be possible not only to evaluate in an objective way the behaviour of the system according to variation of relevant parameters but also to measure the level of satisfaction of users by implementing an appropriate satisfaction function.

In our future work, we will test how much mixing public interaction (based on a kiosk), with a more personal one, based on mobile personal devices improves the satisfaction not only of the user that interacts with a personal device but also the satisfaction of unknown people since it allows tuning the statistical profile.

**Acknowledgments.** We thank Gianni Cozzolongo and Francesco Ambrouso for their contribution in this project.

# References

1. Adomavicius, G., Tuzhilin, A.: Toward the next generation of recommender systems: A survey of the state-of-the-art and possible extensions. IEEE Transactions on Knowledge and Data Engineering 17(6), 734–749 (2005)
2. Burke, R.: Hybrid Recommender Systems: Survey and Experiments. User Modeling and User-Adapted Interaction 12(4), 331–370 (2002)
3. Cavalluzzi, A., De Carolis, B., Pizzutilo, S., Cozzolongo, G.: Interacting with embodied agents in public environments. In: Proceedings of AVI 2004, Gallipoli, Italy, May 2004, pp. 240–243 (2004)
4. Dix, A., Finlay, J., Abowd, G.D., Beale, R.: Human-computer interaction. Pearson Education, London (2004)
5. Elderez, S.: Information encountering: a conceptual framework for accidental information discovery. In: Proceedings of an International Conference on Information Seeking in Context (ISIC), Tampere, Finland, pp. 412–421 (1997)
6. Endrei, M., Ang, J., Arsanjani, A., Chua, S., Comte, P., Krogdahl, P., Luo, M., Newling, T.: Patterns: Service-oriented Architecture and Web Services. IBM Redbook (2004) ISBN 073845317X
7. Goren Bar, D., Glinansky, O.: Family Stereotyping: A Model to Filter TV Programs for Multiple Viewers -. In: Ardissono, L., Buczak, A. (eds.) Proceedings of the 2nd Workshop on Personalization in Future TV - Malaga, Spain, pp. 95–102 (2002)
8. Heckmann, D.: Ubiquitous user modeling. IOS Press, Amsterdam (2005)
9. Joachims, T., Granka, L., Pan, B., Hembrooke, H., Gay, G.: Accurately interpreting click-through data as implicit feedback. In: Proceedings of the 28th Annual international ACM SIGIR Conference on Research and Development in information Retrieval, SIGIR 2005, Salvador, Brazil, August 15-19, 2005, pp. 154–161. ACM, New York (2005)
10. Konstan, J.A., Riedl, J.: Research Resources for Recommender Systems. In: CHI 1999 Workshop Interacting with Recommender, Pittsburgh, Pennsylvania, USA (1999)

11. Maglio, P.P., Campbell, C.S.: Tradeoffs in displaying peripheral information. In: Proceedings of Association for Computing Machinery's Human Factors in Computing Systems, CHI 2000, pp. 241–248 (2000)
12. Masthoff, J.: Group Modeling: Selecting a Sequence of Television Items to Suit a Group of Viewers. User Modeling and User-Adapted Interaction 14(1), 37–85 (2004)
13. McCarthy, J., Anagnost, T.: MusicFX: An arbiter of group preferences for computer supported collaborative workouts. In: Proceedings of the ACM 1998 conference on CSCW, Seattle, WA, pp. 363–372 (1998)
14. O'Conner, M., Cosley, D., Konstanm, J.A., Riedl, J.: PolyLens: a Recommender System for Groups of Users. In: Proceedings of ECSCW 2001, Bonn, Germany, pp. 199–218 (2001)
15. Pizzutilo, S., De Carolis, B., Cozzolongo, G., Ambruoso, F.: A Group Adaptive System in Public Environments. WSEAS Transaction on Systems 4(11), 1883–1890 (2005)

# Author Index